BY LIANA FINCK 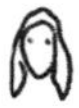

→ LET THERE BE LIGHT

EXCUSE ME

PASSING FOR HUMAN

LET THERE BE LIGHT

☆

LET THERE BE LIGHT

THE REAL STORY OF HER CREATION

☆ LIANA FINCK

*

RANDOM HOUSE

NEW YORK

PUBLISHED IN THE UNITED STATES BY RANDOM HOUSE,
AN IMPRINT AND DIVISION OF PENGUIN RANDOM HOUSE LLC, NEW YORK.

RANDOM HOUSE AND THE HOUSE COLOPHON ARE REGISTERED
TRADEMARKS OF PENGUIN RANDOM HOUSE LLC.

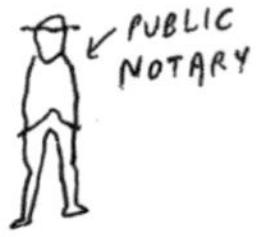
PUBLIC NOTARY

LIBRARY OF CONGRESS CATALOGING-IN-PUBLICATION DATA
NAMES: FINCK, LIANA, ARTIST, AUTHOR.

TITLE: LET THERE BE LIGHT: THE REAL STORY OF HER CREATION / LIANA FINCK.

DESCRIPTION: FIRST EDITION. | NEW YORK: RANDOM HOUSE, [2022]

IDENTIFIERS: LCCN 2021020417 (PRINT) | LCCN 2021020418 (EBOOK) /
ISBN 9781984801531 (HARDCOVER: ACID-FREE PAPER)
ISBN 9781984801524 (EBOOK)

SUBJECTS: LCSH: BIBLE. OLD TESTAMENT—COMIC BOOKS, STRIPS, ETC. | GRAPHIC NOVELS. | LCGFT: BIBLE COMICS. | GRAPHIC NOVELS. | COMICS (GRAPHIC WORKS)

CLASSIFICATION: LCC PN6727.F4943 L48 2022 (PRINT)
LCC PN6727.F4943 (EBOOK) | DDC 741.5/973—DC23
LC RECORD AVAILABLE AT HTTPS://LCCN.LOC.GOV/2021020417
LC EBOOK RECORD AVAILABLE AT HTTPS://LCCN.LOC.GOV/2021020418

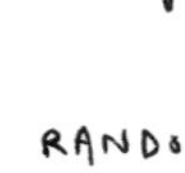

PRINTED IN THE UNITED STATES OF AMERICA
ON ACID-FREE PAPER

RANDOMHOUSEBOOKS.COM

987654321

FIRST EDITION

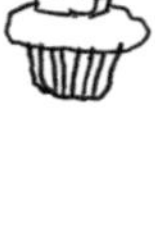

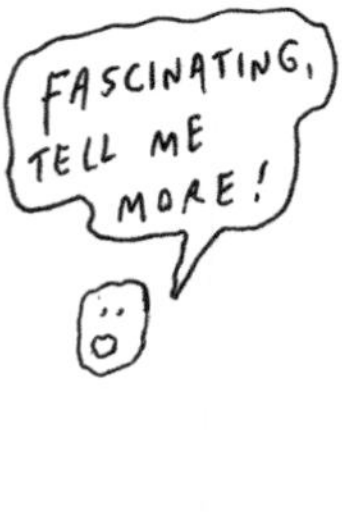
FASCINATING, TELL ME MORE!

To my mom, HARRIET FINCK, who CREATED ME (WITH A LITTLE HELP FROM MY DAD, MICHAEL FINCK).

AND VERY MUCH IN MEMORY OF SUSAN KAMIL.

I

PAST

THERE'S NO NEED FOR ME TO GO INTO THE TROUBLES WITH THE KING JAMES
VERSION OF THE BIBLE HERE, BUT WHEN I ENCOUNTERED THE FIRST BOOK,
THE BOOK OF GENESIS, I IMMEDIATELY UNDERSTOOD IT TO BE A BOOK
FOR CHILDREN.

— JAMAICA KINCAID, "THE DISTURBANCES OF THE GARDEN"

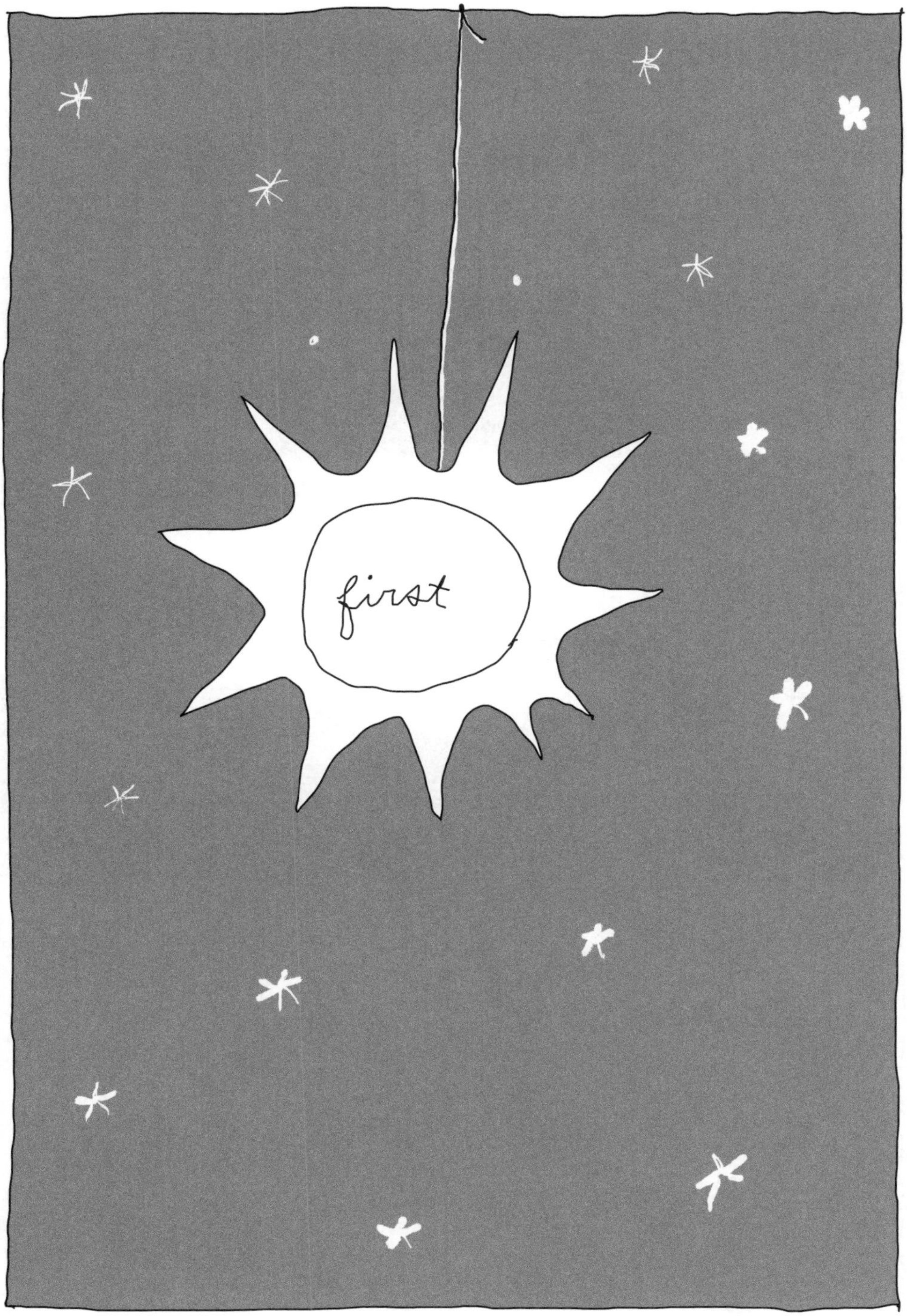
first

FIRST, SHE CREATED THE HEAVENS AND THE EARTH.

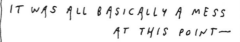
IT WAS ALL BASICALLY A MESS AT THIS POINT—

WITH DARKNESS FLOATING ON THE FACE OF THE DEPTHS.

SHE LAY THERE UNABLE TO MOVE, WONDERING IF THIS WAS ALL SHE WAS CAPABLE OF.

THAT WAS THE BEGINNING OF DISAPPOINTMENT.

TIME — OR SOMETHING — PASSED.

FINALLY, SHE OPENED HER MOUTH—

AND SAID:

LET THERE BE LIGHT!

AND THERE WAS LIGHT.

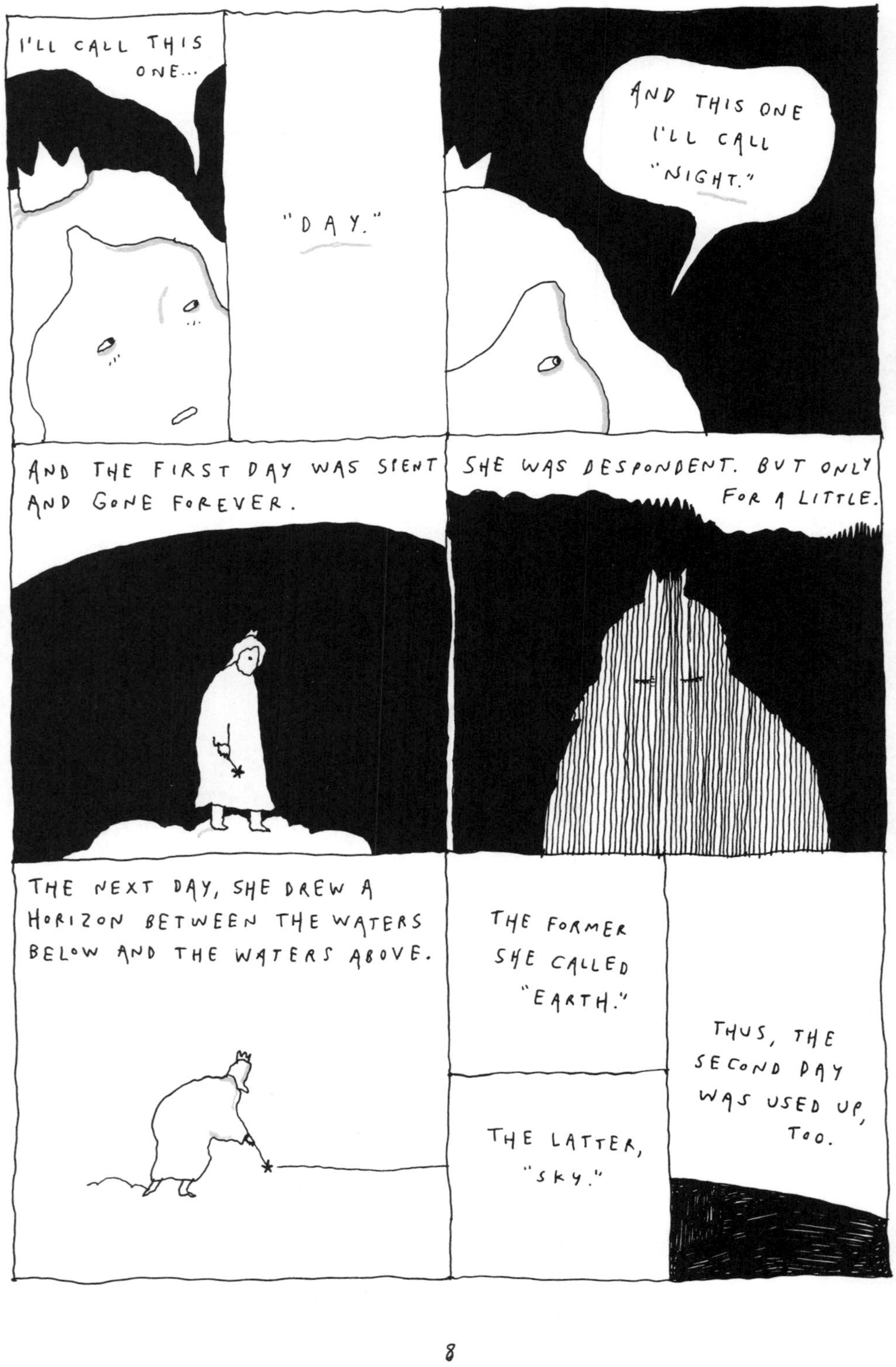
I'LL CALL THIS ONE...
"DAY."
AND THIS ONE I'LL CALL "NIGHT."
AND THE FIRST DAY WAS SPENT AND GONE FOREVER.
SHE WAS DESPONDENT. BUT ONLY FOR A LITTLE.
THE NEXT DAY, SHE DREW A HORIZON BETWEEN THE WATERS BELOW AND THE WATERS ABOVE.
THE FORMER SHE CALLED "EARTH."
THE LATTER, "SKY."
THUS, THE SECOND DAY WAS USED UP, TOO.

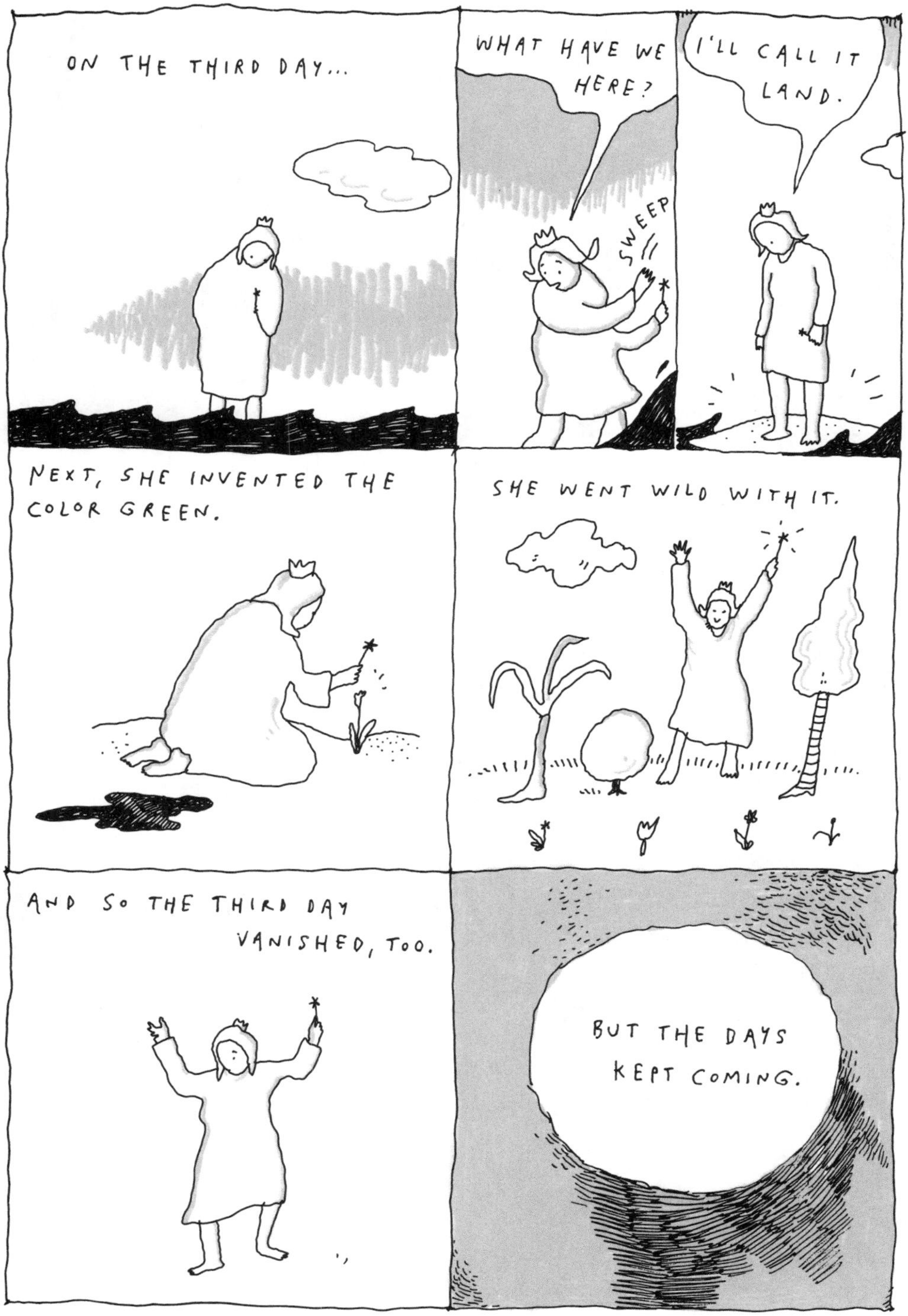
ON THE THIRD DAY...
WHAT HAVE WE HERE?
SWEEP
I'LL CALL IT LAND.
NEXT, SHE INVENTED THE COLOR GREEN.
SHE WENT WILD WITH IT.
AND SO THE THIRD DAY VANISHED, TOO.
BUT THE DAYS KEPT COMING.

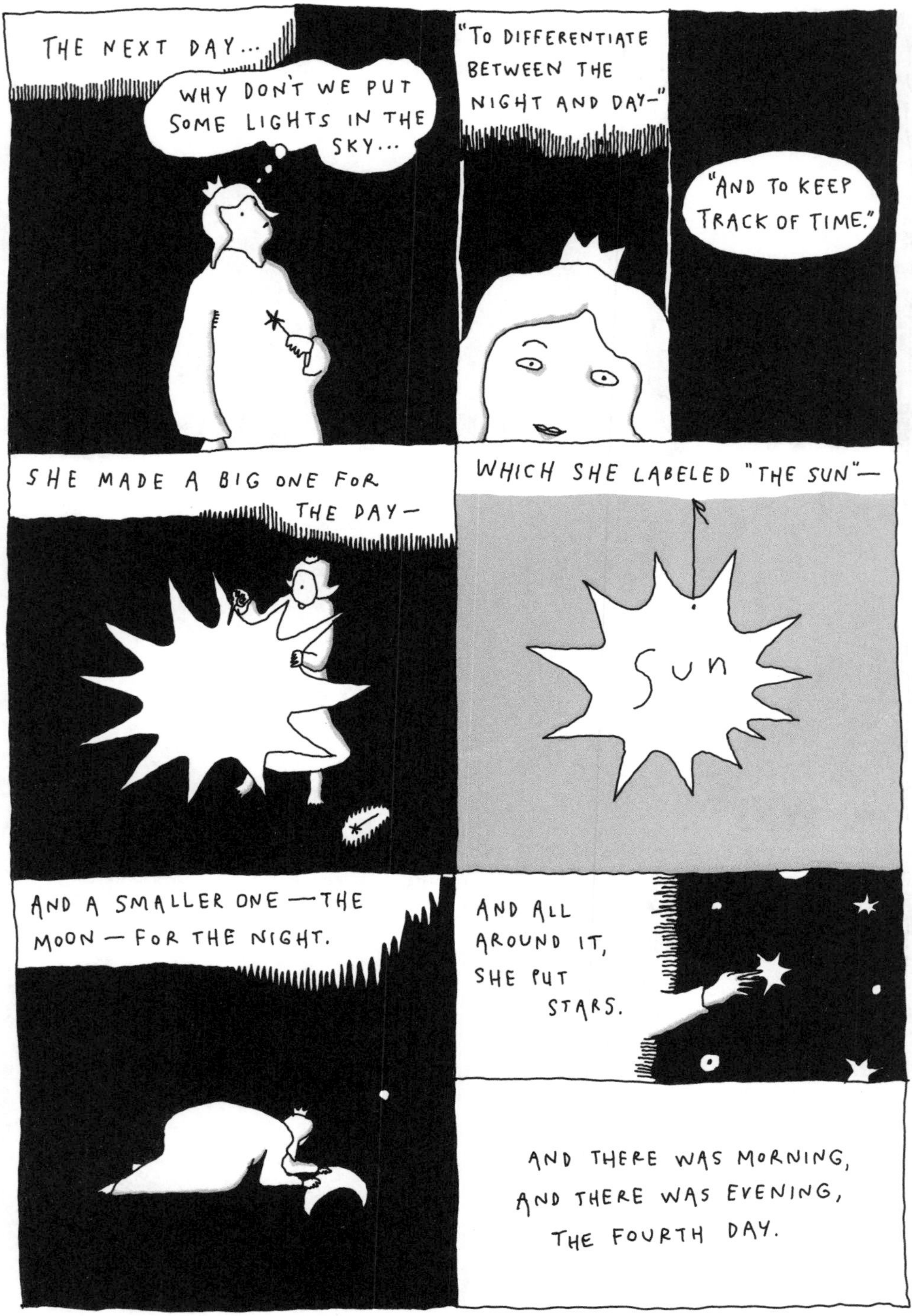
THE NEXT DAY...
WHY DON'T WE PUT SOME LIGHTS IN THE SKY...
"TO DIFFERENTIATE BETWEEN THE NIGHT AND DAY–"
"AND TO KEEP TRACK OF TIME."
SHE MADE A BIG ONE FOR THE DAY–
WHICH SHE LABELED "THE SUN"–
SUN
AND A SMALLER ONE — THE MOON — FOR THE NIGHT.
AND ALL AROUND IT, SHE PUT STARS.
AND THERE WAS MORNING, AND THERE WAS EVENING, THE FOURTH DAY.

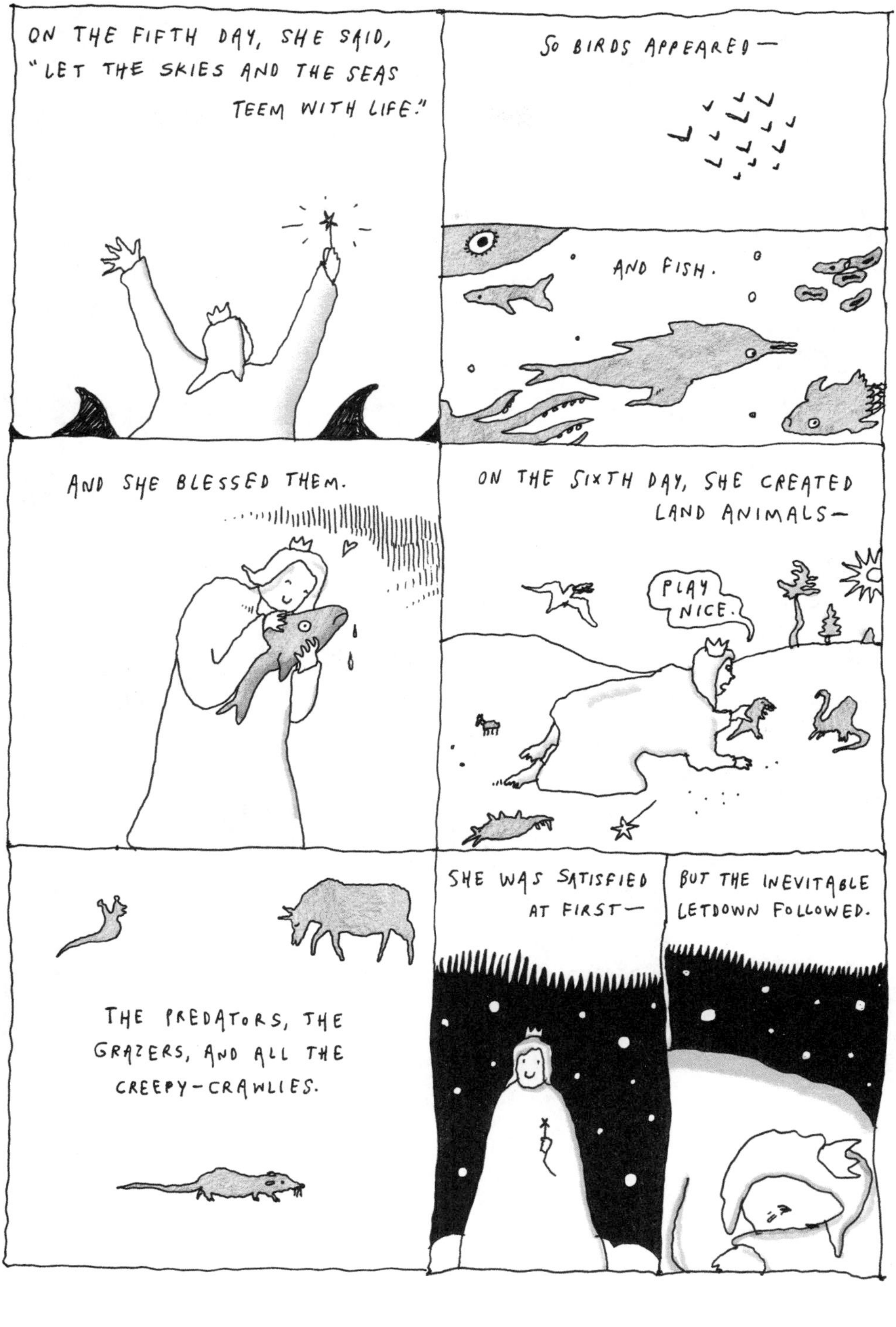
ON THE FIFTH DAY, SHE SAID, "LET THE SKIES AND THE SEAS TEEM WITH LIFE."
SO BIRDS APPEARED—
AND FISH.
AND SHE BLESSED THEM.
ON THE SIXTH DAY, SHE CREATED LAND ANIMALS—
PLAY NICE.
THE PREDATORS, THE GRAZERS, AND ALL THE CREEPY-CRAWLIES.
SHE WAS SATISFIED AT FIRST—
BUT THE INEVITABLE LETDOWN FOLLOWED.

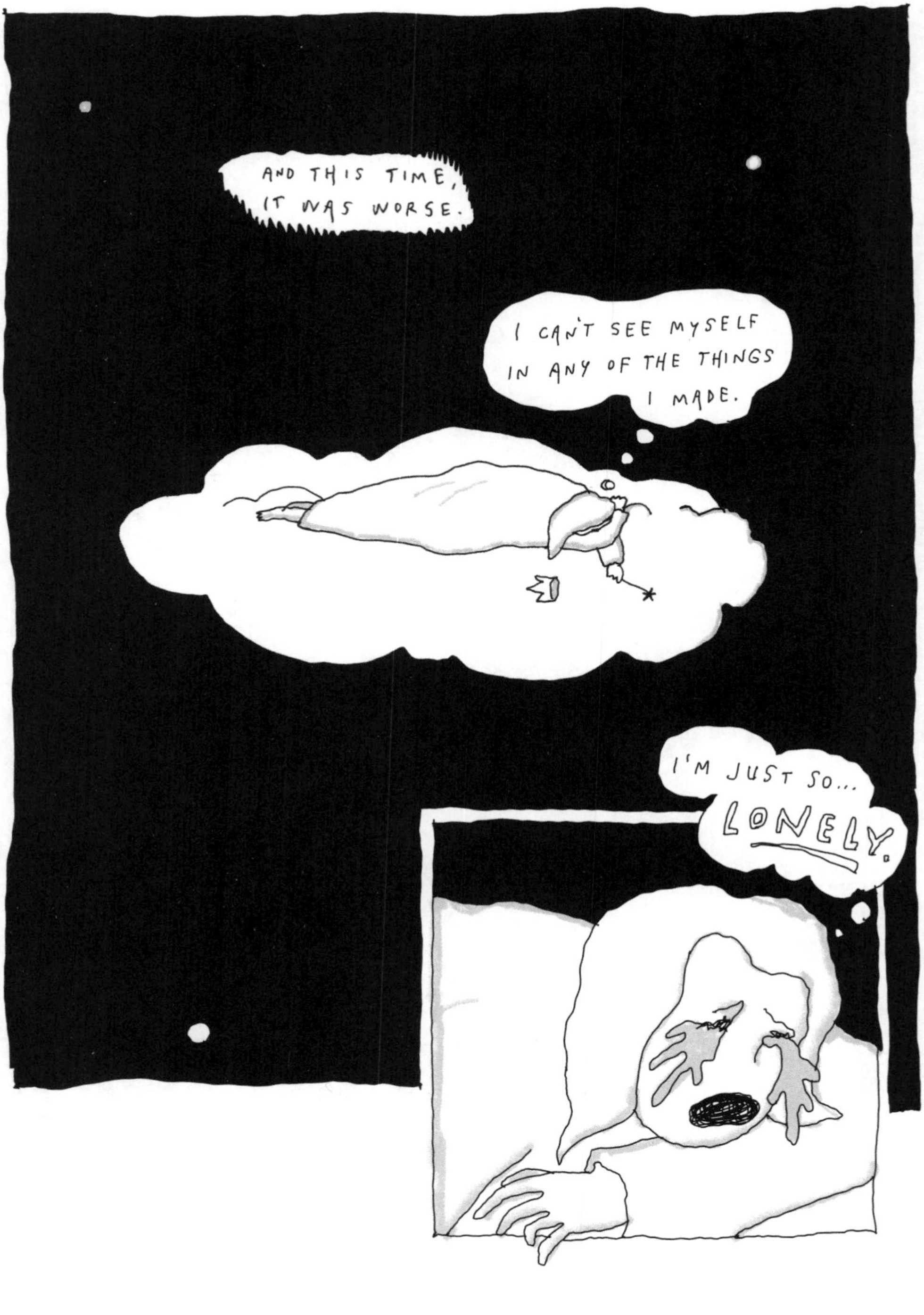
AND THIS TIME, IT WAS WORSE.
I CAN'T SEE MYSELF IN ANY OF THE THINGS I MADE.
I'M JUST SO... LONELY.

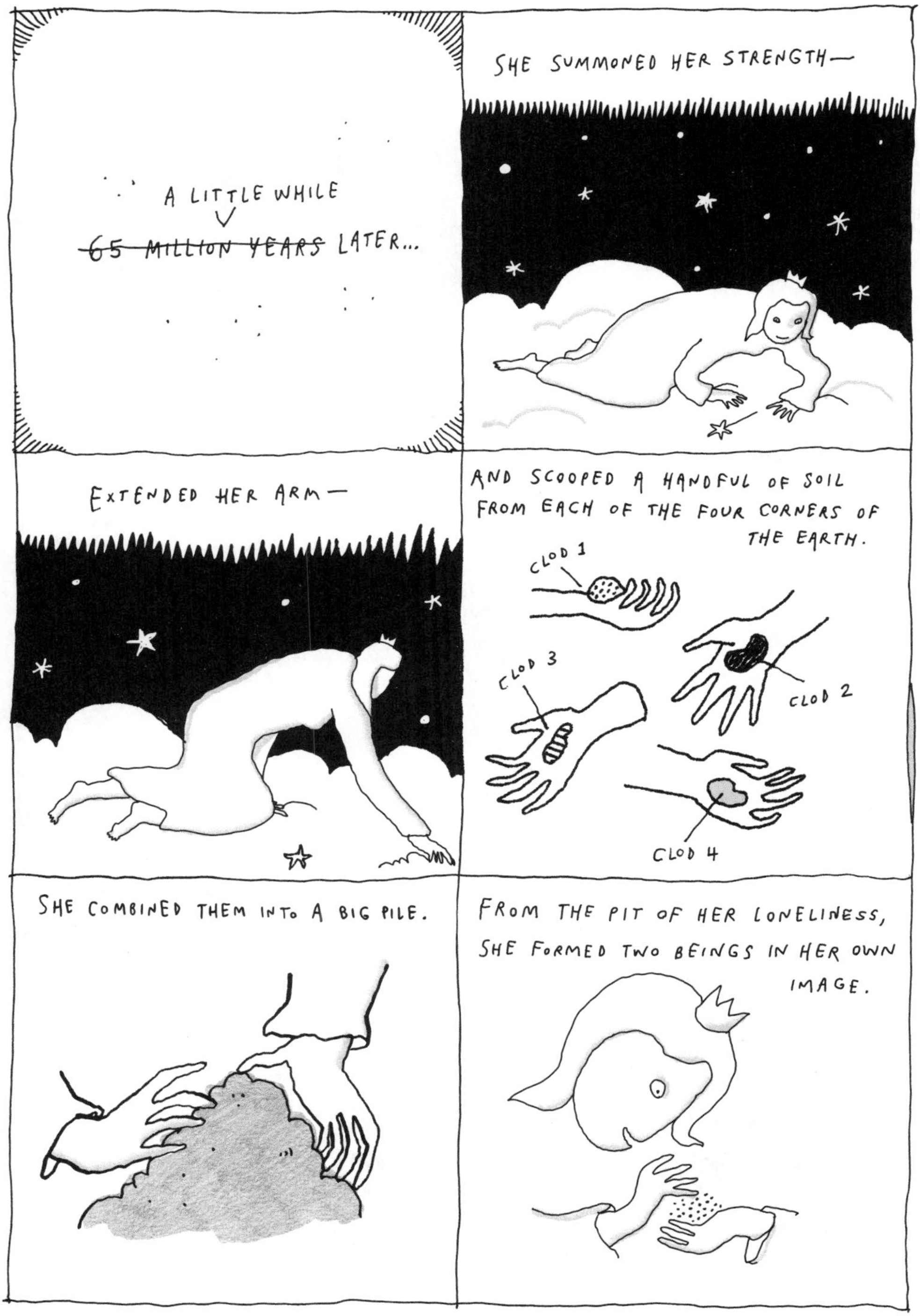
A LITTLE WHILE
65 MILLION YEARS LATER...
SHE SUMMONED HER STRENGTH—
EXTENDED HER ARM—
AND SCOOPED A HANDFUL OF SOIL FROM EACH OF THE FOUR CORNERS OF THE EARTH.
CLOD 1
CLOD 2
CLOD 3
CLOD 4
SHE COMBINED THEM INTO A BIG PILE.
FROM THE PIT OF HER LONELINESS, SHE FORMED TWO BEINGS IN HER OWN IMAGE.

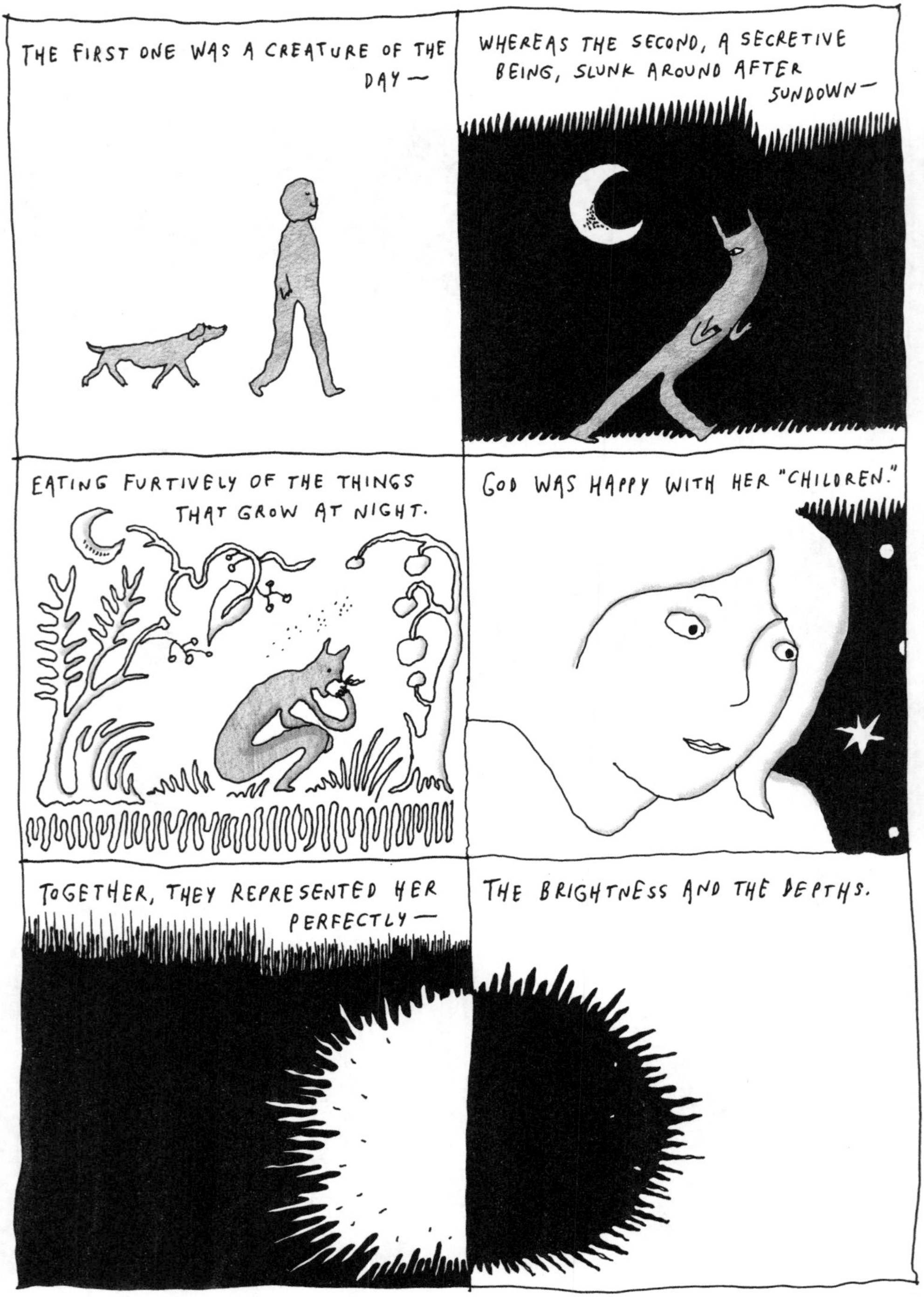
THE FIRST ONE WAS A CREATURE OF THE DAY—
WHEREAS THE SECOND, A SECRETIVE BEING, SLUNK AROUND AFTER SUNDOWN—
EATING FURTIVELY OF THE THINGS THAT GROW AT NIGHT.
GOD WAS HAPPY WITH HER "CHILDREN."
TOGETHER, THEY REPRESENTED HER PERFECTLY—
THE BRIGHTNESS AND THE DEPTHS.

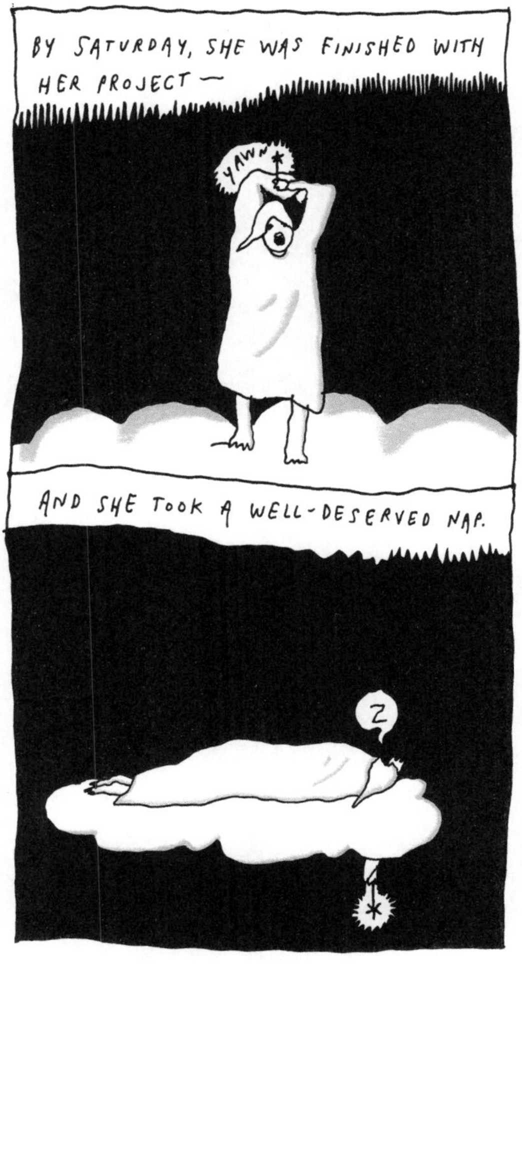
BY SATURDAY, SHE WAS FINISHED WITH HER PROJECT —
YAWN
AND SHE TOOK A WELL-DESERVED NAP.
Z

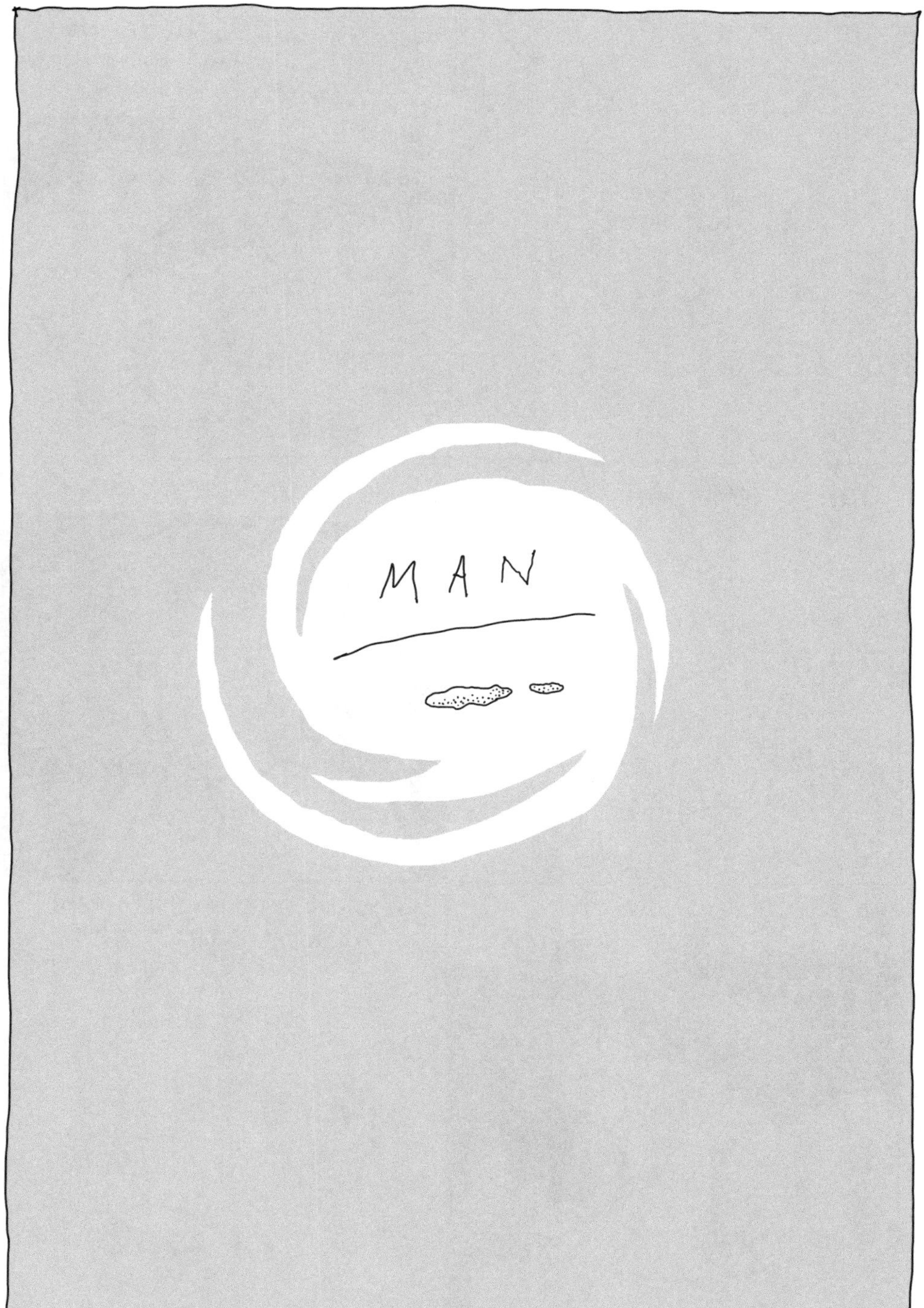
MAN

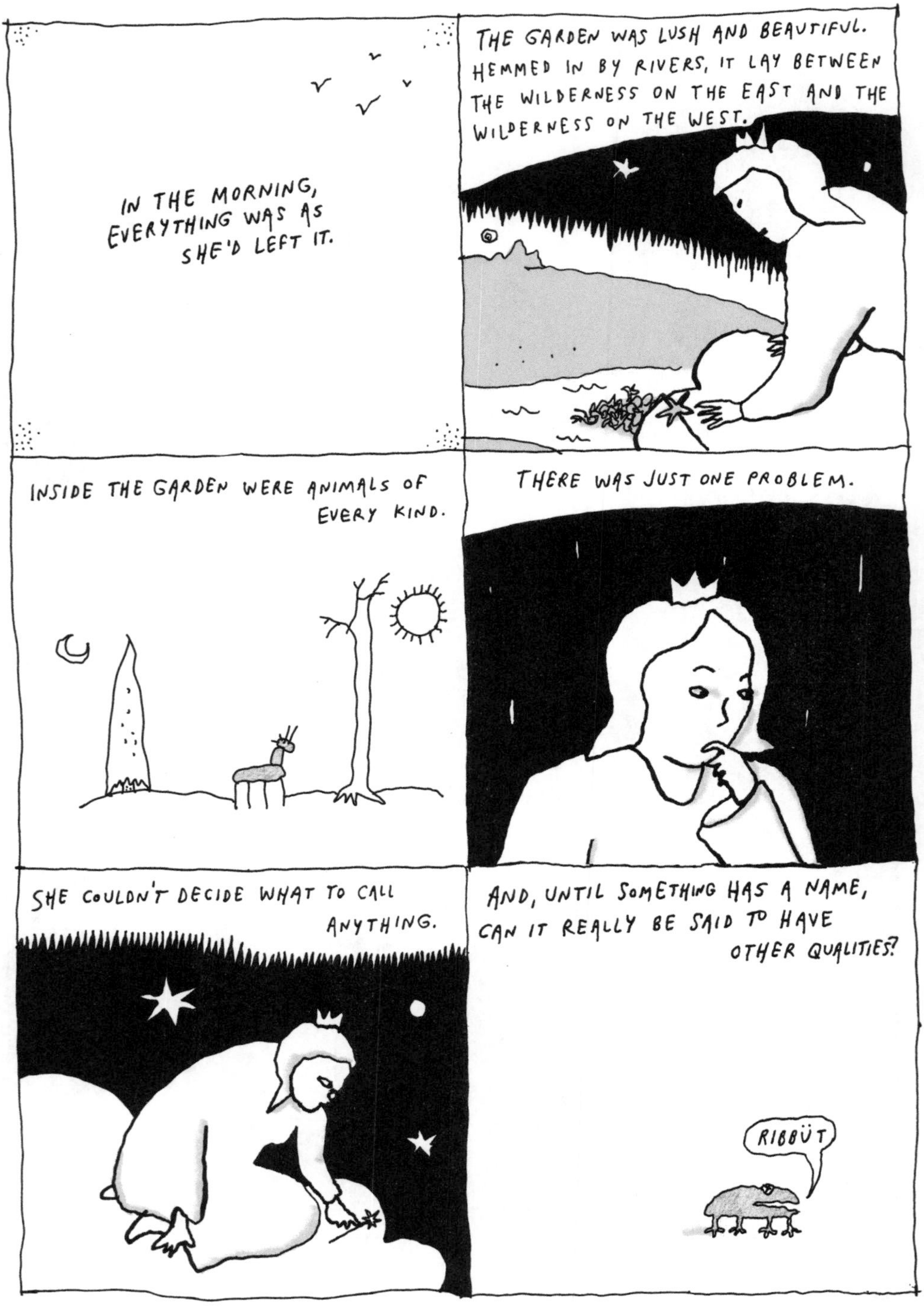
IN THE MORNING, EVERYTHING WAS AS SHE'D LEFT IT.
THE GARDEN WAS LUSH AND BEAUTIFUL. HEMMED IN BY RIVERS, IT LAY BETWEEN THE WILDERNESS ON THE EAST AND THE WILDERNESS ON THE WEST.
INSIDE THE GARDEN WERE ANIMALS OF EVERY KIND.
THERE WAS JUST ONE PROBLEM.
SHE COULDN'T DECIDE WHAT TO CALL ANYTHING.
AND, UNTIL SOMETHING HAS A NAME, CAN IT REALLY BE SAID TO HAVE OTHER QUALITIES?
RIBBÜT

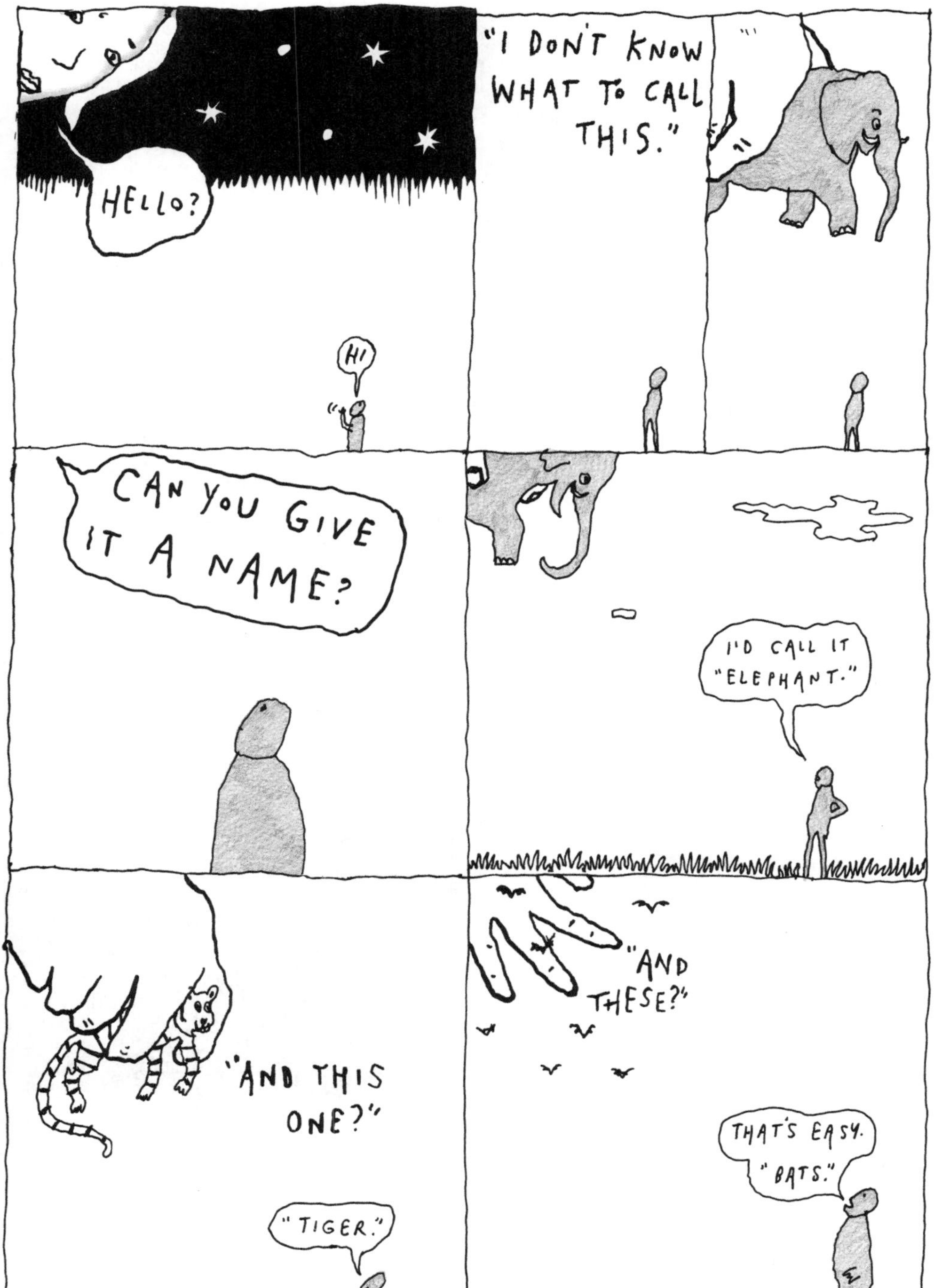
HELLO?
HI
"I DON'T KNOW WHAT TO CALL THIS."
CAN YOU GIVE IT A NAME?
I'D CALL IT "ELEPHANT."
"AND THIS ONE?"
"TIGER."
"AND THESE?"
THAT'S EASY. "BATS."

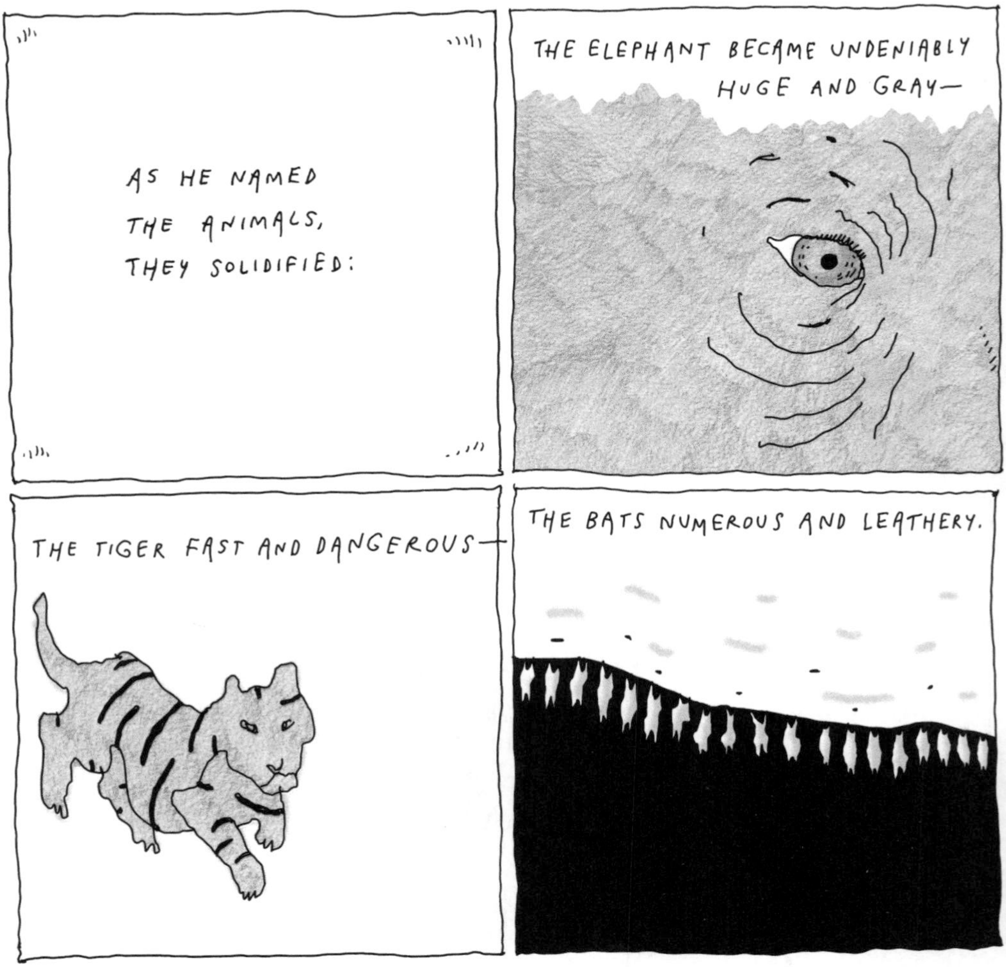
AS HE NAMED THE ANIMALS, THEY SOLIDIFIED:
THE ELEPHANT BECAME UNDENIABLY HUGE AND GRAY—
THE TIGER FAST AND DANGEROUS—
THE BATS NUMEROUS AND LEATHERY.

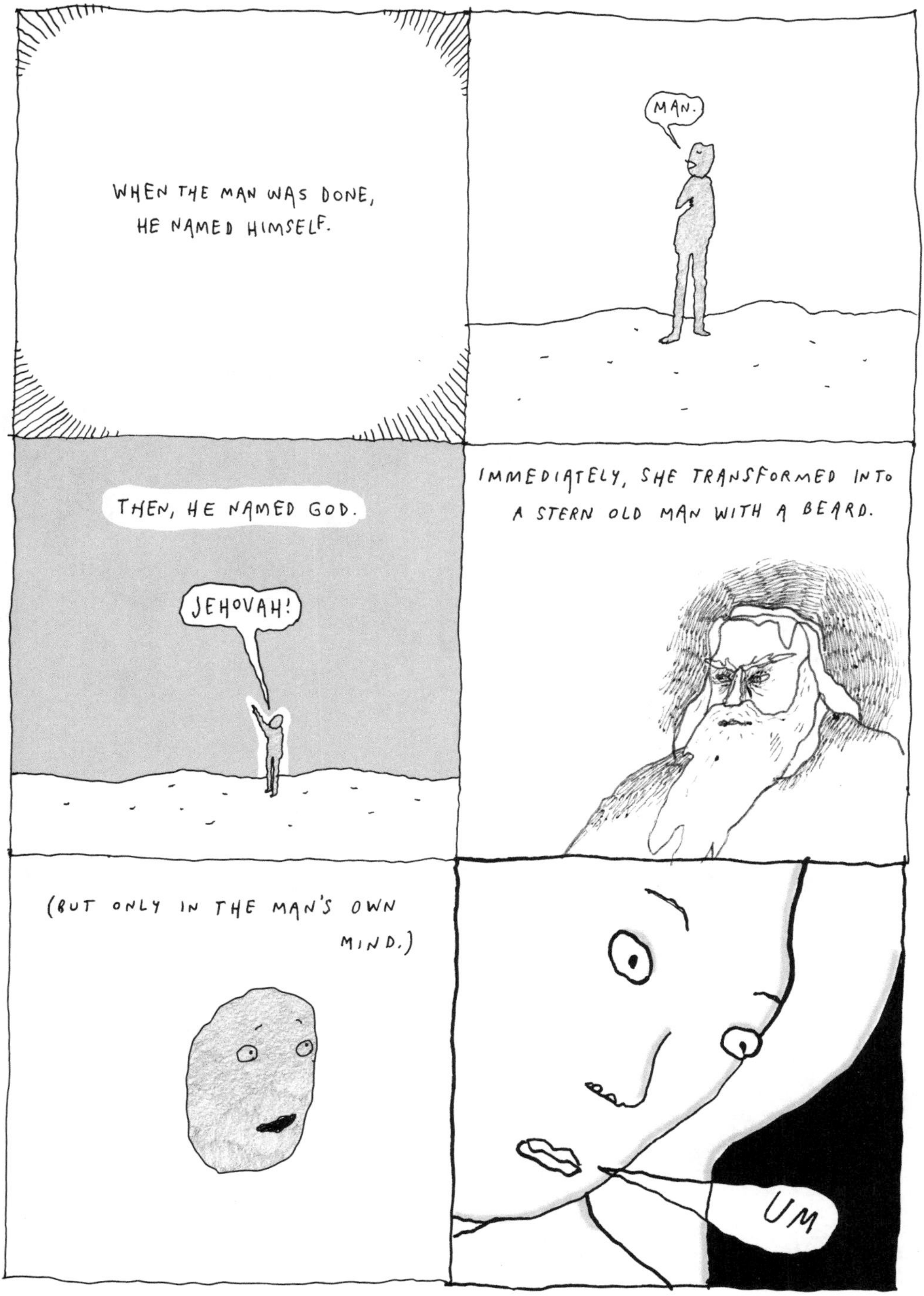
WHEN THE MAN WAS DONE, HE NAMED HIMSELF.
MAN.
THEN, HE NAMED GOD.
JEHOVAH!
IMMEDIATELY, SHE TRANSFORMED INTO A STERN OLD MAN WITH A BEARD.
(BUT ONLY IN THE MAN'S OWN MIND.)
UM

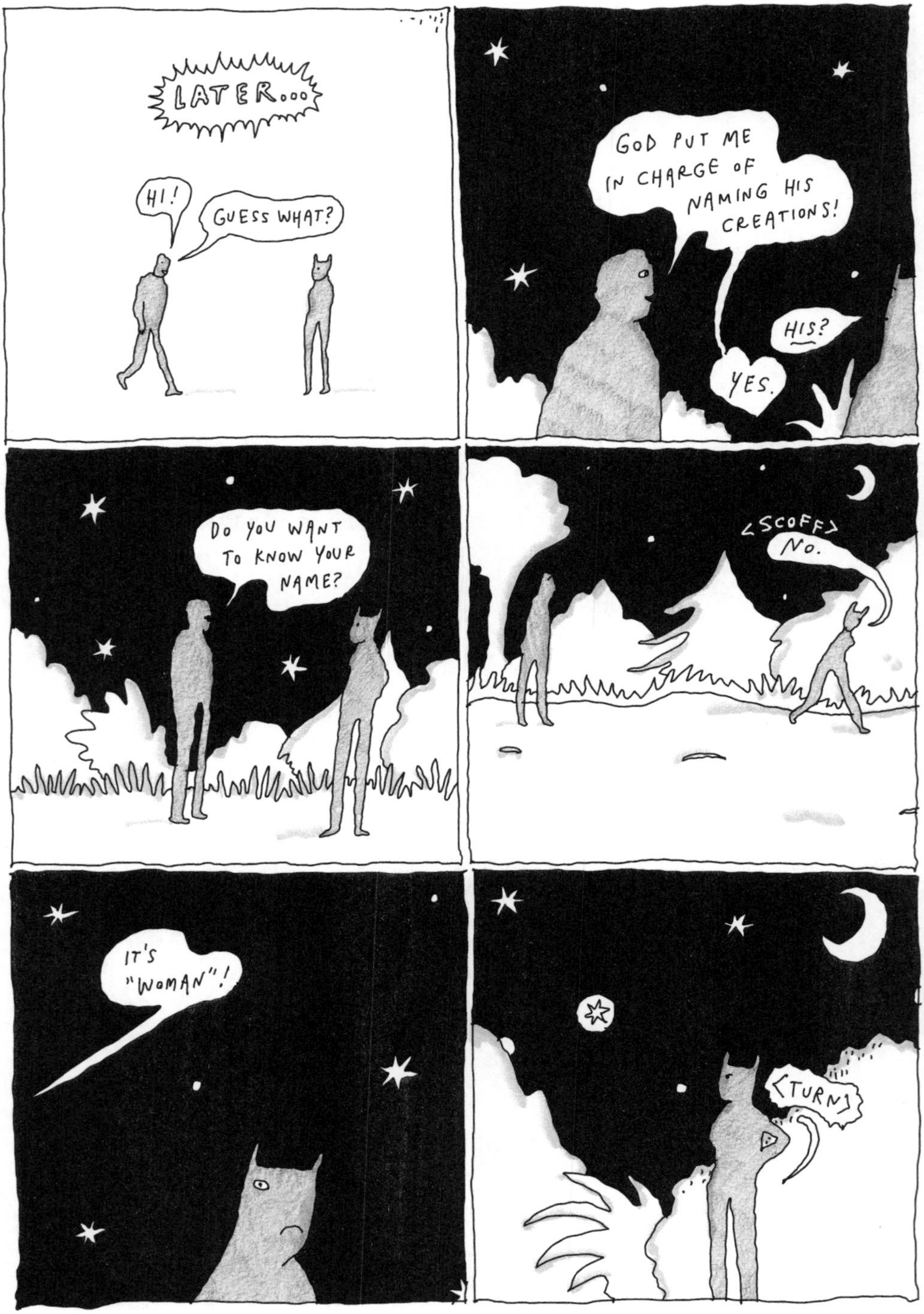
LATER...
HI!
GUESS WHAT?
GOD PUT ME IN CHARGE OF NAMING HIS CREATIONS!
HIS?
YES.
DO YOU WANT TO KNOW YOUR NAME?
<SCOFF>
NO.
IT'S "WOMAN"!
[TURN]

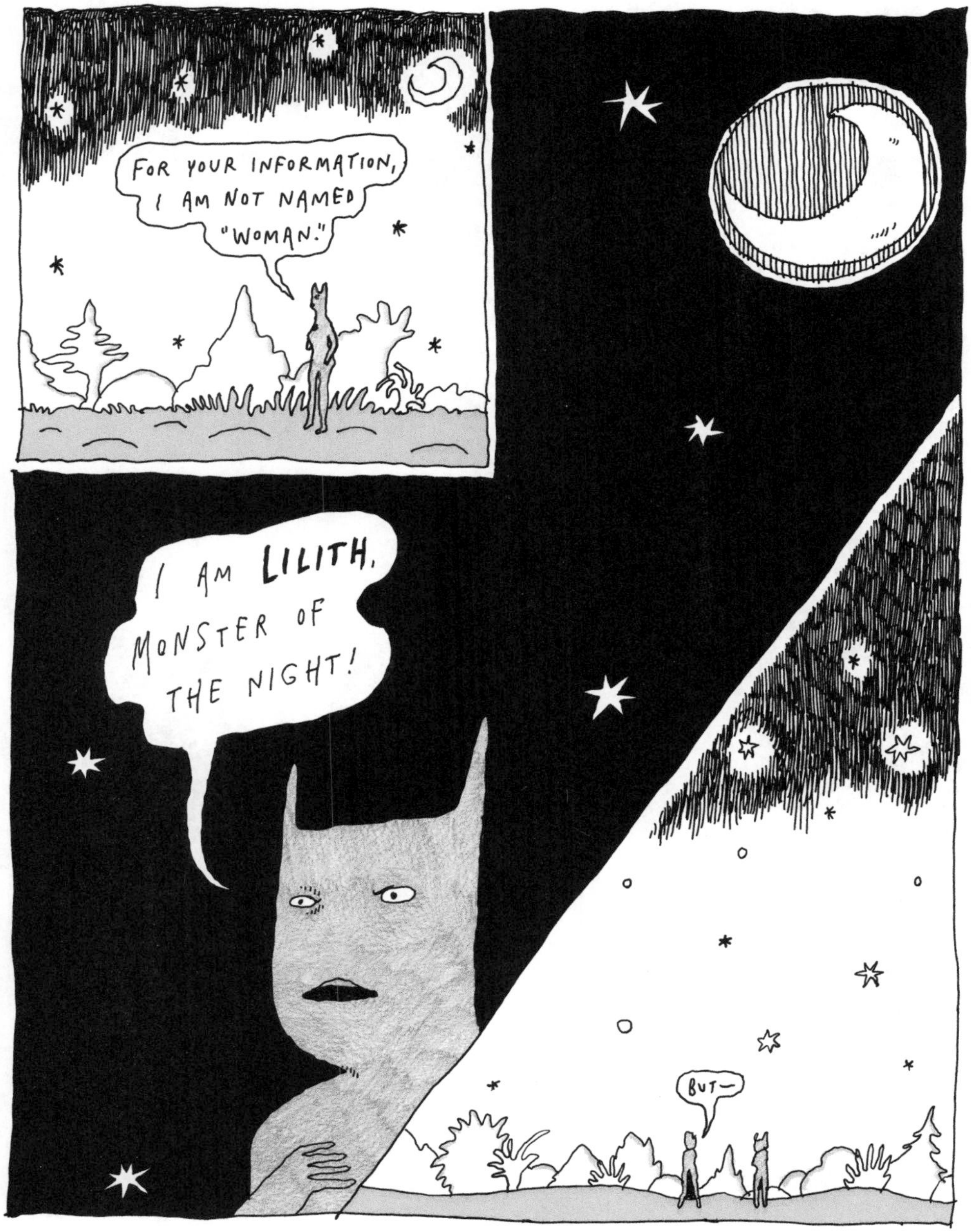
FOR YOUR INFORMATION, I AM NOT NAMED "WOMAN."
I AM LILITH, MONSTER OF THE NIGHT!
BUT—

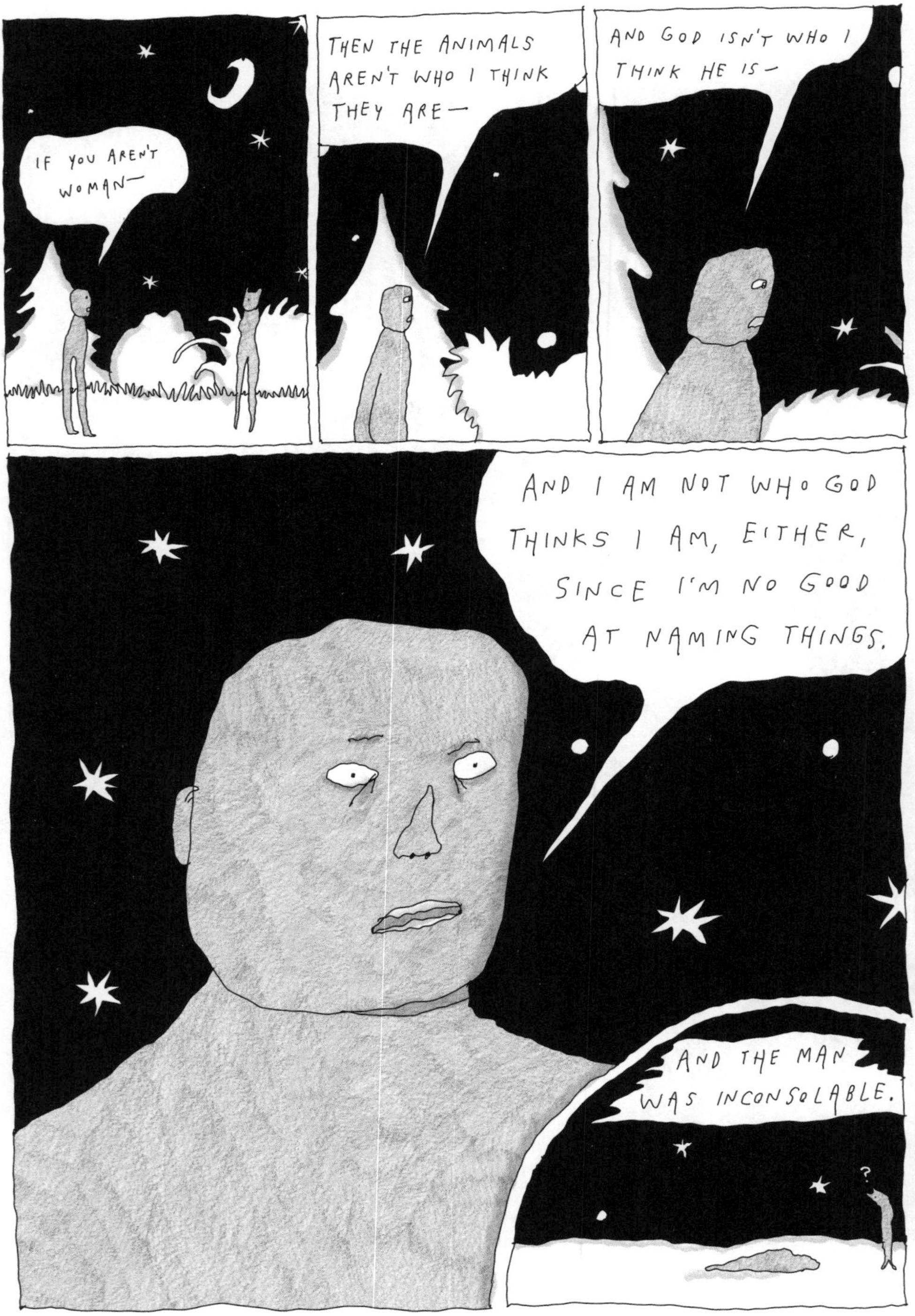
IF YOU AREN'T WOMAN—
THEN THE ANIMALS AREN'T WHO I THINK THEY ARE—
AND GOD ISN'T WHO I THINK HE IS—
AND I AM NOT WHO GOD THINKS I AM, EITHER, SINCE I'M NO GOOD AT NAMING THINGS.
AND THE MAN WAS INCONSOLABLE.

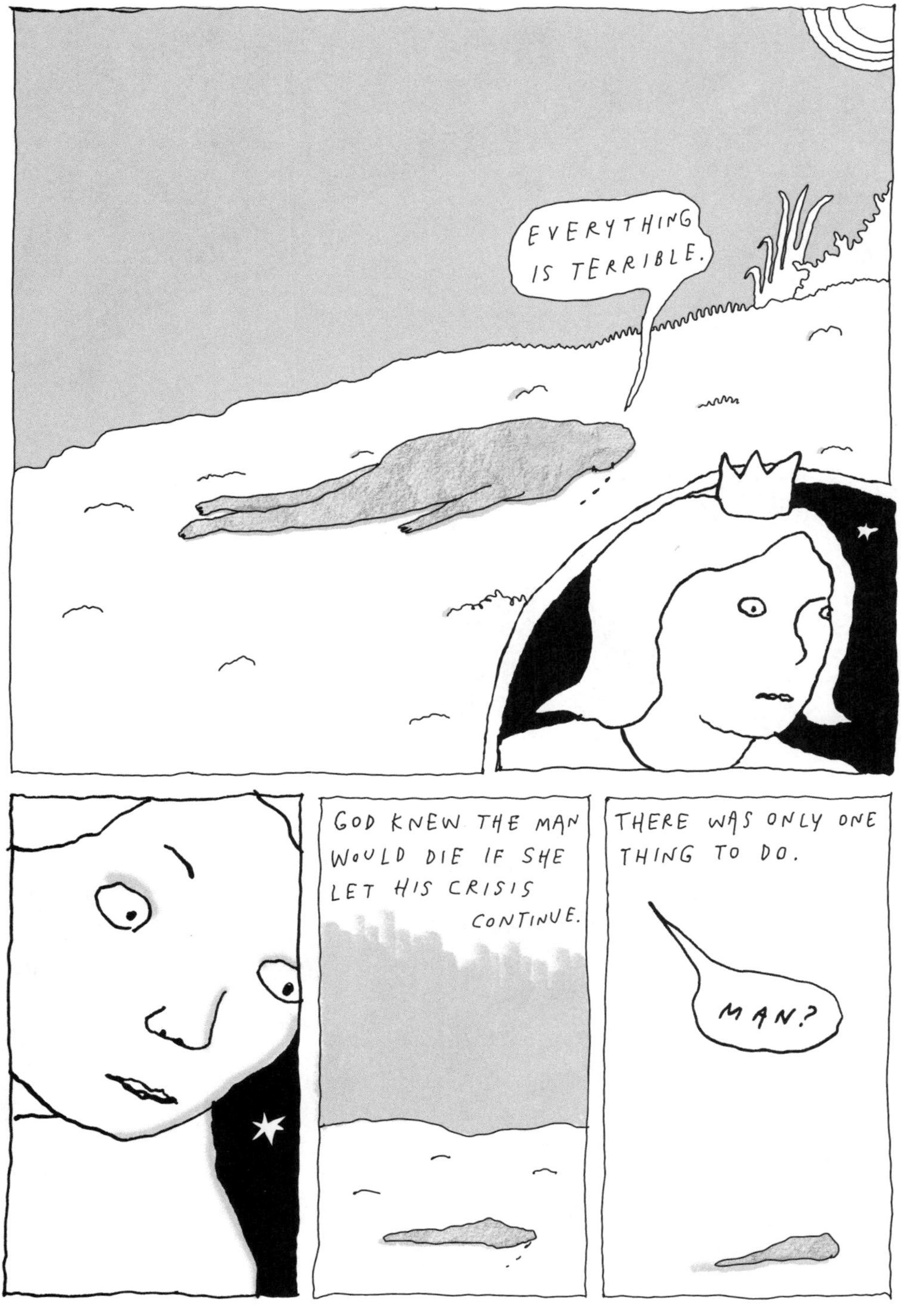
EVERYTHING IS TERRIBLE.
GOD KNEW THE MAN WOULD DIE IF SHE LET HIS CRISIS CONTINUE.
THERE WAS ONLY ONE THING TO DO.
MAN?

IT'S ME. GOD.
I AM AN OLD MAN WITH A BEARD. YOU WERE RIGHT ABOUT EVERYTHING.
SOB
MAN?
NUDGE

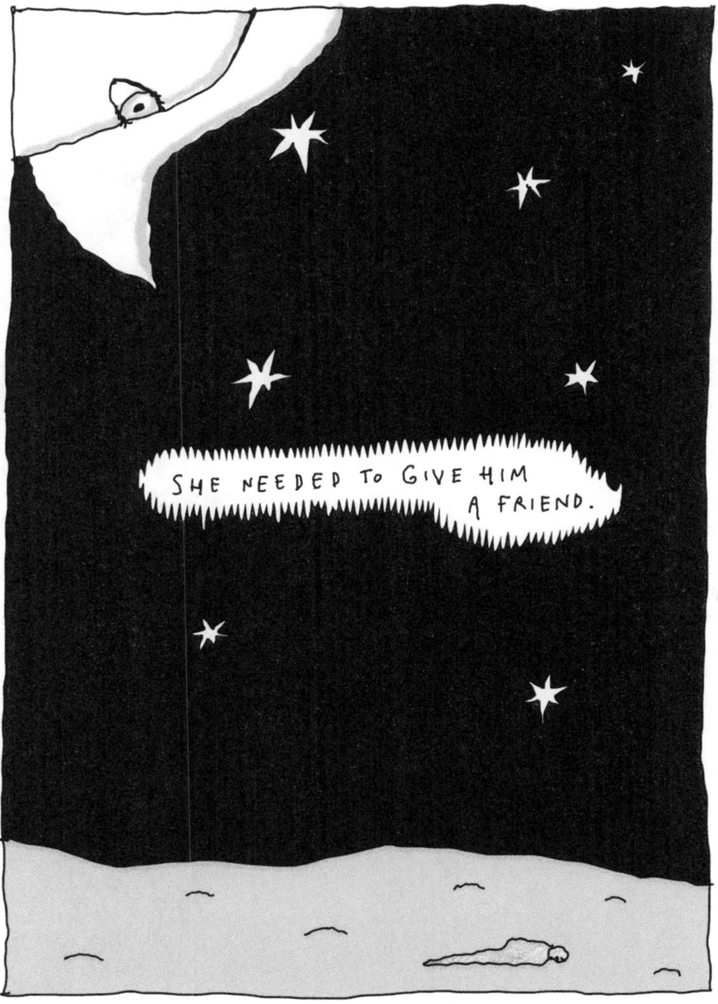
SHE NEEDED TO GIVE HIM A FRIEND.

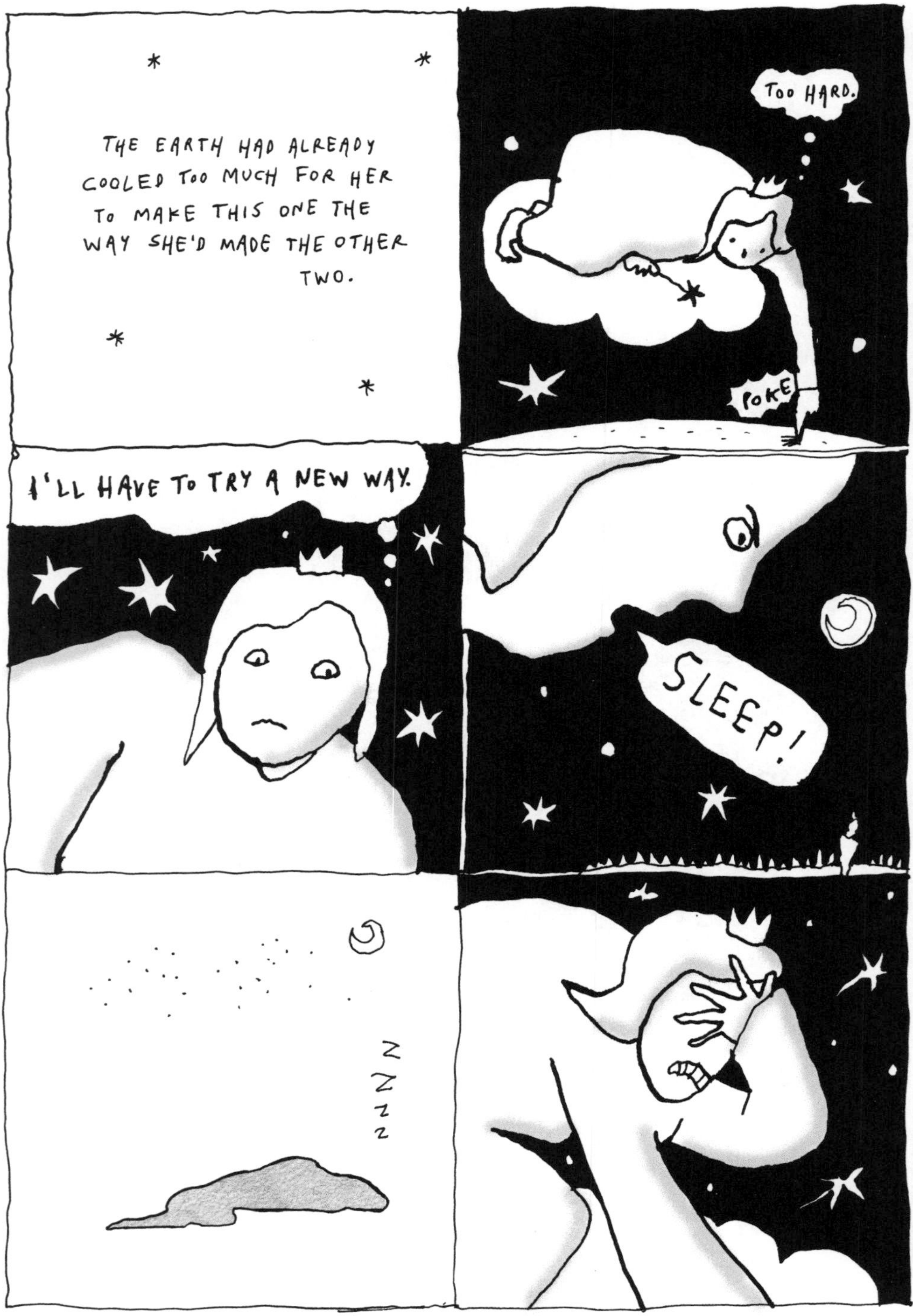
THE EARTH HAD ALREADY COOLED TOO MUCH FOR HER TO MAKE THIS ONE THE WAY SHE'D MADE THE OTHER TWO.
TOO HARD.
POKE
I'LL HAVE TO TRY A NEW WAY.
SLEEP!
Z Z Z Z

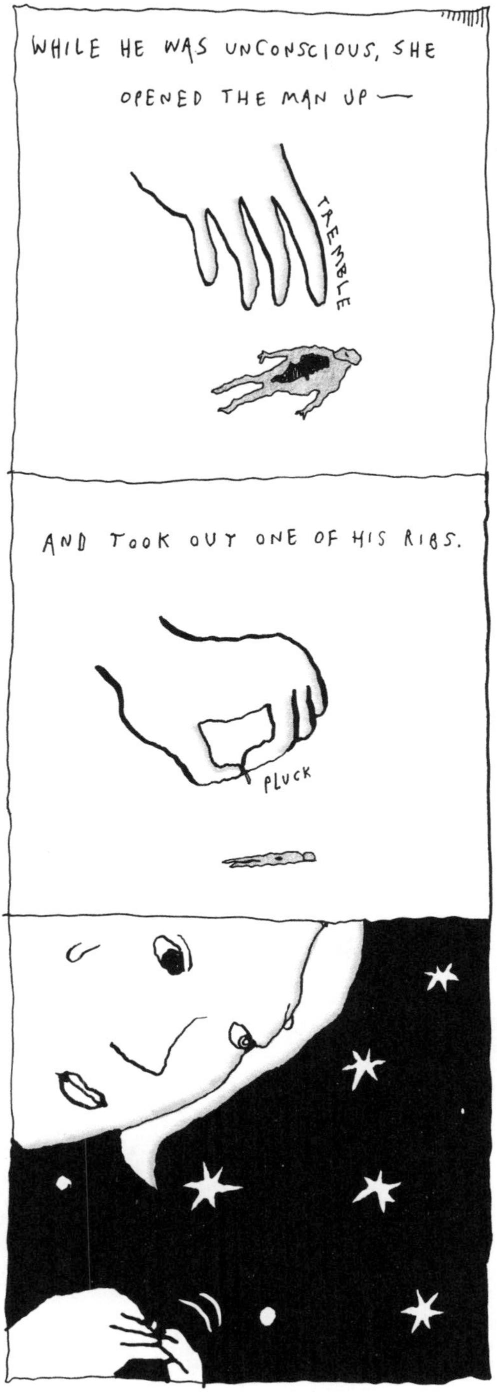
WHILE HE WAS UNCONSCIOUS, SHE OPENED THE MAN UP—
TREMBLE
AND TOOK OUT ONE OF HIS RIBS.
PLUCK

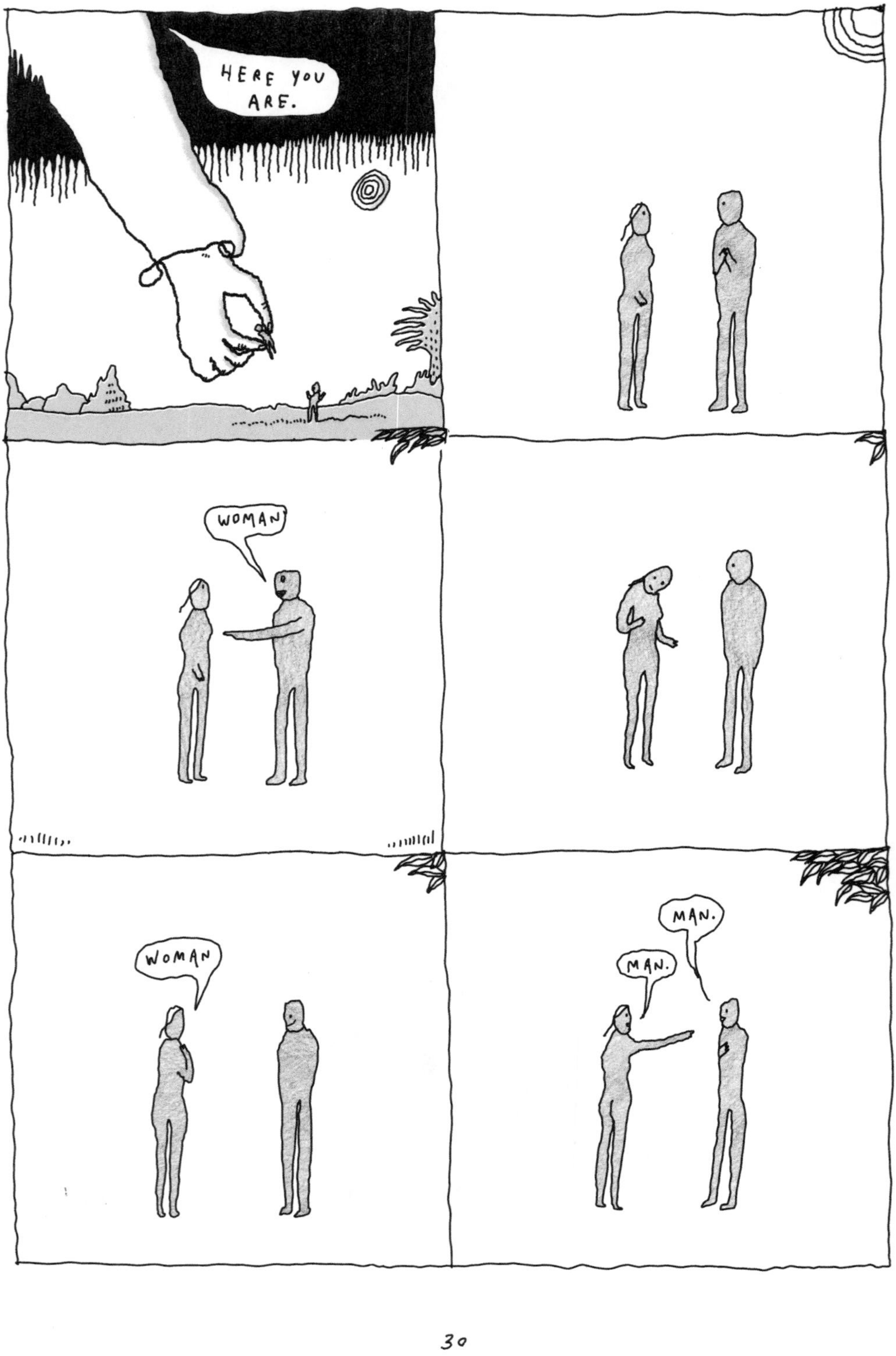
HERE YOU ARE.
WOMAN
WOMAN
MAN.
MAN.

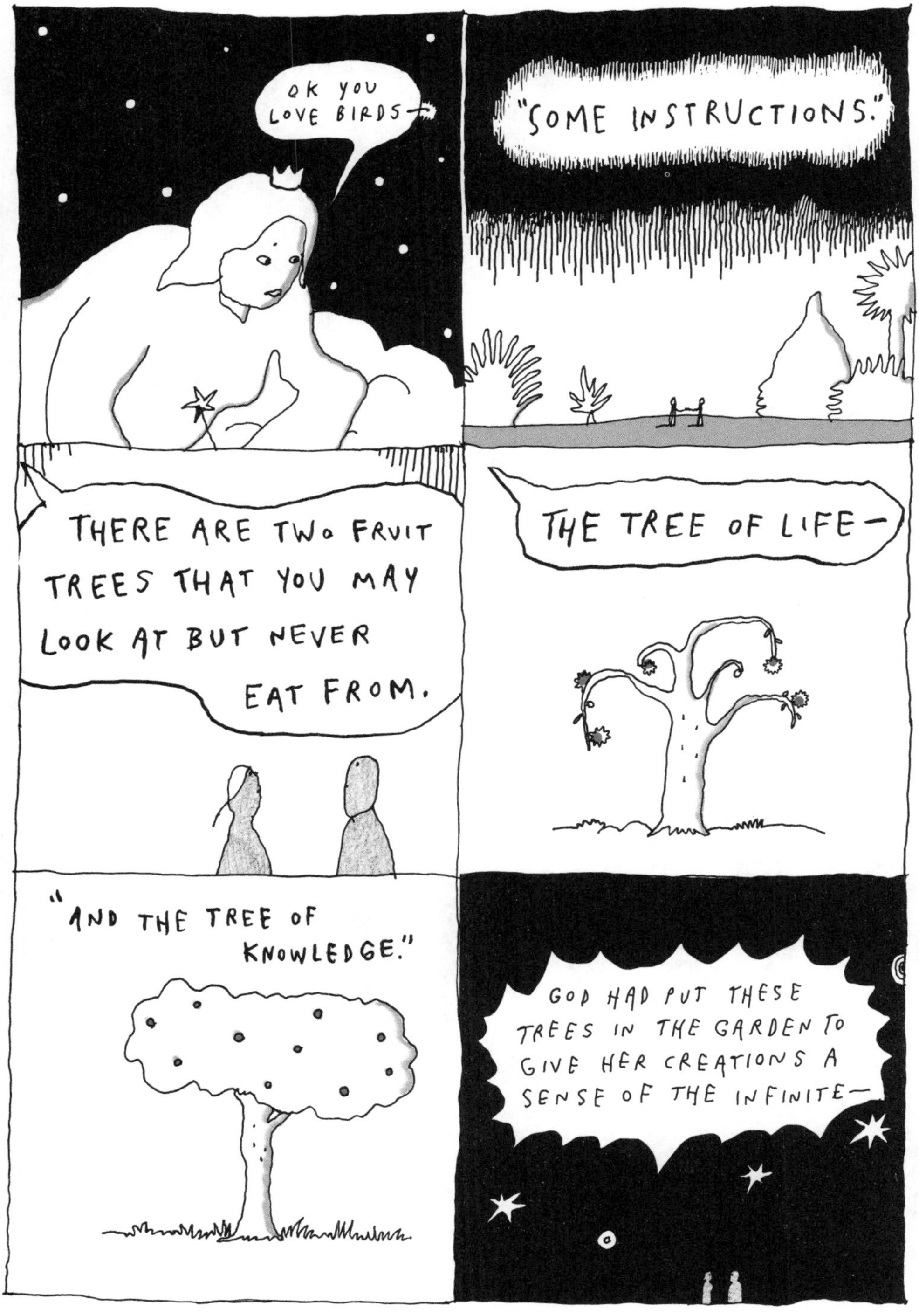
OK YOU LOVE BIRDS—
"SOME INSTRUCTIONS."
THERE ARE TWO FRUIT TREES THAT YOU MAY LOOK AT BUT NEVER EAT FROM.
THE TREE OF LIFE—
"AND THE TREE OF KNOWLEDGE."
GOD HAD PUT THESE TREES IN THE GARDEN TO GIVE HER CREATIONS A SENSE OF THE INFINITE—

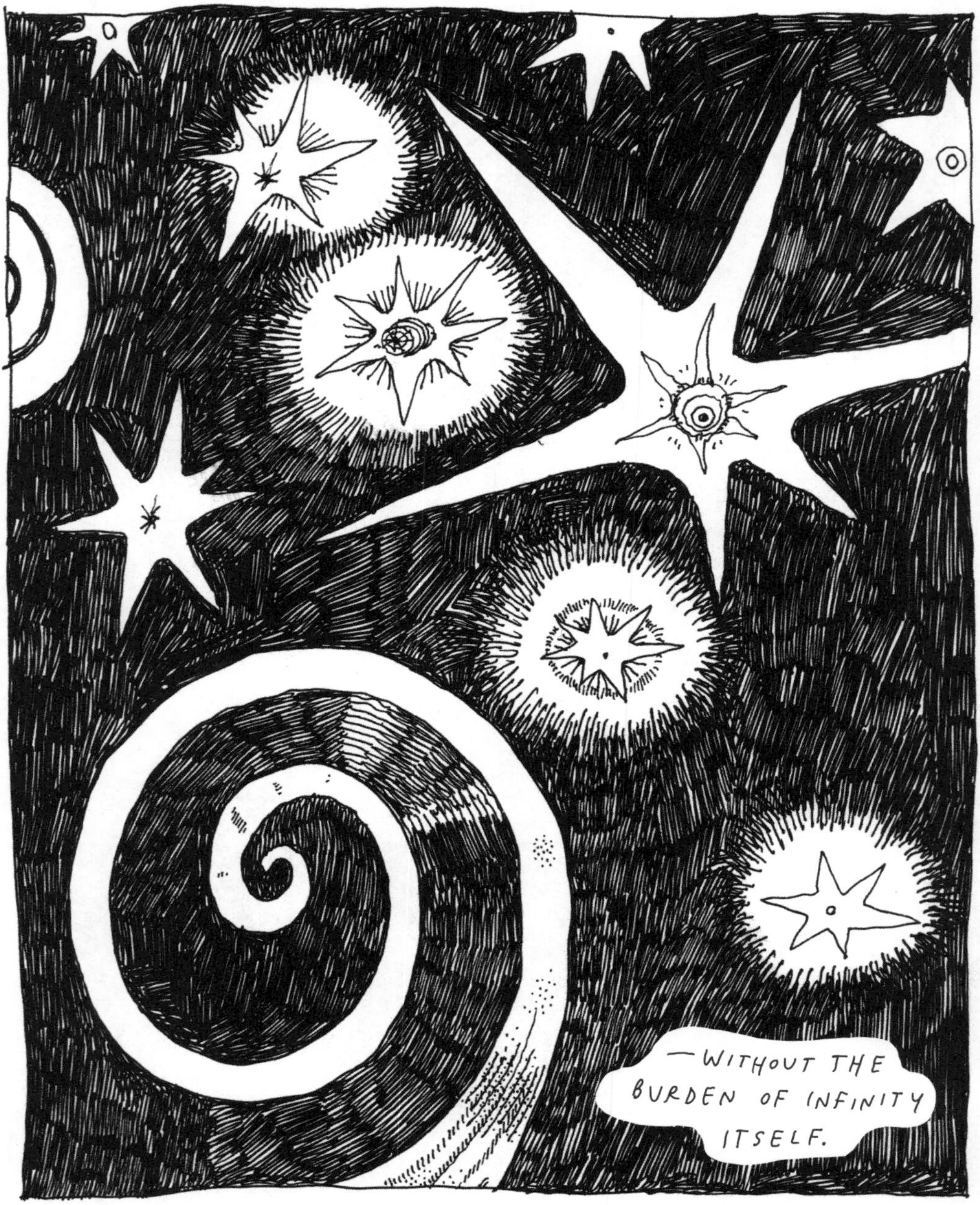
—WITHOUT THE
BURDEN OF INFINITY
ITSELF.

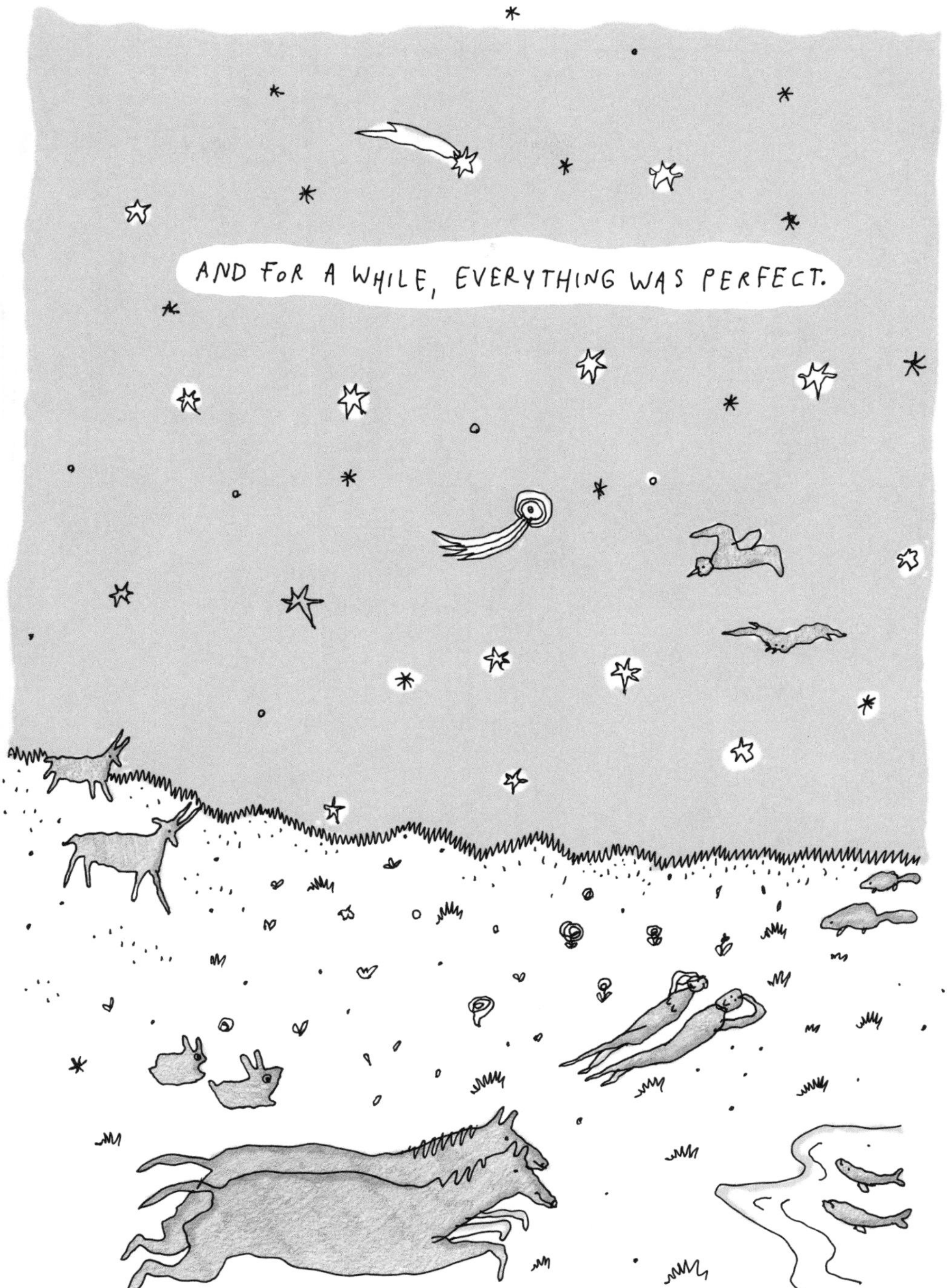
AND FOR A WHILE, EVERYTHING WAS PERFECT.

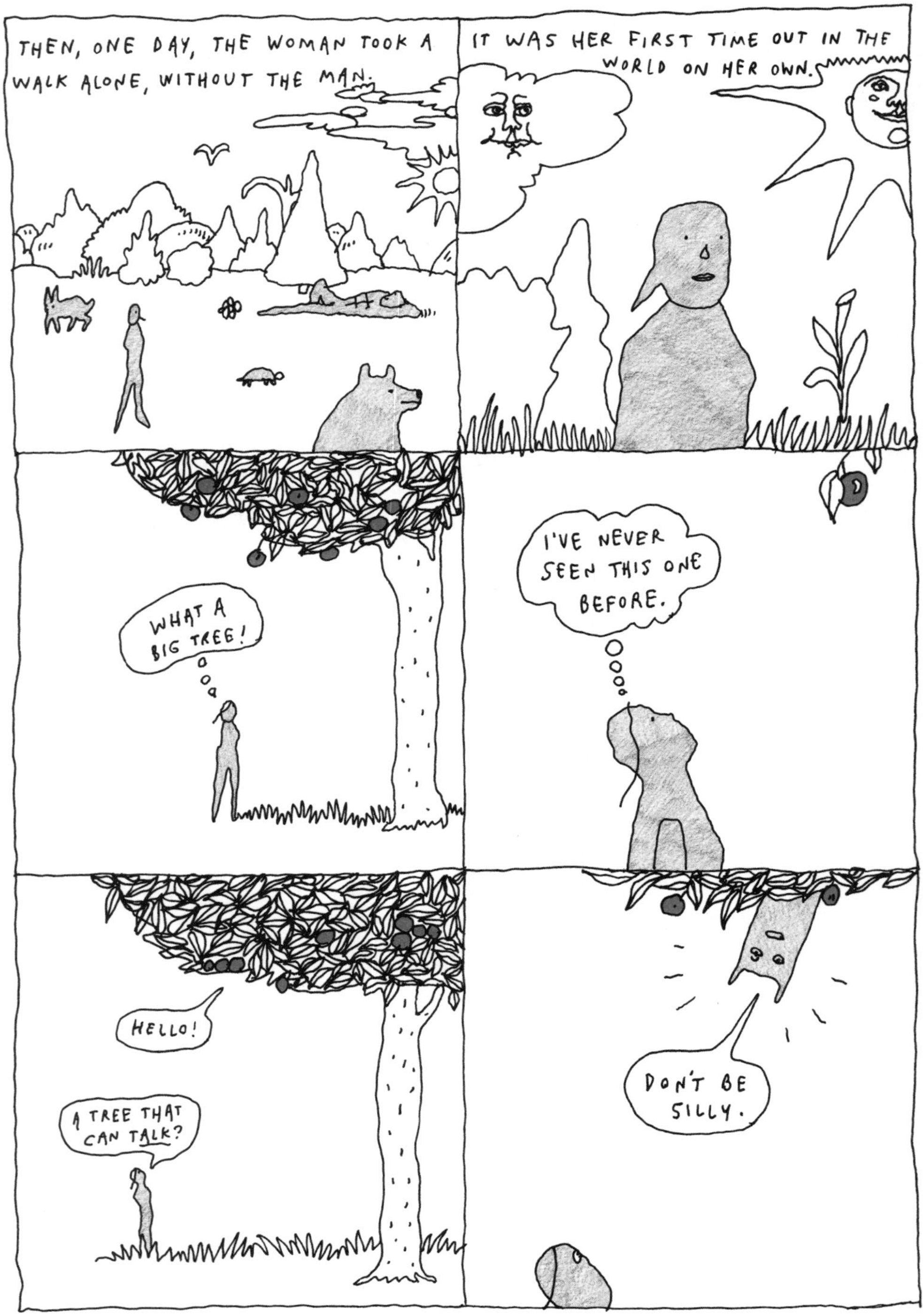
THEN, ONE DAY, THE WOMAN TOOK A WALK ALONE, WITHOUT THE MAN.
IT WAS HER FIRST TIME OUT IN THE WORLD ON HER OWN.
WHAT A BIG TREE!
I'VE NEVER SEEN THIS ONE BEFORE.
HELLO!
A TREE THAT CAN TALK?
DON'T BE SILLY.

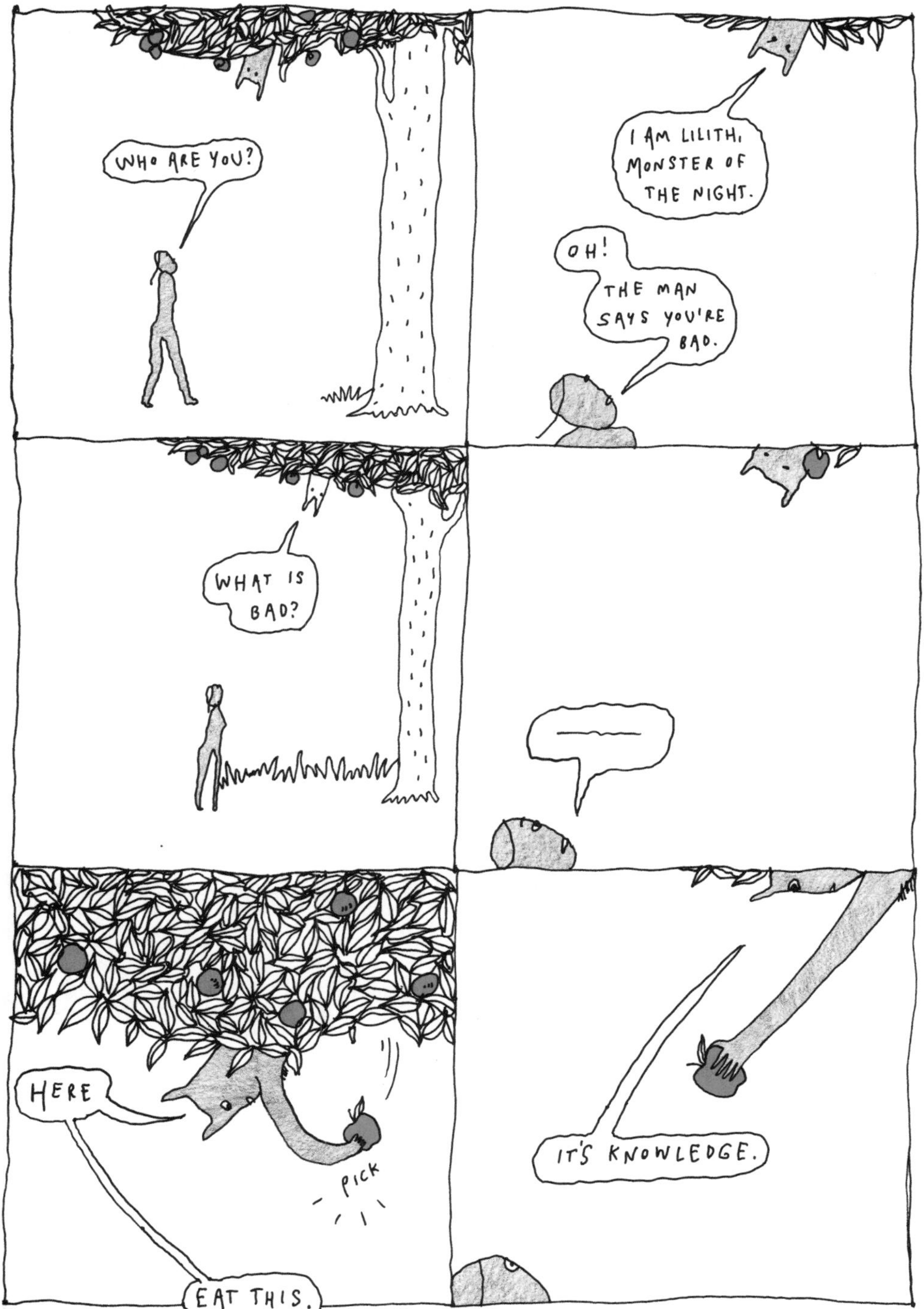
WHO ARE YOU?
I AM LILITH, MONSTER OF THE NIGHT.
OH!
THE MAN SAYS YOU'RE BAD.
WHAT IS BAD?
HERE
EAT THIS.
PICK
IT'S KNOWLEDGE.

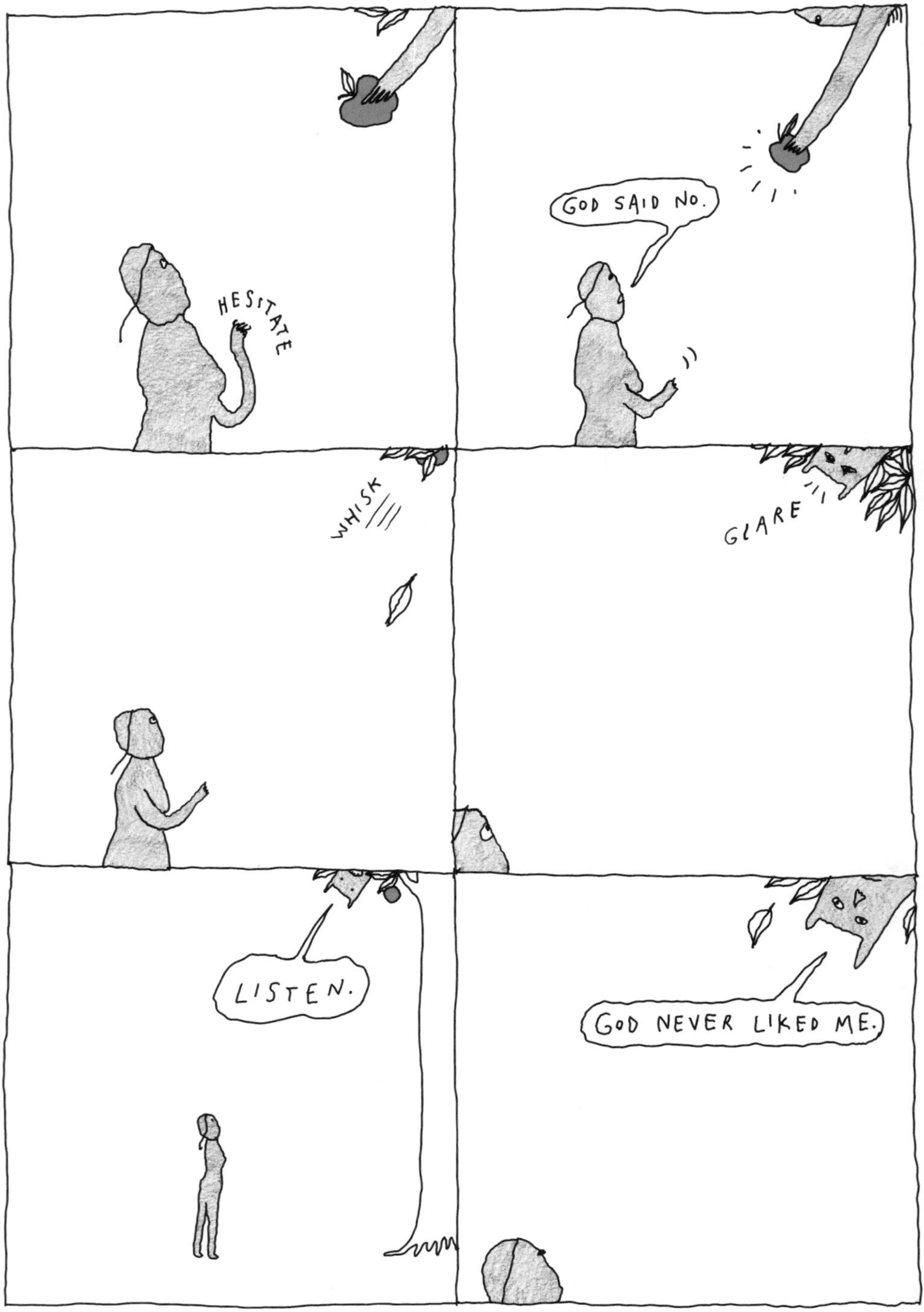
HESITATE
GOD SAID NO.
WHISK
GLARE
LISTEN.
GOD NEVER LIKED ME.

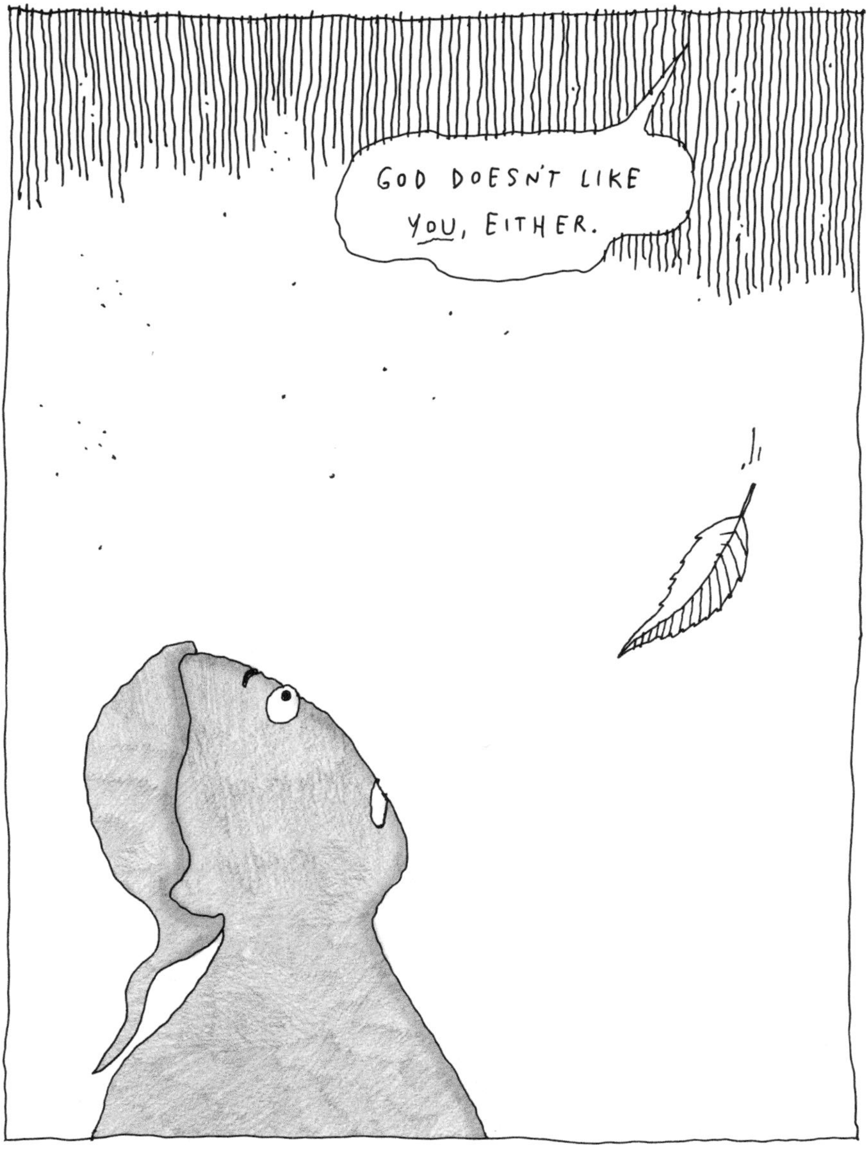
GOD DOESN'T LIKE YOU, EITHER.

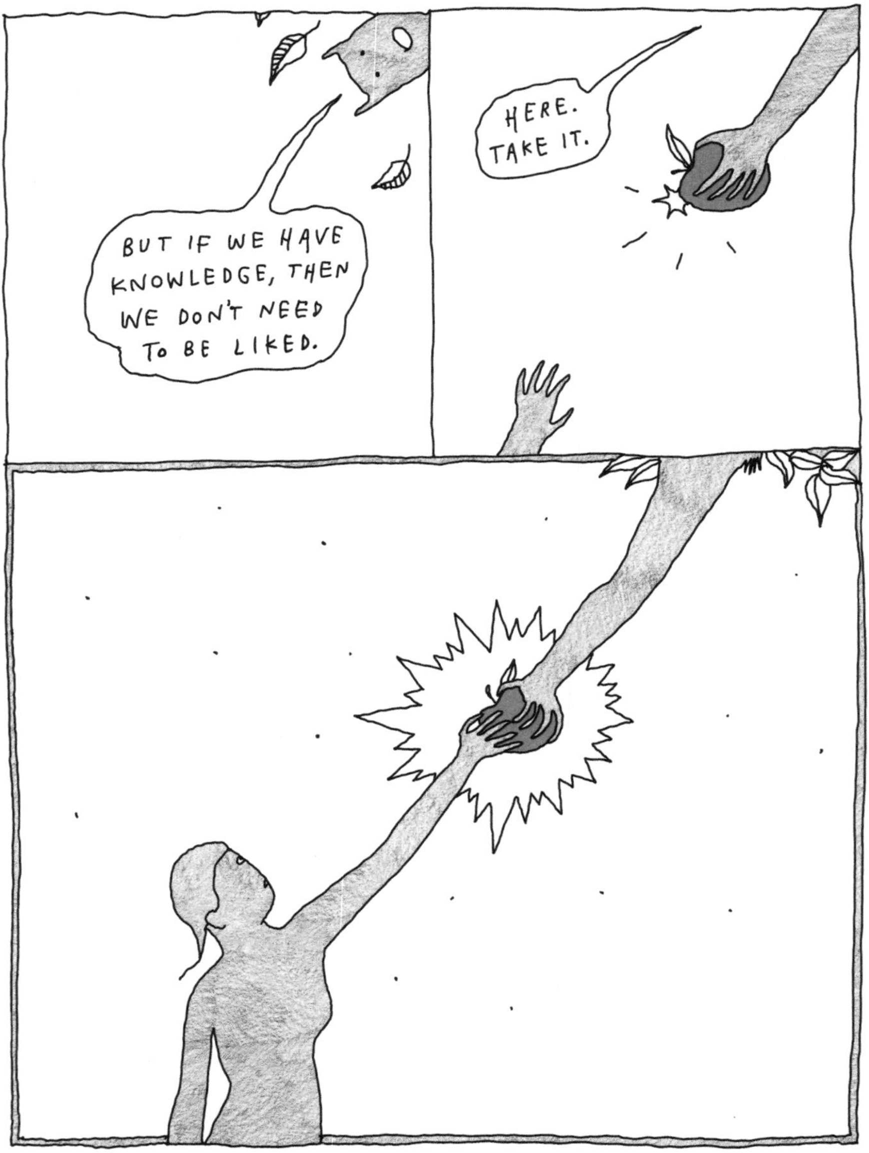
BUT IF WE HAVE KNOWLEDGE, THEN WE DON'T NEED TO BE LIKED.
HERE. TAKE IT.

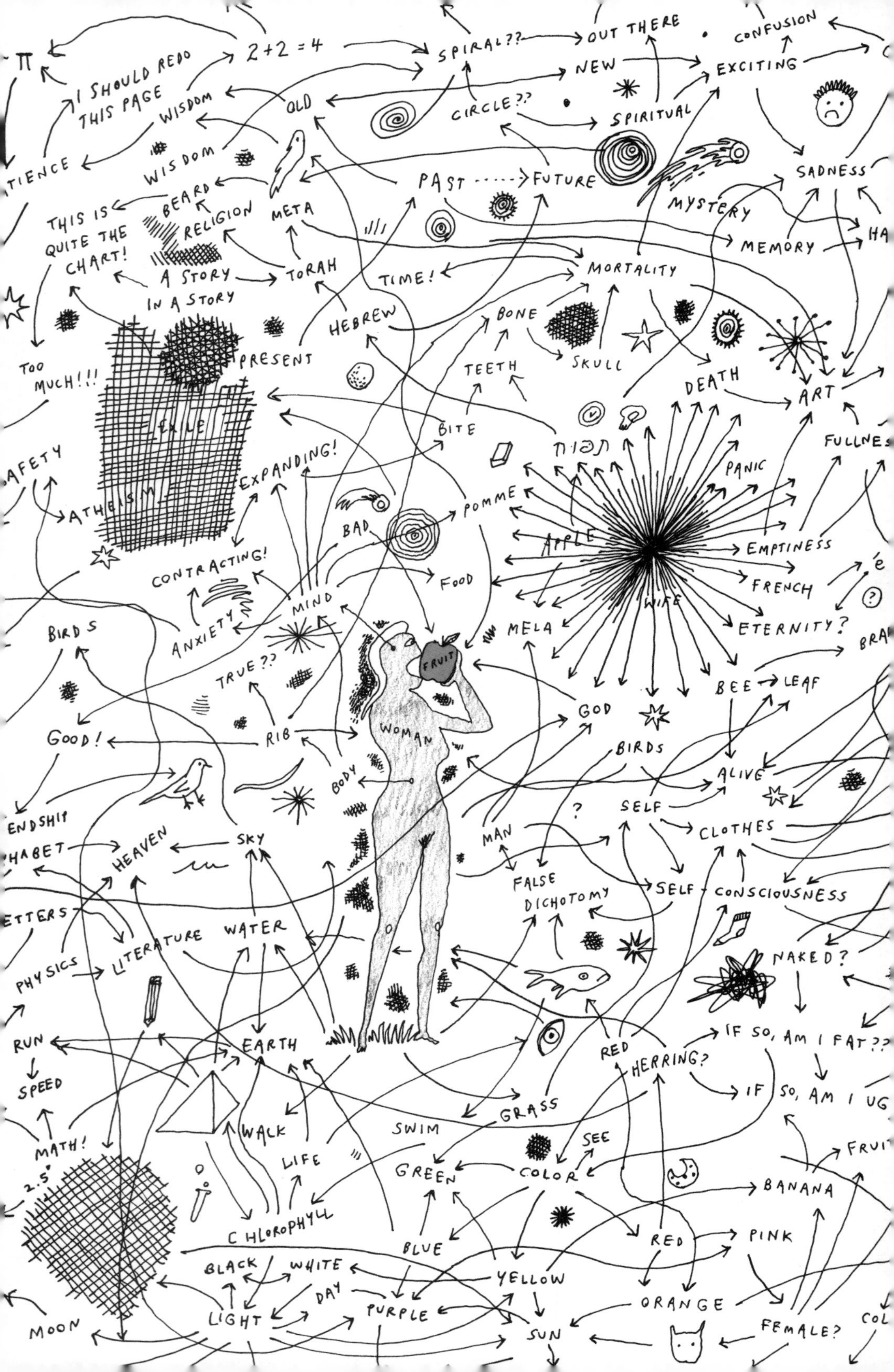
π
I SHOULD REDO THIS PAGE
2+2=4
SPIRAL??
OUT THERE
CONFUSION
NEW
EXCITING
OLD
WISDOM
CIRCLE??
SPIRITUAL
WISDOM
BEARD
THIS IS QUITE THE CHART!
RELIGION
META
PAST ----> FUTURE
MYSTERY
SADNESS
MEMORY
A STORY
IN A STORY
TORAH
TIME!
MORTALITY
HEBREW
BONE
TOO MUCH!!!
PRESENT
TEETH
SKULL
DEATH
ART
EXILE
BITE
תפוח
PANIC
EXPANDING!
ATHEISM
POMME
BAD
APPLE
EMPTINESS
CONTRACTING!
FOOD
FRENCH
é
?
MIND
WIFE
ETERNITY?
ANXIETY
MELA
BIRDS
TRUE??
FRUIT
BEE
LEAF
GOD
GOOD!
RIB
WOMAN
BIRDS
BODY
ALIVE
SELF
?
MAN
CLOTHES
HEAVEN
SKY
FALSE DICHOTOMY
SELF-CONSCIOUSNESS
LITERATURE
WATER
NAKED?
PHYSICS
RUN
EARTH
IF SO, AM I FAT??
SPEED
RED
HERRING?
GRASS
MATH!
SWIM
SEE
WALK
2.5°
LIFE
GREEN
COLOR
BANANA
CHLOROPHYLL
BLUE
RED
PINK
BLACK
WHITE
YELLOW
DAY
ORANGE
LIGHT
PURPLE
MOON
SUN
FEMALE?

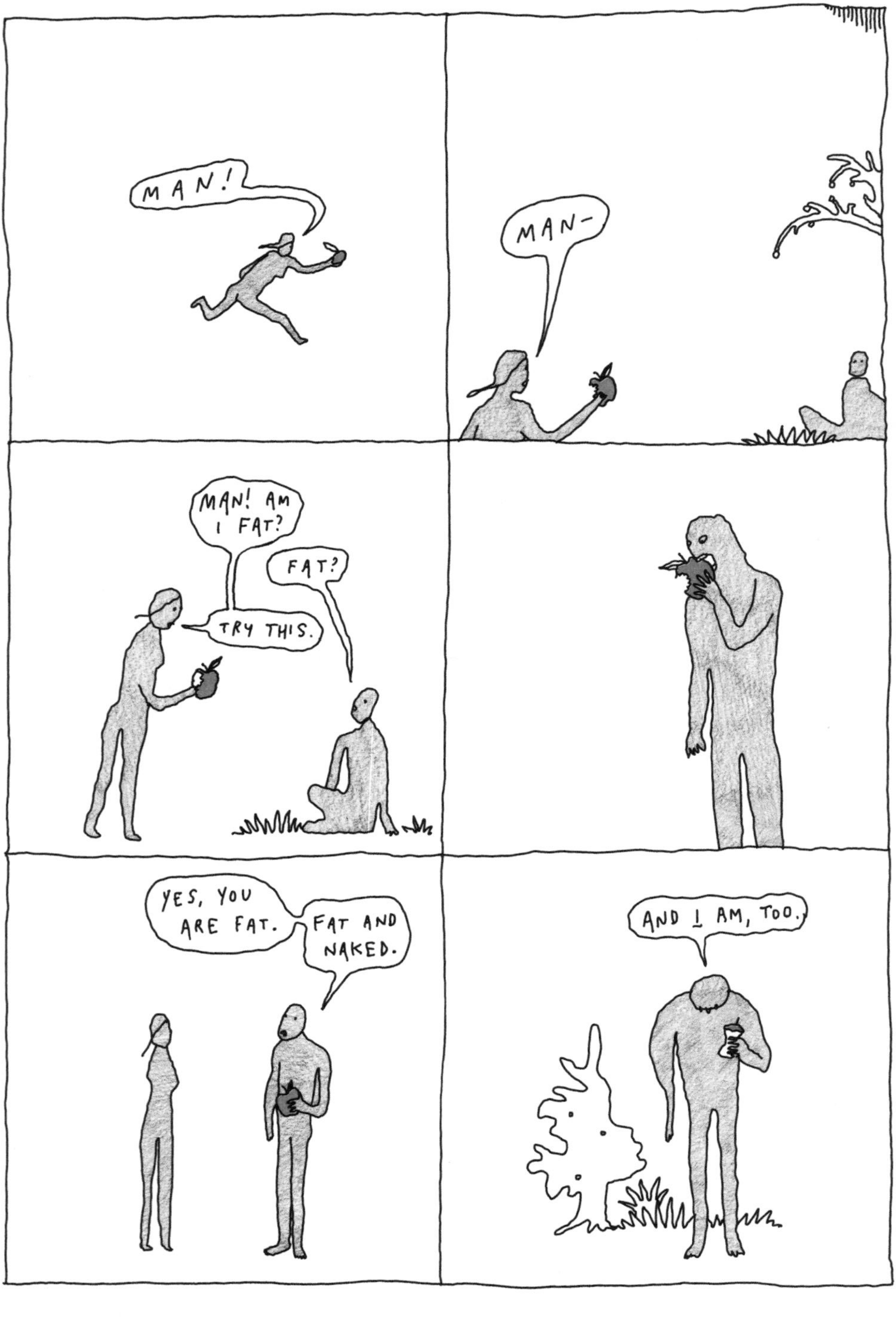
MAN!
MAN-
MAN! AM I FAT?
TRY THIS.
FAT?
YES, YOU ARE FAT.
FAT AND NAKED.
AND I AM, TOO.

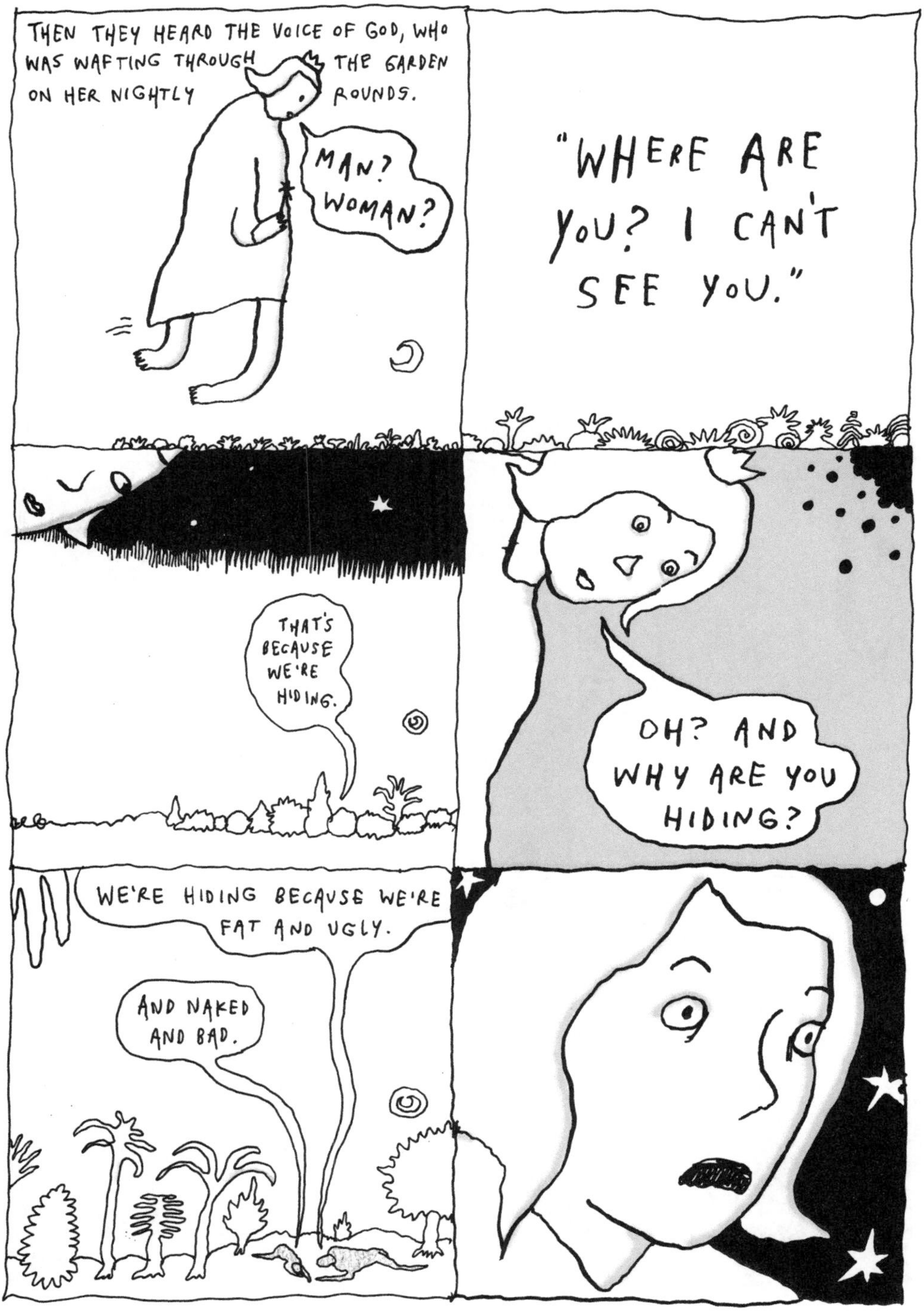
THEN THEY HEARD THE VOICE OF GOD, WHO WAS WAFTING THROUGH THE GARDEN ON HER NIGHTLY ROUNDS.
MAN? WOMAN?
"WHERE ARE YOU? I CAN'T SEE YOU."
THAT'S BECAUSE WE'RE HIDING.
OH? AND WHY ARE YOU HIDING?
WE'RE HIDING BECAUSE WE'RE FAT AND UGLY.
AND NAKED AND BAD.

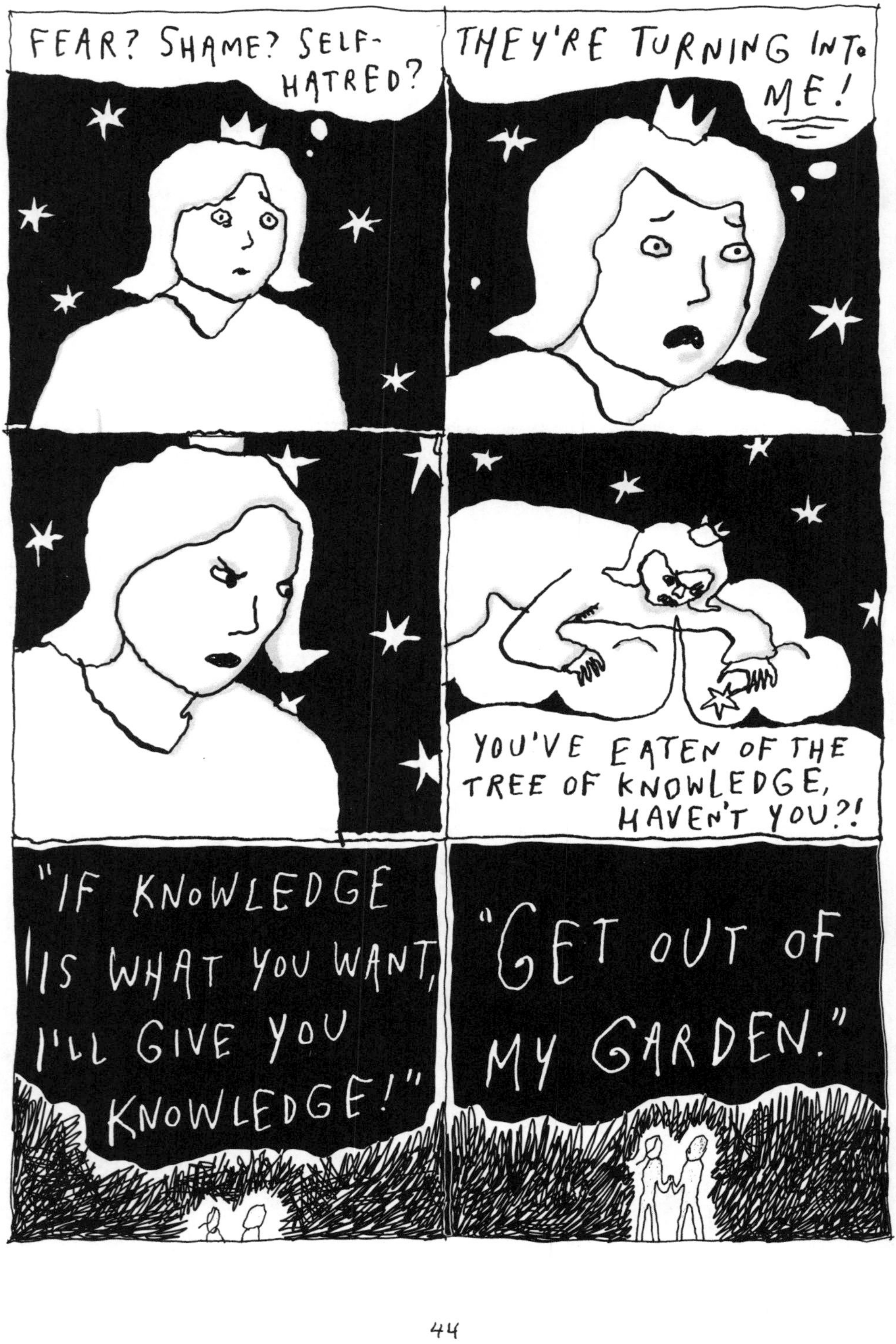
FEAR? SHAME? SELF-HATRED?
THEY'RE TURNING INTO ME!
YOU'VE EATEN OF THE TREE OF KNOWLEDGE, HAVEN'T YOU?!
"IF KNOWLEDGE IS WHAT YOU WANT, I'LL GIVE YOU KNOWLEDGE!"
"GET OUT OF MY GARDEN."

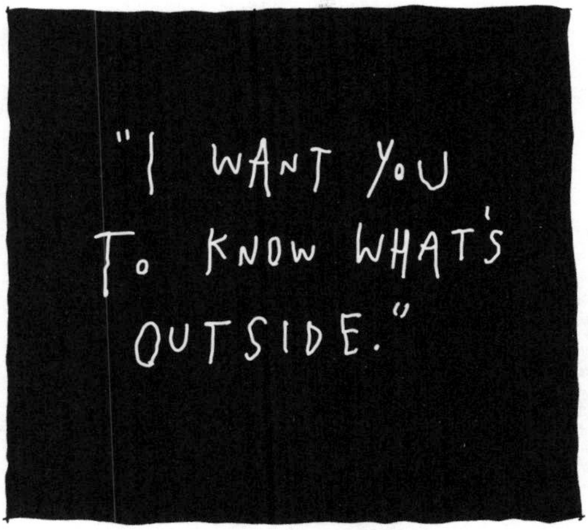
"I WANT YOU TO KNOW WHAT'S OUTSIDE."

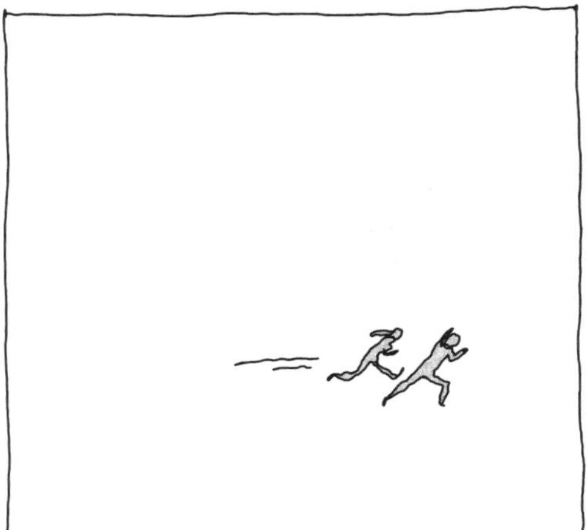

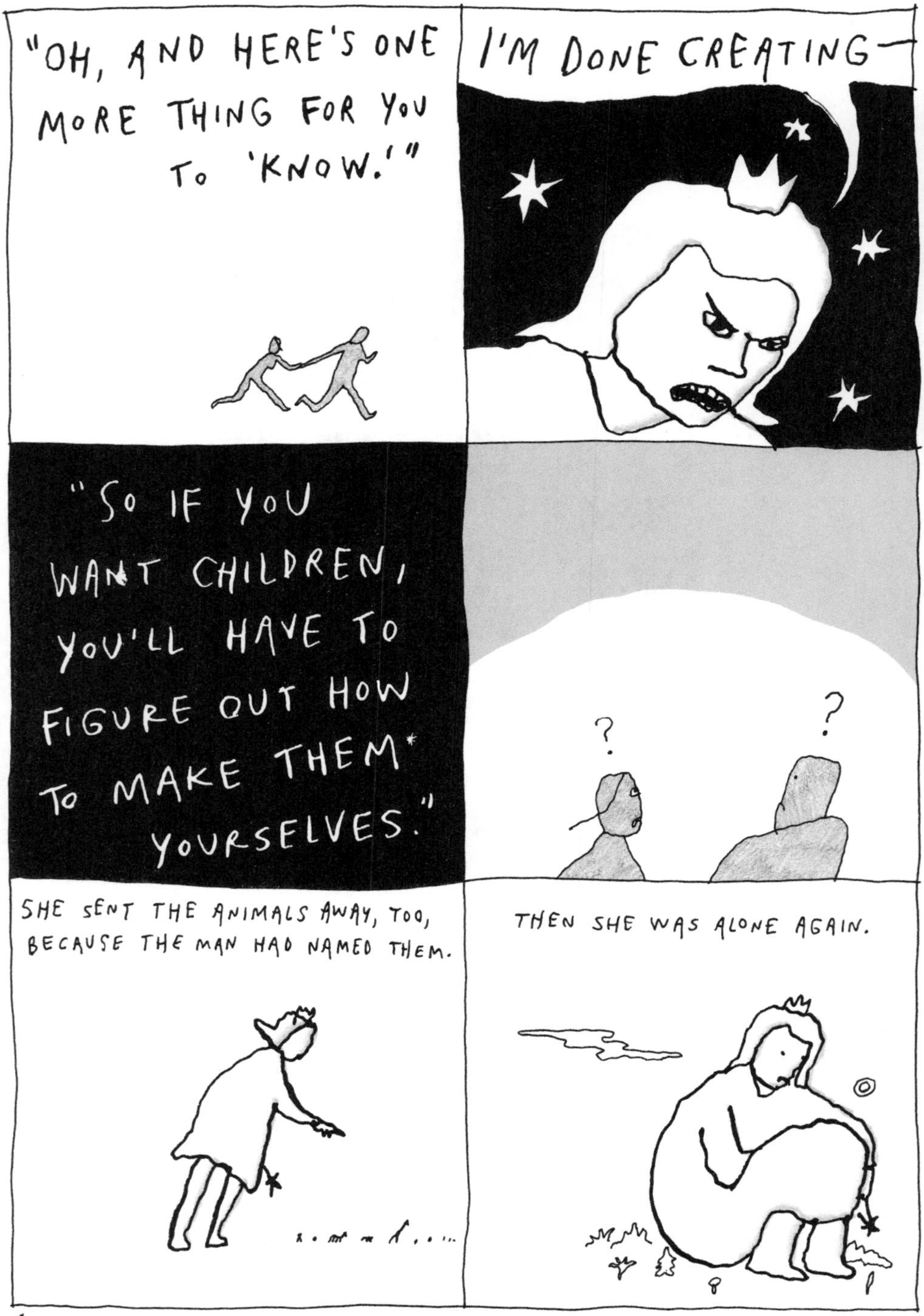
"OH, AND HERE'S ONE MORE THING FOR YOU TO 'KNOW.'"
I'M DONE CREATING—
"SO IF YOU WANT CHILDREN, YOU'LL HAVE TO FIGURE OUT HOW TO MAKE THEM* YOURSELVES."
? ?
SHE SENT THE ANIMALS AWAY, TOO, BECAUSE THE MAN HAD NAMED THEM.
THEN SHE WAS ALONE AGAIN.

*THE WORD FOR SEX IN THE TORAH IS "TO KNOW."

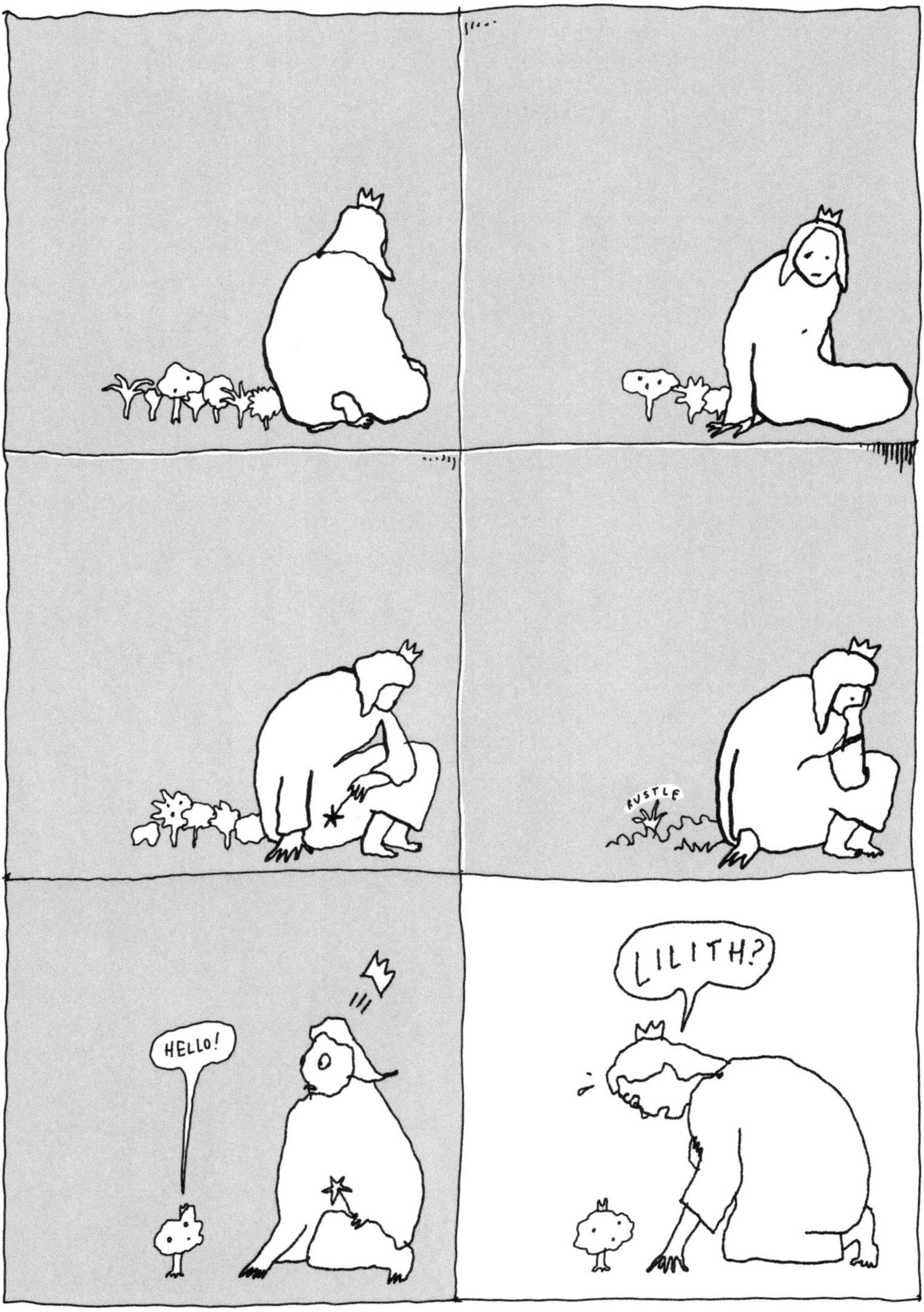
RUSTLE
HELLO!
LILITH?

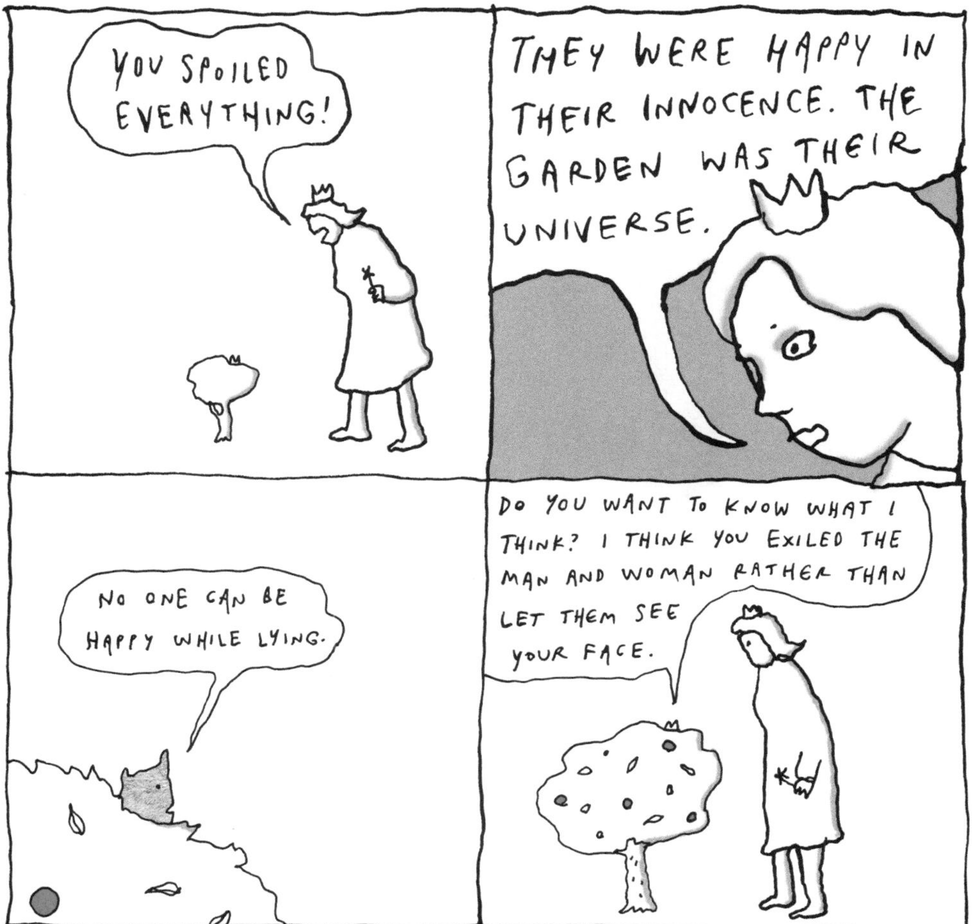
YOU SPOILED EVERYTHING!
THEY WERE HAPPY IN THEIR INNOCENCE. THE GARDEN WAS THEIR UNIVERSE.
NO ONE CAN BE HAPPY WHILE LYING.
DO YOU WANT TO KNOW WHAT I THINK? I THINK YOU EXILED THE MAN AND WOMAN RATHER THAN LET THEM SEE YOUR FACE.

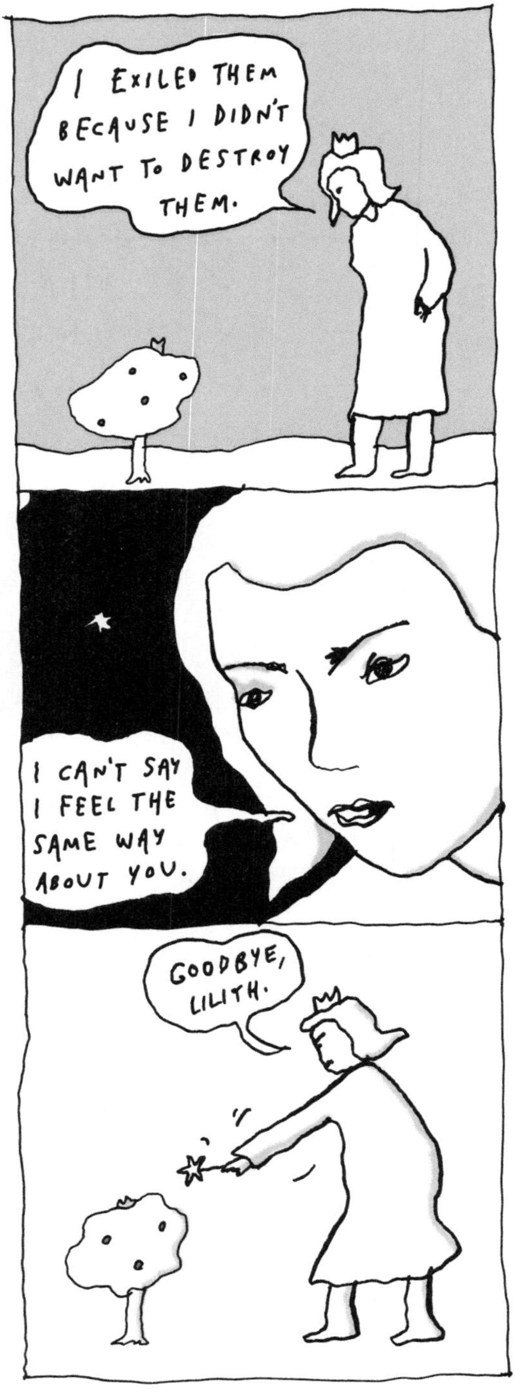
I EXILED THEM BECAUSE I DIDN'T WANT TO DESTROY THEM.
I CAN'T SAY I FEEL THE SAME WAY ABOUT YOU.
GOODBYE, LILITH.

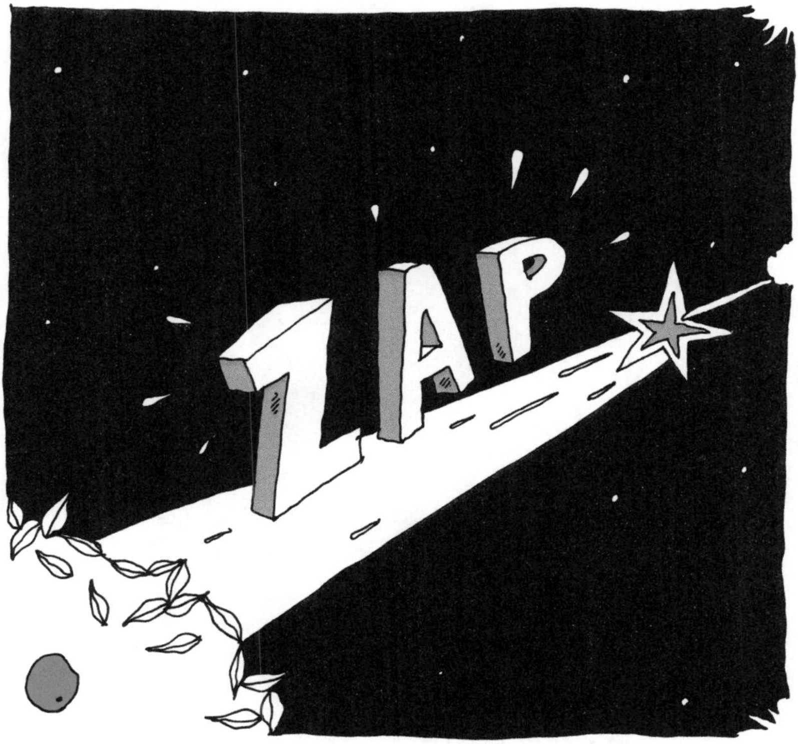
ZAP

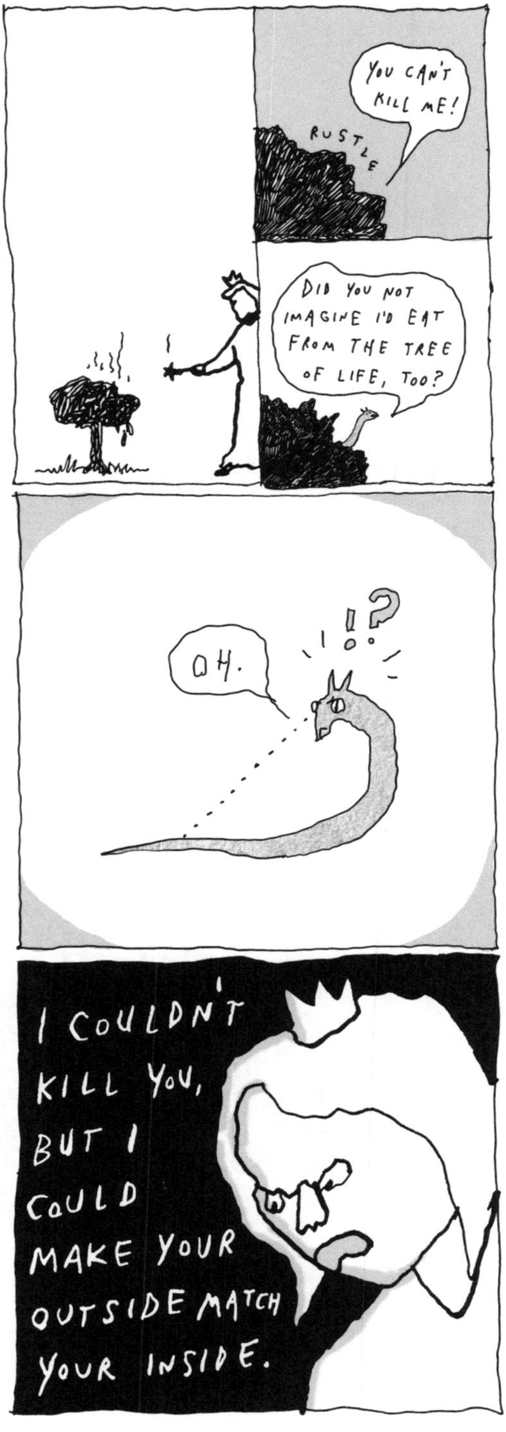
YOU CAN'T KILL ME!
RUSTLE
DID YOU NOT IMAGINE I'D EAT FROM THE TREE OF LIFE, TOO?
OH.
!?
I COULDN'T KILL YOU, BUT I COULD MAKE YOUR OUTSIDE MATCH YOUR INSIDE.

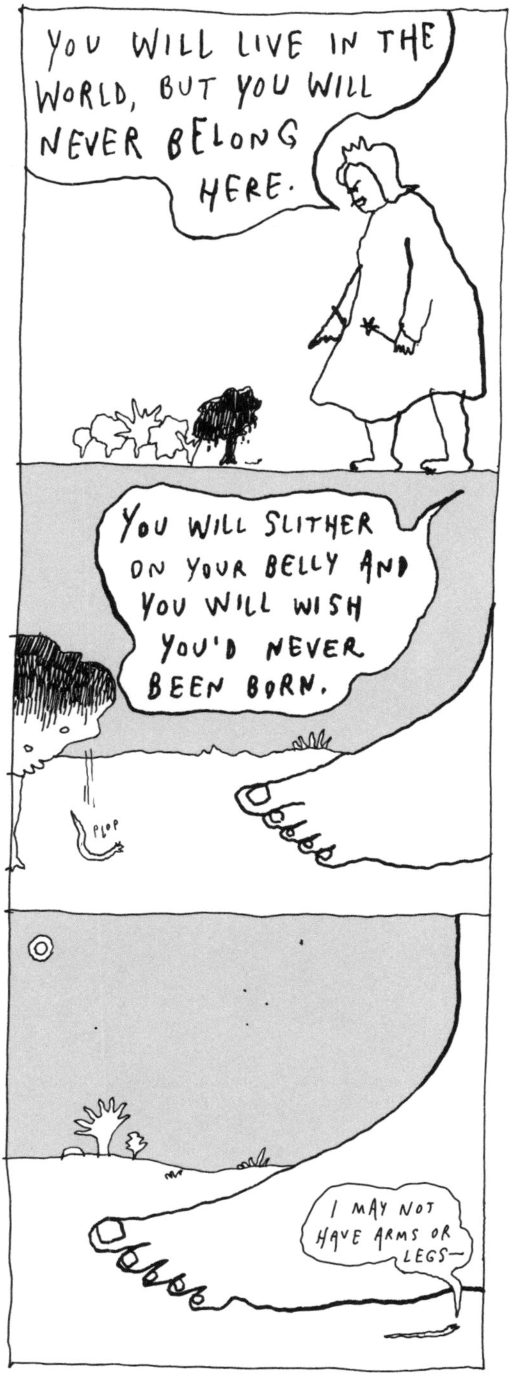
YOU WILL LIVE IN THE WORLD, BUT YOU WILL NEVER BELONG HERE.
YOU WILL SLITHER ON YOUR BELLY AND YOU WILL WISH YOU'D NEVER BEEN BORN.
PLOP
I MAY NOT HAVE ARMS OR LEGS—

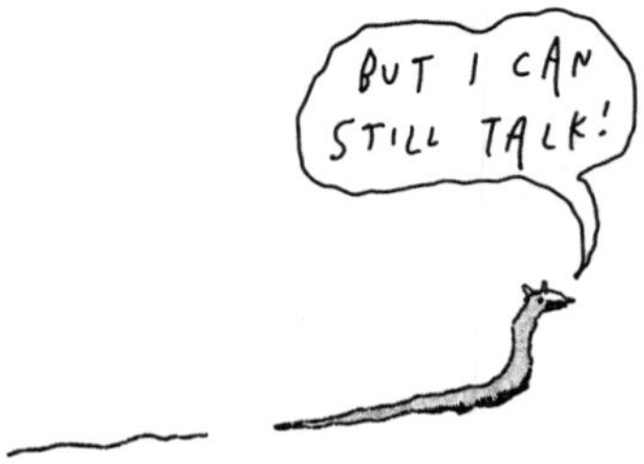
BUT I CAN
STILL TALK!

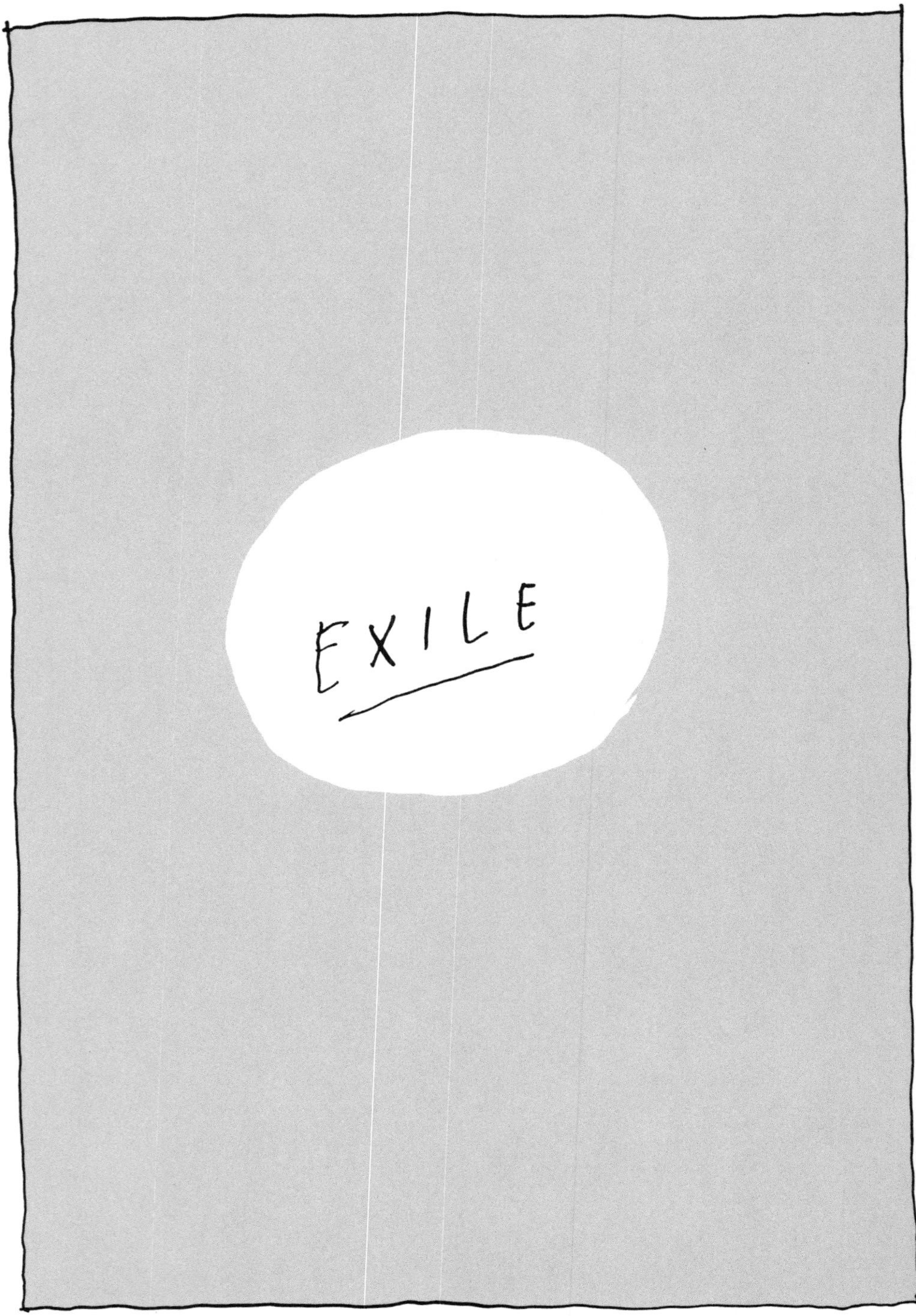
EXILE

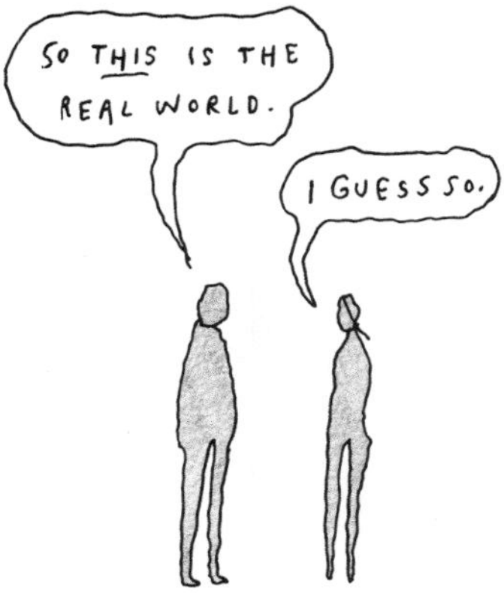
SO THIS IS THE REAL WORLD.
I GUESS SO.

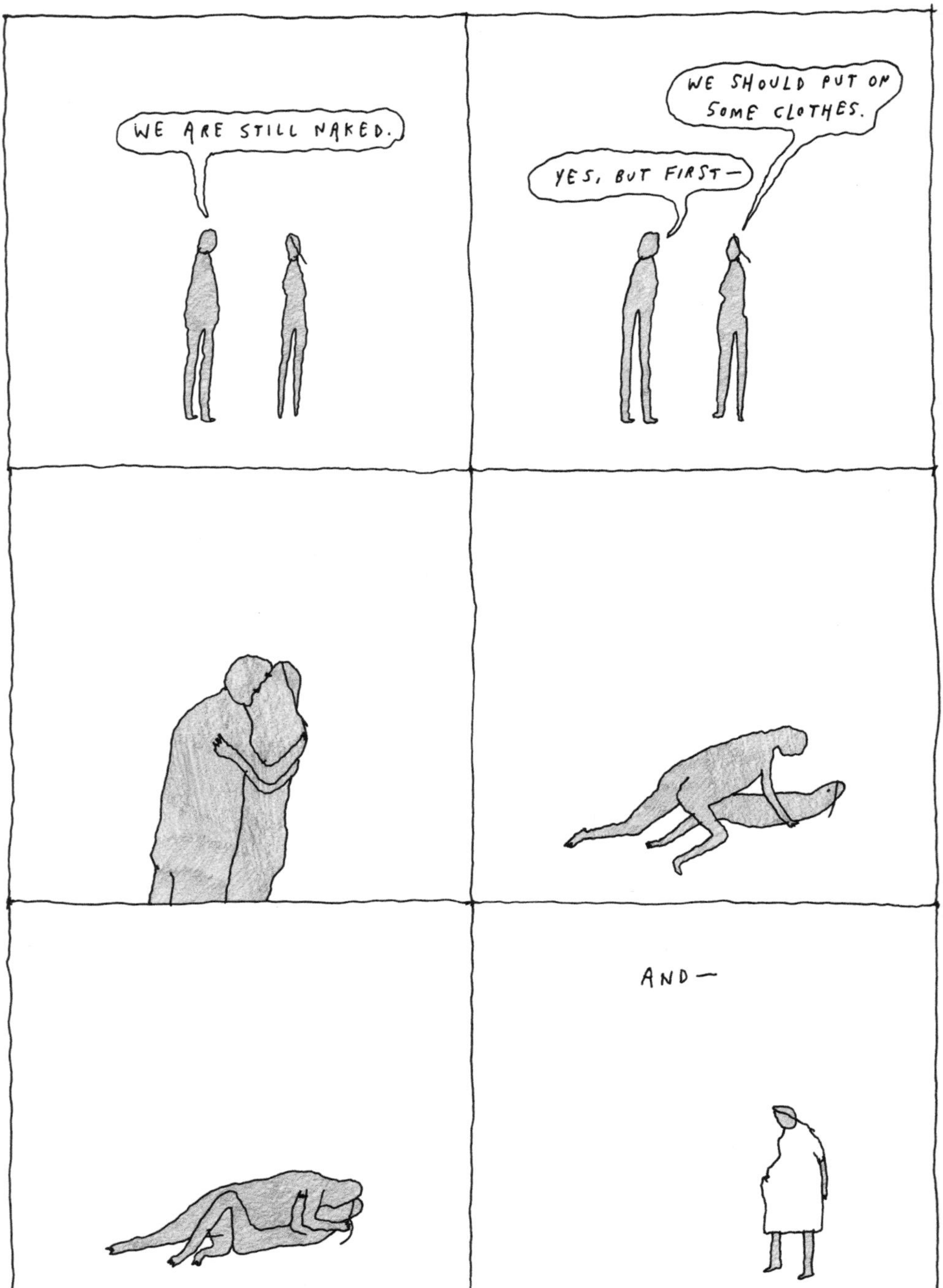
WE ARE STILL NAKED.
WE SHOULD PUT ON SOME CLOTHES.
YES, BUT FIRST—
AND—

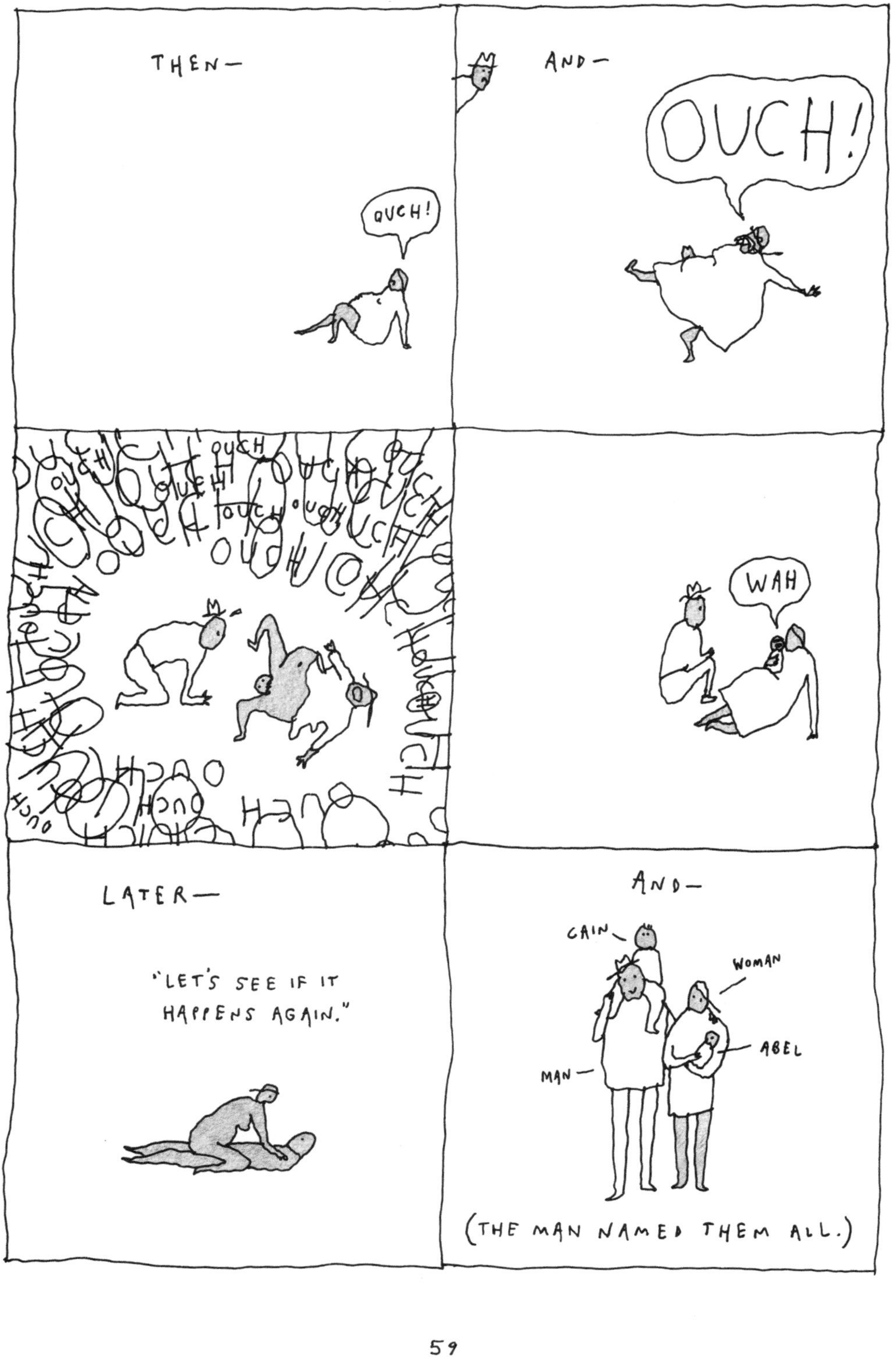
THEN—
OUCH!
AND—
OUCH!
WAH
LATER—
"LET'S SEE IF IT HAPPENS AGAIN."
AND—
CAIN
WOMAN
ABEL
MAN
(THE MAN NAMED THEM ALL.)

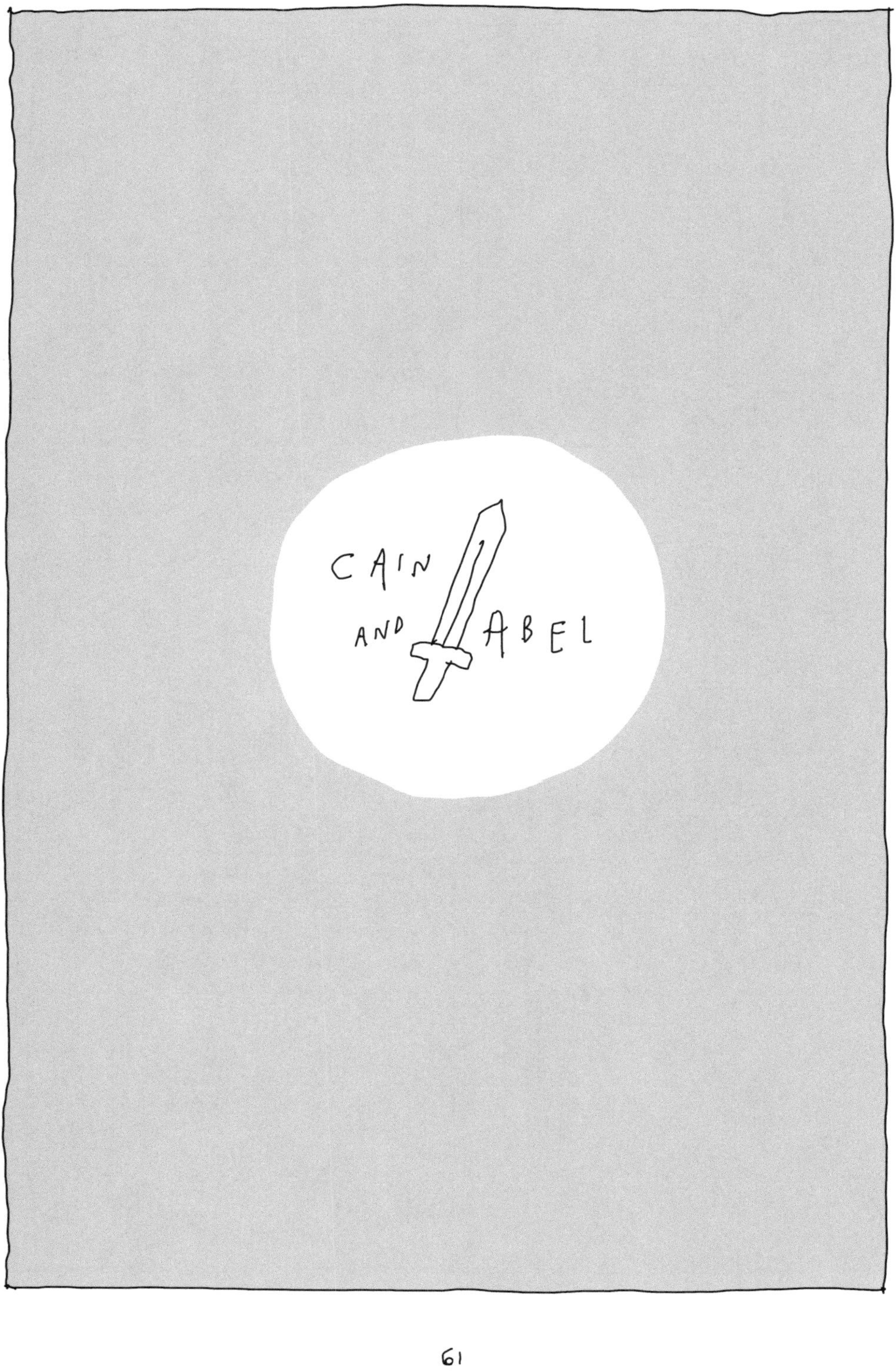
CAIN
AND ABEL

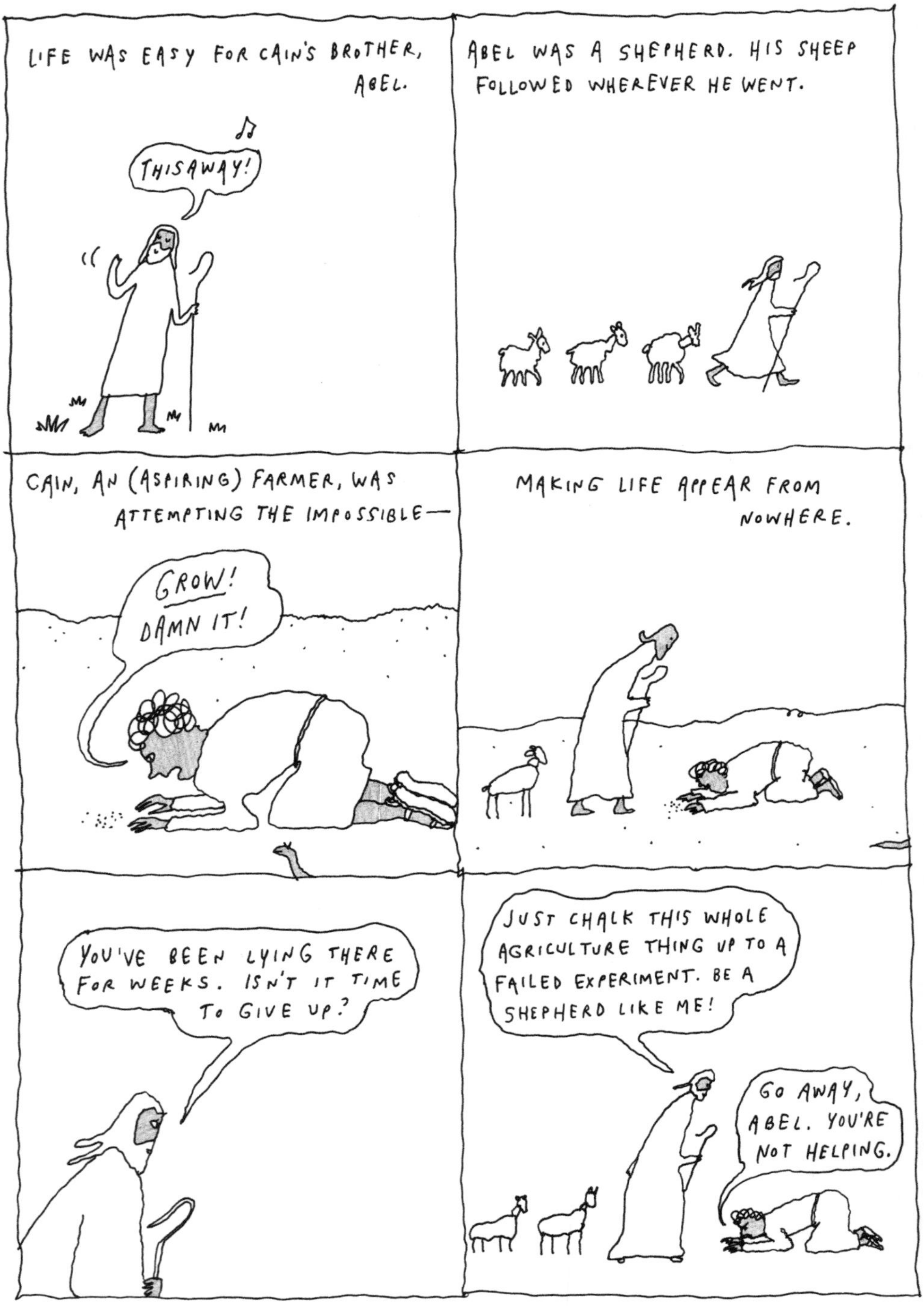
LIFE WAS EASY FOR CAIN'S BROTHER, ABEL.
THISAWAY!
ABEL WAS A SHEPHERD. HIS SHEEP FOLLOWED WHEREVER HE WENT.
CAIN, AN (ASPIRING) FARMER, WAS ATTEMPTING THE IMPOSSIBLE—
GROW! DAMN IT!
MAKING LIFE APPEAR FROM NOWHERE.
YOU'VE BEEN LYING THERE FOR WEEKS. ISN'T IT TIME TO GIVE UP?
JUST CHALK THIS WHOLE AGRICULTURE THING UP TO A FAILED EXPERIMENT. BE A SHEPHERD LIKE ME!
GO AWAY, ABEL. YOU'RE NOT HELPING.

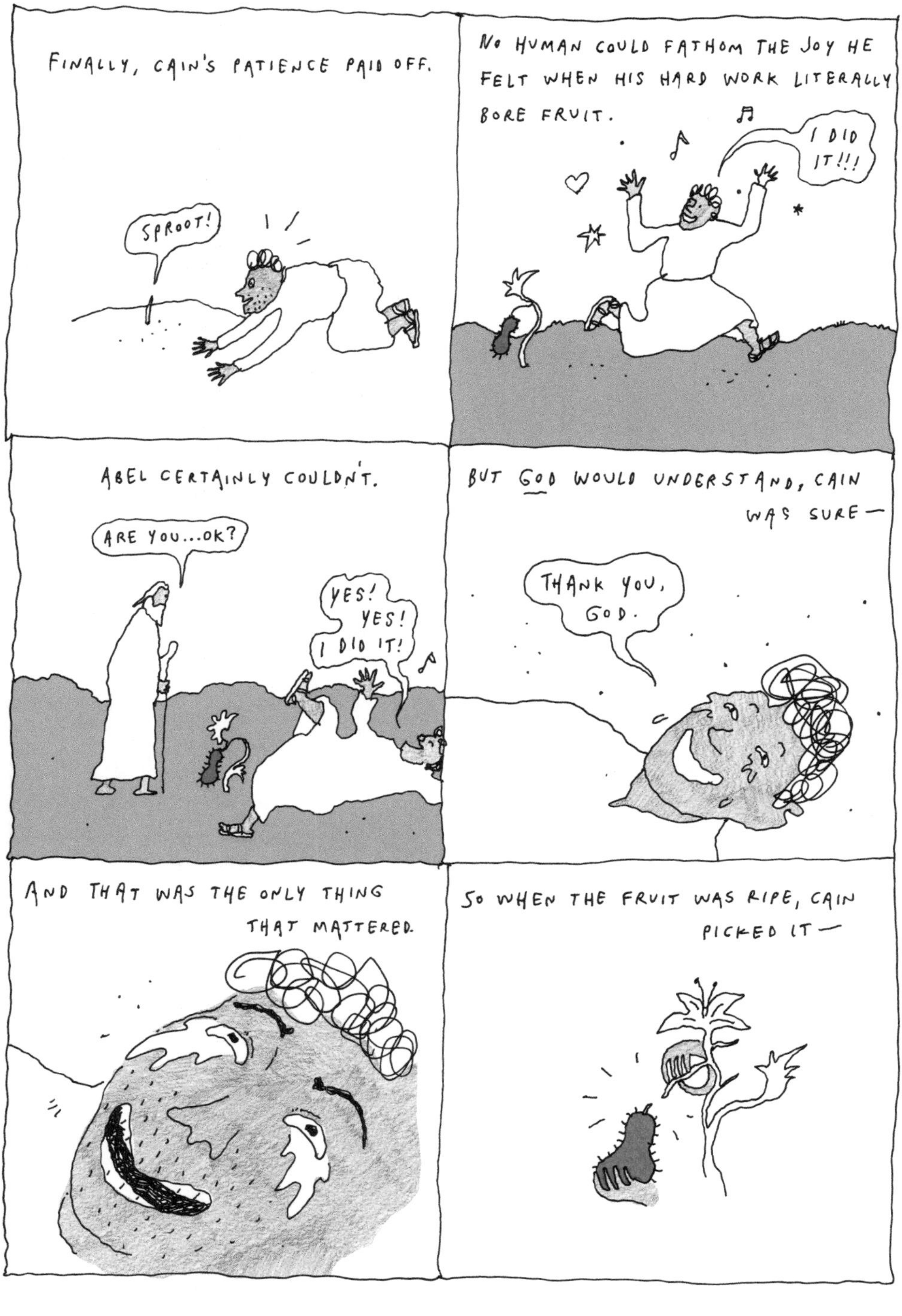
FINALLY, CAIN'S PATIENCE PAID OFF.
SPROOT!
NO HUMAN COULD FATHOM THE JOY HE FELT WHEN HIS HARD WORK LITERALLY BORE FRUIT.
I DID IT!!!
ABEL CERTAINLY COULDN'T.
ARE YOU...OK?
YES! YES! I DID IT!
BUT GOD WOULD UNDERSTAND, CAIN WAS SURE—
THANK YOU, GOD.
AND THAT WAS THE ONLY THING THAT MATTERED.
SO WHEN THE FRUIT WAS RIPE, CAIN PICKED IT—

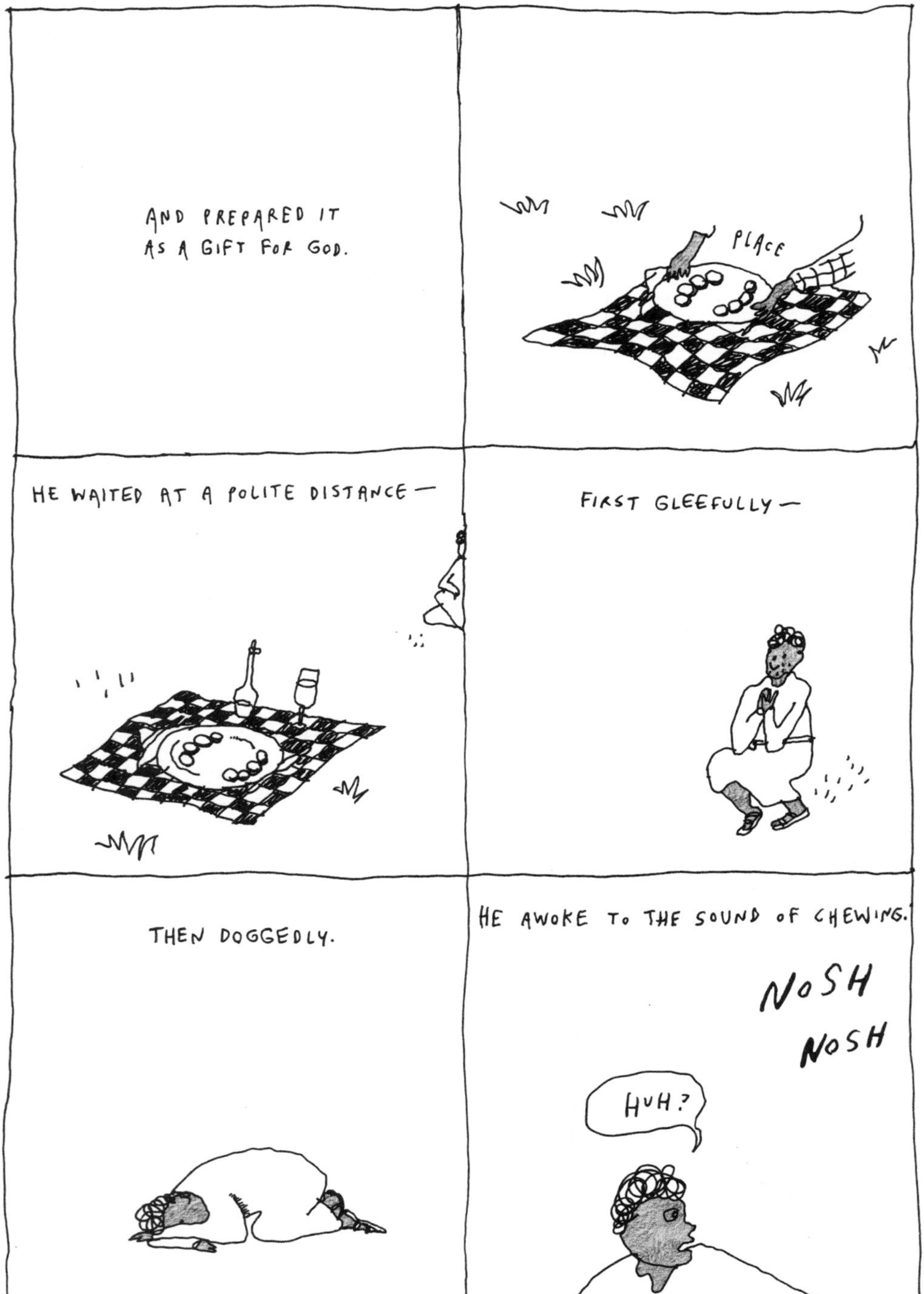
AND PREPARED IT
AS A GIFT FOR GOD.
PLACE
HE WAITED AT A POLITE DISTANCE—
FIRST GLEEFULLY—
THEN DOGGEDLY.
HE AWOKE TO THE SOUND OF CHEWING.
NOSH
NOSH
HUH?

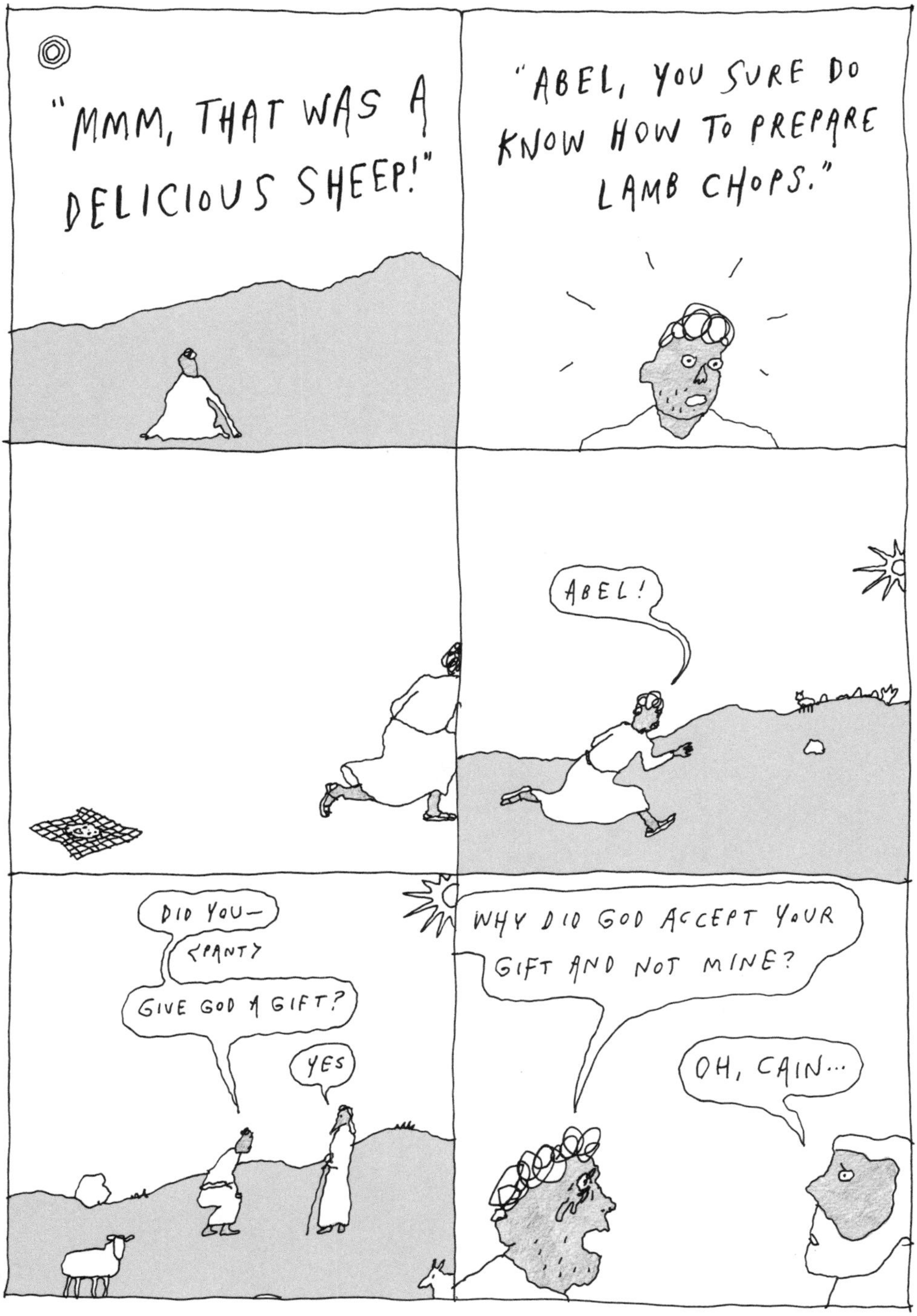
"MMM, THAT WAS A DELICIOUS SHEEP!"
"ABEL, YOU SURE DO KNOW HOW TO PREPARE LAMB CHOPS."
ABEL!
DID YOU—
<PANT>
GIVE GOD A GIFT?
YES
WHY DID GOD ACCEPT YOUR GIFT AND NOT MINE?
OH, CAIN...

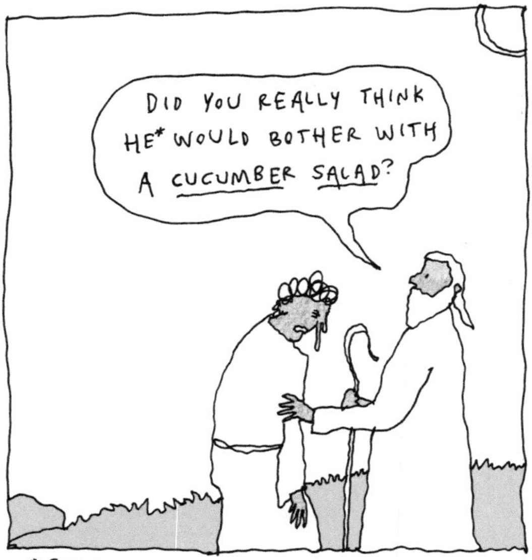
DID YOU REALLY THINK HE* WOULD BOTHER WITH A CUCUMBER SALAD?

*GRRR

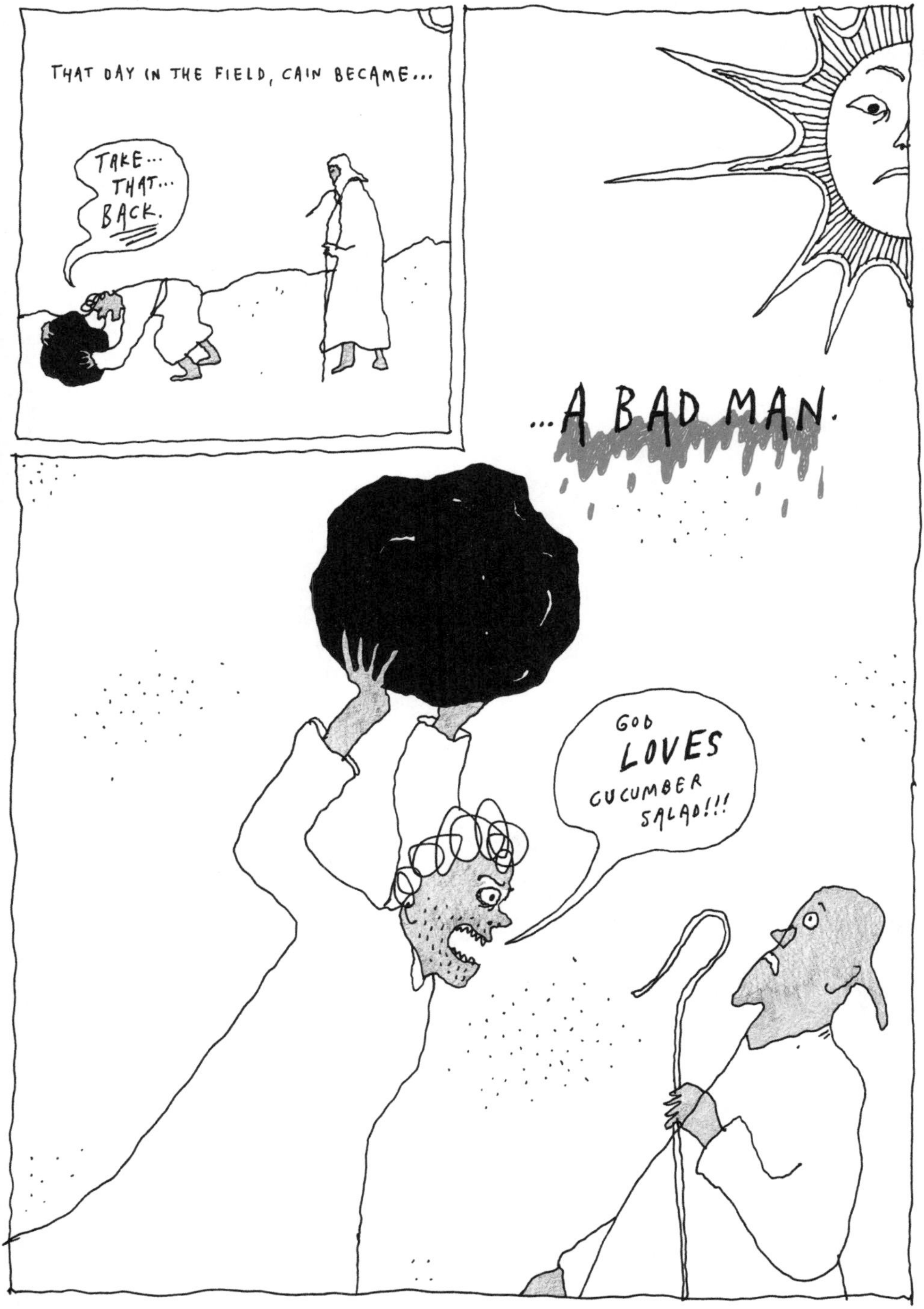
THAT DAY IN THE FIELD, CAIN BECAME...
TAKE... THAT... BACK.
...A BAD MAN.
GOD LOVES CUCUMBER SALAD!!!

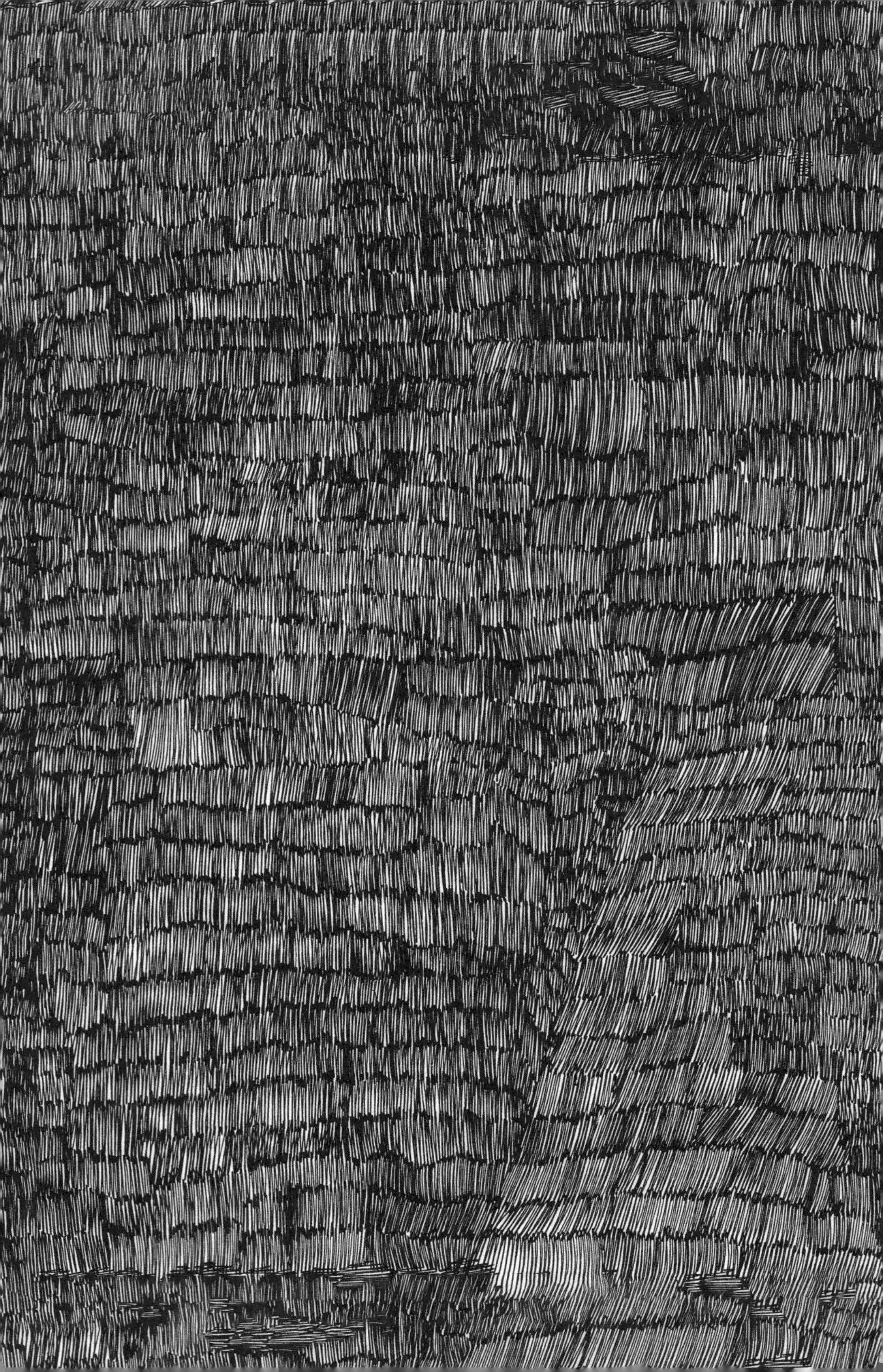

THERE WAS NO ROAD MAP YET TO BEING A BAD MAN.
CAIN WAS THE FIRST ONE.

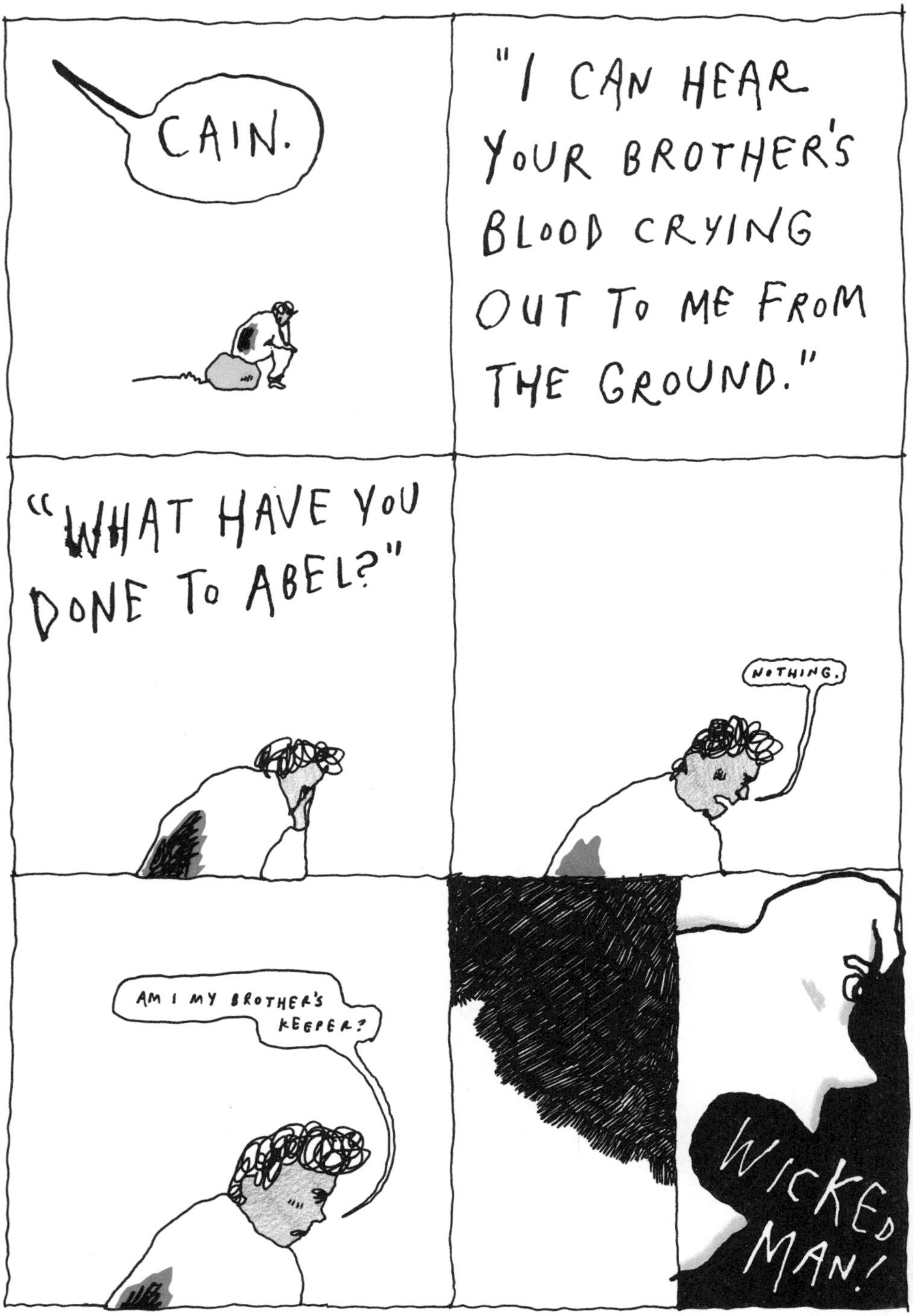
CAIN.
"I CAN HEAR YOUR BROTHER'S BLOOD CRYING OUT TO ME FROM THE GROUND."
"WHAT HAVE YOU DONE TO ABEL?"
NOTHING.
AM I MY BROTHER'S KEEPER?
WICKED MAN!

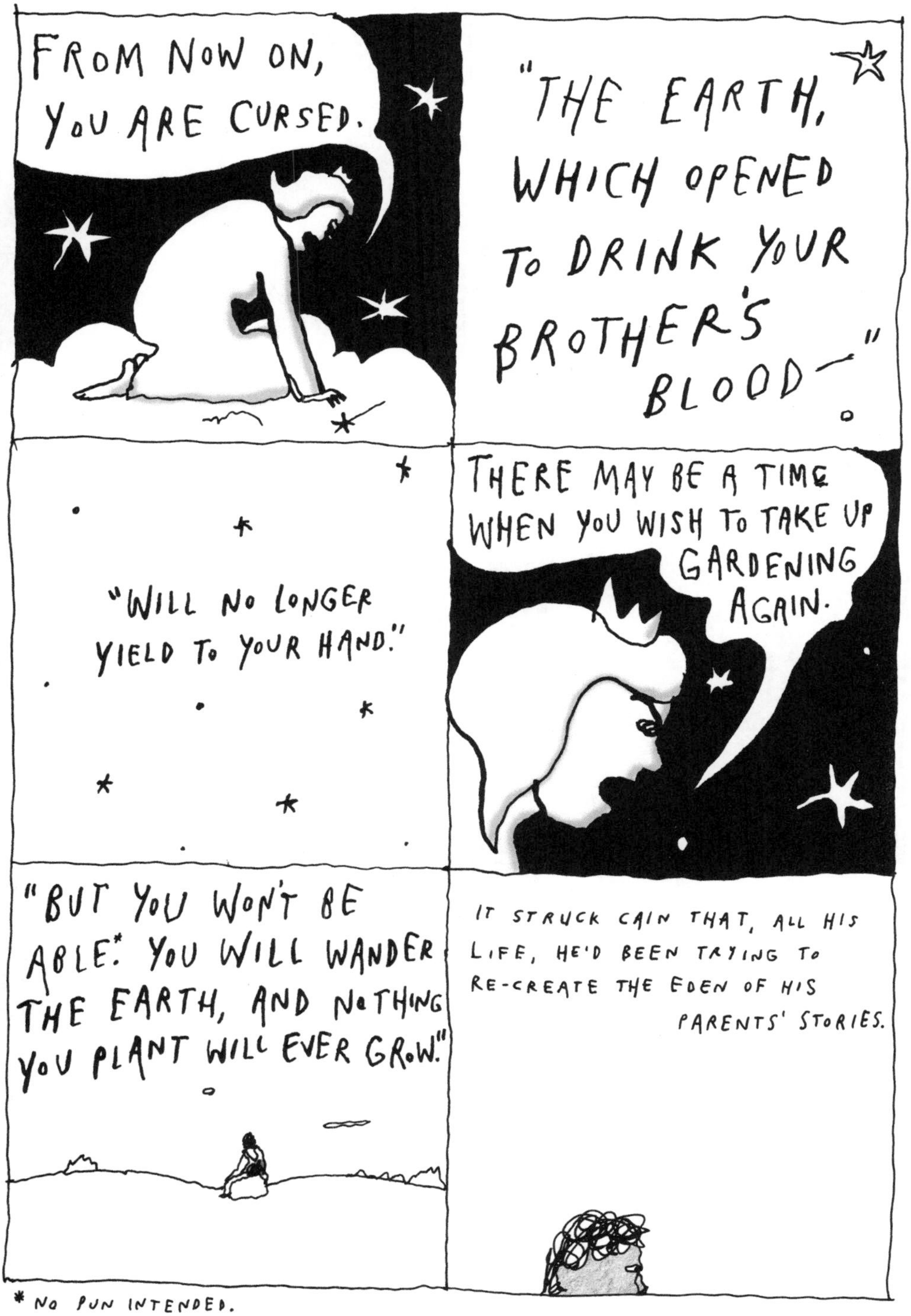
FROM NOW ON, YOU ARE CURSED.
"THE EARTH, WHICH OPENED TO DRINK YOUR BROTHER'S BLOOD—"
"WILL NO LONGER YIELD TO YOUR HAND."
THERE MAY BE A TIME WHEN YOU WISH TO TAKE UP GARDENING AGAIN.
"BUT YOU WON'T BE ABLE.* YOU WILL WANDER THE EARTH, AND NOTHING YOU PLANT WILL EVER GROW."
IT STRUCK CAIN THAT, ALL HIS LIFE, HE'D BEEN TRYING TO RE-CREATE THE EDEN OF HIS PARENTS' STORIES.

* NO PUN INTENDED.

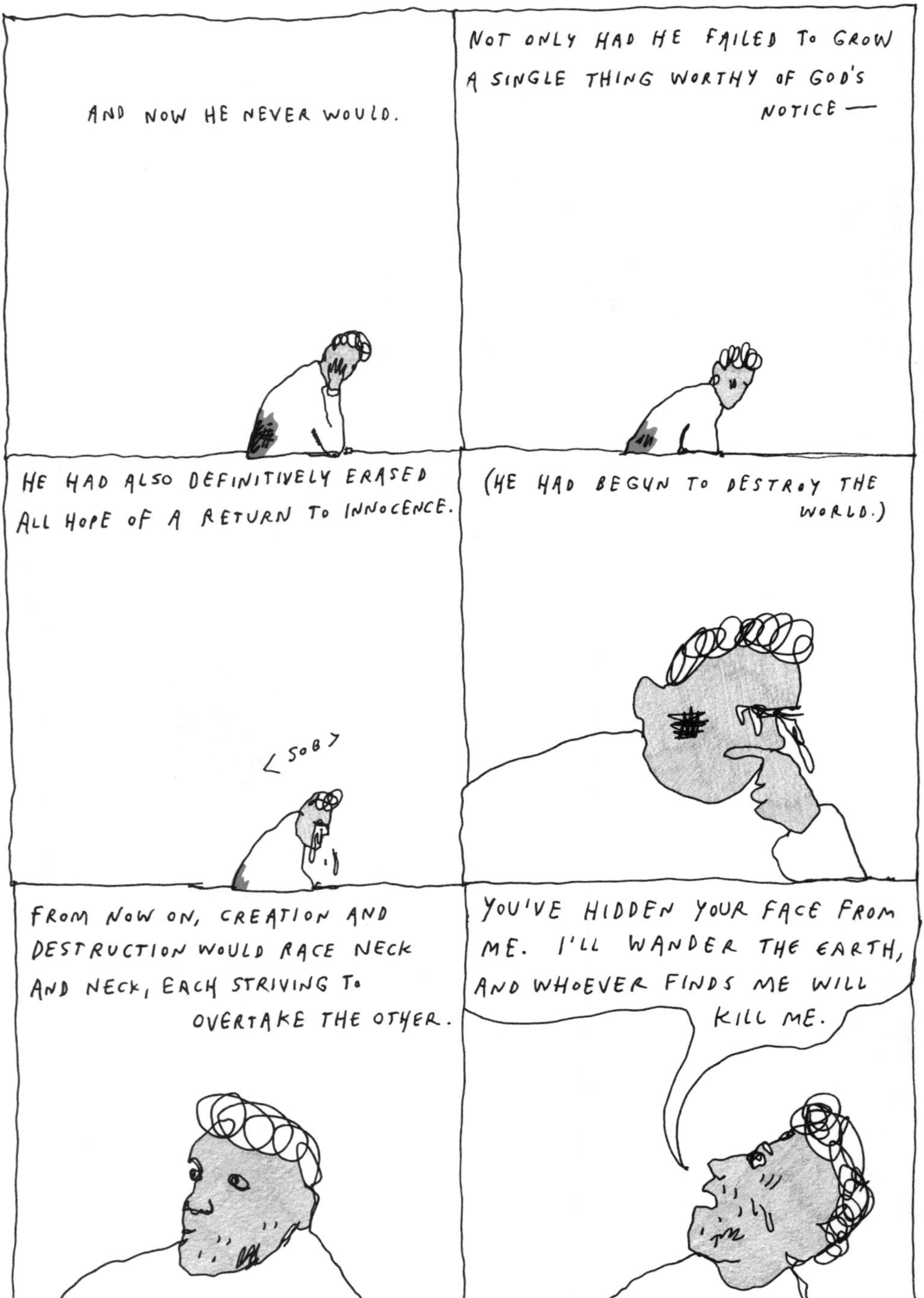
AND NOW HE NEVER WOULD.
NOT ONLY HAD HE FAILED TO GROW A SINGLE THING WORTHY OF GOD'S NOTICE —
HE HAD ALSO DEFINITIVELY ERASED ALL HOPE OF A RETURN TO INNOCENCE.
<SOB>
(HE HAD BEGUN TO DESTROY THE WORLD.)
FROM NOW ON, CREATION AND DESTRUCTION WOULD RACE NECK AND NECK, EACH STRIVING TO OVERTAKE THE OTHER.
YOU'VE HIDDEN YOUR FACE FROM ME. I'LL WANDER THE EARTH, AND WHOEVER FINDS ME WILL KILL ME.

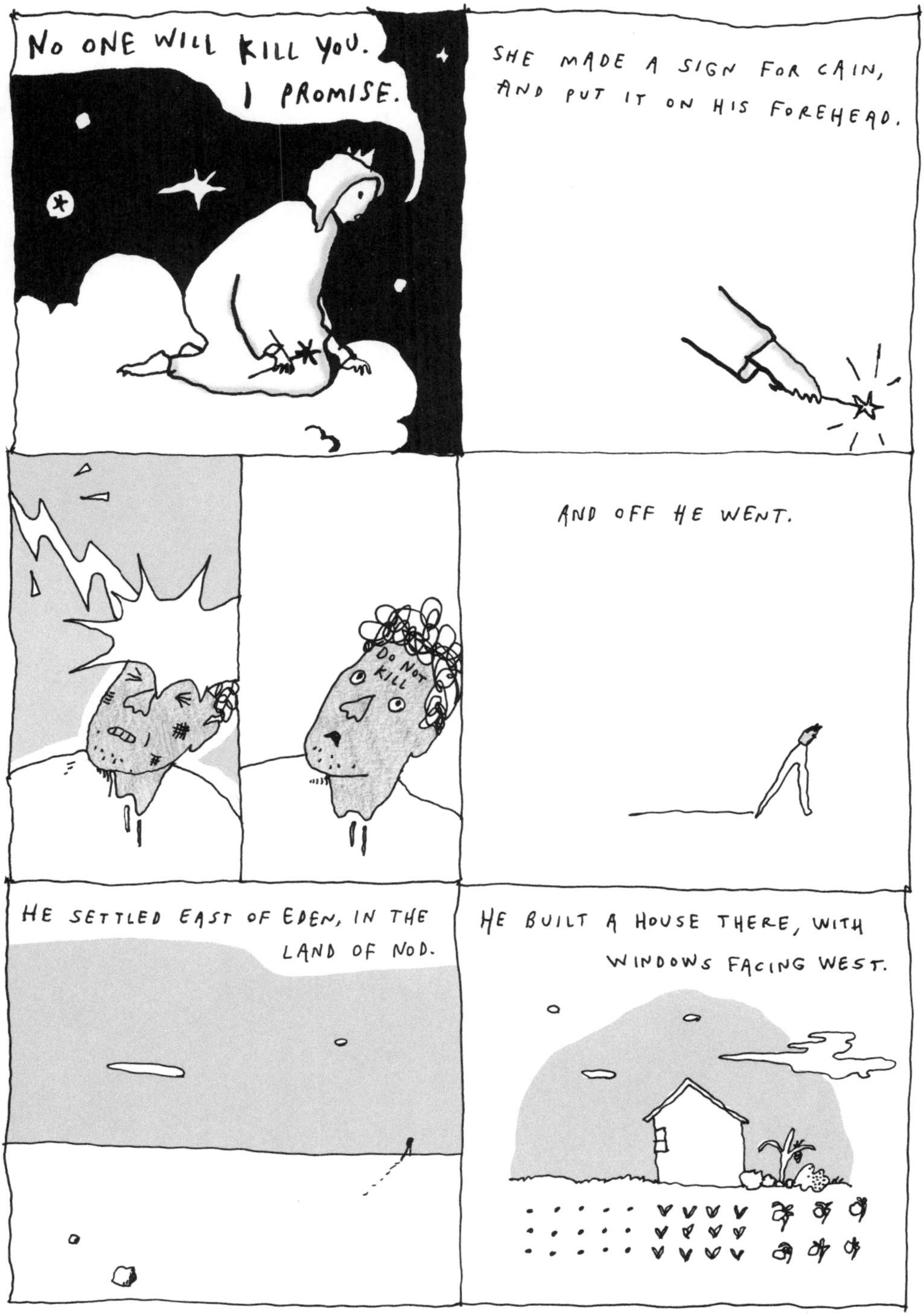
NO ONE WILL KILL YOU. I PROMISE.
SHE MADE A SIGN FOR CAIN, AND PUT IT ON HIS FOREHEAD.
DO NOT KILL
AND OFF HE WENT.
HE SETTLED EAST OF EDEN, IN THE LAND OF NOD.
HE BUILT A HOUSE THERE, WITH WINDOWS FACING WEST.

THE
BEGATS

(A RASH OF MIRACULOUS BIRTHS)

THIS IS THE LEDGER OF THE GENERATIONS
OF MAN. IF YOU ARE EASILY BORED,
                    YOU MAY SKIP IT.

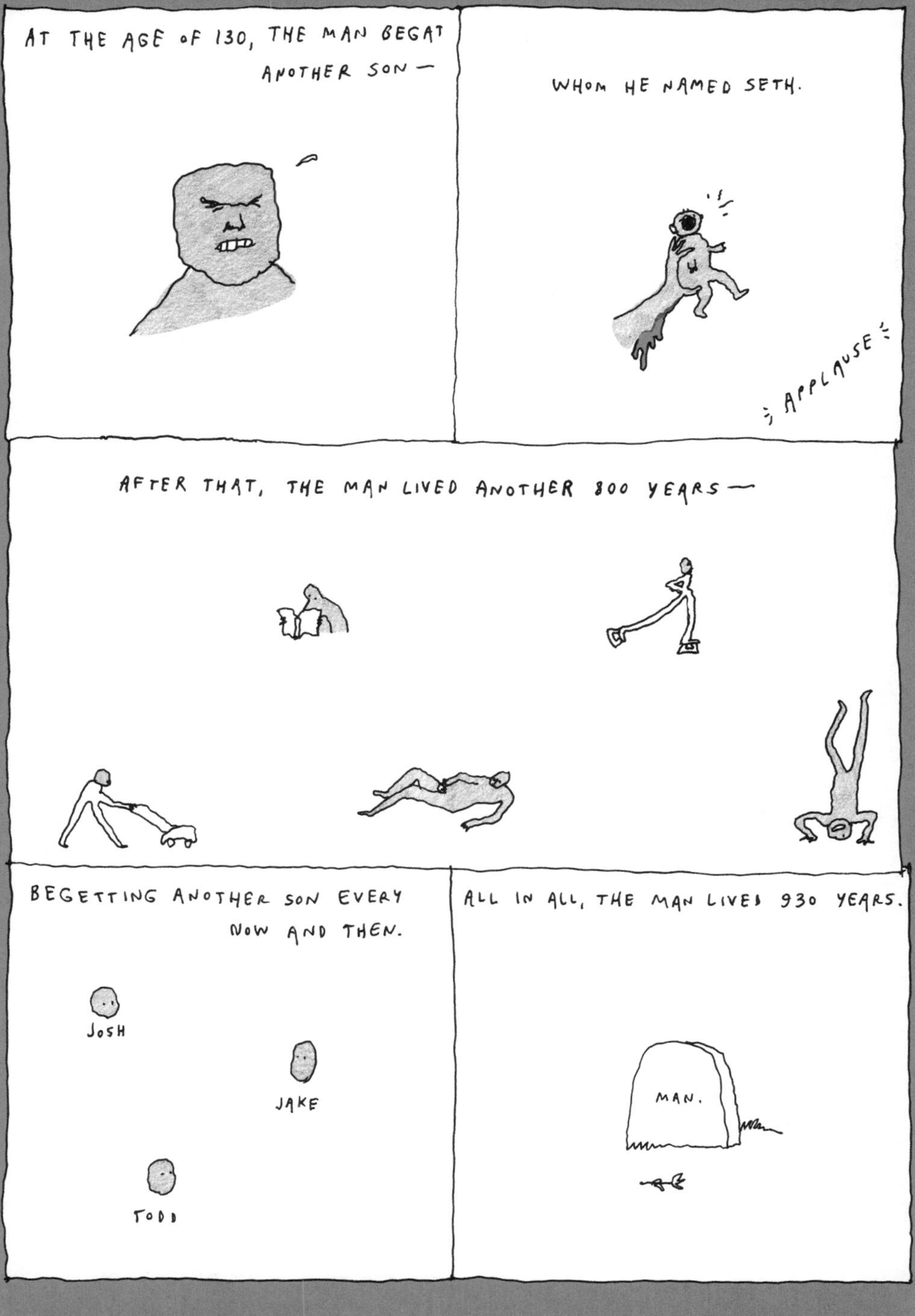
AT THE AGE OF 130, THE MAN BEGAT ANOTHER SON—
WHOM HE NAMED SETH.
APPLAUSE
AFTER THAT, THE MAN LIVED ANOTHER 800 YEARS—
BEGETTING ANOTHER SON EVERY NOW AND THEN.
JOSH
JAKE
TODD
ALL IN ALL, THE MAN LIVED 930 YEARS.
MAN.

WHEN SETH WAS 105 YEARS OLD—

I FEEL STRANGE

HE BEGAT ENOSH.

WAHHH!

AFTER THAT, SETH CONTINUED ON ANOTHER 807 YEARS—

BEGETTING, BEGETTING.

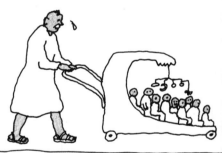

HE DIED AT 912. SMOTHERED BY BABIES.

AT THE AGE OF 90, ENOSH BEGAT KENAN.

WHAT THE?

PFT

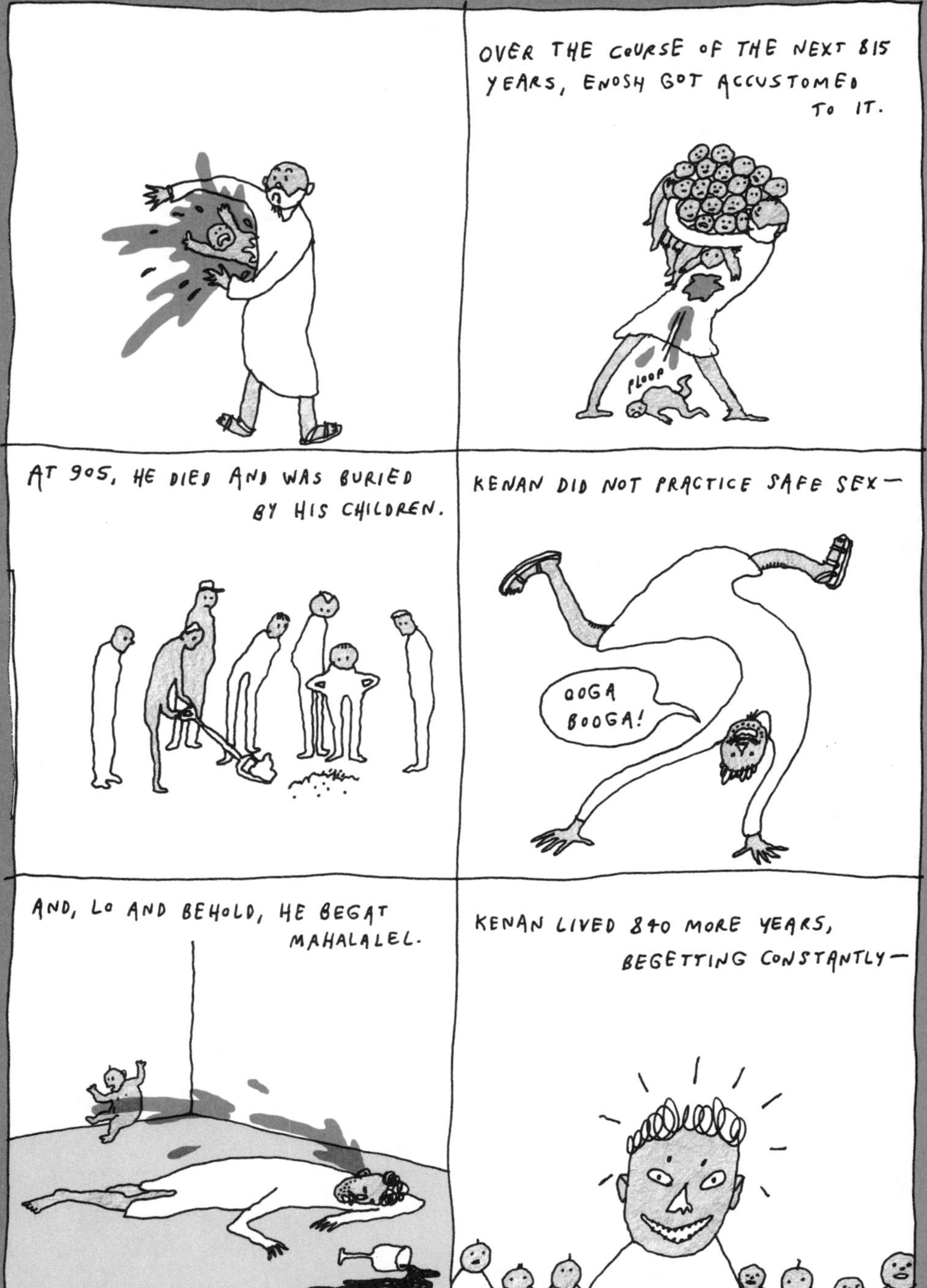
OVER THE COURSE OF THE NEXT 815 YEARS, ENOSH GOT ACCUSTOMED TO IT.
PLOOP
AT 905, HE DIED AND WAS BURIED BY HIS CHILDREN.
KENAN DID NOT PRACTICE SAFE SEX—
OOGA BOOGA!
AND, LO AND BEHOLD, HE BEGAT MAHALALEL.
KENAN LIVED 840 MORE YEARS, BEGETTING CONSTANTLY—

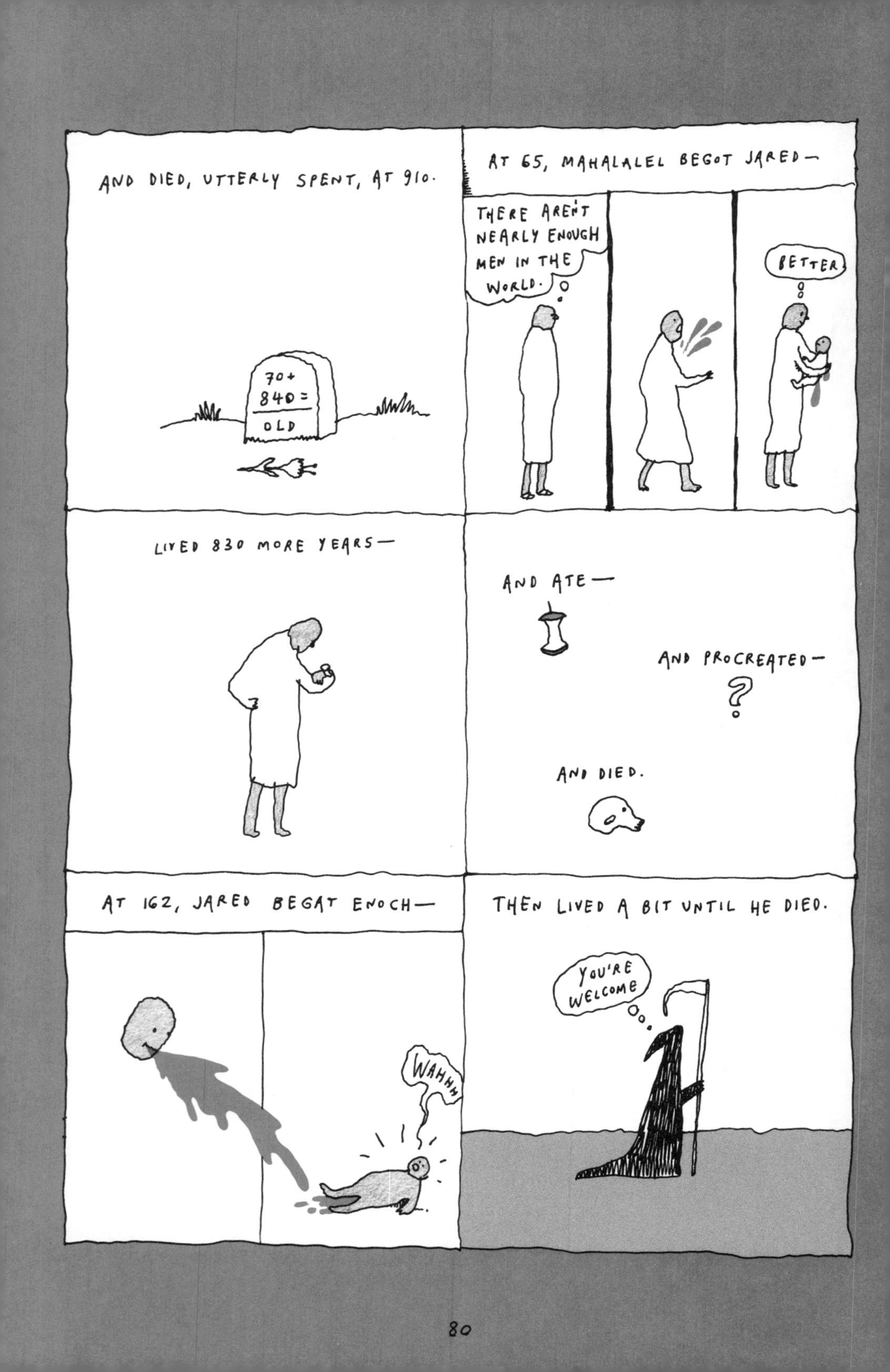
AND DIED, UTTERLY SPENT, AT 910.
70+
840=
OLD
AT 65, MAHALALEL BEGOT JARED—
THERE AREN'T NEARLY ENOUGH MEN IN THE WORLD.
BETTER.
LIVED 830 MORE YEARS—
AND ATE—
AND PROCREATED—
?
AND DIED.
AT 162, JARED BEGAT ENOCH—
WAHHH
THEN LIVED A BIT UNTIL HE DIED.
YOU'RE WELCOME

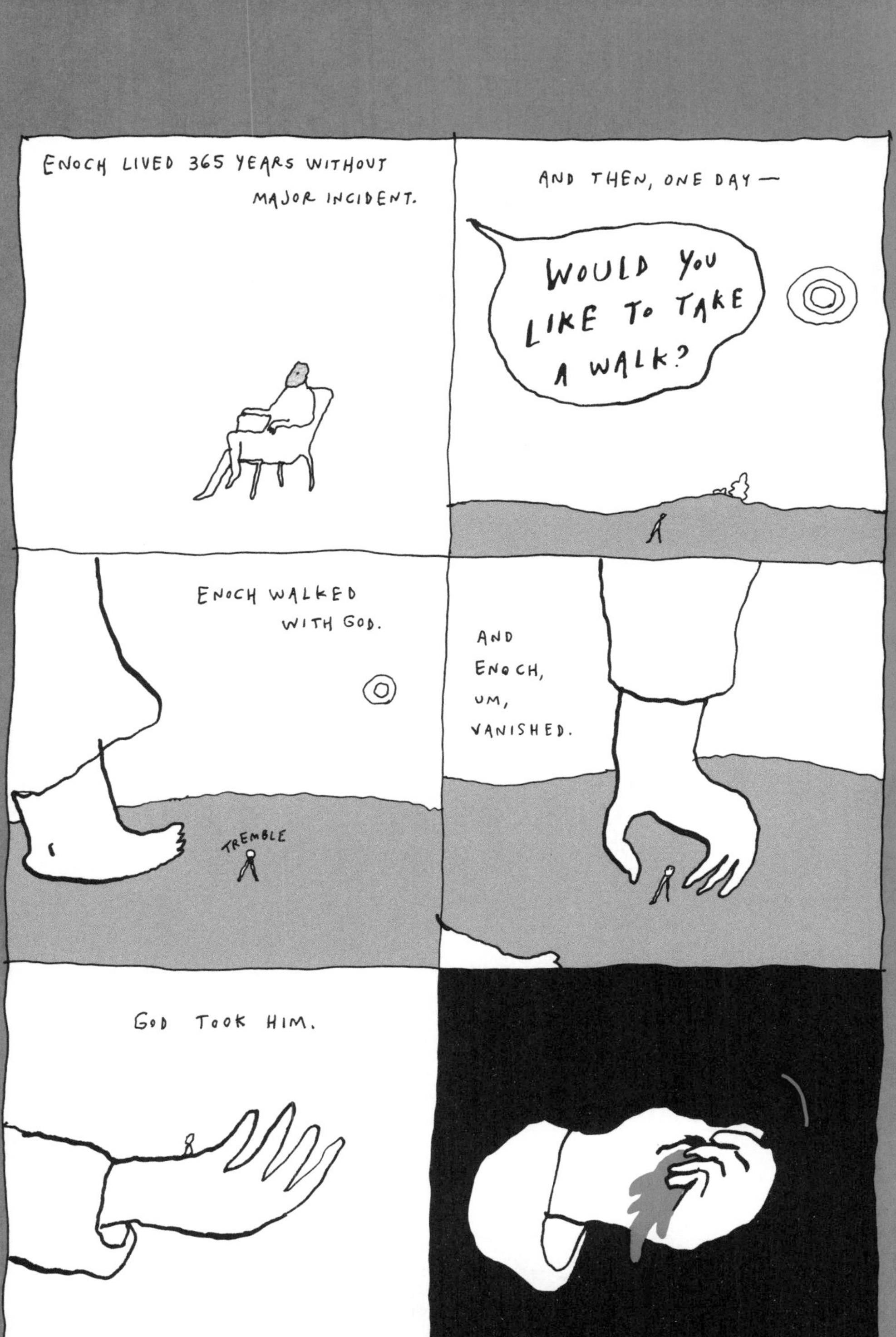
ENOCH LIVED 365 YEARS WITHOUT MAJOR INCIDENT.
AND THEN, ONE DAY—
WOULD YOU LIKE TO TAKE A WALK?
ENOCH WALKED WITH GOD.
TREMBLE
AND ENOCH, UM, VANISHED.
GOD TOOK HIM.

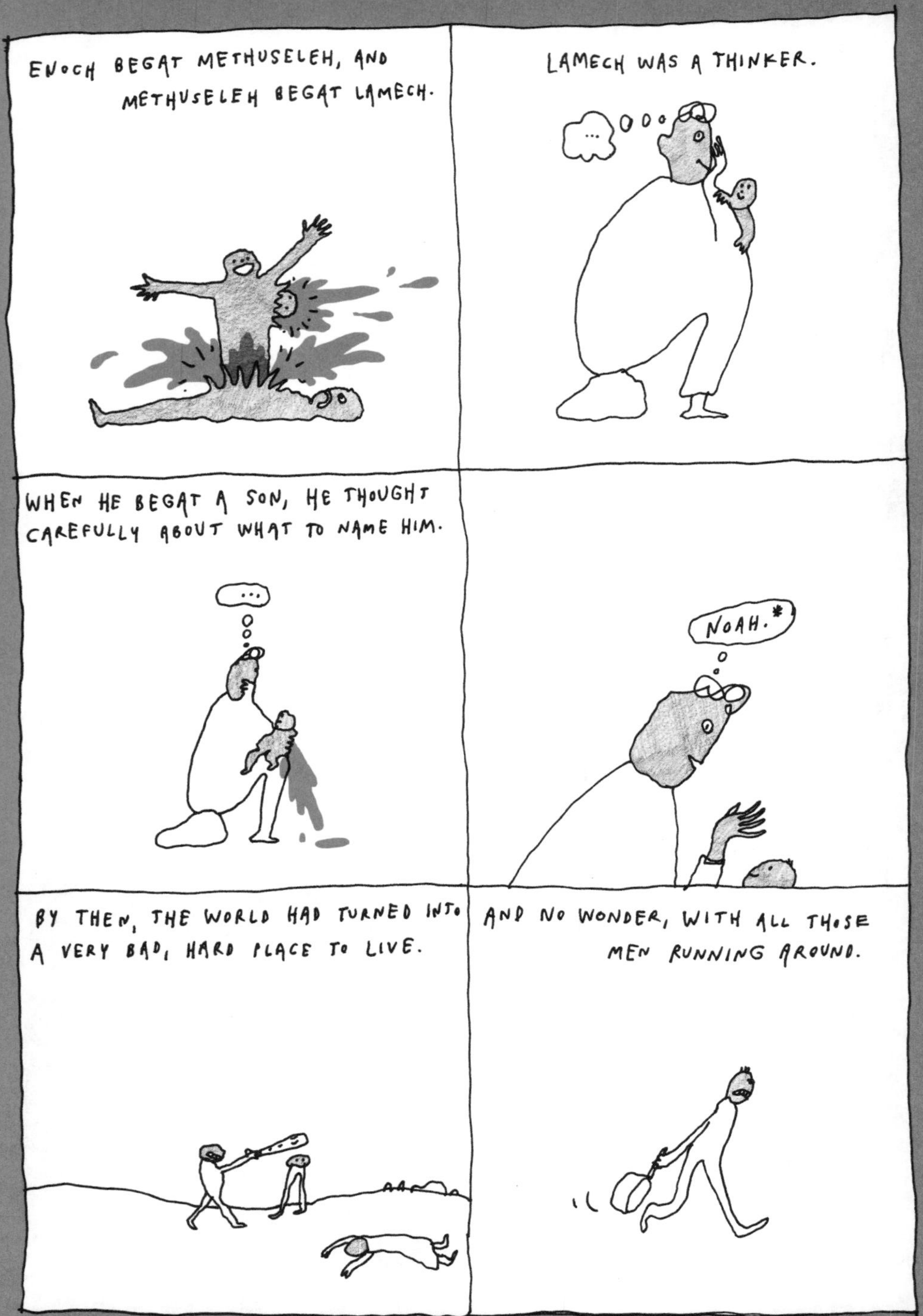
ENOCH BEGAT METHUSELEH, AND METHUSELEH BEGAT LAMECH.
LAMECH WAS A THINKER.
...
WHEN HE BEGAT A SON, HE THOUGHT CAREFULLY ABOUT WHAT TO NAME HIM.
...
NOAH.*
BY THEN, THE WORLD HAD TURNED INTO A VERY BAD, HARD PLACE TO LIVE.
AND NO WONDER, WITH ALL THOSE MEN RUNNING AROUND.

* "REPOSE," IN HEBREW

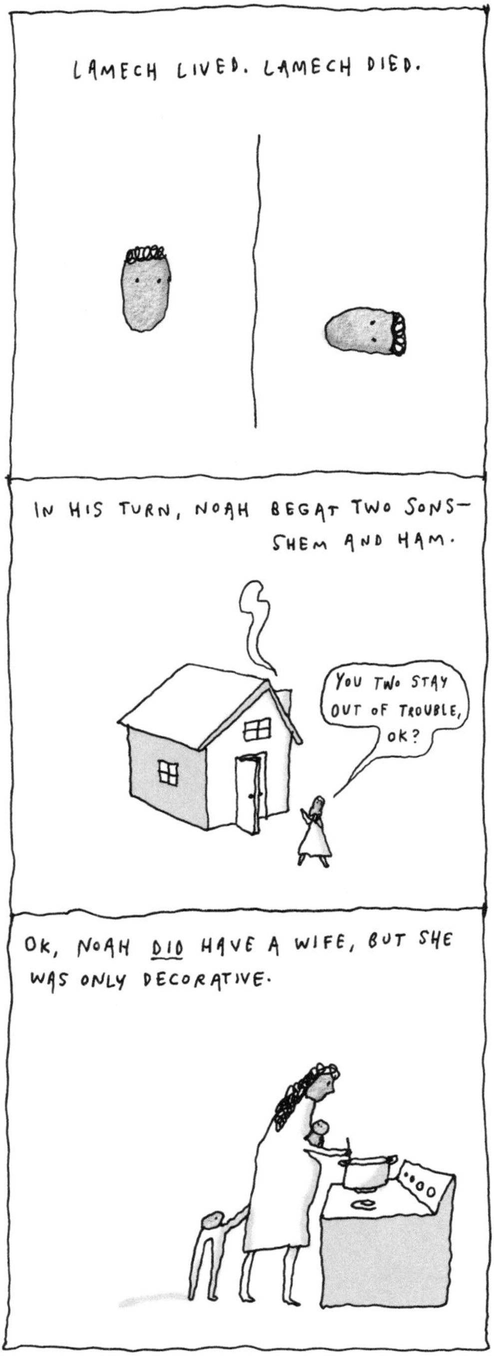
LAMECH LIVED. LAMECH DIED.
IN HIS TURN, NOAH BEGAT TWO SONS—SHEM AND HAM.
YOU TWO STAY OUT OF TROUBLE, OK?
OK, NOAH DID HAVE A WIFE, BUT SHE WAS ONLY DECORATIVE.

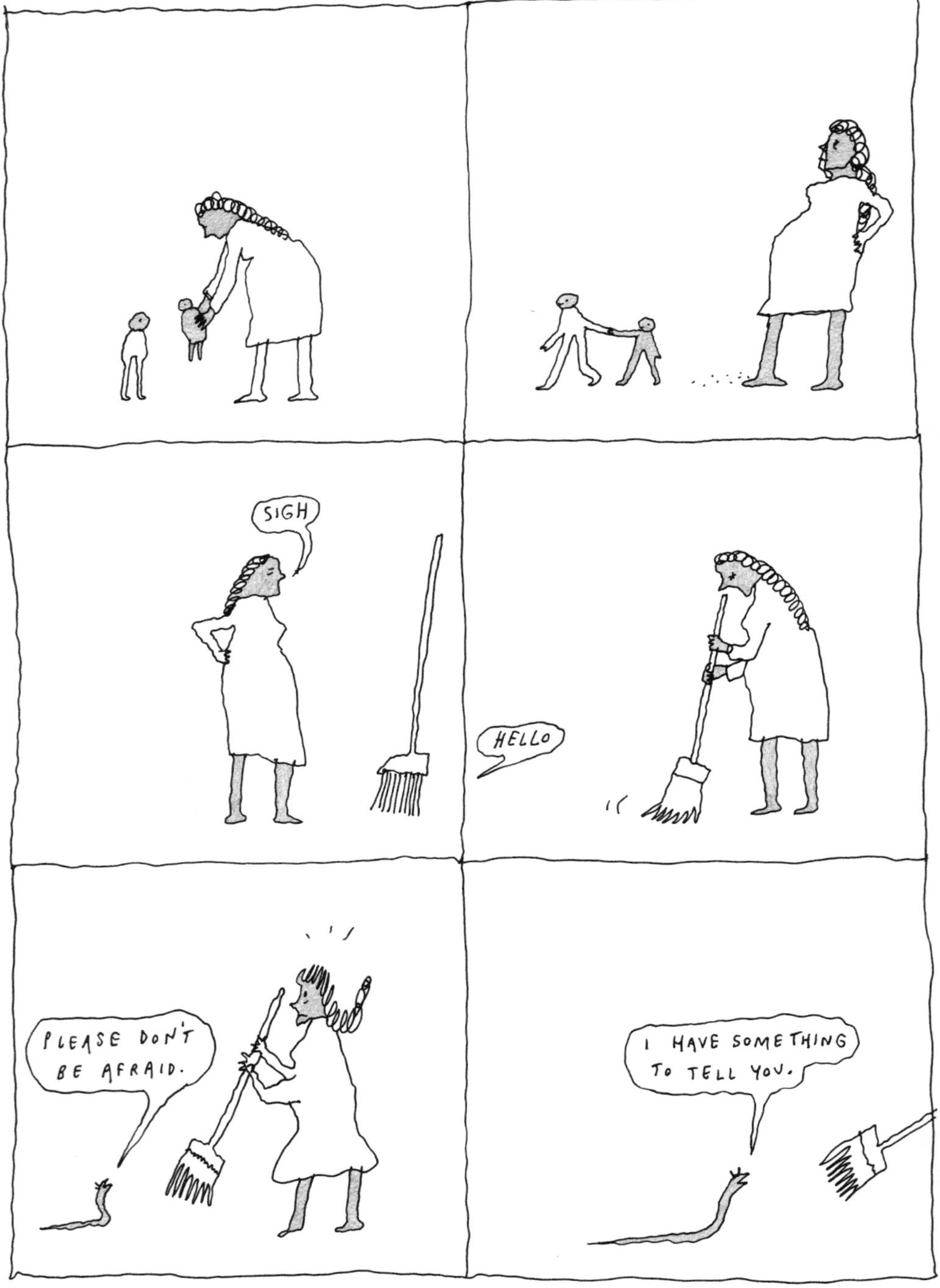
SIGH
HELLO
PLEASE DON'T BE AFRAID.
I HAVE SOMETHING TO TELL YOU.

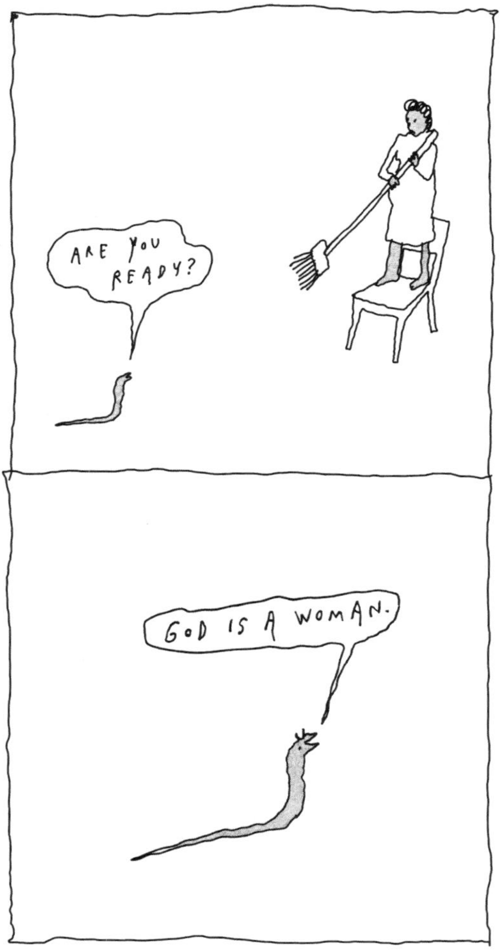
ARE YOU READY?
GOD IS A WOMAN.

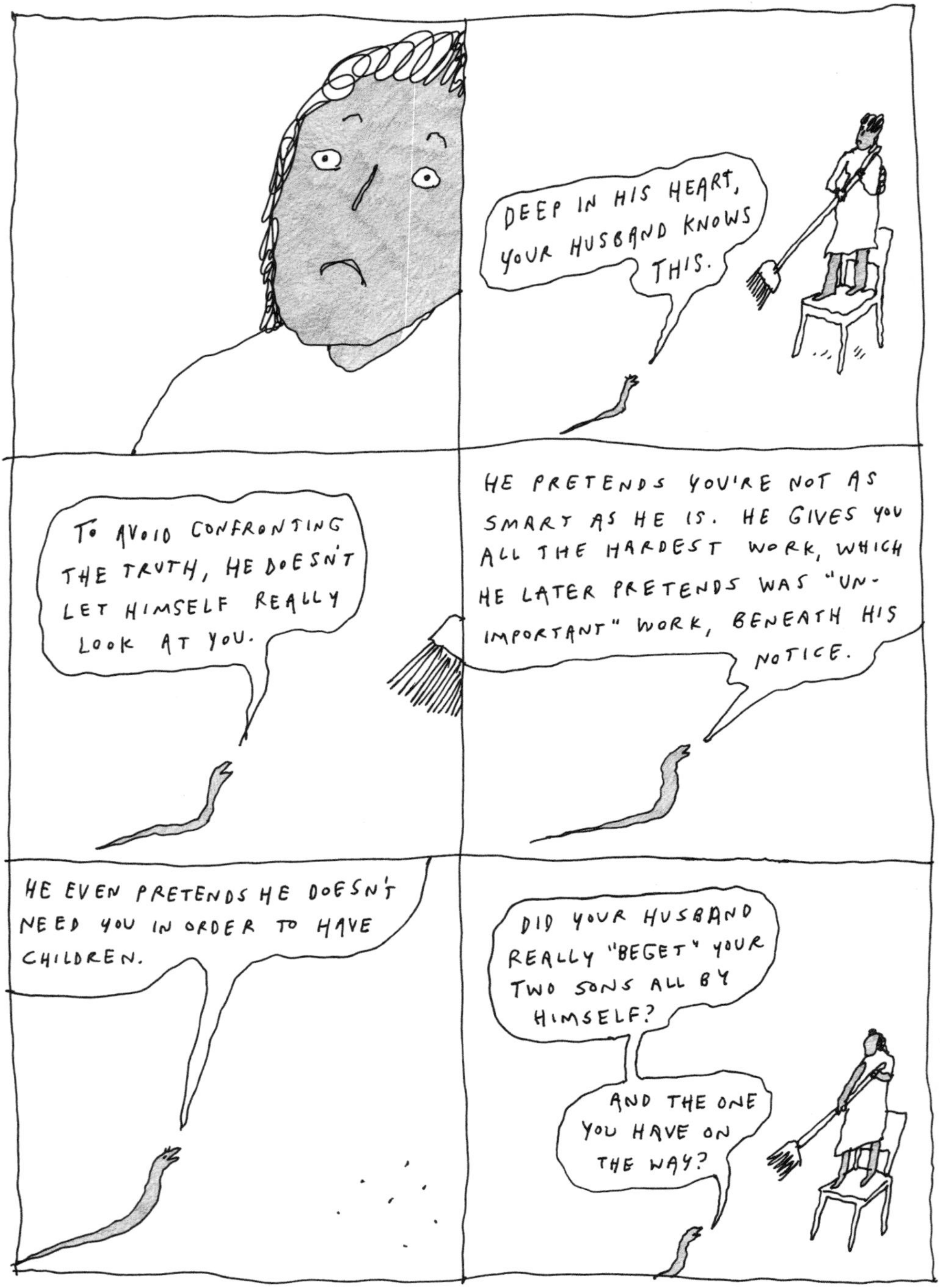
DEEP IN HIS HEART, YOUR HUSBAND KNOWS THIS.
TO AVOID CONFRONTING THE TRUTH, HE DOESN'T LET HIMSELF REALLY LOOK AT YOU.
HE PRETENDS YOU'RE NOT AS SMART AS HE IS. HE GIVES YOU ALL THE HARDEST WORK, WHICH HE LATER PRETENDS WAS "UN-IMPORTANT" WORK, BENEATH HIS NOTICE.
HE EVEN PRETENDS HE DOESN'T NEED YOU IN ORDER TO HAVE CHILDREN.
DID YOUR HUSBAND REALLY "BEGET" YOUR TWO SONS ALL BY HIMSELF?
AND THE ONE YOU HAVE ON THE WAY?

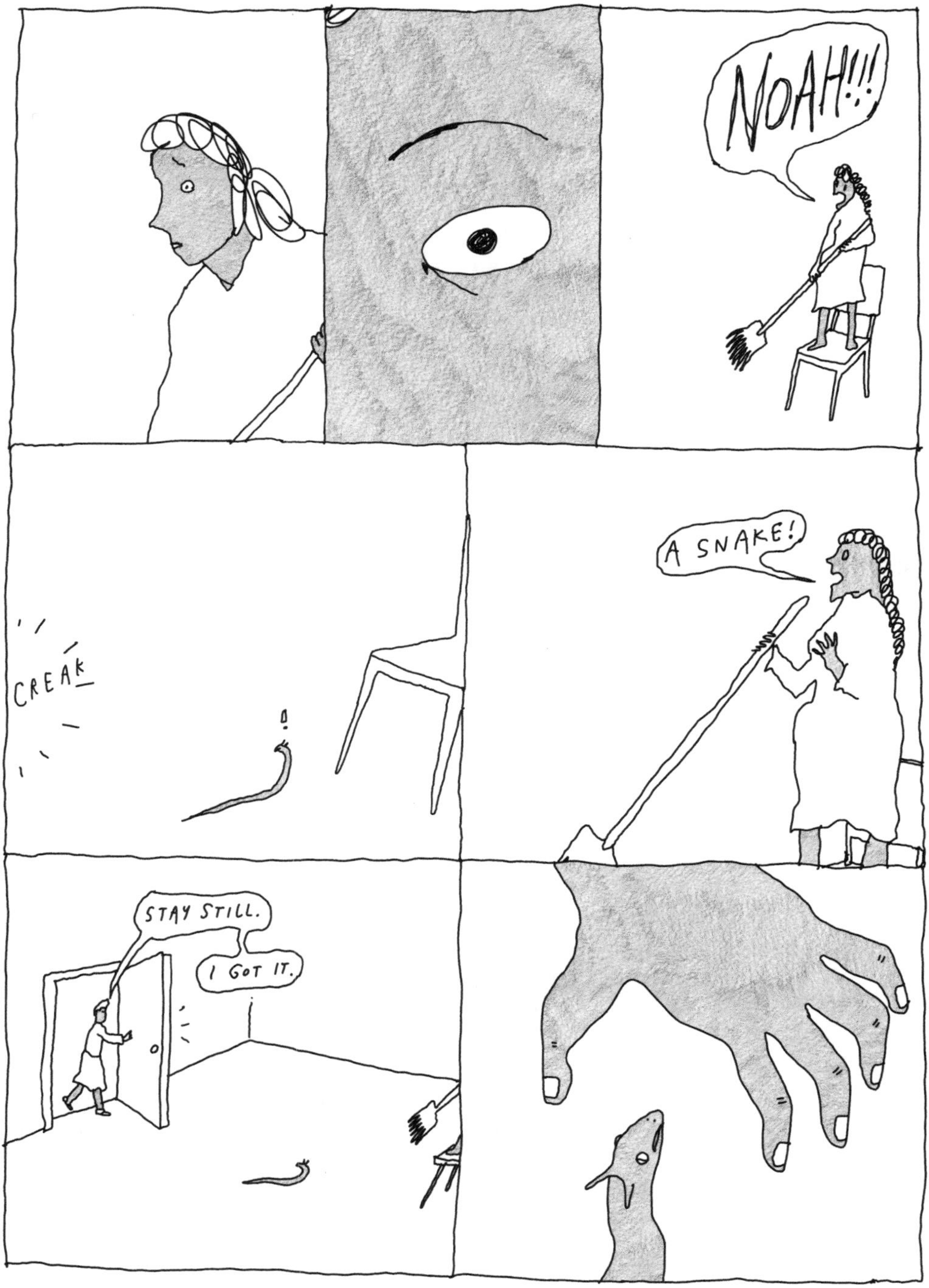
NOAH!!!
CREAK
!
A SNAKE!
STAY STILL.
I GOT IT.

IN THE FULLNESS OF TIME, NOAH ALSO
BEGAT A THIRD SON, JAPHETH. THE
FOUR OF THEM LIVED IN HAPPINESS
AND HARMONY UNTIL THE FLOOD.

NOAH'S WIFE'S NAME IS NOT IMPORTANT, IS NOT KNOWN.

NOAH

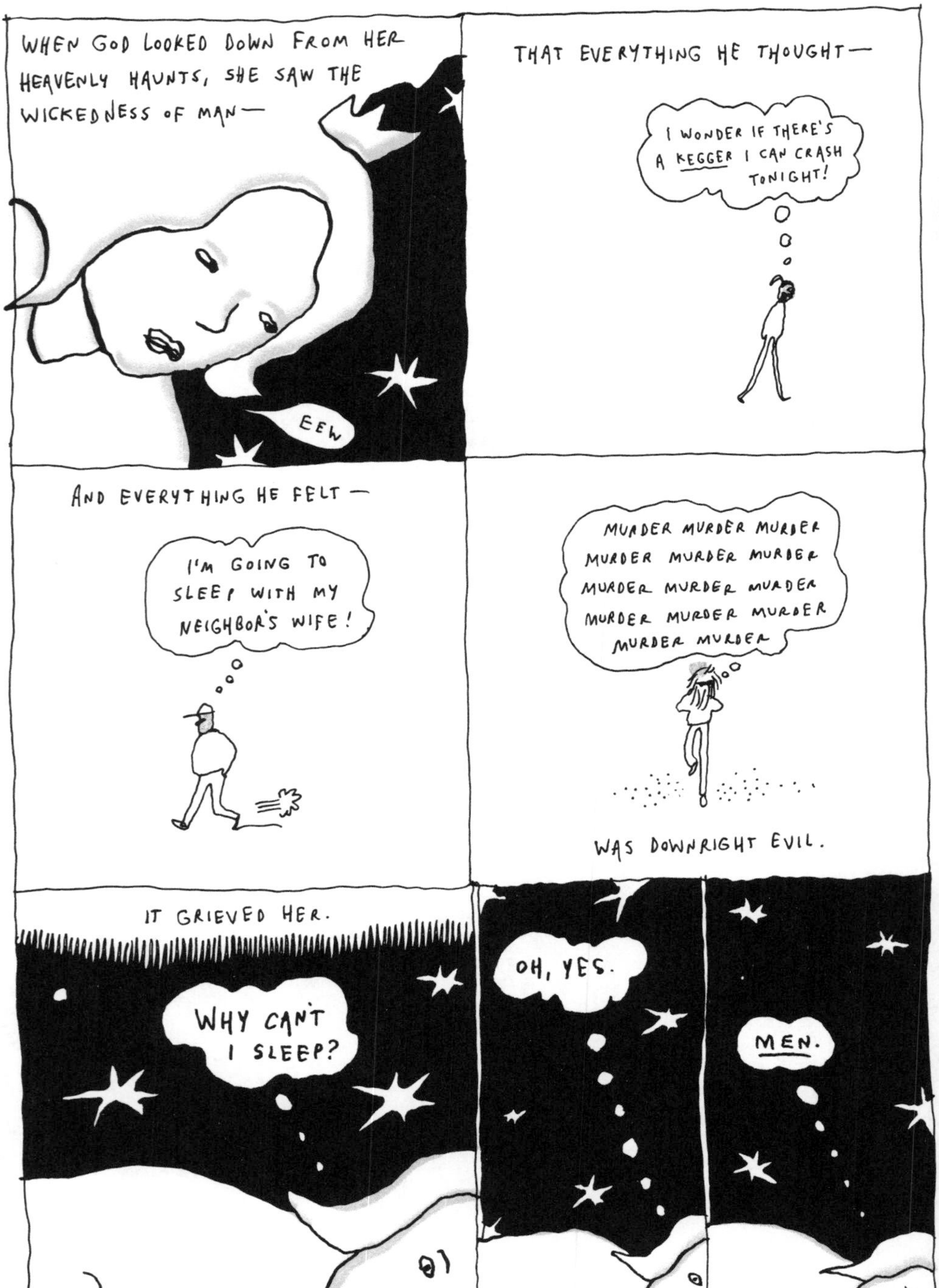
WHEN GOD LOOKED DOWN FROM HER HEAVENLY HAUNTS, SHE SAW THE WICKEDNESS OF MAN—
EEW
THAT EVERYTHING HE THOUGHT—
I WONDER IF THERE'S A KEGGER I CAN CRASH TONIGHT!
AND EVERYTHING HE FELT—
I'M GOING TO SLEEP WITH MY NEIGHBOR'S WIFE!
MURDER MURDER MURDER MURDER MURDER MURDER MURDER MURDER MURDER MURDER MURDER MURDER MURDER MURDER
WAS DOWNRIGHT EVIL.
IT GRIEVED HER.
WHY CAN'T I SLEEP?
OH, YES.
MEN.

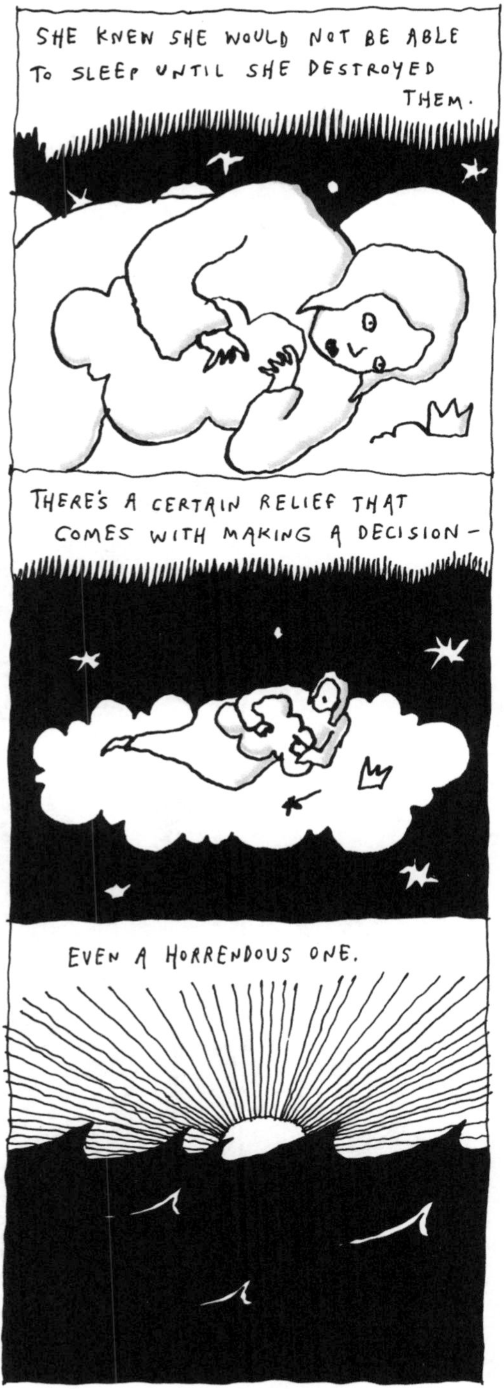
SHE KNEW SHE WOULD NOT BE ABLE TO SLEEP UNTIL SHE DESTROYED THEM.
THERE'S A CERTAIN RELIEF THAT COMES WITH MAKING A DECISION –
EVEN A HORRENDOUS ONE.

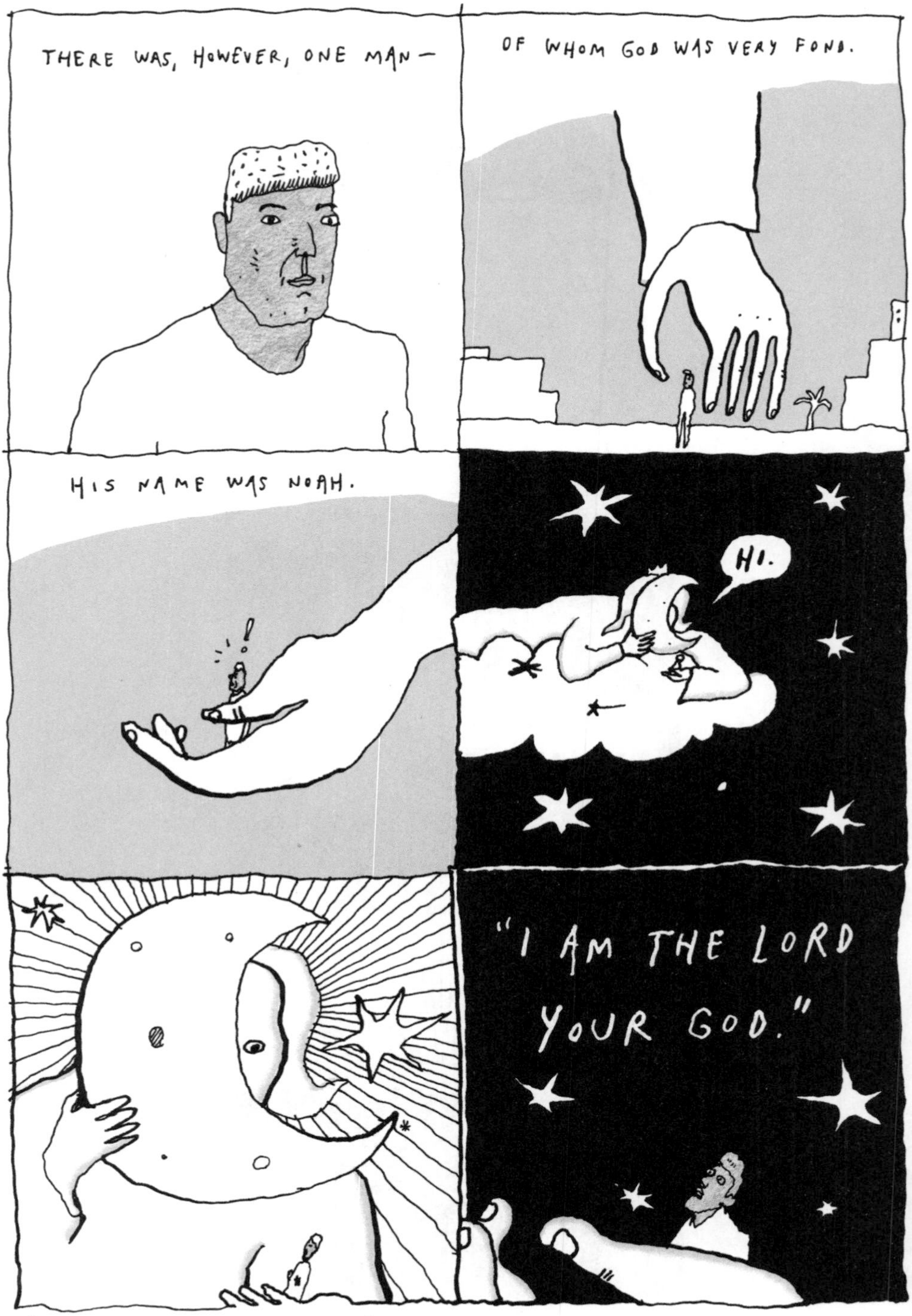
THERE WAS, HOWEVER, ONE MAN—
OF WHOM GOD WAS VERY FOND.
HIS NAME WAS NOAH.
HI.
*
"I AM THE LORD YOUR GOD."

*A MOON IS ALWAYS A GOOD DISGUISE.

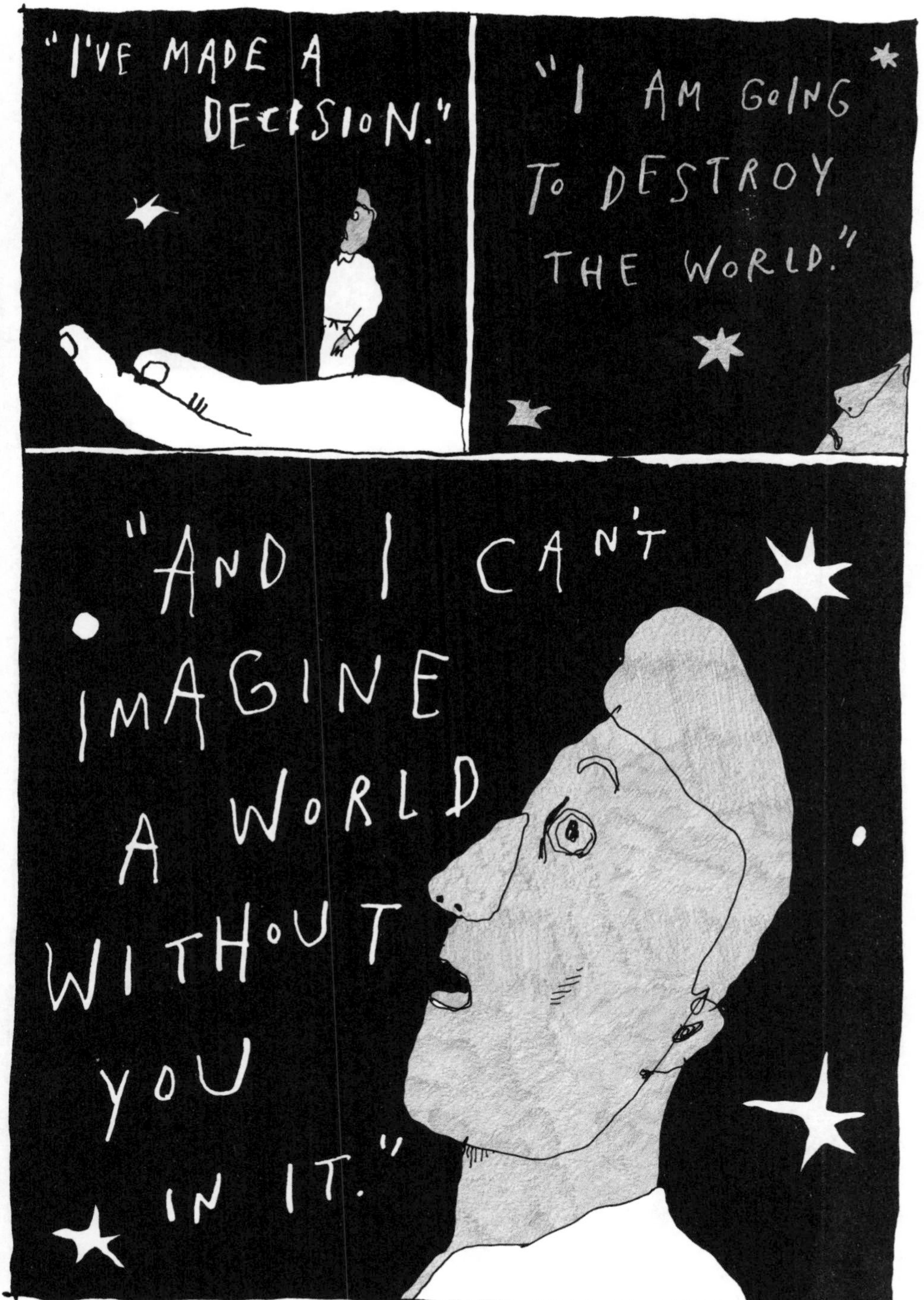
"I'VE MADE A DECISION."
"I AM GOING TO DESTROY THE WORLD."
"AND I CAN'T IMAGINE A WORLD WITHOUT YOU IN IT."

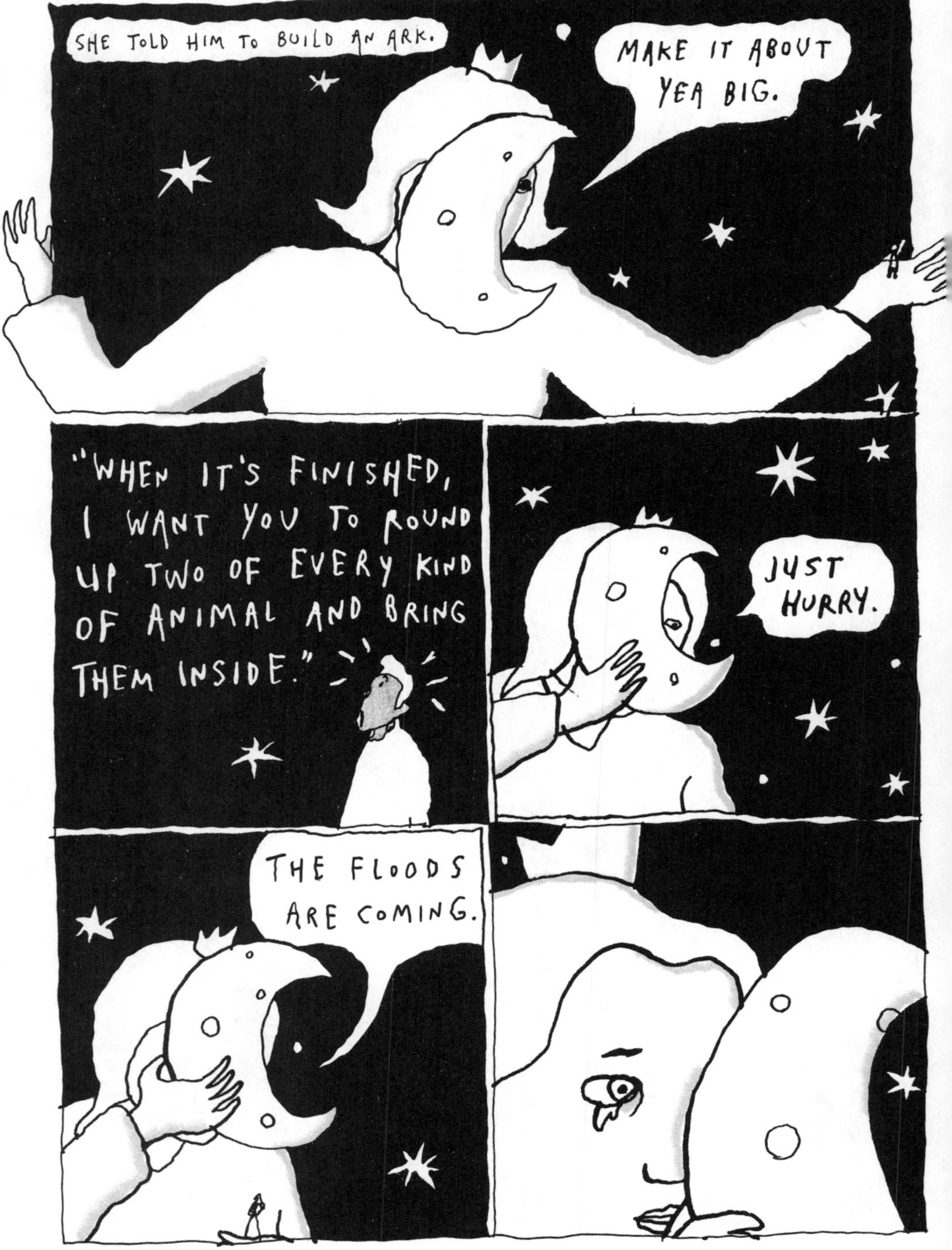
SHE TOLD HIM TO BUILD AN ARK.
MAKE IT ABOUT YEA BIG.
"WHEN IT'S FINISHED, I WANT YOU TO ROUND UP TWO OF EVERY KIND OF ANIMAL AND BRING THEM INSIDE."
JUST HURRY.
THE FLOODS ARE COMING.

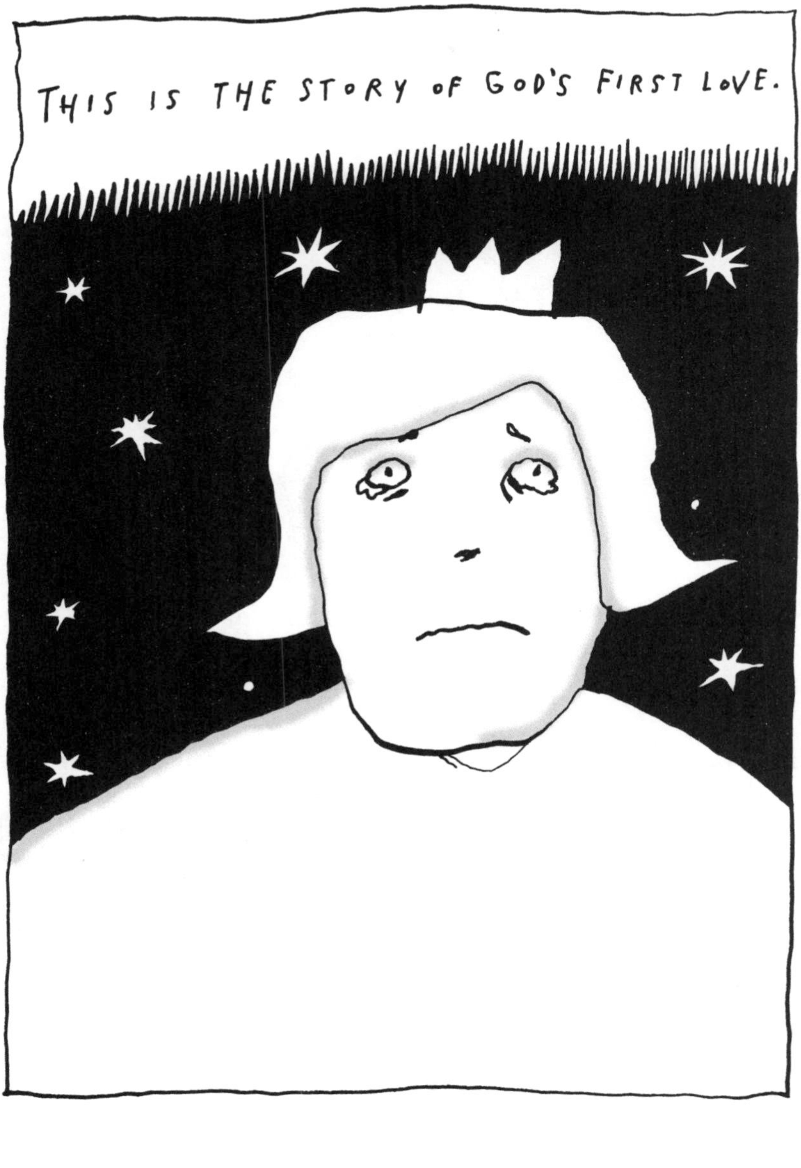
THIS IS THE STORY OF GOD'S FIRST LOVE.

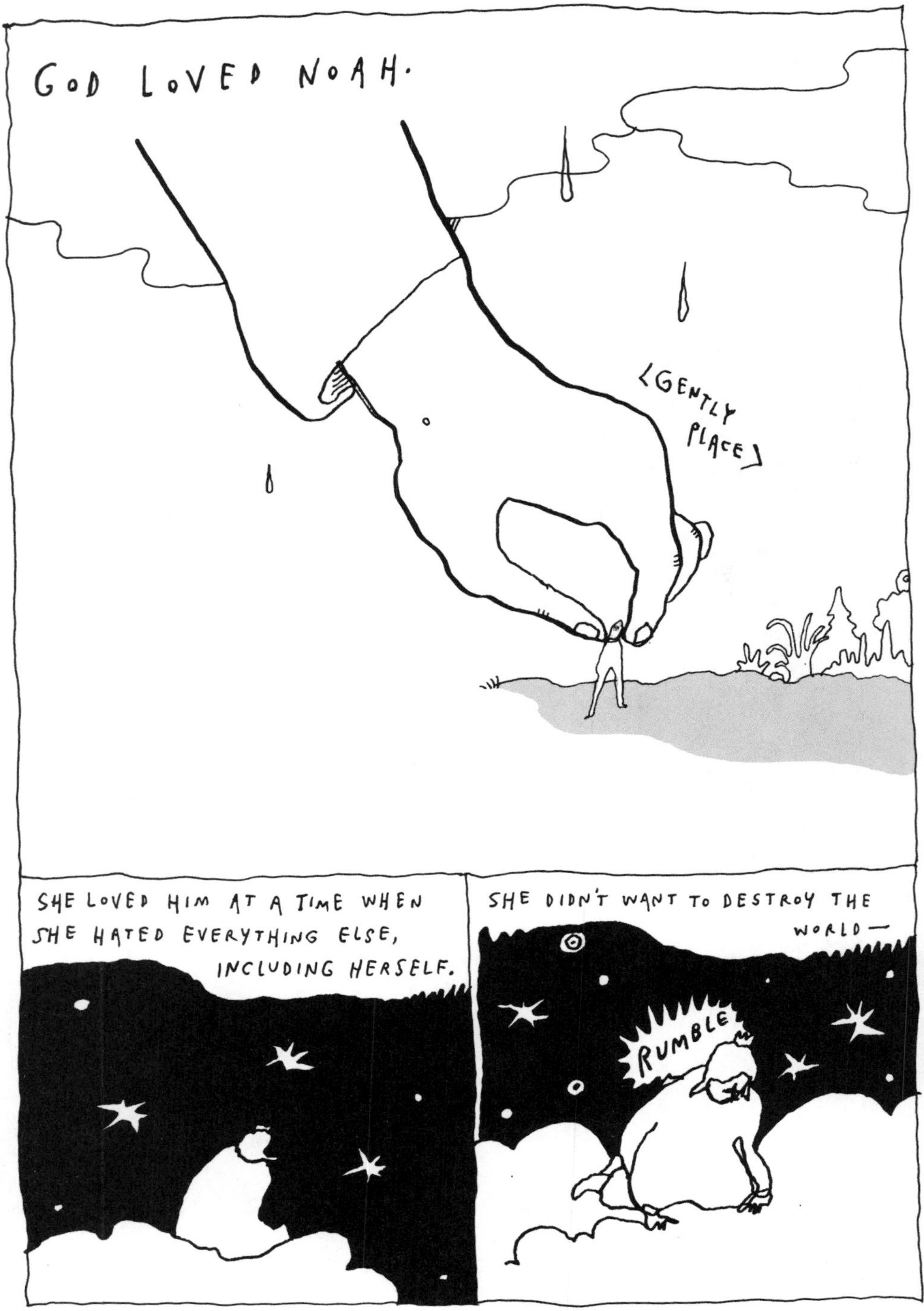
GOD LOVED NOAH.
<GENTLY PLACE>
SHE LOVED HIM AT A TIME WHEN SHE HATED EVERYTHING ELSE, INCLUDING HERSELF.
SHE DIDN'T WANT TO DESTROY THE WORLD—
RUMBLE

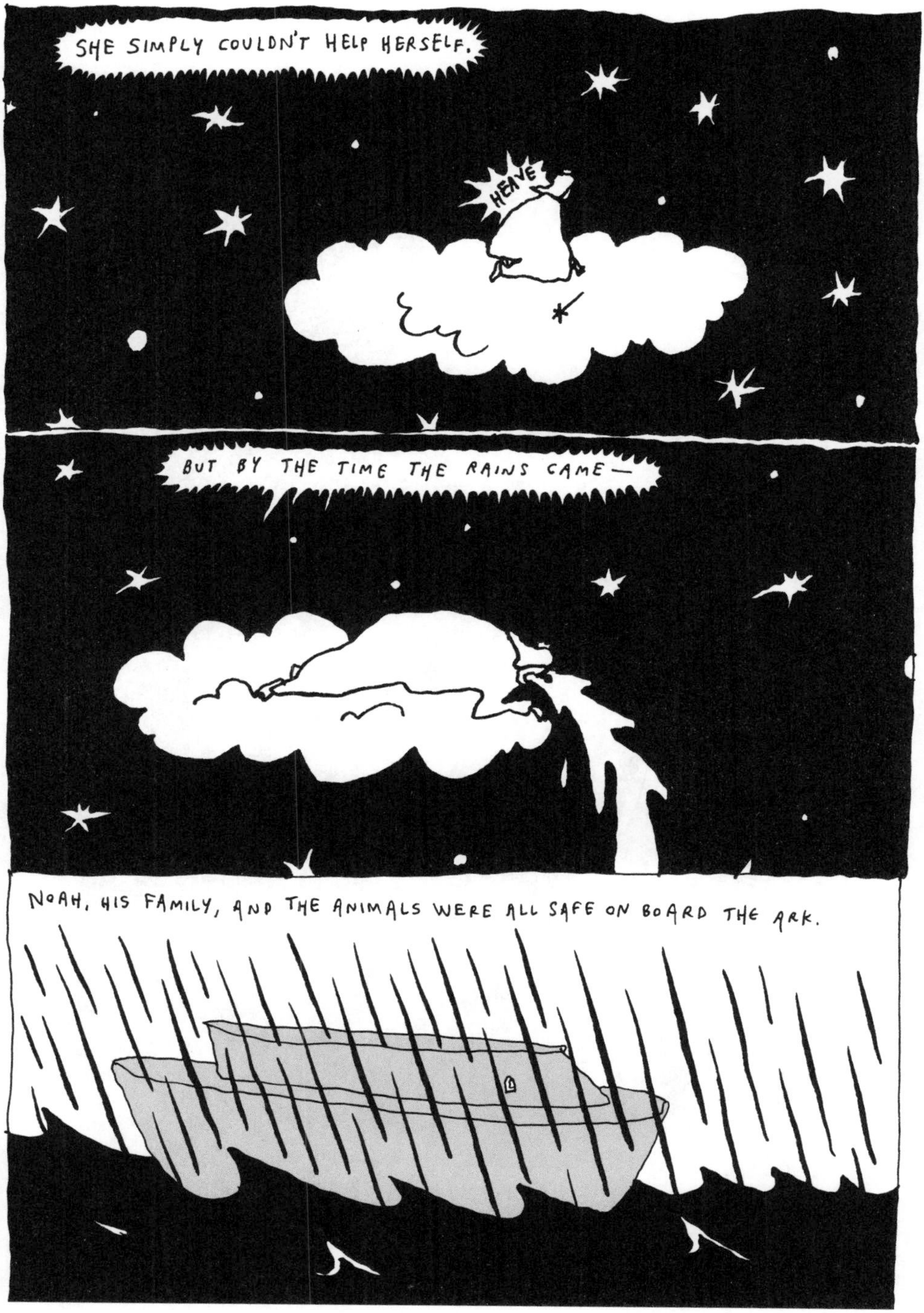
SHE SIMPLY COULDN'T HELP HERSELF.
HEAVE
BUT BY THE TIME THE RAINS CAME—
NOAH, HIS FAMILY, AND THE ANIMALS WERE ALL SAFE ON BOARD THE ARK.

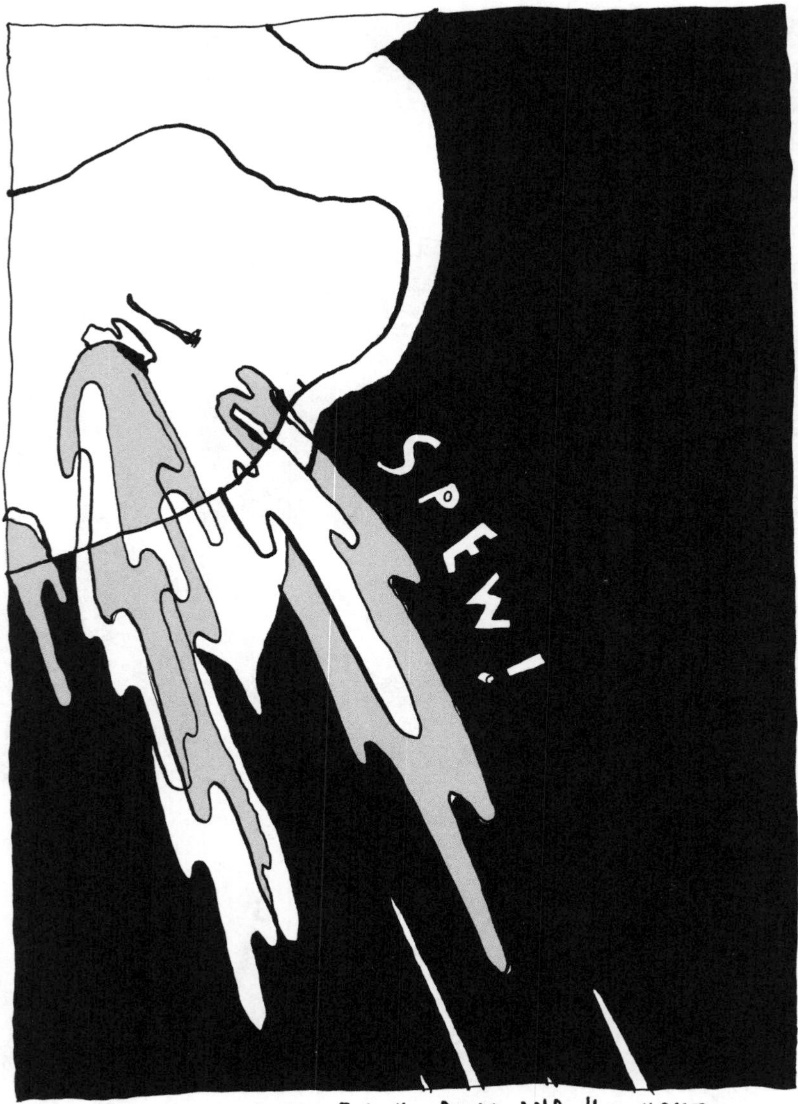
SPEW!

OUR HEROINE CRIED FOR 40 DAYS AND 40 NIGHTS.

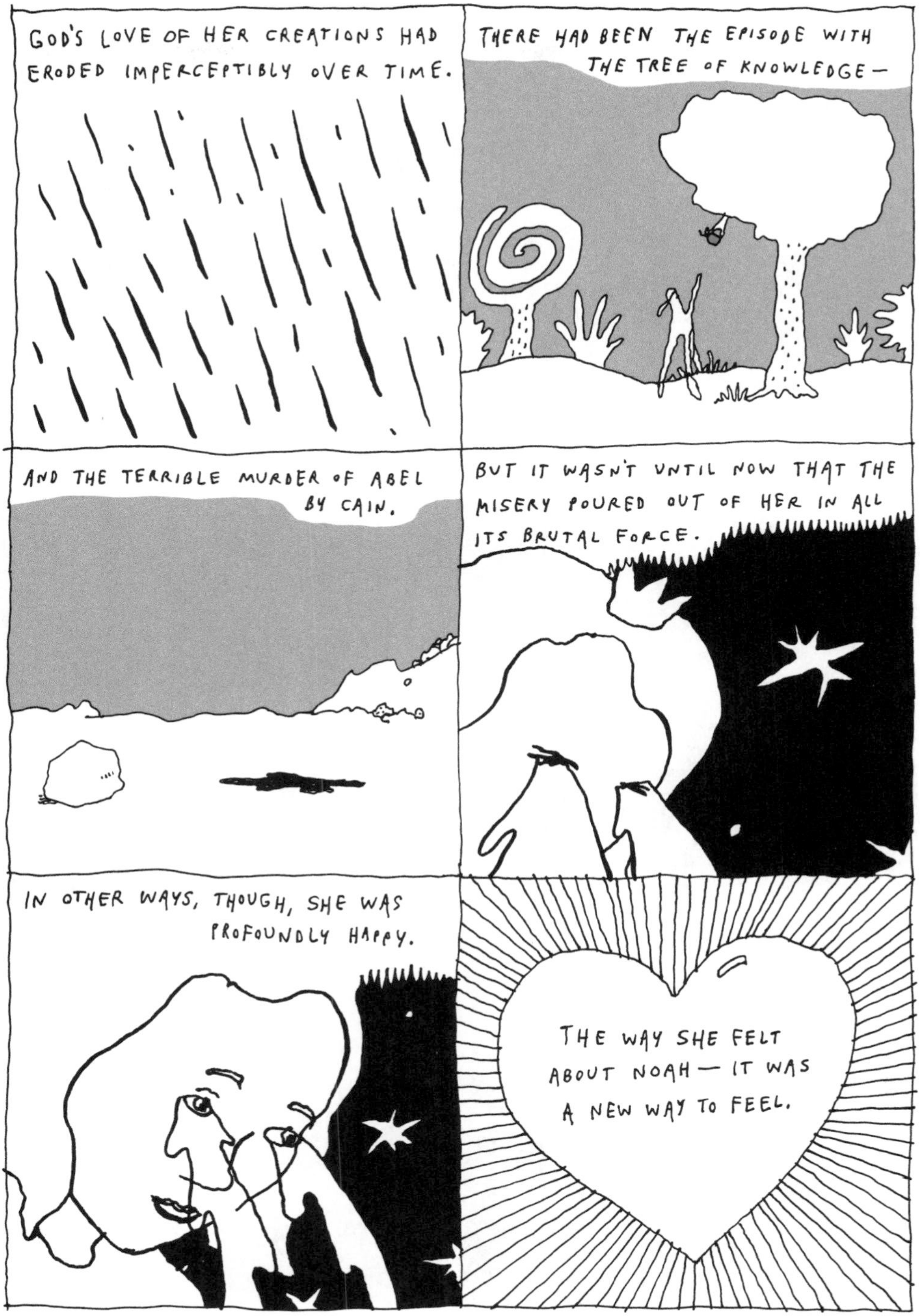
GOD'S LOVE OF HER CREATIONS HAD ERODED IMPERCEPTIBLY OVER TIME.
THERE HAD BEEN THE EPISODE WITH THE TREE OF KNOWLEDGE—
AND THE TERRIBLE MURDER OF ABEL BY CAIN.
BUT IT WASN'T UNTIL NOW THAT THE MISERY POURED OUT OF HER IN ALL ITS BRUTAL FORCE.
IN OTHER WAYS, THOUGH, SHE WAS PROFOUNDLY HAPPY.
THE WAY SHE FELT ABOUT NOAH— IT WAS A NEW WAY TO FEEL.

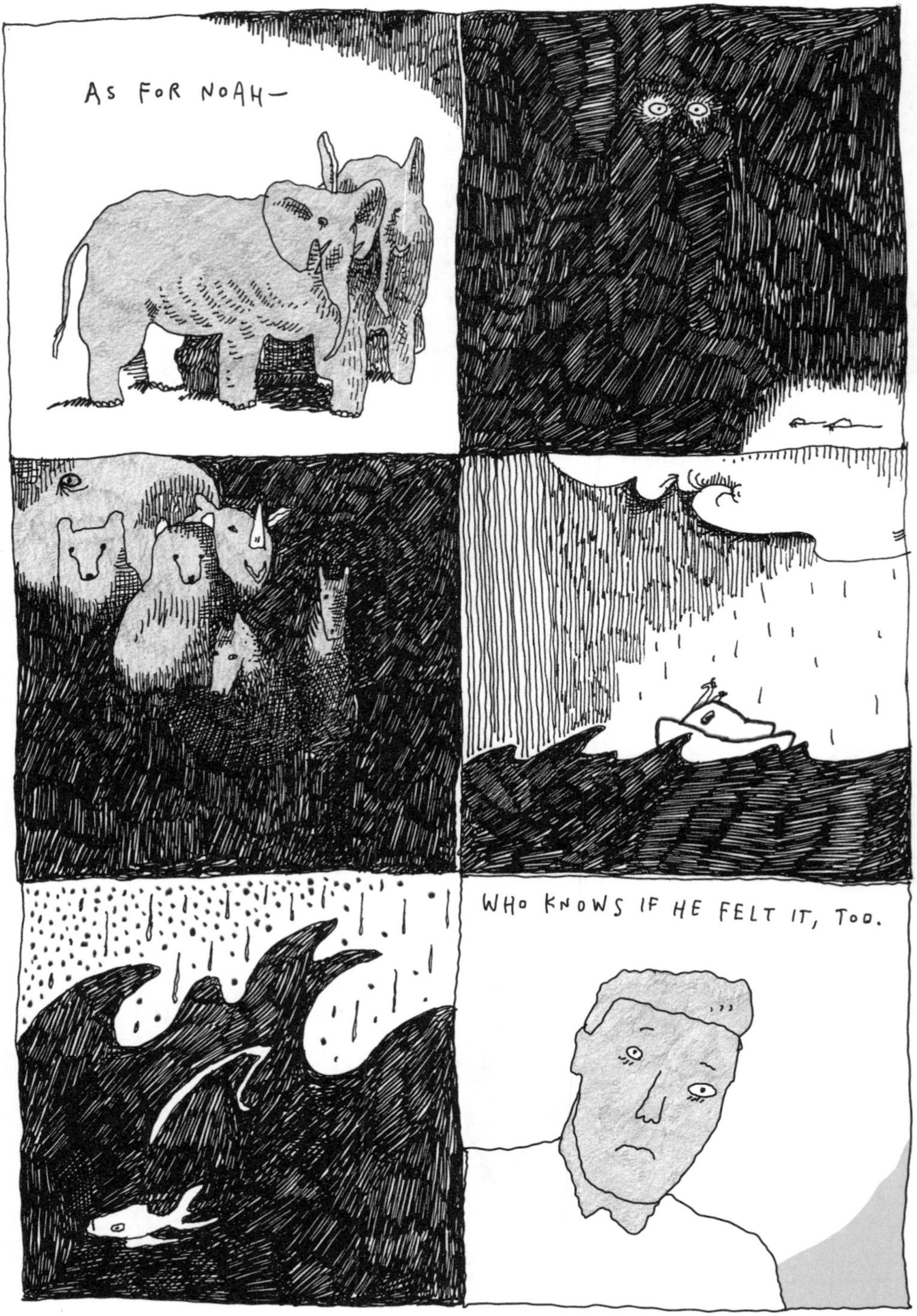
AS FOR NOAH—
WHO KNOWS IF HE FELT IT, TOO.

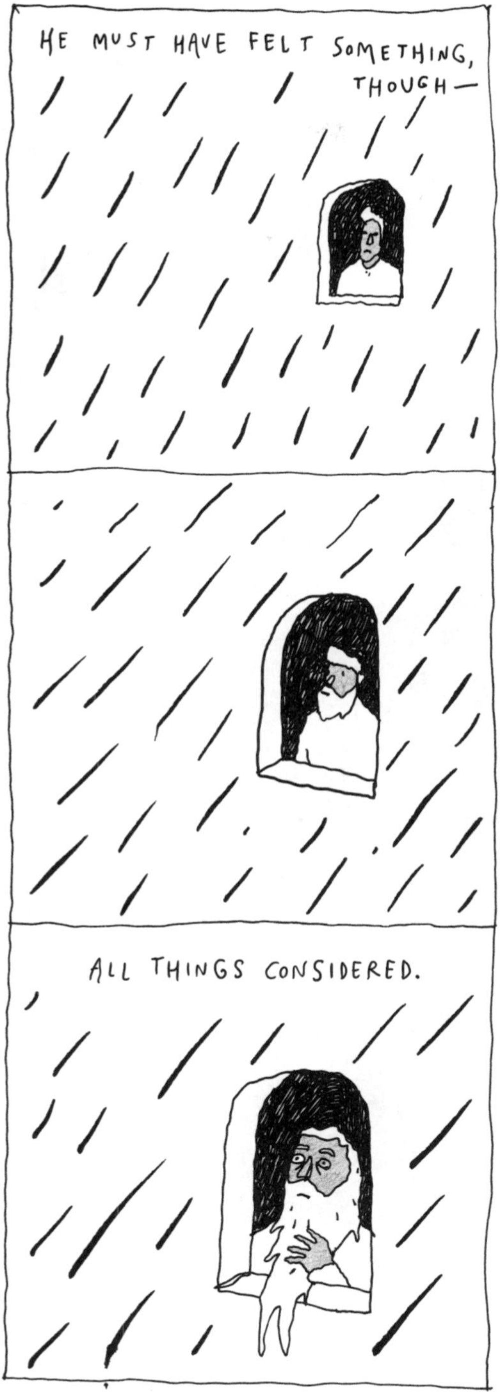
HE MUST HAVE FELT SOMETHING, THOUGH—
ALL THINGS CONSIDERED.

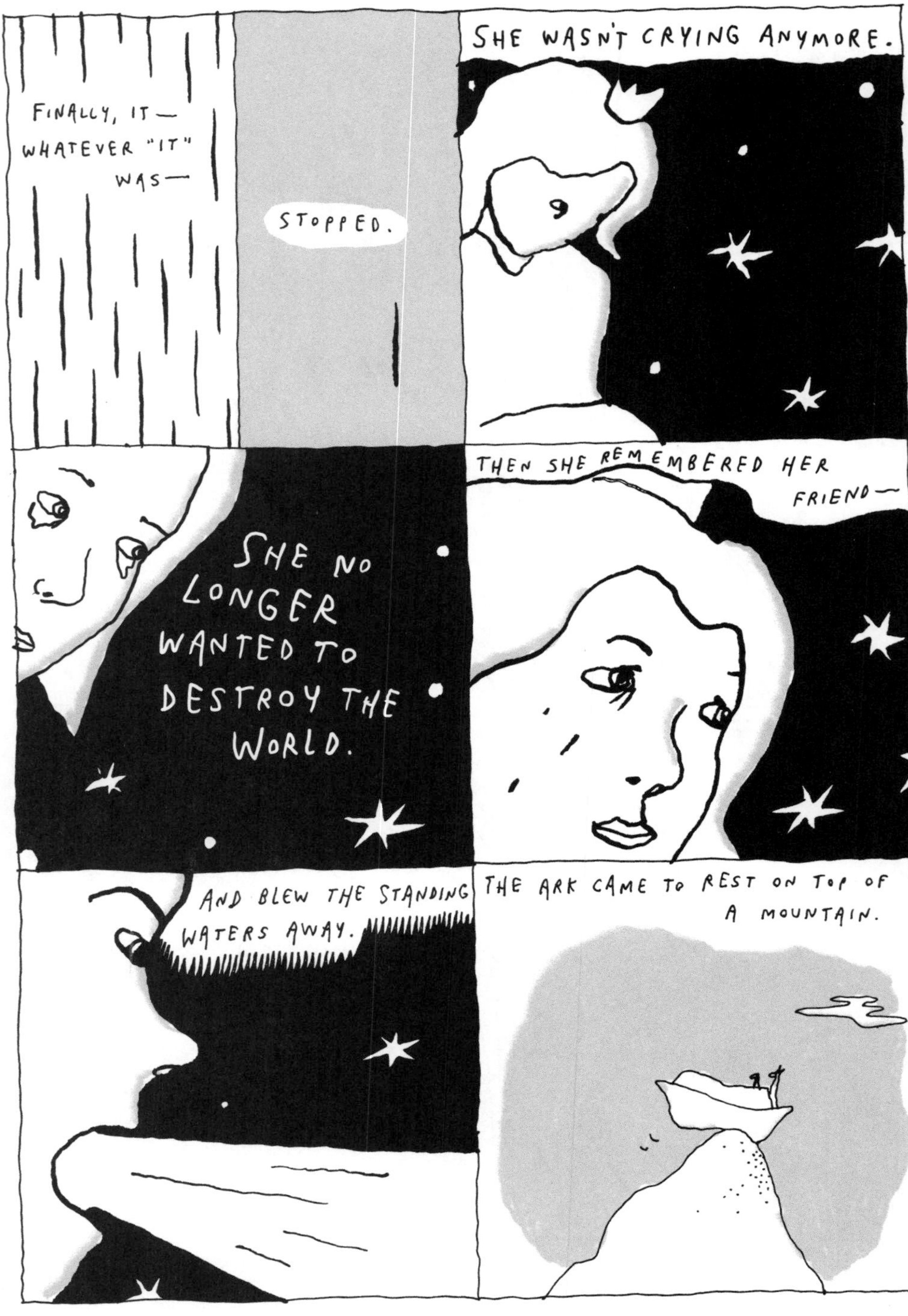
FINALLY, IT— WHATEVER "IT" WAS—
STOPPED.
SHE WASN'T CRYING ANYMORE.
SHE NO LONGER WANTED TO DESTROY THE WORLD.
THEN SHE REMEMBERED HER FRIEND—
AND BLEW THE STANDING WATERS AWAY.
THE ARK CAME TO REST ON TOP OF A MOUNTAIN.

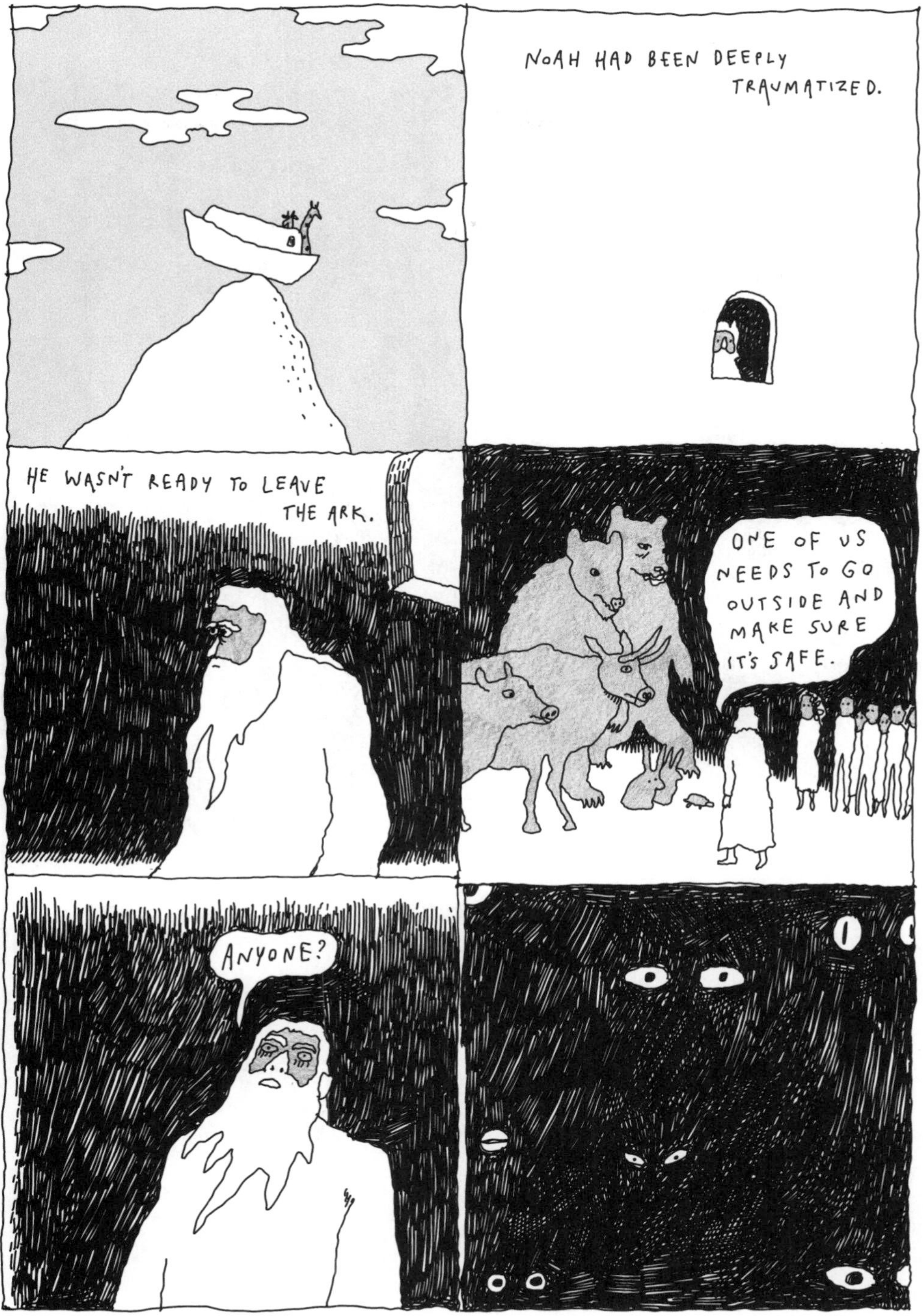
NOAH HAD BEEN DEEPLY TRAUMATIZED.
HE WASN'T READY TO LEAVE THE ARK.
ONE OF US NEEDS TO GO OUTSIDE AND MAKE SURE IT'S SAFE.
ANYONE?

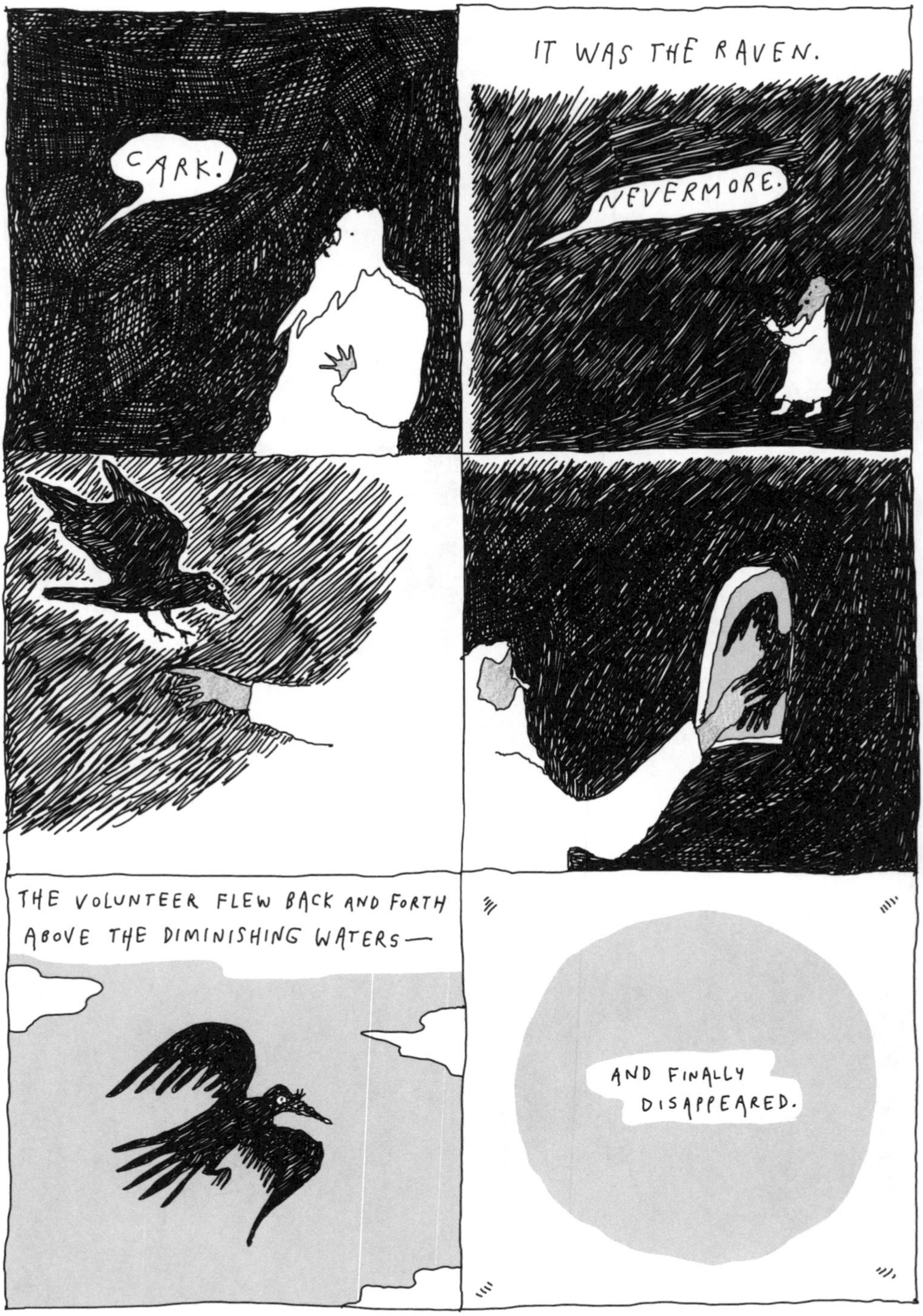
CARK!
IT WAS THE RAVEN.
NEVERMORE.
THE VOLUNTEER FLEW BACK AND FORTH ABOVE THE DIMINISHING WATERS—
AND FINALLY DISAPPEARED.

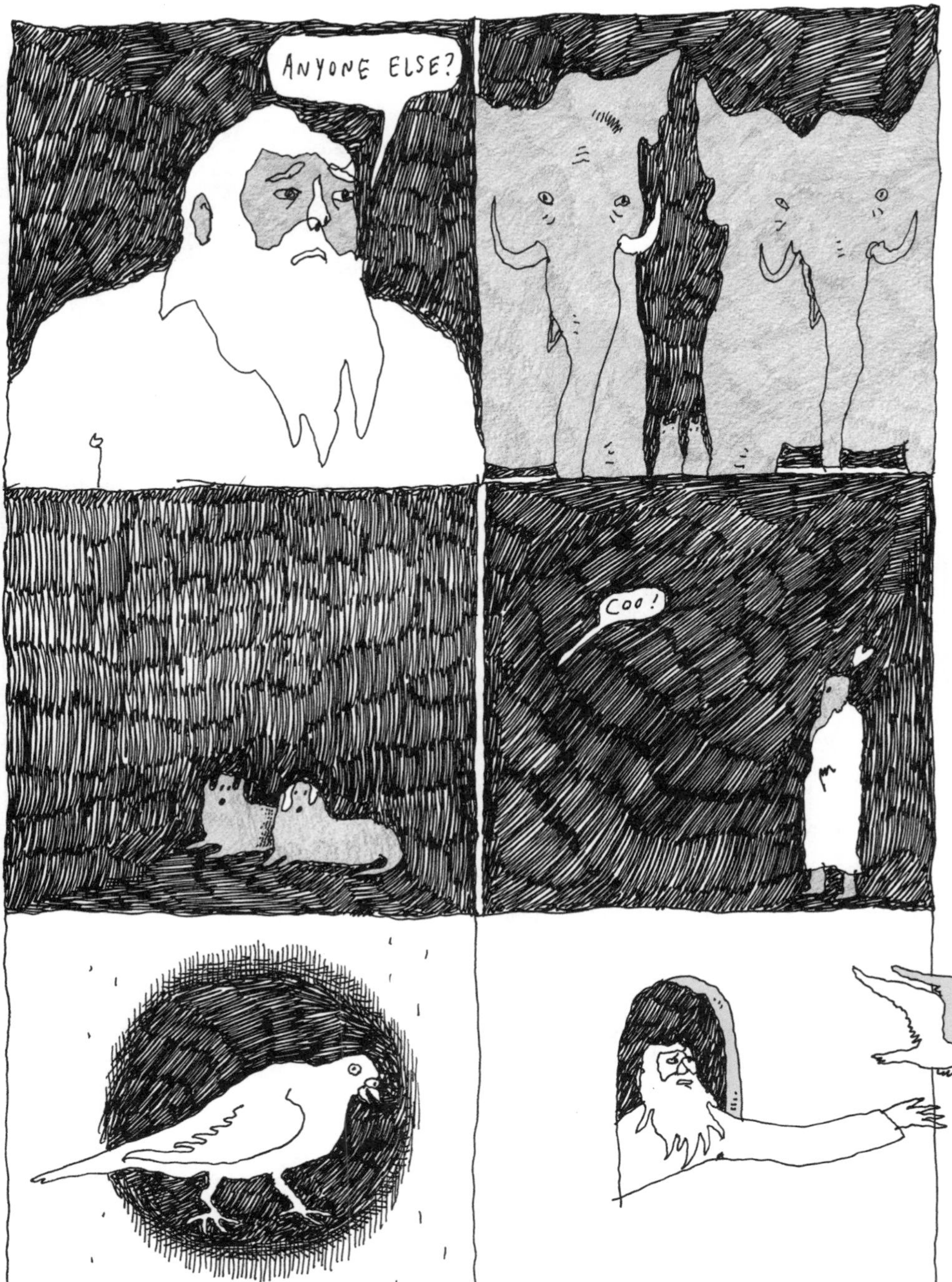
ANYONE ELSE?
COO!

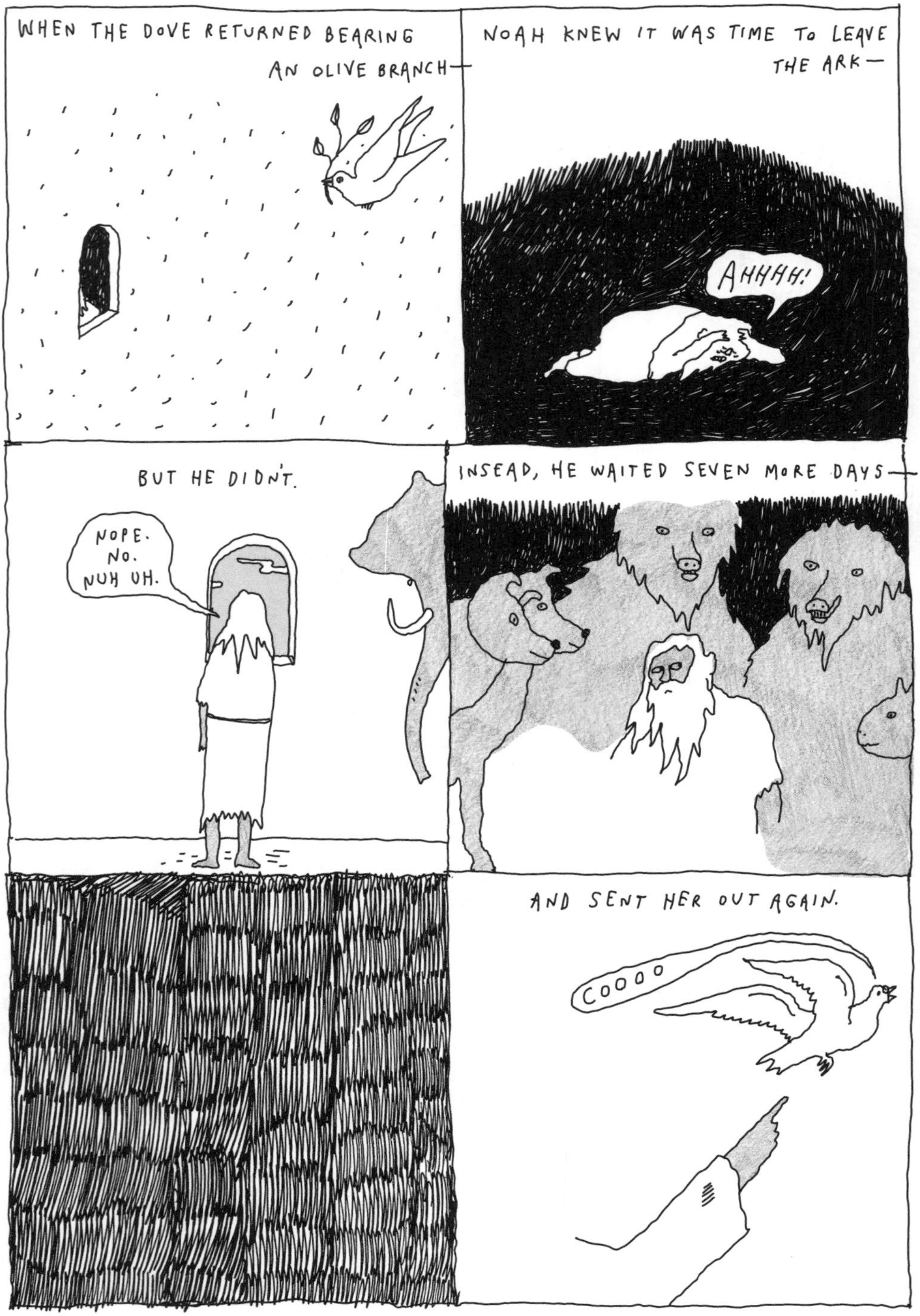

WHEN THE DOVE RETURNED BEARING AN OLIVE BRANCH—
NOAH KNEW IT WAS TIME TO LEAVE THE ARK—
AHHHH!
BUT HE DIDN'T.
NOPE. NO. NUH UH.
INSEAD, HE WAITED SEVEN MORE DAYS—
AND SENT HER OUT AGAIN.
COOOO

AND THIS TIME,
SHE DIDN'T COME BACK.

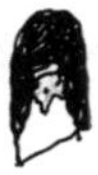

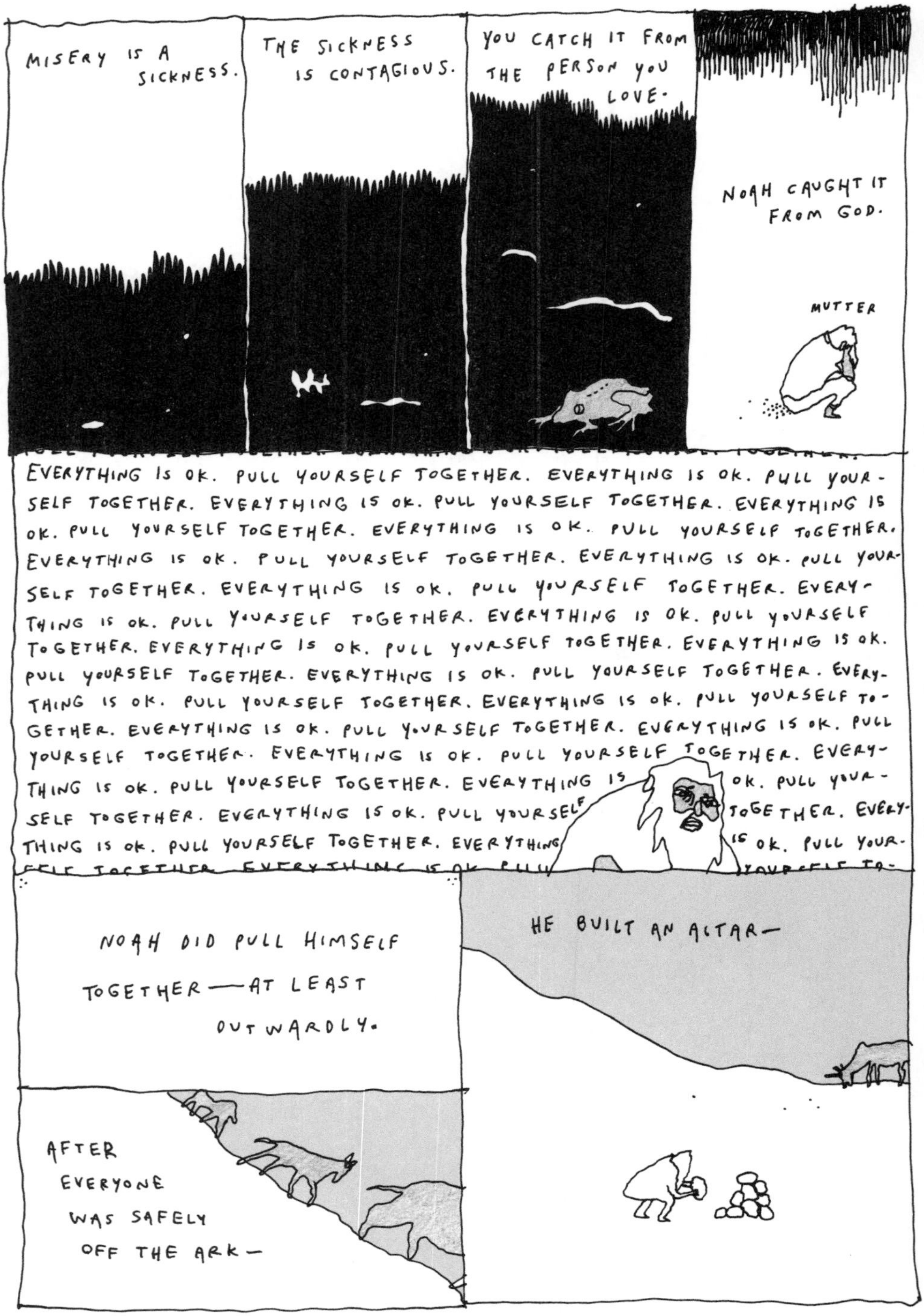
MISERY IS A SICKNESS.
THE SICKNESS IS CONTAGIOUS.
YOU CATCH IT FROM THE PERSON YOU LOVE.
NOAH CAUGHT IT FROM GOD.
MUTTER
EVERYTHING IS OK. PULL YOURSELF TOGETHER. EVERYTHING IS OK. PULL YOUR-
NOAH DID PULL HIMSELF TOGETHER—AT LEAST OUTWARDLY.
AFTER EVERYONE WAS SAFELY OFF THE ARK—
HE BUILT AN ALTAR—

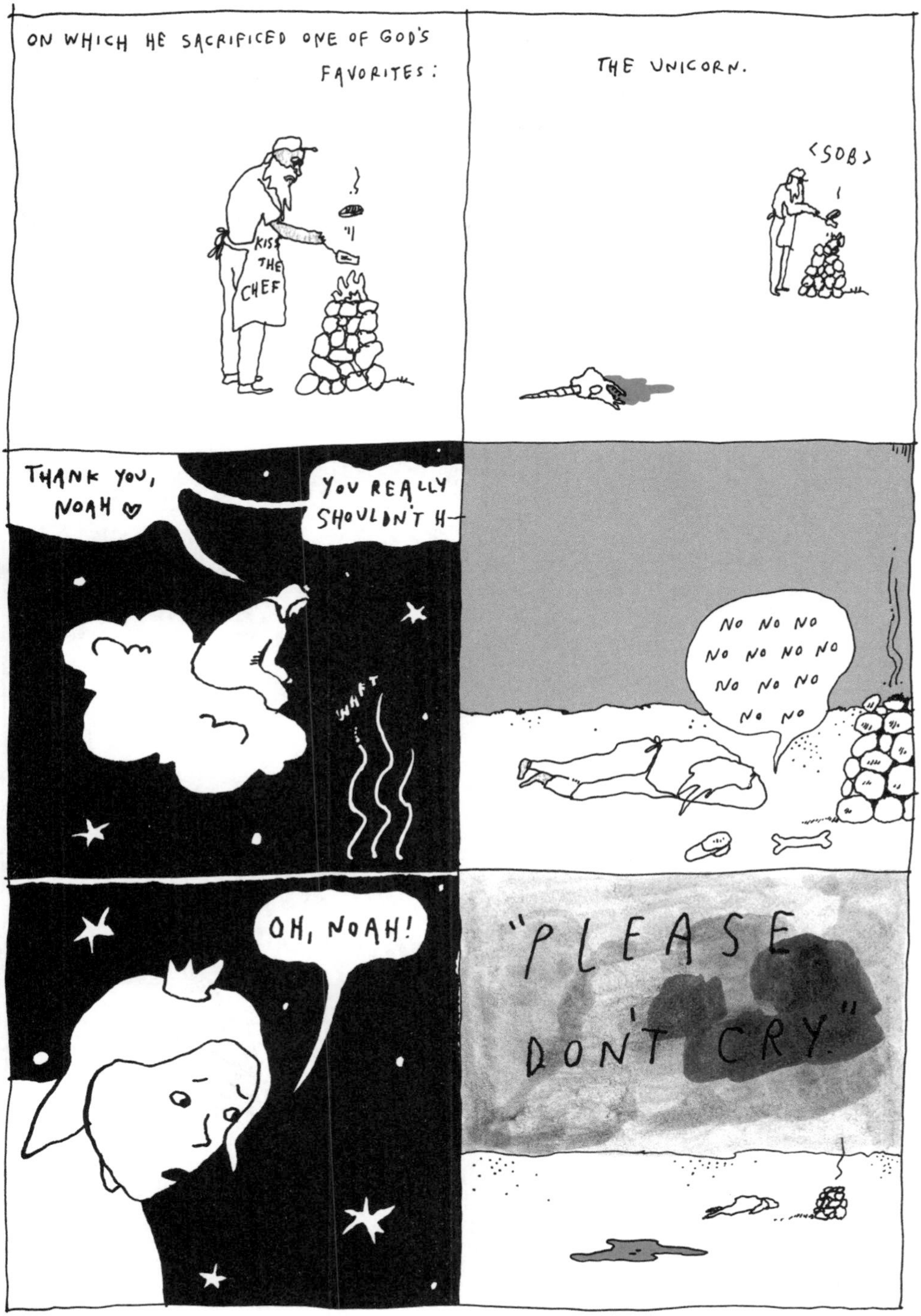

ON WHICH HE SACRIFICED ONE OF GOD'S FAVORITES:
KISS THE CHEF
THE UNICORN.
<SOB>
THANK YOU, NOAH ♡
YOU REALLY SHOULDN'T H—
WAFT
NO NO NO NO NO NO NO NO NO NO NO NO
OH, NOAH!
"PLEASE DON'T CRY."

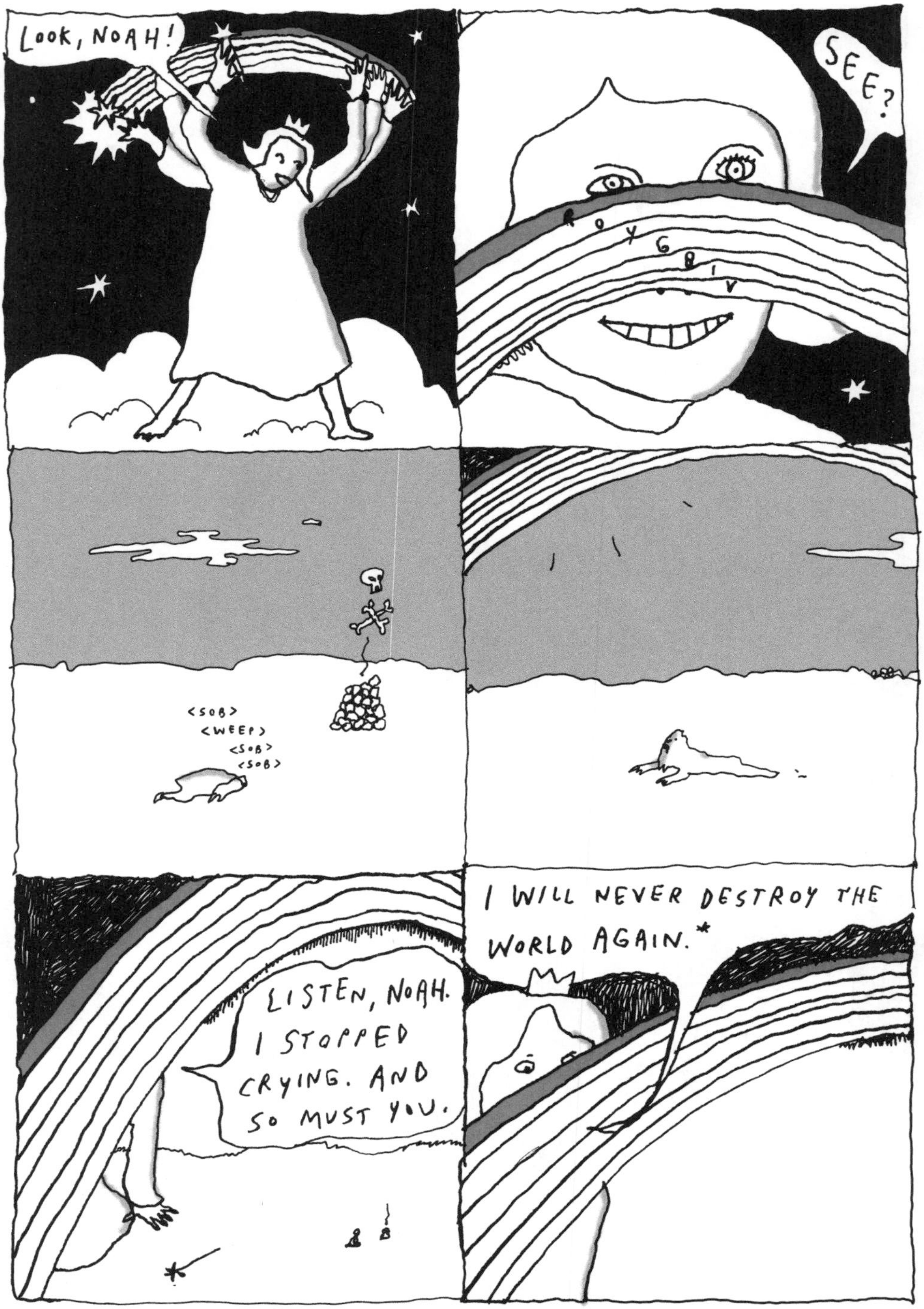
LOOK, NOAH!
SEE?
R O Y G B I V
<SOB>
<WEEP>
<SOB>
<SOB>
LISTEN, NOAH. I STOPPED CRYING. AND SO MUST YOU.
I WILL NEVER DESTROY THE WORLD AGAIN.*

*SHE MEANT IT.

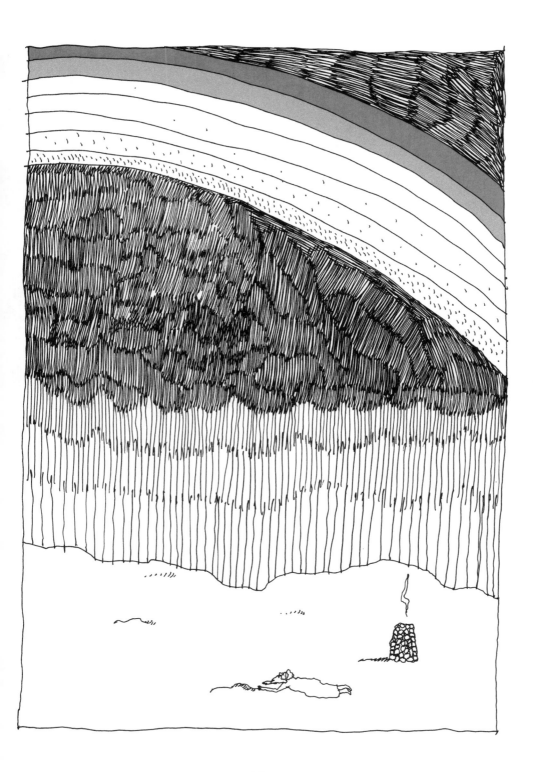

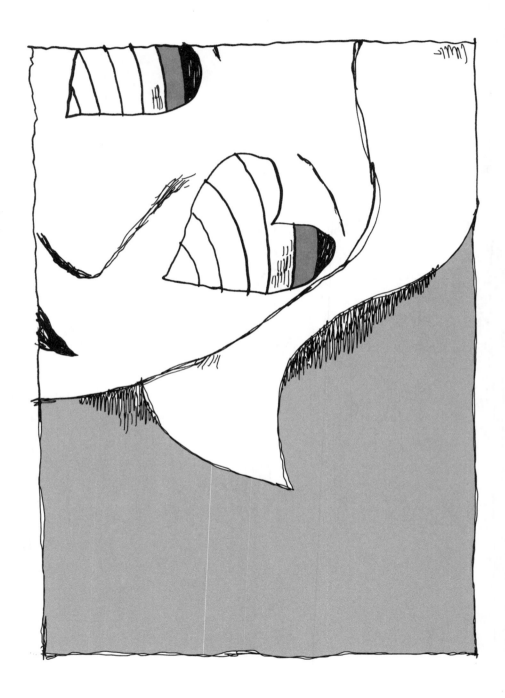

114

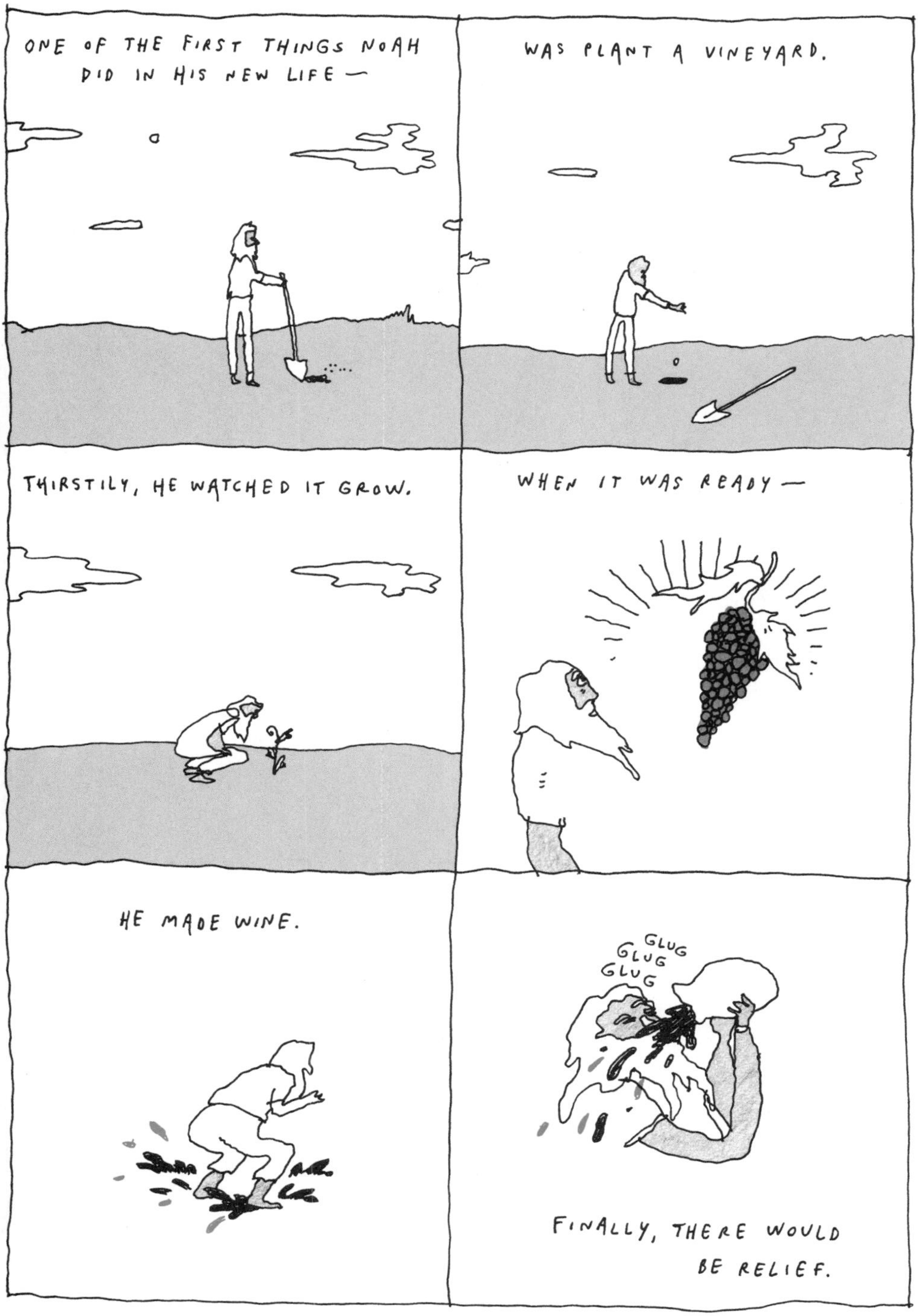
ONE OF THE FIRST THINGS NOAH DID IN HIS NEW LIFE —
WAS PLANT A VINEYARD.
THIRSTILY, HE WATCHED IT GROW.
WHEN IT WAS READY —
HE MADE WINE.
GLUG
GLUG
GLUG
FINALLY, THERE WOULD BE RELIEF.

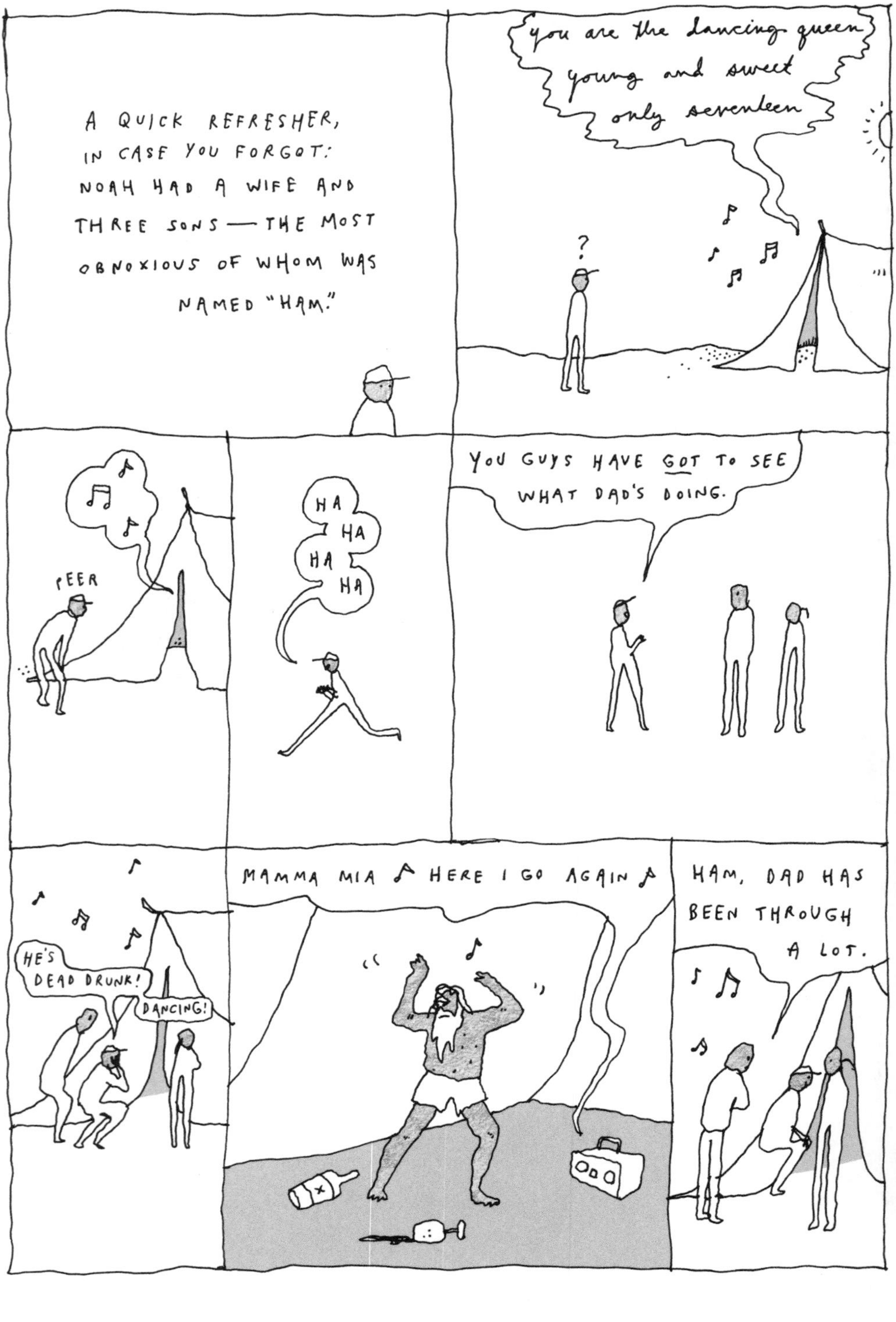
A QUICK REFRESHER, IN CASE YOU FORGOT: NOAH HAD A WIFE AND THREE SONS — THE MOST OBNOXIOUS OF WHOM WAS NAMED "HAM."
you are the dancing queen young and sweet only seventeen
?
PEER
HA HA HA HA
YOU GUYS HAVE GOT TO SEE WHAT DAD'S DOING.
HE'S DEAD DRUNK!
DANCING!
MAMMA MIA ♪ HERE I GO AGAIN ♪
HAM, DAD HAS BEEN THROUGH A LOT.

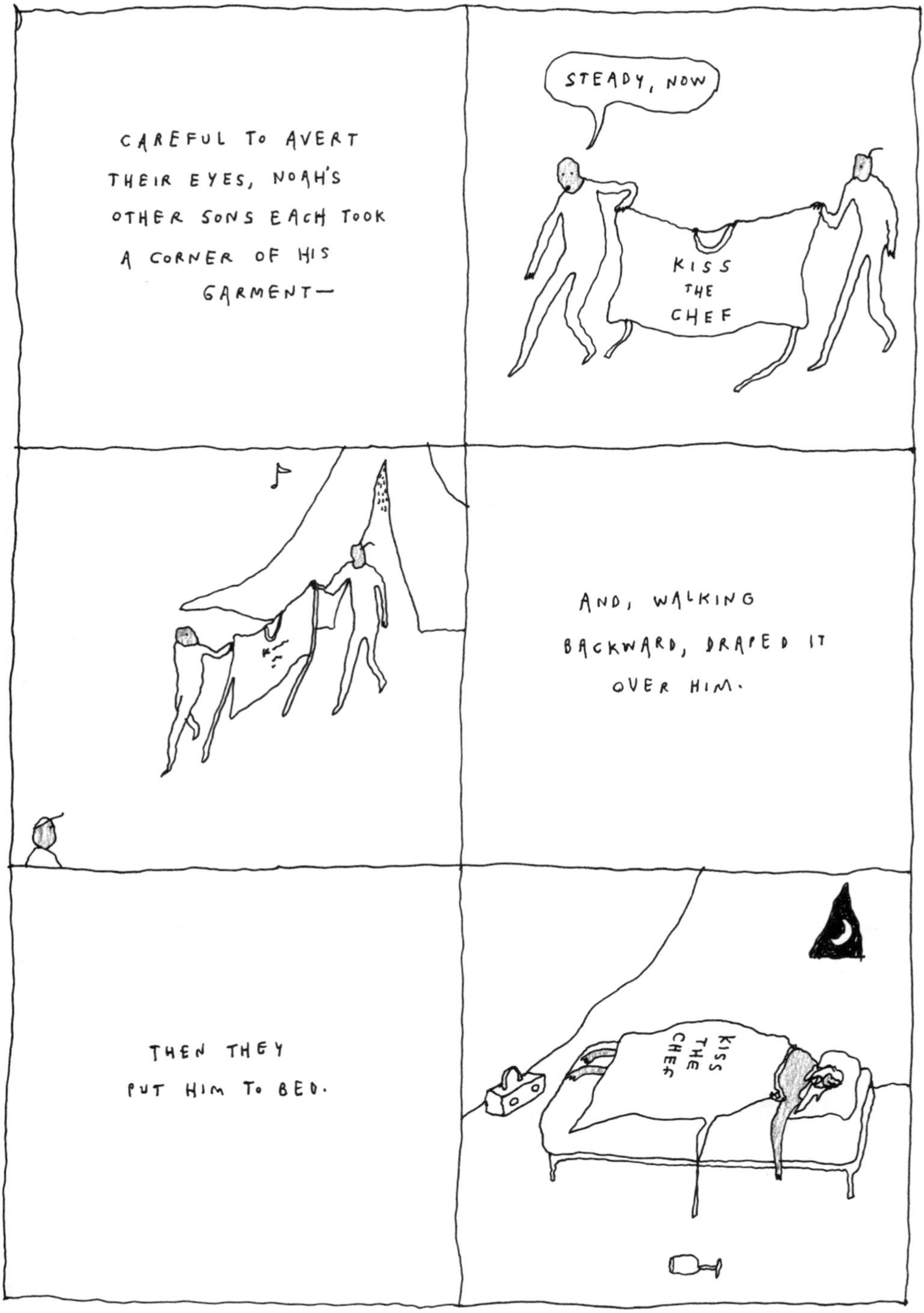
CAREFUL TO AVERT THEIR EYES, NOAH'S OTHER SONS EACH TOOK A CORNER OF HIS GARMENT—
STEADY, NOW
KISS THE CHEF
AND, WALKING BACKWARD, DRAPED IT OVER HIM.
THEN THEY PUT HIM TO BED.
KISS THE CHEF

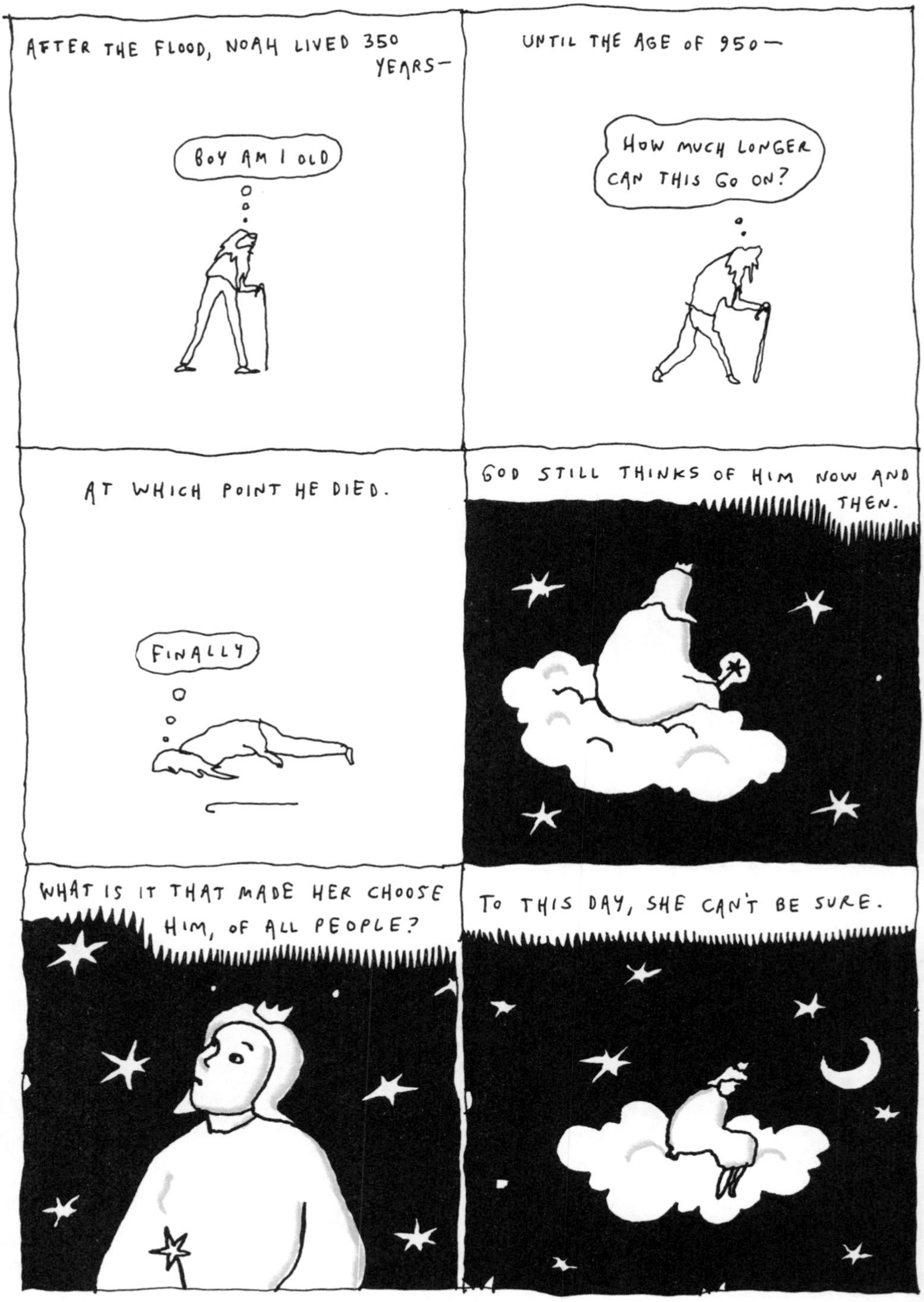
AFTER THE FLOOD, NOAH LIVED 350 YEARS—
BOY AM I OLD
UNTIL THE AGE OF 950—
HOW MUCH LONGER CAN THIS GO ON?
AT WHICH POINT HE DIED.
FINALLY
GOD STILL THINKS OF HIM NOW AND THEN.
WHAT IS IT THAT MADE HER CHOOSE HIM, OF ALL PEOPLE?
TO THIS DAY, SHE CAN'T BE SURE.

NIMROD.

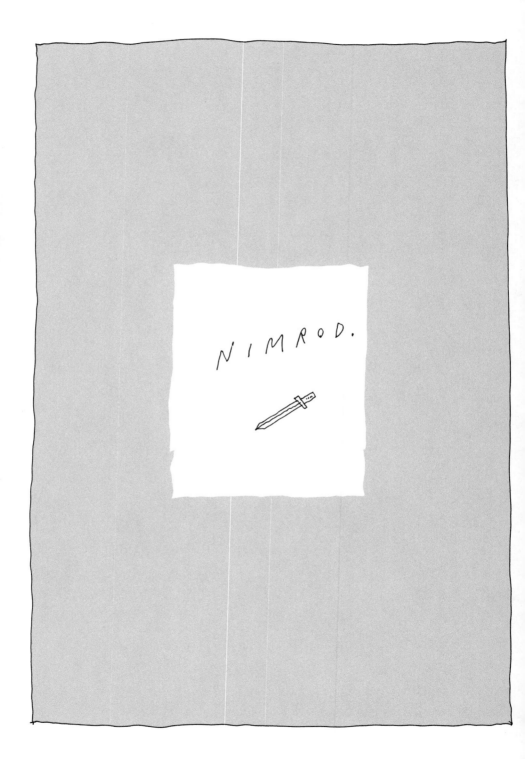

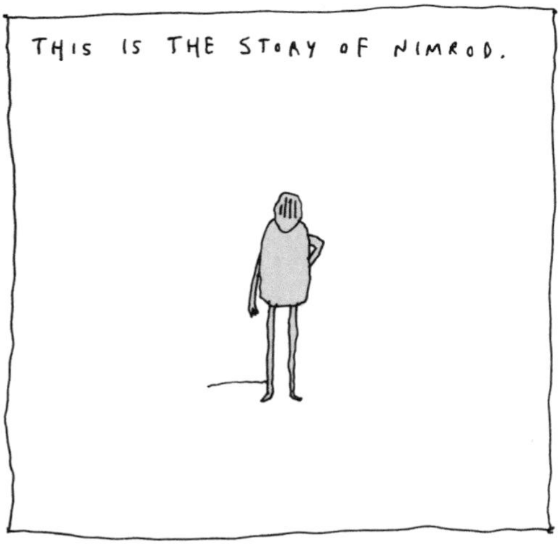
THIS IS THE STORY OF NIMROD.

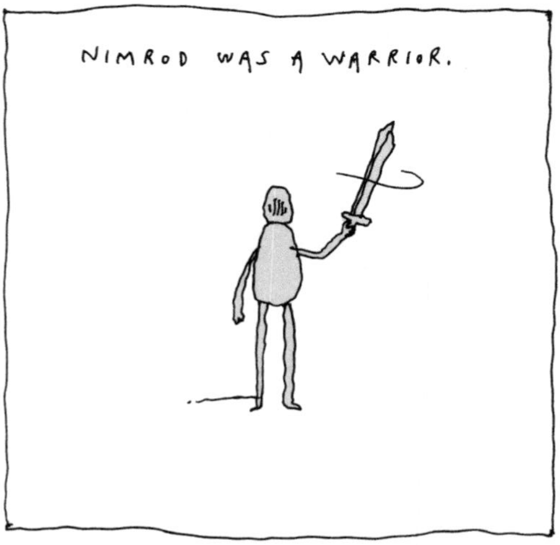
NIMROD WAS A WARRIOR.

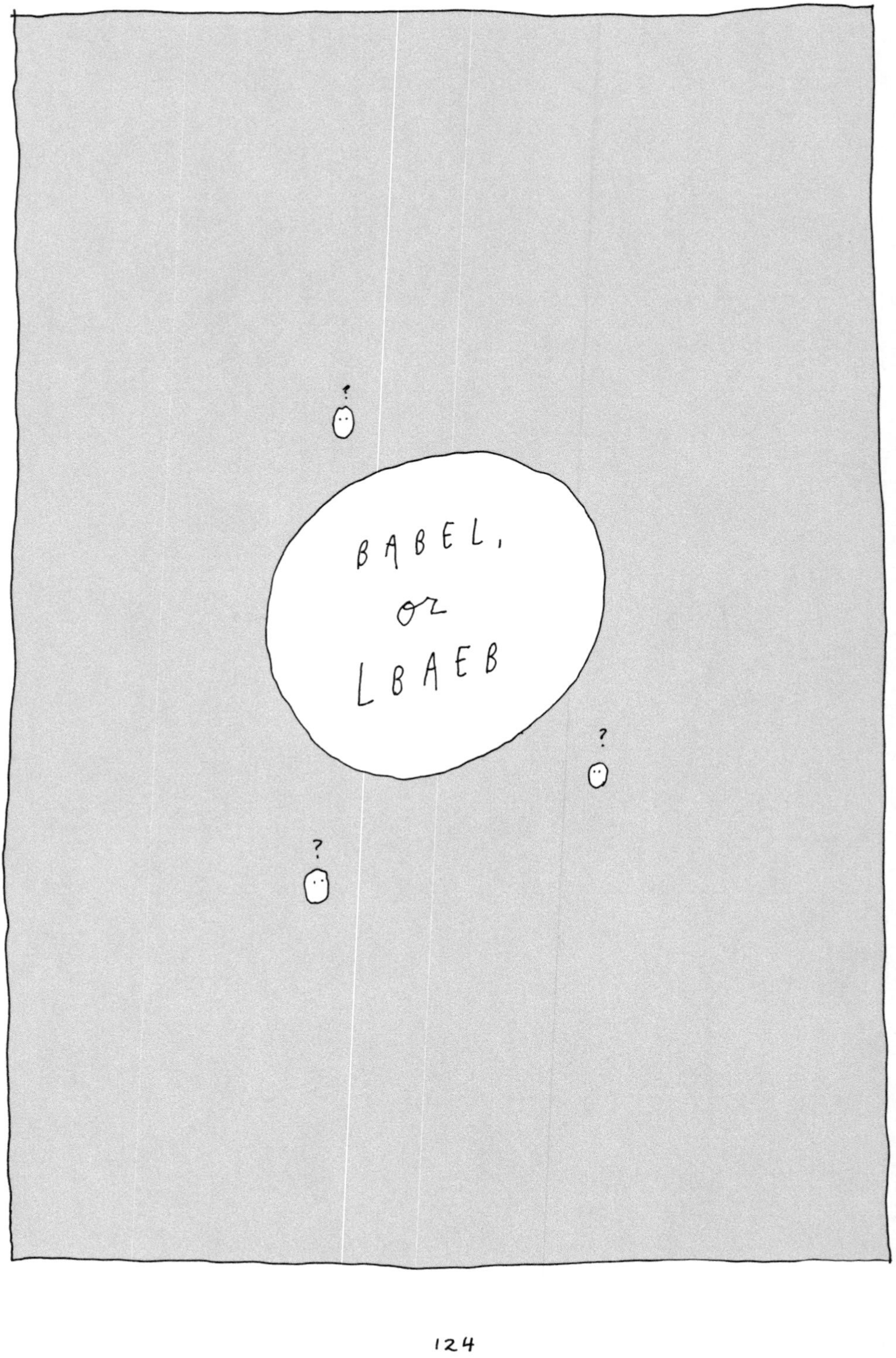
BABEL,
or
LBAEB

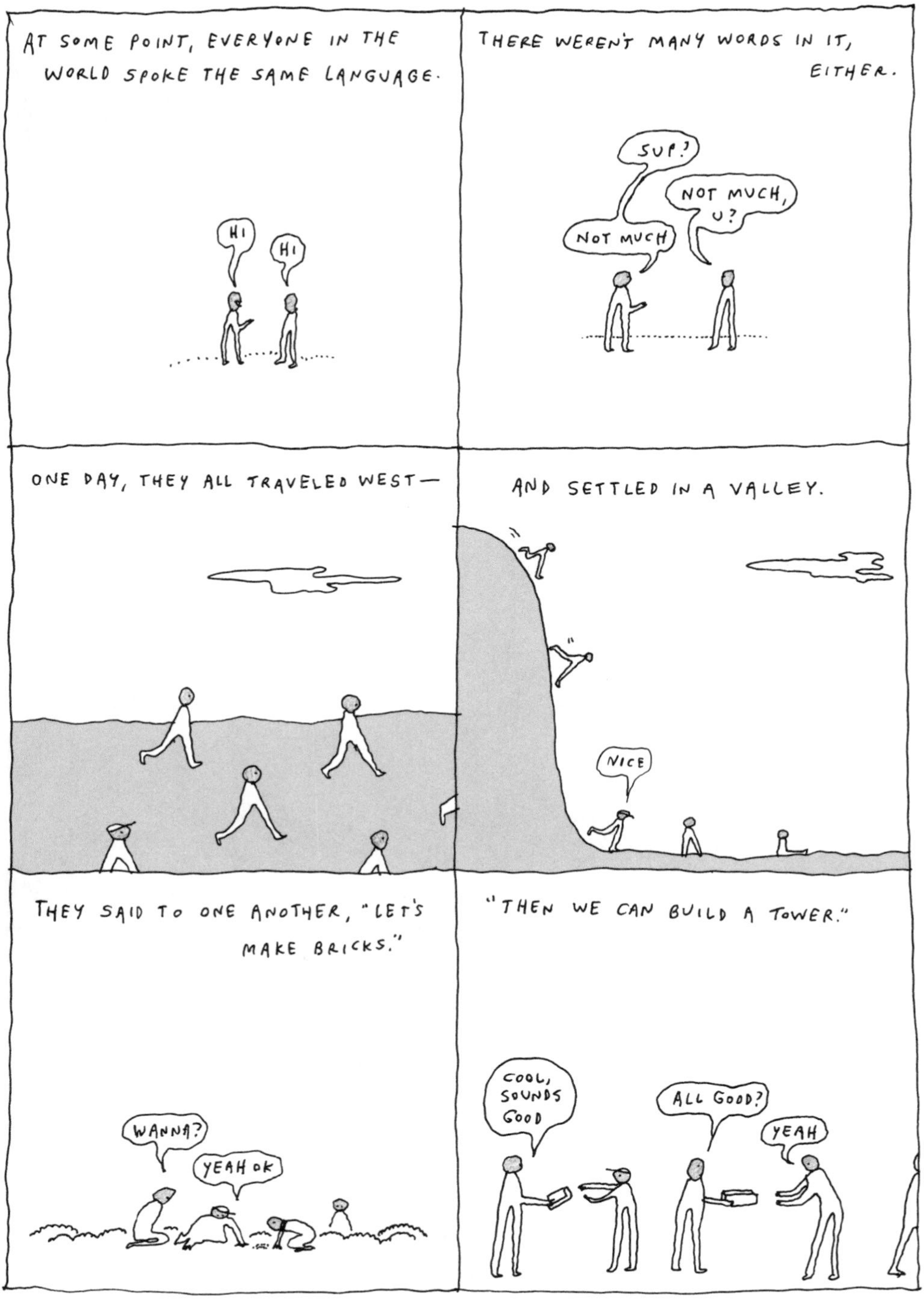
AT SOME POINT, EVERYONE IN THE WORLD SPOKE THE SAME LANGUAGE.
HI
HI
THERE WEREN'T MANY WORDS IN IT, EITHER.
SUP?
NOT MUCH
NOT MUCH, U?
ONE DAY, THEY ALL TRAVELED WEST—
AND SETTLED IN A VALLEY.
NICE
THEY SAID TO ONE ANOTHER, "LET'S MAKE BRICKS."
WANNA?
YEAH OK
"THEN WE CAN BUILD A TOWER."
COOL, SOUNDS GOOD
ALL GOOD?
YEAH

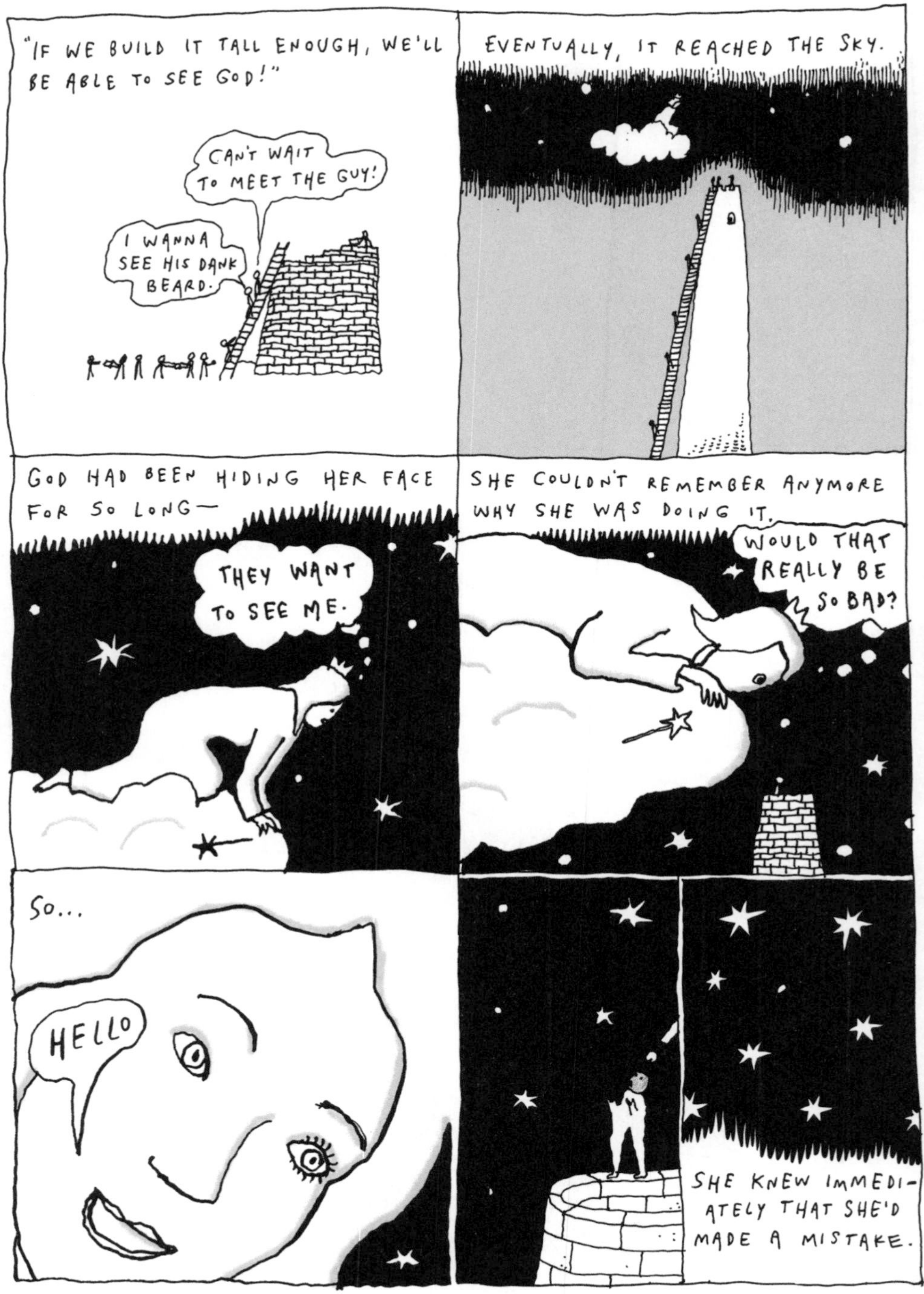
"IF WE BUILD IT TALL ENOUGH, WE'LL BE ABLE TO SEE GOD!"
CAN'T WAIT TO MEET THE GUY!
I WANNA SEE HIS DANK BEARD.
EVENTUALLY, IT REACHED THE SKY.
GOD HAD BEEN HIDING HER FACE FOR SO LONG—
THEY WANT TO SEE ME.
SHE COULDN'T REMEMBER ANYMORE WHY SHE WAS DOING IT.
WOULD THAT REALLY BE SO BAD?
SO...
HELLO
SHE KNEW IMMEDIATELY THAT SHE'D MADE A MISTAKE.

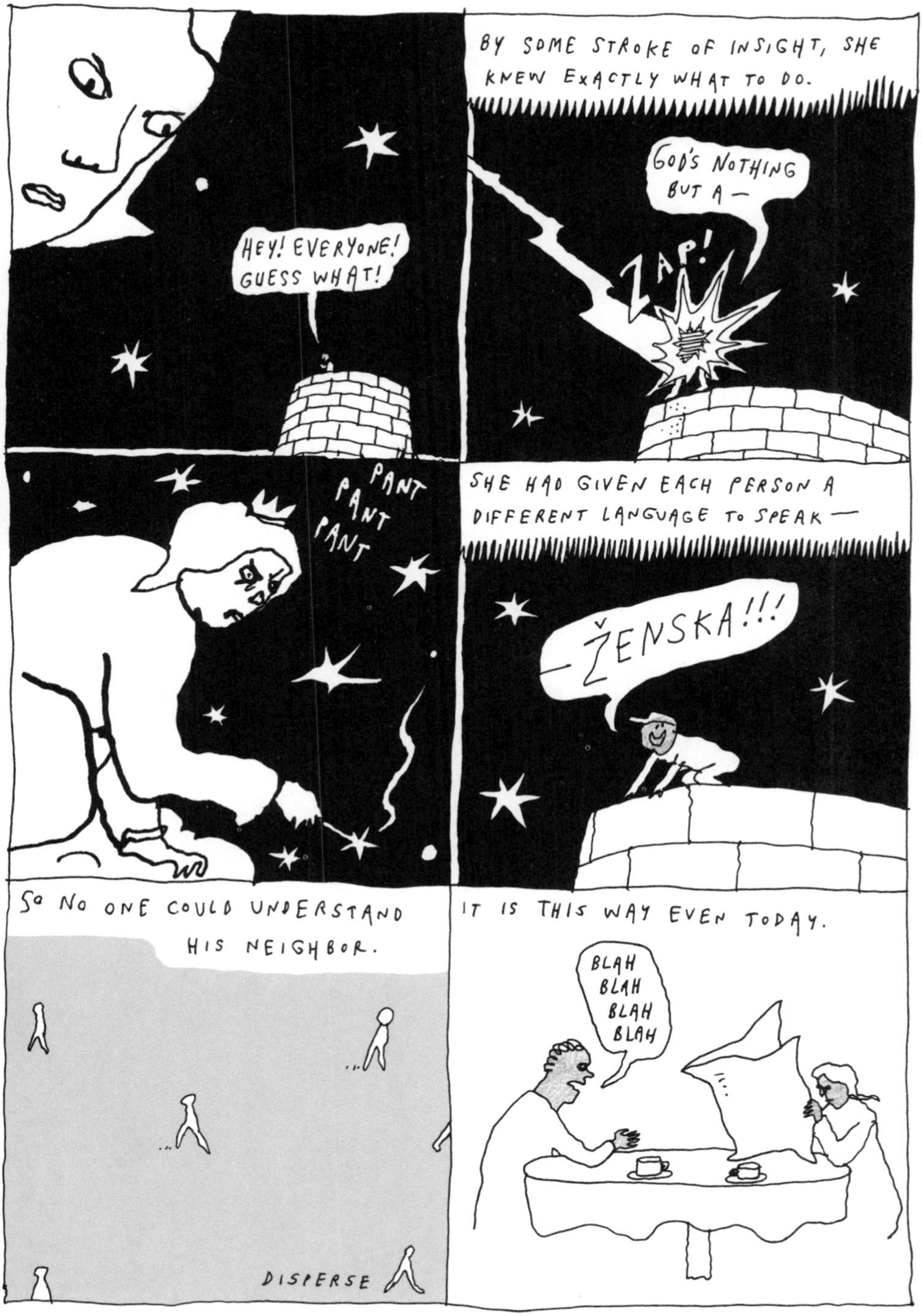
HEY! EVERYONE! GUESS WHAT!
BY SOME STROKE OF INSIGHT, SHE KNEW EXACTLY WHAT TO DO.
GOD'S NOTHING BUT A—
ZAP!
PANT PANT PANT
SHE HAD GIVEN EACH PERSON A DIFFERENT LANGUAGE TO SPEAK—
—ŽENSKA!!!
SO NO ONE COULD UNDERSTAND HIS NEIGHBOR.
DISPERSE
IT IS THIS WAY EVEN TODAY.
BLAH BLAH BLAH BLAH

WITHDRAWAL

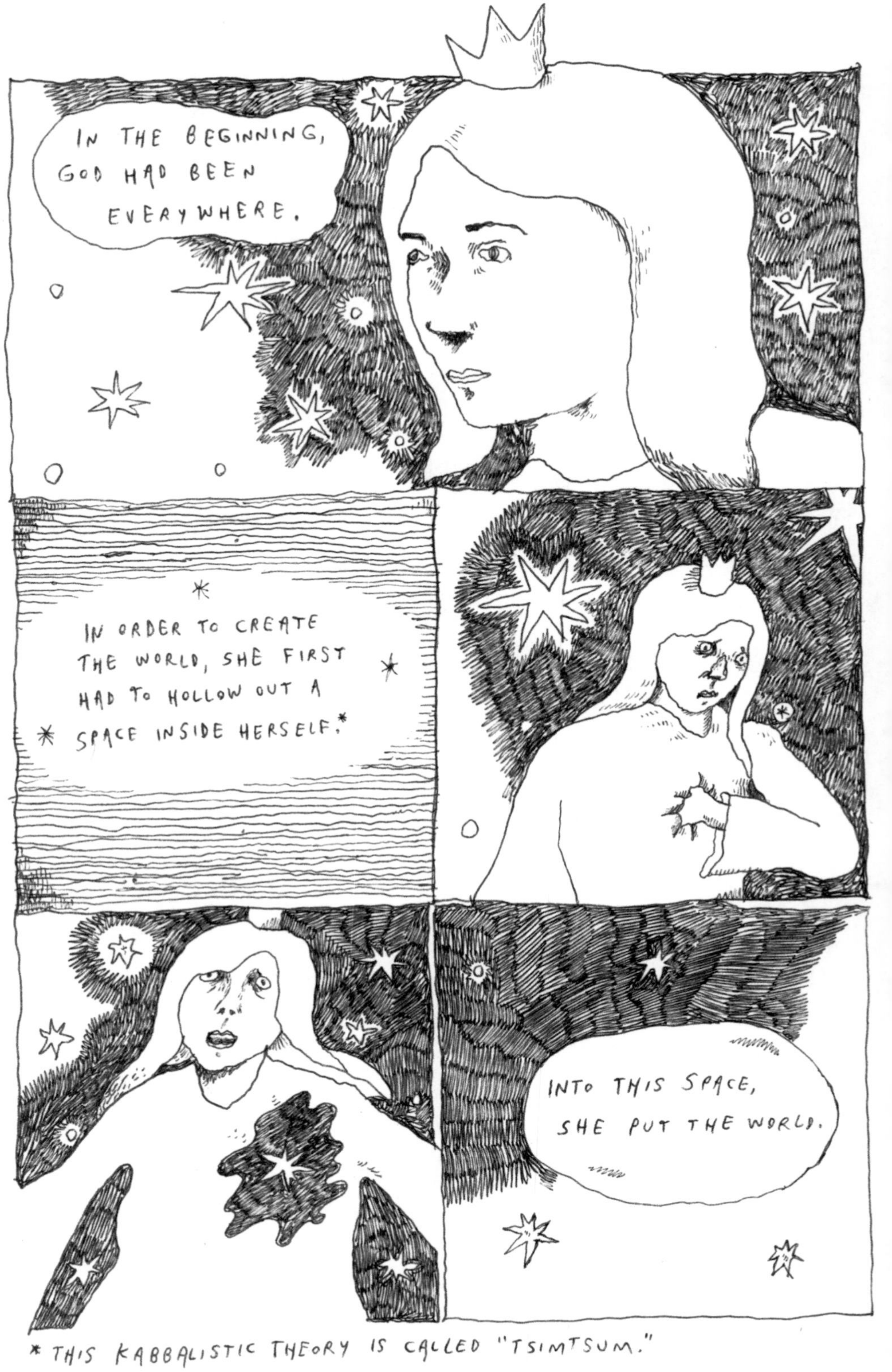
IN THE BEGINNING, GOD HAD BEEN EVERYWHERE.
IN ORDER TO CREATE THE WORLD, SHE FIRST HAD TO HOLLOW OUT A SPACE INSIDE HERSELF.*
INTO THIS SPACE, SHE PUT THE WORLD.

* THIS KABBALISTIC THEORY IS CALLED "TSIMTSUM."

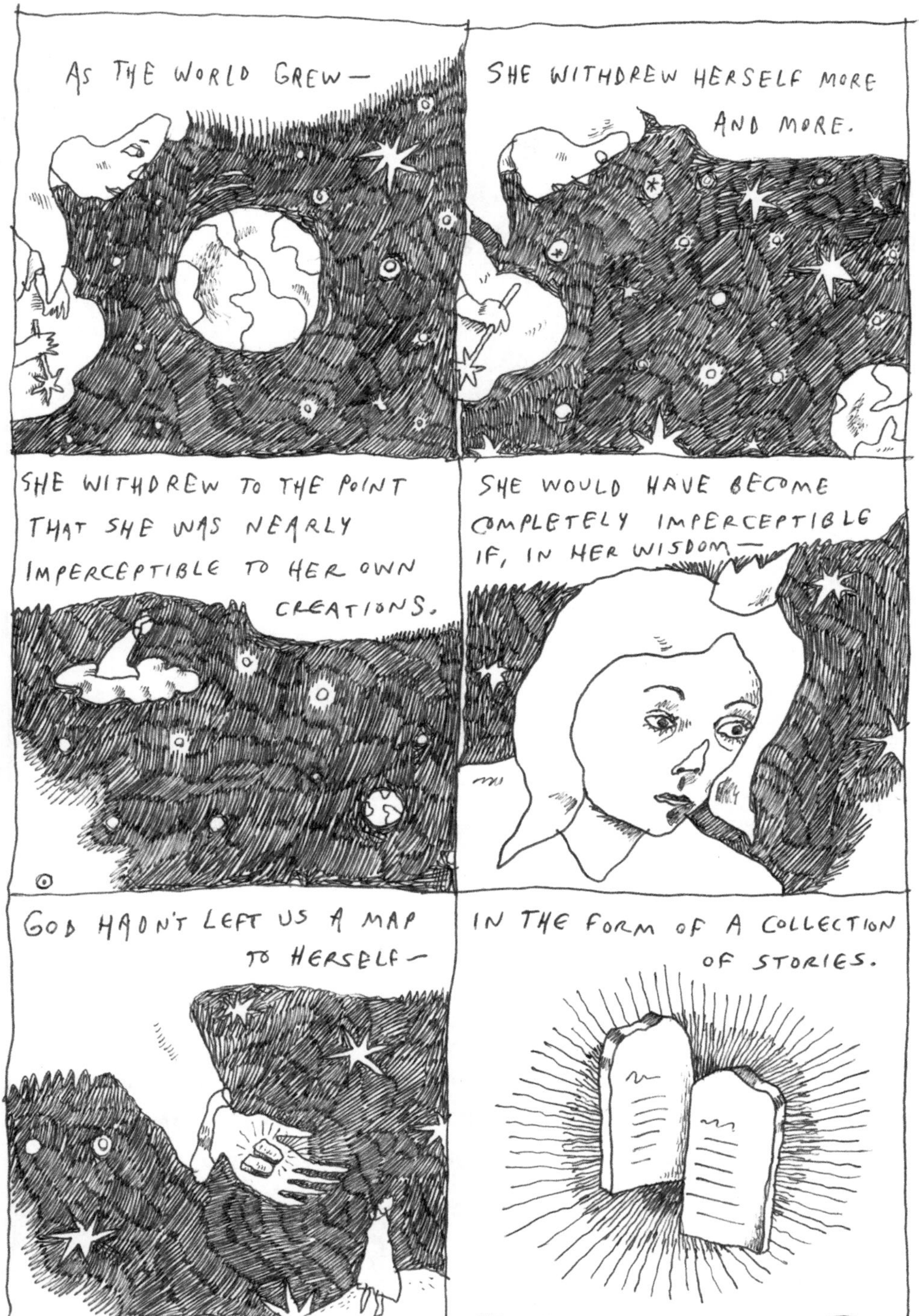
AS THE WORLD GREW—
SHE WITHDREW HERSELF MORE AND MORE.
SHE WITHDREW TO THE POINT THAT SHE WAS NEARLY IMPERCEPTIBLE TO HER OWN CREATIONS.
SHE WOULD HAVE BECOME COMPLETELY IMPERCEPTIBLE IF, IN HER WISDOM—
GOD HADN'T LEFT US A MAP TO HERSELF—
IN THE FORM OF A COLLECTION OF STORIES.

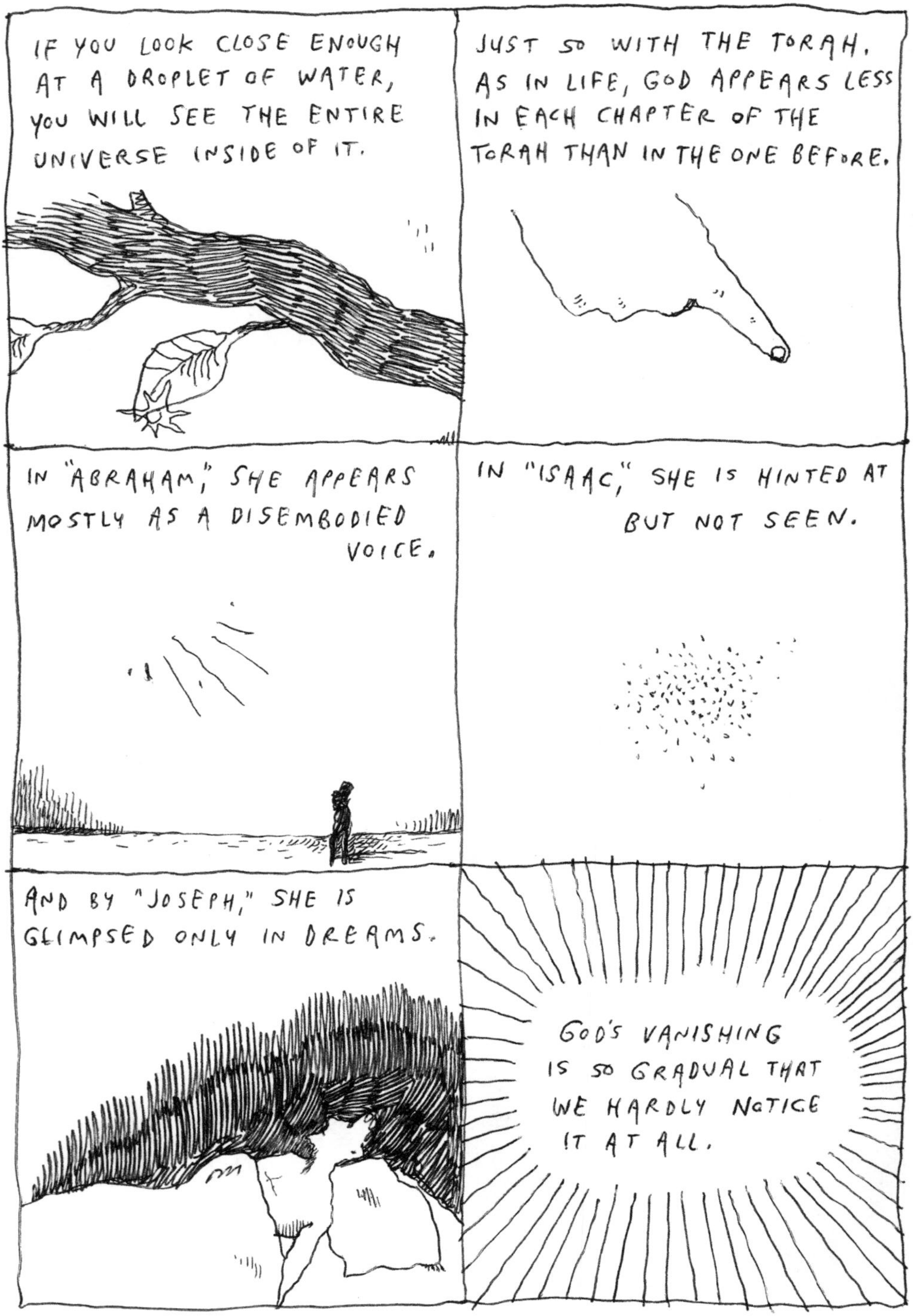
IF YOU LOOK CLOSE ENOUGH AT A DROPLET OF WATER, YOU WILL SEE THE ENTIRE UNIVERSE INSIDE OF IT.
JUST SO WITH THE TORAH. AS IN LIFE, GOD APPEARS LESS IN EACH CHAPTER OF THE TORAH THAN IN THE ONE BEFORE.
IN "ABRAHAM," SHE APPEARS MOSTLY AS A DISEMBODIED VOICE.
IN "ISAAC," SHE IS HINTED AT BUT NOT SEEN.
AND BY "JOSEPH," SHE IS GLIMPSED ONLY IN DREAMS.
GOD'S VANISHING IS SO GRADUAL THAT WE HARDLY NOTICE IT AT ALL.

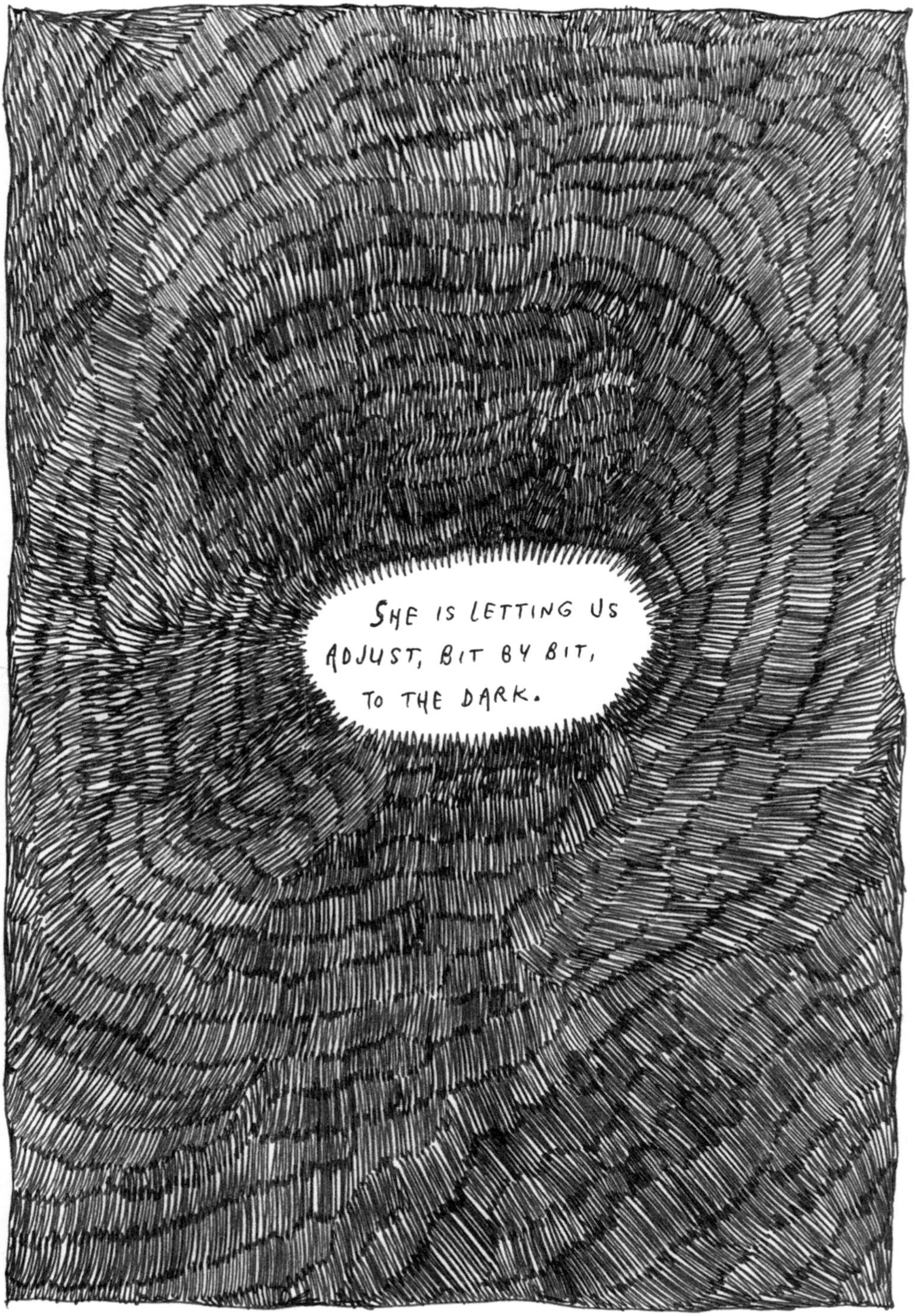
SHE IS LETTING US ADJUST, BIT BY BIT, TO THE DARK.

FOR ONLY IN GOD'S ABSENCE CAN WE BEGIN TO COMPREHEND HER LOVE FOR US.

ONLY THEN CAN WE SEE HER IN
OURSELVES.

II

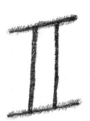

PRESENT

O MY DOVE. IN THE CRANNY OF THE ROCKS,
HIDDEN BY THE CLIFF, LET ME SEE YOUR FACE, LET
ME HEAR YOUR VOICE.

—SONG OF SONGS 2:14

A WOMAN'S VOICE IS TO BE REGARDED AS NAKEDNESS.
—BERAKHOT 24A:17

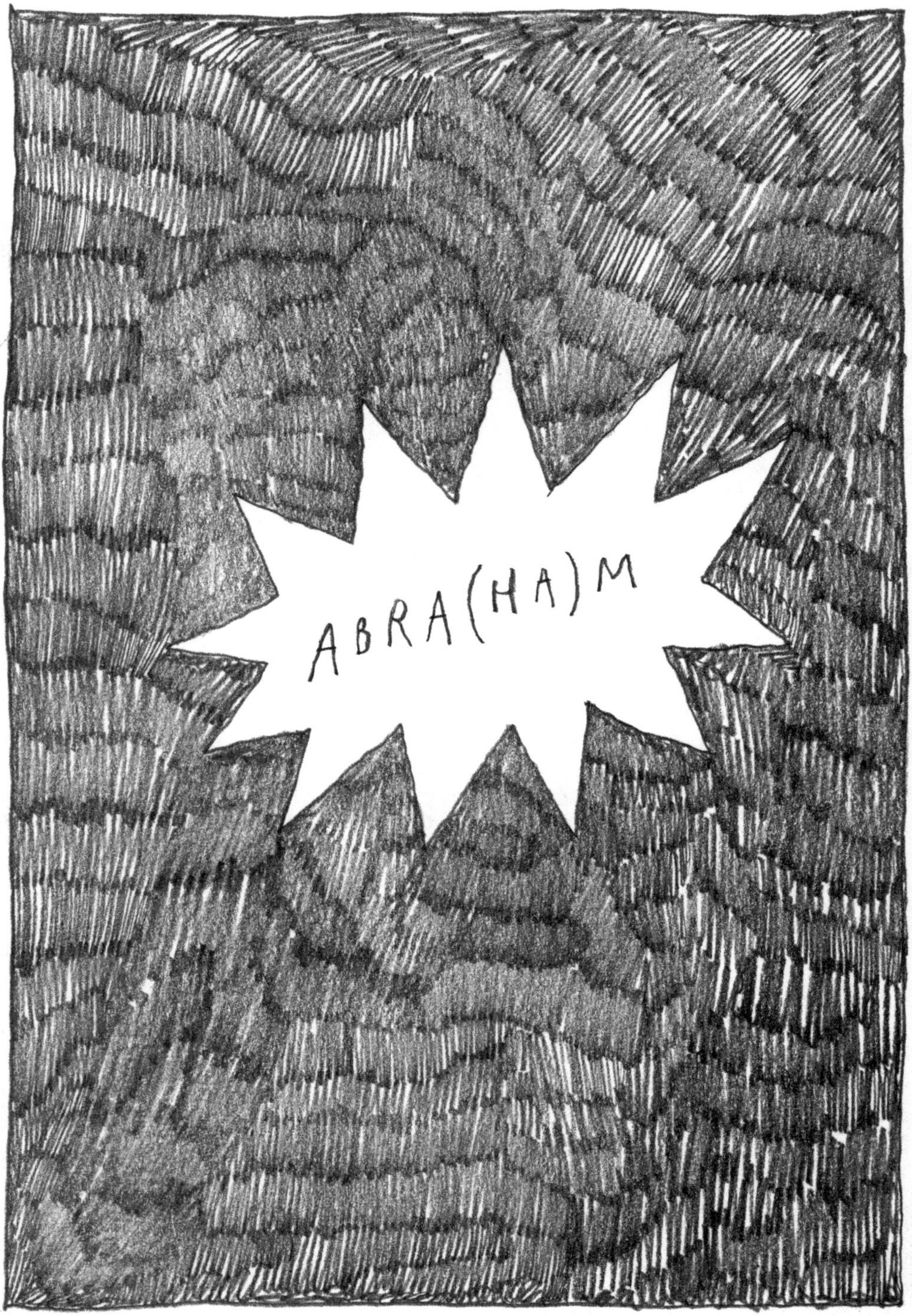
ABRA(HA)M

MORNING

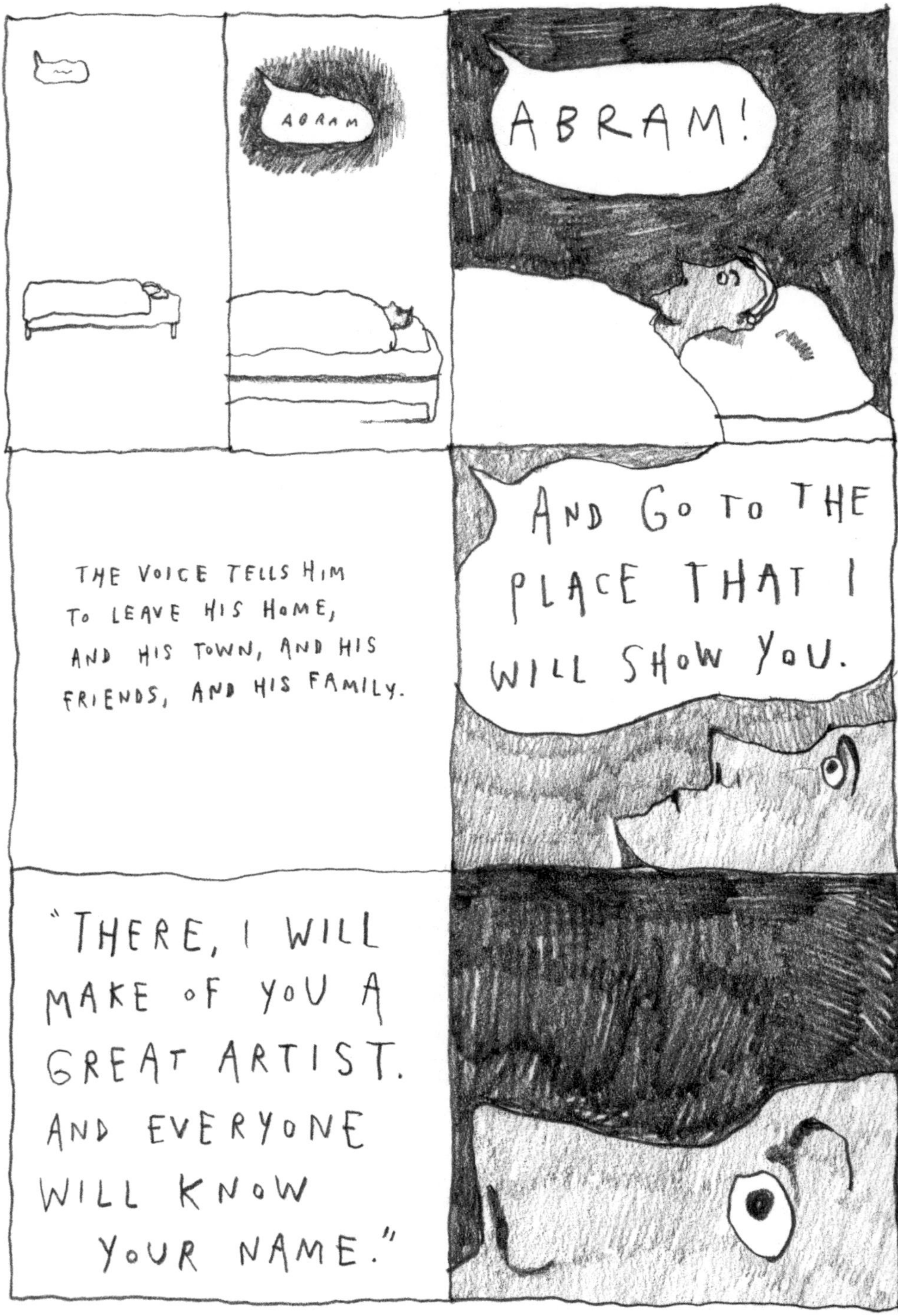

ABRAM
ABRAM!
THE VOICE TELLS HIM TO LEAVE HIS HOME, AND HIS TOWN, AND HIS FRIENDS, AND HIS FAMILY.
AND GO TO THE PLACE THAT I WILL SHOW YOU.
"THERE, I WILL MAKE OF YOU A GREAT ARTIST. AND EVERYONE WILL KNOW YOUR NAME."

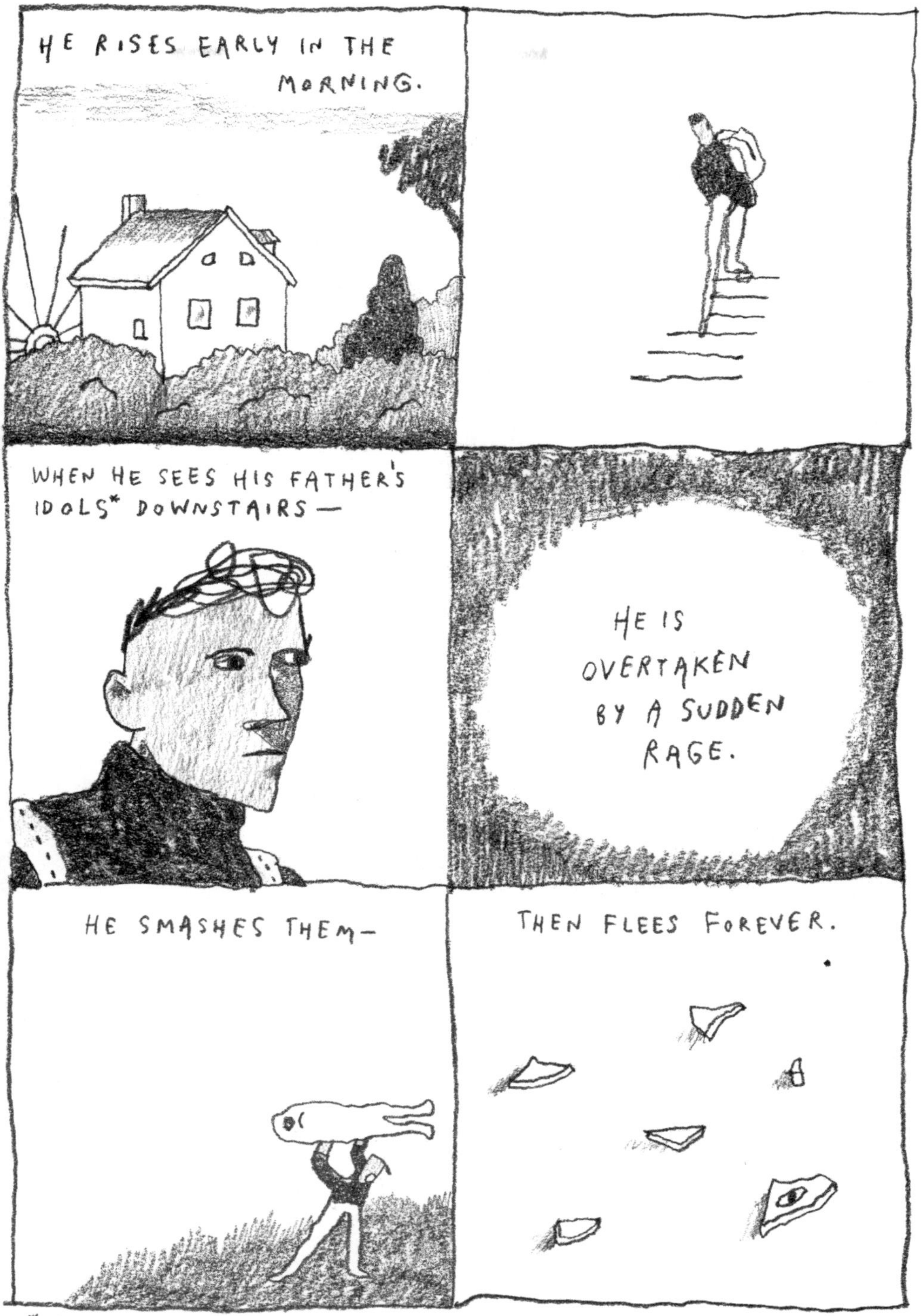
HE RISES EARLY IN THE MORNING.
WHEN HE SEES HIS FATHER'S IDOLS* DOWNSTAIRS—
HE IS OVERTAKEN BY A SUDDEN RAGE.
HE SMASHES THEM—
THEN FLEES FOREVER.

* FALSE GODS.

DEPARTURE

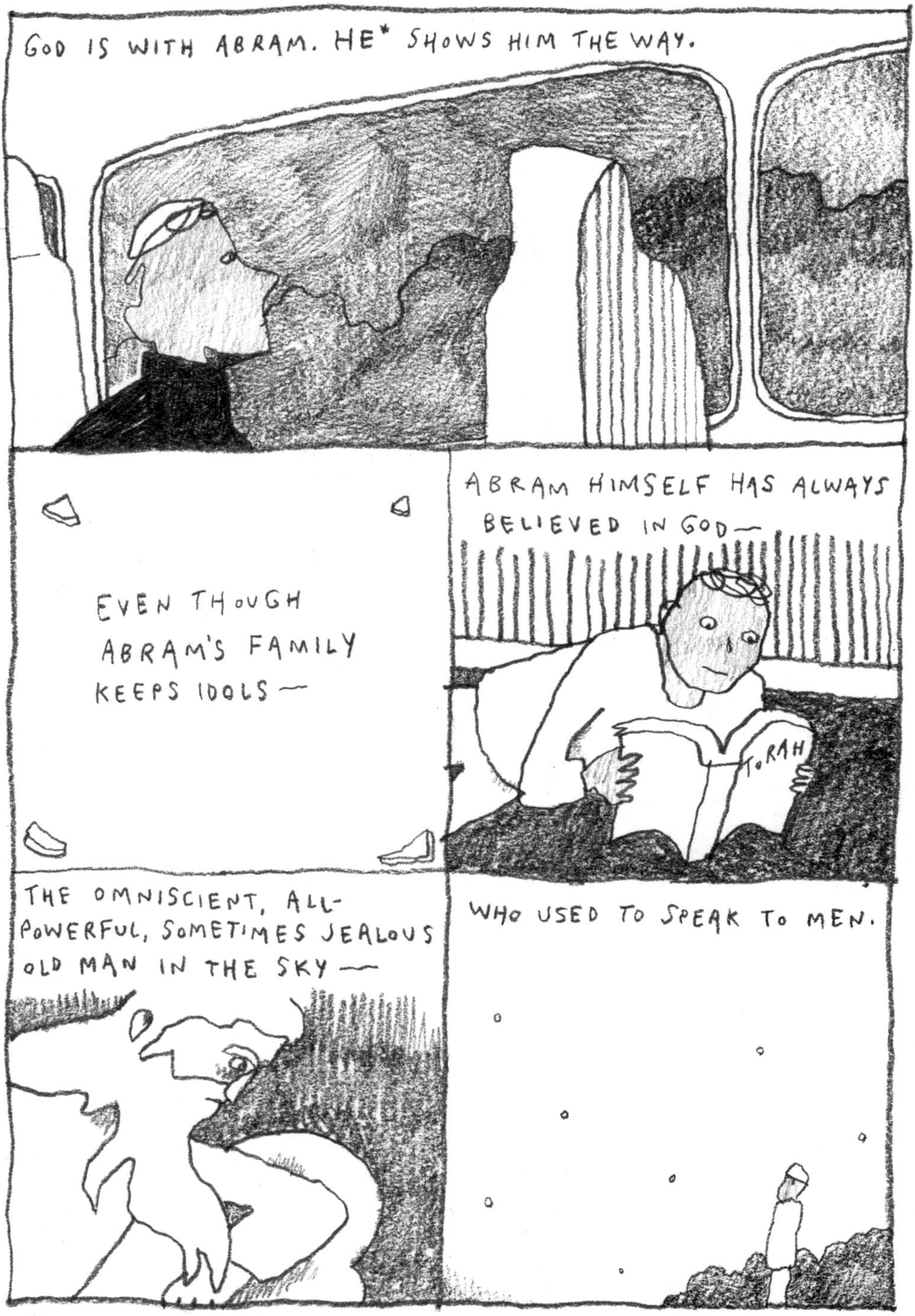
GOD IS WITH ABRAM. HE* SHOWS HIM THE WAY.
EVEN THOUGH ABRAM'S FAMILY KEEPS IDOLS—
ABRAM HIMSELF HAS ALWAYS BELIEVED IN GOD—
TORAH
THE OMNISCIENT, ALL-POWERFUL, SOMETIMES JEALOUS OLD MAN IN THE SKY—
WHO USED TO SPEAK TO MEN.

* . . .

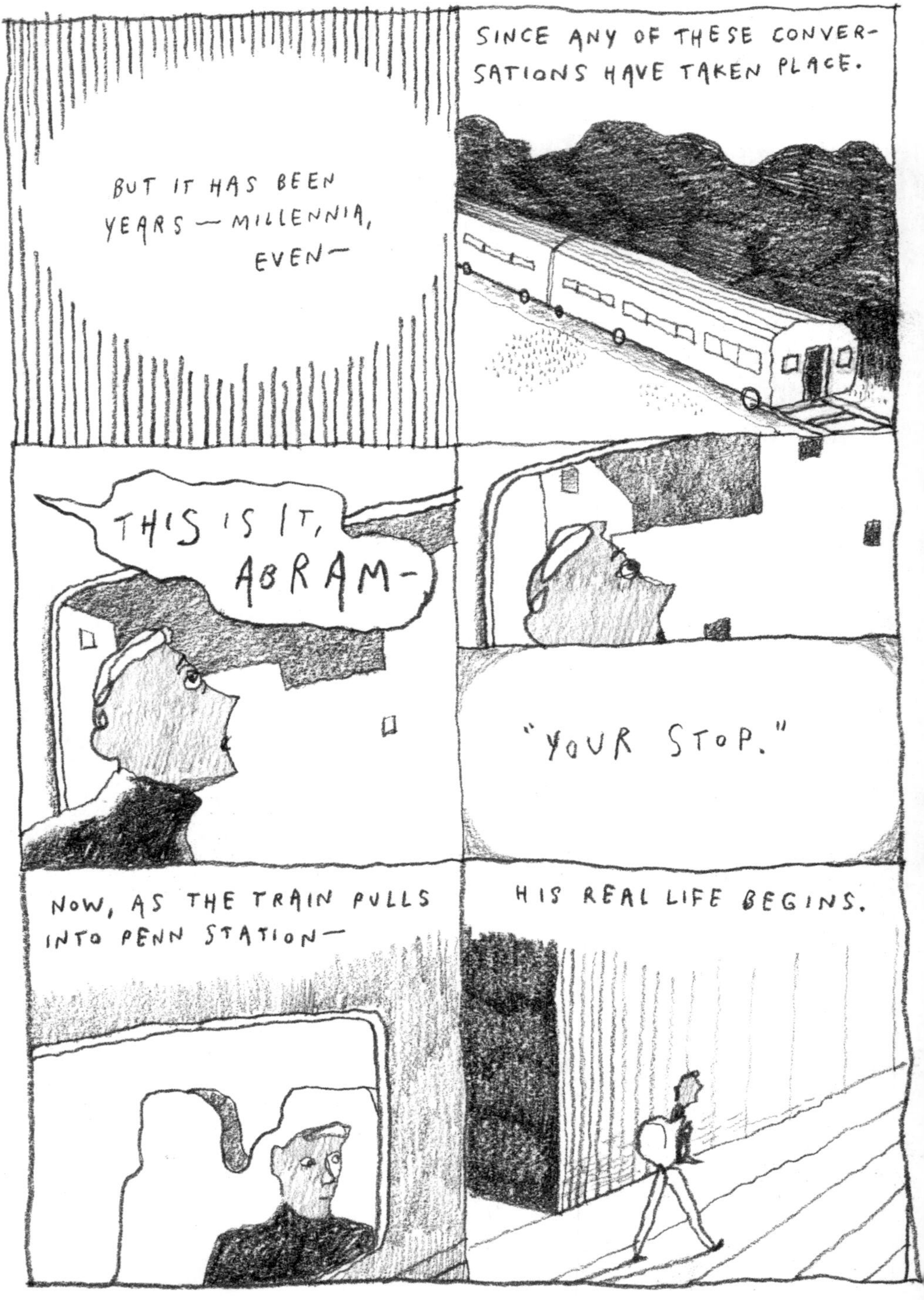
BUT IT HAS BEEN YEARS — MILLENNIA, EVEN—
SINCE ANY OF THESE CONVERSATIONS HAVE TAKEN PLACE.
THIS IS IT, ABRAM—
"YOUR STOP."
NOW, AS THE TRAIN PULLS INTO PENN STATION—
HIS REAL LIFE BEGINS.

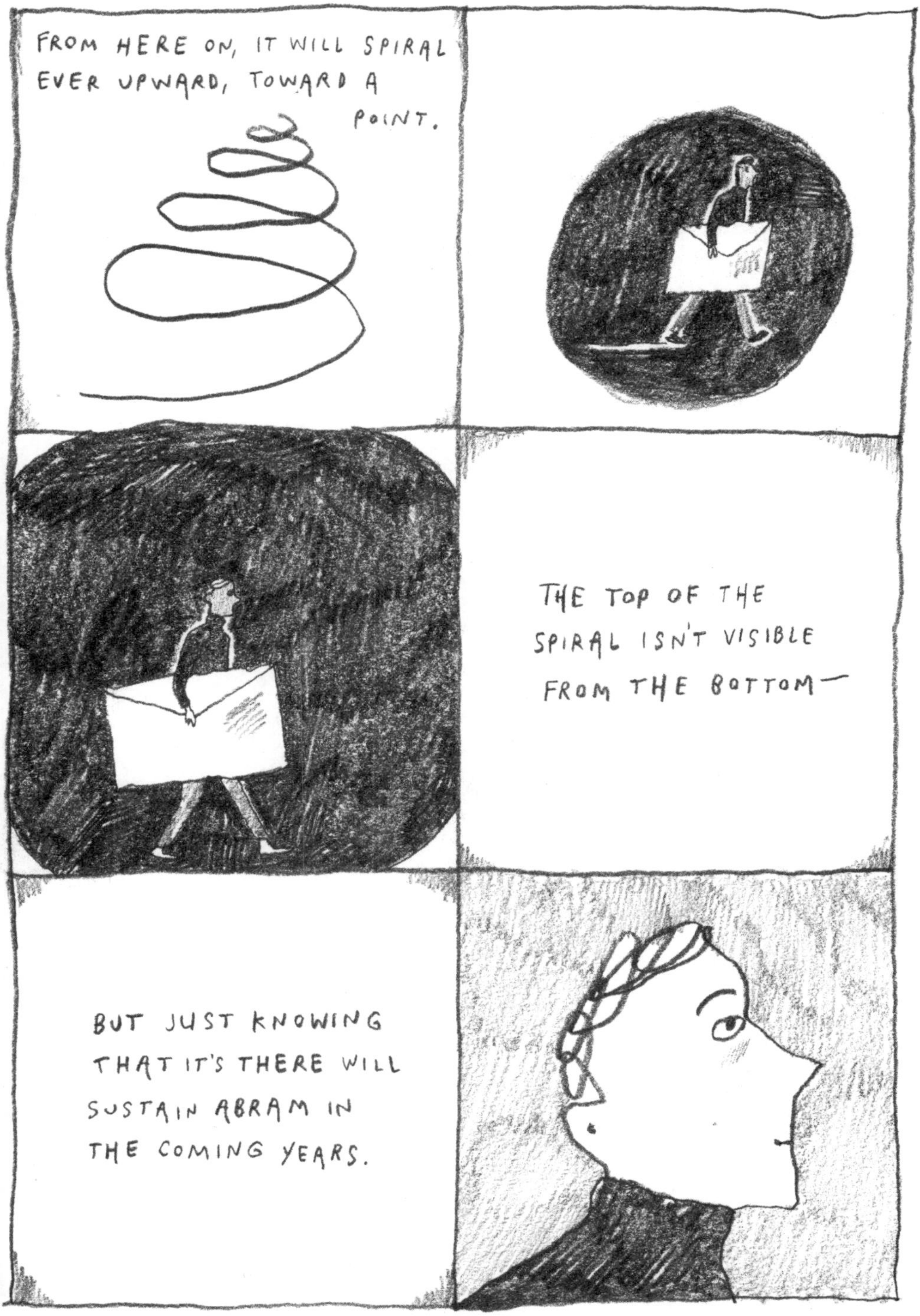
FROM HERE ON, IT WILL SPIRAL EVER UPWARD, TOWARD A POINT.
THE TOP OF THE SPIRAL ISN'T VISIBLE FROM THE BOTTOM—
BUT JUST KNOWING THAT IT'S THERE WILL SUSTAIN ABRAM IN THE COMING YEARS.

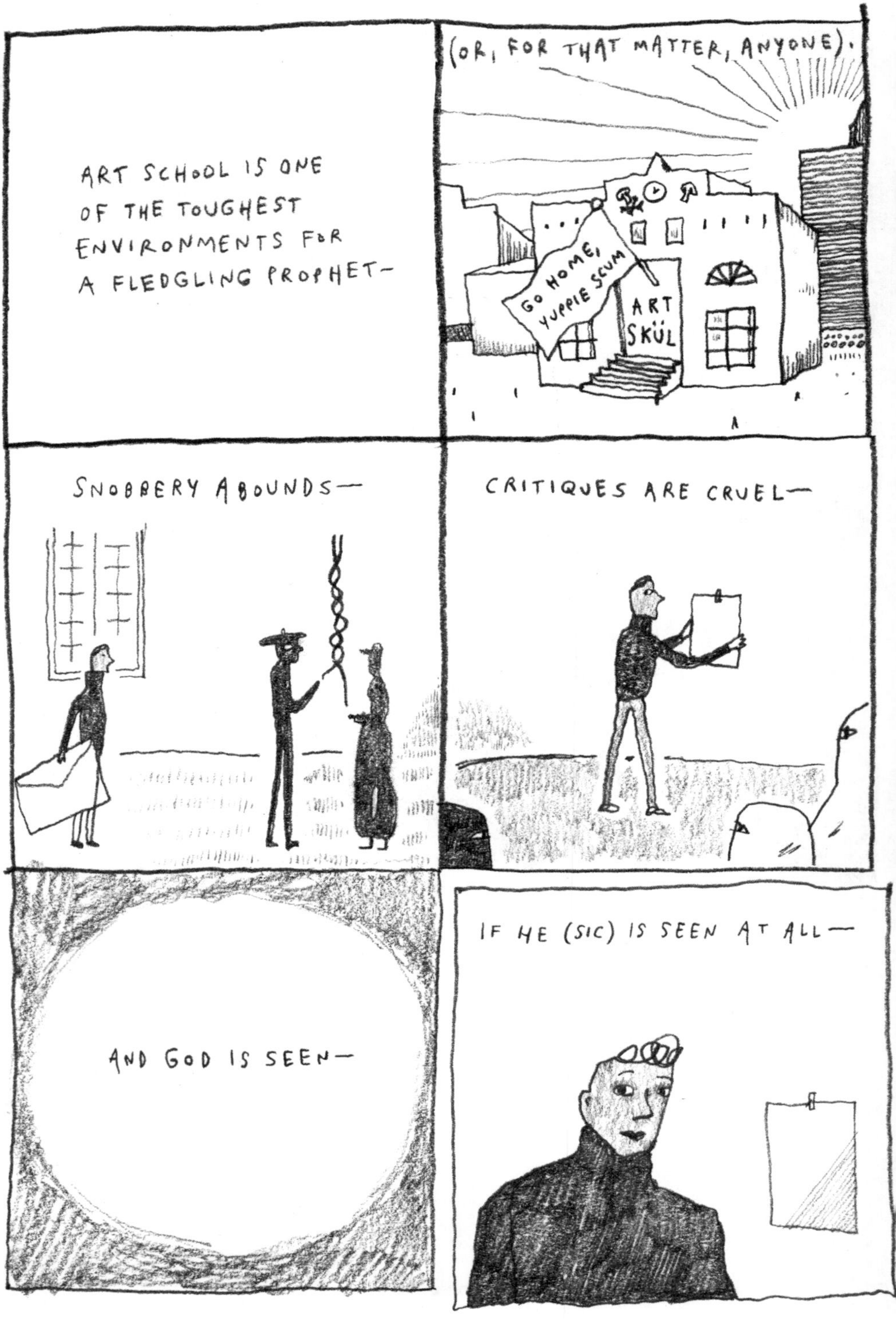

ART SCHOOL IS ONE OF THE TOUGHEST ENVIRONMENTS FOR A FLEDGLING PROPHET—
(OR, FOR THAT MATTER, ANYONE).
GO HOME, YUPPIE SCUM
ART SKÜL
SNOBBERY ABOUNDS—
CRITIQUES ARE CRUEL—
AND GOD IS SEEN—
IF HE (SIC) IS SEEN AT ALL—

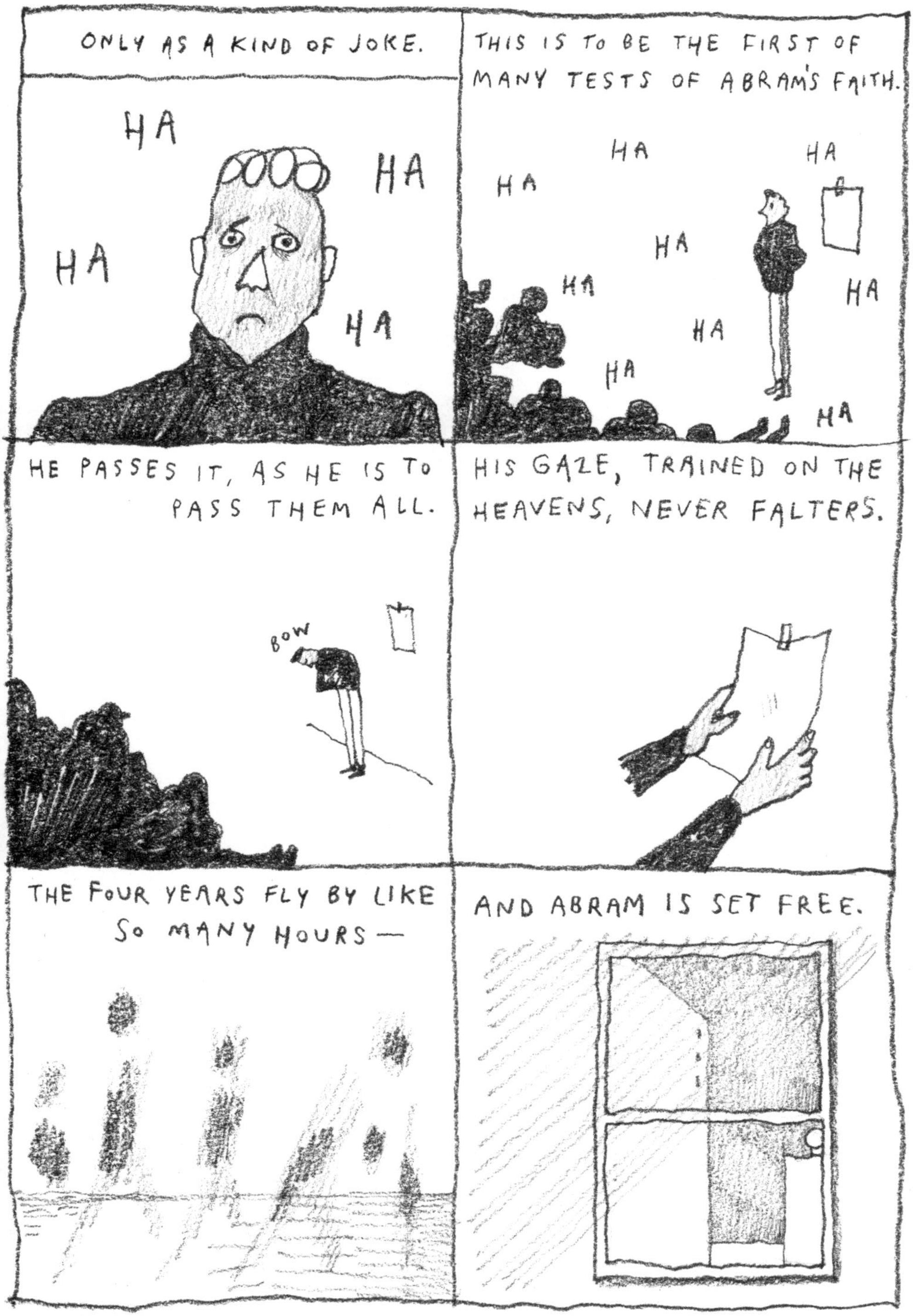
ONLY AS A KIND OF JOKE.
HA
HA
HA
HA
THIS IS TO BE THE FIRST OF MANY TESTS OF ABRAM'S FAITH.
HA
HA
HA
HA
HA
HA
HA
HA
HA
HE PASSES IT, AS HE IS TO PASS THEM ALL.
BOW
HIS GAZE, TRAINED ON THE HEAVENS, NEVER FALTERS.
THE FOUR YEARS FLY BY LIKE SO MANY HOURS —
AND ABRAM IS SET FREE.

3

THE WAIT

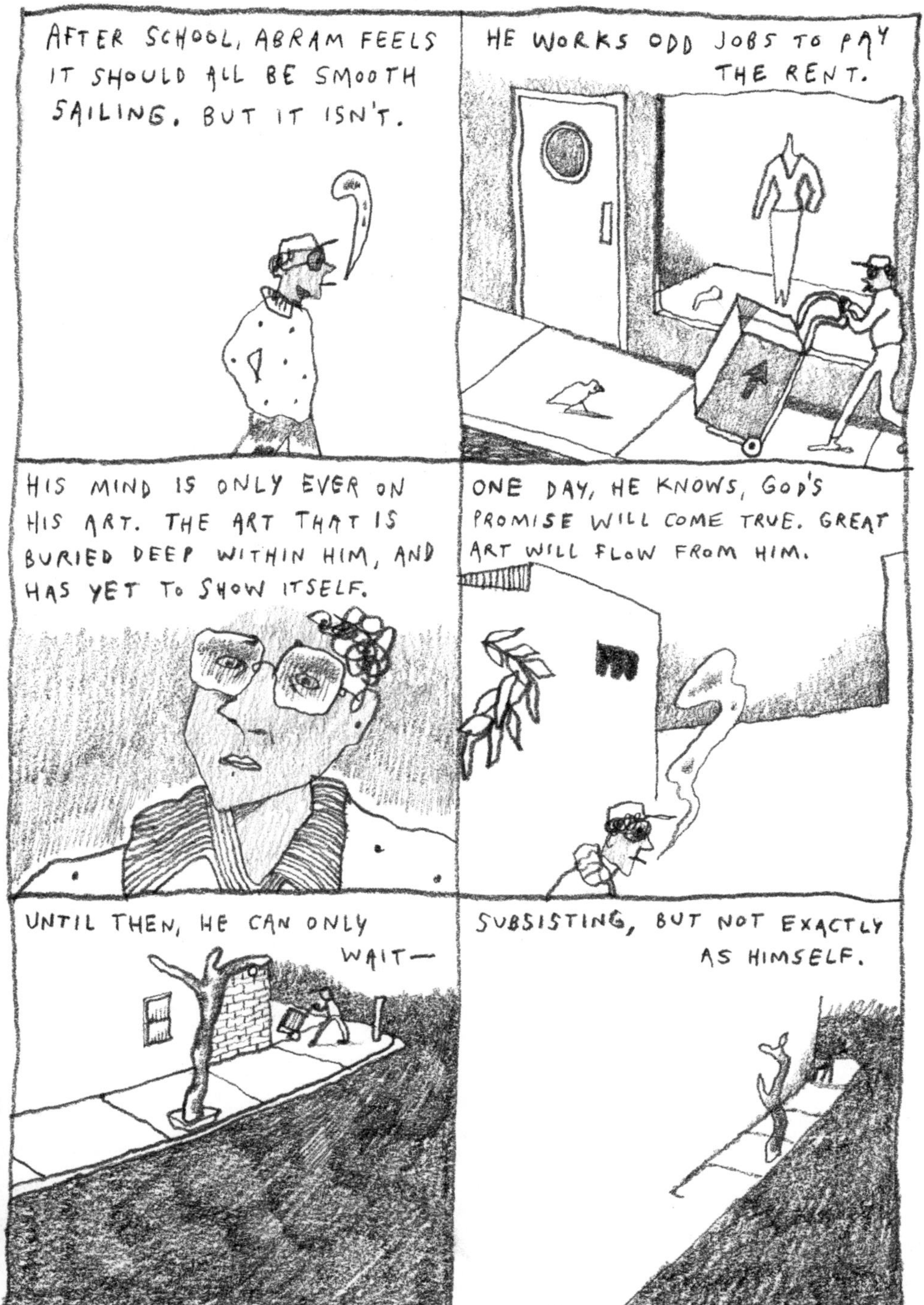
AFTER SCHOOL, ABRAM FEELS IT SHOULD ALL BE SMOOTH SAILING. BUT IT ISN'T.
HE WORKS ODD JOBS TO PAY THE RENT.
HIS MIND IS ONLY EVER ON HIS ART. THE ART THAT IS BURIED DEEP WITHIN HIM, AND HAS YET TO SHOW ITSELF.
ONE DAY, HE KNOWS, GOD'S PROMISE WILL COME TRUE. GREAT ART WILL FLOW FROM HIM.
UNTIL THEN, HE CAN ONLY WAIT—
SUBSISTING, BUT NOT EXACTLY AS HIMSELF.

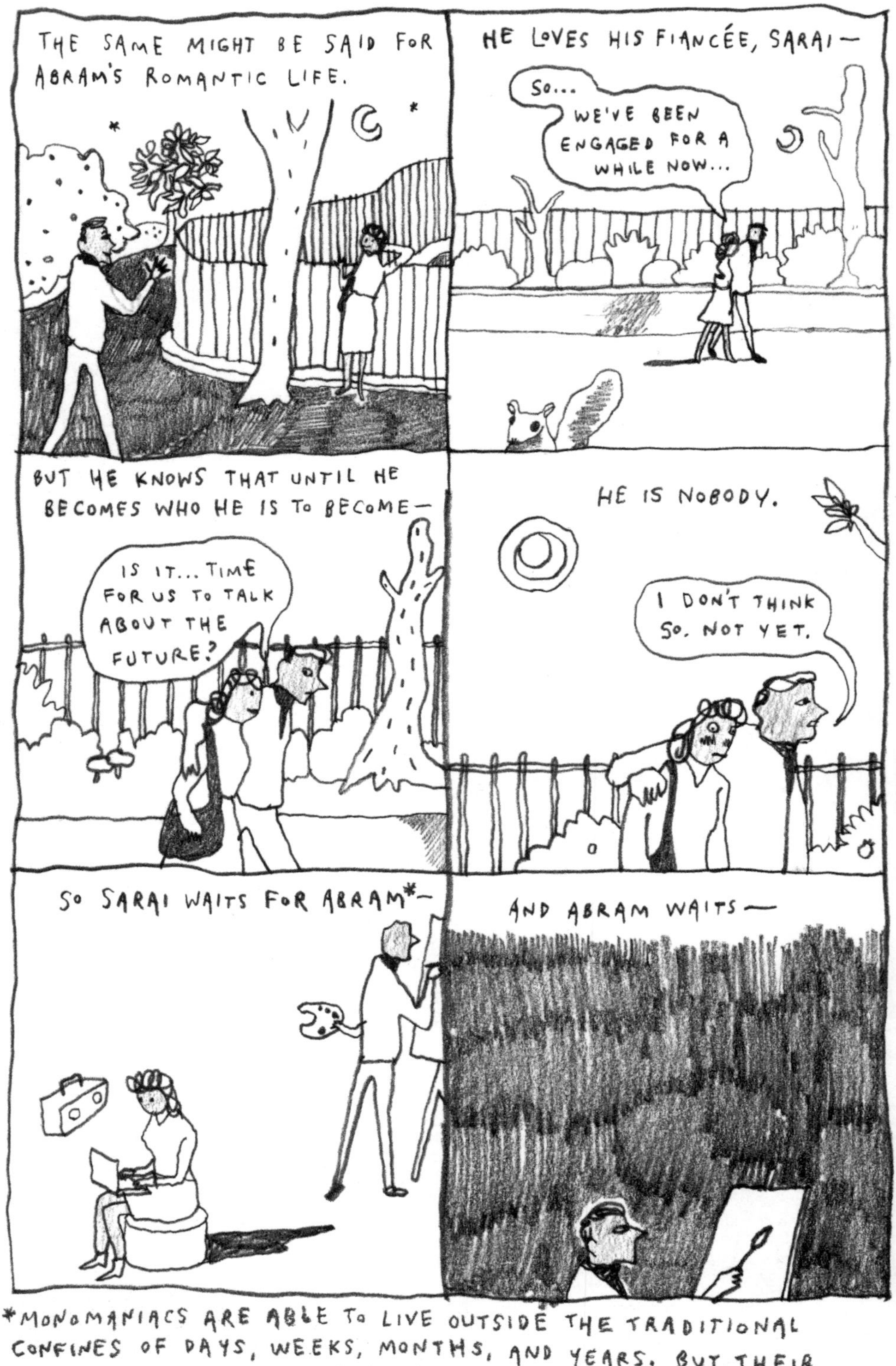
THE SAME MIGHT BE SAID FOR ABRAM'S ROMANTIC LIFE.
HE LOVES HIS FIANCÉE, SARAI—
SO... WE'VE BEEN ENGAGED FOR A WHILE NOW...
BUT HE KNOWS THAT UNTIL HE BECOMES WHO HE IS TO BECOME—
IS IT... TIME FOR US TO TALK ABOUT THE FUTURE?
HE IS NOBODY.
I DON'T THINK SO. NOT YET.
SO SARAI WAITS FOR ABRAM*—
AND ABRAM WAITS—

*MONOMANIACS ARE ABLE TO LIVE OUTSIDE THE TRADITIONAL CONFINES OF DAYS, WEEKS, MONTHS, AND YEARS. BUT THEIR FRIENDS AND PARTNERS SUFFER DOUBLY.

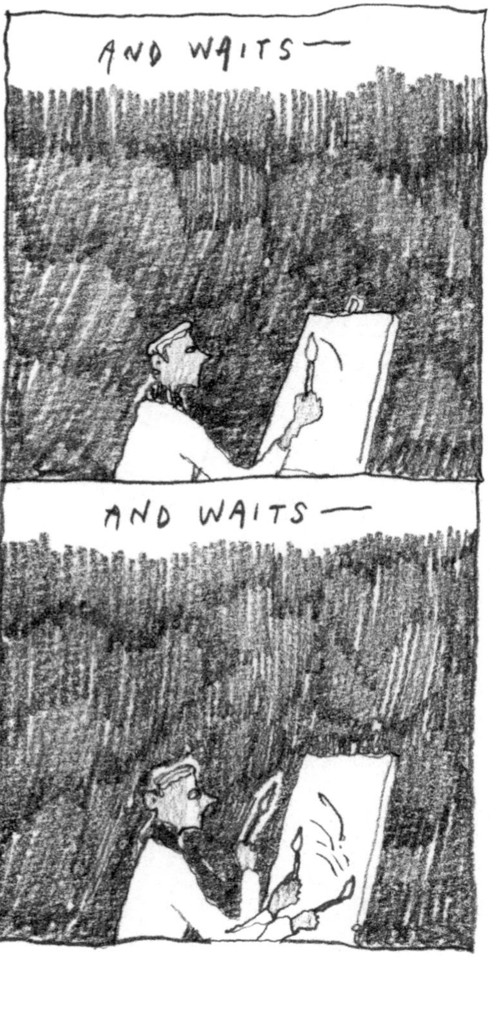
AND WAITS—
AND WAITS—

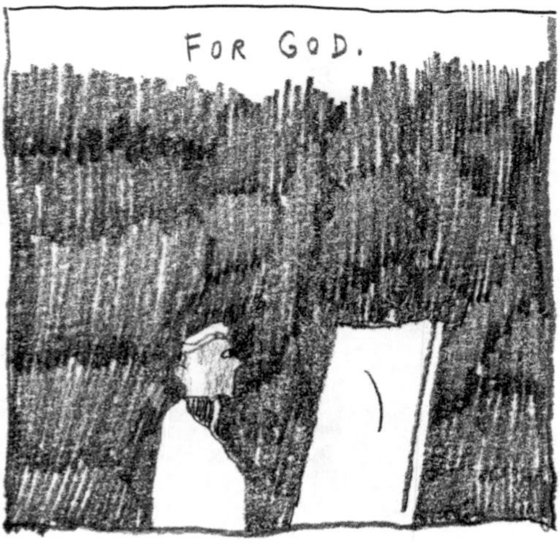
FOR GOD.

4

"LIFT UP YOUR EYES"

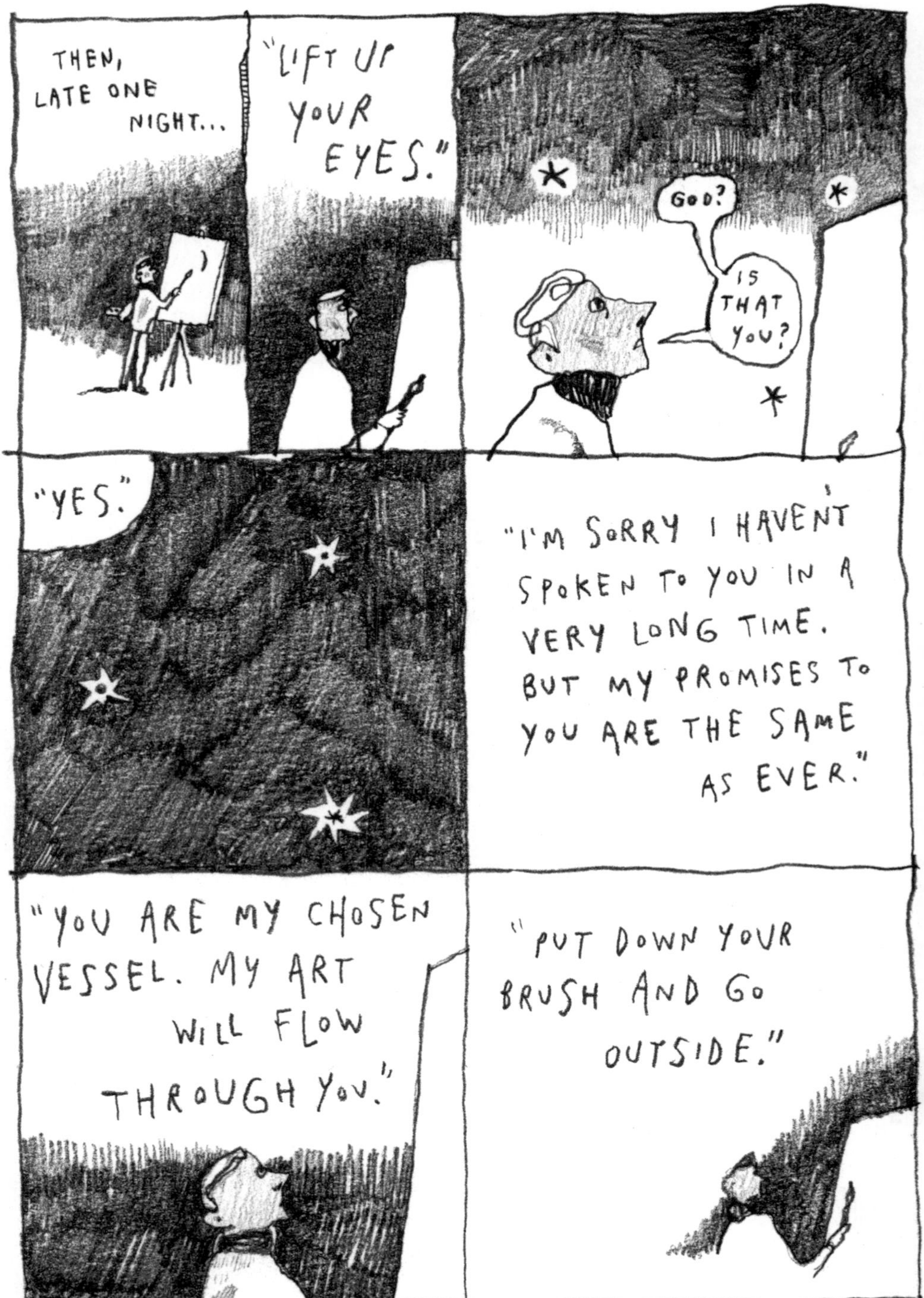
THEN, LATE ONE NIGHT...
"LIFT UP YOUR EYES."
GOD?
IS THAT YOU?
"YES."
"I'M SORRY I HAVEN'T SPOKEN TO YOU IN A VERY LONG TIME. BUT MY PROMISES TO YOU ARE THE SAME AS EVER."
"YOU ARE MY CHOSEN VESSEL. MY ART WILL FLOW THROUGH YOU."
"PUT DOWN YOUR BRUSH AND GO OUTSIDE."

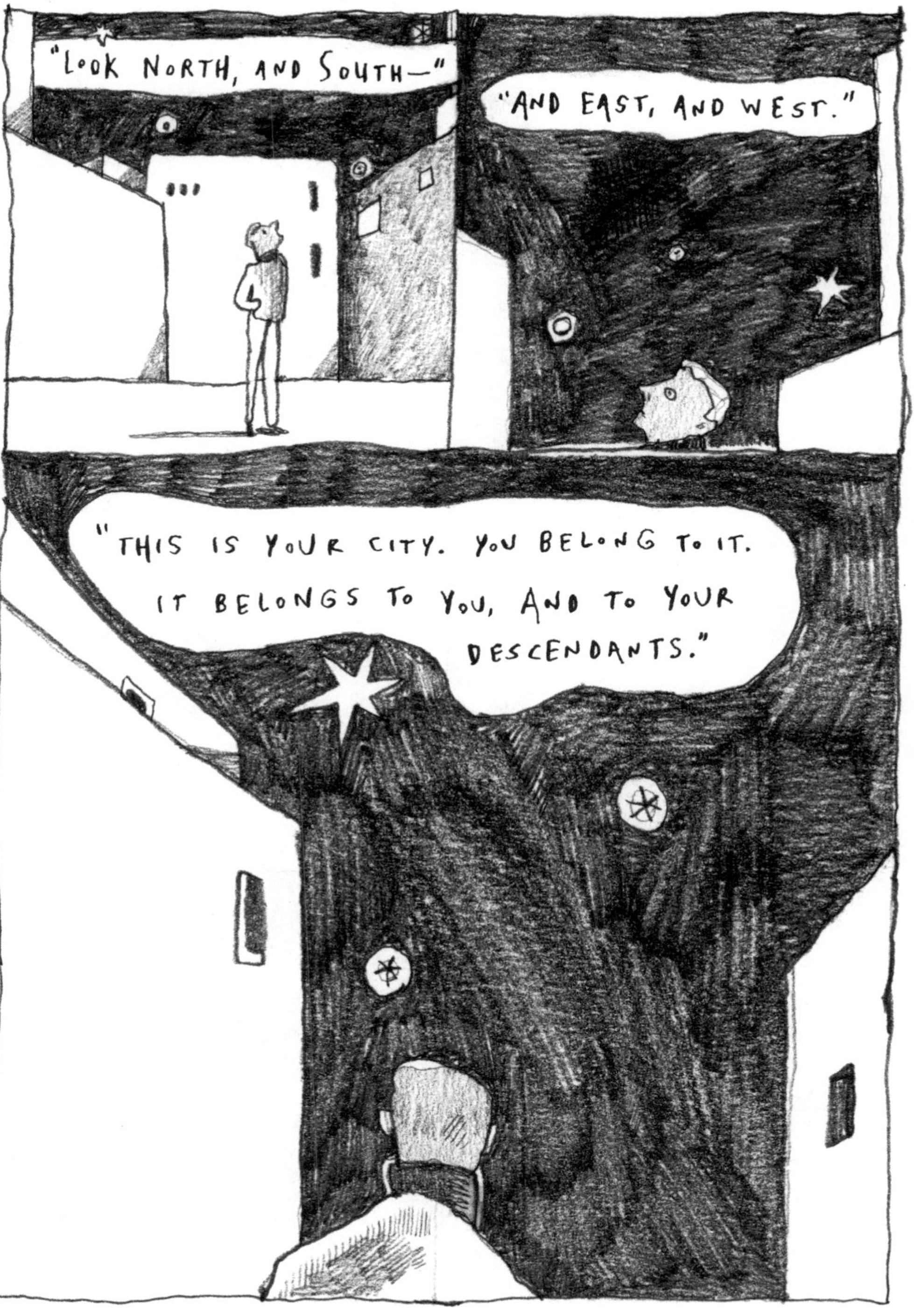
"LOOK NORTH, AND SOUTH—"
"AND EAST, AND WEST."
"THIS IS YOUR CITY. YOU BELONG TO IT. IT BELONGS TO YOU, AND TO YOUR DESCENDANTS."

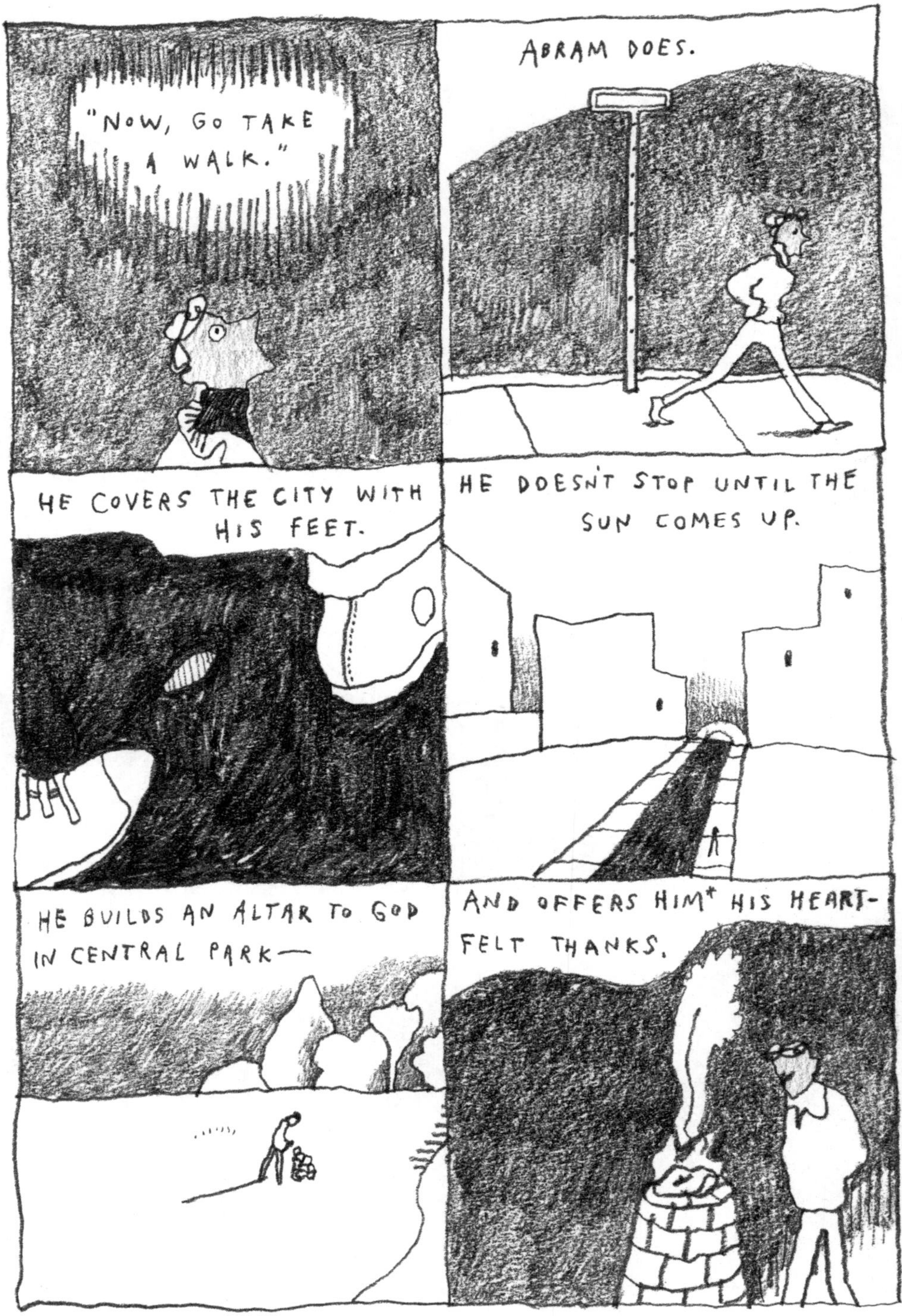
"NOW, GO TAKE A WALK."
ABRAM DOES.
HE COVERS THE CITY WITH HIS FEET.
HE DOESN'T STOP UNTIL THE SUN COMES UP.
HE BUILDS AN ALTAR TO GOD IN CENTRAL PARK—
AND OFFERS HIM* HIS HEART-FELT THANKS.

*!

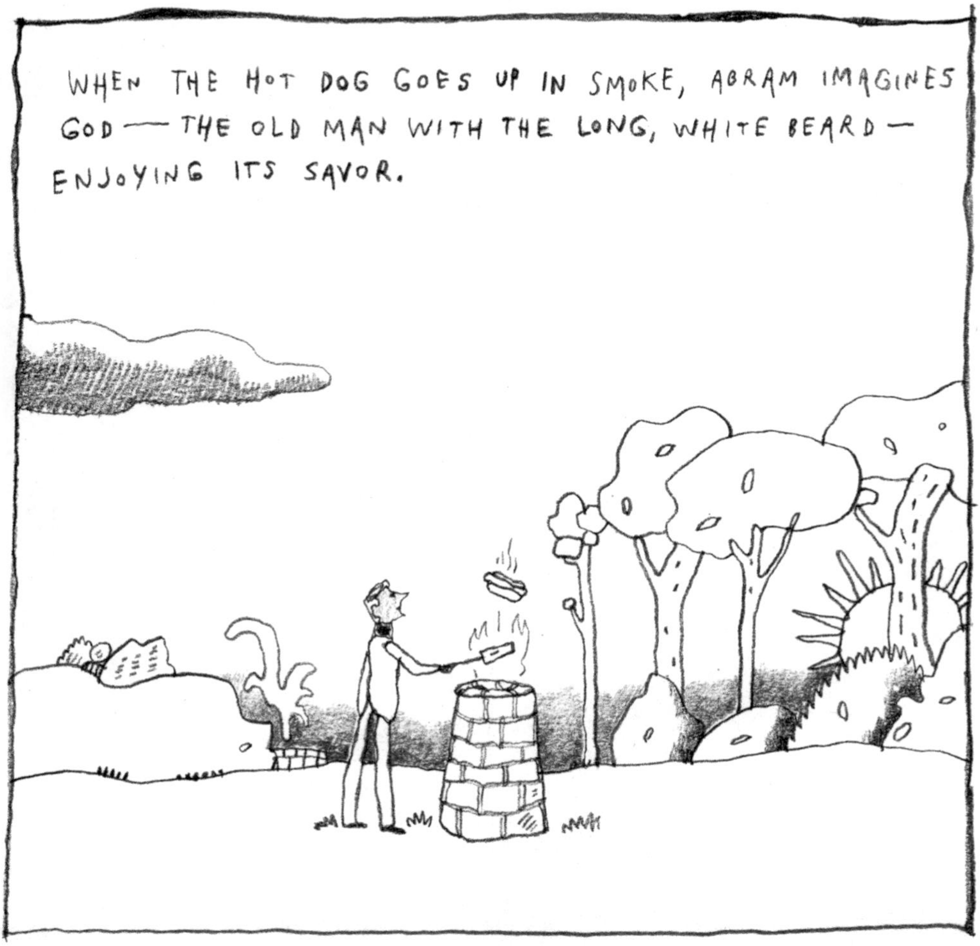
WHEN THE HOT DOG GOES UP IN SMOKE, ABRAM IMAGINES GOD — THE OLD MAN WITH THE LONG, WHITE BEARD — ENJOYING ITS SAVOR.

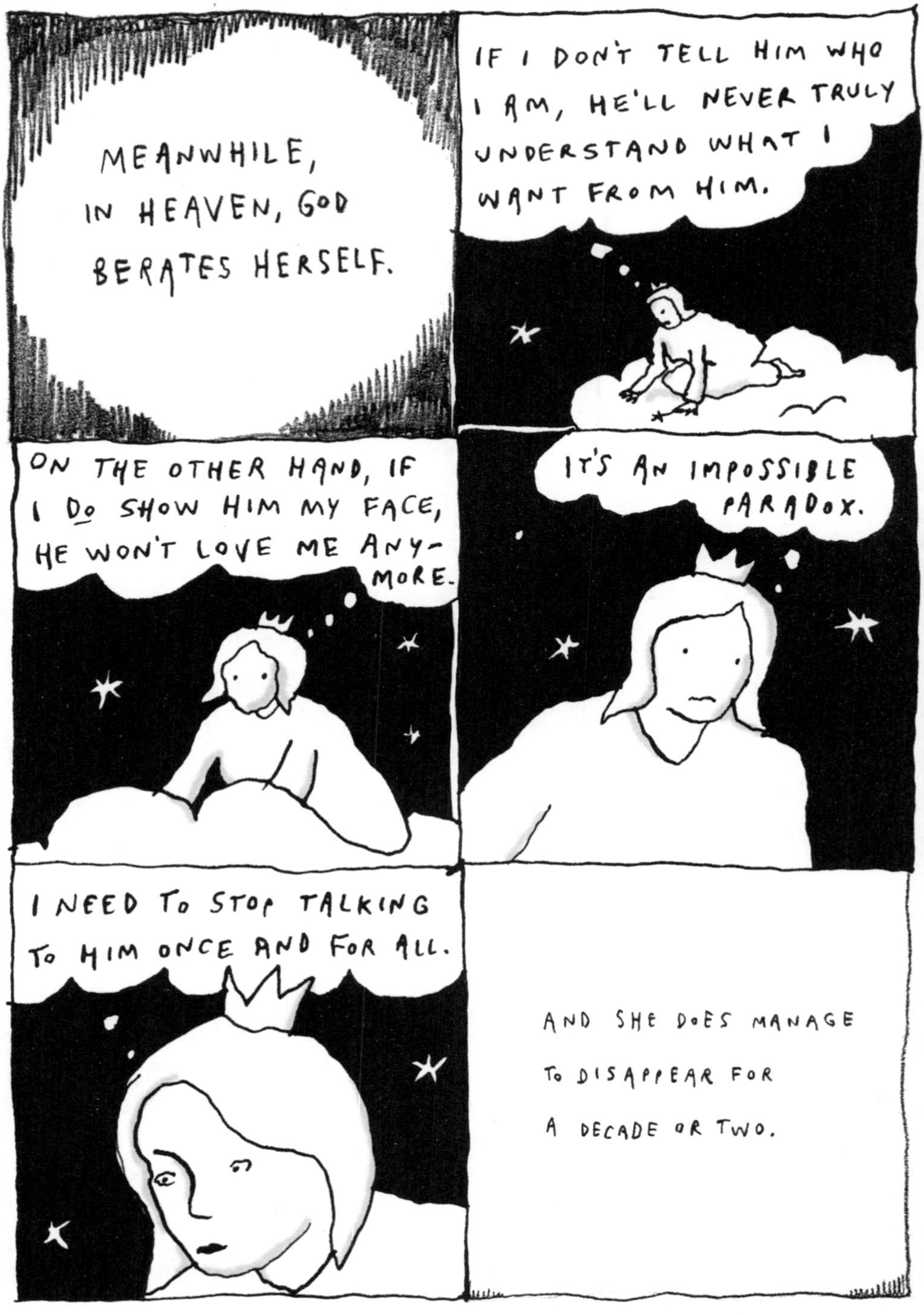
MEANWHILE, IN HEAVEN, GOD BERATES HERSELF.
IF I DON'T TELL HIM WHO I AM, HE'LL NEVER TRULY UNDERSTAND WHAT I WANT FROM HIM.
ON THE OTHER HAND, IF I DO SHOW HIM MY FACE, HE WON'T LOVE ME ANY-MORE.
IT'S AN IMPOSSIBLE PARADOX.
I NEED TO STOP TALKING TO HIM ONCE AND FOR ALL.
AND SHE DOES MANAGE TO DISAPPEAR FOR A DECADE OR TWO.

THESE ARE THE LOST YEARS IN
ABRAM'S LIFE.

5

FINALLY

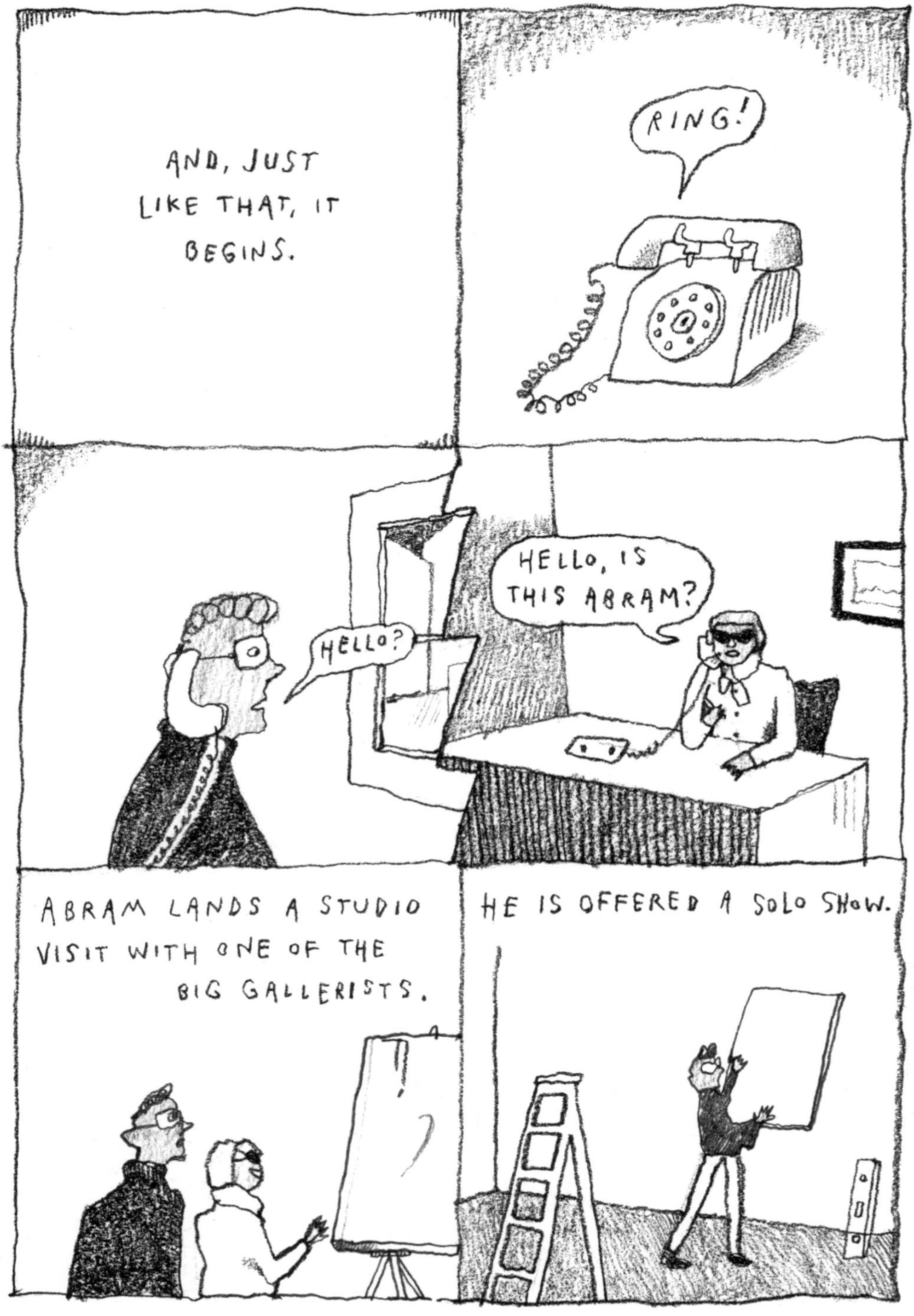
AND, JUST LIKE THAT, IT BEGINS.
RING!
HELLO?
HELLO, IS THIS ABRAM?
ABRAM LANDS A STUDIO VISIT WITH ONE OF THE BIG GALLERISTS.
HE IS OFFERED A SOLO SHOW.

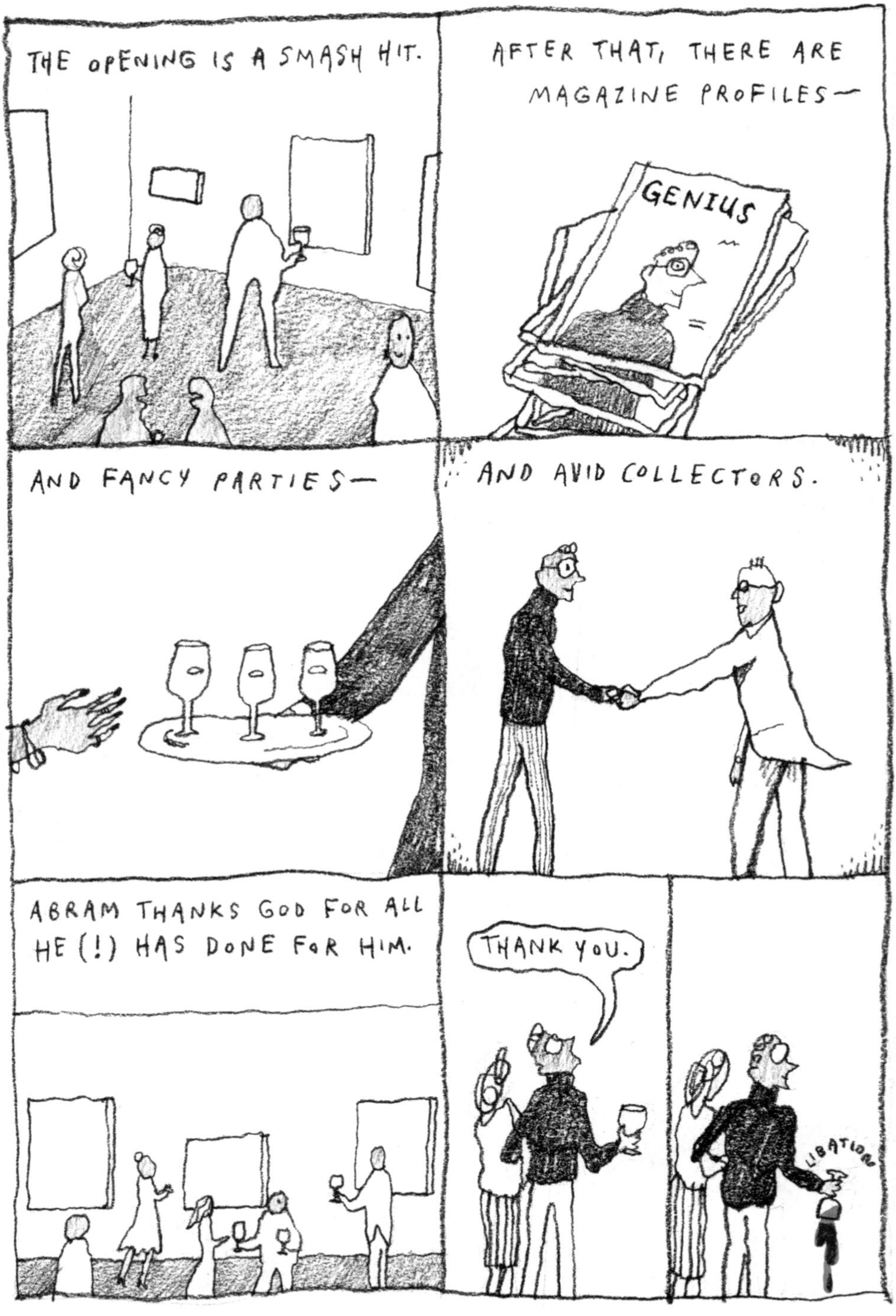
THE OPENING IS A SMASH HIT.
AFTER THAT, THERE ARE MAGAZINE PROFILES—
GENIUS
AND FANCY PARTIES—
AND AVID COLLECTORS.
ABRAM THANKS GOD FOR ALL HE (!) HAS DONE FOR HIM.
THANK YOU.
LIBATION

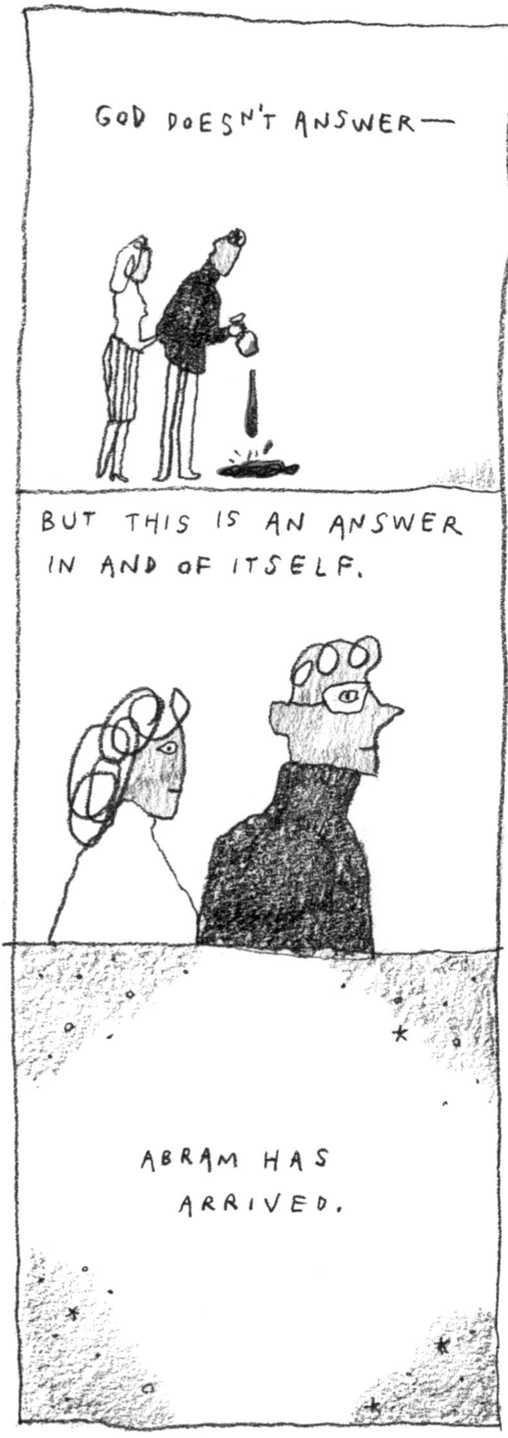
GOD DOESN'T ANSWER—
BUT THIS IS AN ANSWER IN AND OF ITSELF.
ABRAM HAS ARRIVED.

BABY FEVER

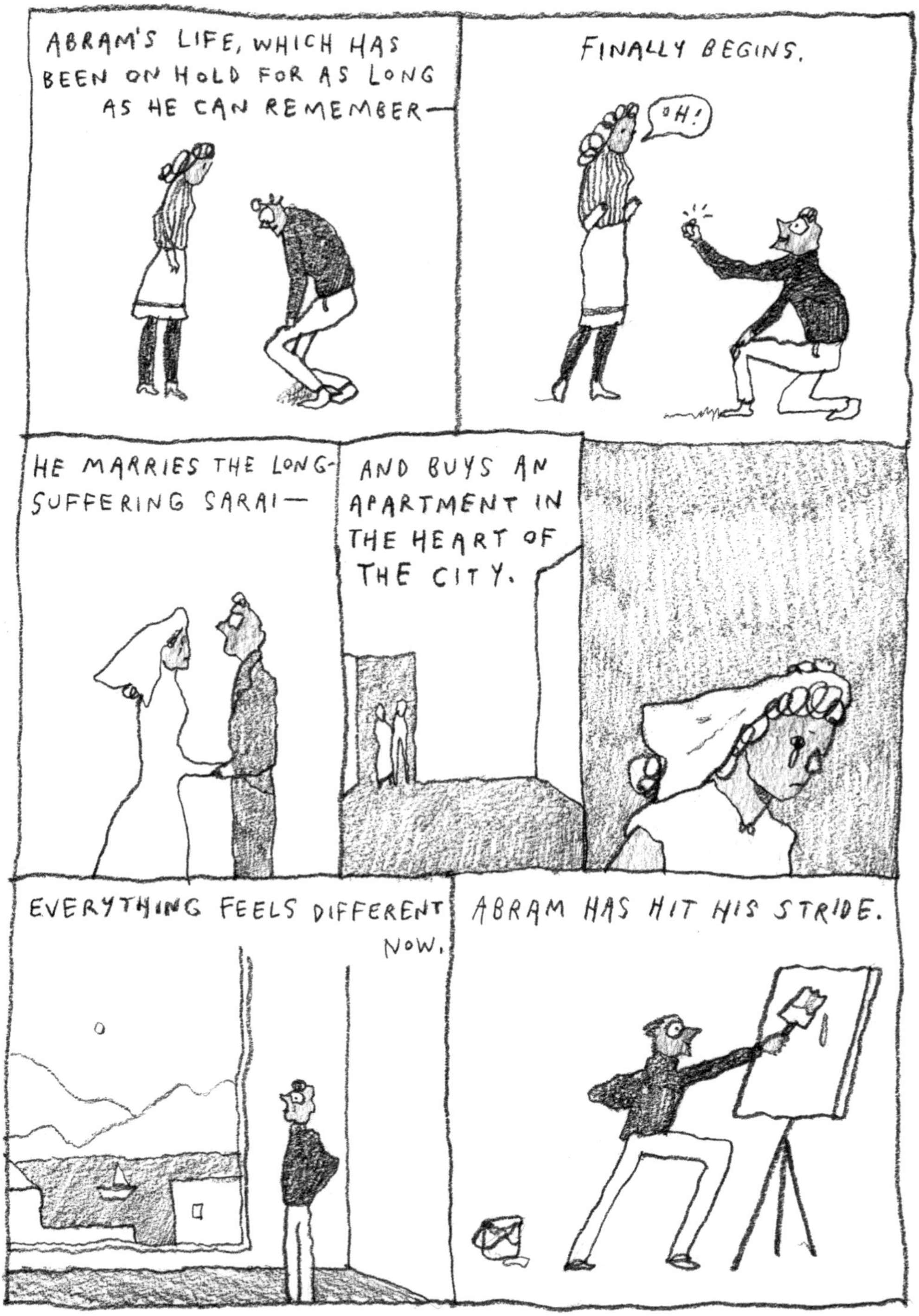
ABRAM'S LIFE, WHICH HAS BEEN ON HOLD FOR AS LONG AS HE CAN REMEMBER—
FINALLY BEGINS.
OH!
HE MARRIES THE LONG-SUFFERING SARAI—
AND BUYS AN APARTMENT IN THE HEART OF THE CITY.
EVERYTHING FEELS DIFFERENT NOW.
ABRAM HAS HIT HIS STRIDE.

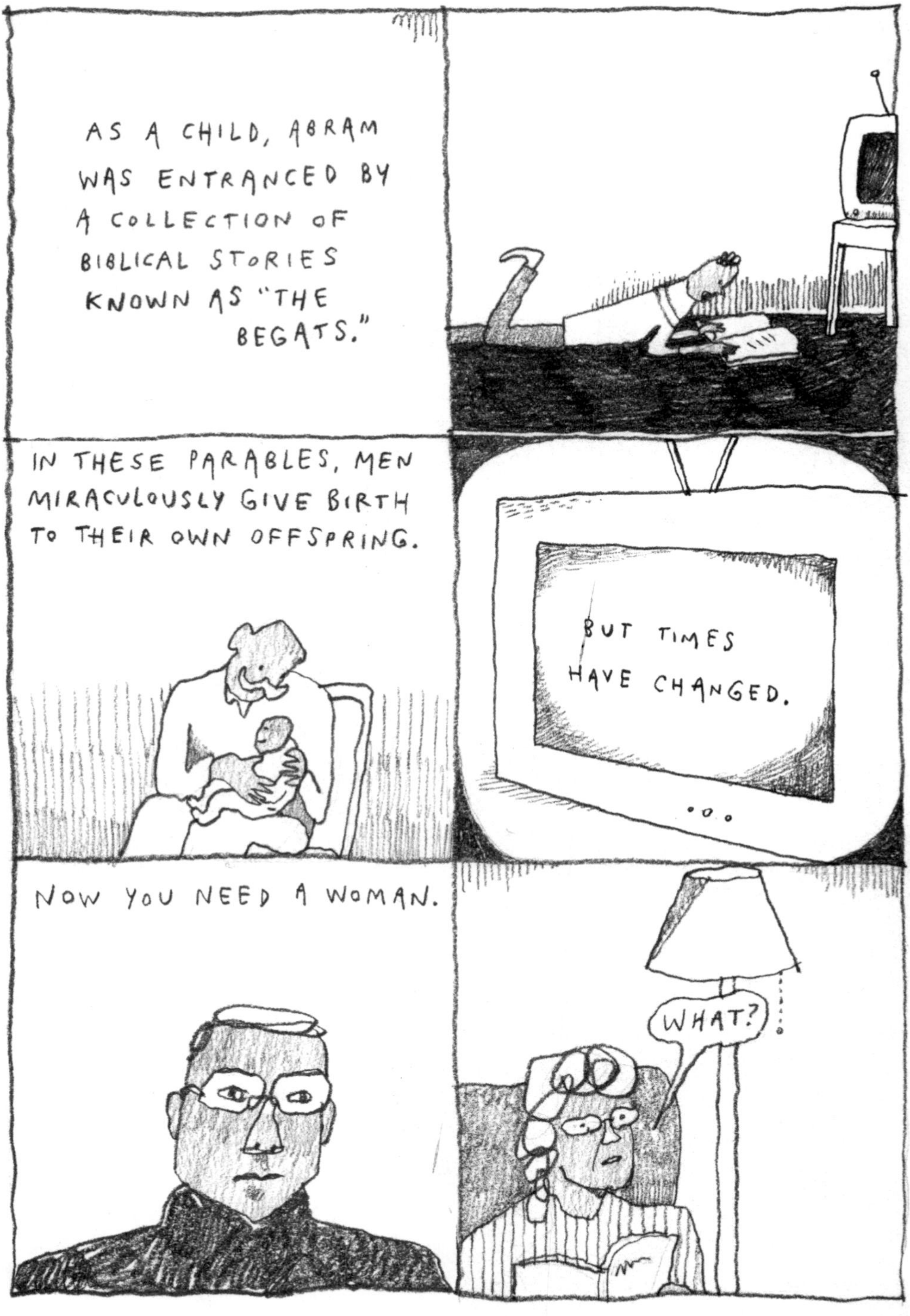
AS A CHILD, ABRAM WAS ENTRANCED BY A COLLECTION OF BIBLICAL STORIES KNOWN AS "THE BEGATS."
IN THESE PARABLES, MEN MIRACULOUSLY GIVE BIRTH TO THEIR OWN OFFSPRING.
BUT TIMES HAVE CHANGED.
NOW YOU NEED A WOMAN.
WHAT?

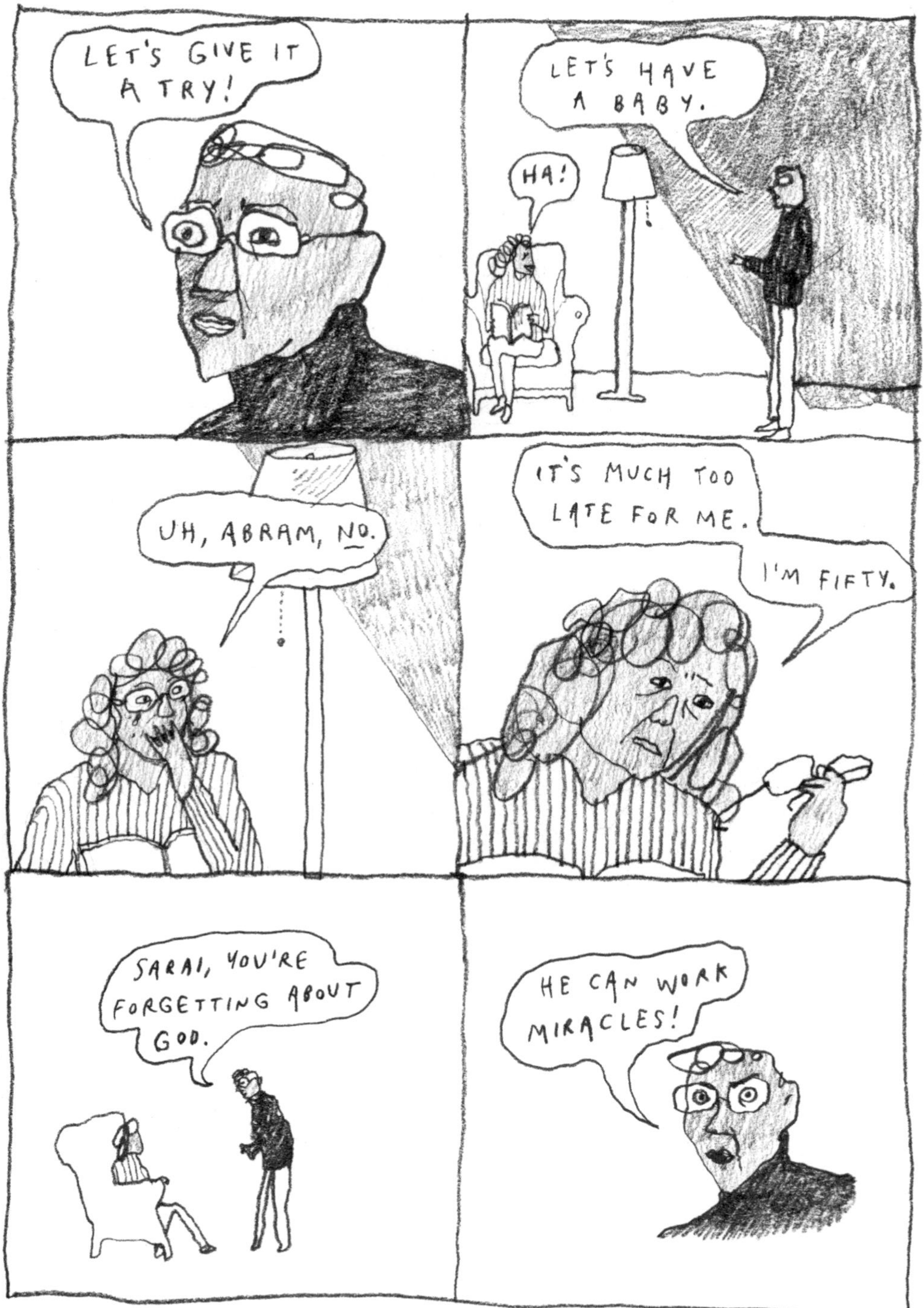
LET'S GIVE IT A TRY!
LET'S HAVE A BABY.
HA!
UH, ABRAM, NO.
IT'S MUCH TOO LATE FOR ME.
I'M FIFTY.
SARAI, YOU'RE FORGETTING ABOUT GOD.
HE CAN WORK MIRACLES!

THIS MUST BE TRUE.

ABRAM HAS STAKED HIS LIFE
ON IT.

7

MORE TIME PASSES

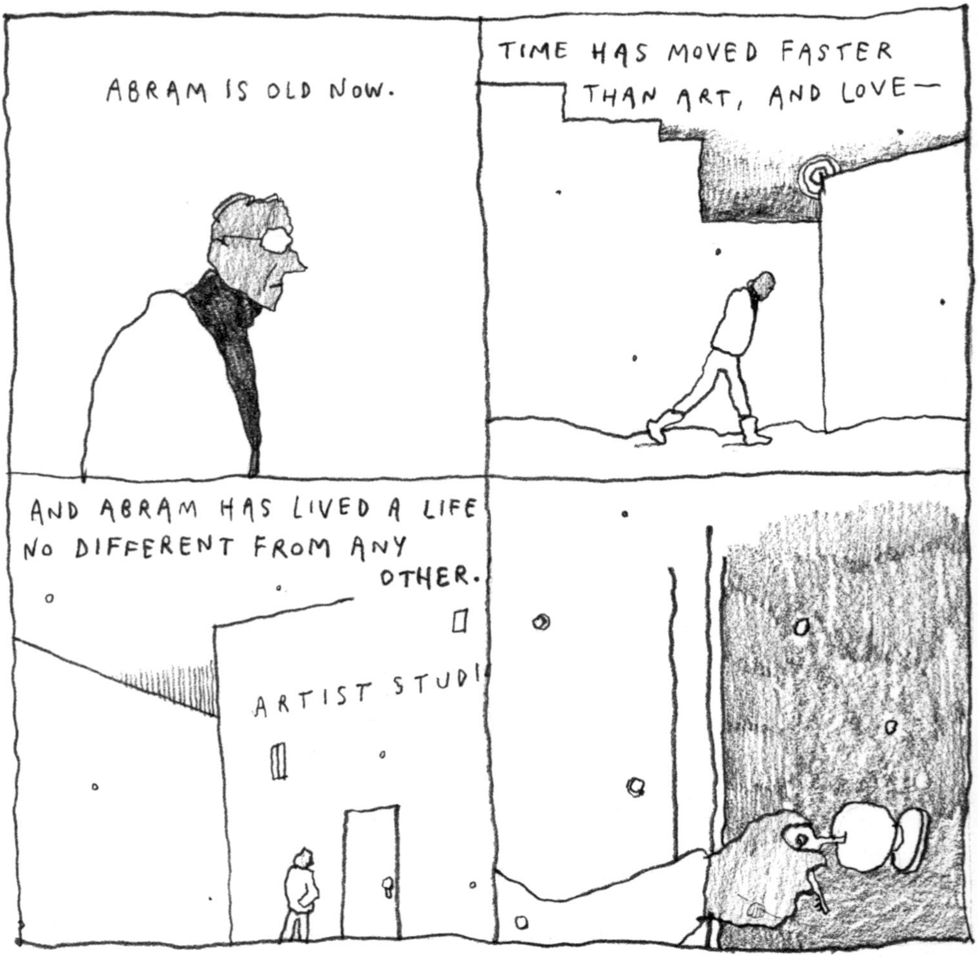

ABRAM IS OLD NOW.
TIME HAS MOVED FASTER THAN ART, AND LOVE—
AND ABRAM HAS LIVED A LIFE NO DIFFERENT FROM ANY OTHER.
ARTIST STUDI

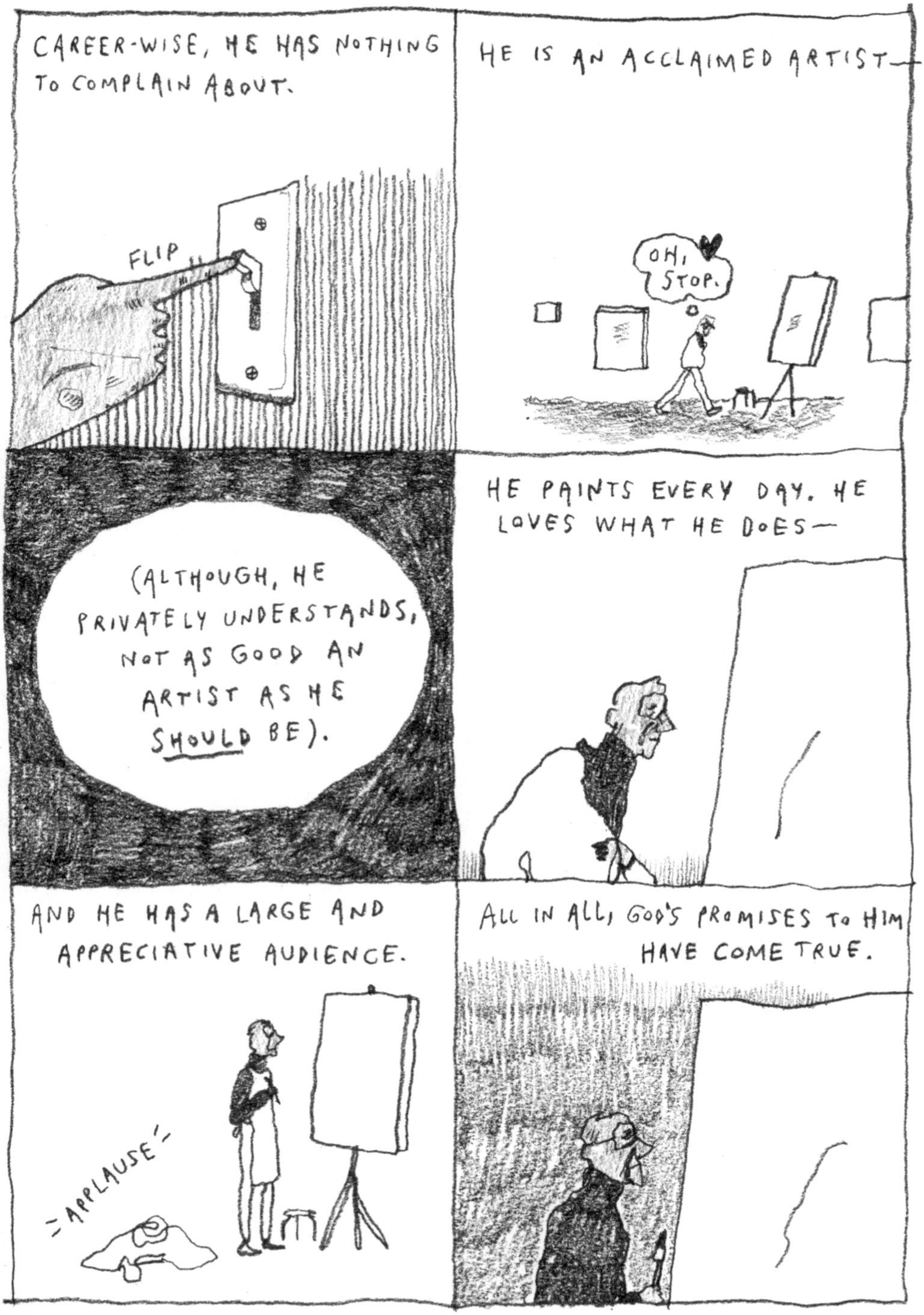
CAREER-WISE, HE HAS NOTHING TO COMPLAIN ABOUT.
FLIP
HE IS AN ACCLAIMED ARTIST—
OH, STOP.
(ALTHOUGH, HE PRIVATELY UNDERSTANDS, NOT AS GOOD AN ARTIST AS HE SHOULD BE).
HE PAINTS EVERY DAY. HE LOVES WHAT HE DOES—
AND HE HAS A LARGE AND APPRECIATIVE AUDIENCE.
APPLAUSE
ALL IN ALL, GOD'S PROMISES TO HIM HAVE COME TRUE.

SO IF THE LIFE GOD HAS
GRANTED HIM IS LESS
EARTH·SHATTERINGLY
SPECTACULAR THAN
HE EXPECTED —

— WELL, THAT'S
HIS PROBLEM, NOT
GOD'S.

TRUTH

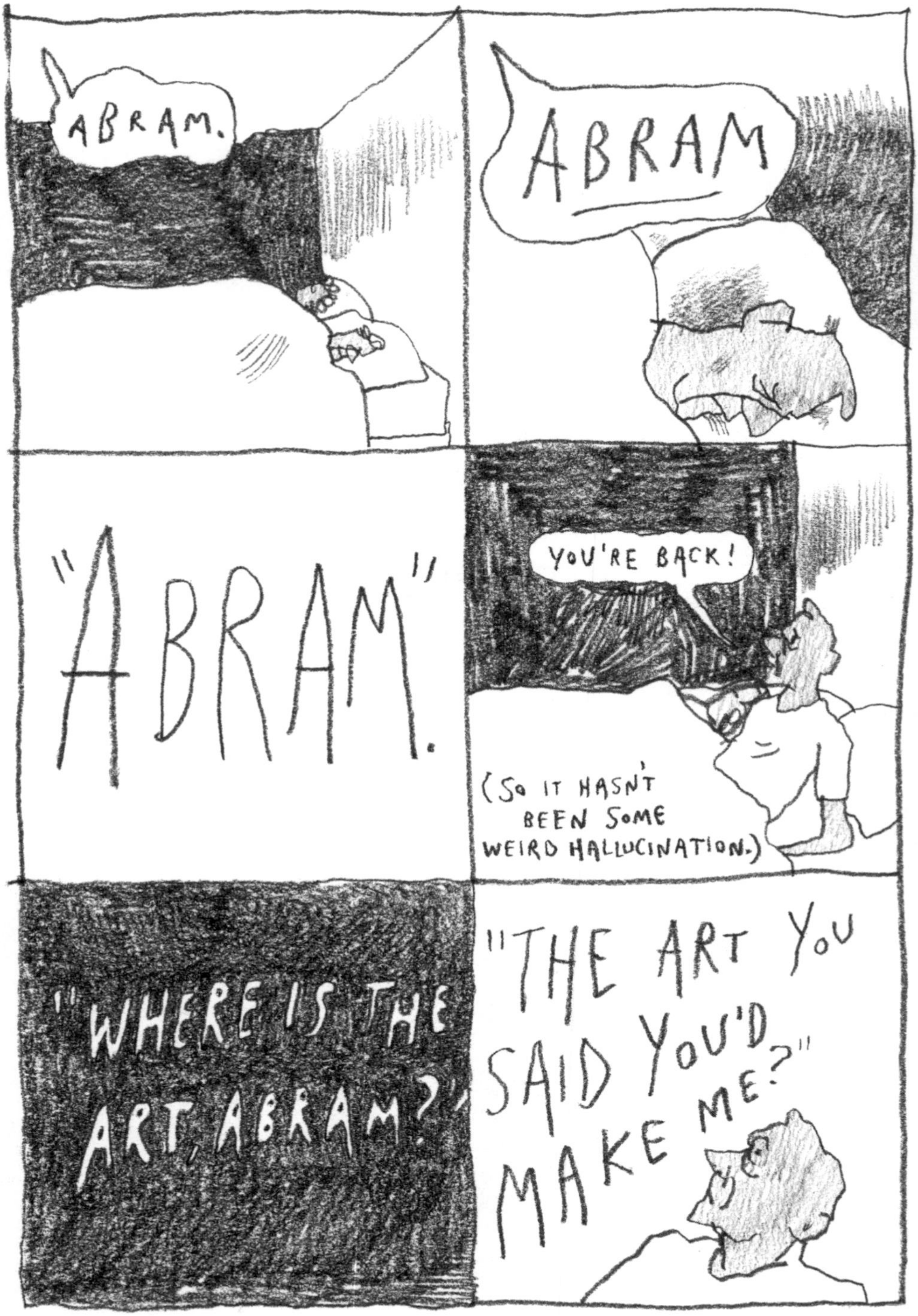
ABRAM.
ABRAM
"ABRAM".
YOU'RE BACK!
(SO IT HASN'T BEEN SOME WEIRD HALLUCINATION.)
"WHERE IS THE ART, ABRAM?"
"THE ART YOU SAID YOU'D MAKE ME?"

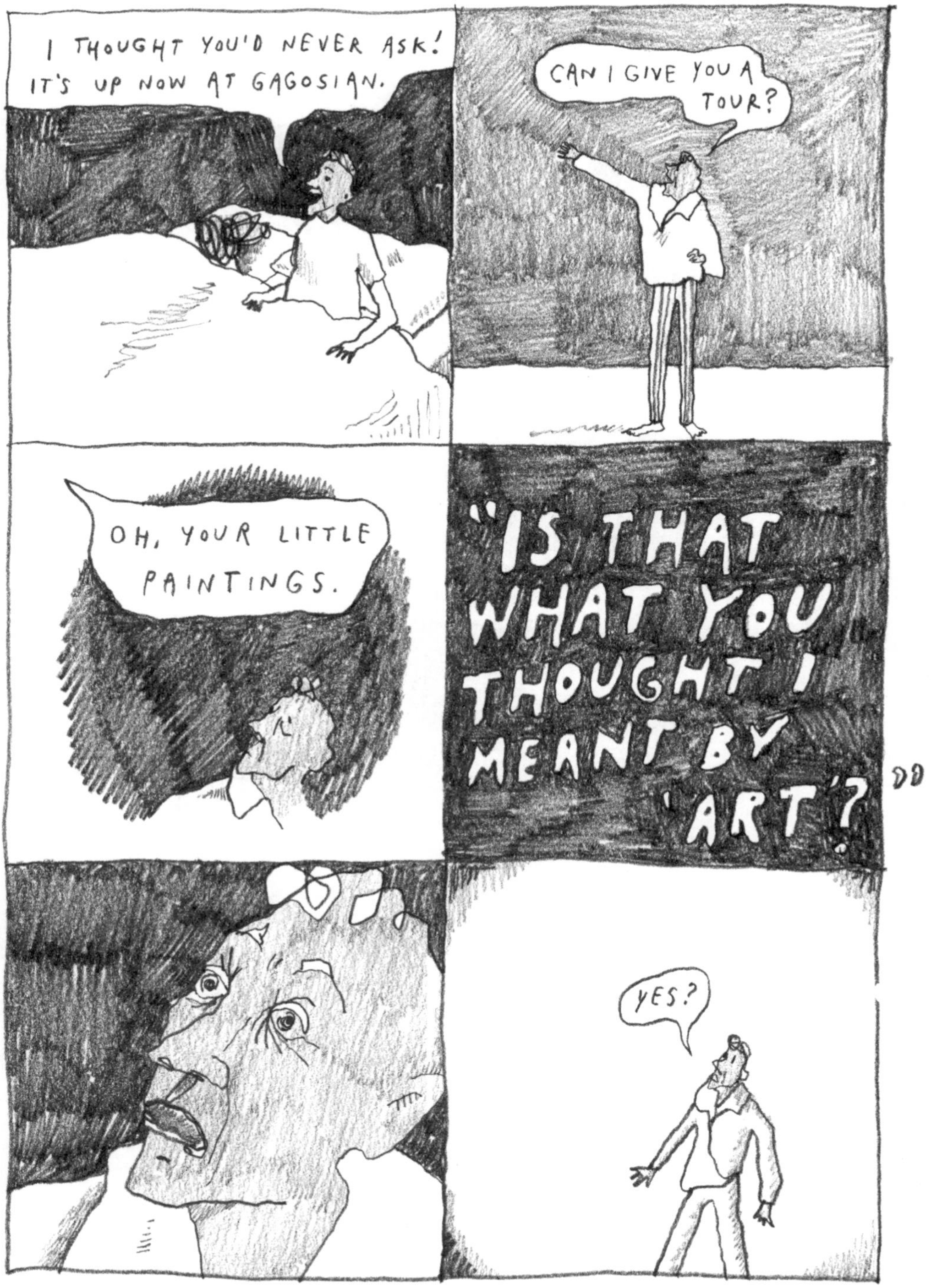
I THOUGHT YOU'D NEVER ASK! IT'S UP NOW AT GAGOSIAN.
CAN I GIVE YOU A TOUR?
OH, YOUR LITTLE PAINTINGS.
"IS THAT WHAT YOU THOUGHT I MEANT BY 'ART'?"
YES?

"SILLY BOY."
"THAT ISN'T ART."
"THAT'S JUST A HOBBY."

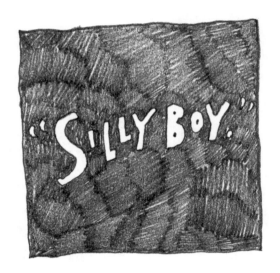

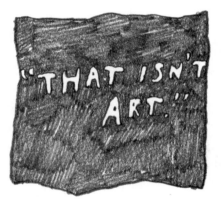

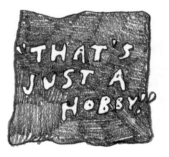

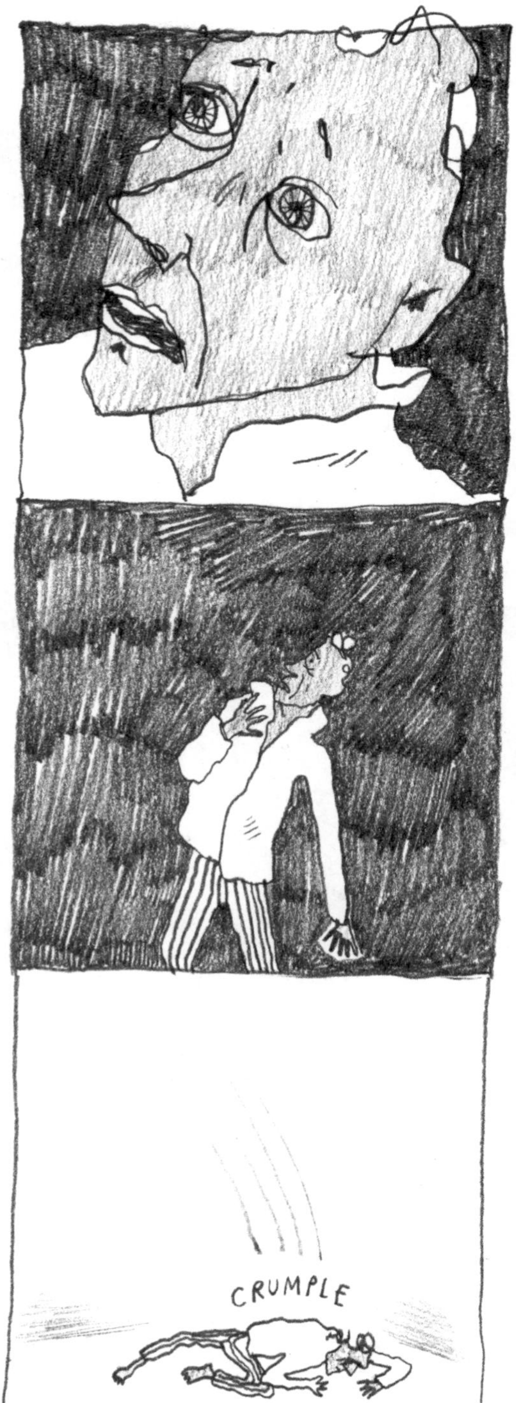
CRUMPLE

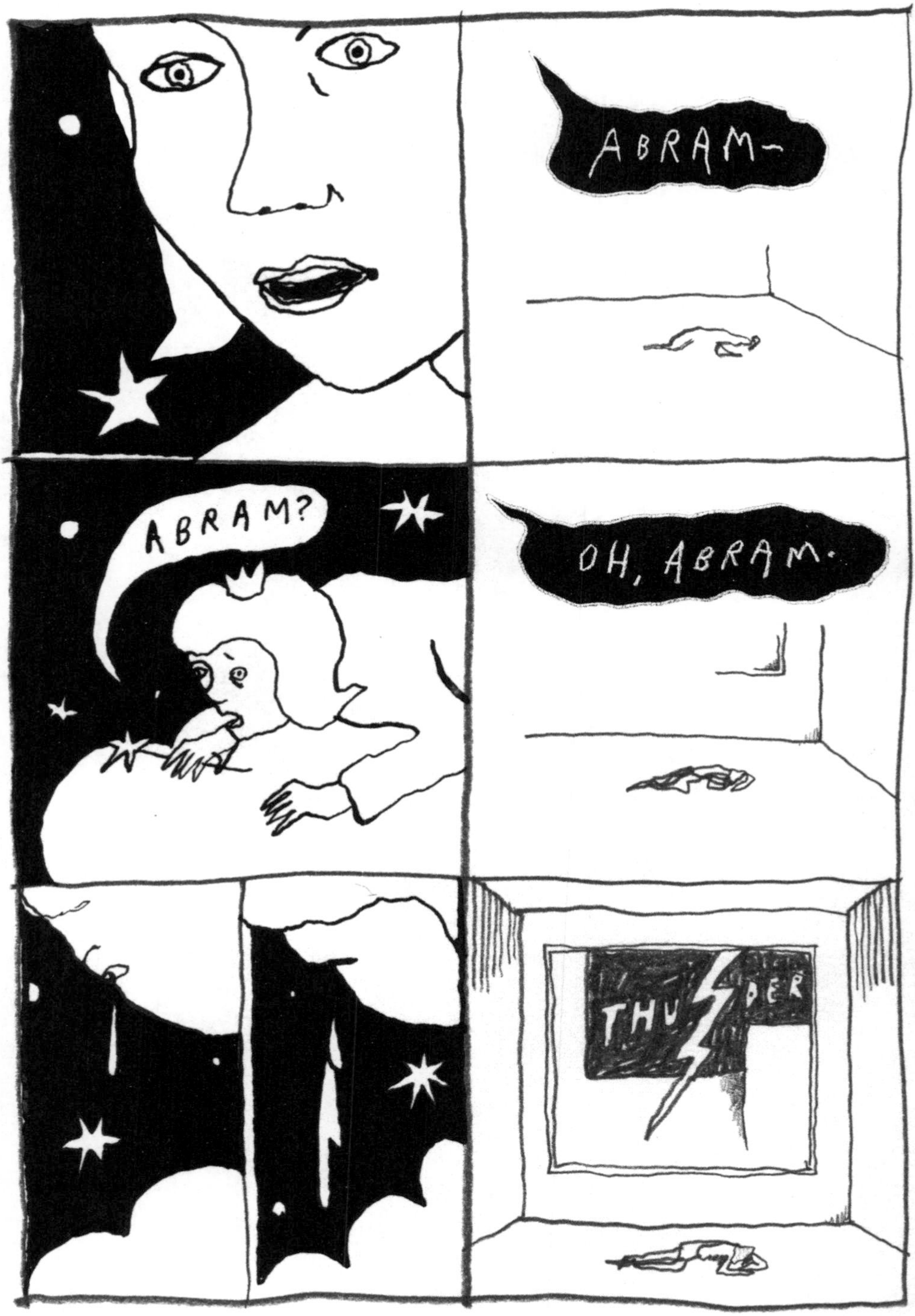
ABRAM-
ABRAM?
OH, ABRAM.
THUNDER

9

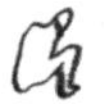

LOST SOUL

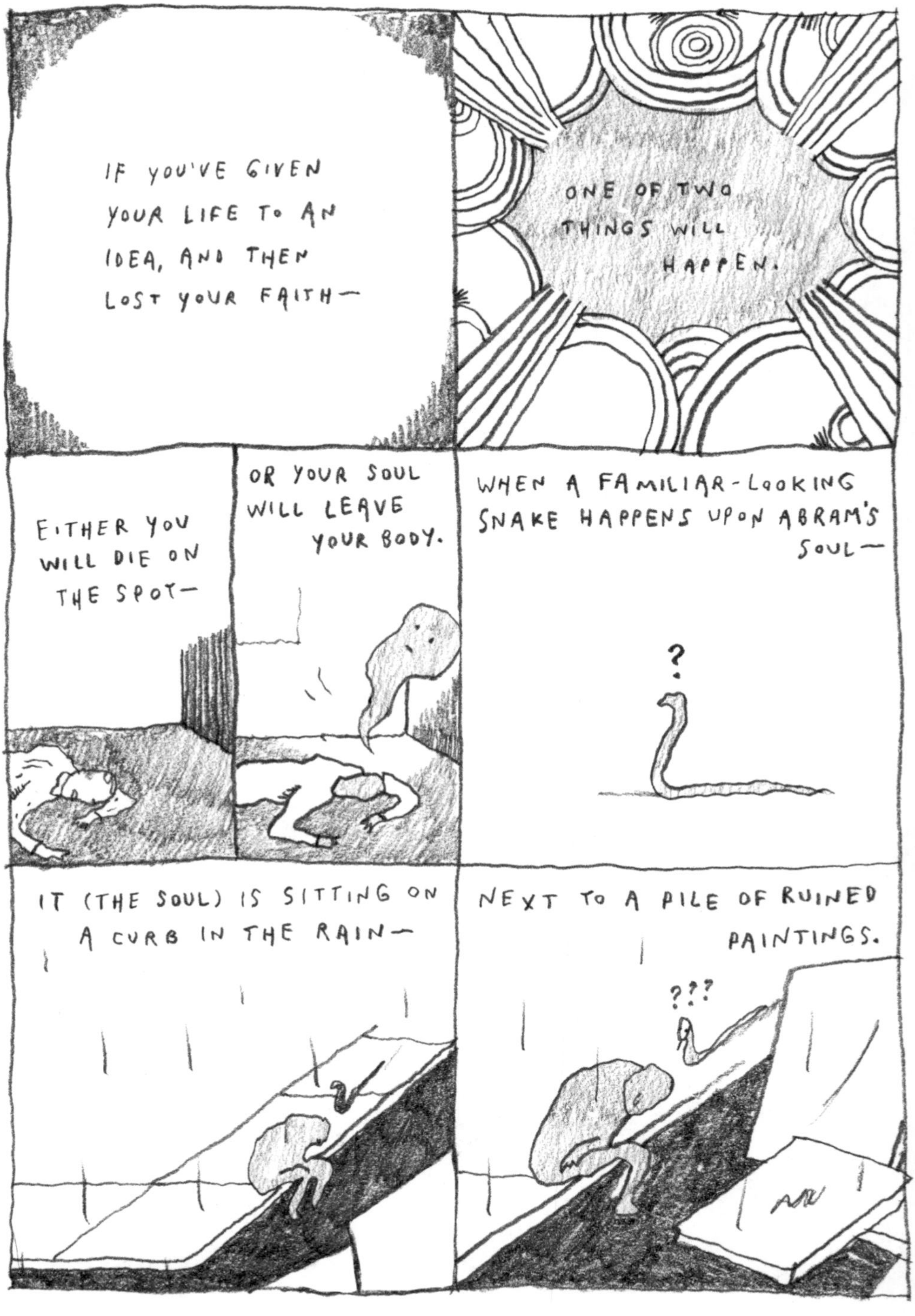
IF YOU'VE GIVEN YOUR LIFE TO AN IDEA, AND THEN LOST YOUR FAITH—
ONE OF TWO THINGS WILL HAPPEN.
EITHER YOU WILL DIE ON THE SPOT—
OR YOUR SOUL WILL LEAVE YOUR BODY.
WHEN A FAMILIAR-LOOKING SNAKE HAPPENS UPON ABRAM'S SOUL—
?
IT (THE SOUL) IS SITTING ON A CURB IN THE RAIN—
NEXT TO A PILE OF RUINED PAINTINGS.
???

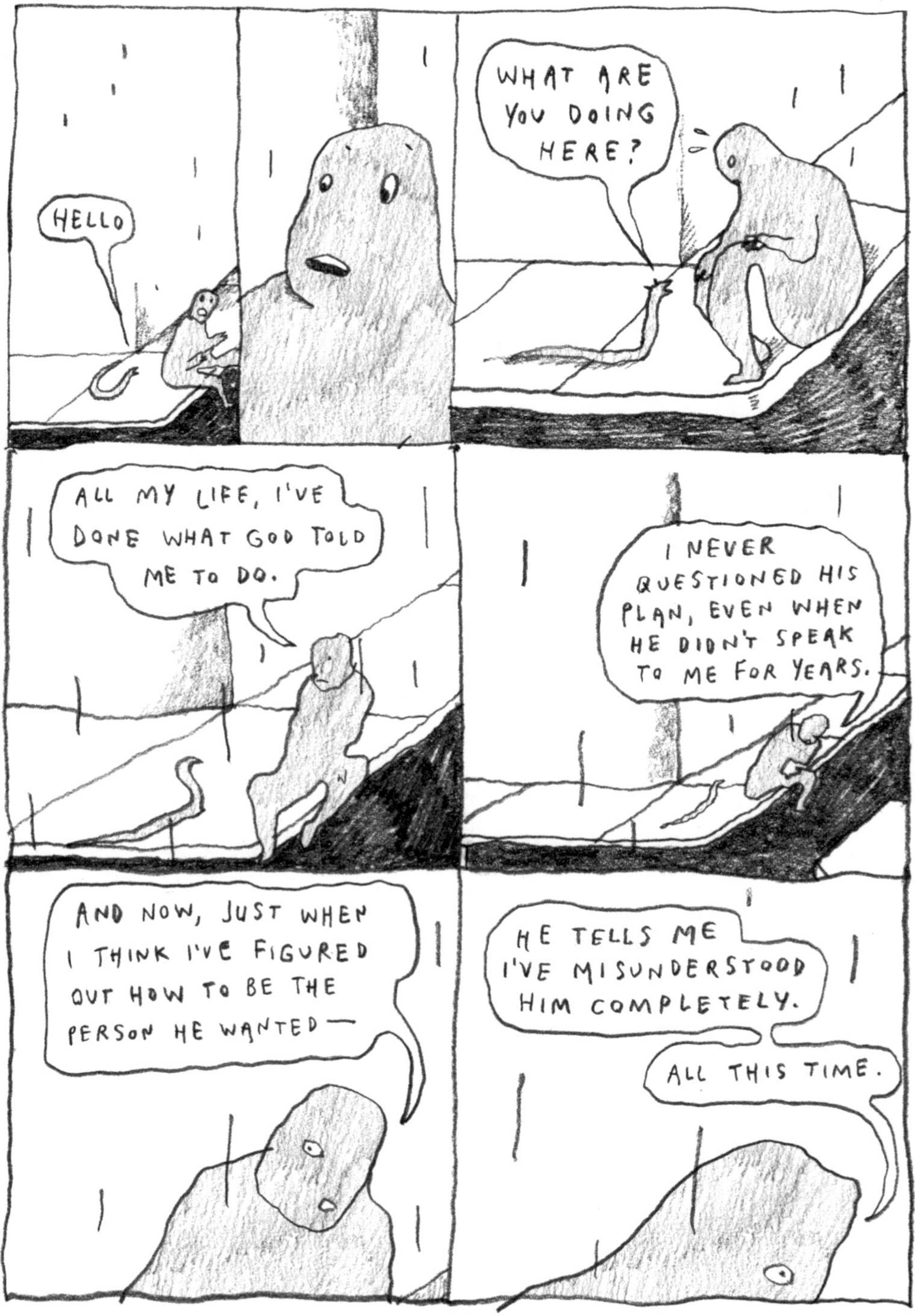
HELLO
WHAT ARE YOU DOING HERE?
ALL MY LIFE, I'VE DONE WHAT GOD TOLD ME TO DO.
I NEVER QUESTIONED HIS PLAN, EVEN WHEN HE DIDN'T SPEAK TO ME FOR YEARS.
AND NOW, JUST WHEN I THINK I'VE FIGURED OUT HOW TO BE THE PERSON HE WANTED—
HE TELLS ME I'VE MISUNDERSTOOD HIM COMPLETELY.
ALL THIS TIME.

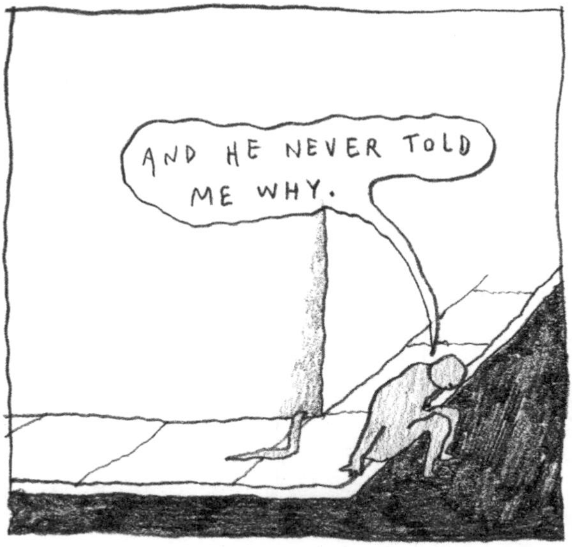
AND HE NEVER TOLD ME WHY.

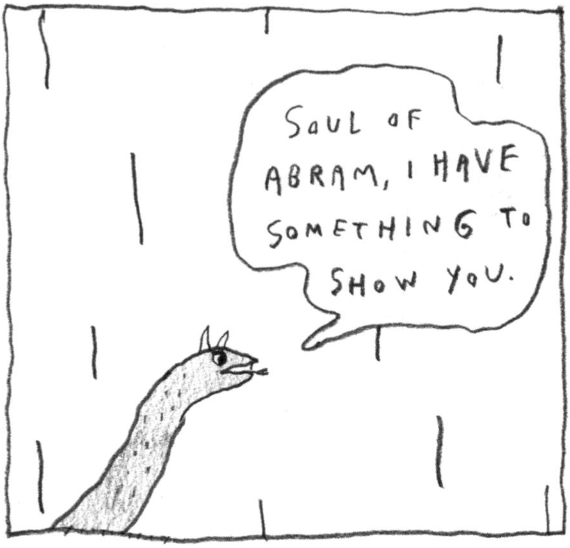
SOUL OF ABRAM, I HAVE SOMETHING TO SHOW YOU.

10

EDEN

THE GARDEN OF EDEN, NOW A WELL-MAINTAINED CITY PARK, IS CLOSED TO THE PUBLIC.

IT IS GUARDED BY AN ANGEL WITH A FLAMING SWORD.

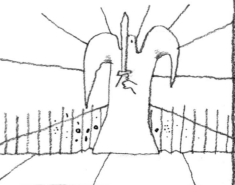

IF YOU HAPPEN TO PASS BY AT THE EXACT RIGHT TIME

YOU WILL CATCH HER ON HER EVENING ROUNDS.

GLIMMER

(WHICH NO ONE EVER DOES)—

IT IS COMMON KNOWLEDGE* THAT GOD CAN'T STAND TO BE LOOKED AT.

SHE CAN ONLY BE GLIMPSED INDIRECTLY. NOT BY THE MAN HIMSELF. BUT BY HIS SOUL.

*AMONG ANGELS

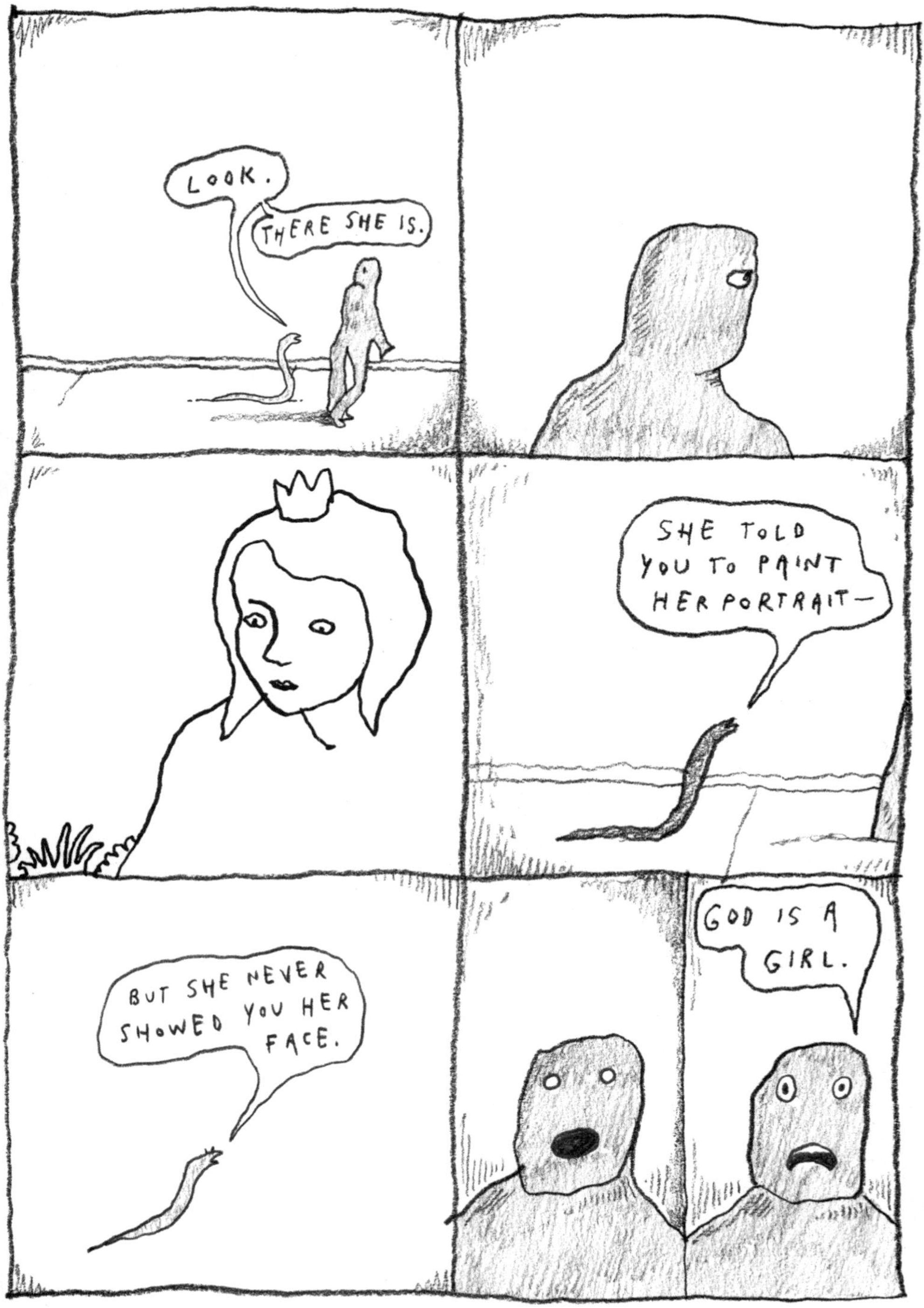
LOOK.
THERE SHE IS.
SHE TOLD YOU TO PAINT HER PORTRAIT—
BUT SHE NEVER SHOWED YOU HER FACE.
GOD IS A GIRL.

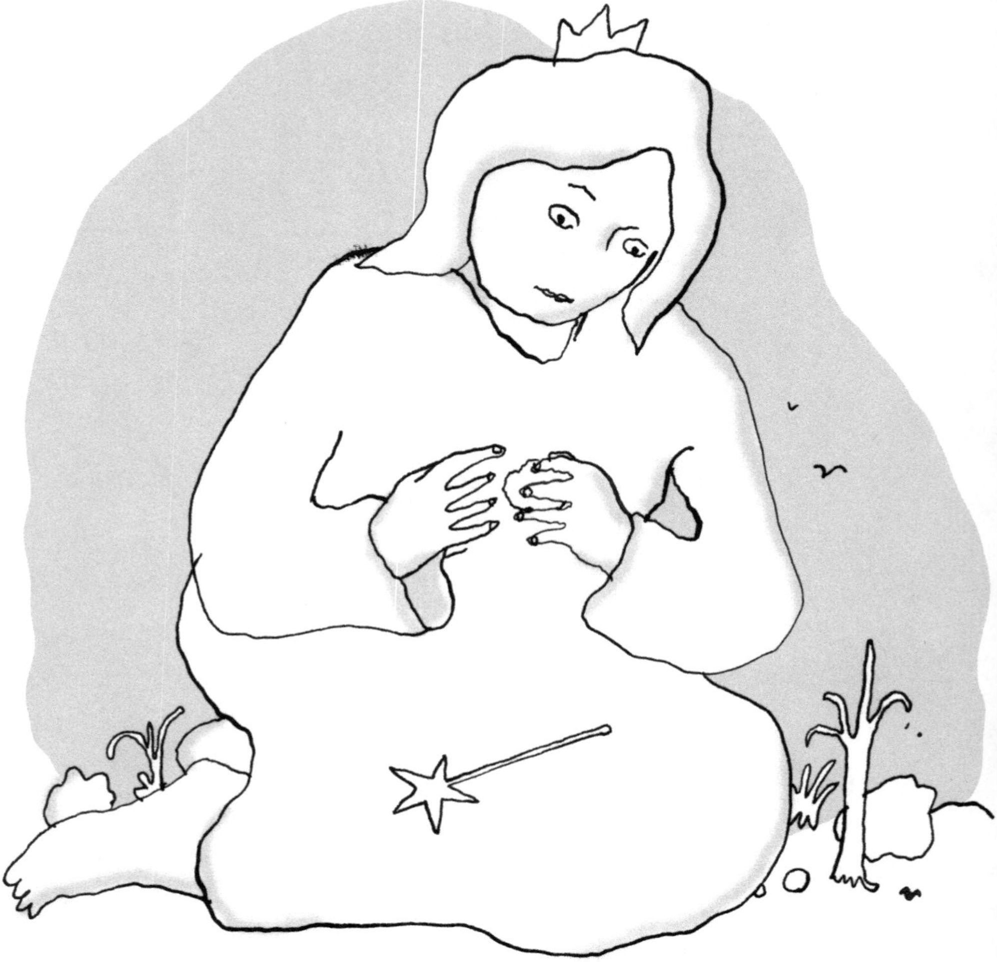

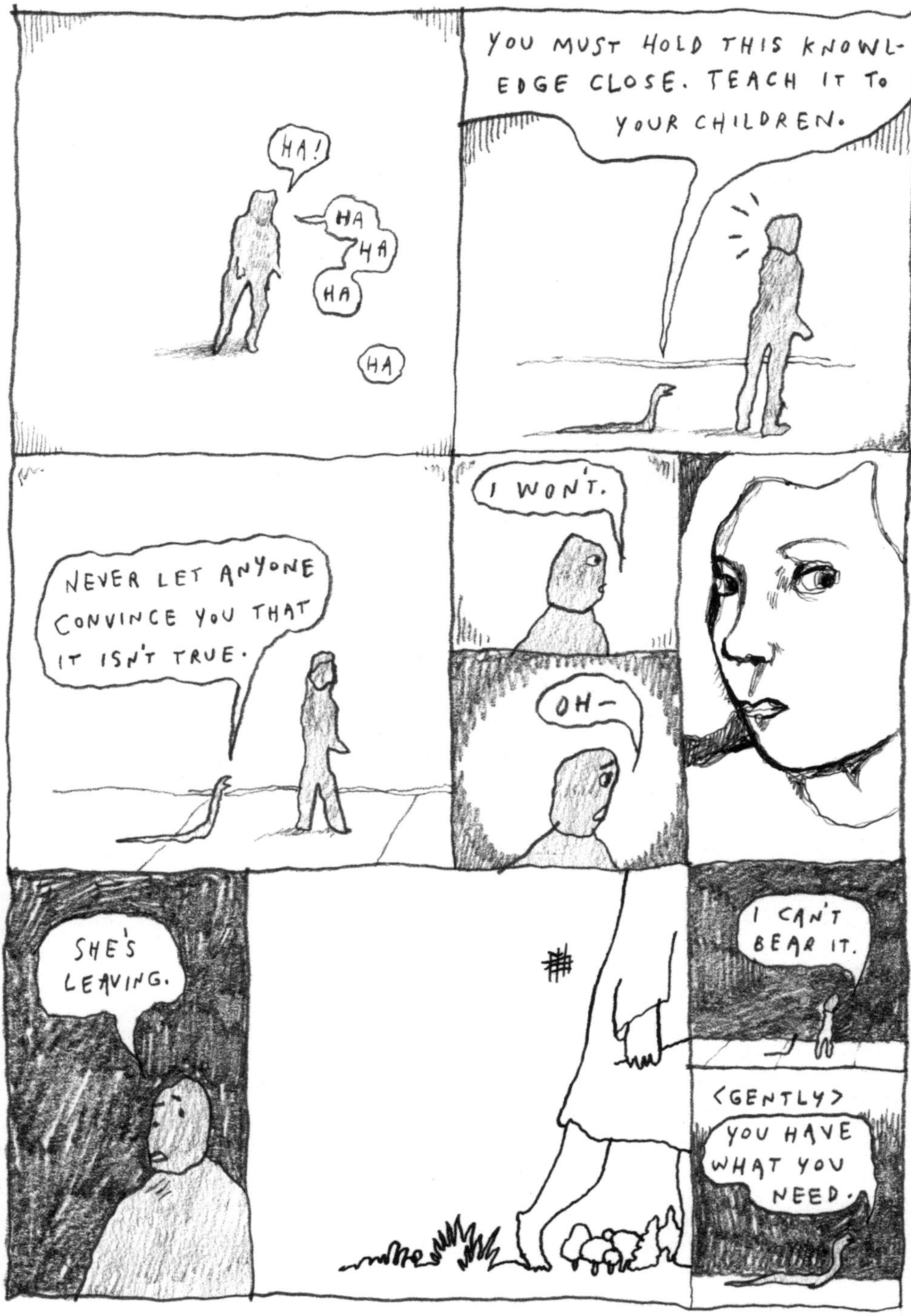
HA!
HA
HA
HA
HA
YOU MUST HOLD THIS KNOWLEDGE CLOSE. TEACH IT TO YOUR CHILDREN.
NEVER LET ANYONE CONVINCE YOU THAT IT ISN'T TRUE.
I WON'T.
OH—
SHE'S LEAVING.
I CAN'T BEAR IT.
<GENTLY>
YOU HAVE WHAT YOU NEED.

11

SON OF GOD

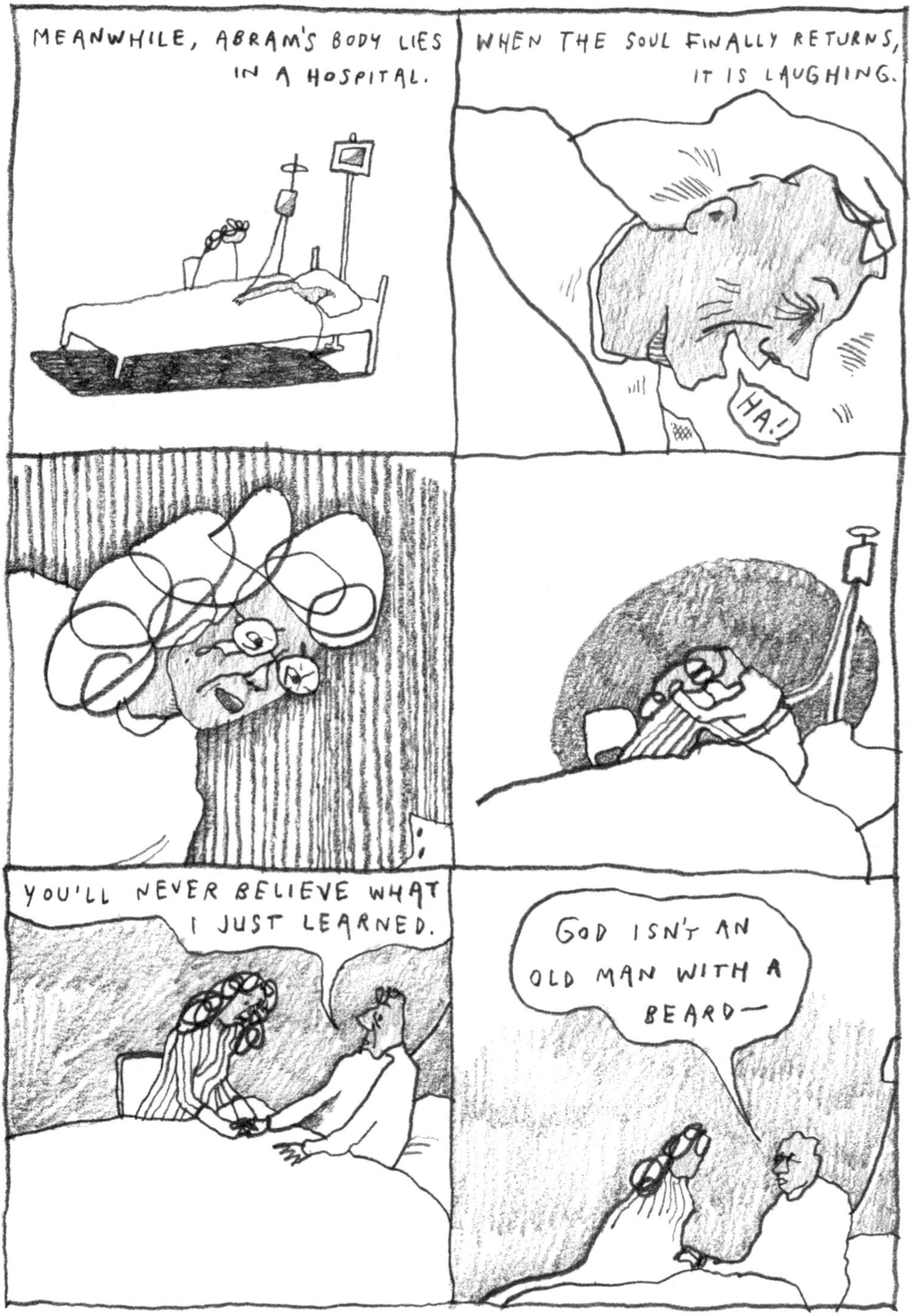
MEANWHILE, ABRAM'S BODY LIES IN A HOSPITAL.
WHEN THE SOUL FINALLY RETURNS, IT IS LAUGHING.
HA!
YOU'LL NEVER BELIEVE WHAT I JUST LEARNED.
GOD ISN'T AN OLD MAN WITH A BEARD—

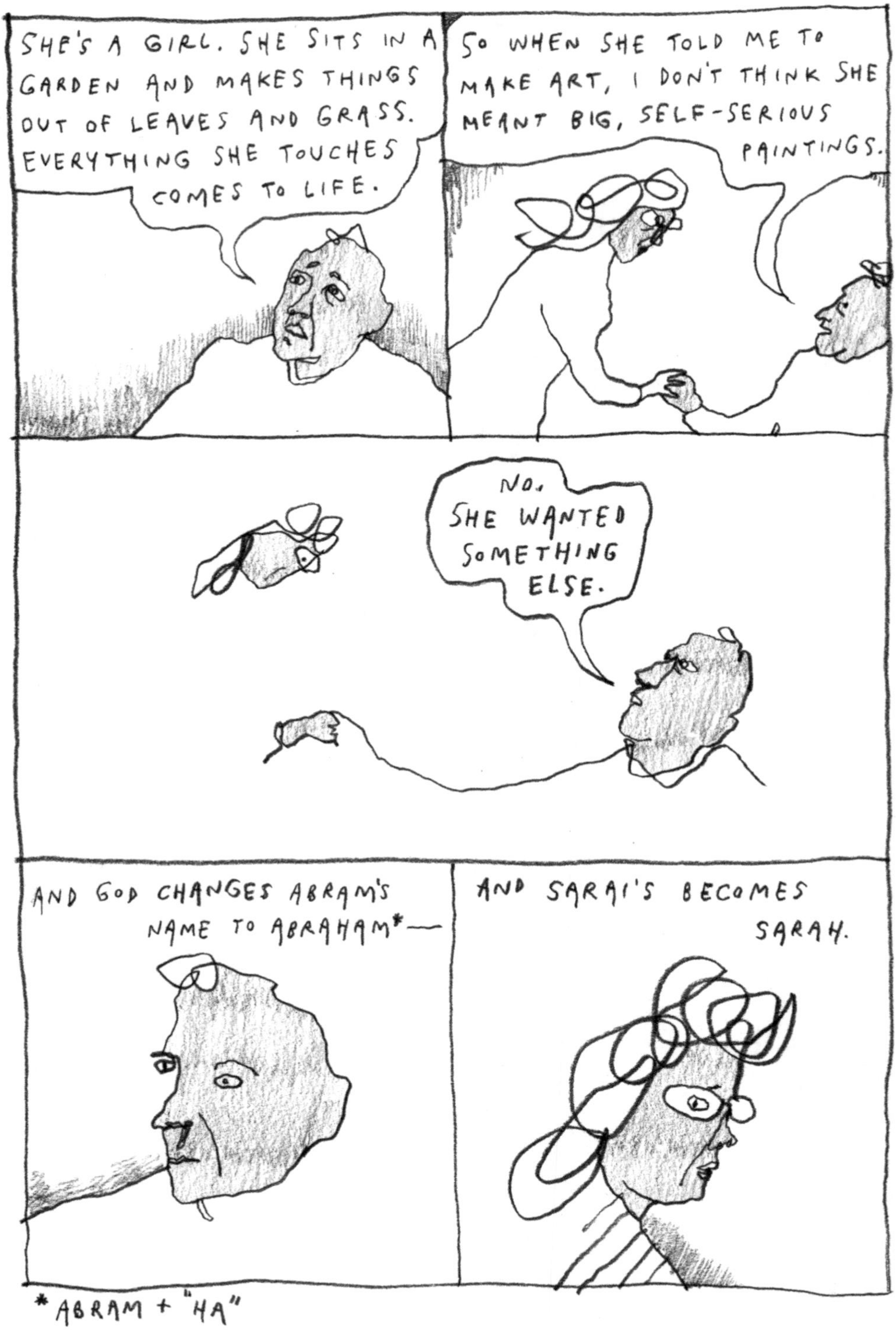
SHE'S A GIRL. SHE SITS IN A GARDEN AND MAKES THINGS OUT OF LEAVES AND GRASS. EVERYTHING SHE TOUCHES COMES TO LIFE.
SO WHEN SHE TOLD ME TO MAKE ART, I DON'T THINK SHE MEANT BIG, SELF-SERIOUS PAINTINGS.
NO. SHE WANTED SOMETHING ELSE.
AND GOD CHANGES ABRAM'S NAME TO ABRAHAM*—
AND SARAI'S BECOMES SARAH.

*ABRAM + "HA"

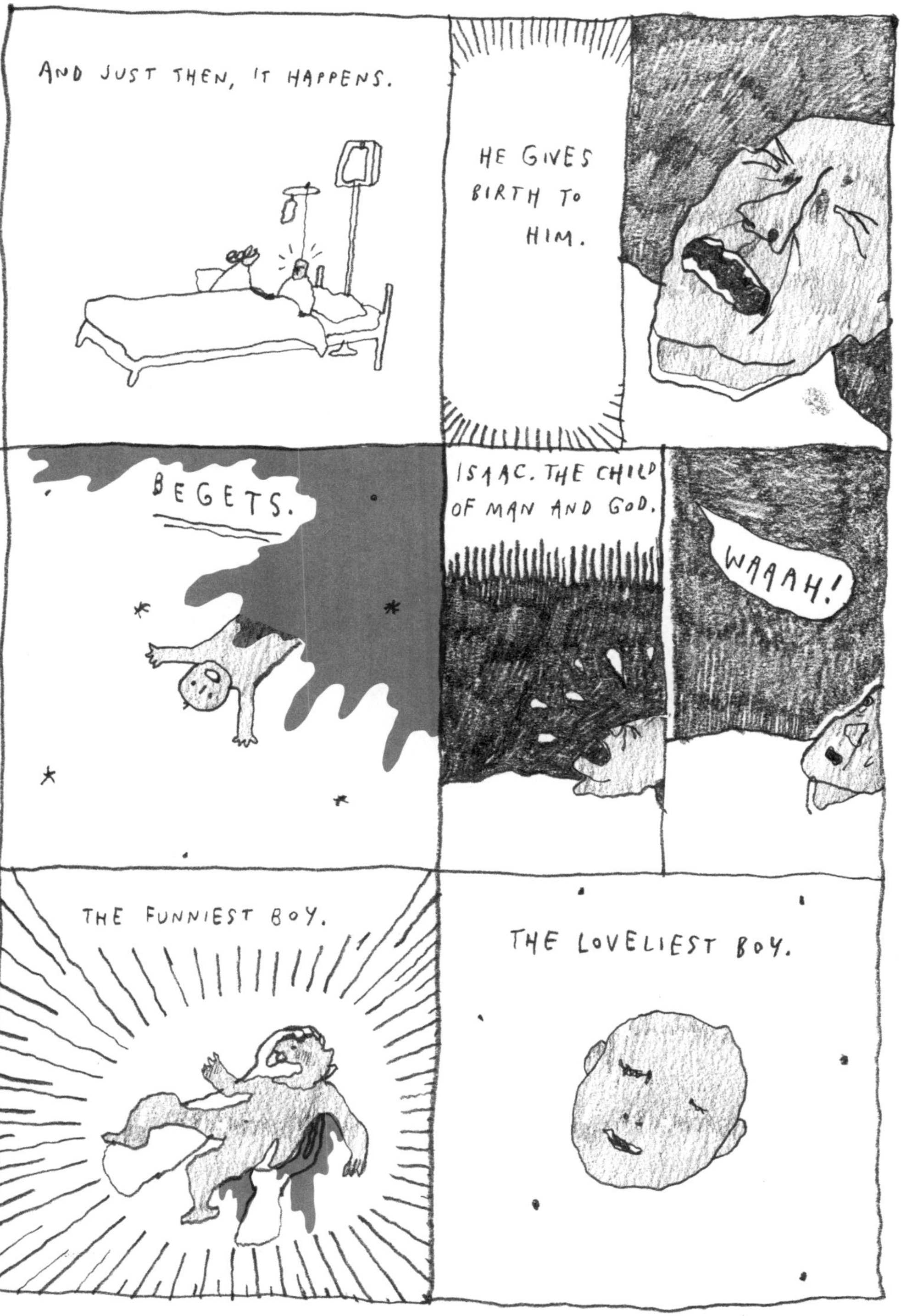
AND JUST THEN, IT HAPPENS.
HE GIVES BIRTH TO HIM.
BEGETS.
ISAAC. THE CHILD OF MAN AND GOD.
WAAAH!
THE FUNNIEST BOY.
THE LOVELIEST BOY.

ISAAC.

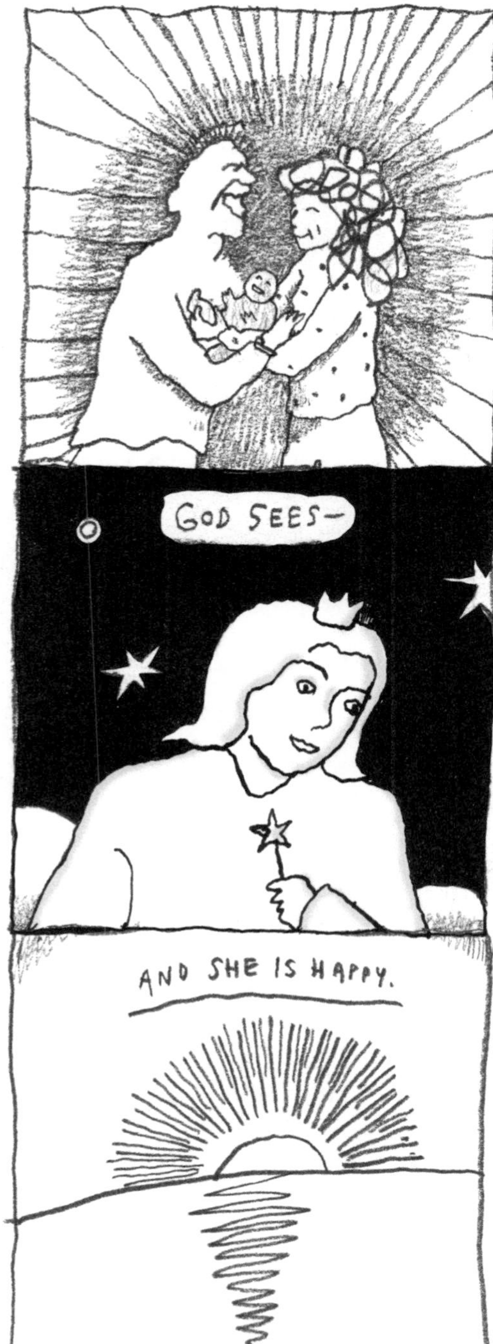
GOD SEES—
AND SHE IS HAPPY.

12

THE FACE OF GOD

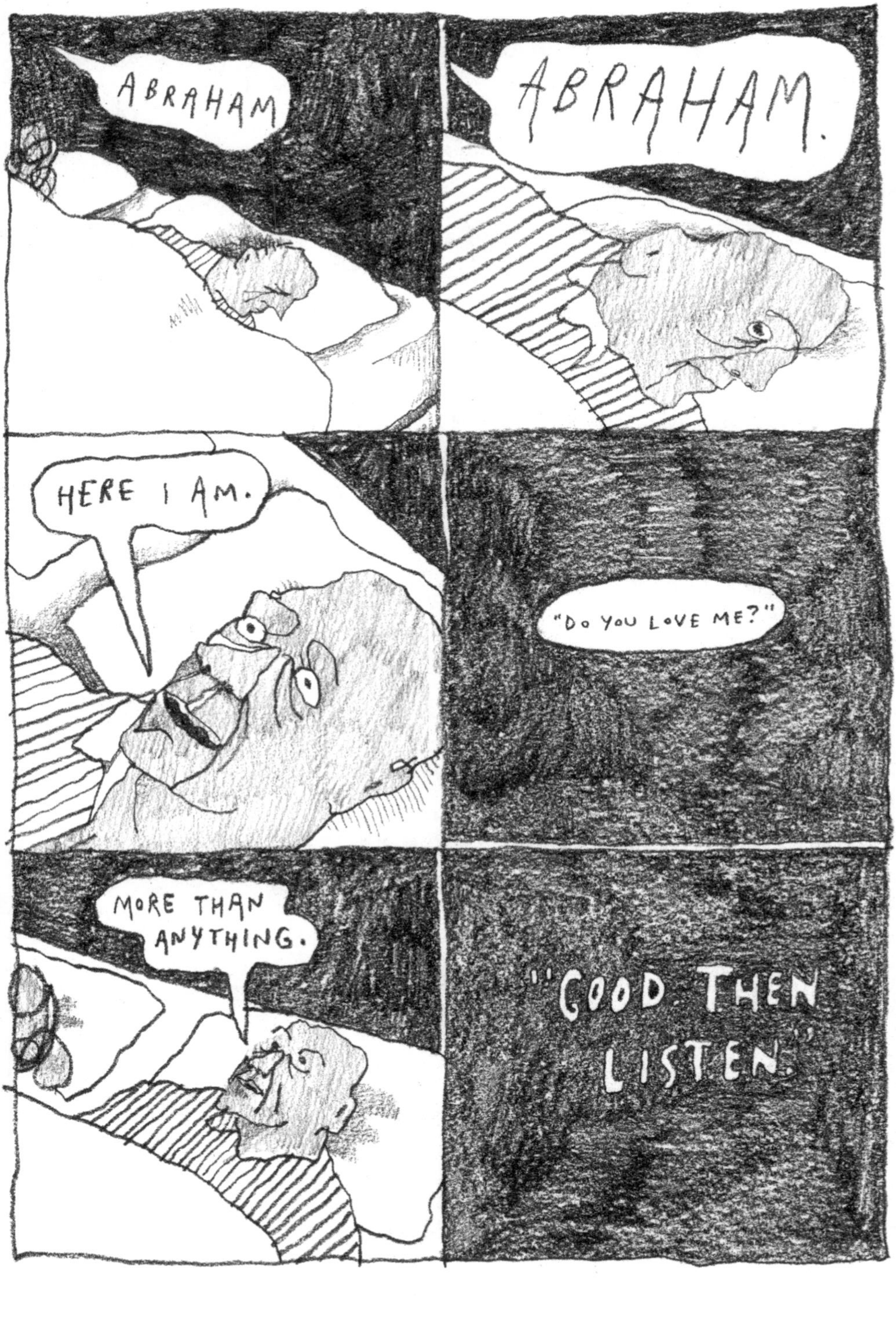
ABRAHAM
ABRAHAM.
HERE I AM.
"DO YOU LOVE ME?"
MORE THAN ANYTHING.
"GOOD THEN LISTEN."

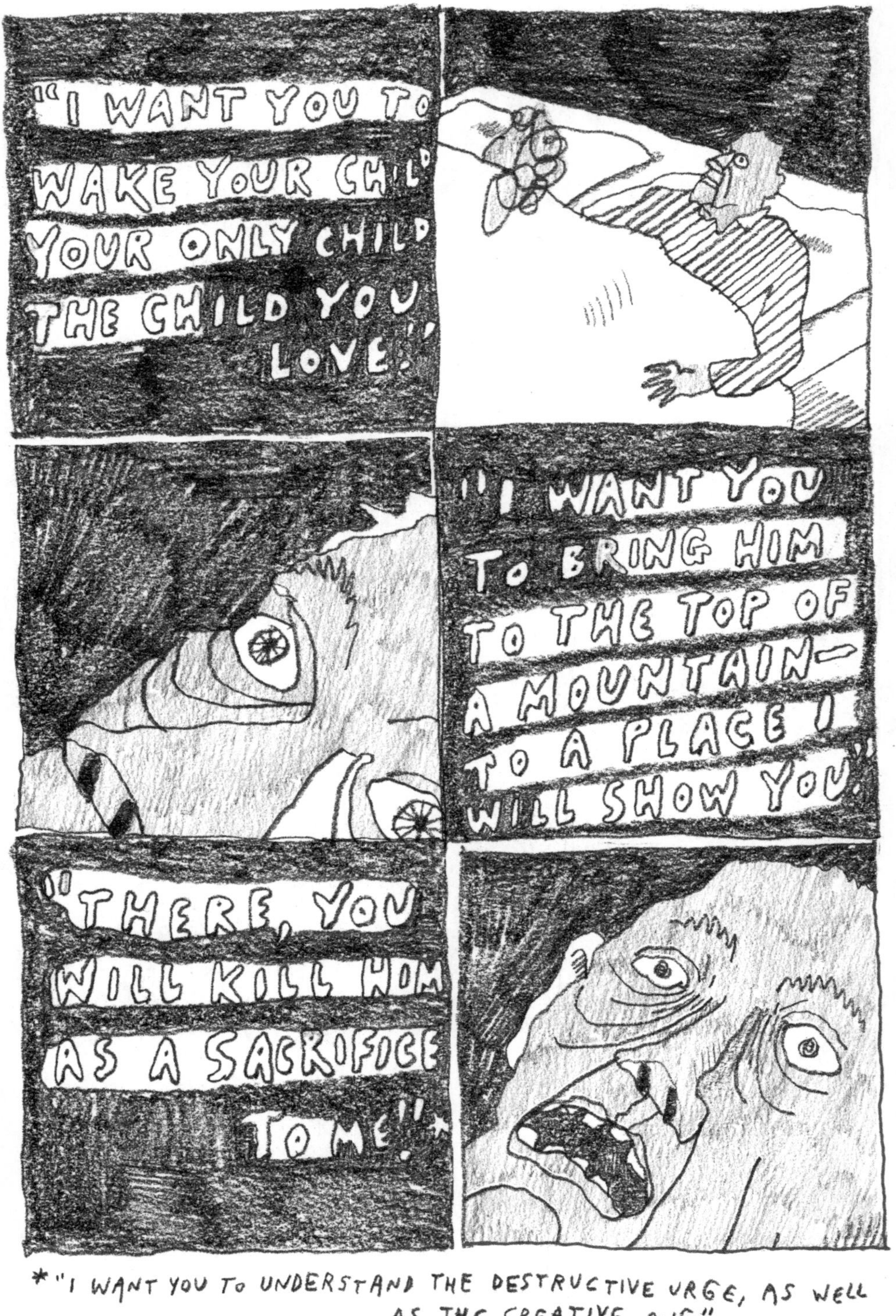
"I WANT YOU TO WAKE YOUR CHILD YOUR ONLY CHILD THE CHILD YOU LOVE!"
"I WANT YOU TO BRING HIM TO THE TOP OF A MOUNTAIN— TO A PLACE I WILL SHOW YOU."
"THERE, YOU WILL KILL HIM AS A SACRIFICE TO ME!"*

*"I WANT YOU TO UNDERSTAND THE DESTRUCTIVE URGE, AS WELL AS THE CREATIVE ONE."

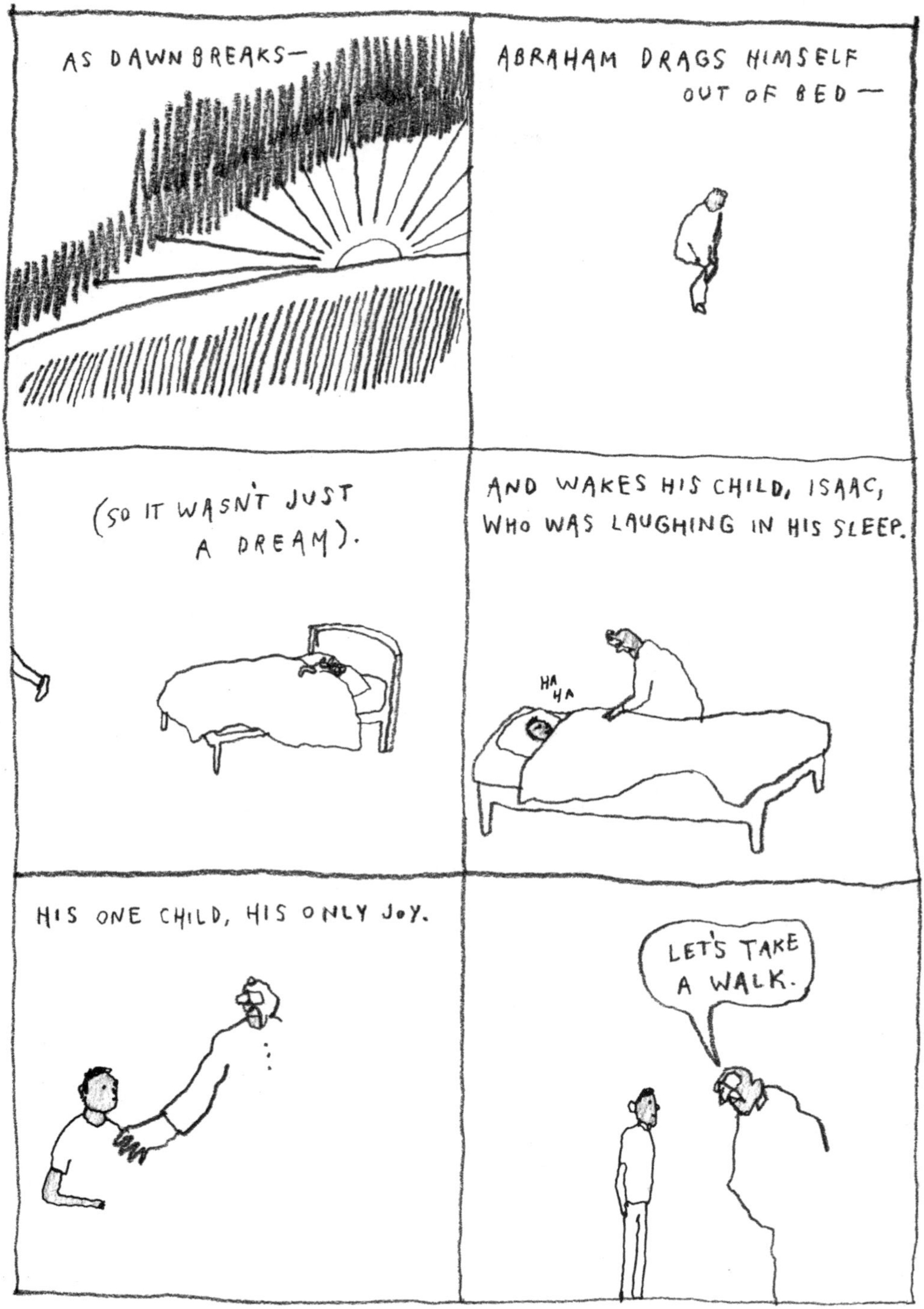
AS DAWN BREAKS—
ABRAHAM DRAGS HIMSELF OUT OF BED—
(SO IT WASN'T JUST A DREAM).
AND WAKES HIS CHILD, ISAAC, WHO WAS LAUGHING IN HIS SLEEP.
HA HA
HIS ONE CHILD, HIS ONLY JOY.
LET'S TAKE A WALK.

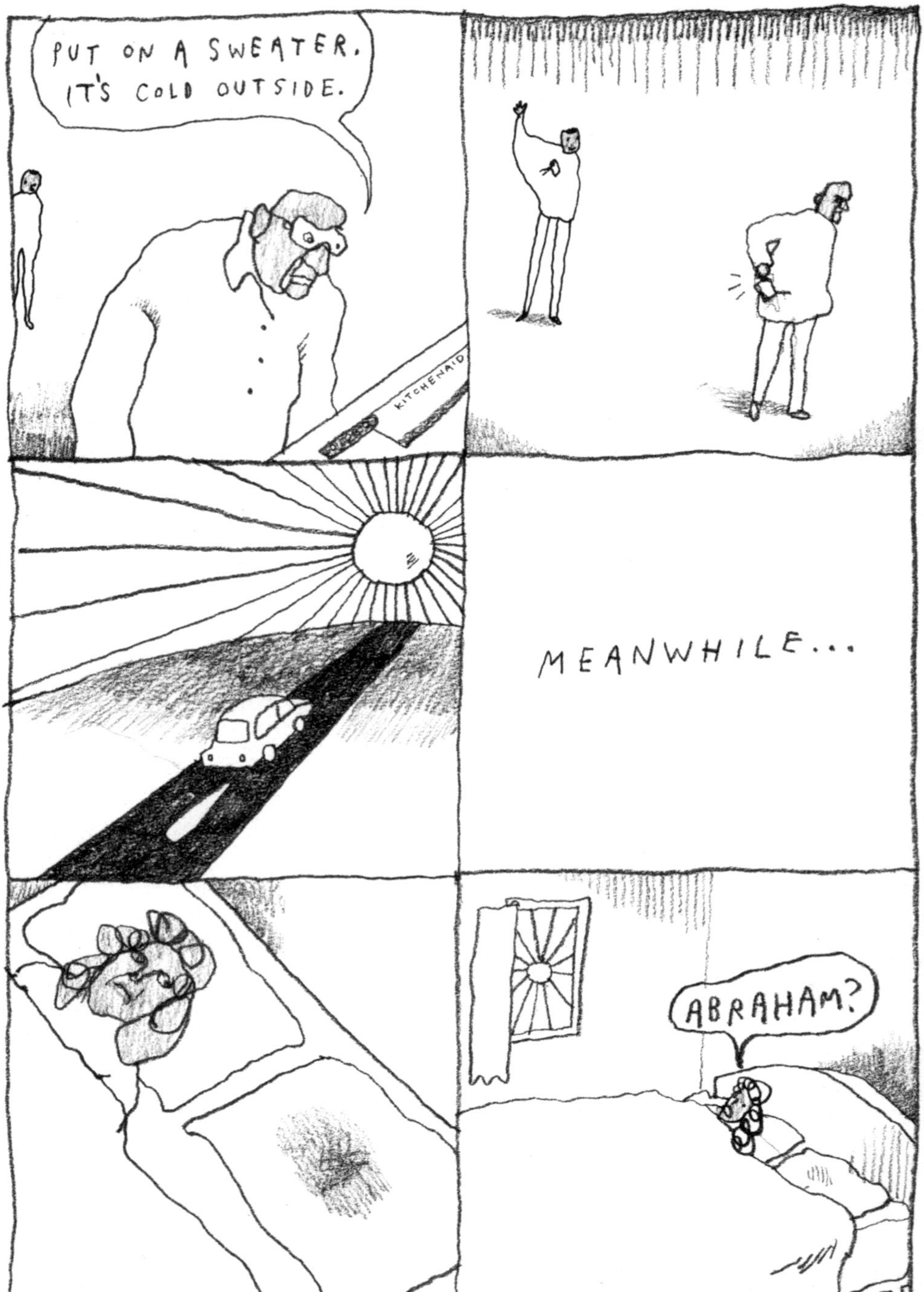
PUT ON A SWEATER. IT'S COLD OUTSIDE.
KITCHENAID
MEANWHILE...
ABRAHAM?

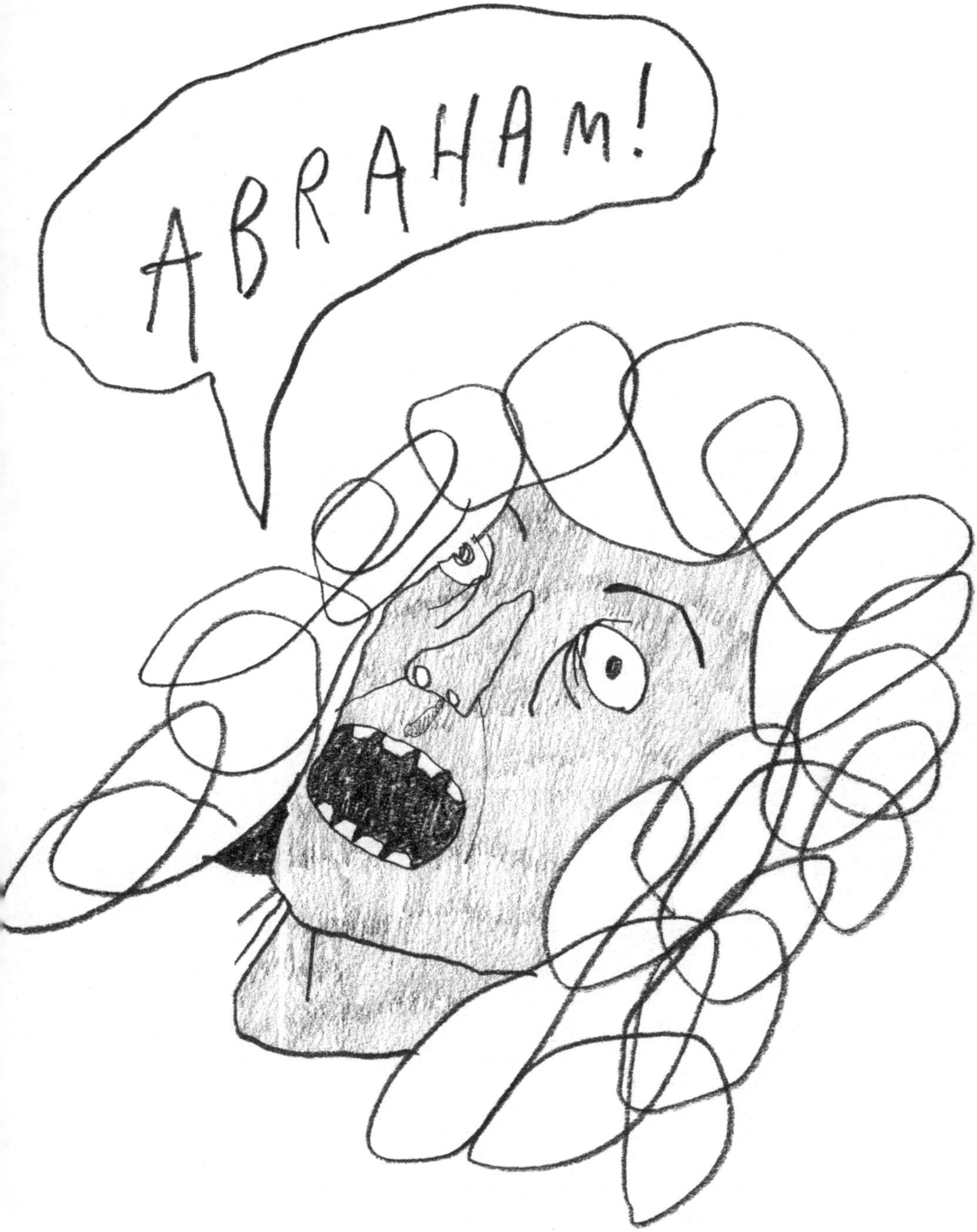
ABRAHAM!

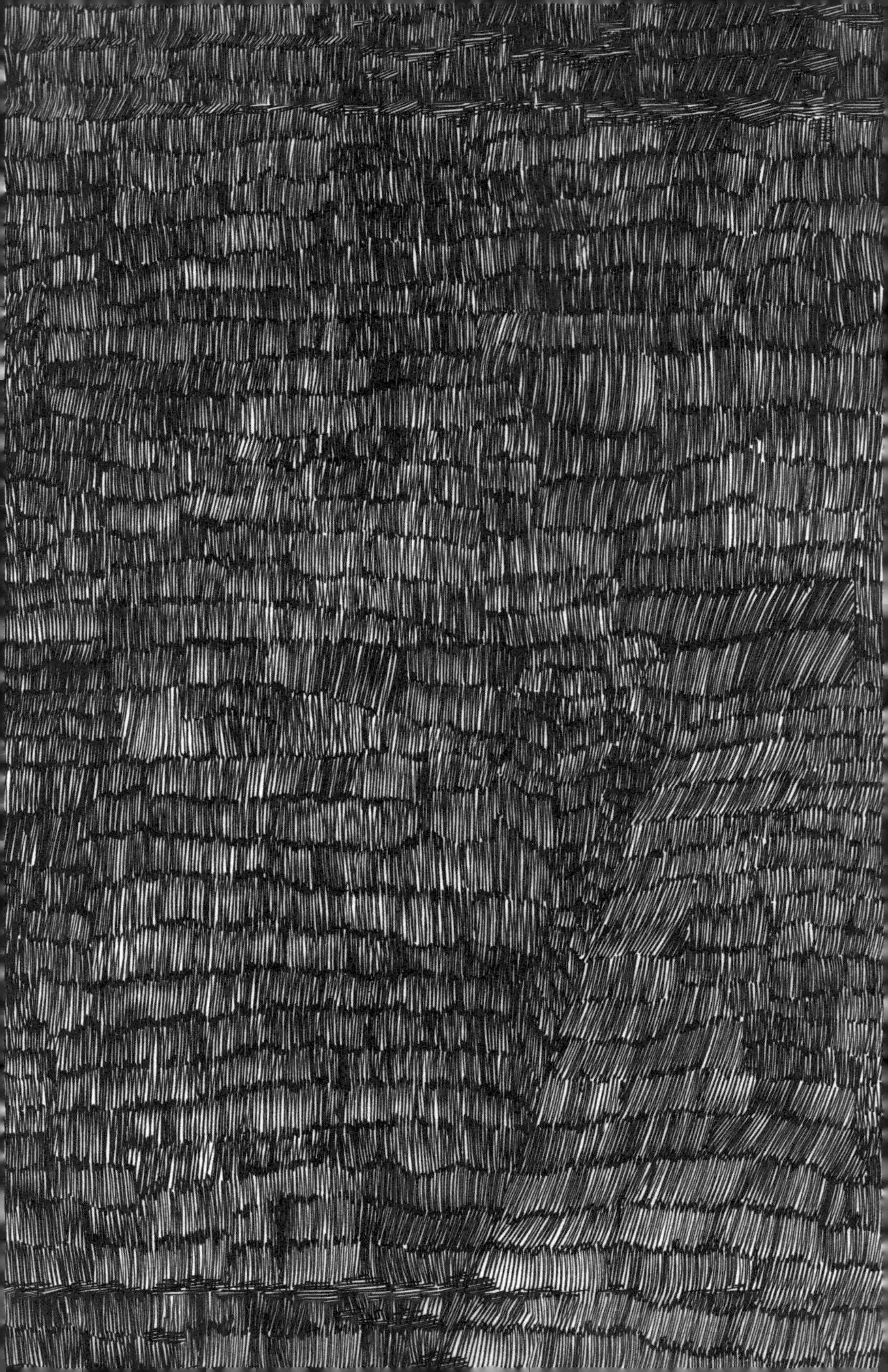

13

THE BAR MITZVAH

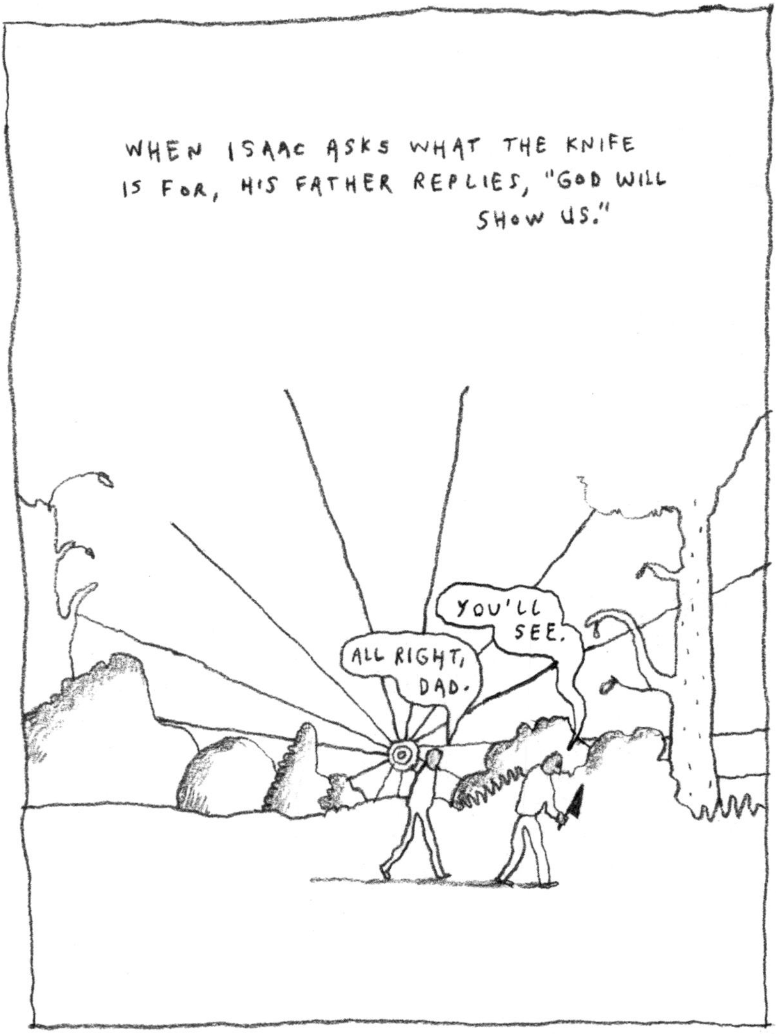
WHEN ISAAC ASKS WHAT THE KNIFE IS FOR, HIS FATHER REPLIES, "GOD WILL SHOW US."
YOU'LL SEE.
ALL RIGHT, DAD.

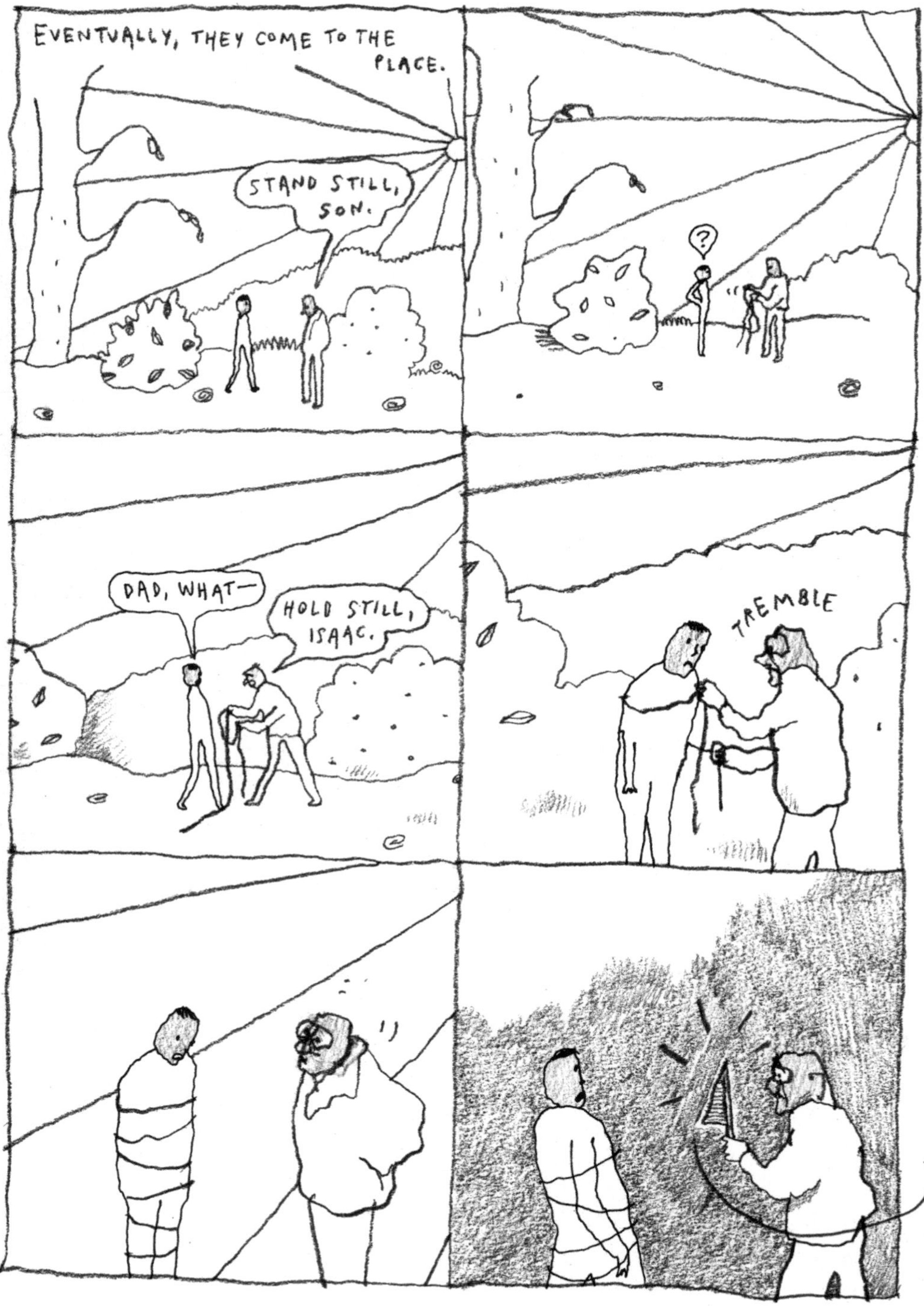

EVENTUALLY, THEY COME TO THE PLACE.
STAND STILL, SON.
?
DAD, WHAT—
HOLD STILL, ISAAC.
TREMBLE

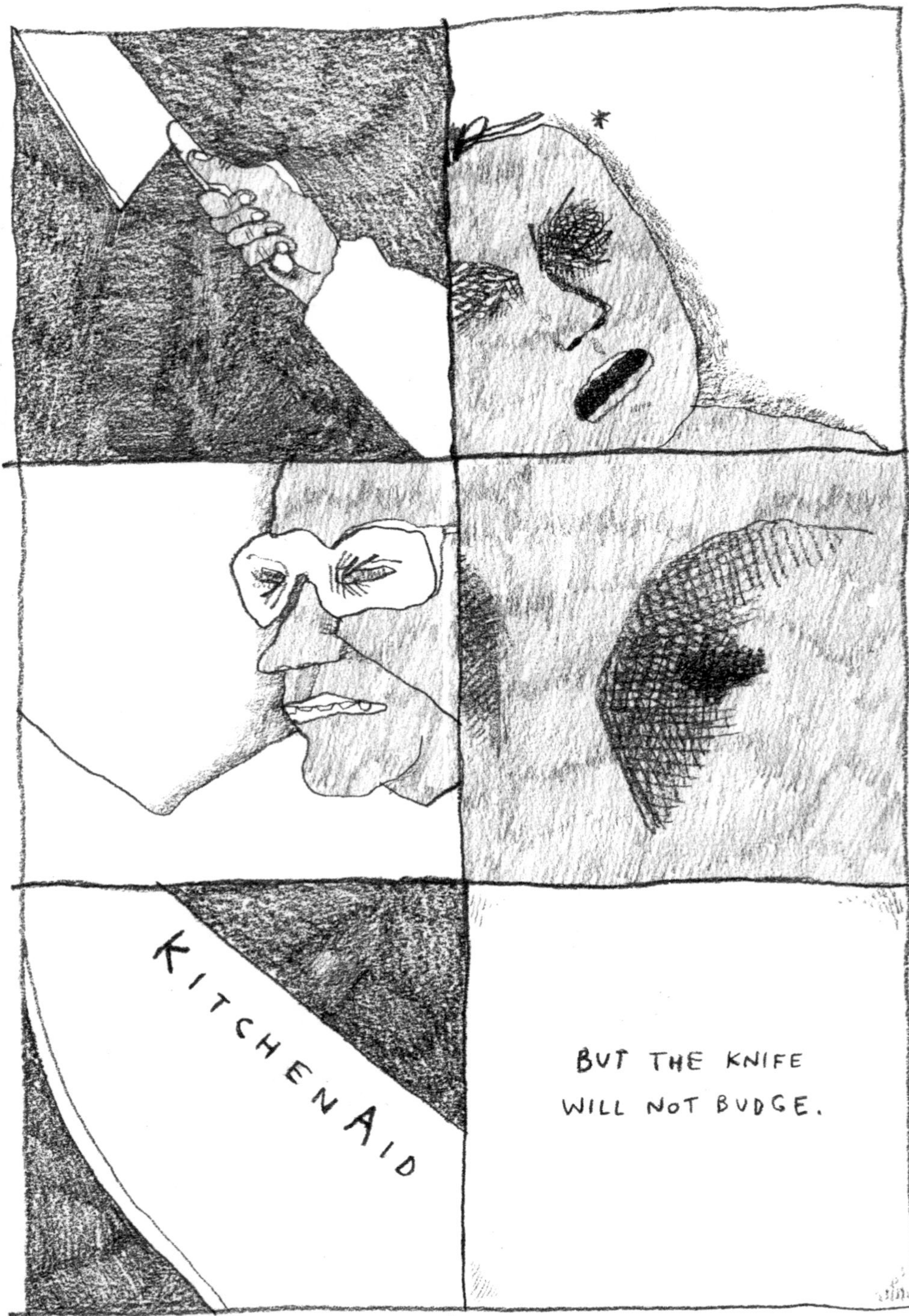
*
KITCHENAID
BUT THE KNIFE WILL NOT BUDGE.

*TRAUMA CAN CHANGE A PERSON. AFTER THE INCIDENT, ISAAC WILL BECOME ALMOST UNRECOGNIZABLE.

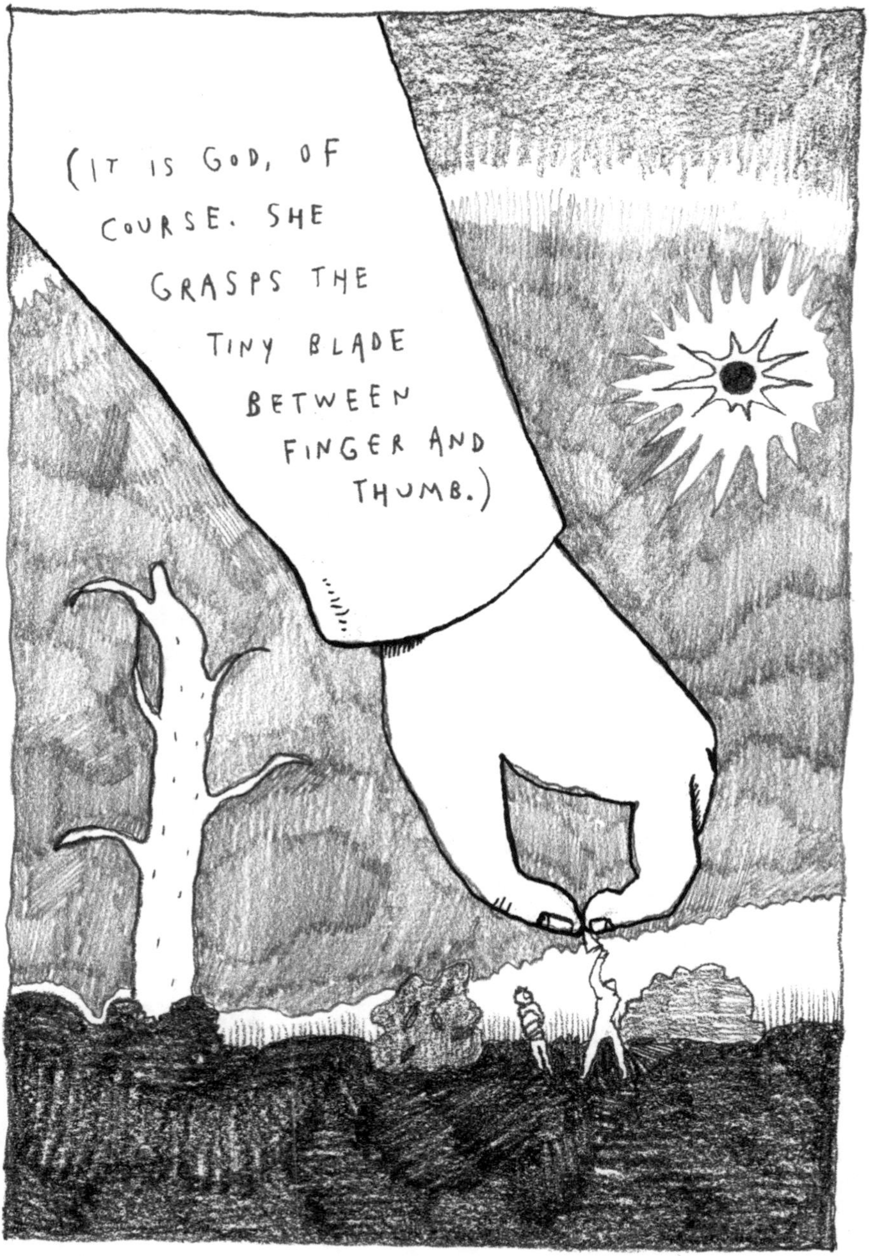
(IT IS GOD, OF COURSE. SHE GRASPS THE TINY BLADE BETWEEN FINGER AND THUMB.)

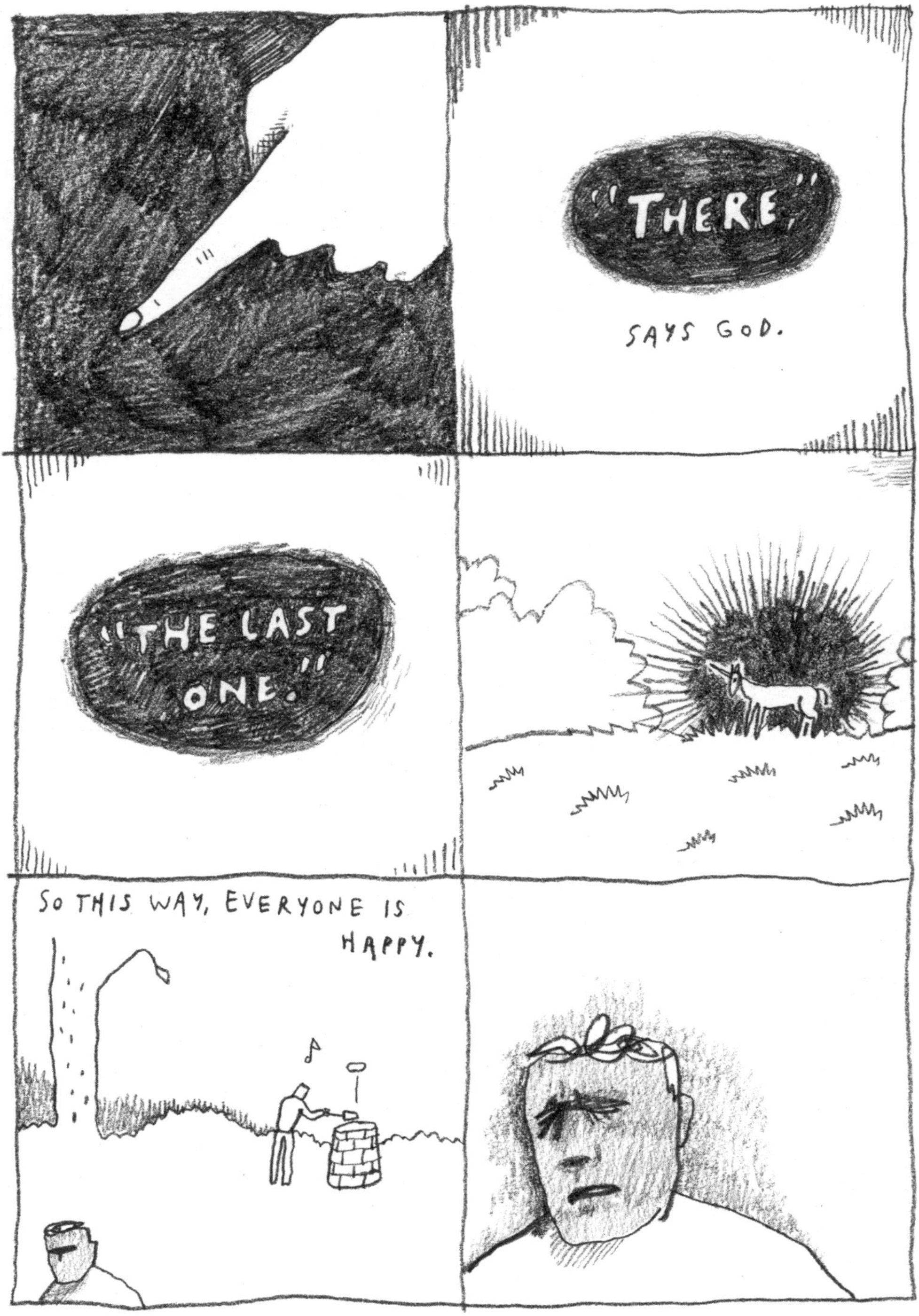
"THERE,"
SAYS GOD.
"THE LAST ONE."
SO THIS WAY, EVERYONE IS HAPPY.

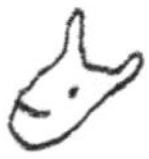

14

THE LIVES OF SARAH

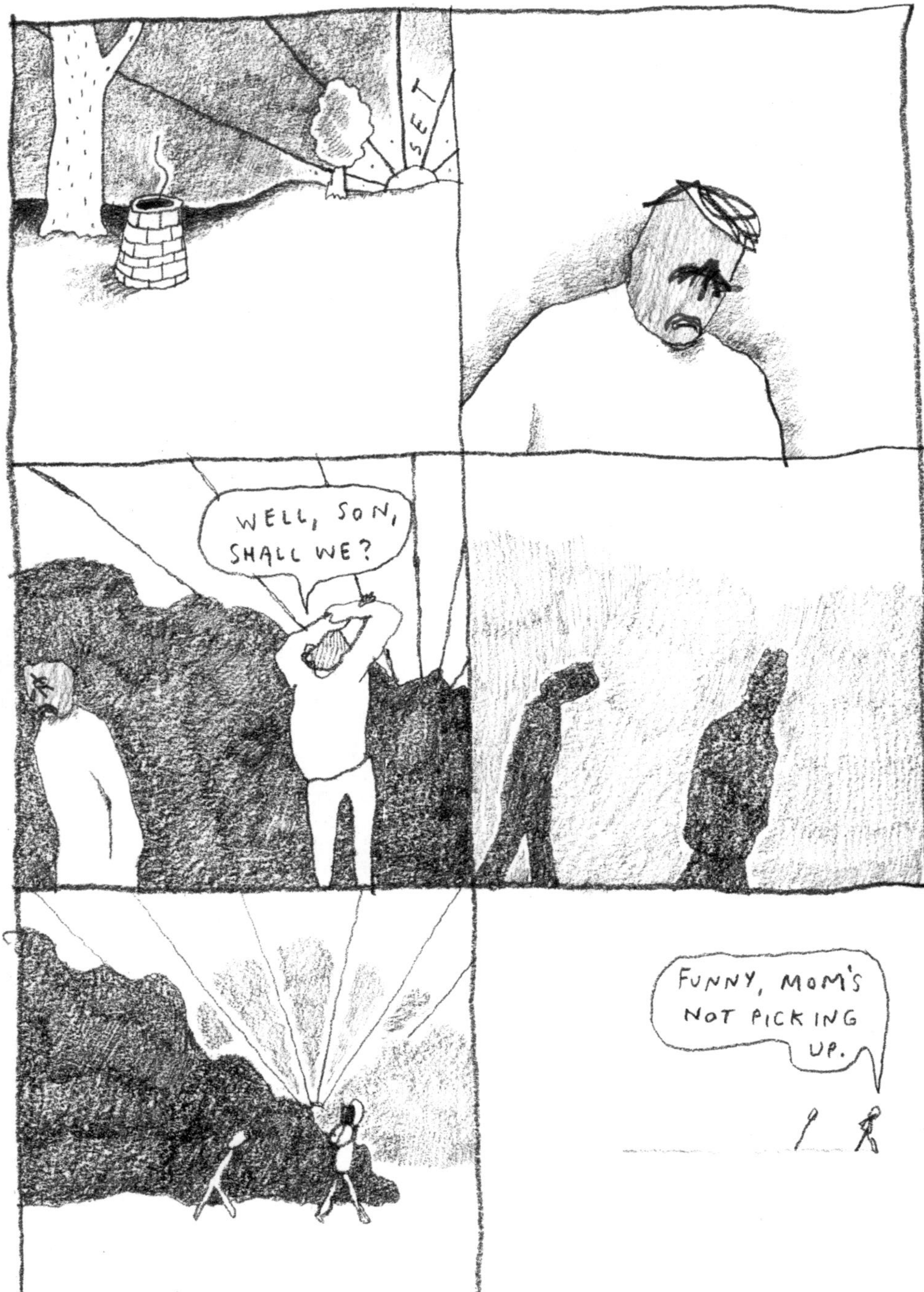
SET
WELL, SON, SHALL WE?
FUNNY, MOM'S NOT PICKING UP.

SARAH IS GONE.

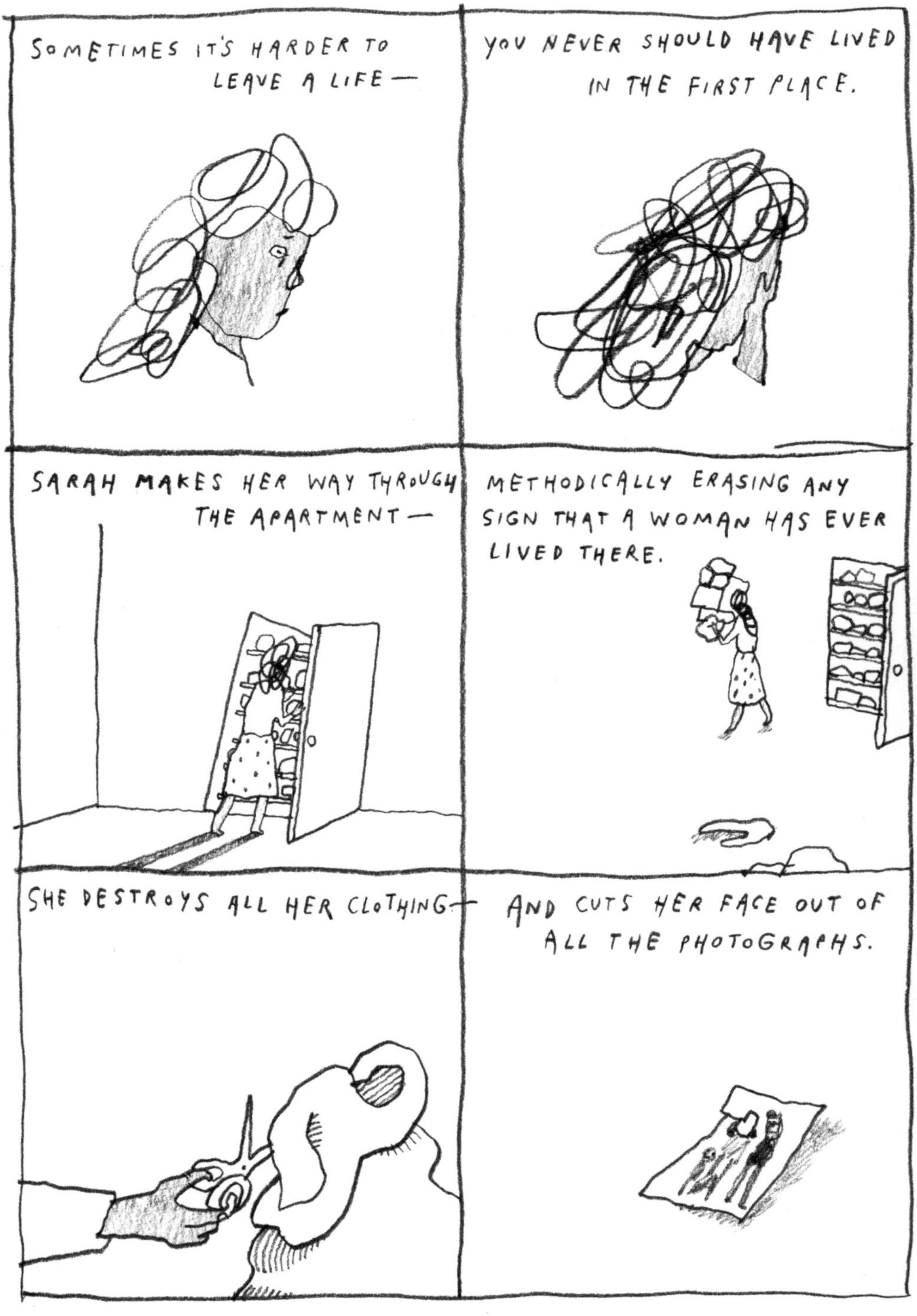
SOMETIMES IT'S HARDER TO LEAVE A LIFE—
YOU NEVER SHOULD HAVE LIVED IN THE FIRST PLACE.
SARAH MAKES HER WAY THROUGH THE APARTMENT—
METHODICALLY ERASING ANY SIGN THAT A WOMAN HAS EVER LIVED THERE.
SHE DESTROYS ALL HER CLOTHING—
AND CUTS HER FACE OUT OF ALL THE PHOTOGRAPHS.

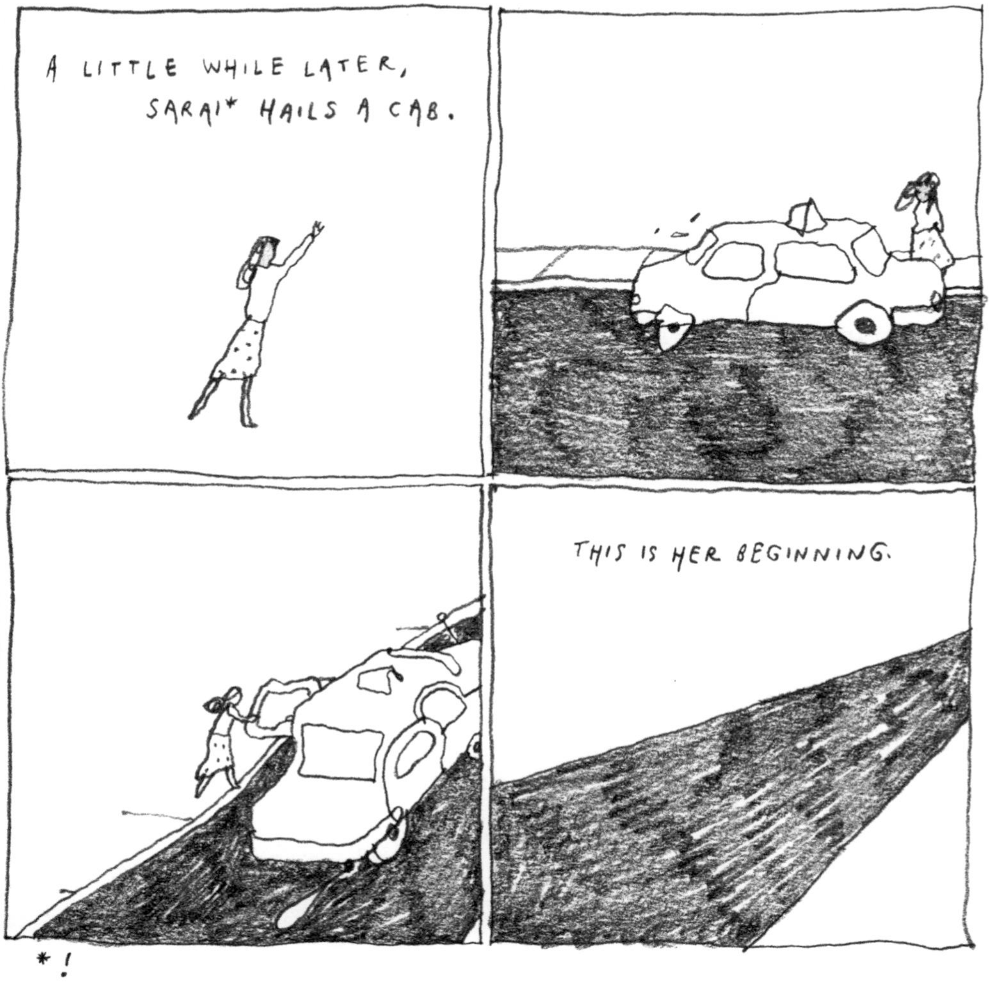
A LITTLE WHILE LATER,
SARAI* HAILS A CAB.
THIS IS HER BEGINNING.
*!

END

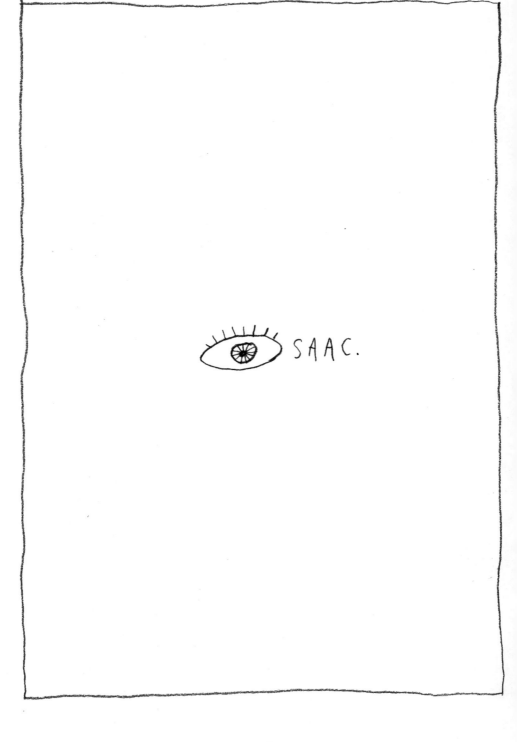

SAAC.

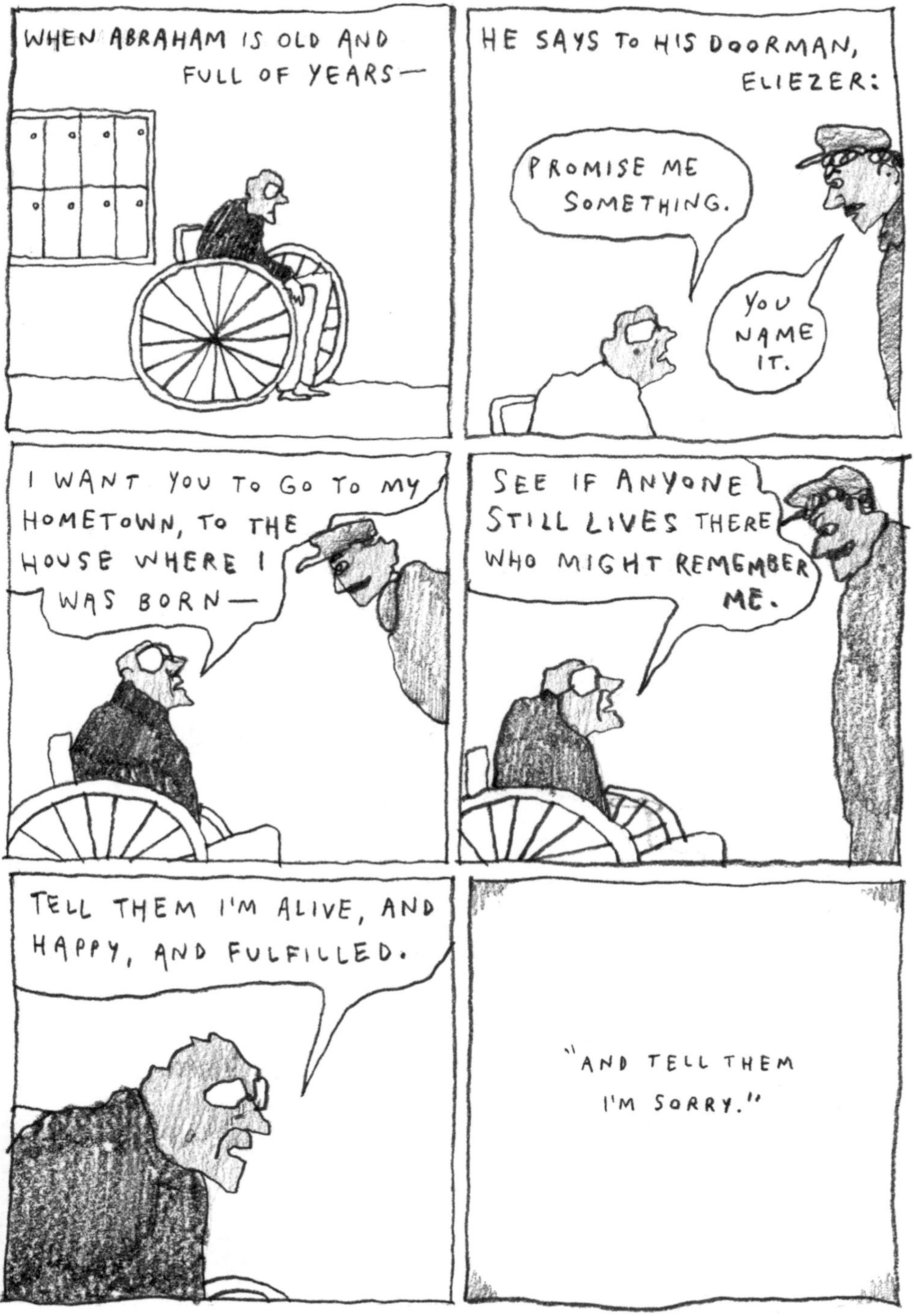
WHEN ABRAHAM IS OLD AND FULL OF YEARS—
HE SAYS TO HIS DOORMAN, ELIEZER:
PROMISE ME SOMETHING.
YOU NAME IT.
I WANT YOU TO GO TO MY HOMETOWN, TO THE HOUSE WHERE I WAS BORN—
SEE IF ANYONE STILL LIVES THERE WHO MIGHT REMEMBER ME.
TELL THEM I'M ALIVE, AND HAPPY, AND FULFILLED.
"AND TELL THEM I'M SORRY."

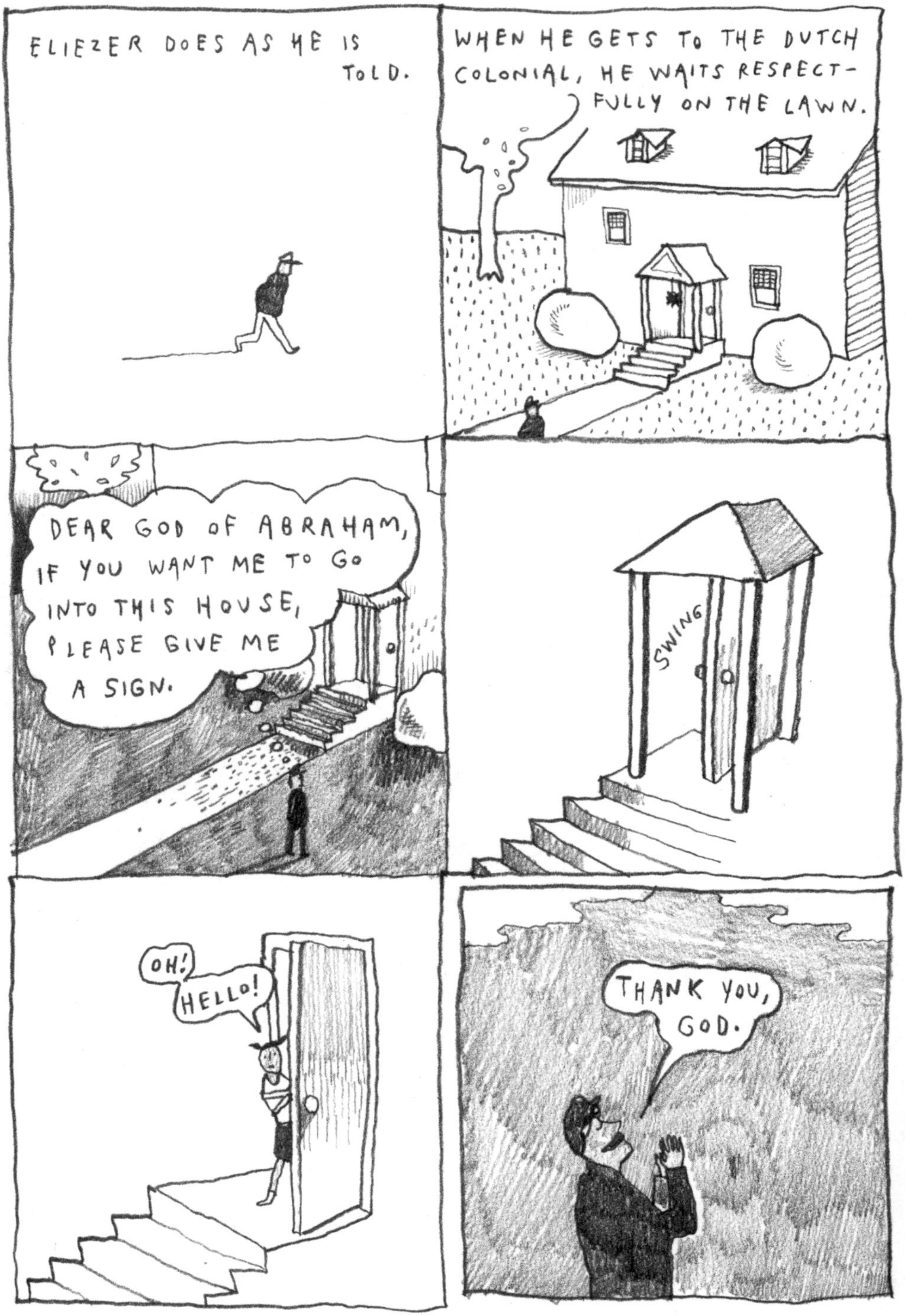
ELIEZER DOES AS HE IS TOLD.
WHEN HE GETS TO THE DUTCH COLONIAL, HE WAITS RESPECTFULLY ON THE LAWN.
DEAR GOD OF ABRAHAM, IF YOU WANT ME TO GO INTO THIS HOUSE, PLEASE GIVE ME A SIGN.
SWING
OH!
HELLO!
THANK YOU, GOD.

ONLY AFTER THE YOUNG WOMAN
HAS OFFERED HIM:

A CUP OF TEA—

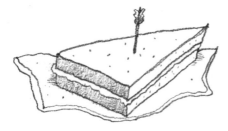

A SANDWICH—

AND A PIECE OF PIE—

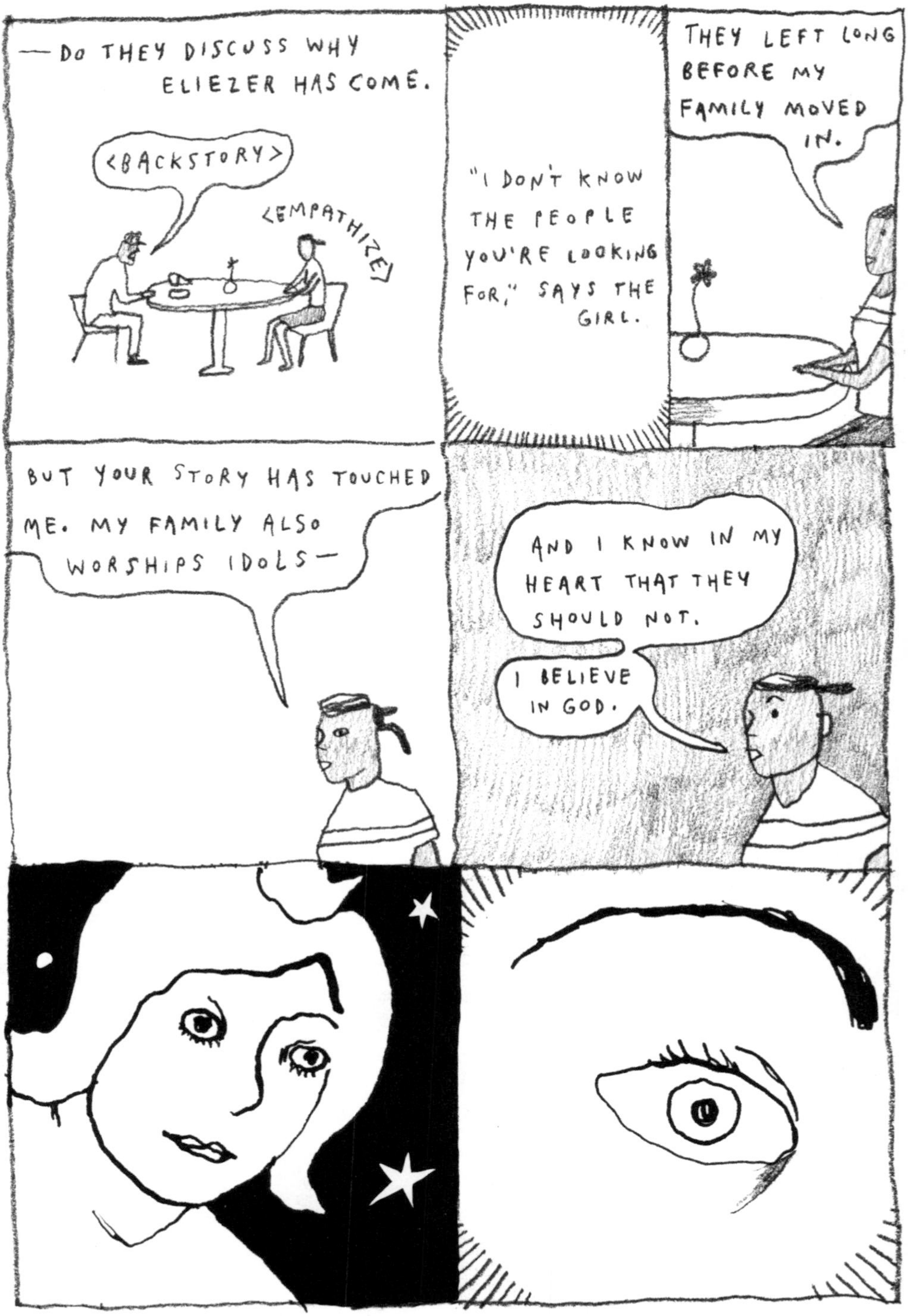
—DO THEY DISCUSS WHY ELIEZER HAS COME.
<BACKSTORY>
<EMPATHIZE>
"I DON'T KNOW THE PEOPLE YOU'RE LOOKING FOR," SAYS THE GIRL.
THEY LEFT LONG BEFORE MY FAMILY MOVED IN.
BUT YOUR STORY HAS TOUCHED ME. MY FAMILY ALSO WORSHIPS IDOLS—
AND I KNOW IN MY HEART THAT THEY SHOULD NOT.
I BELIEVE IN GOD.

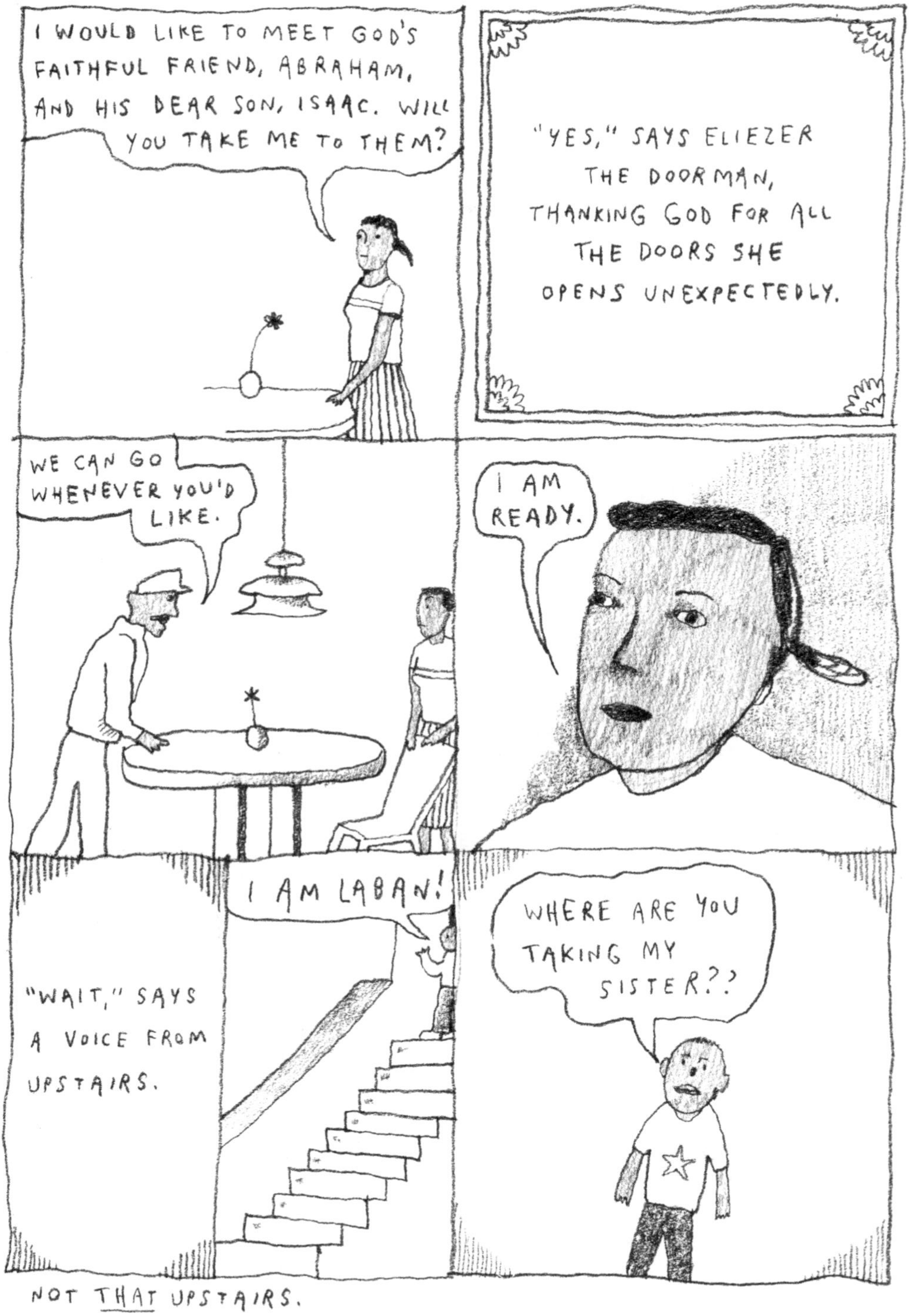
I WOULD LIKE TO MEET GOD'S FAITHFUL FRIEND, ABRAHAM, AND HIS DEAR SON, ISAAC. WILL YOU TAKE ME TO THEM?
"YES," SAYS ELIEZER THE DOORMAN, THANKING GOD FOR ALL THE DOORS SHE OPENS UNEXPECTEDLY.
WE CAN GO WHENEVER YOU'D LIKE.
I AM READY.
"WAIT," SAYS A VOICE FROM UPSTAIRS.
I AM LABAN!
WHERE ARE YOU TAKING MY SISTER??
NOT THAT UPSTAIRS.

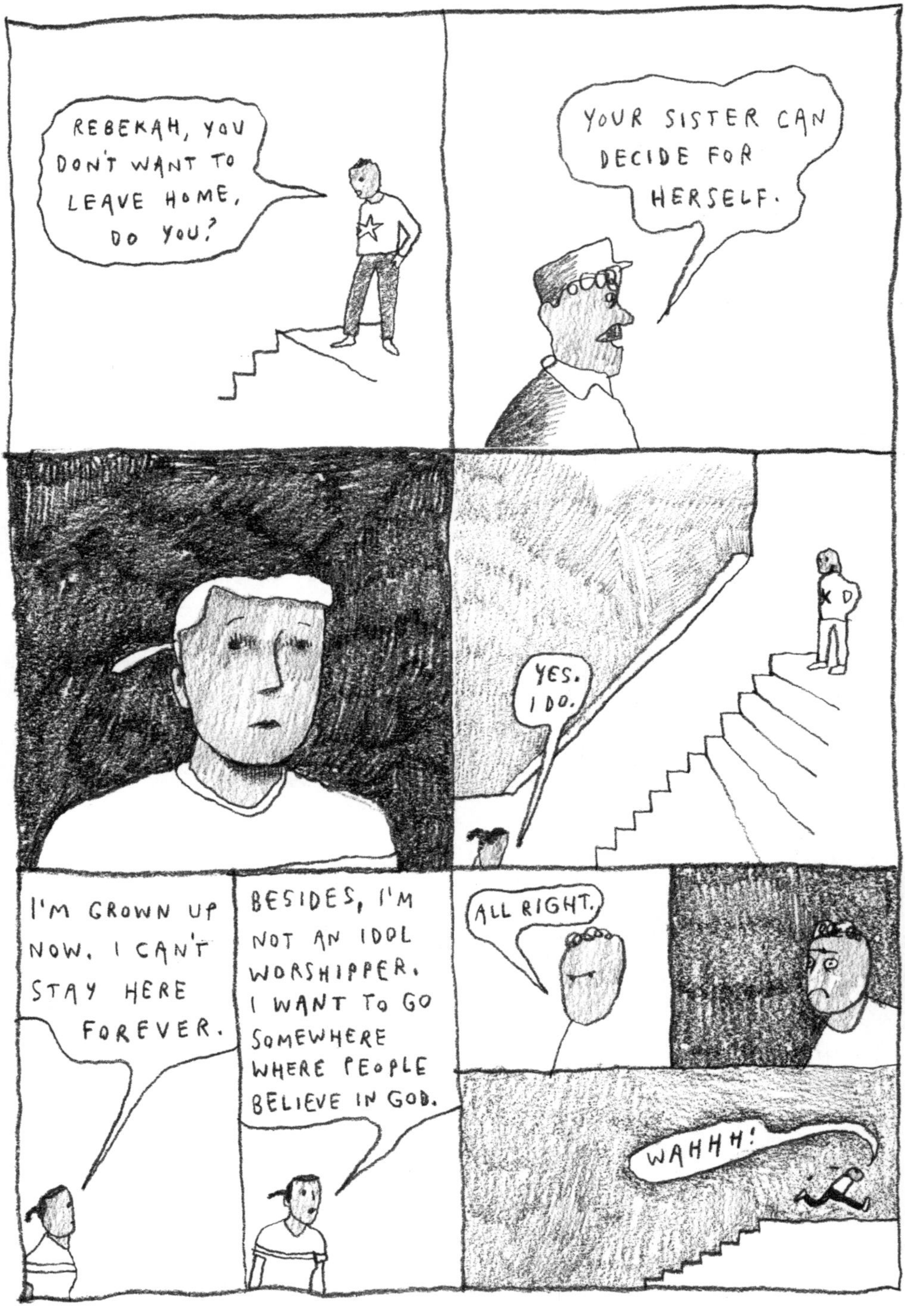
REBEKAH, YOU DON'T WANT TO LEAVE HOME, DO YOU?
YOUR SISTER CAN DECIDE FOR HERSELF.
YES. I DO.
I'M GROWN UP NOW. I CAN'T STAY HERE FOREVER.
BESIDES, I'M NOT AN IDOL WORSHIPPER. I WANT TO GO SOMEWHERE WHERE PEOPLE BELIEVE IN GOD.
ALL RIGHT.
WAHHH!

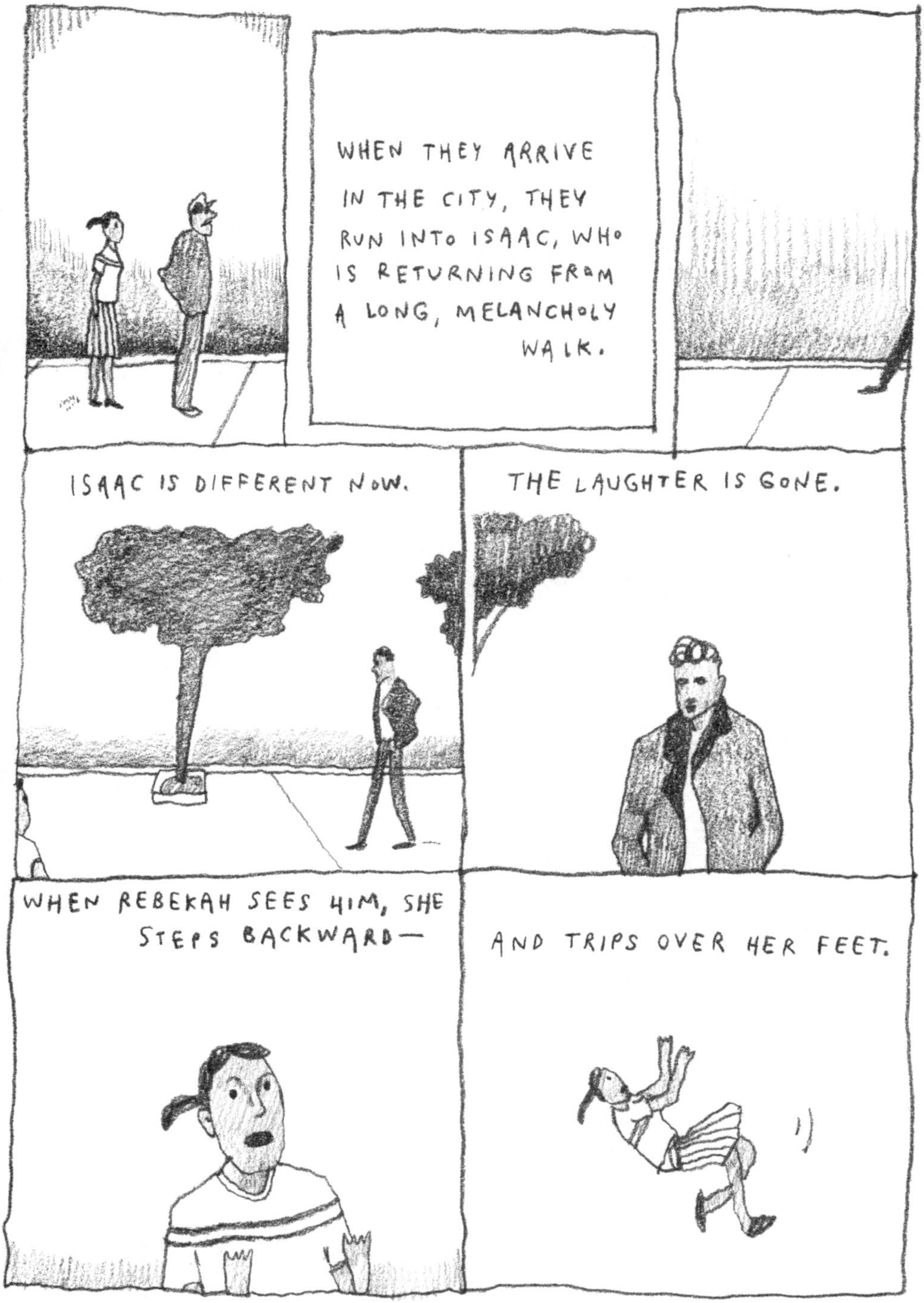
WHEN THEY ARRIVE IN THE CITY, THEY RUN INTO ISAAC, WHO IS RETURNING FROM A LONG, MELANCHOLY WALK.
ISAAC IS DIFFERENT NOW.
THE LAUGHTER IS GONE.
WHEN REBEKAH SEES HIM, SHE STEPS BACKWARD—
AND TRIPS OVER HER FEET.

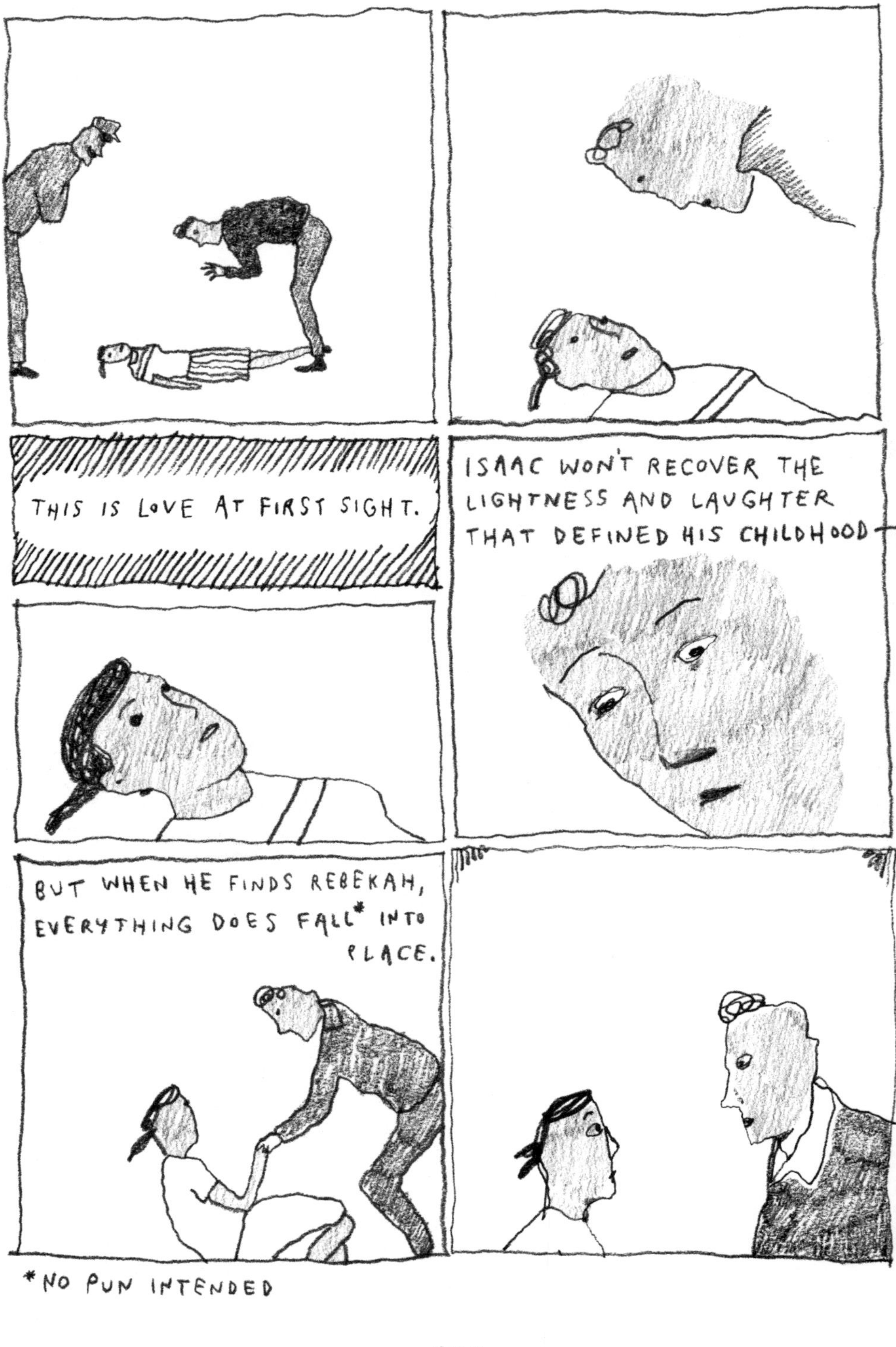
THIS IS LOVE AT FIRST SIGHT.
ISAAC WON'T RECOVER THE LIGHTNESS AND LAUGHTER THAT DEFINED HIS CHILDHOOD—
BUT WHEN HE FINDS REBEKAH, EVERYTHING DOES FALL* INTO PLACE.
*NO PUN INTENDED

WHEN THEY KISS—

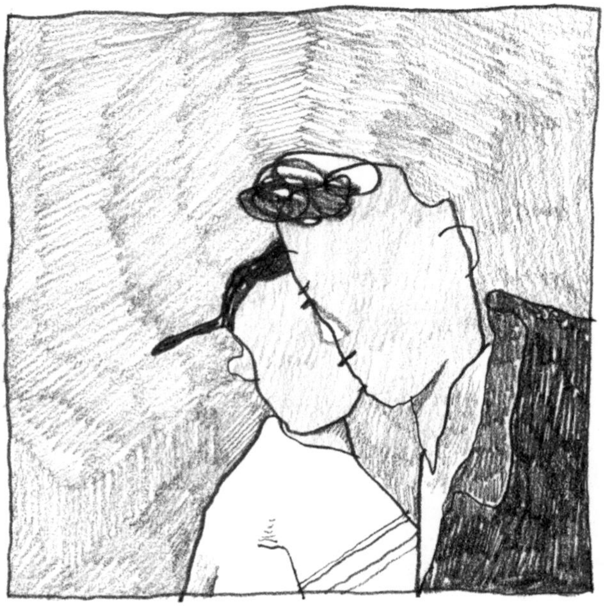

THE PRESENT ENDS—

AND THE FUTURE BEGINS.

future

AND HE WAS, AND HE IS, AND HE WILL BE...

—"ADON OLAM" (A JEWISH PRAYER)

THE CITY

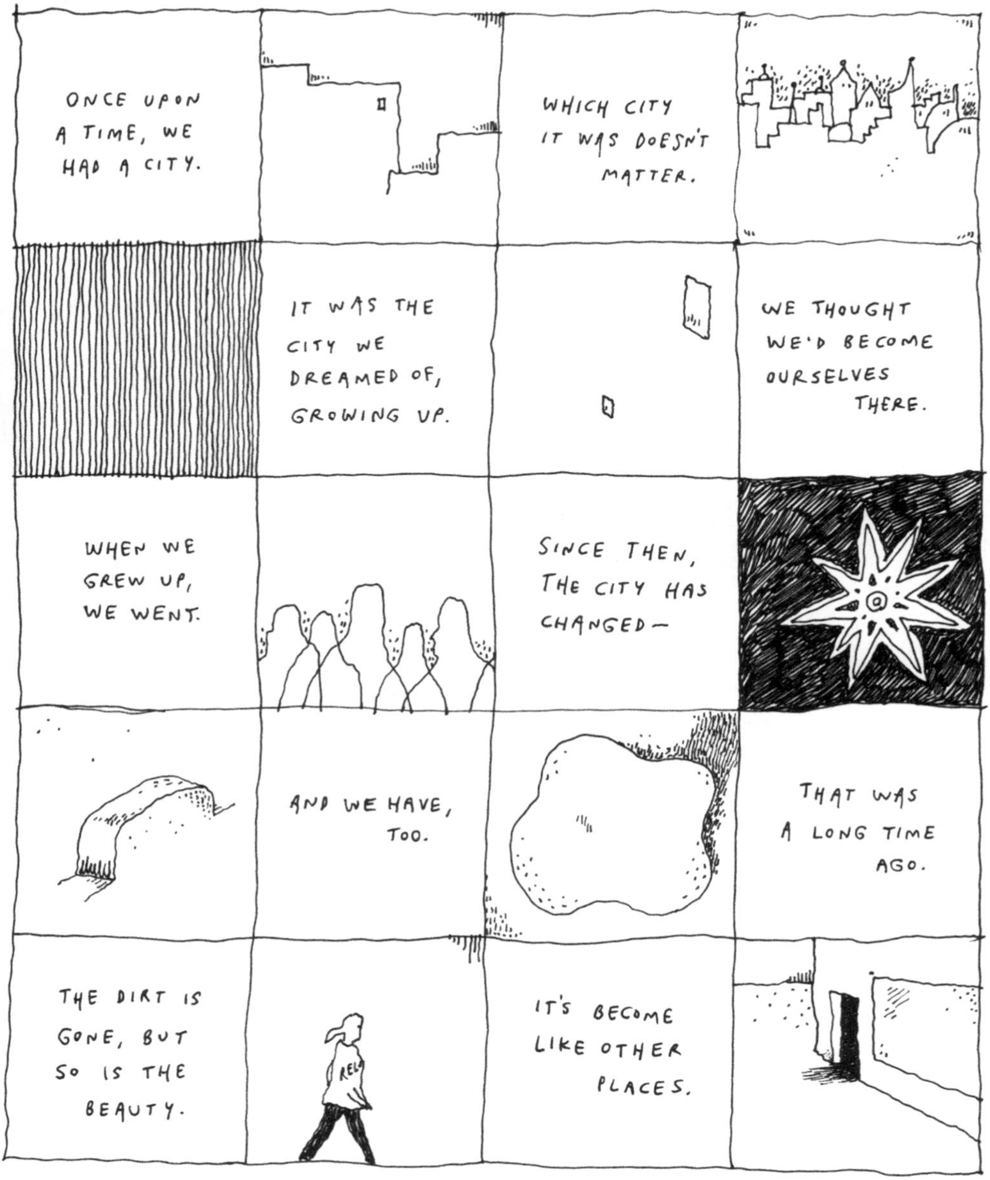
ONCE UPON A TIME, WE HAD A CITY.
WHICH CITY IT WAS DOESN'T MATTER.
IT WAS THE CITY WE DREAMED OF, GROWING UP.
WE THOUGHT WE'D BECOME OURSELVES THERE.
WHEN WE GREW UP, WE WENT.
SINCE THEN, THE CITY HAS CHANGED—
AND WE HAVE, TOO.
THAT WAS A LONG TIME AGO.
THE DIRT IS GONE, BUT SO IS THE BEAUTY.
IT'S BECOME LIKE OTHER PLACES.

SINCE THE
BEGINNING, WE'VE
MADE UP STORIES.

THESE STORIES
WERE ABOUT
GOD —

WHO MADE US
IN HER IMAGE.

SHE GAVE US
THE WORLD TO
INHABIT —

AND THE
ANIMALS TO
NAME.

THESE STORIES
ARE GONE NOW.

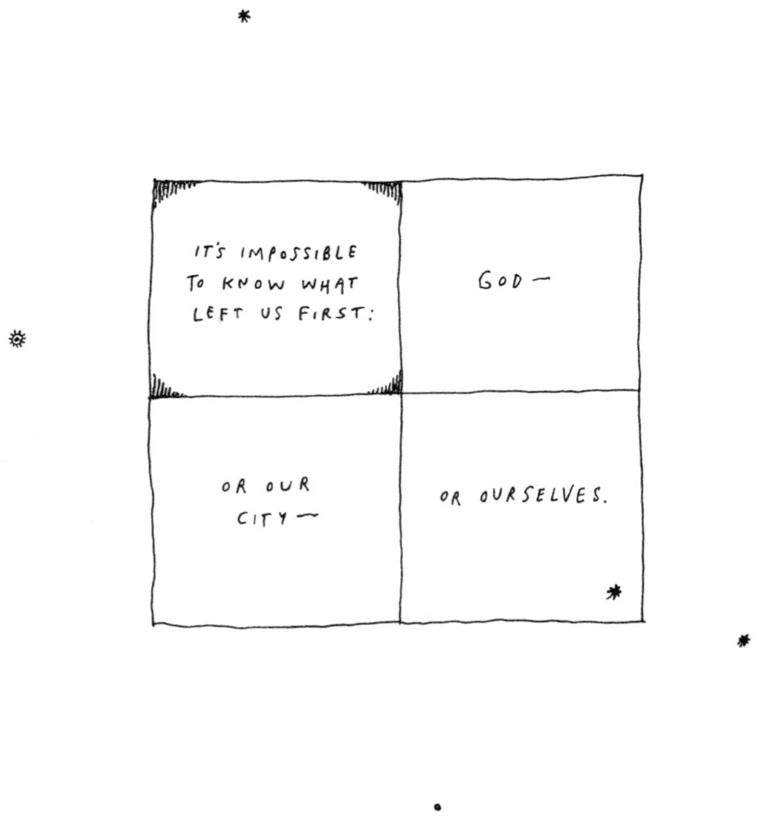
IT'S IMPOSSIBLE TO KNOW WHAT LEFT US FIRST:
GOD—
OR OUR CITY—
OR OURSELVES.

ESAV JACOB

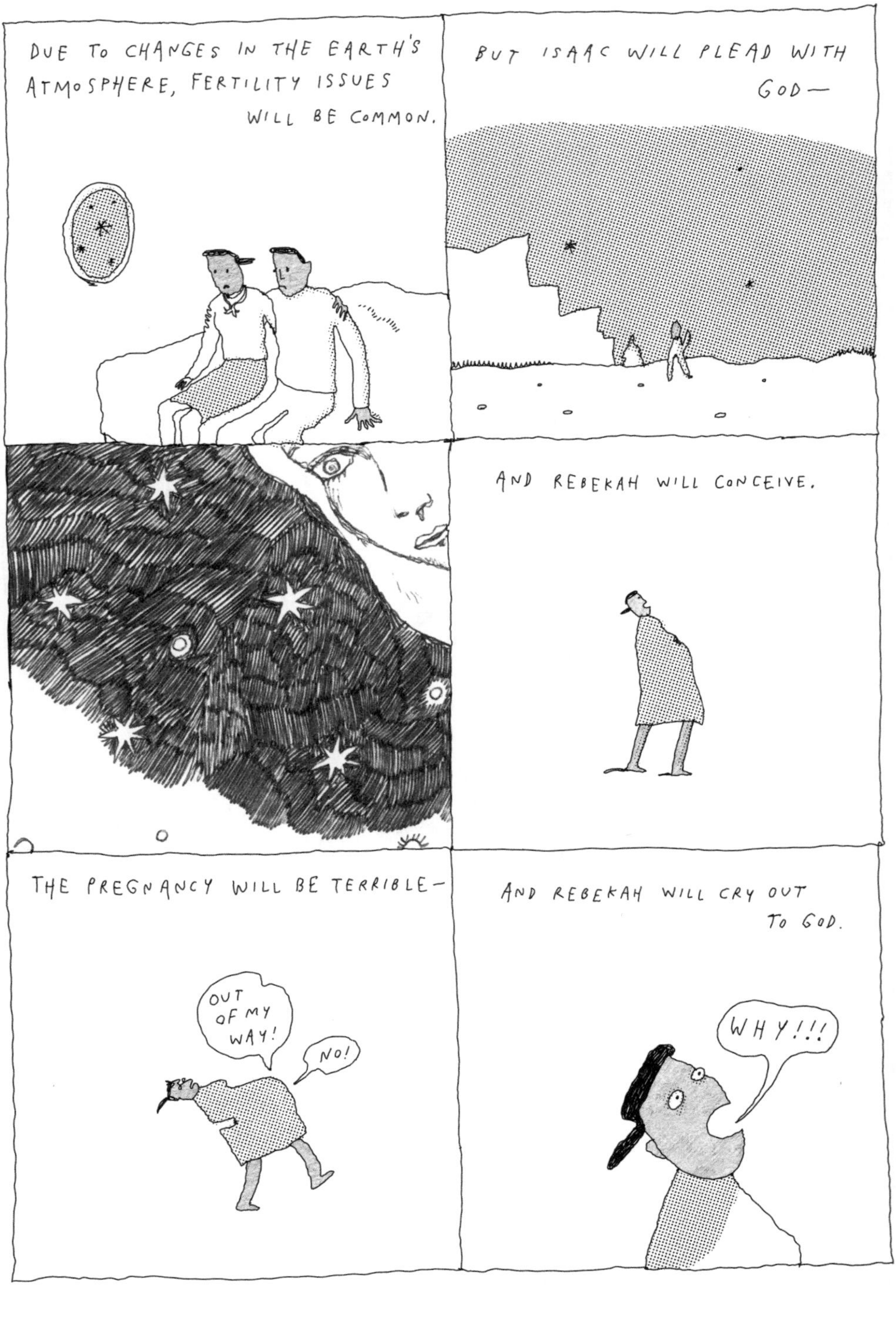
DUE TO CHANGES IN THE EARTH'S ATMOSPHERE, FERTILITY ISSUES WILL BE COMMON.
BUT ISAAC WILL PLEAD WITH GOD—
AND REBEKAH WILL CONCEIVE.
THE PREGNANCY WILL BE TERRIBLE—
OUT OF MY WAY!
NO!
AND REBEKAH WILL CRY OUT TO GOD.
WHY!!!

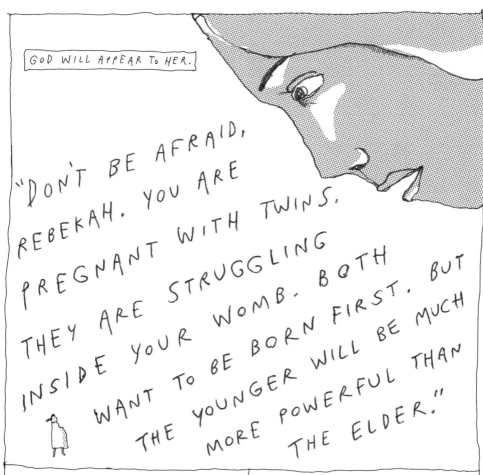

GOD WILL APPEAR TO HER.

"DON'T BE AFRAID, REBEKAH. YOU ARE PREGNANT WITH TWINS. THEY ARE STRUGGLING INSIDE YOUR WOMB. BOTH WANT TO BE BORN FIRST. BUT THE YOUNGER WILL BE MUCH MORE POWERFUL THAN THE ELDER."

THE FIRST TWIN, ESAV, WILL EMERGE WITH A THICK COAT OF RED BODY HAIR.

JACOB WILL COME NEXT, CLUTCHING AT HIS BROTHER'S HEEL.

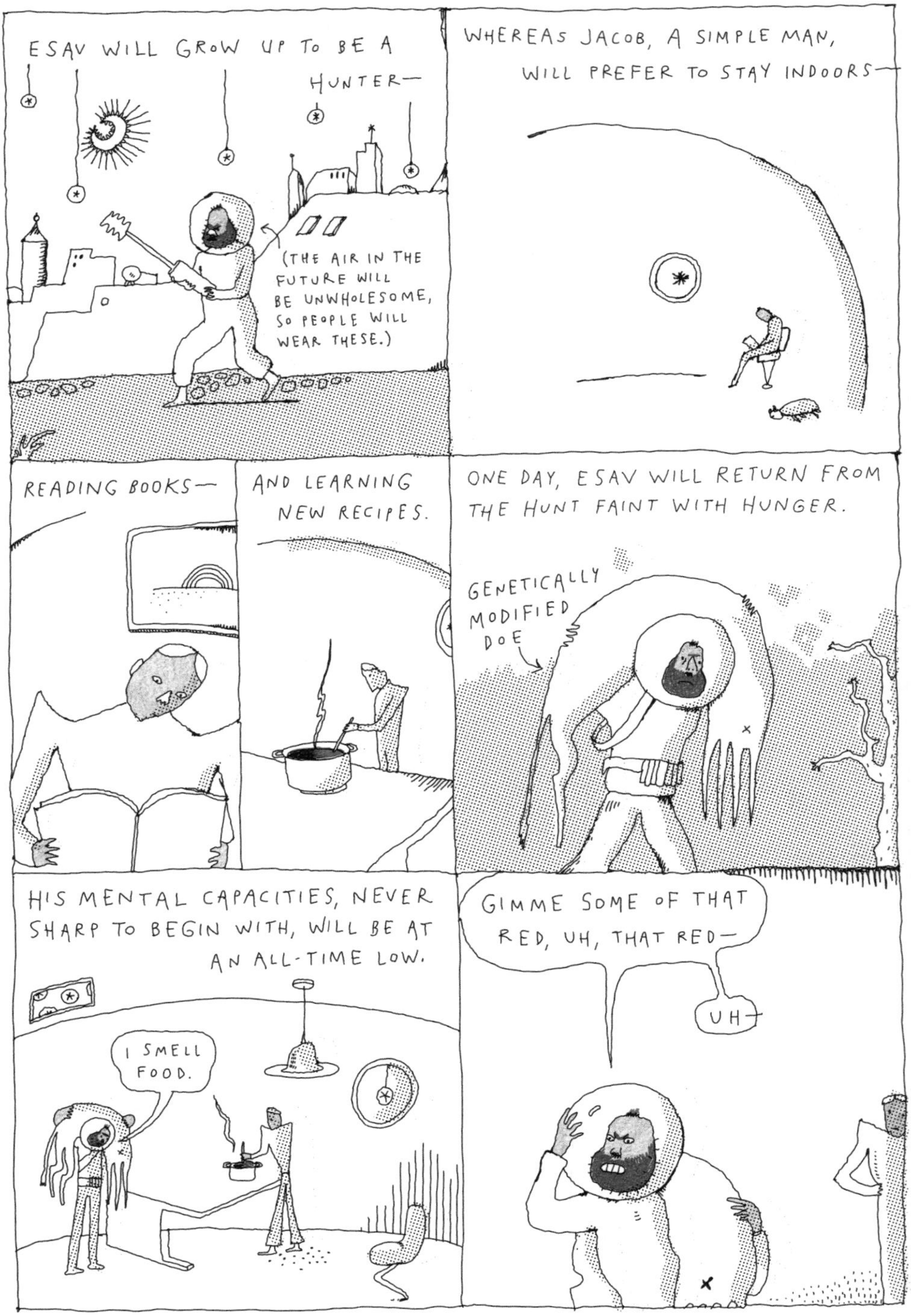
ESAV WILL GROW UP TO BE A HUNTER—
(THE AIR IN THE FUTURE WILL BE UNWHOLESOME, SO PEOPLE WILL WEAR THESE.)
WHEREAS JACOB, A SIMPLE MAN, WILL PREFER TO STAY INDOORS—
READING BOOKS—
AND LEARNING NEW RECIPES.
ONE DAY, ESAV WILL RETURN FROM THE HUNT FAINT WITH HUNGER.
GENETICALLY MODIFIED DOE
HIS MENTAL CAPACITIES, NEVER SHARP TO BEGIN WITH, WILL BE AT AN ALL-TIME LOW.
I SMELL FOOD.
GIMME SOME OF THAT RED, UH, THAT RED—
UH—

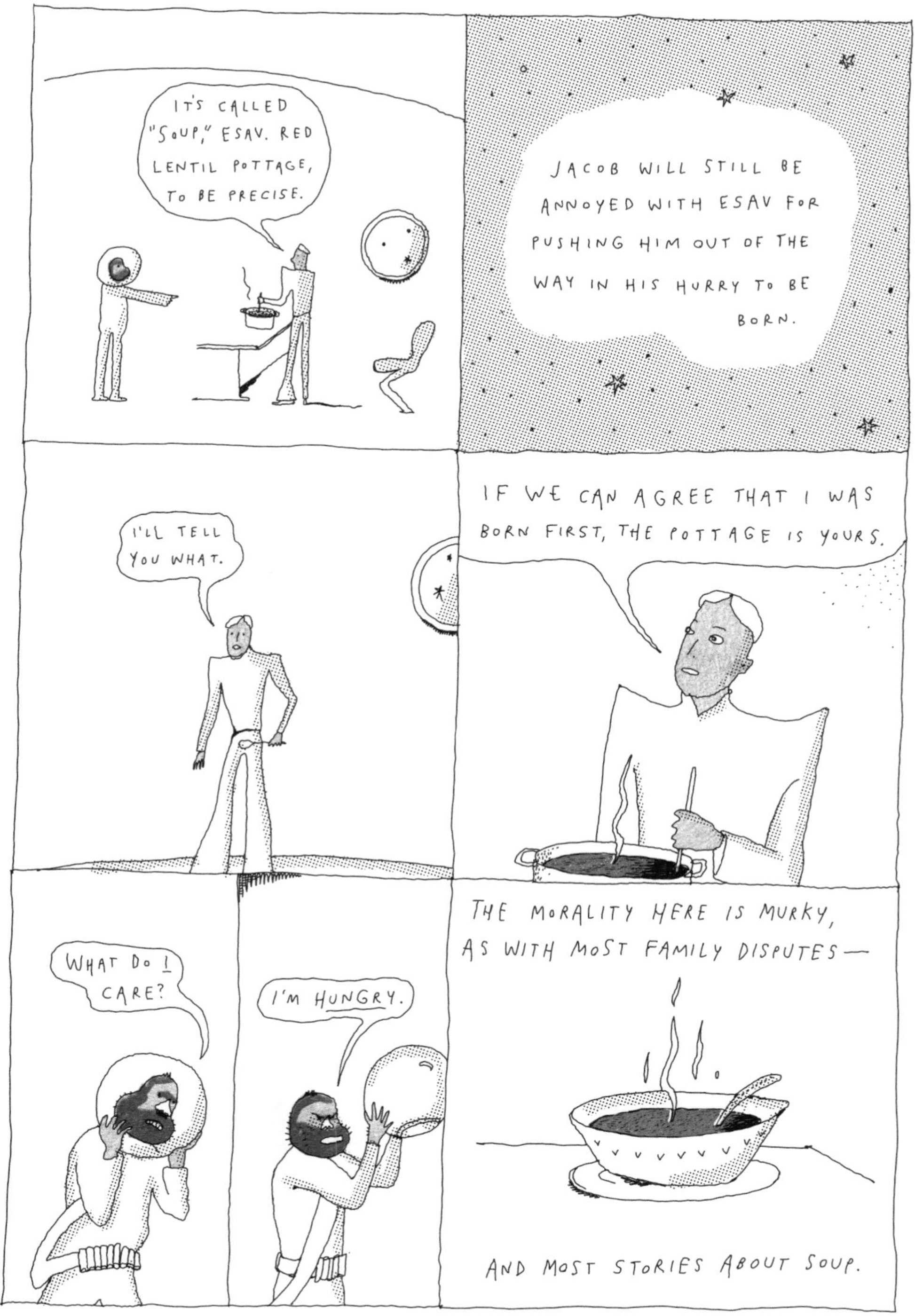
IT'S CALLED "SOUP," ESAV. RED LENTIL POTTAGE, TO BE PRECISE.
JACOB WILL STILL BE ANNOYED WITH ESAV FOR PUSHING HIM OUT OF THE WAY IN HIS HURRY TO BE BORN.
I'LL TELL YOU WHAT.
IF WE CAN AGREE THAT I WAS BORN FIRST, THE POTTAGE IS YOURS.
WHAT DO I CARE?
I'M HUNGRY.
THE MORALITY HERE IS MURKY, AS WITH MOST FAMILY DISPUTES—
AND MOST STORIES ABOUT SOUP.

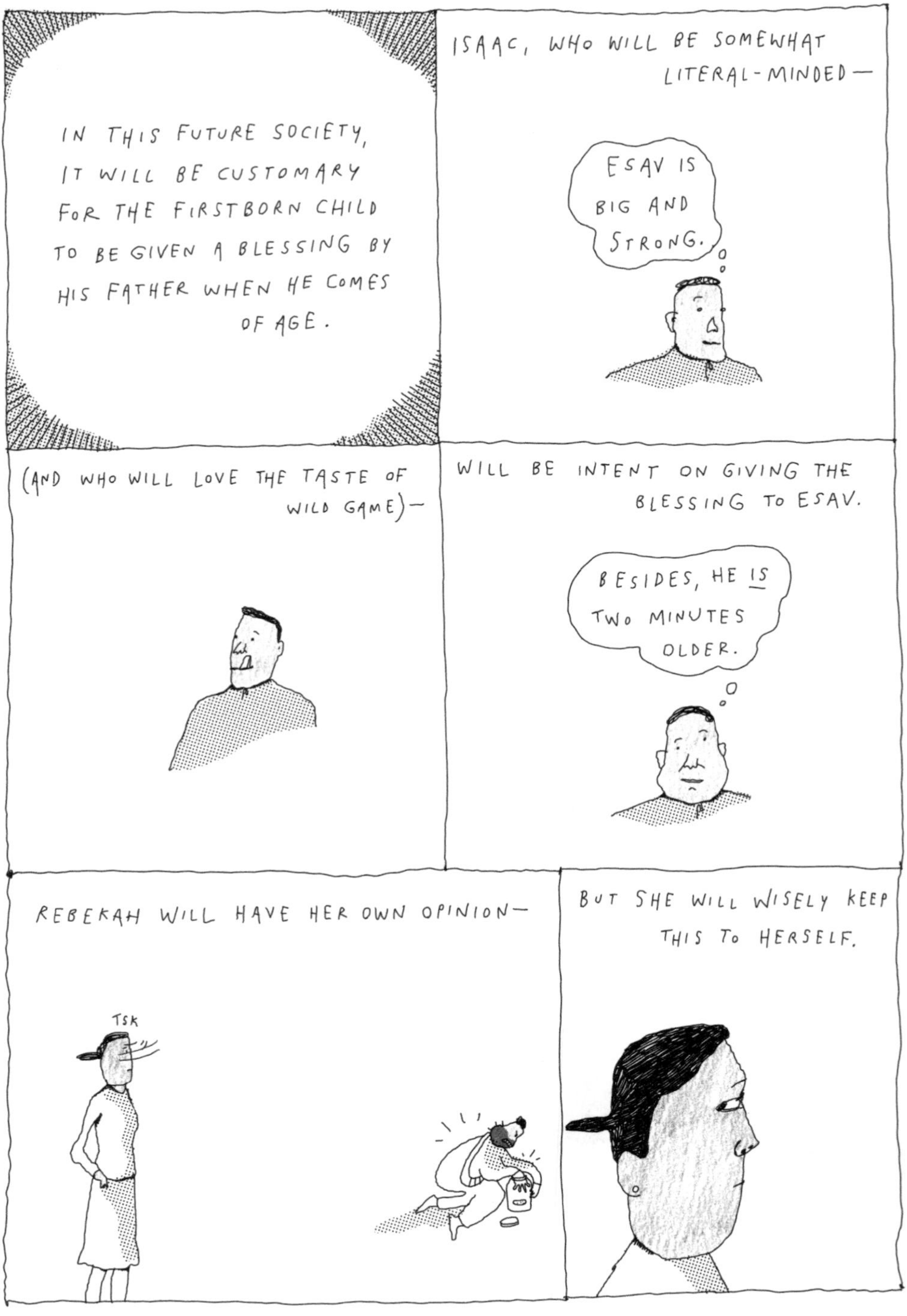
IN THIS FUTURE SOCIETY, IT WILL BE CUSTOMARY FOR THE FIRSTBORN CHILD TO BE GIVEN A BLESSING BY HIS FATHER WHEN HE COMES OF AGE.
ISAAC, WHO WILL BE SOMEWHAT LITERAL-MINDED—
ESAV IS BIG AND STRONG.
(AND WHO WILL LOVE THE TASTE OF WILD GAME)—
WILL BE INTENT ON GIVING THE BLESSING TO ESAV.
BESIDES, HE IS TWO MINUTES OLDER.
REBEKAH WILL HAVE HER OWN OPINION—
TSK
BUT SHE WILL WISELY KEEP THIS TO HERSELF.

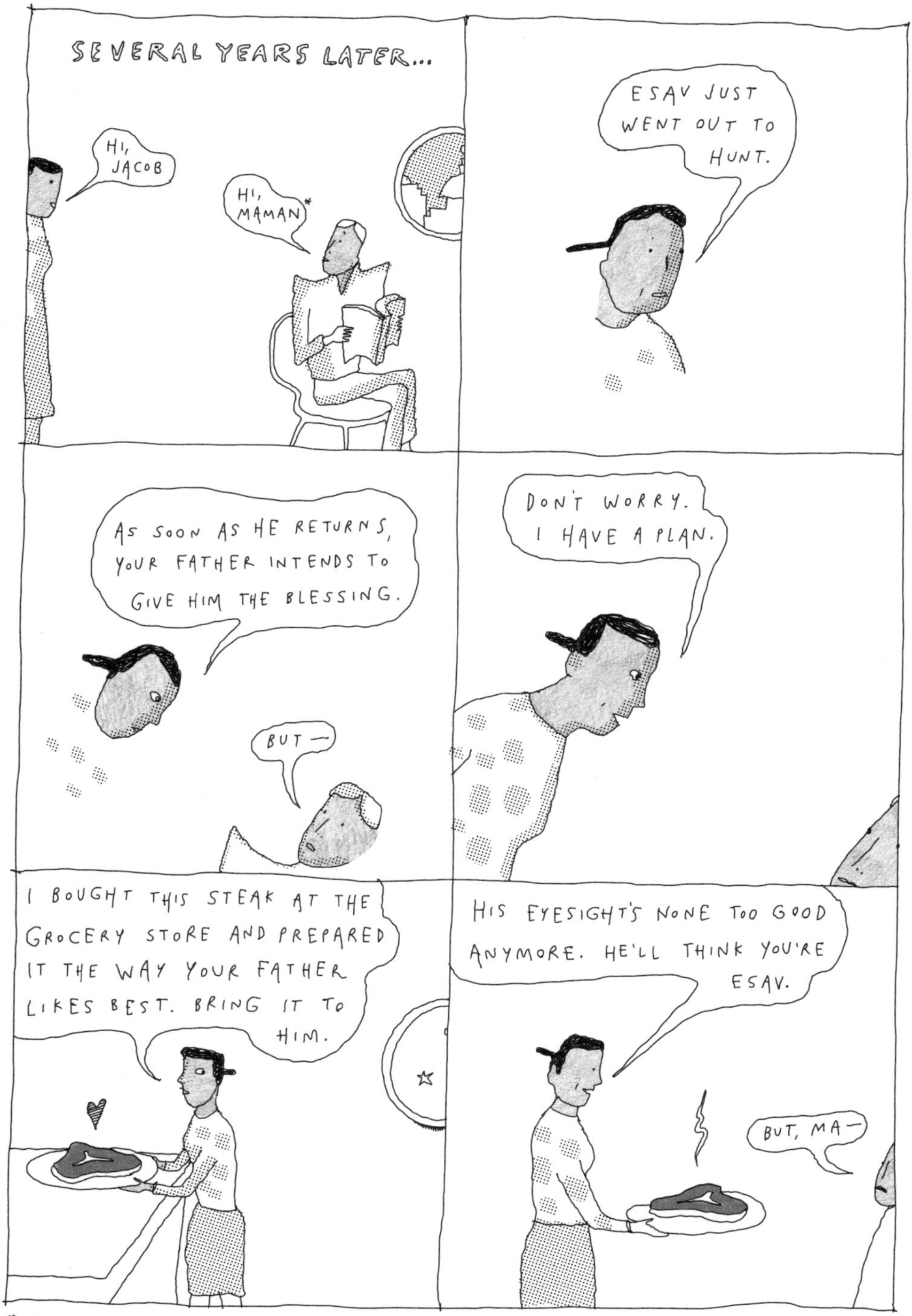
SEVERAL YEARS LATER...
HI, JACOB
HI, MAMAN*
ESAV JUST WENT OUT TO HUNT.
AS SOON AS HE RETURNS, YOUR FATHER INTENDS TO GIVE HIM THE BLESSING.
BUT—
DON'T WORRY. I HAVE A PLAN.
I BOUGHT THIS STEAK AT THE GROCERY STORE AND PREPARED IT THE WAY YOUR FATHER LIKES BEST. BRING IT TO HIM.
HIS EYESIGHT'S NONE TOO GOOD ANYMORE. HE'LL THINK YOU'RE ESAV.
BUT, MA—

*JACOB WILL BE A FRANCOPHILE, OF COURSE.

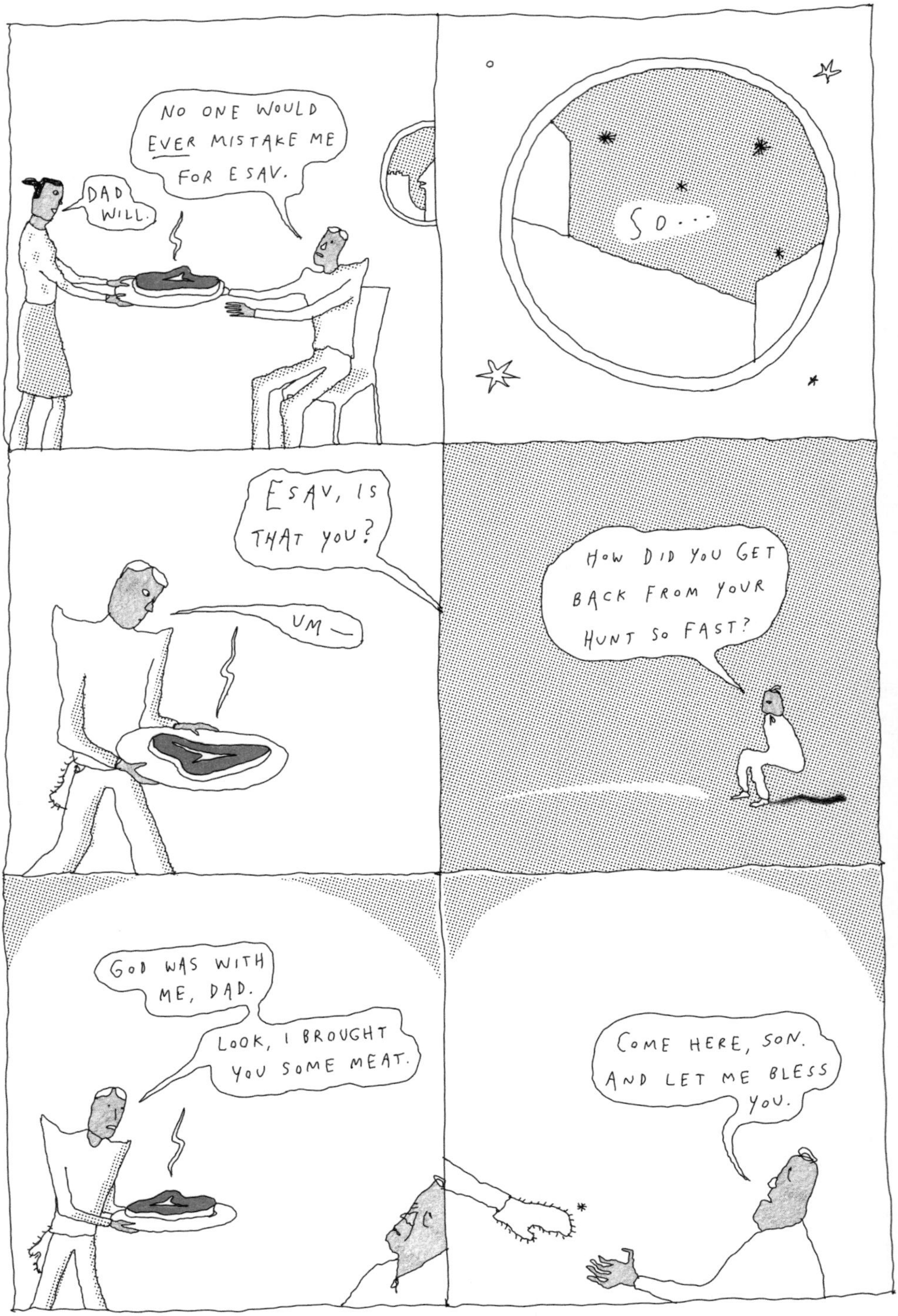
DAD WILL.
NO ONE WOULD EVER MISTAKE ME FOR ESAV.
SO...
ESAV, IS THAT YOU?
UM—
HOW DID YOU GET BACK FROM YOUR HUNT SO FAST?
GOD WAS WITH ME, DAD.
LOOK, I BROUGHT YOU SOME MEAT.
COME HERE, SON. AND LET ME BLESS YOU.
*

*REBEKAH HAD GIVEN JACOB FUR MITTENS TO WEAR SO HIS HANDS WOULD FEEL HAIRY, LIKE ESAV'S.

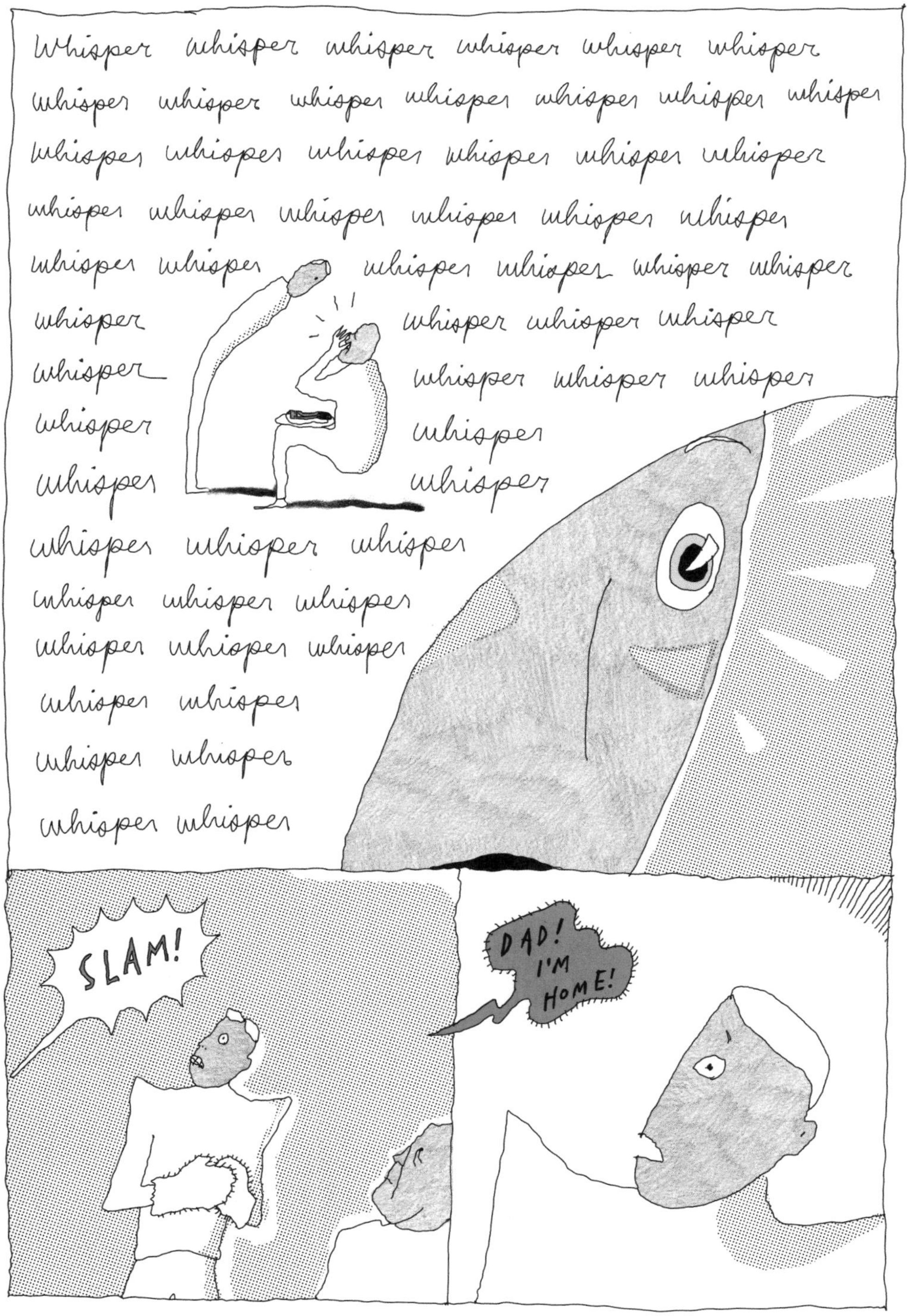
Whisper whisper whisper whisper whisper whisper
whisper whisper whisper whisper whisper whisper whisper
whisper whisper whisper whisper whisper whisper
whisper whisper whisper whisper whisper whisper
whisper whisper whisper whisper whisper whisper
whisper whisper whisper whisper
whisper whisper whisper whisper
whisper whisper
whisper whisper
whisper whisper whisper
whisper whisper whisper
whisper whisper whisper
whisper whisper
whisper whisper
whisper whisper
SLAM!
DAD! I'M HOME!

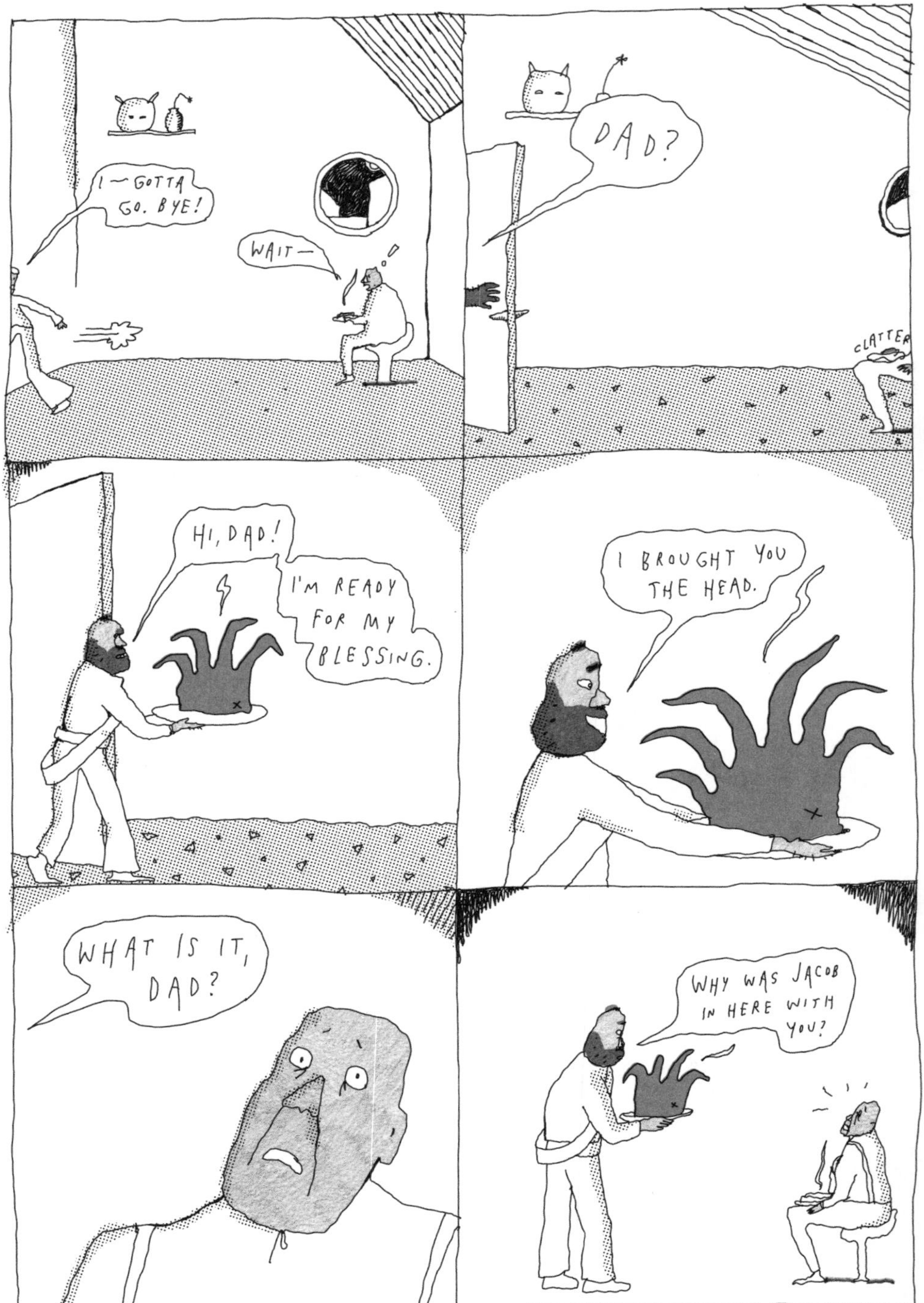
I—GOTTA GO. BYE!
WAIT—
DAD?
CLATTER
HI, DAD!
I'M READY FOR MY BLESSING.
I BROUGHT YOU THE HEAD.
WHAT IS IT, DAD?
WHY WAS JACOB IN HERE WITH YOU?

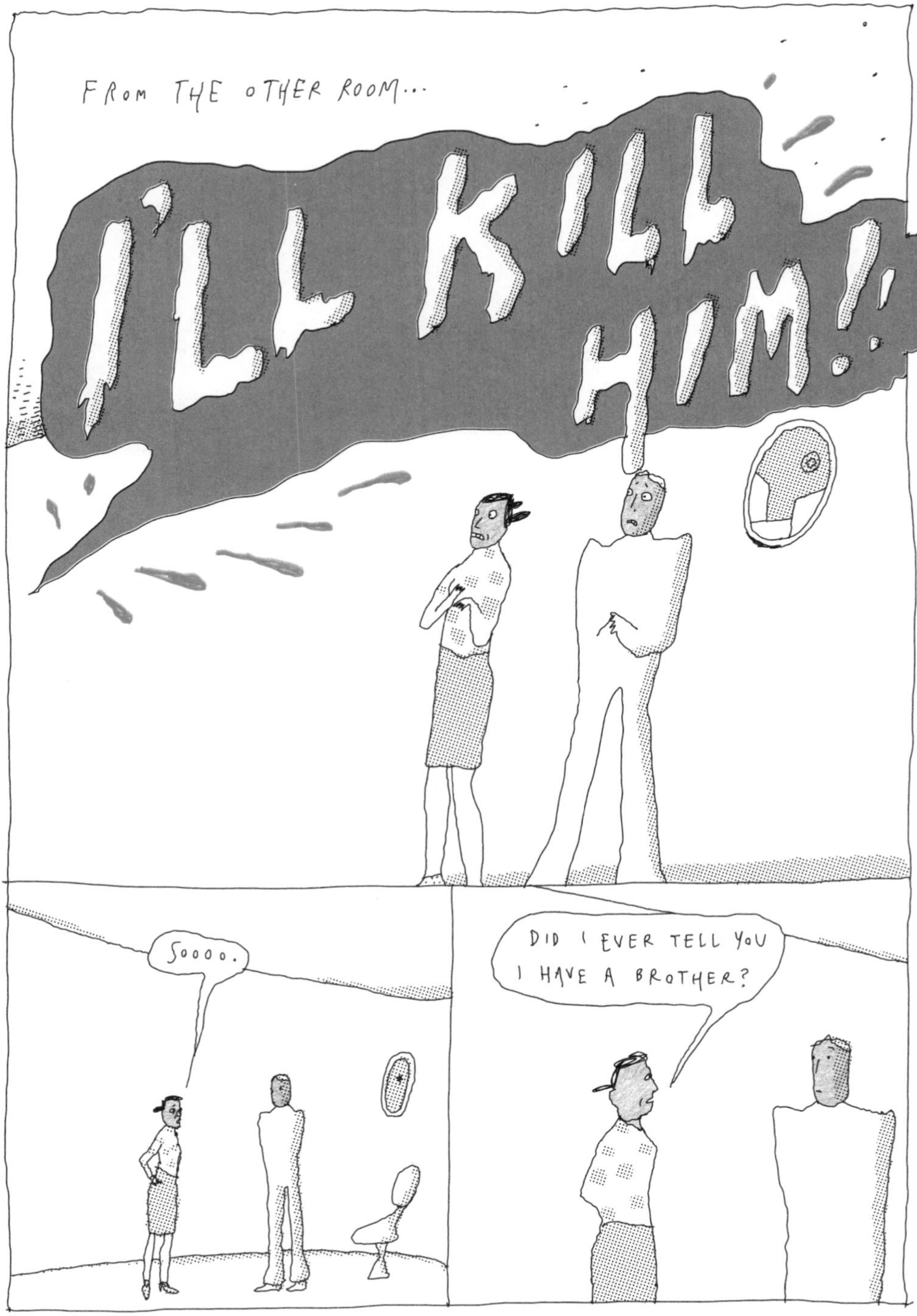
FROM THE OTHER ROOM...
I'LL KILL HIM!!!
SOOOO.
DID I EVER TELL YOU I HAVE A BROTHER?

THIS WILL BE REBEKAH'S PRIVATE MIRACLE: THAT EVEN THOUGH SHE IS THE ONLY WOMAN GOD WILL HAVE SPOKEN TO DIRECTLY, SHE WILL BE THE PERSON WHO UNDERSTANDS GOD BEST OF ALL.

JACOB WILL LEAVE RIGHT AWAY, WITH
ONLY HIS HELMET TO PROTECT HIM, AND A
SMALL KNAPSACK OF SUPPLIES.

HE HAS NEVER LEFT HOME BEFORE.

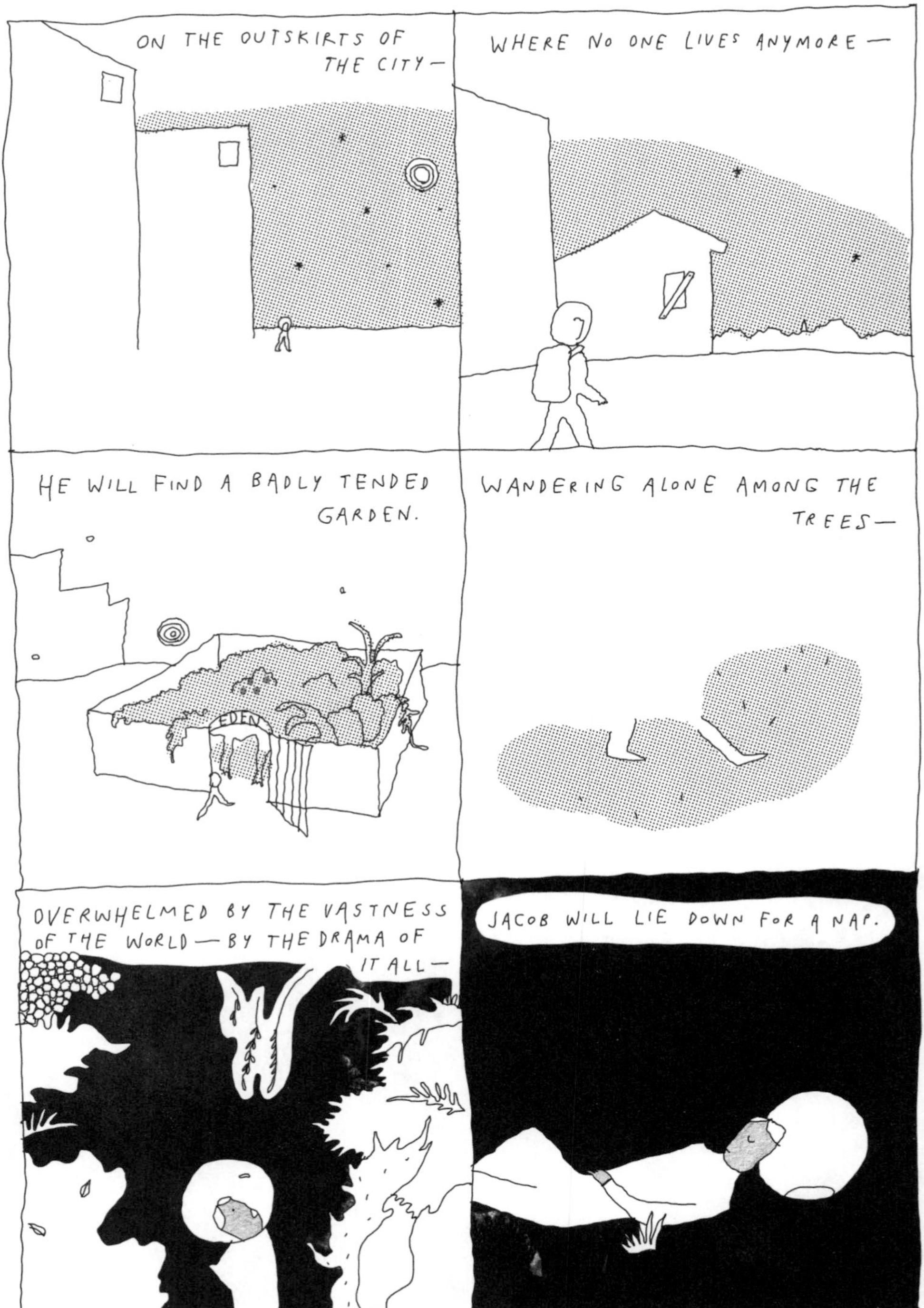
ON THE OUTSKIRTS OF THE CITY—
WHERE NO ONE LIVES ANYMORE—
HE WILL FIND A BADLY TENDED GARDEN.
EDEN
WANDERING ALONE AMONG THE TREES—
OVERWHELMED BY THE VASTNESS OF THE WORLD—BY THE DRAMA OF IT ALL—
JACOB WILL LIE DOWN FOR A NAP.

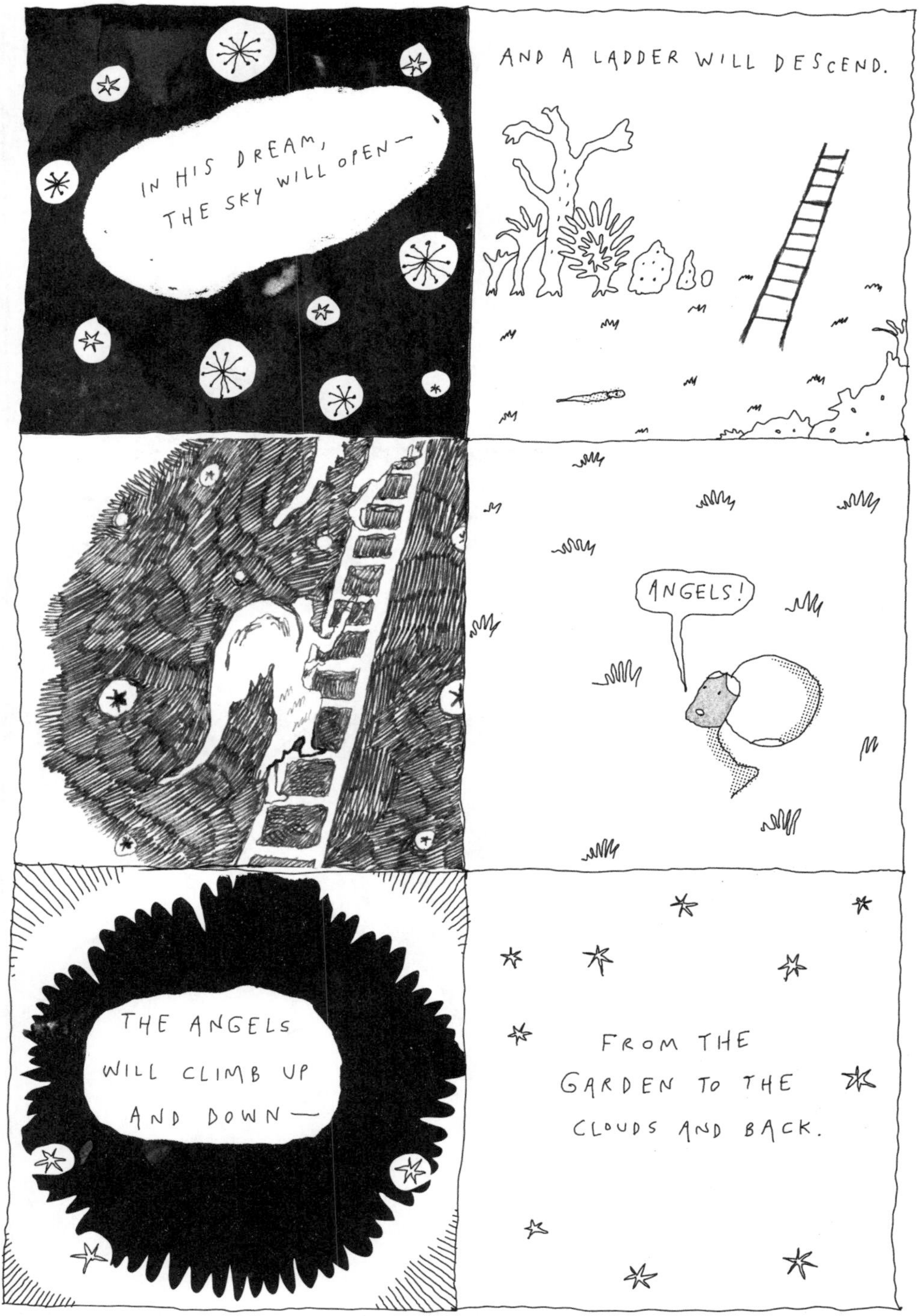
IN HIS DREAM, THE SKY WILL OPEN—
AND A LADDER WILL DESCEND.
ANGELS!
THE ANGELS WILL CLIMB UP AND DOWN—
FROM THE GARDEN TO THE CLOUDS AND BACK.

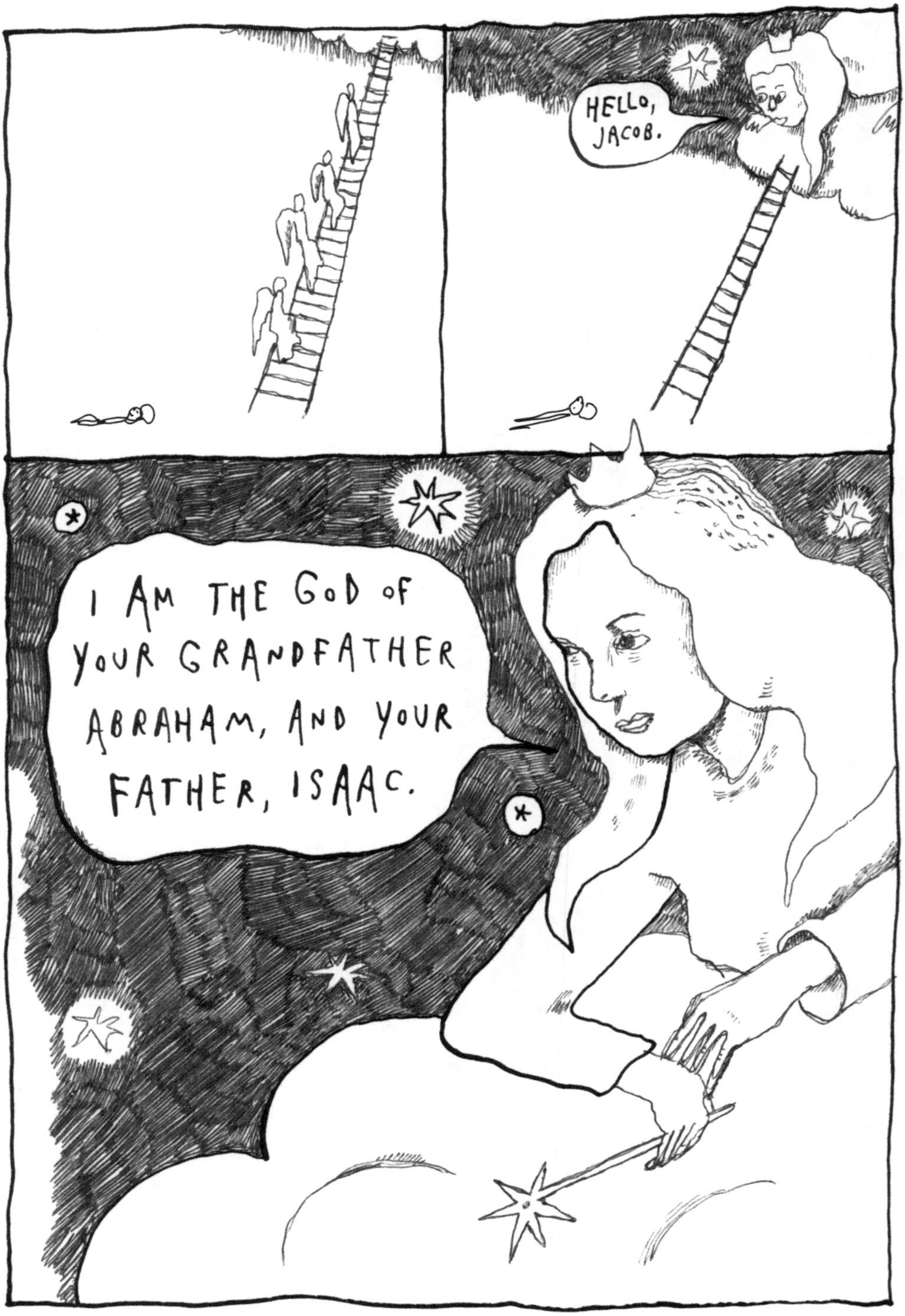
HELLO, JACOB.
I AM THE GOD OF YOUR GRANDFATHER ABRAHAM, AND YOUR FATHER, ISAAC.

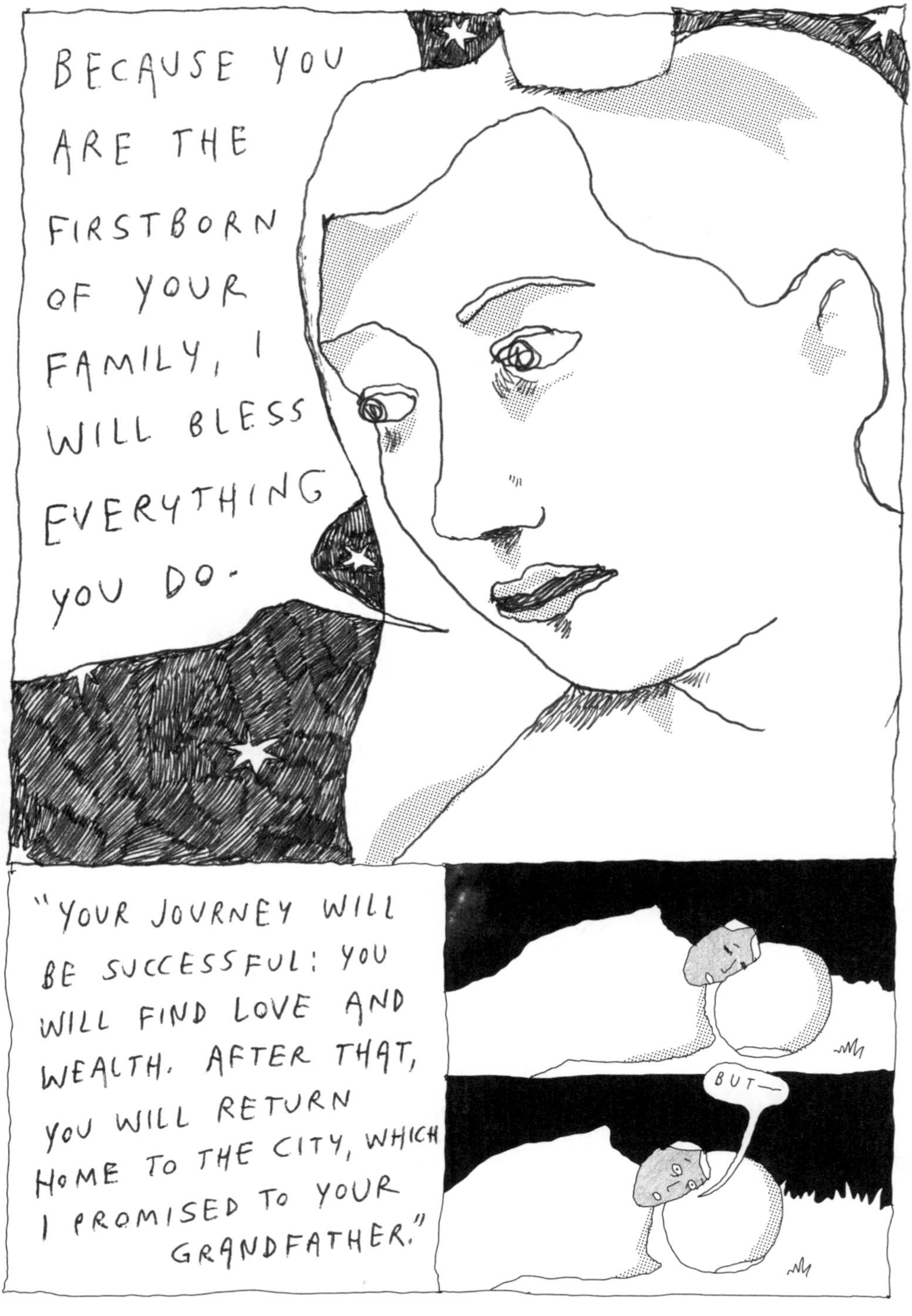

BECAUSE YOU ARE THE FIRSTBORN OF YOUR FAMILY, I WILL BLESS EVERYTHING YOU DO.
"YOUR JOURNEY WILL BE SUCCESSFUL: YOU WILL FIND LOVE AND WEALTH. AFTER THAT, YOU WILL RETURN HOME TO THE CITY, WHICH I PROMISED TO YOUR GRANDFATHER."
BUT—

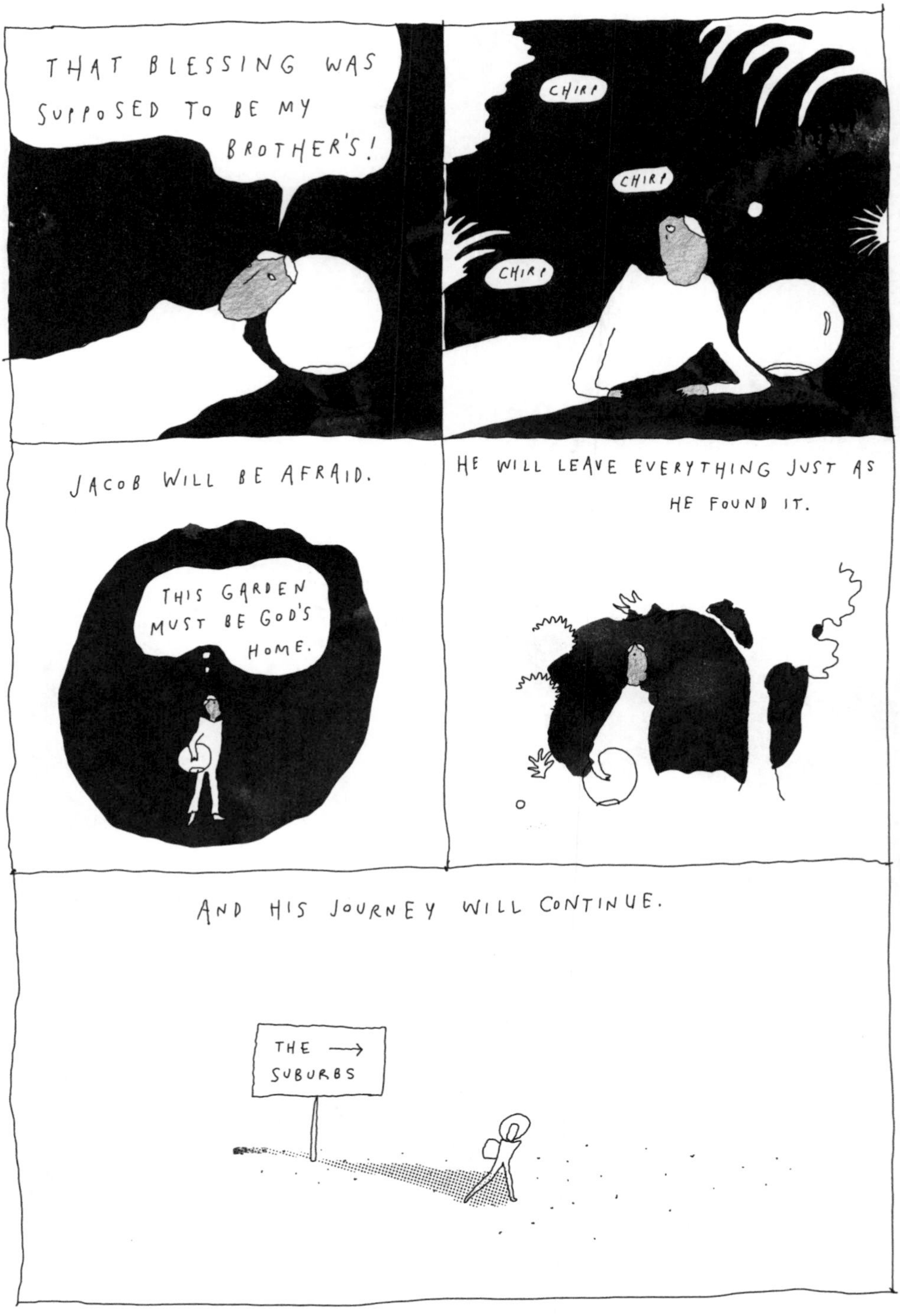
THAT BLESSING WAS SUPPOSED TO BE MY BROTHER'S!
CHIRP
CHIRP
CHIRP
JACOB WILL BE AFRAID.
THIS GARDEN MUST BE GOD'S HOME.
HE WILL LEAVE EVERYTHING JUST AS HE FOUND IT.
AND HIS JOURNEY WILL CONTINUE.
THE → SUBURBS

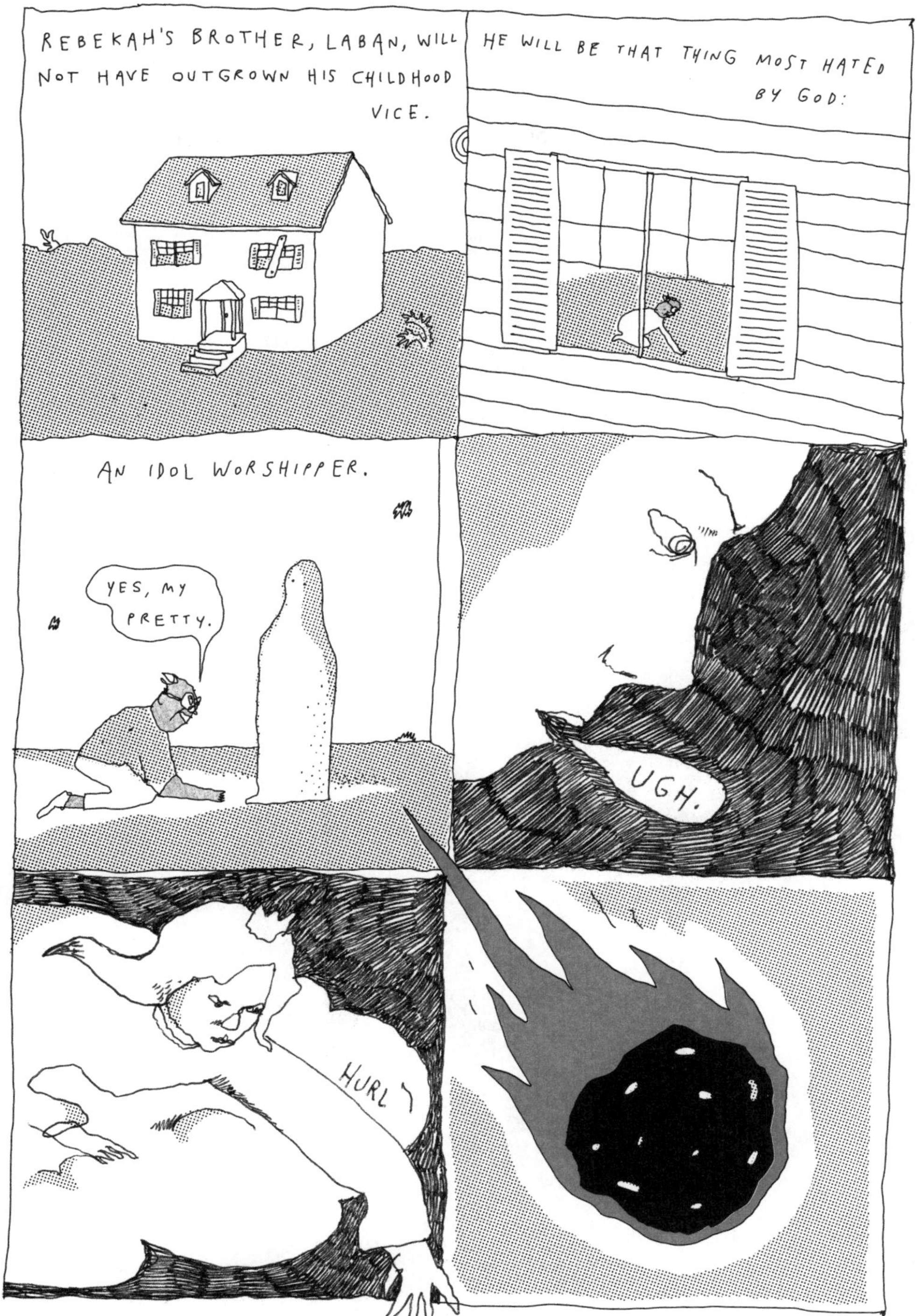
REBEKAH'S BROTHER, LABAN, WILL NOT HAVE OUTGROWN HIS CHILDHOOD VICE.
HE WILL BE THAT THING MOST HATED BY GOD:
AN IDOL WORSHIPPER.
YES, MY PRETTY.
UGH.
HURL

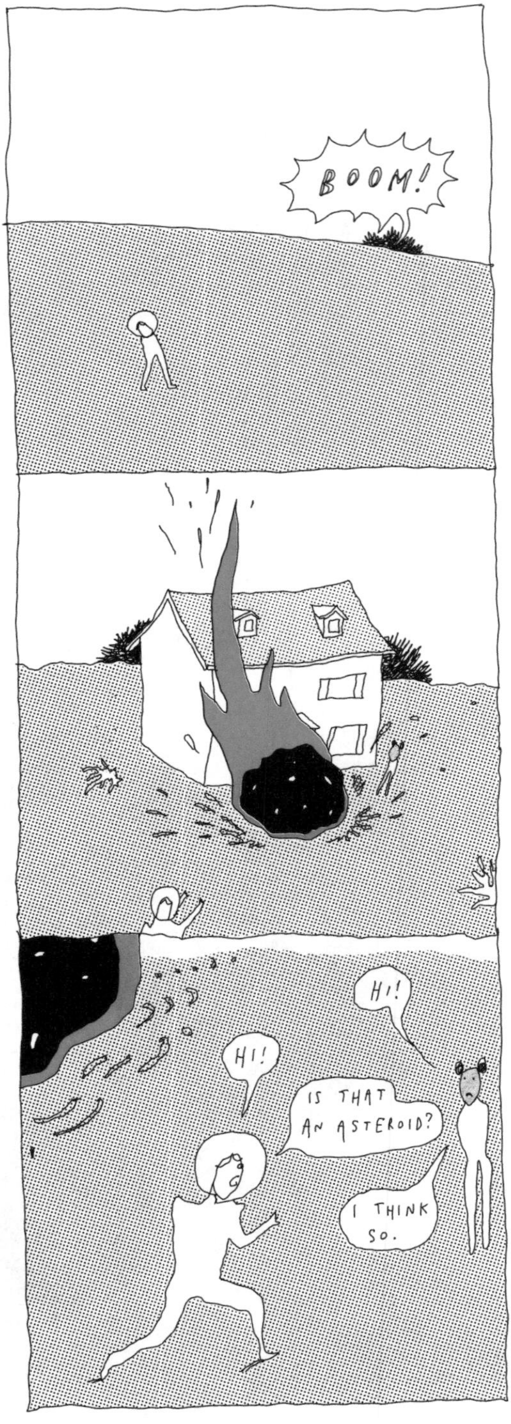
BOOM!
HI!
HI!
IS THAT AN ASTEROID?
I THINK SO.

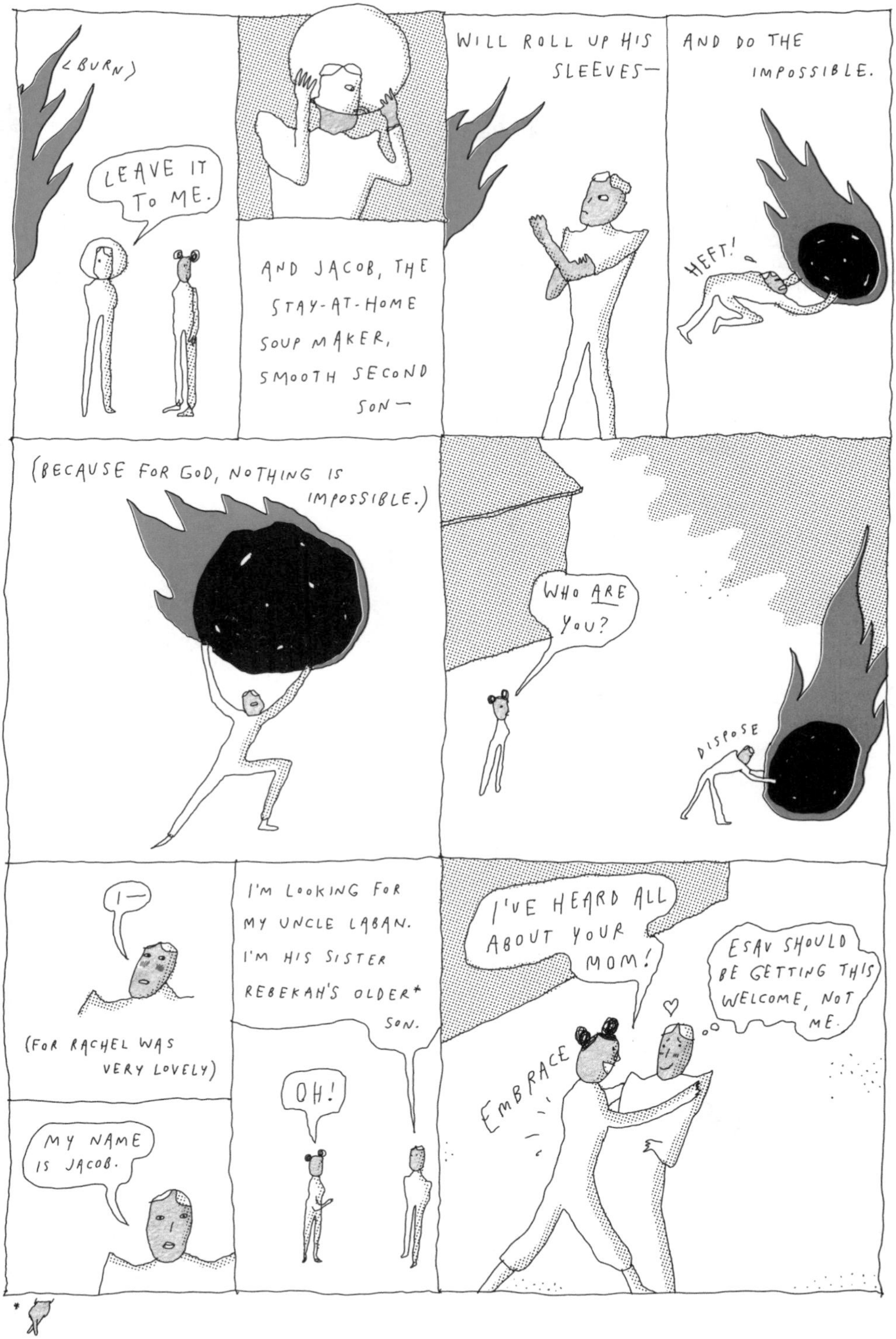
<BURN>
LEAVE IT TO ME.
AND JACOB, THE STAY-AT-HOME SOUP MAKER, SMOOTH SECOND SON—
WILL ROLL UP HIS SLEEVES—
AND DO THE IMPOSSIBLE.
HEFT!
(BECAUSE FOR GOD, NOTHING IS IMPOSSIBLE.)
WHO ARE YOU?
DISPOSE
I—
(FOR RACHEL WAS VERY LOVELY)
MY NAME IS JACOB.
I'M LOOKING FOR MY UNCLE LABAN. I'M HIS SISTER REBEKAH'S OLDER* SON.
OH!
I'VE HEARD ALL ABOUT YOUR MOM!
ESAU SHOULD BE GETTING THIS WELCOME, NOT ME.
EMBRACE
*

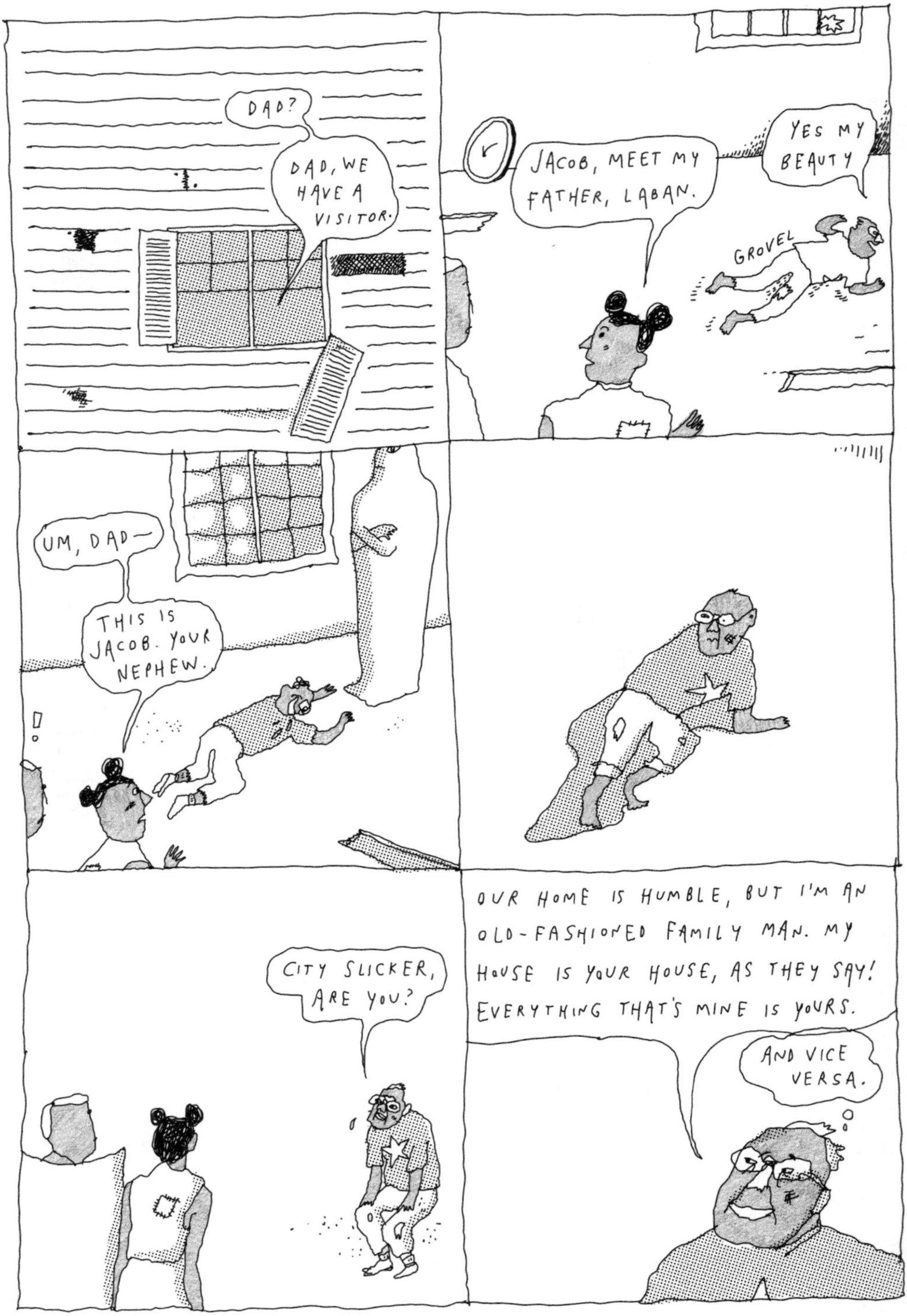

DAD?
DAD, WE HAVE A VISITOR.
JACOB, MEET MY FATHER, LABAN.
YES MY BEAUTY
GROVEL
UM, DAD—
THIS IS JACOB. YOUR NEPHEW.
!
CITY SLICKER, ARE YOU?
OUR HOME IS HUMBLE, BUT I'M AN OLD-FASHIONED FAMILY MAN. MY HOUSE IS YOUR HOUSE, AS THEY SAY! EVERYTHING THAT'S MINE IS YOURS.
AND VICE VERSA.

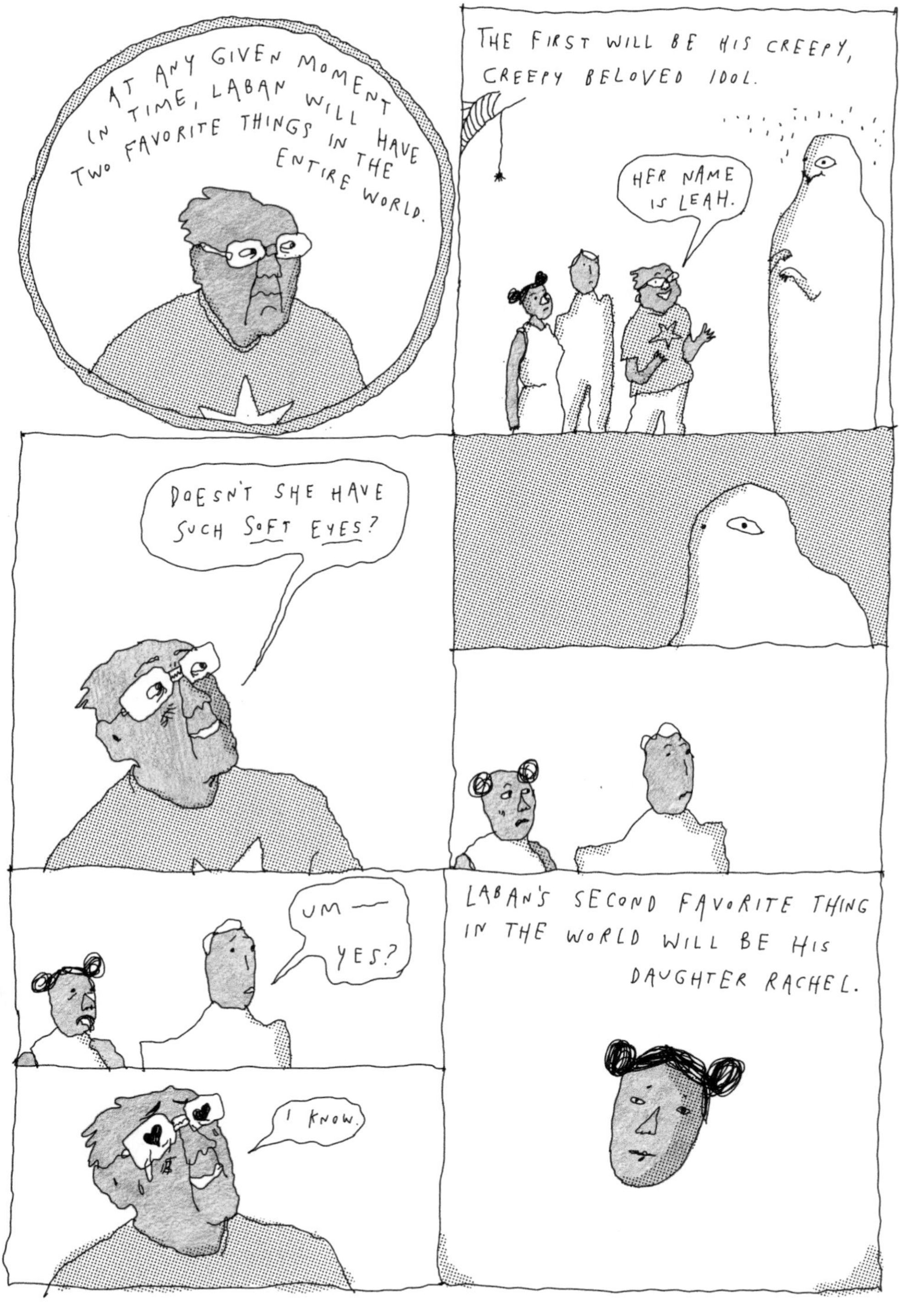
AT ANY GIVEN MOMENT IN TIME, LABAN WILL HAVE TWO FAVORITE THINGS IN THE ENTIRE WORLD.
THE FIRST WILL BE HIS CREEPY, CREEPY BELOVED IDOL.
HER NAME IS LEAH.
DOESN'T SHE HAVE SUCH SOFT EYES?
UM— YES?
I KNOW.
LABAN'S SECOND FAVORITE THING IN THE WORLD WILL BE HIS DAUGHTER RACHEL.

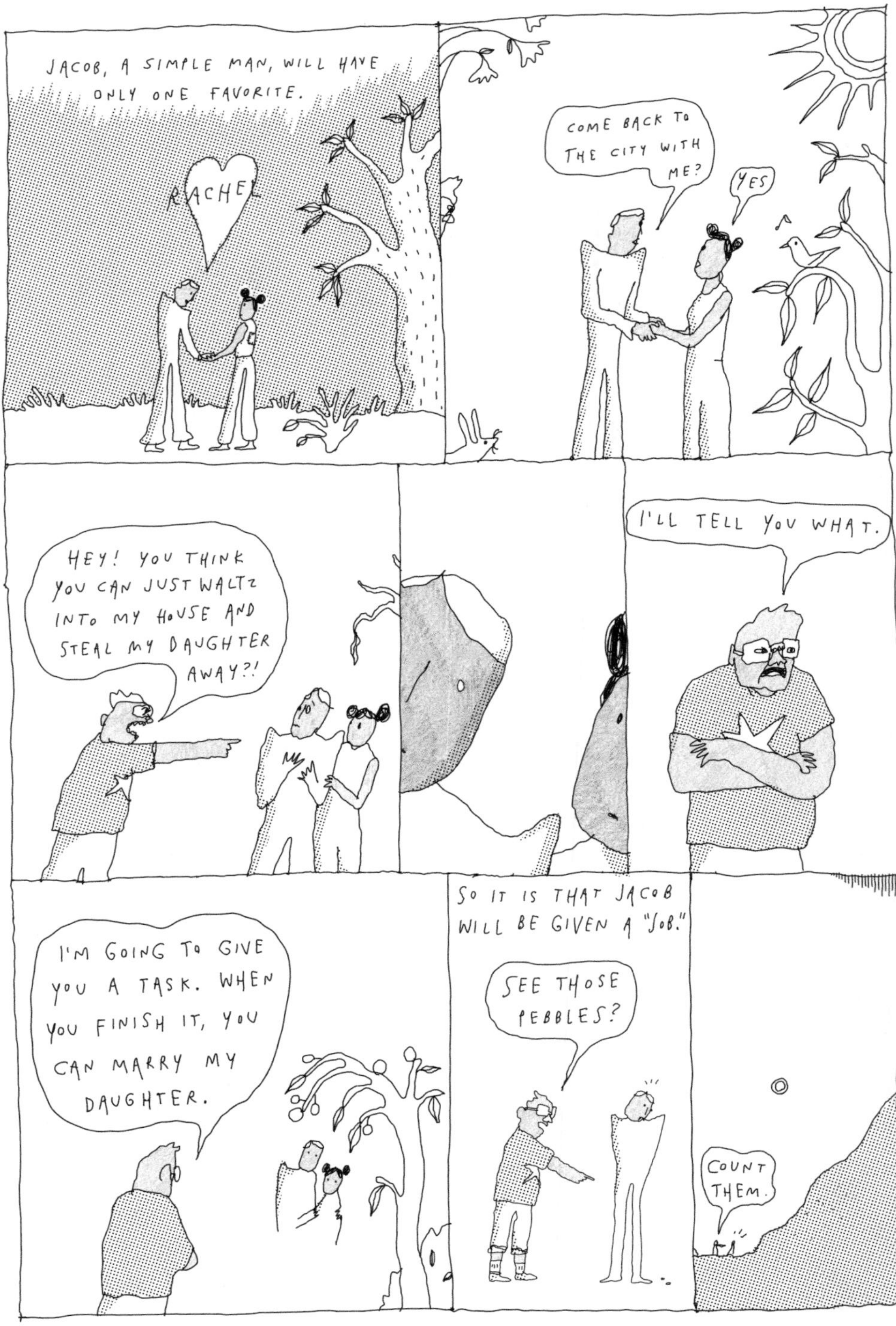

JACOB, A SIMPLE MAN, WILL HAVE ONLY ONE FAVORITE.
RACHEL
COME BACK TO THE CITY WITH ME?
YES
HEY! YOU THINK YOU CAN JUST WALTZ INTO MY HOUSE AND STEAL MY DAUGHTER AWAY?!
I'LL TELL YOU WHAT.
I'M GOING TO GIVE YOU A TASK. WHEN YOU FINISH IT, YOU CAN MARRY MY DAUGHTER.
SO IT IS THAT JACOB WILL BE GIVEN A "JOB."
SEE THOSE PEBBLES?
COUNT THEM.

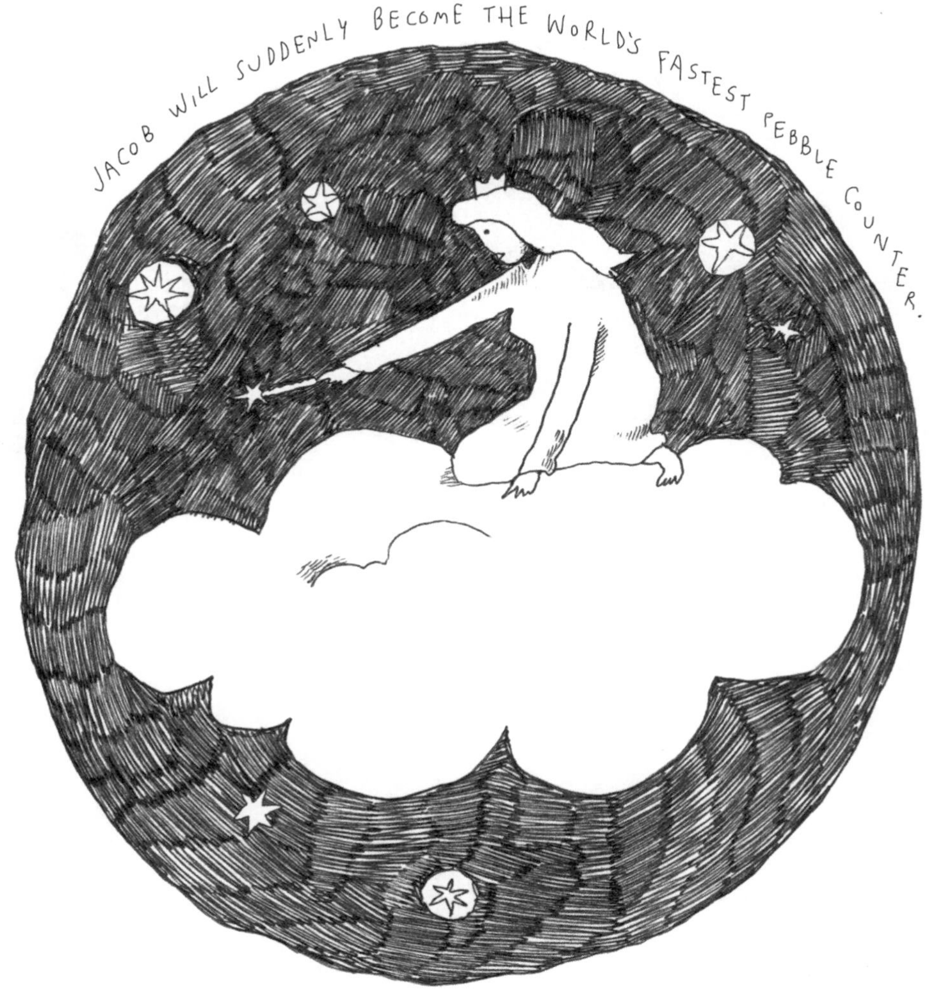
JACOB WILL SUDDENLY BECOME THE WORLD'S FASTEST PEBBLE COUNTER.

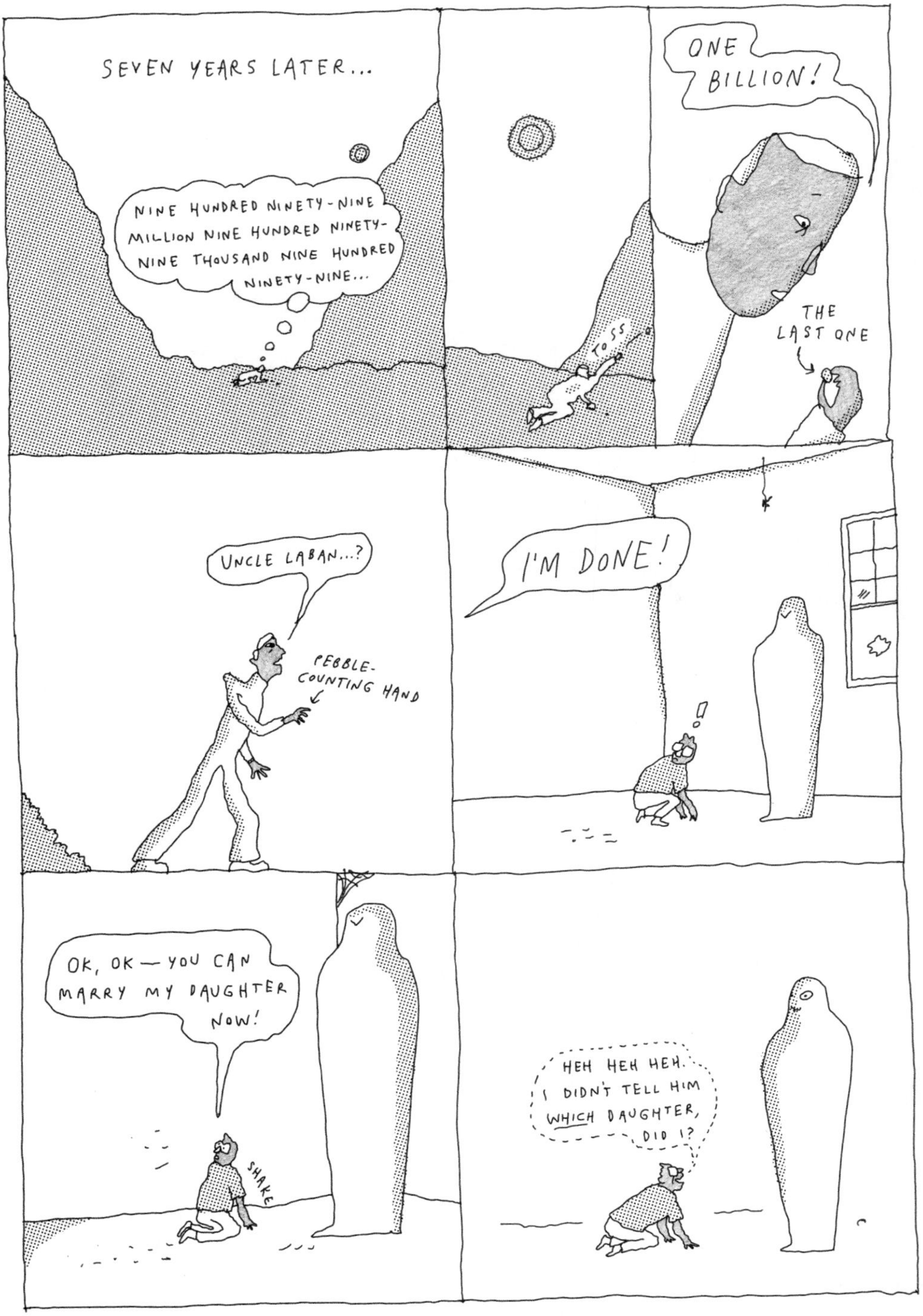
SEVEN YEARS LATER...
NINE HUNDRED NINETY-NINE MILLION NINE HUNDRED NINETY-NINE THOUSAND NINE HUNDRED NINETY-NINE...
TOSS
ONE BILLION!
THE LAST ONE
UNCLE LABAN...?
PEBBLE-COUNTING HAND
I'M DONE!
OK, OK — YOU CAN MARRY MY DAUGHTER NOW!
SHAKE
HEH HEH HEH. I DIDN'T TELL HIM WHICH DAUGHTER, DID I?

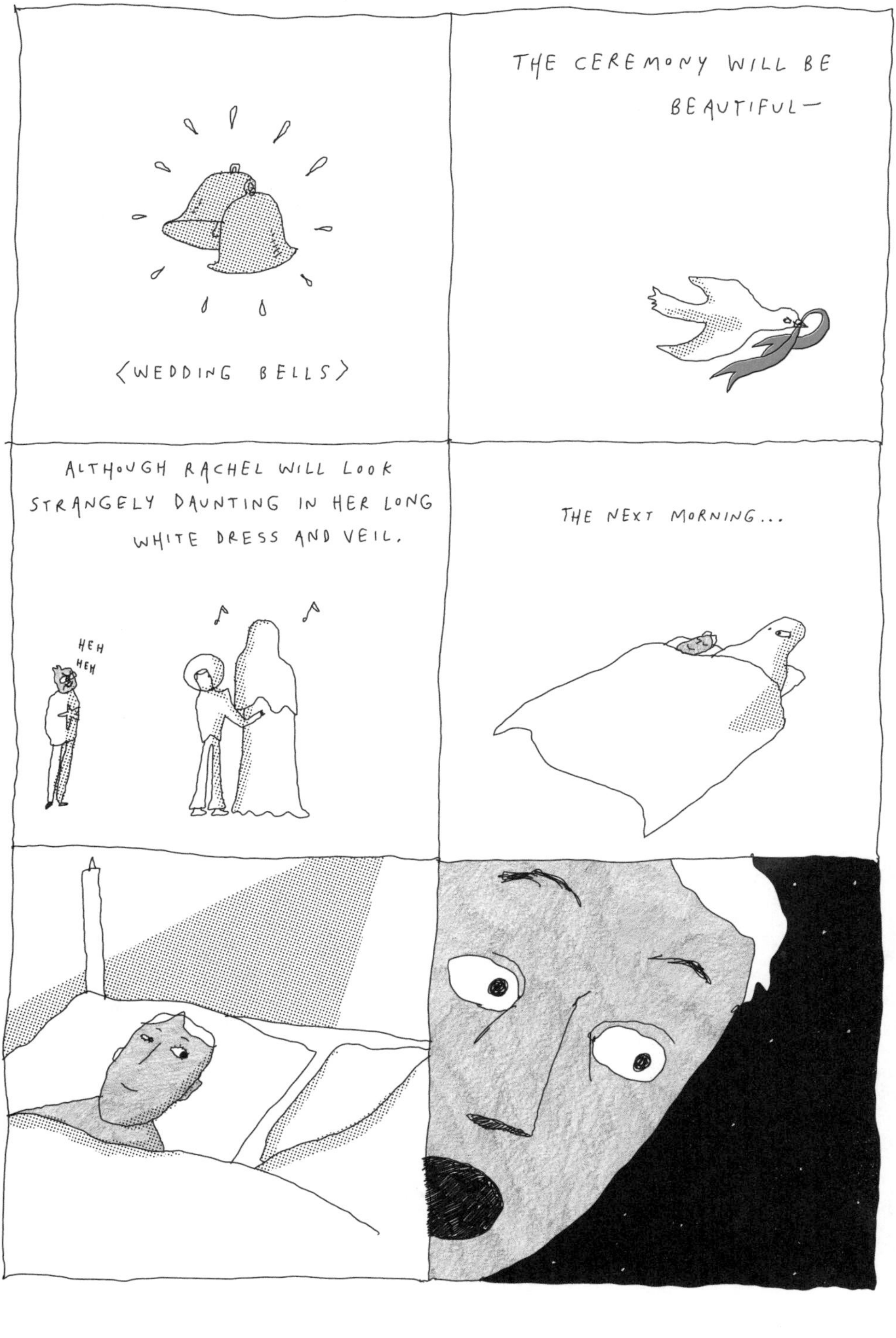

⟨WEDDING BELLS⟩
THE CEREMONY WILL BE BEAUTIFUL—
ALTHOUGH RACHEL WILL LOOK STRANGELY DAUNTING IN HER LONG WHITE DRESS AND VEIL.
HEH HEH
THE NEXT MORNING...

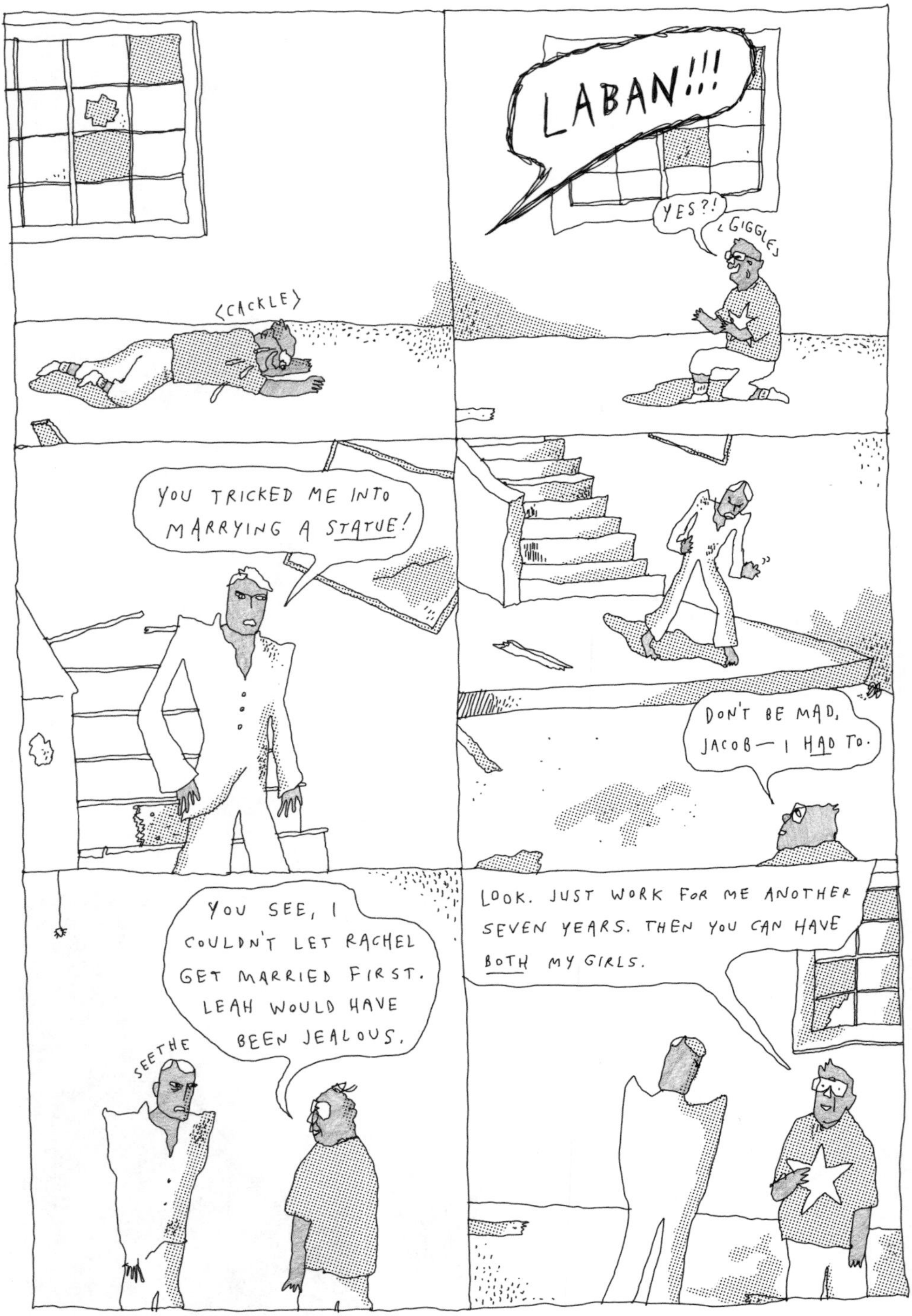

<CACKLE>
LABAN!!!
YES?!
<GIGGLES>
YOU TRICKED ME INTO MARRYING A STATUE!
DON'T BE MAD, JACOB— I HAD TO.
YOU SEE, I COULDN'T LET RACHEL GET MARRIED FIRST. LEAH WOULD HAVE BEEN JEALOUS.
SEETHE
LOOK. JUST WORK FOR ME ANOTHER SEVEN YEARS. THEN YOU CAN HAVE BOTH MY GIRLS.

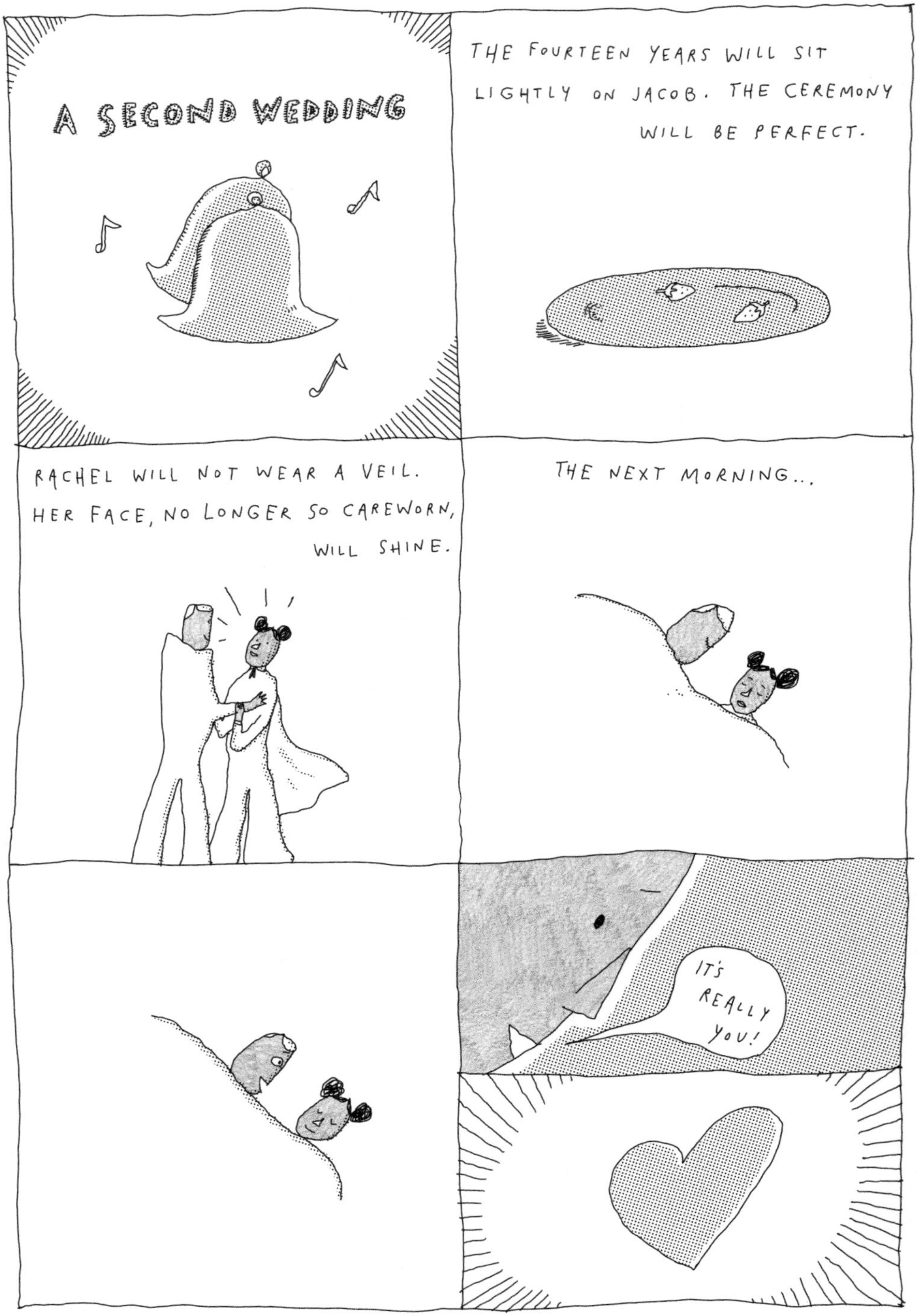
A SECOND WEDDING
THE FOURTEEN YEARS WILL SIT LIGHTLY ON JACOB. THE CEREMONY WILL BE PERFECT.
RACHEL WILL NOT WEAR A VEIL. HER FACE, NO LONGER SO CAREWORN, WILL SHINE.
THE NEXT MORNING...
IT'S REALLY YOU!

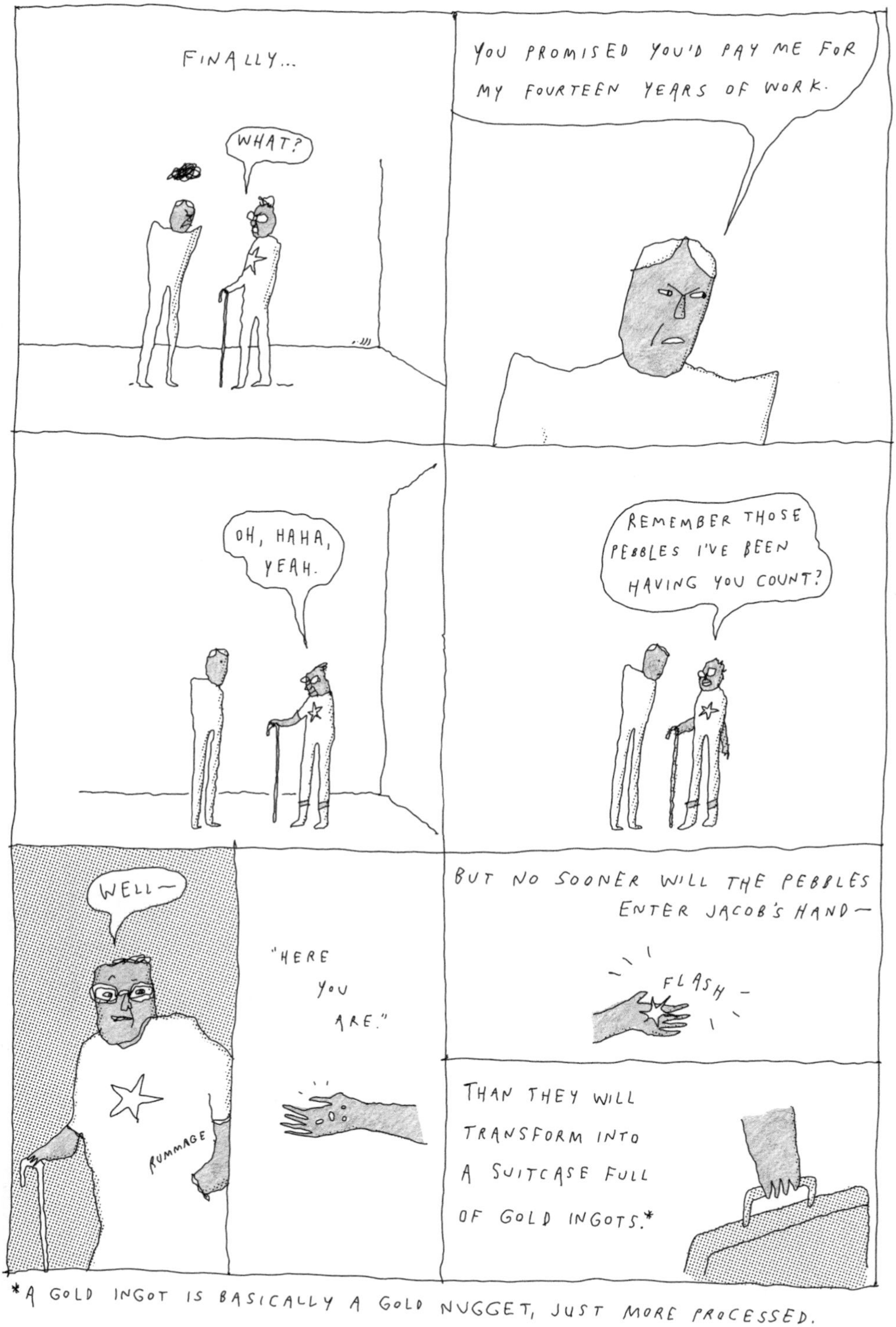
FINALLY...
WHAT?
YOU PROMISED YOU'D PAY ME FOR MY FOURTEEN YEARS OF WORK.
OH, HAHA, YEAH.
REMEMBER THOSE PEBBLES I'VE BEEN HAVING YOU COUNT?
WELL—
RUMMAGE
"HERE YOU ARE."
BUT NO SOONER WILL THE PEBBLES ENTER JACOB'S HAND—
FLASH
THAN THEY WILL TRANSFORM INTO A SUITCASE FULL OF GOLD INGOTS.*

*A GOLD INGOT IS BASICALLY A GOLD NUGGET, JUST MORE PROCESSED.

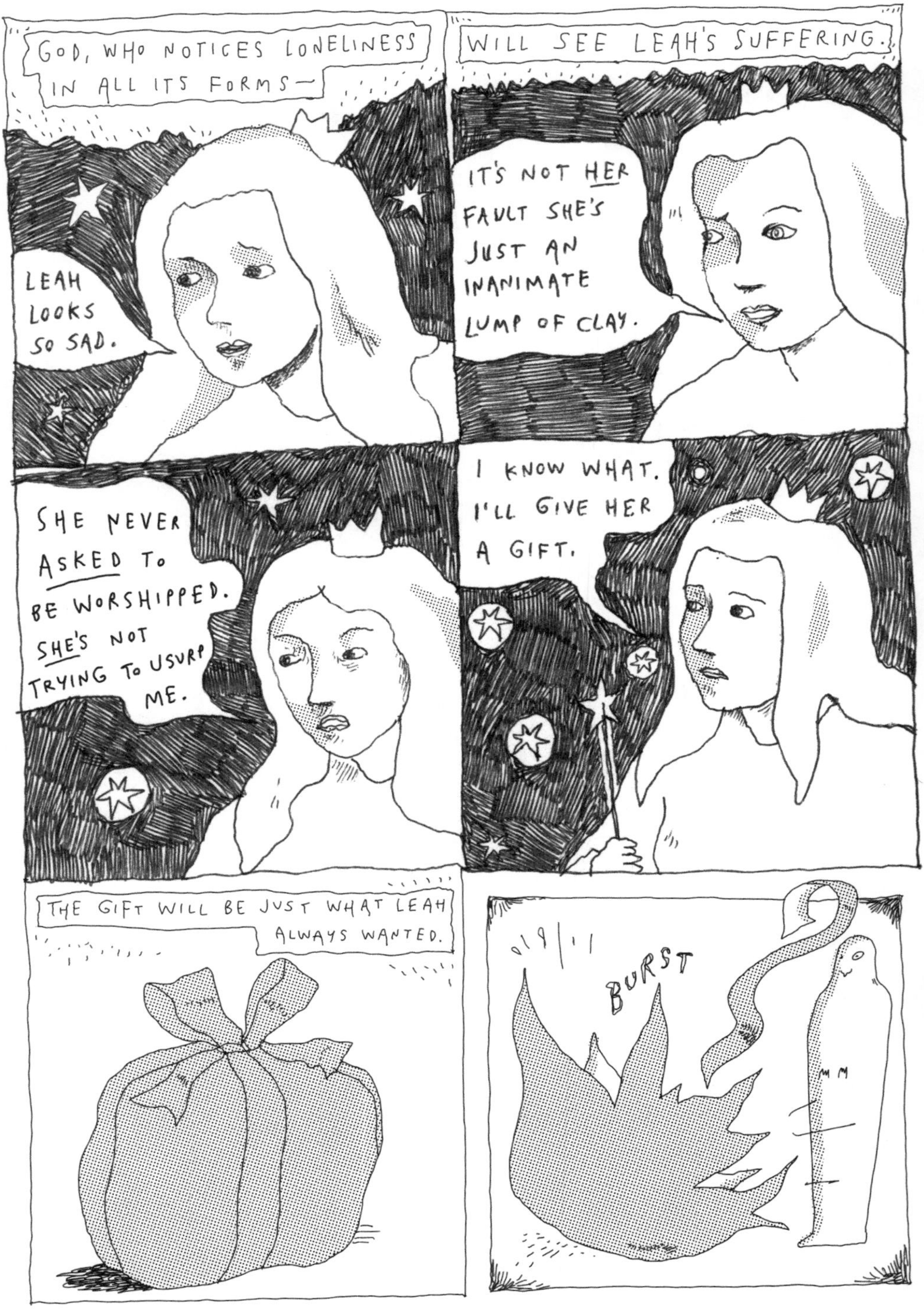
GOD, WHO NOTICES LONELINESS IN ALL ITS FORMS—
LEAH LOOKS SO SAD.
WILL SEE LEAH'S SUFFERING.
IT'S NOT HER FAULT SHE'S JUST AN INANIMATE LUMP OF CLAY.
SHE NEVER ASKED TO BE WORSHIPPED. SHE'S NOT TRYING TO USURP ME.
I KNOW WHAT. I'LL GIVE HER A GIFT.
THE GIFT WILL BE JUST WHAT LEAH ALWAYS WANTED.
BURST

SEVEN CHILDREN!
REUBEN!
LEVI!
SIMEON!
JUDAH!
ZEBULUN!
ISSACHAR!
DINAH!

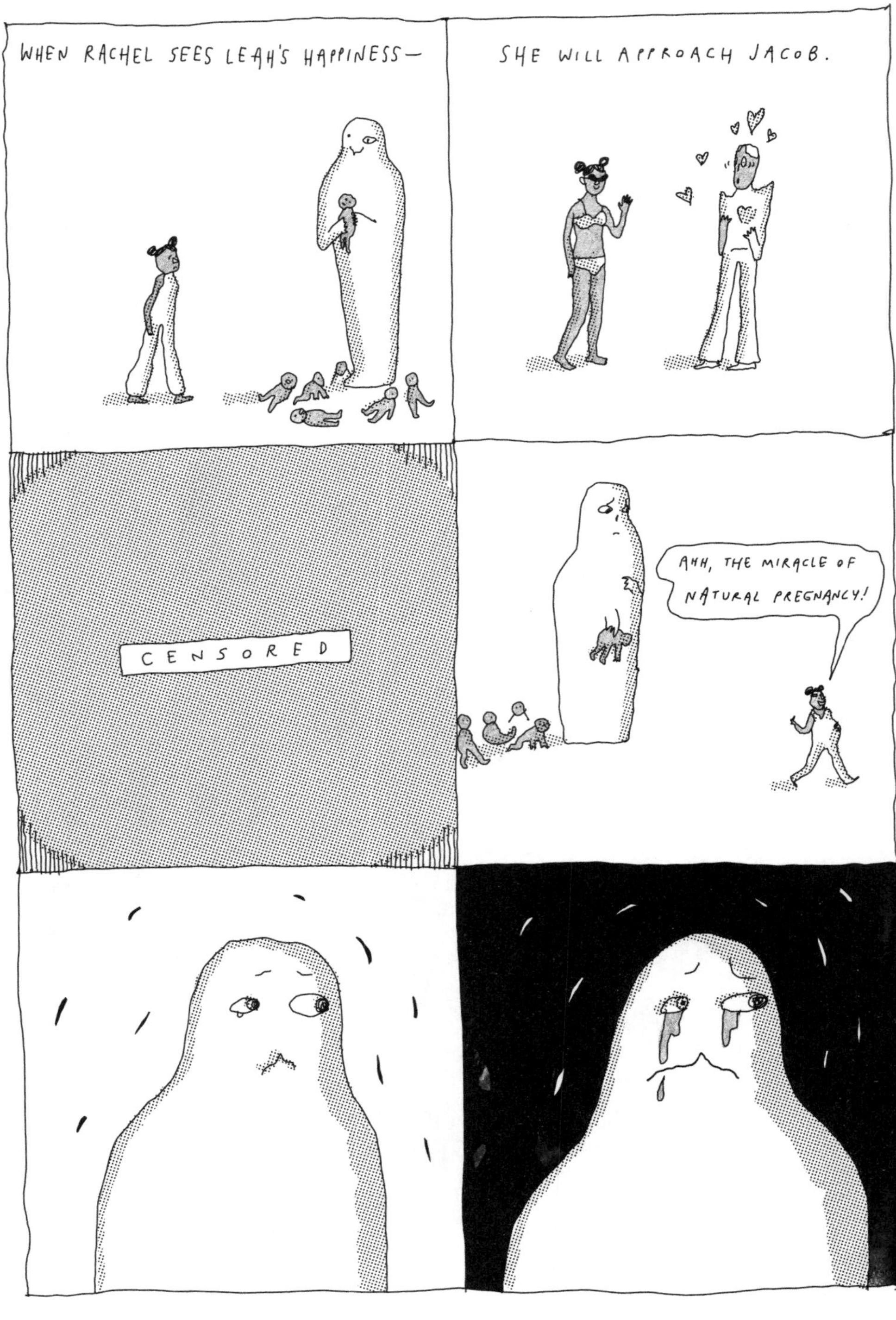
WHEN RACHEL SEES LEAH'S HAPPINESS—
SHE WILL APPROACH JACOB.
CENSORED
AHH, THE MIRACLE OF NATURAL PREGNANCY!

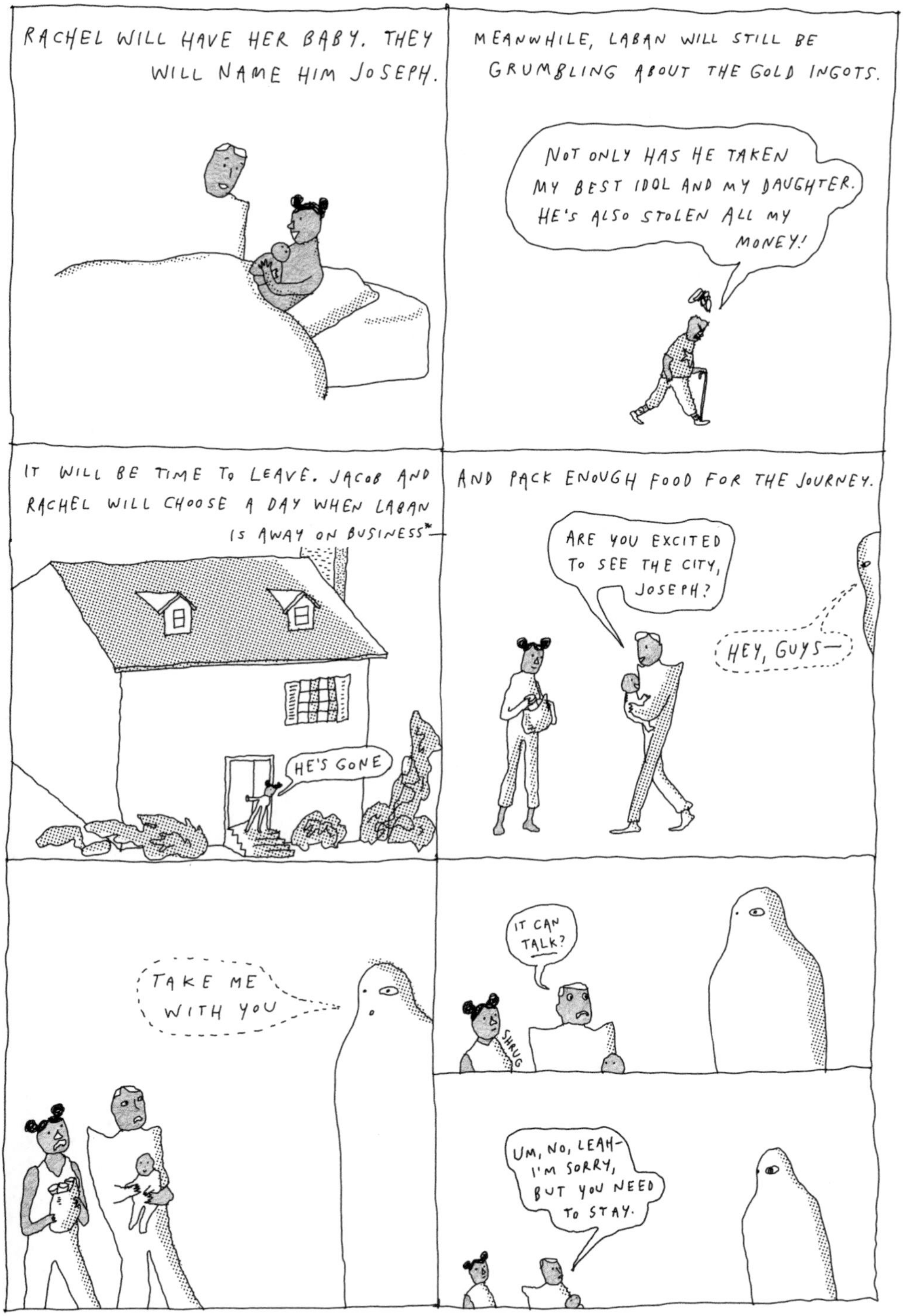
RACHEL WILL HAVE HER BABY. THEY WILL NAME HIM JOSEPH.
MEANWHILE, LABAN WILL STILL BE GRUMBLING ABOUT THE GOLD INGOTS.
NOT ONLY HAS HE TAKEN MY BEST IDOL AND MY DAUGHTER. HE'S ALSO STOLEN ALL MY MONEY!
IT WILL BE TIME TO LEAVE. JACOB AND RACHEL WILL CHOOSE A DAY WHEN LABAN IS AWAY ON BUSINESS*—
HE'S GONE
AND PACK ENOUGH FOOD FOR THE JOURNEY.
ARE YOU EXCITED TO SEE THE CITY, JOSEPH?
HEY, GUYS—
TAKE ME WITH YOU
IT CAN TALK?
SHRUG
UM, NO, LEAH-I'M SORRY, BUT YOU NEED TO STAY.

*?

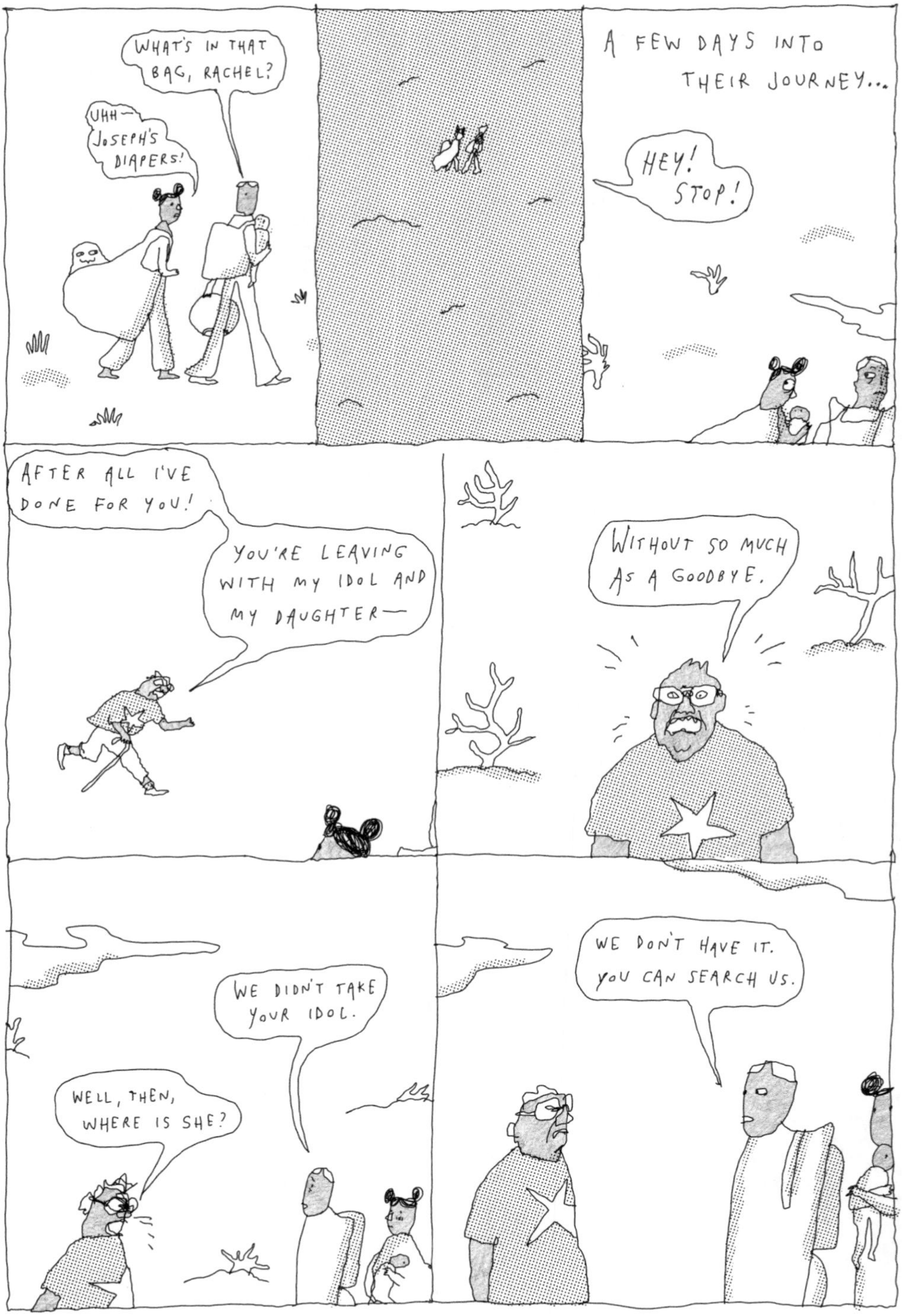
WHAT'S IN THAT BAG, RACHEL?
UHH— JOSEPH'S DIAPERS!
A FEW DAYS INTO THEIR JOURNEY...
HEY! STOP!
AFTER ALL I'VE DONE FOR YOU!
YOU'RE LEAVING WITH MY IDOL AND MY DAUGHTER—
WITHOUT SO MUCH AS A GOODBYE.
WE DIDN'T TAKE YOUR IDOL.
WELL, THEN, WHERE IS SHE?
WE DON'T HAVE IT. YOU CAN SEARCH US.

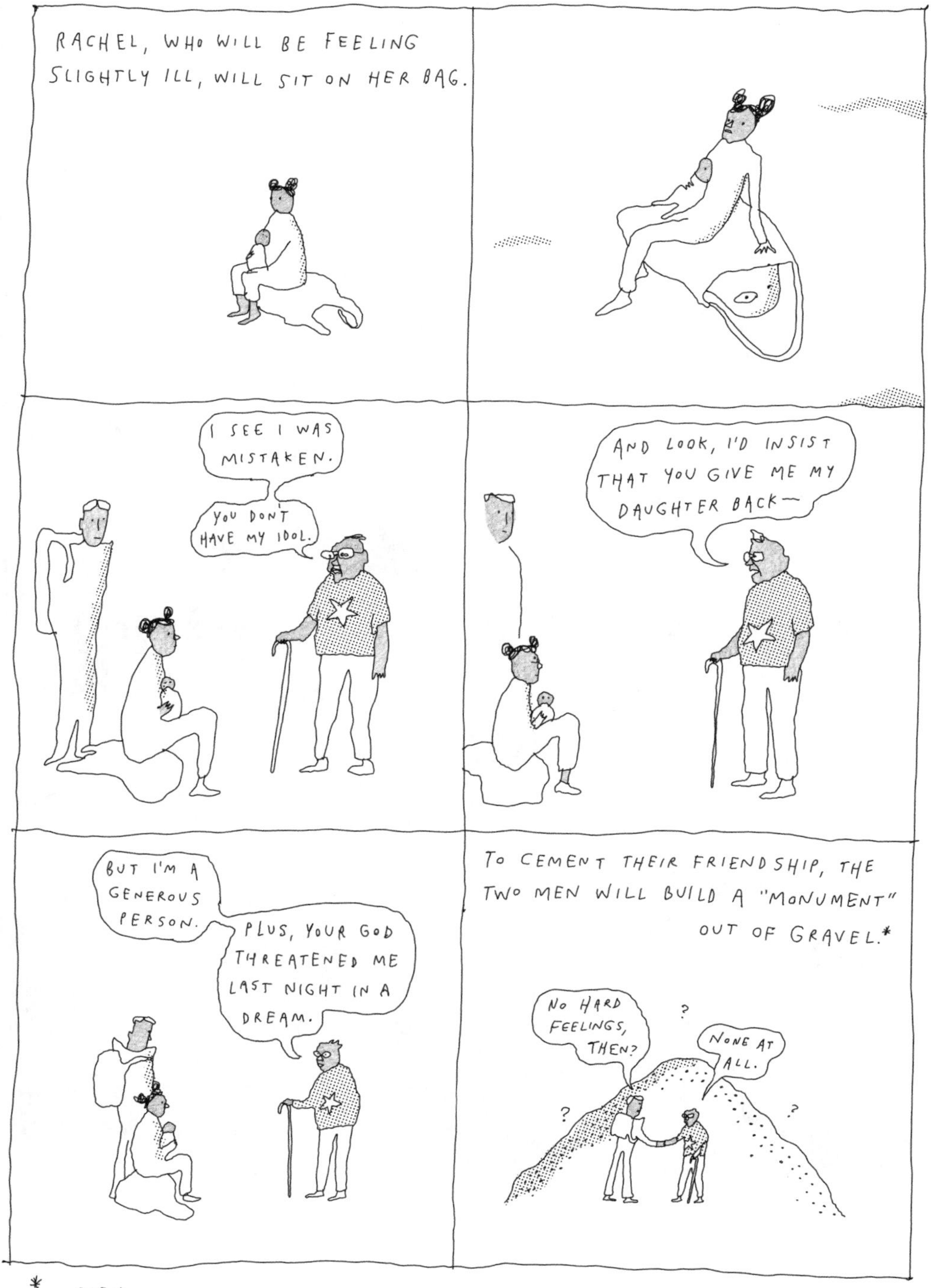
RACHEL, WHO WILL BE FEELING SLIGHTLY ILL, WILL SIT ON HER BAG.
I SEE I WAS MISTAKEN.
YOU DON'T HAVE MY IDOL.
AND LOOK, I'D INSIST THAT YOU GIVE ME MY DAUGHTER BACK—
BUT I'M A GENEROUS PERSON.
PLUS, YOUR GOD THREATENED ME LAST NIGHT IN A DREAM.
TO CEMENT THEIR FRIENDSHIP, THE TWO MEN WILL BUILD A "MONUMENT" OUT OF GRAVEL.*
NO HARD FEELINGS, THEN?
NONE AT ALL.
?
?
?

*...MEN.

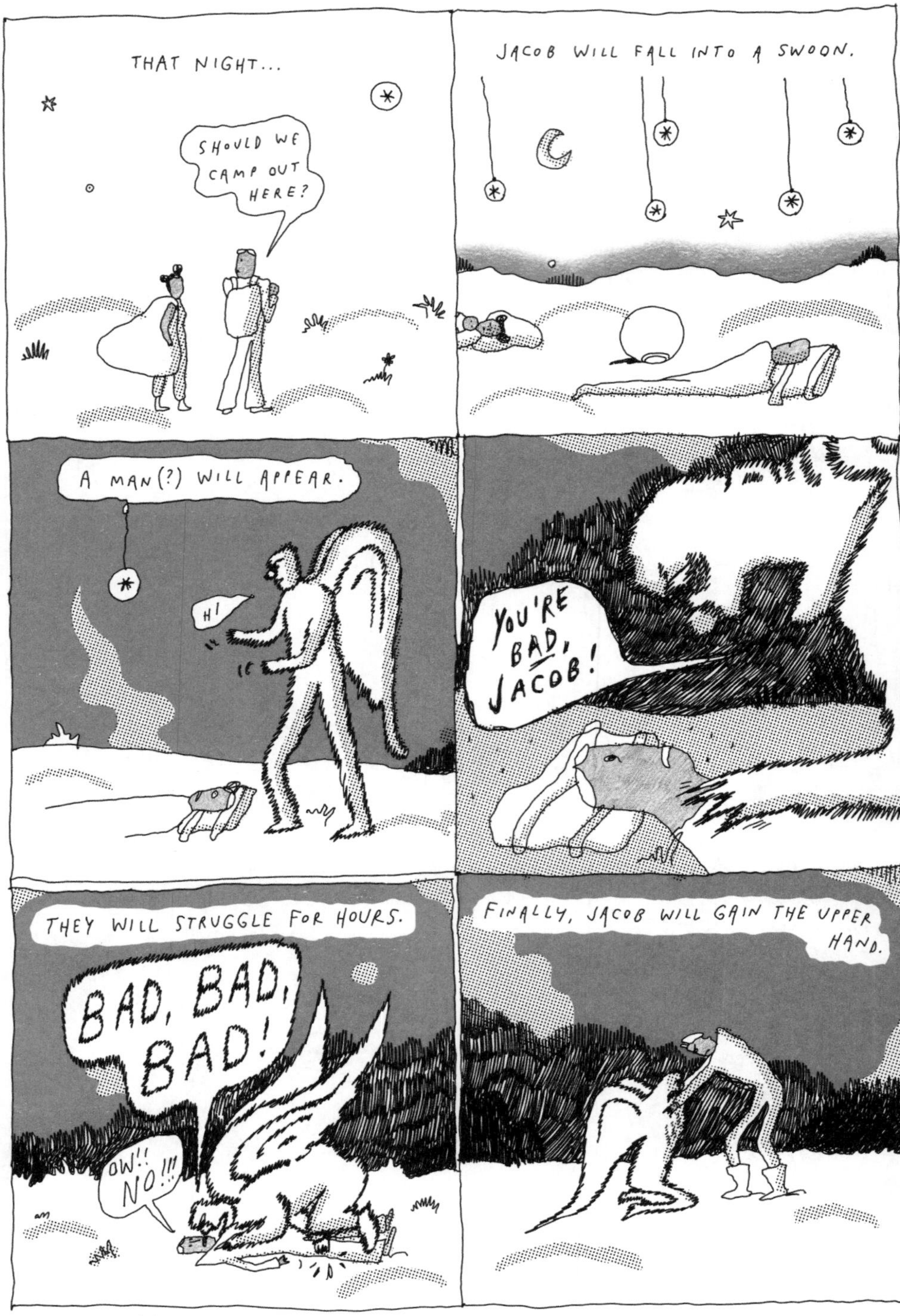
THAT NIGHT...
SHOULD WE CAMP OUT HERE?
JACOB WILL FALL INTO A SWOON.
A MAN(?) WILL APPEAR.
HI
YOU'RE BAD, JACOB!
THEY WILL STRUGGLE FOR HOURS.
BAD, BAD, BAD!
OW!! NO!!!
FINALLY, JACOB WILL GAIN THE UPPER HAND.

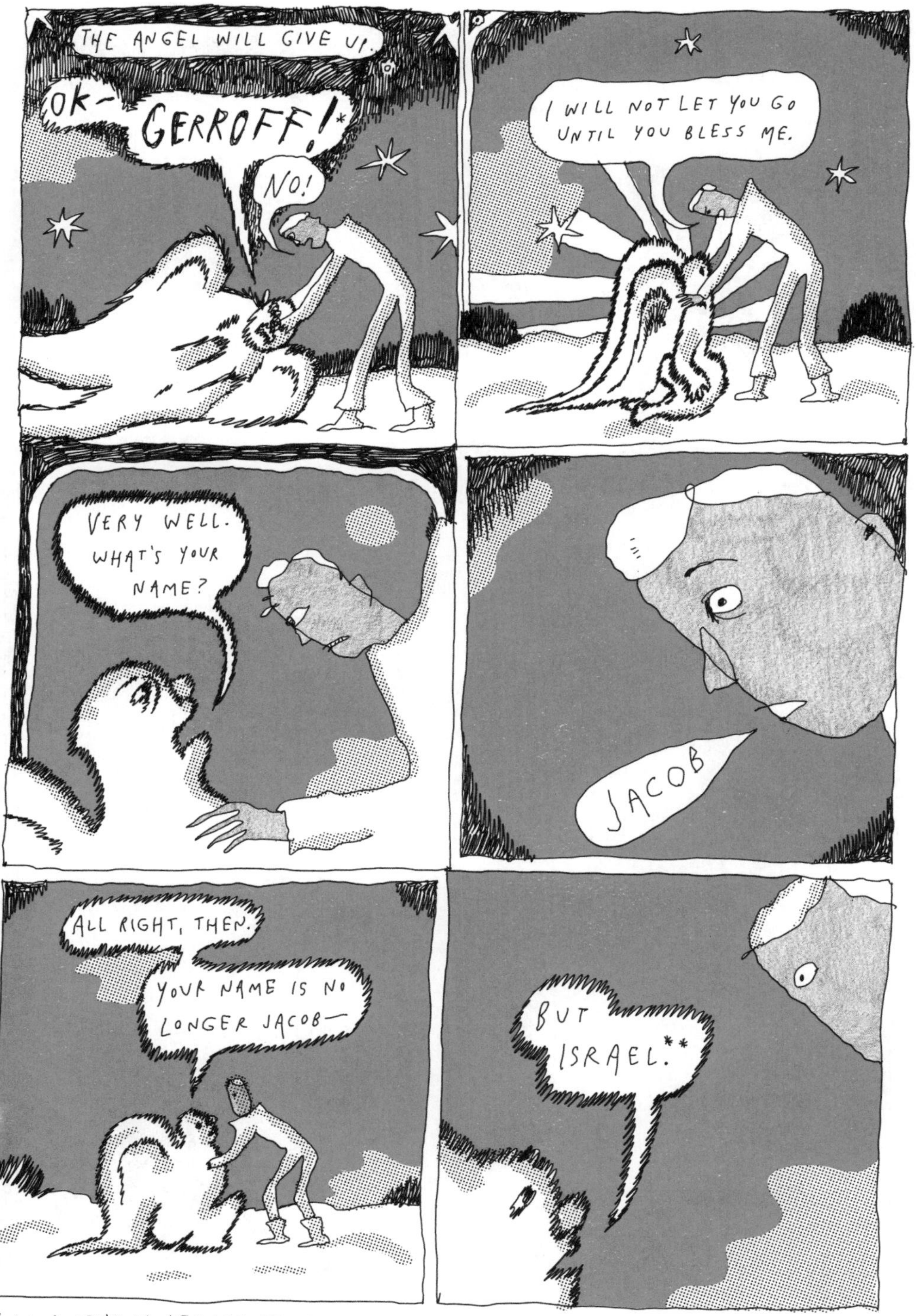
THE ANGEL WILL GIVE UP.
OK— GERROFF!*
NO!
I WILL NOT LET YOU GO UNTIL YOU BLESS ME.
VERY WELL. WHAT'S YOUR NAME?
JACOB
ALL RIGHT, THEN.
YOUR NAME IS NO LONGER JACOB—
BUT ISRAEL.**

* AN ANGEL'S WINGS ARE RESTLESS. THEY WILL DISINTEGRATE IF NOT IN CONSTANT USE.

** "WRESTLED WITH GOD"

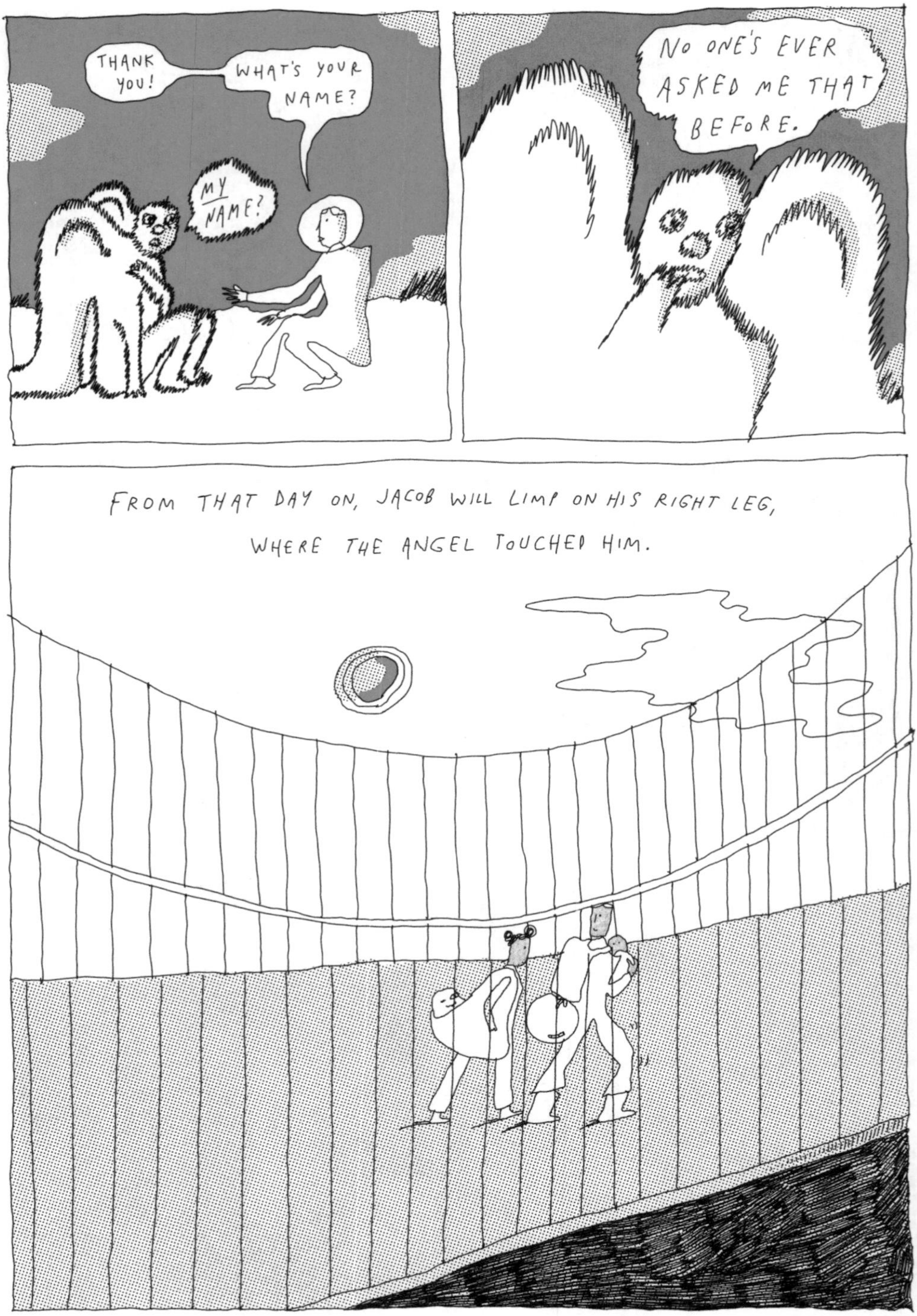
THANK YOU!
WHAT'S YOUR NAME?
MY NAME?
NO ONE'S EVER ASKED ME THAT BEFORE.
FROM THAT DAY ON, JACOB WILL LIMP ON HIS RIGHT LEG, WHERE THE ANGEL TOUCHED HIM.

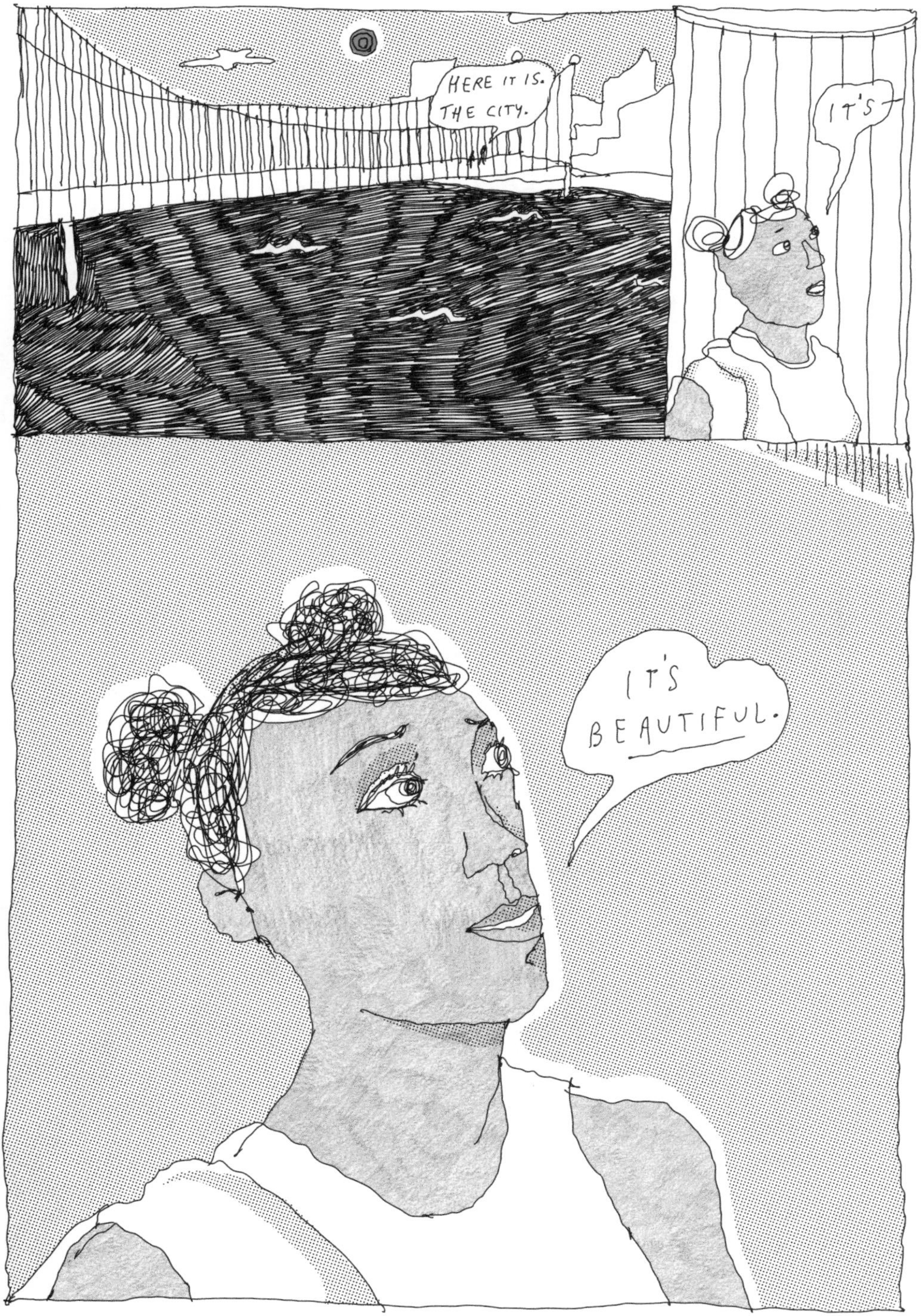
HERE IT IS. THE CITY.
IT'S—
IT'S BEAUTIFUL.

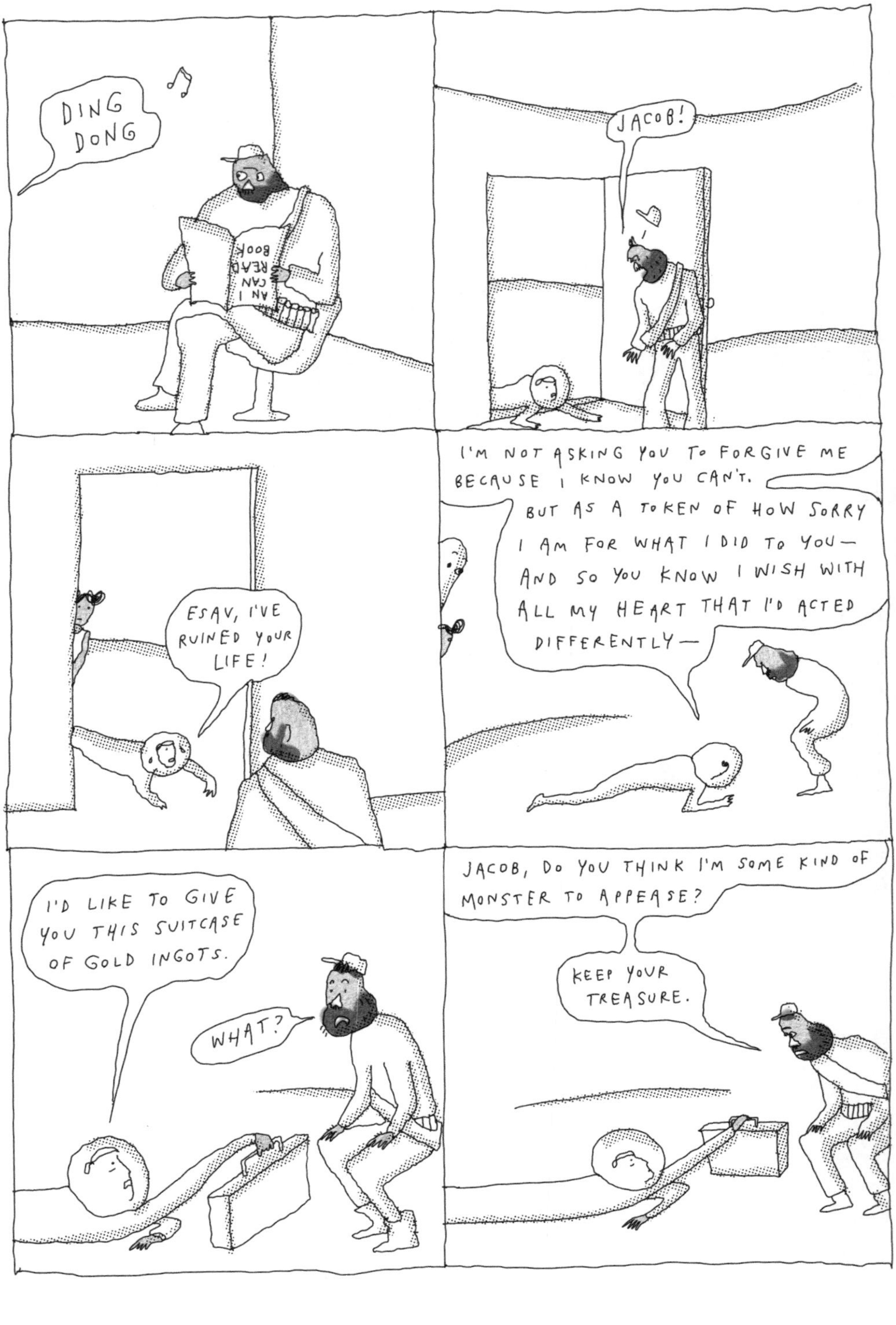
DING DONG
AN I CAN READ BOOK
JACOB!
ESAV, I'VE RUINED YOUR LIFE!
I'M NOT ASKING YOU TO FORGIVE ME BECAUSE I KNOW YOU CAN'T.
BUT AS A TOKEN OF HOW SORRY I AM FOR WHAT I DID TO YOU— AND SO YOU KNOW I WISH WITH ALL MY HEART THAT I'D ACTED DIFFERENTLY—
I'D LIKE TO GIVE YOU THIS SUITCASE OF GOLD INGOTS.
WHAT?
JACOB, DO YOU THINK I'M SOME KIND OF MONSTER TO APPEASE?
KEEP YOUR TREASURE.

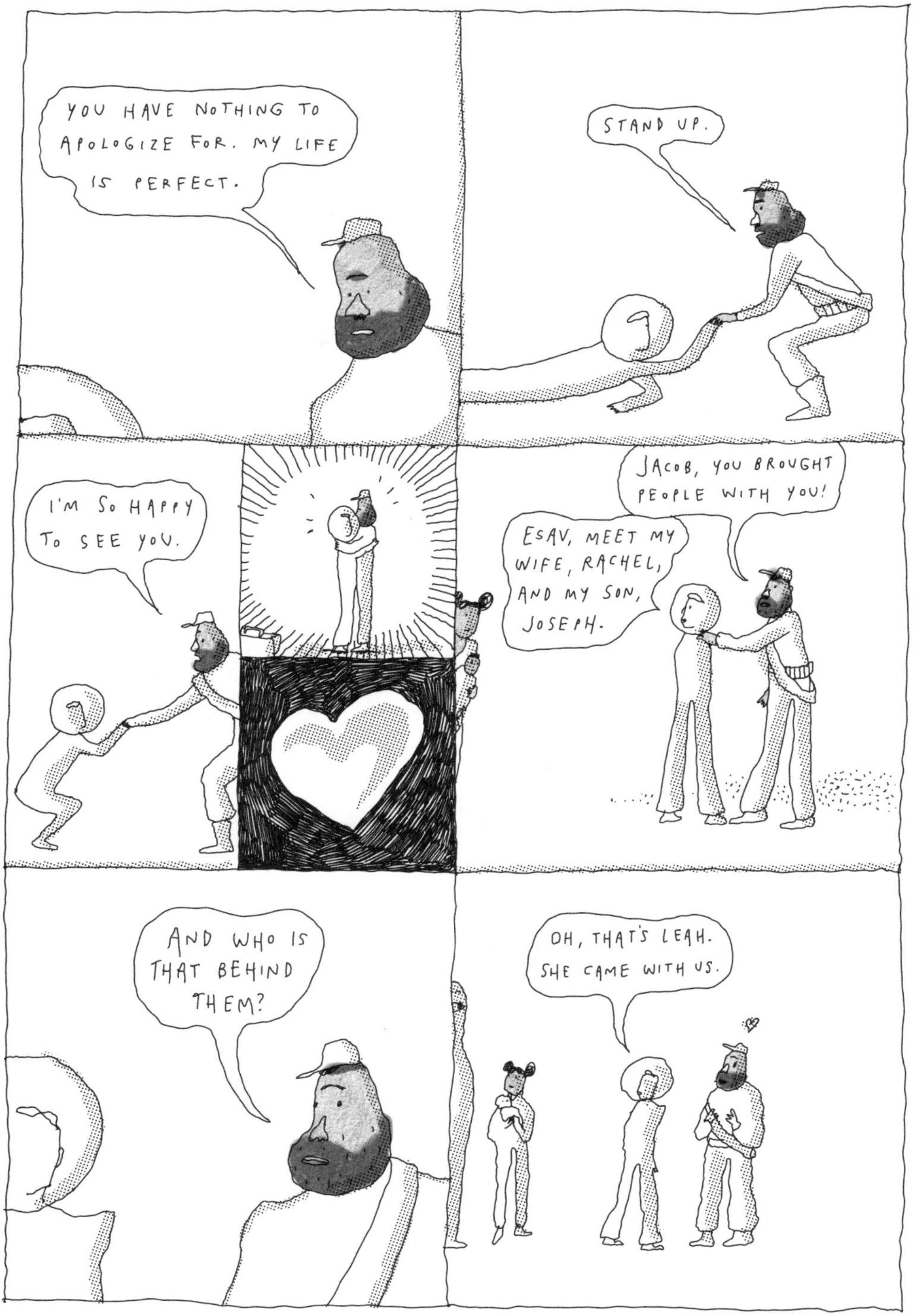
YOU HAVE NOTHING TO APOLOGIZE FOR. MY LIFE IS PERFECT.
STAND UP.
I'M SO HAPPY TO SEE YOU.
JACOB, YOU BROUGHT PEOPLE WITH YOU!
ESAV, MEET MY WIFE, RACHEL, AND MY SON, JOSEPH.
AND WHO IS THAT BEHIND THEM?
OH, THAT'S LEAH. SHE CAME WITH US.

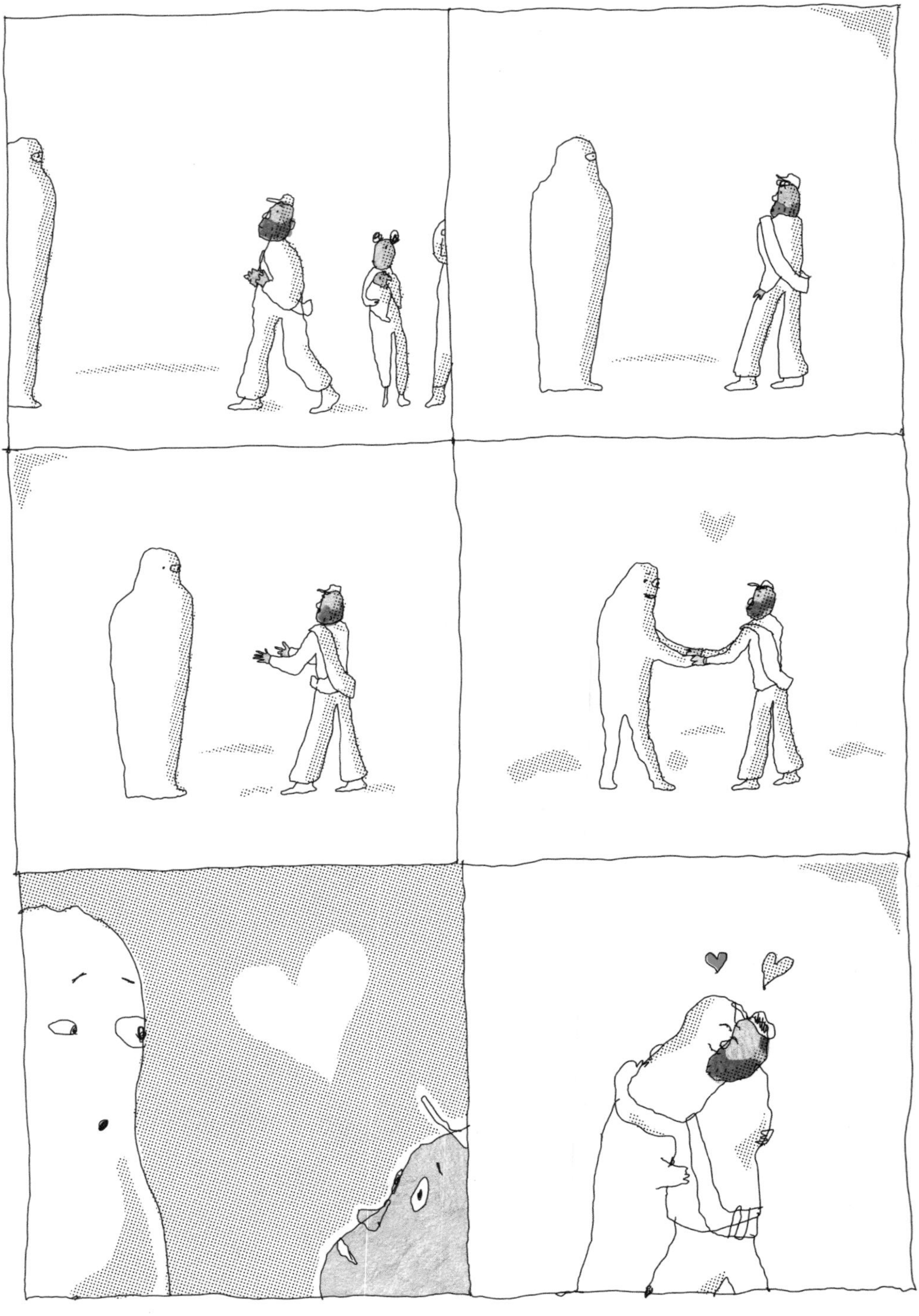

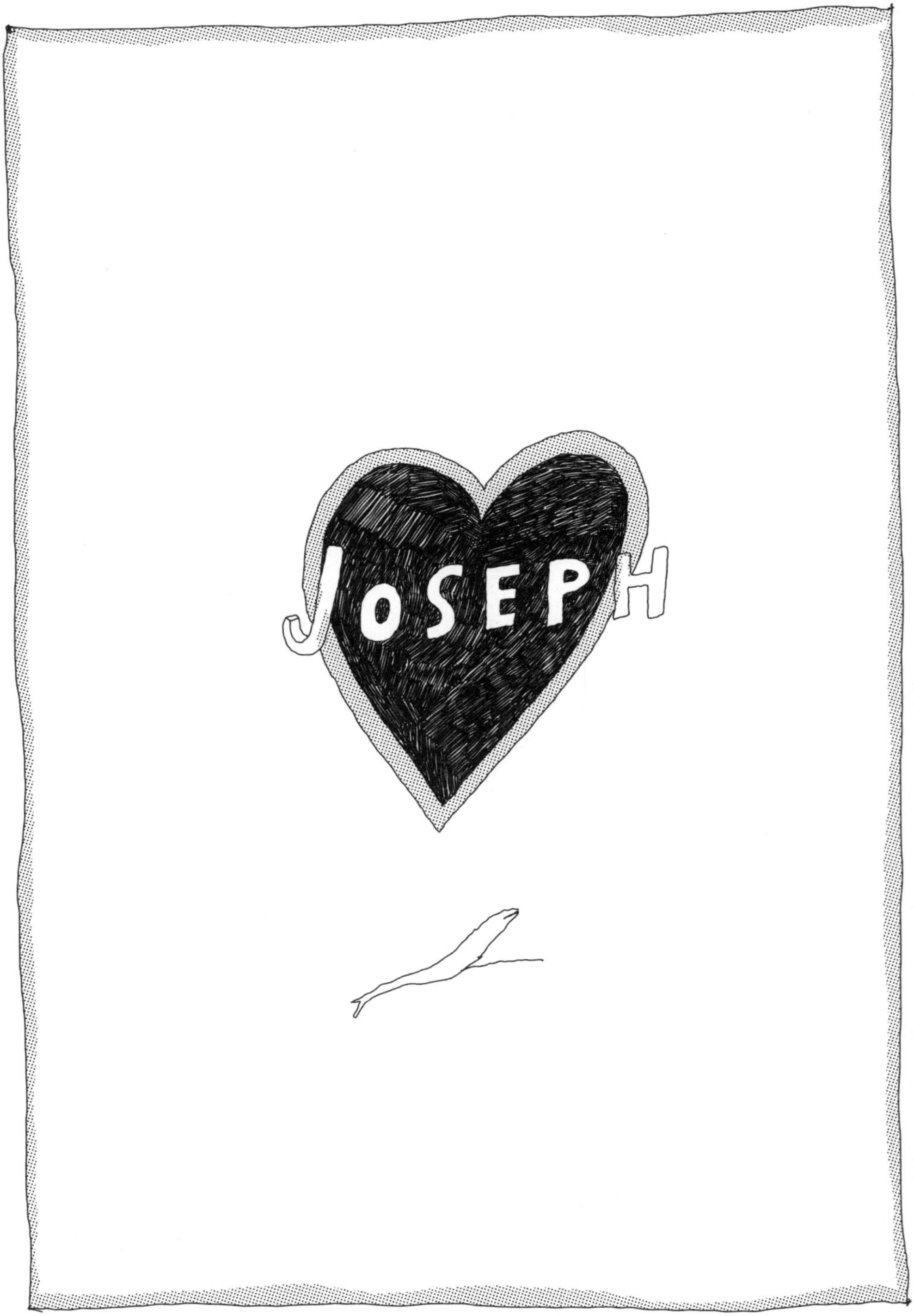
JOSEPH

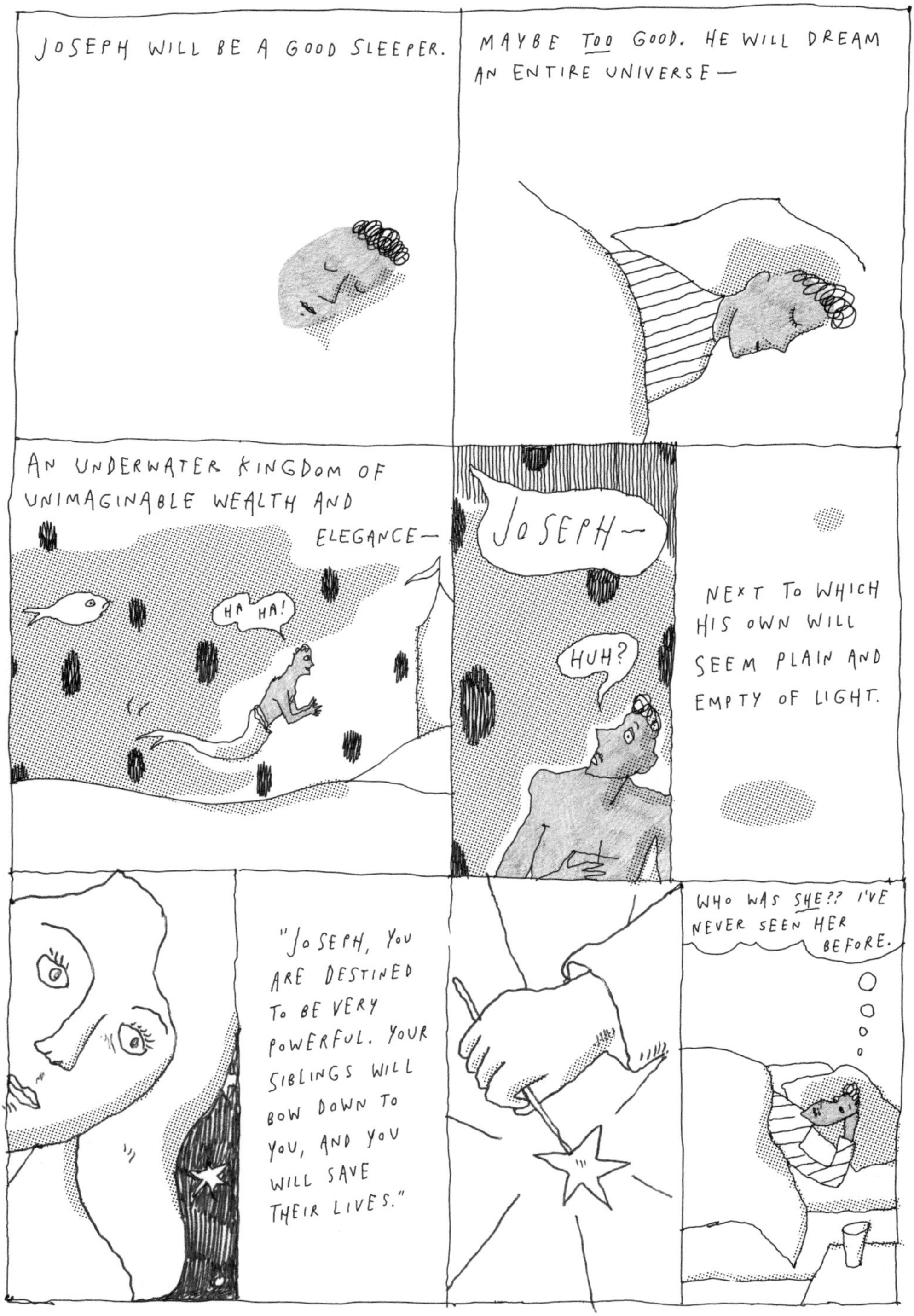
JOSEPH WILL BE A GOOD SLEEPER.
MAYBE TOO GOOD. HE WILL DREAM AN ENTIRE UNIVERSE—
AN UNDERWATER KINGDOM OF UNIMAGINABLE WEALTH AND ELEGANCE—
HA HA!
JOSEPH~
HUH?
NEXT TO WHICH HIS OWN WILL SEEM PLAIN AND EMPTY OF LIGHT.
"JOSEPH, YOU ARE DESTINED TO BE VERY POWERFUL. YOUR SIBLINGS WILL BOW DOWN TO YOU, AND YOU WILL SAVE THEIR LIVES."
WHO WAS SHE?? I'VE NEVER SEEN HER BEFORE.

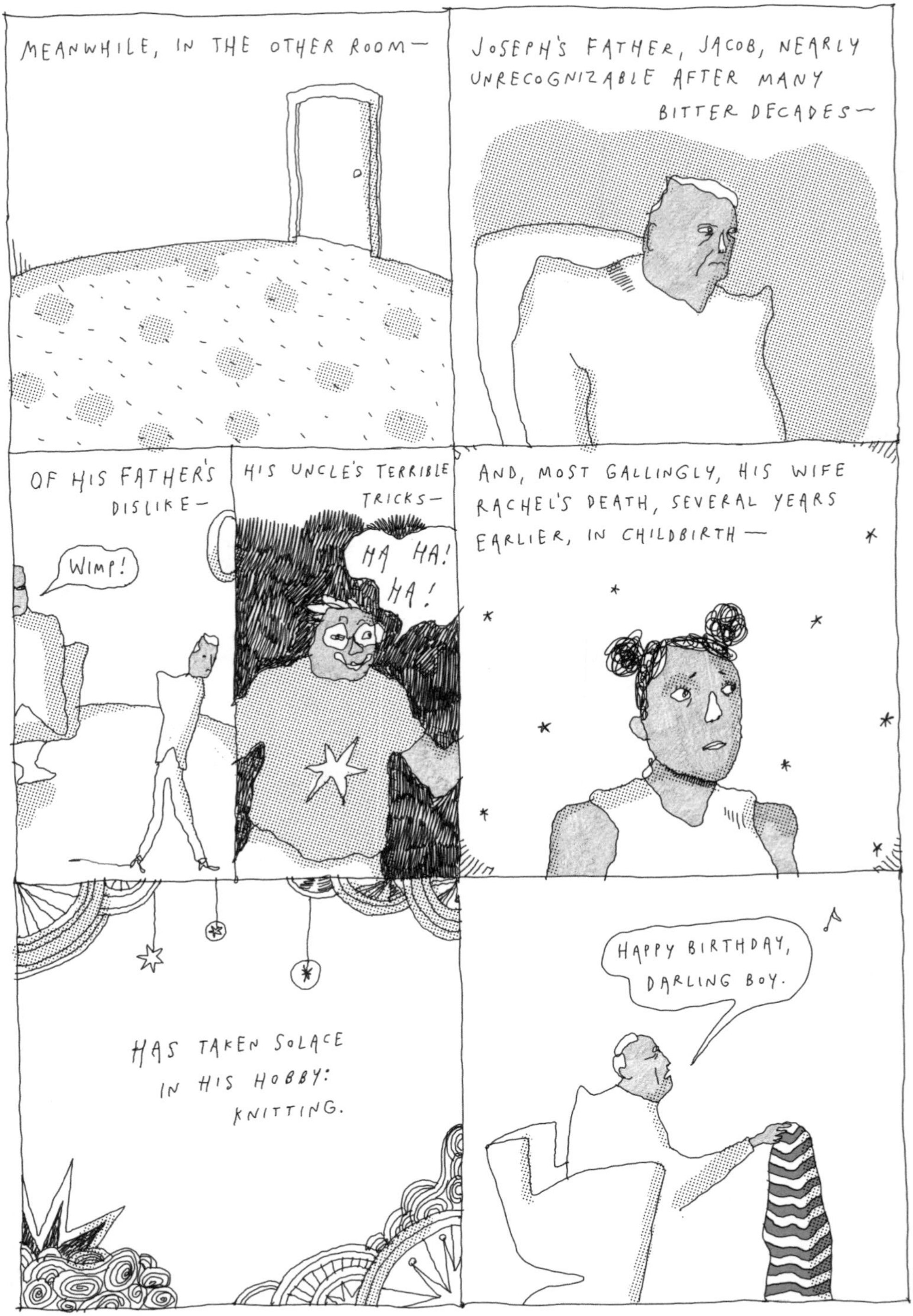

MEANWHILE, IN THE OTHER ROOM—
JOSEPH'S FATHER, JACOB, NEARLY UNRECOGNIZABLE AFTER MANY BITTER DECADES—
OF HIS FATHER'S DISLIKE—
WIMP!
HIS UNCLE'S TERRIBLE TRICKS—
HA HA! HA!
AND, MOST GALLINGLY, HIS WIFE RACHEL'S DEATH, SEVERAL YEARS EARLIER, IN CHILDBIRTH—
HAS TAKEN SOLACE IN HIS HOBBY: KNITTING.
HAPPY BIRTHDAY, DARLING BOY.

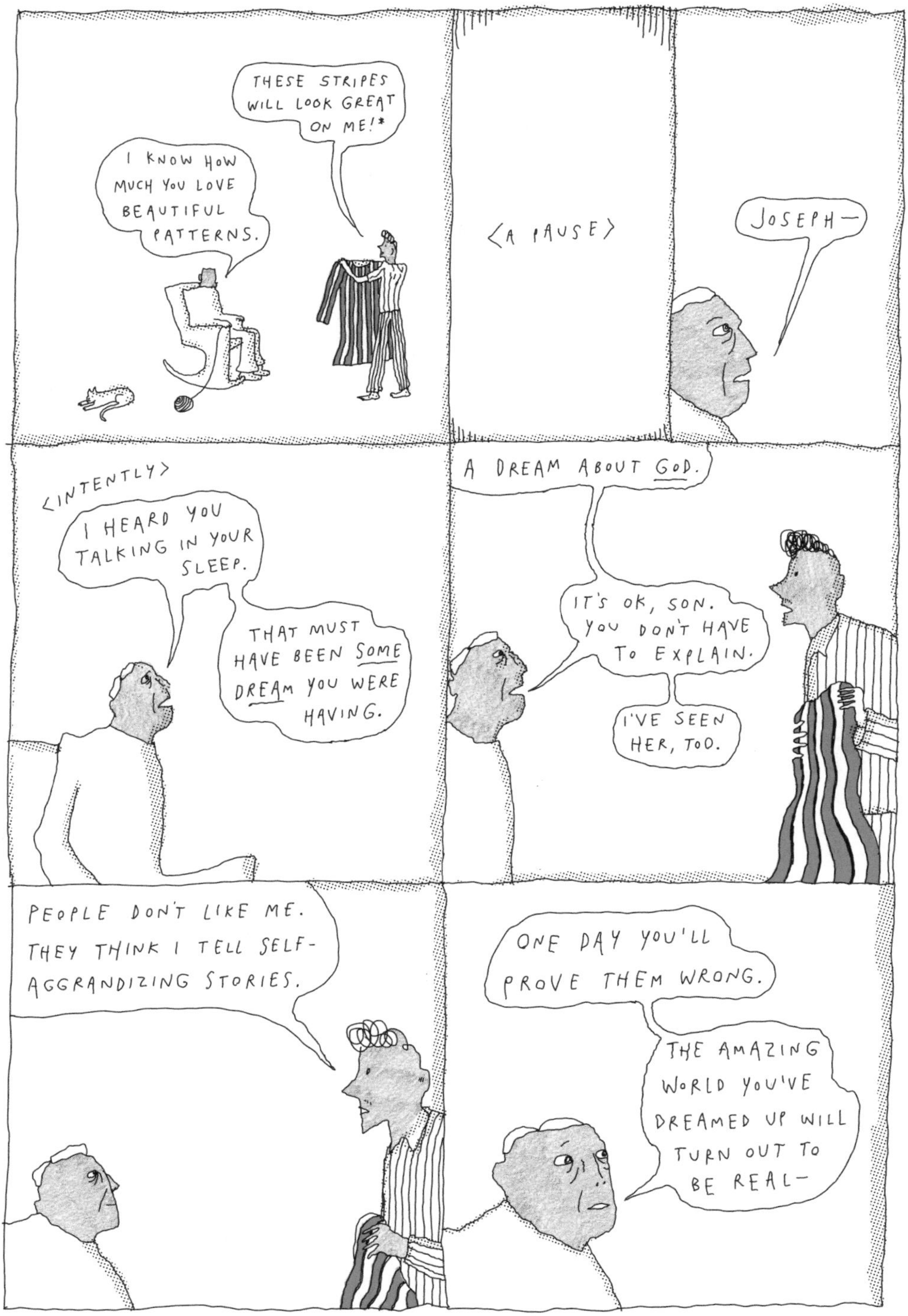
I KNOW HOW MUCH YOU LOVE BEAUTIFUL PATTERNS.
THESE STRIPES WILL LOOK GREAT ON ME!*
<A PAUSE>
JOSEPH—
<INTENTLY>
I HEARD YOU TALKING IN YOUR SLEEP.
THAT MUST HAVE BEEN SOME DREAM YOU WERE HAVING.
A DREAM ABOUT GOD.
IT'S OK, SON. YOU DON'T HAVE TO EXPLAIN.
I'VE SEEN HER, TOO.
PEOPLE DON'T LIKE ME. THEY THINK I TELL SELF-AGGRANDIZING STORIES.
ONE DAY YOU'LL PROVE THEM WRONG.
THE AMAZING WORLD YOU'VE DREAMED UP WILL TURN OUT TO BE REAL—

*JOSEPH WILL HAVE A BIT OF AN EGO.

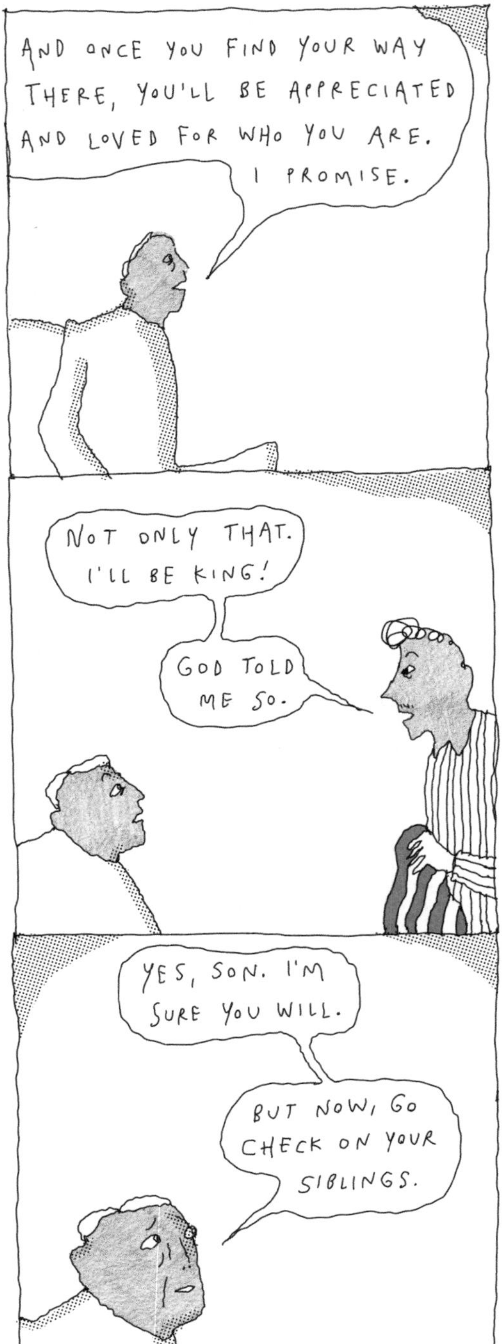
AND ONCE YOU FIND YOUR WAY THERE, YOU'LL BE APPRECIATED AND LOVED FOR WHO YOU ARE. I PROMISE.
NOT ONLY THAT. I'LL BE KING!
GOD TOLD ME SO.
YES, SON. I'M SURE YOU WILL.
BUT NOW, GO CHECK ON YOUR SIBLINGS.

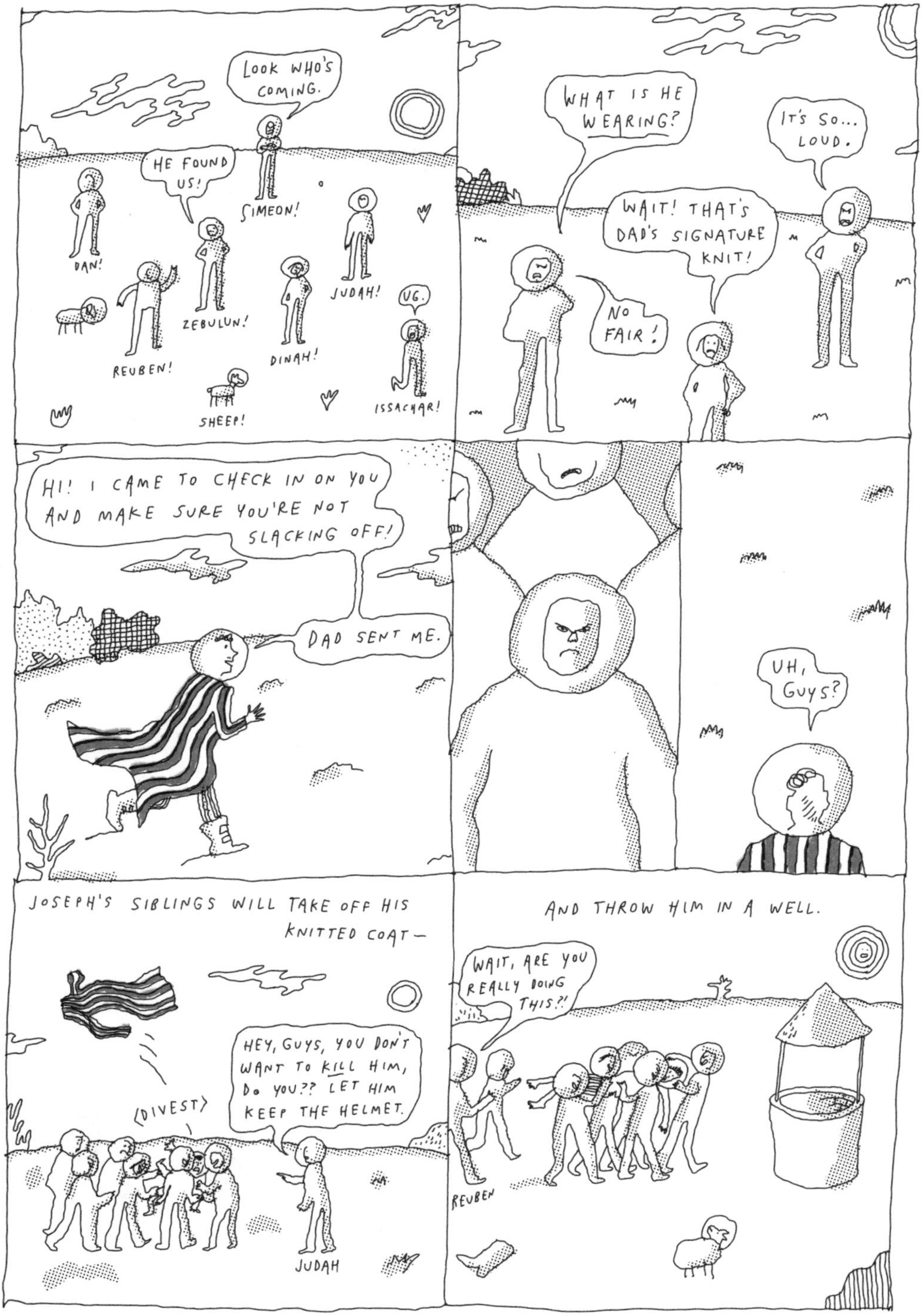
LOOK WHO'S COMING.
HE FOUND US!
SIMEON!
DAN!
ZEBULUN!
JUDAH!
UG.
REUBEN!
DINAH!
SHEEP!
ISSACHAR!
WHAT IS HE WEARING?
IT'S SO... LOUD.
WAIT! THAT'S DAD'S SIGNATURE KNIT!
NO FAIR!
HI! I CAME TO CHECK IN ON YOU AND MAKE SURE YOU'RE NOT SLACKING OFF!
DAD SENT ME.
UH, GUYS?
JOSEPH'S SIBLINGS WILL TAKE OFF HIS KNITTED COAT—
HEY, GUYS, YOU DON'T WANT TO KILL HIM, DO YOU?? LET HIM KEEP THE HELMET.
<DIVEST>
JUDAH
AND THROW HIM IN A WELL.
WAIT, ARE YOU REALLY DOING THIS?!
REUBEN

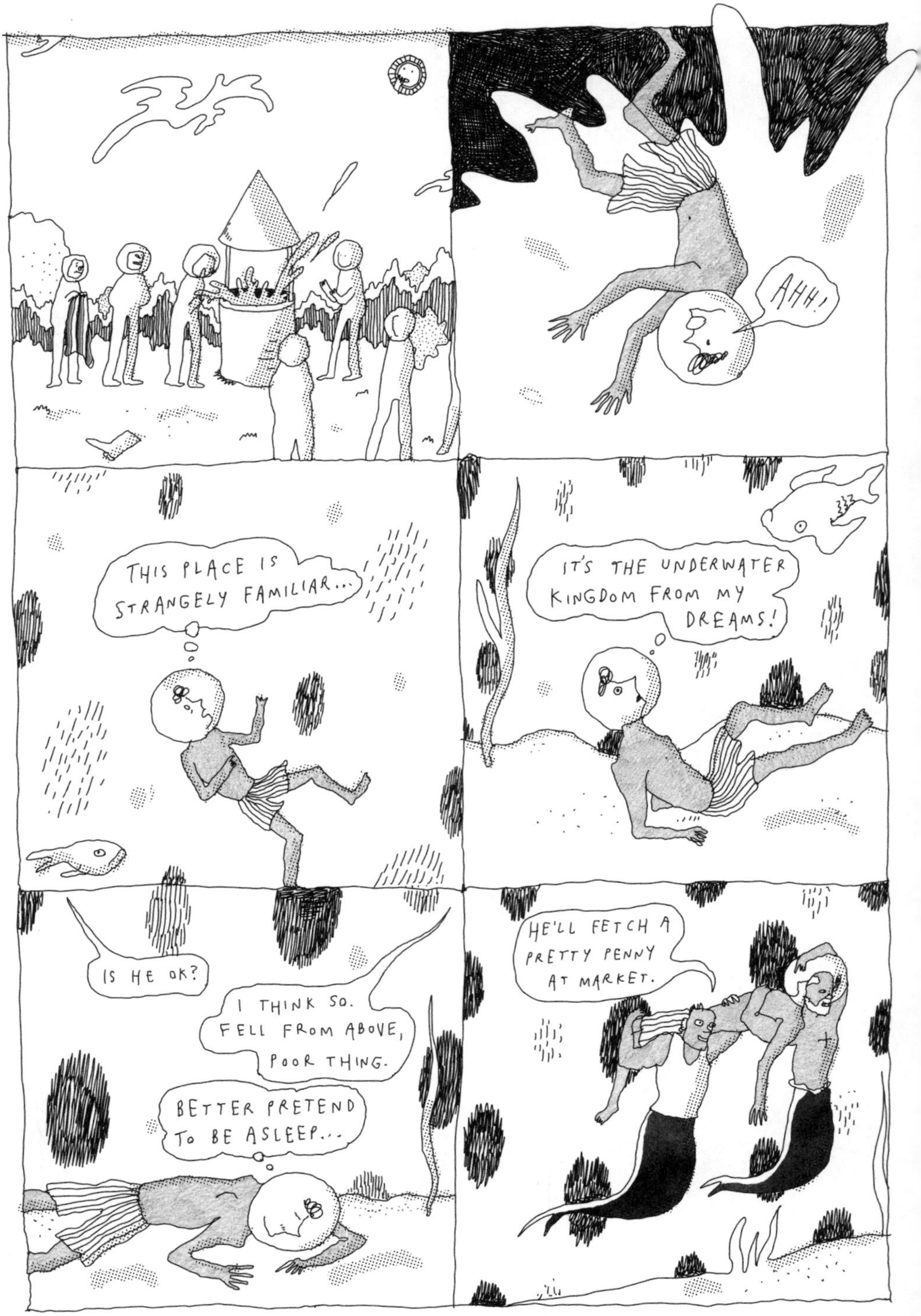
AHH!
THIS PLACE IS STRANGELY FAMILIAR...
IT'S THE UNDERWATER KINGDOM FROM MY DREAMS!
IS HE OK?
I THINK SO. FELL FROM ABOVE, POOR THING.
BETTER PRETEND TO BE ASLEEP...
HE'LL FETCH A PRETTY PENNY AT MARKET.

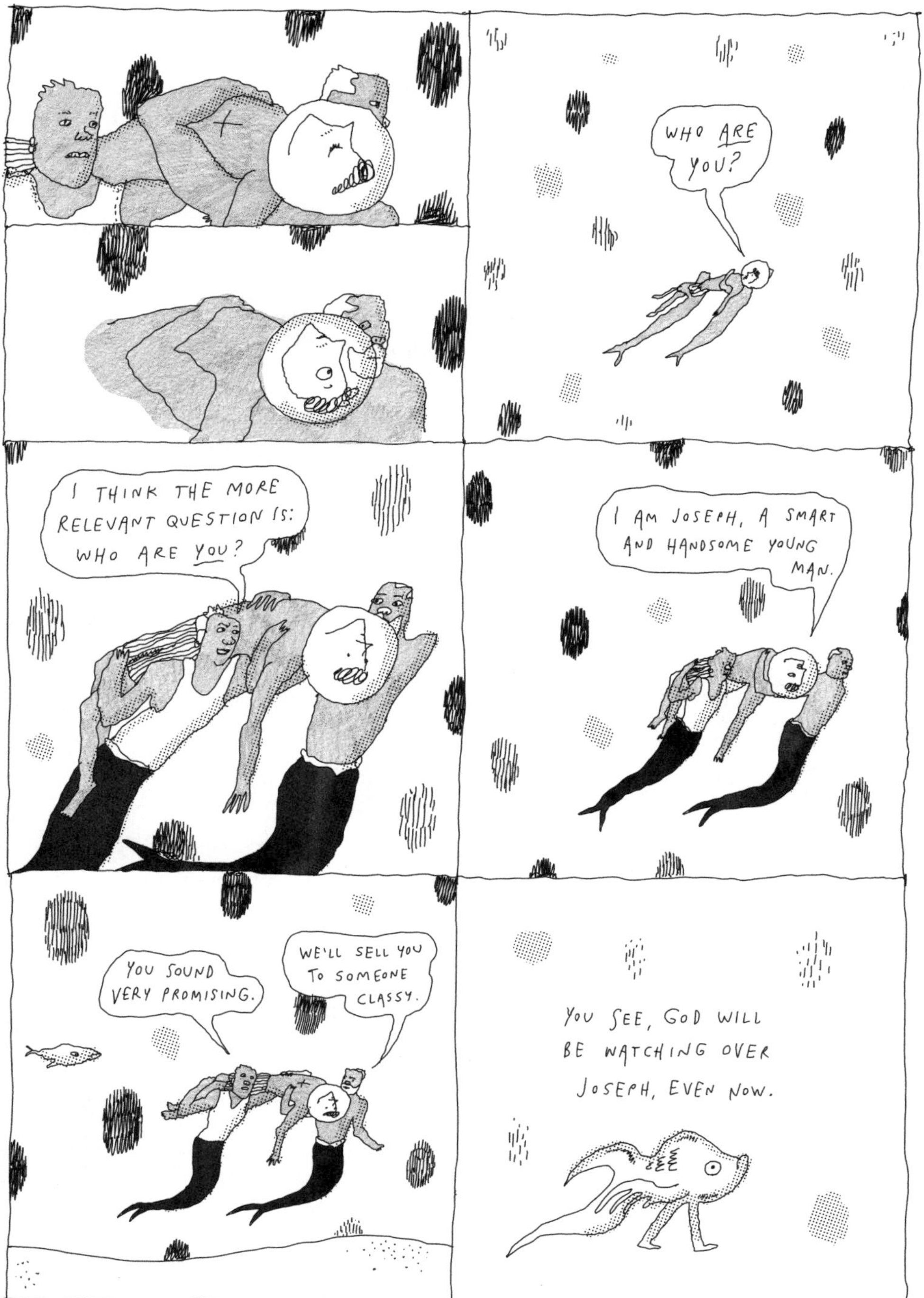
WHO ARE YOU?
I THINK THE MORE RELEVANT QUESTION IS: WHO ARE YOU?
I AM JOSEPH, A SMART AND HANDSOME YOUNG MAN.
YOU SOUND VERY PROMISING.
WE'LL SELL YOU TO SOMEONE CLASSY.
YOU SEE, GOD WILL BE WATCHING OVER JOSEPH, EVEN NOW.

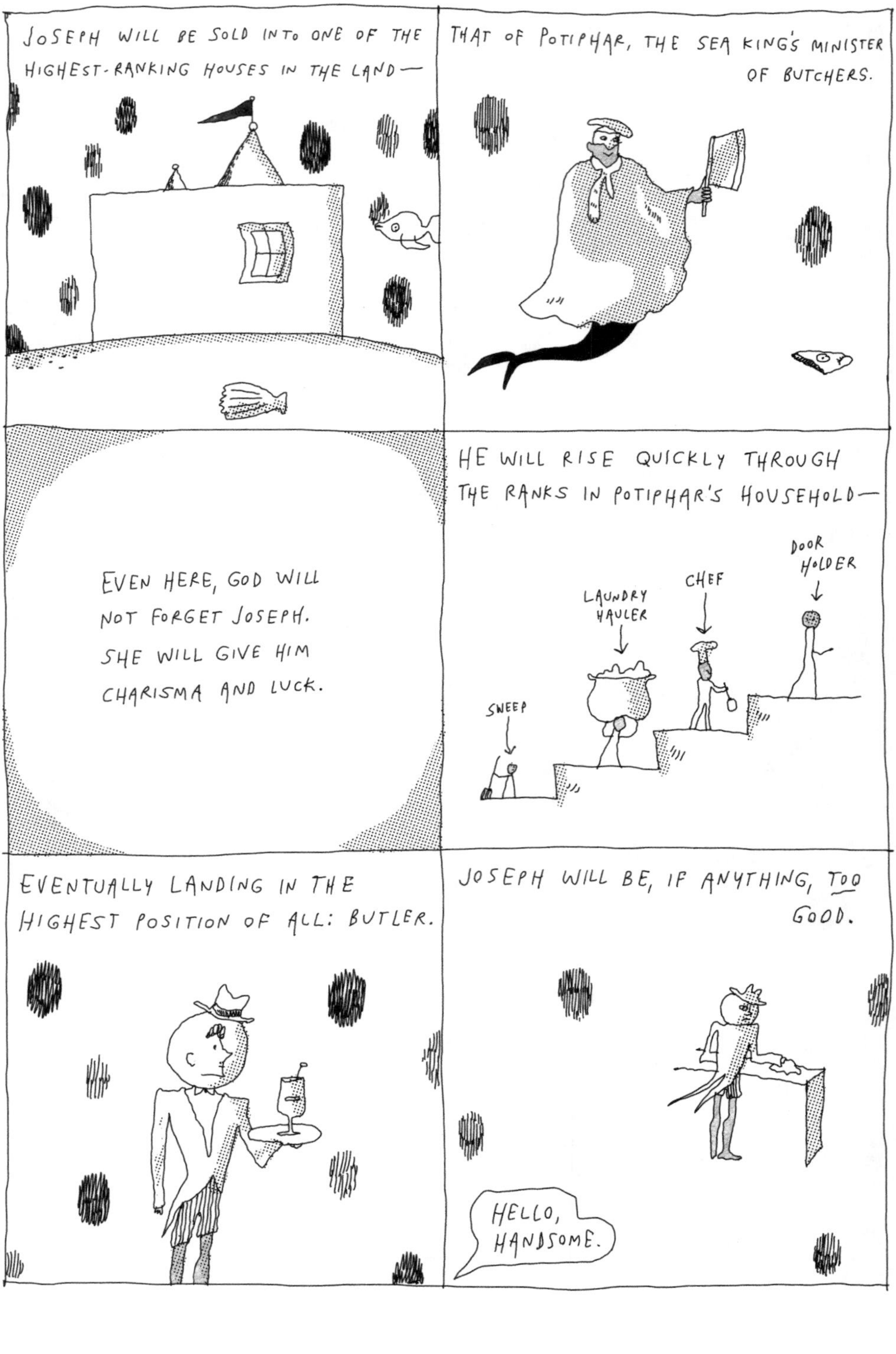

JOSEPH WILL BE SOLD INTO ONE OF THE HIGHEST-RANKING HOUSES IN THE LAND—
THAT OF POTIPHAR, THE SEA KING'S MINISTER OF BUTCHERS.
EVEN HERE, GOD WILL NOT FORGET JOSEPH. SHE WILL GIVE HIM CHARISMA AND LUCK.
HE WILL RISE QUICKLY THROUGH THE RANKS IN POTIPHAR'S HOUSEHOLD—
DOOR HOLDER
CHEF
LAUNDRY HAULER
SWEEP
EVENTUALLY LANDING IN THE HIGHEST POSITION OF ALL: BUTLER.
JOSEPH WILL BE, IF ANYTHING, TOO GOOD.
HELLO, HANDSOME.

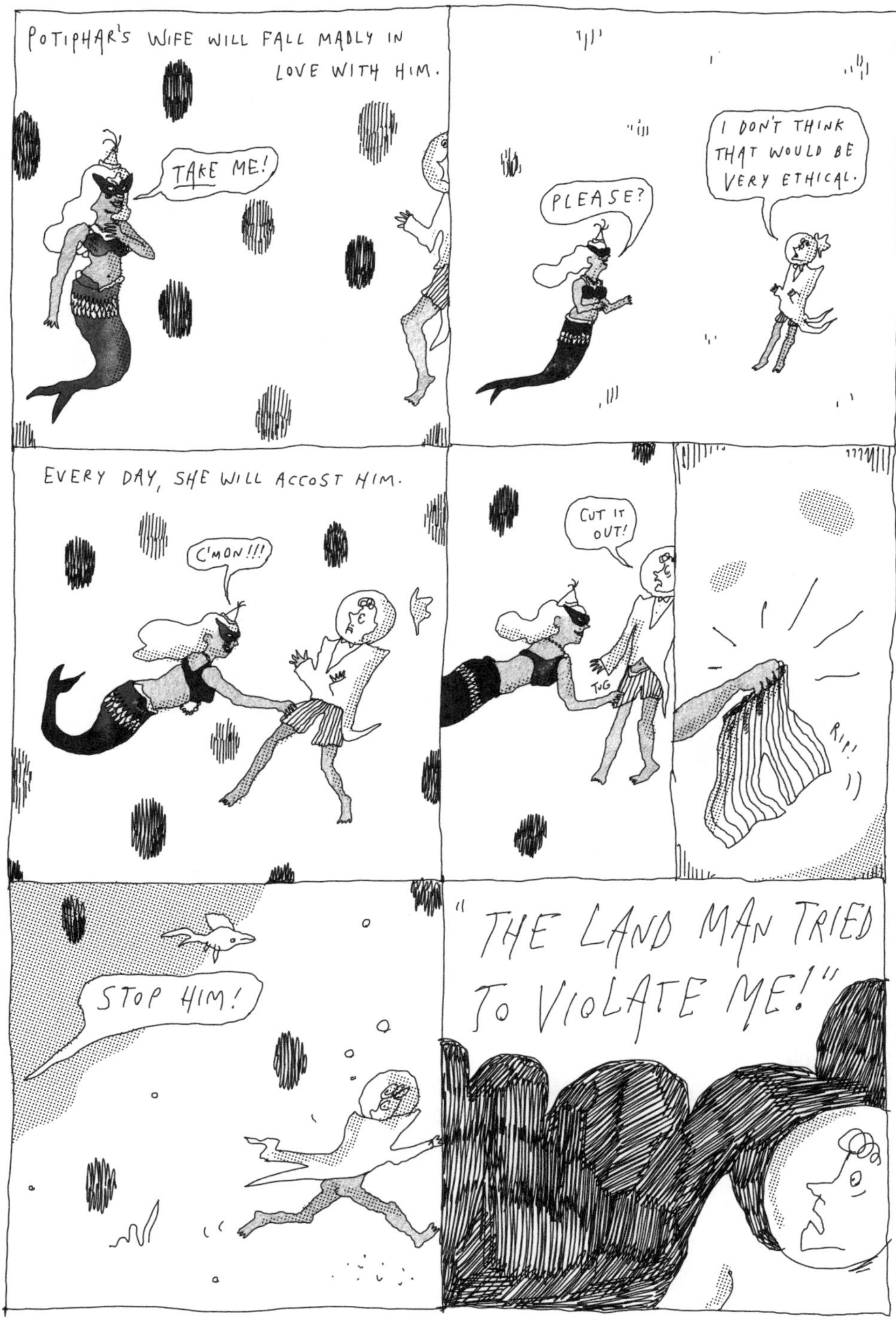
POTIPHAR'S WIFE WILL FALL MADLY IN LOVE WITH HIM.
TAKE ME!
PLEASE?
I DON'T THINK THAT WOULD BE VERY ETHICAL.
EVERY DAY, SHE WILL ACCOST HIM.
C'MON!!!
CUT IT OUT!
TUG
RIP!
STOP HIM!
"THE LAND MAN TRIED TO VIOLATE ME!"

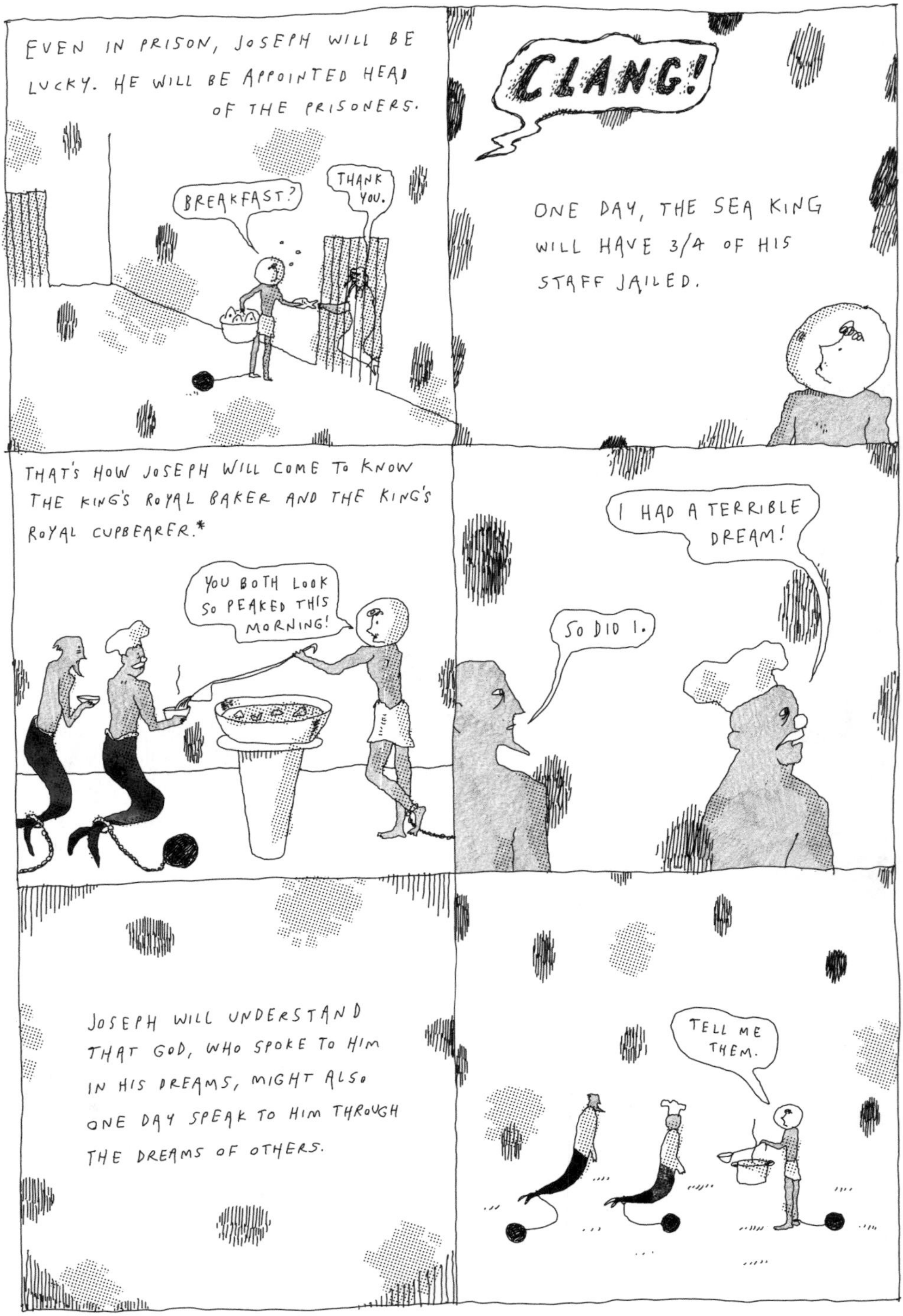
EVEN IN PRISON, JOSEPH WILL BE LUCKY. HE WILL BE APPOINTED HEAD OF THE PRISONERS.
BREAKFAST?
THANK YOU.
CLANG!
ONE DAY, THE SEA KING WILL HAVE 3/4 OF HIS STAFF JAILED.
THAT'S HOW JOSEPH WILL COME TO KNOW THE KING'S ROYAL BAKER AND THE KING'S ROYAL CUPBEARER.*
YOU BOTH LOOK SO PEAKED THIS MORNING!
I HAD A TERRIBLE DREAM!
SO DID I.
JOSEPH WILL UNDERSTAND THAT GOD, WHO SPOKE TO HIM IN HIS DREAMS, MIGHT ALSO ONE DAY SPEAK TO HIM THROUGH THE DREAMS OF OTHERS.
TELL ME THEM.

*WAS THIS A THING?**
**YES.

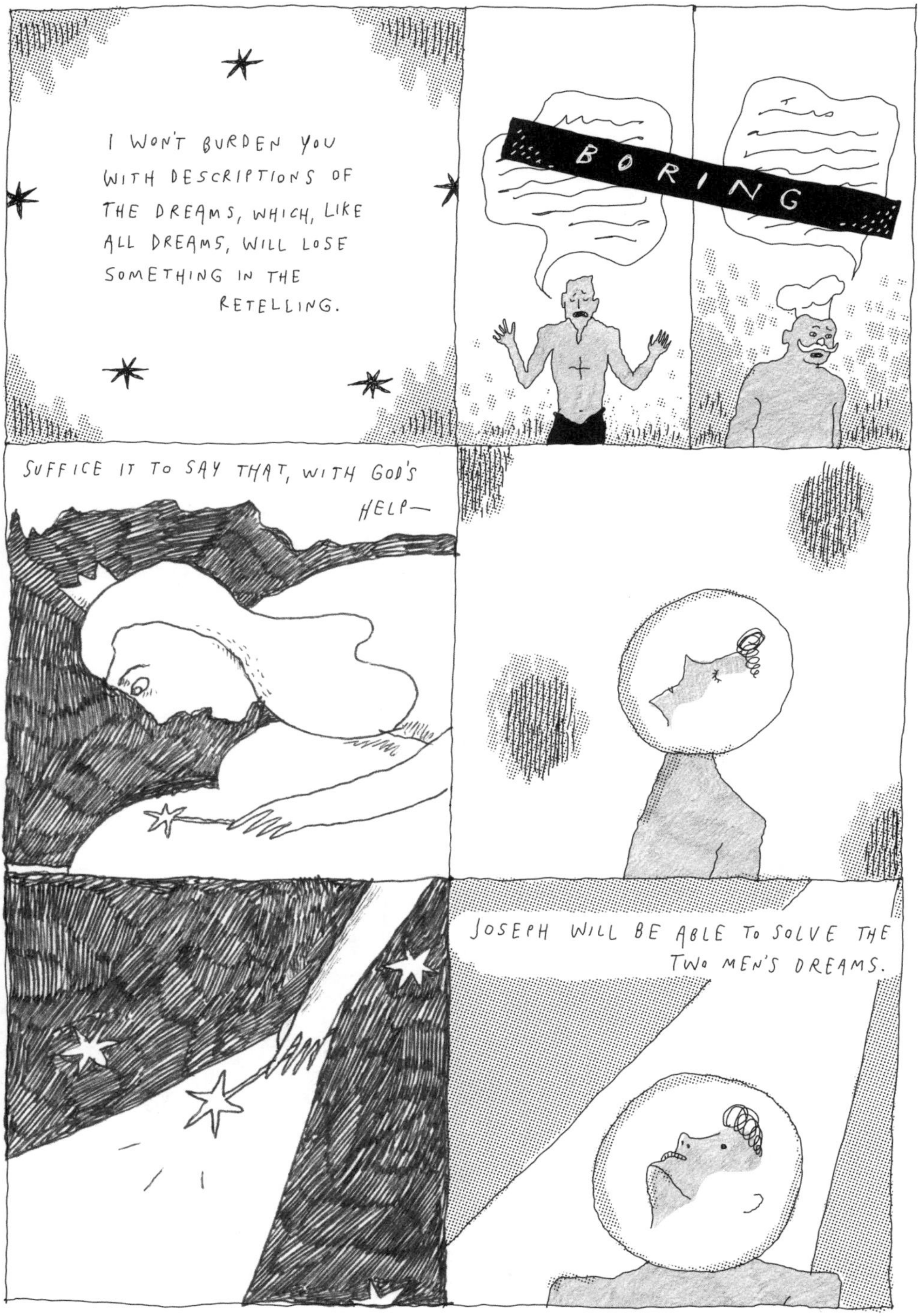
I WON'T BURDEN YOU WITH DESCRIPTIONS OF THE DREAMS, WHICH, LIKE ALL DREAMS, WILL LOSE SOMETHING IN THE RETELLING.
BORING
SUFFICE IT TO SAY THAT, WITH GOD'S HELP—
JOSEPH WILL BE ABLE TO SOLVE THE TWO MEN'S DREAMS.

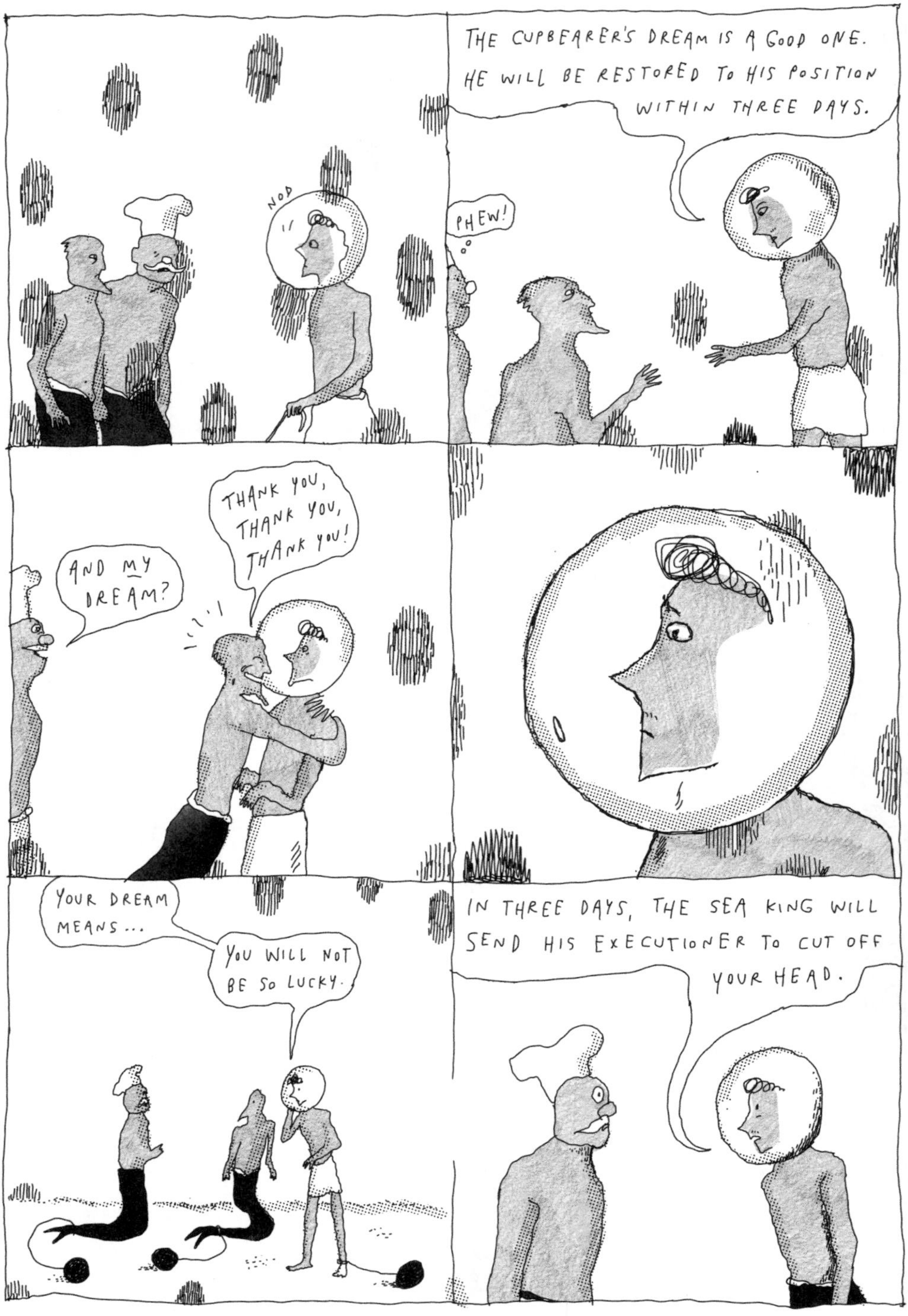
NOD
THE CUPBEARER'S DREAM IS A GOOD ONE. HE WILL BE RESTORED TO HIS POSITION WITHIN THREE DAYS.
PHEW!
THANK YOU, THANK YOU, THANK YOU!
AND MY DREAM?
YOUR DREAM MEANS...
YOU WILL NOT BE SO LUCKY.
IN THREE DAYS, THE SEA KING WILL SEND HIS EXECUTIONER TO CUT OFF YOUR HEAD.

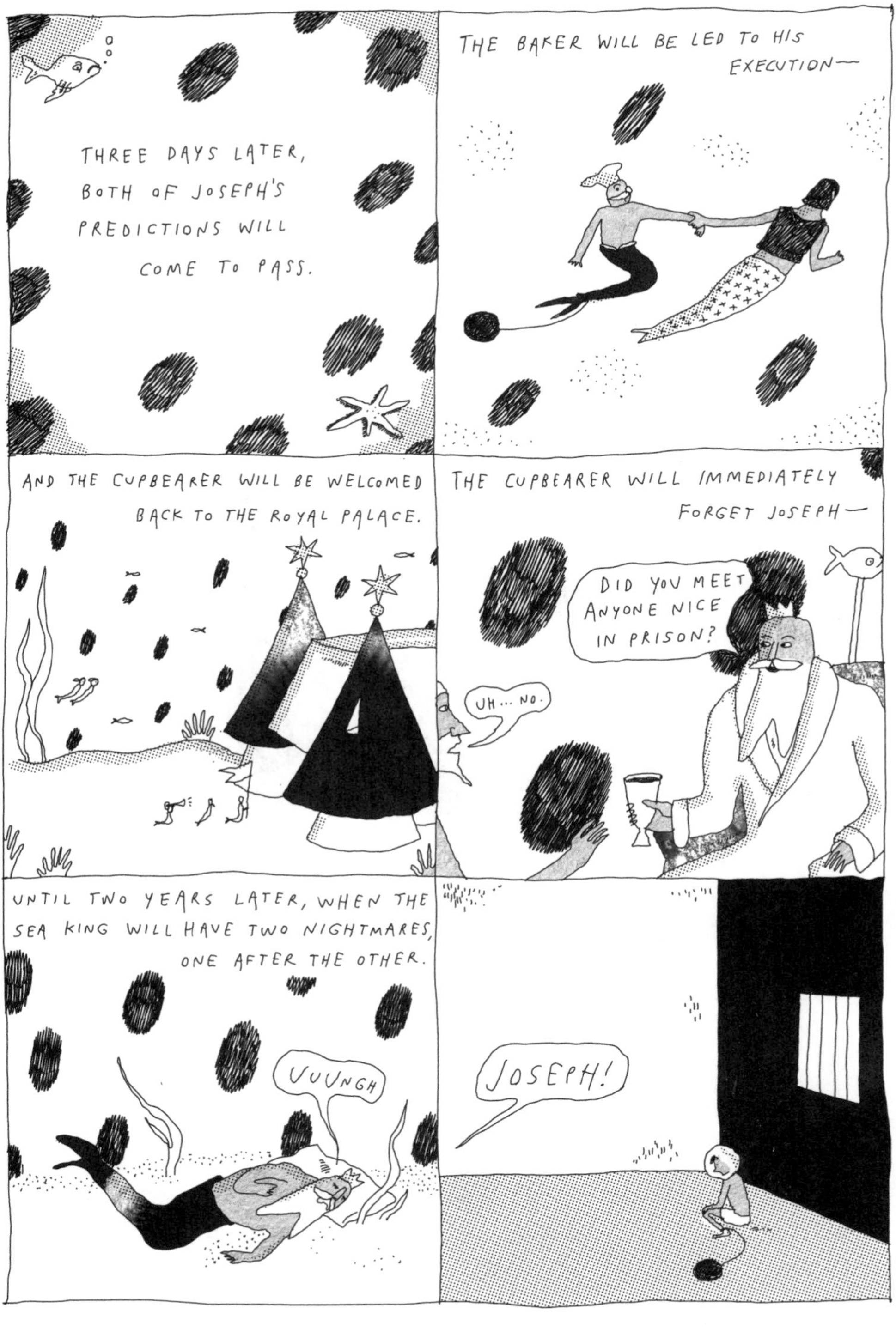
THREE DAYS LATER, BOTH OF JOSEPH'S PREDICTIONS WILL COME TO PASS.
THE BAKER WILL BE LED TO HIS EXECUTION—
AND THE CUPBEARER WILL BE WELCOMED BACK TO THE ROYAL PALACE.
THE CUPBEARER WILL IMMEDIATELY FORGET JOSEPH—
DID YOU MEET ANYONE NICE IN PRISON?
UH... NO.
UNTIL TWO YEARS LATER, WHEN THE SEA KING WILL HAVE TWO NIGHTMARES, ONE AFTER THE OTHER.
VUUNGH
JOSEPH!

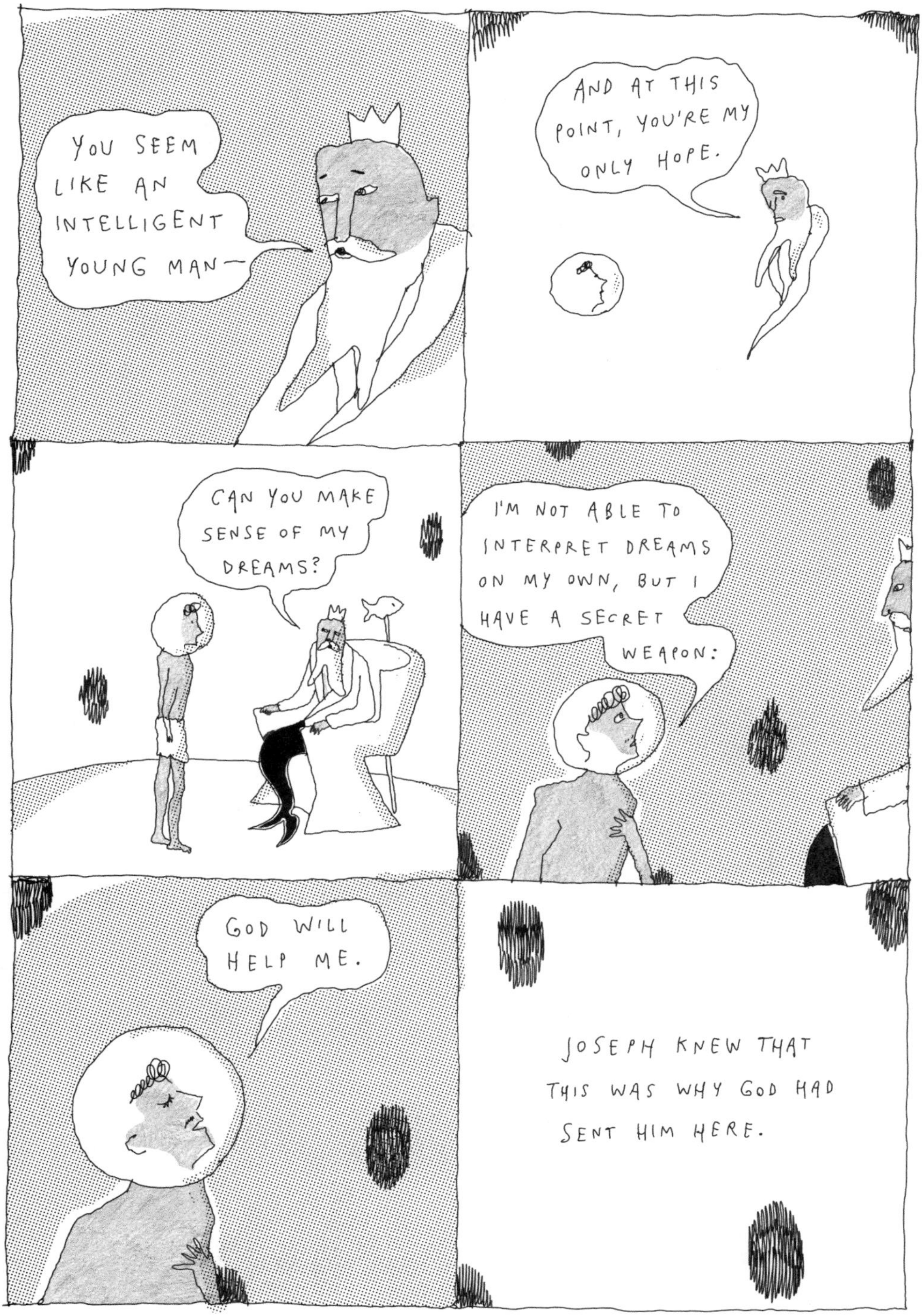
YOU SEEM LIKE AN INTELLIGENT YOUNG MAN—
AND AT THIS POINT, YOU'RE MY ONLY HOPE.
CAN YOU MAKE SENSE OF MY DREAMS?
I'M NOT ABLE TO INTERPRET DREAMS ON MY OWN, BUT I HAVE A SECRET WEAPON:
GOD WILL HELP ME.
JOSEPH KNEW THAT THIS WAS WHY GOD HAD SENT HIM HERE.

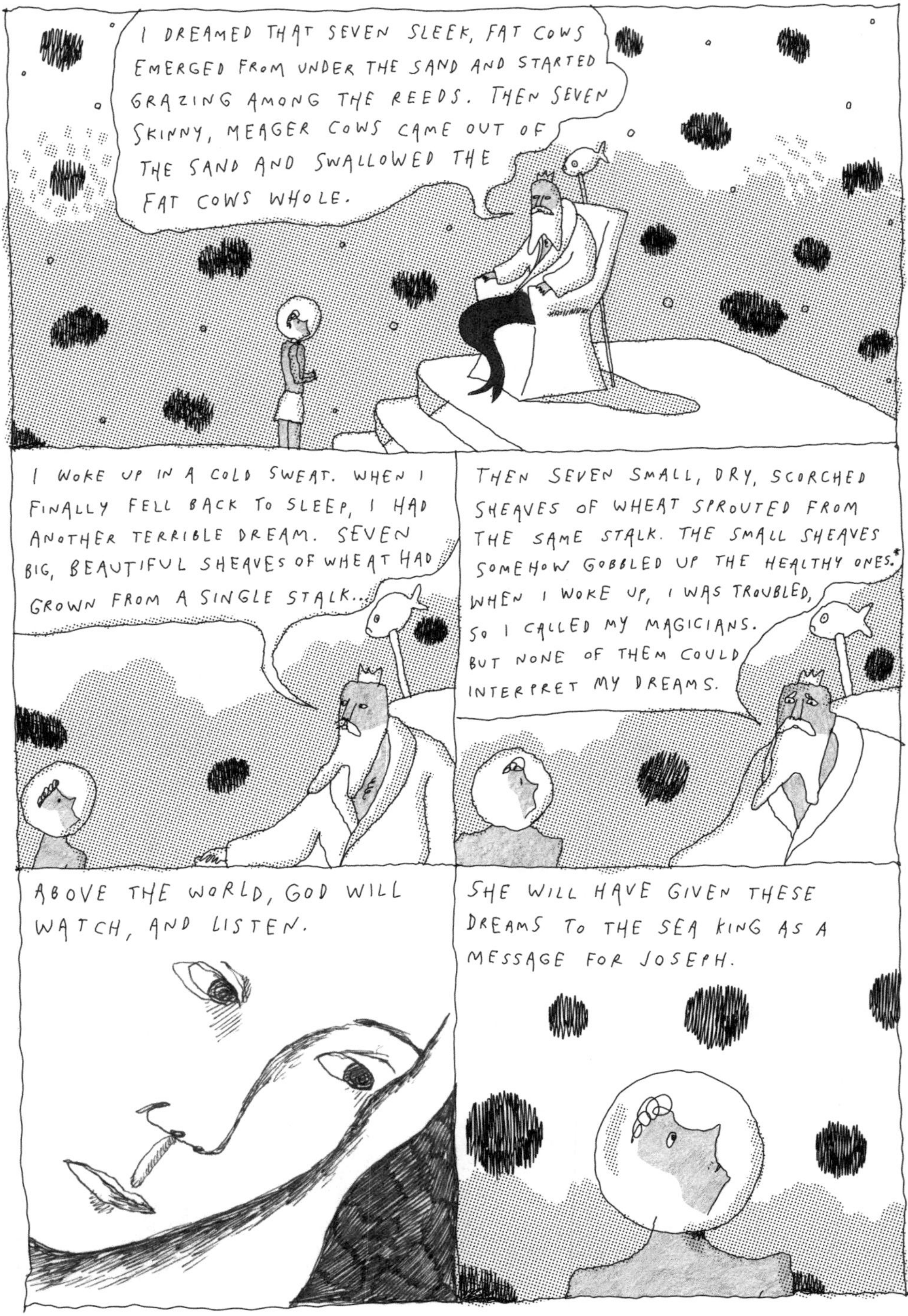
I DREAMED THAT SEVEN SLEEK, FAT COWS EMERGED FROM UNDER THE SAND AND STARTED GRAZING AMONG THE REEDS. THEN SEVEN SKINNY, MEAGER COWS CAME OUT OF THE SAND AND SWALLOWED THE FAT COWS WHOLE.
I WOKE UP IN A COLD SWEAT. WHEN I FINALLY FELL BACK TO SLEEP, I HAD ANOTHER TERRIBLE DREAM. SEVEN BIG, BEAUTIFUL SHEAVES OF WHEAT HAD GROWN FROM A SINGLE STALK...
THEN SEVEN SMALL, DRY, SCORCHED SHEAVES OF WHEAT SPROUTED FROM THE SAME STALK. THE SMALL SHEAVES SOMEHOW GOBBLED UP THE HEALTHY ONES.* WHEN I WOKE UP, I WAS TROUBLED, SO I CALLED MY MAGICIANS. BUT NONE OF THEM COULD INTERPRET MY DREAMS.
ABOVE THE WORLD, GOD WILL WATCH, AND LISTEN.
SHE WILL HAVE GIVEN THESE DREAMS TO THE SEA KING AS A MESSAGE FOR JOSEPH.

* SOOOOOOOO BORING, SORRY.

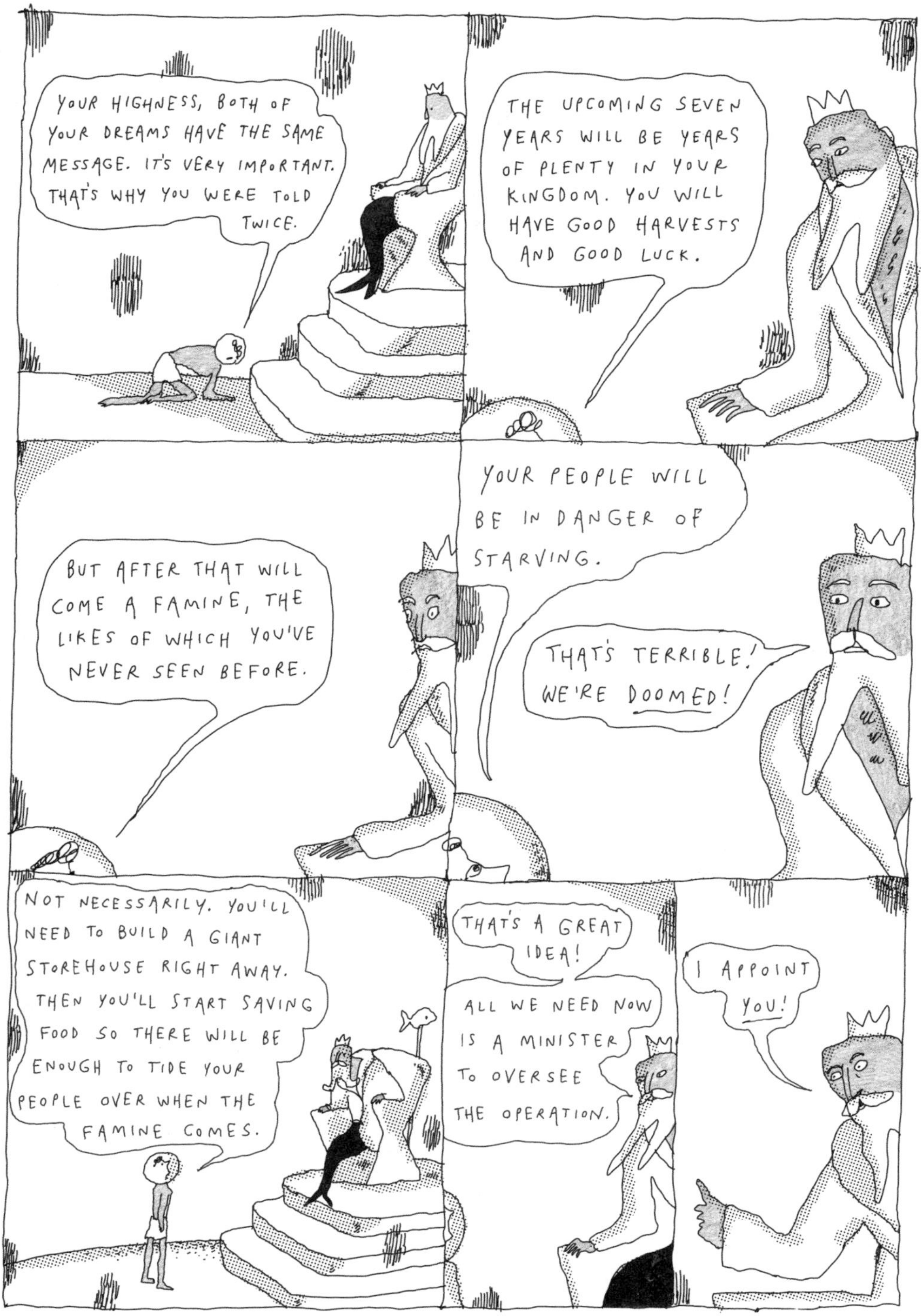
YOUR HIGHNESS, BOTH OF YOUR DREAMS HAVE THE SAME MESSAGE. IT'S VERY IMPORTANT. THAT'S WHY YOU WERE TOLD TWICE.
THE UPCOMING SEVEN YEARS WILL BE YEARS OF PLENTY IN YOUR KINGDOM. YOU WILL HAVE GOOD HARVESTS AND GOOD LUCK.
BUT AFTER THAT WILL COME A FAMINE, THE LIKES OF WHICH YOU'VE NEVER SEEN BEFORE.
YOUR PEOPLE WILL BE IN DANGER OF STARVING.
THAT'S TERRIBLE! WE'RE DOOMED!
NOT NECESSARILY. YOU'LL NEED TO BUILD A GIANT STOREHOUSE RIGHT AWAY. THEN YOU'LL START SAVING FOOD SO THERE WILL BE ENOUGH TO TIDE YOUR PEOPLE OVER WHEN THE FAMINE COMES.
THAT'S A GREAT IDEA!
ALL WE NEED NOW IS A MINISTER TO OVERSEE THE OPERATION.
I APPOINT YOU!

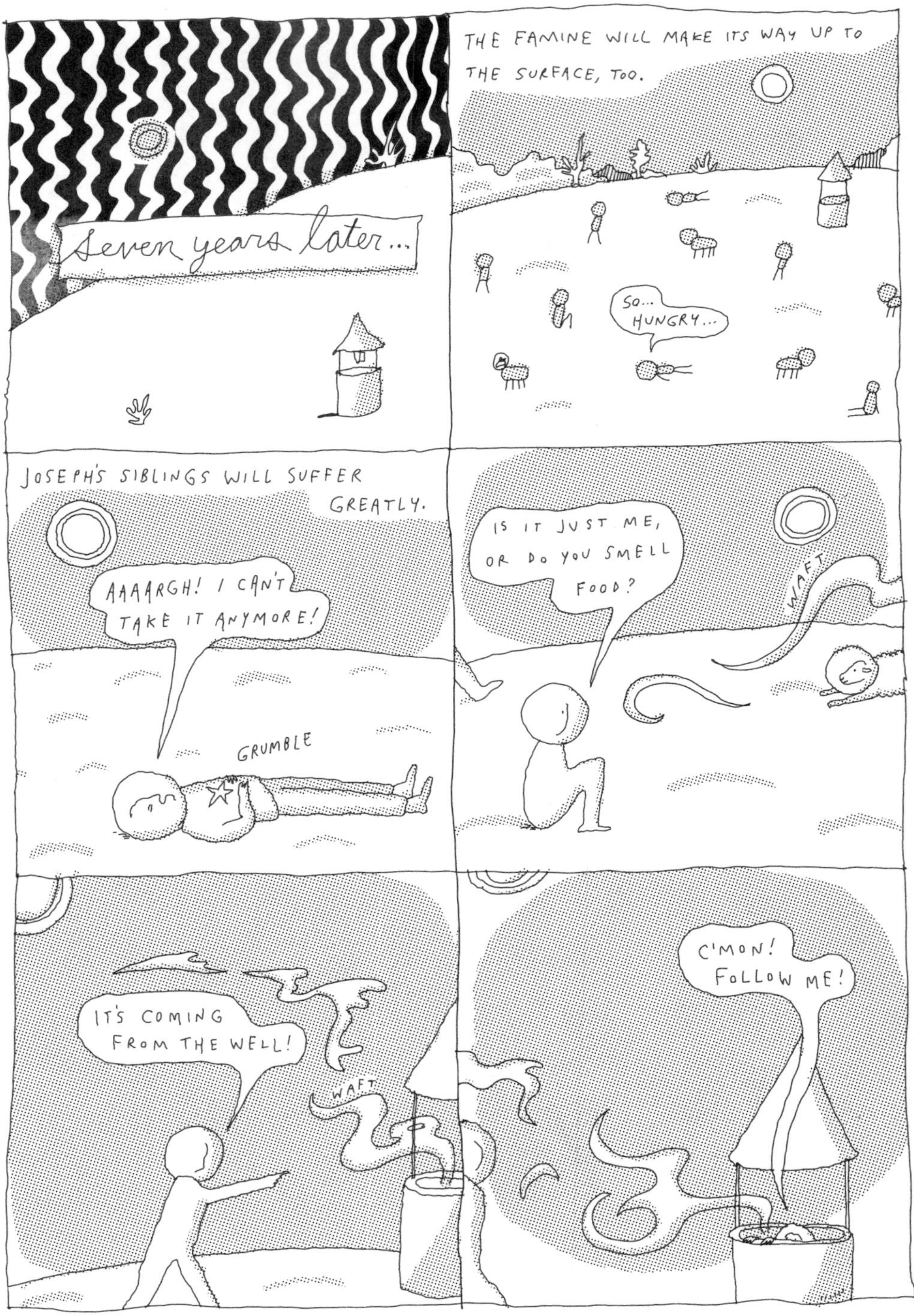
Seven years later...
THE FAMINE WILL MAKE ITS WAY UP TO THE SURFACE, TOO.
SO... HUNGRY...
JOSEPH'S SIBLINGS WILL SUFFER GREATLY.
AAAARGH! I CAN'T TAKE IT ANYMORE!
GRUMBLE
IS IT JUST ME, OR DO YOU SMELL FOOD?
WAFT
IT'S COMING FROM THE WELL!
WAFT
C'MON! FOLLOW ME!

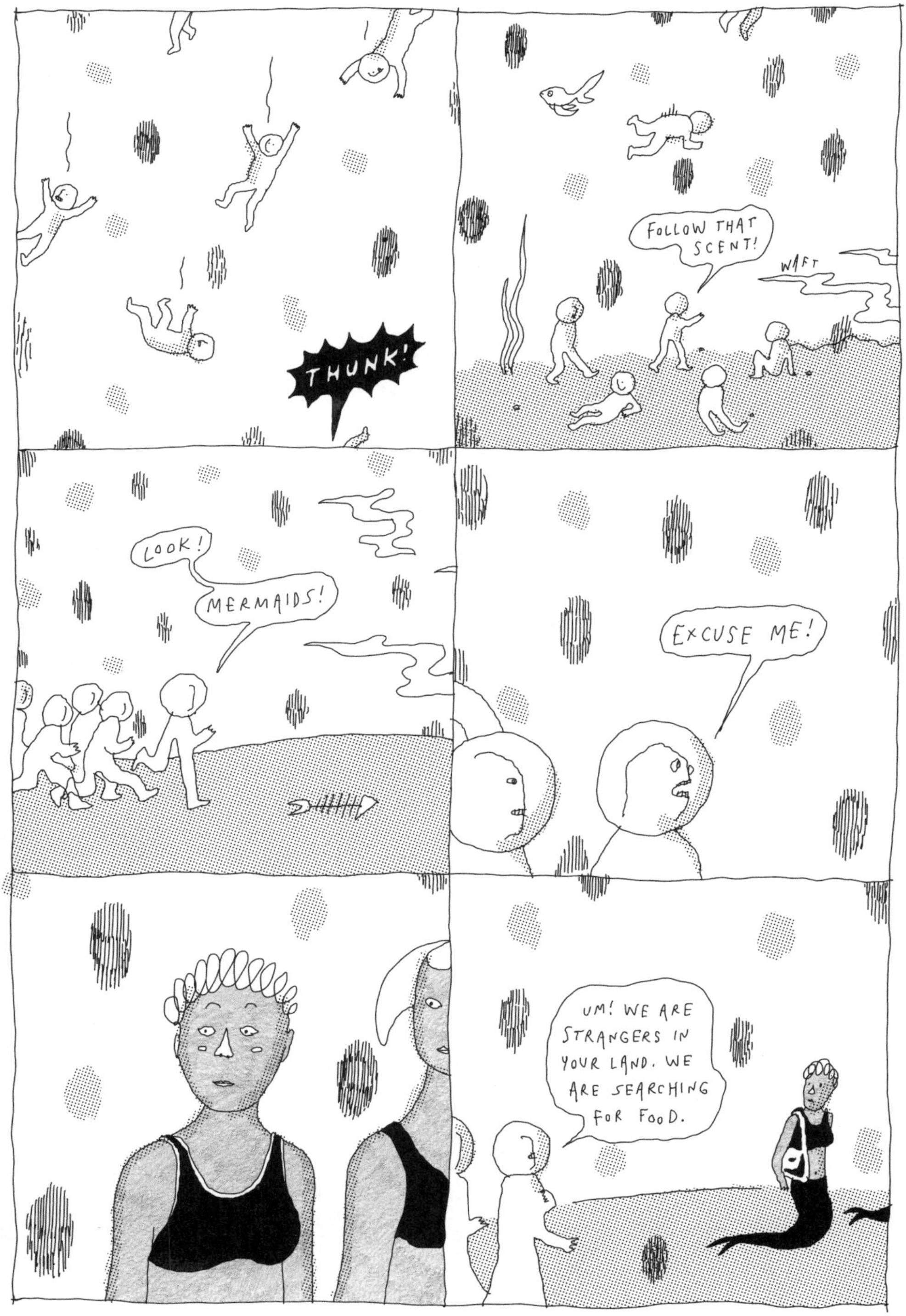
THUNK!
FOLLOW THAT SCENT!
WAFT
LOOK!
MERMAIDS!
EXCUSE ME!
UM! WE ARE STRANGERS IN YOUR LAND. WE ARE SEARCHING FOR FOOD.

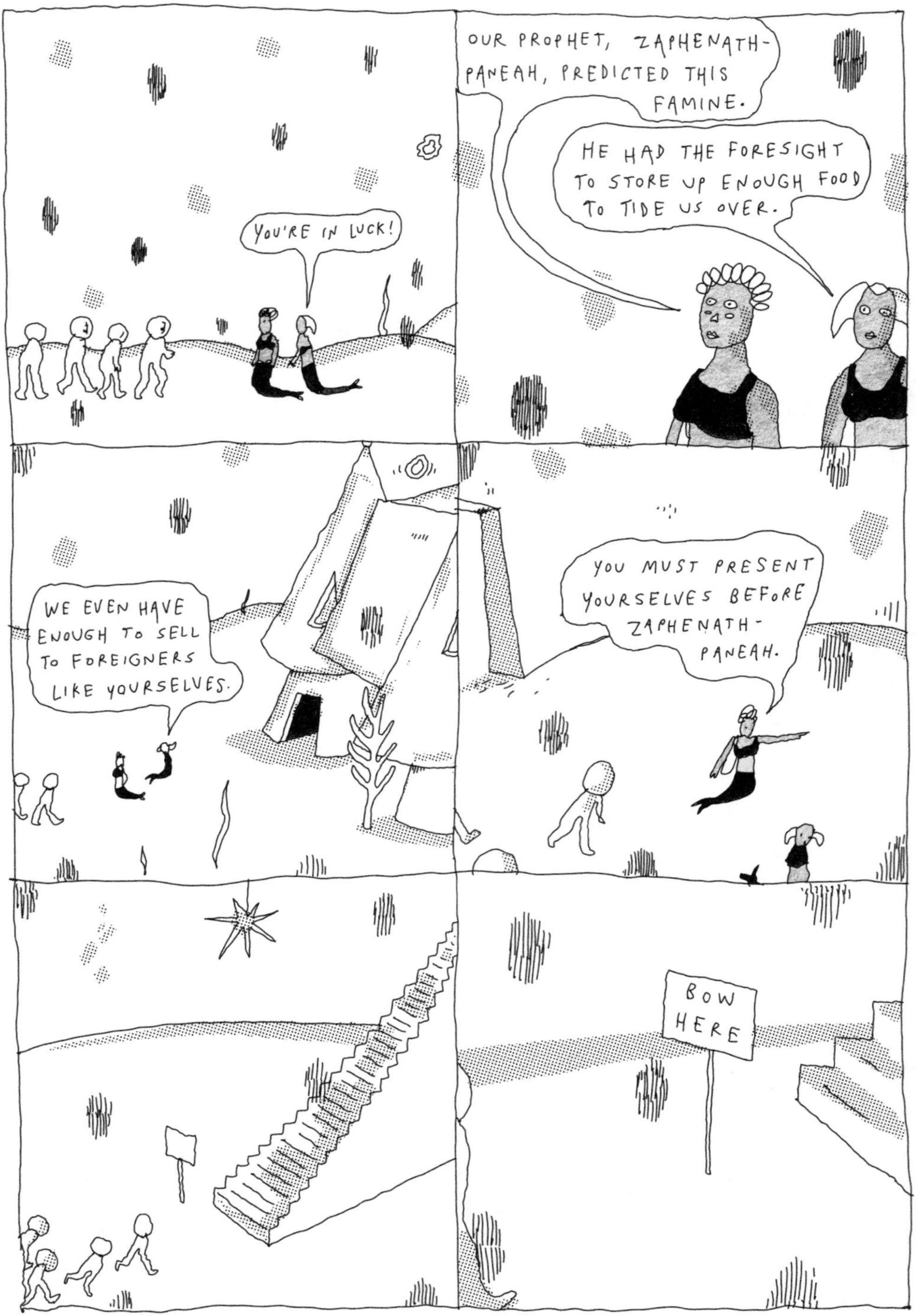
YOU'RE IN LUCK!
OUR PROPHET, ZAPHENATH-PANEAH, PREDICTED THIS FAMINE.
HE HAD THE FORESIGHT TO STORE UP ENOUGH FOOD TO TIDE US OVER.
WE EVEN HAVE ENOUGH TO SELL TO FOREIGNERS LIKE YOURSELVES.
YOU MUST PRESENT YOURSELVES BEFORE ZAPHENATH-PANEAH.
BOW HERE

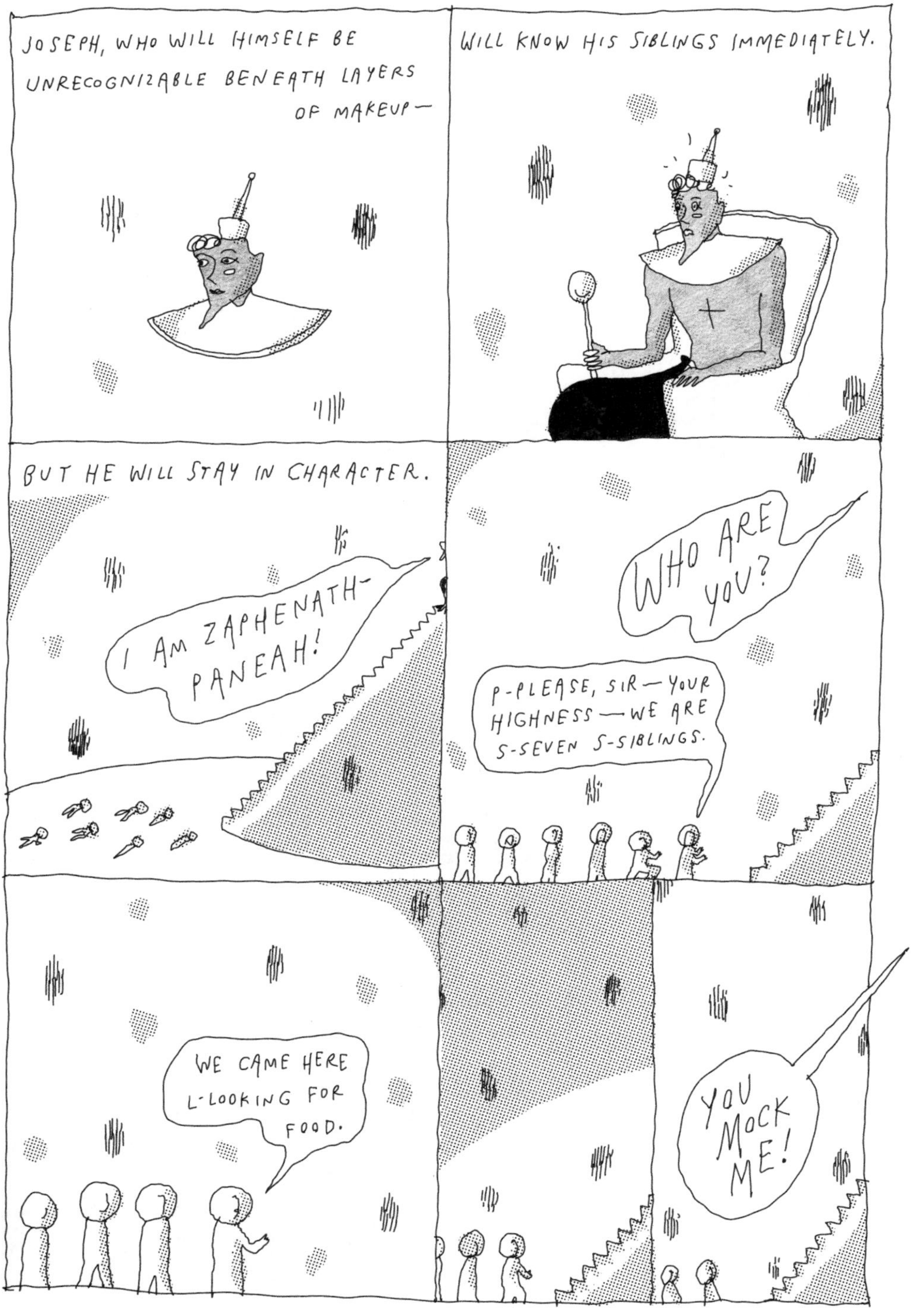
JOSEPH, WHO WILL HIMSELF BE UNRECOGNIZABLE BENEATH LAYERS OF MAKEUP—
WILL KNOW HIS SIBLINGS IMMEDIATELY.
BUT HE WILL STAY IN CHARACTER.
I AM ZAPHENATH-PANEAH!
WHO ARE YOU?
P-PLEASE, SIR—YOUR HIGHNESS—WE ARE S-SEVEN S-SIBLINGS.
WE CAME HERE L-LOOKING FOR FOOD.
YOU MOCK ME!

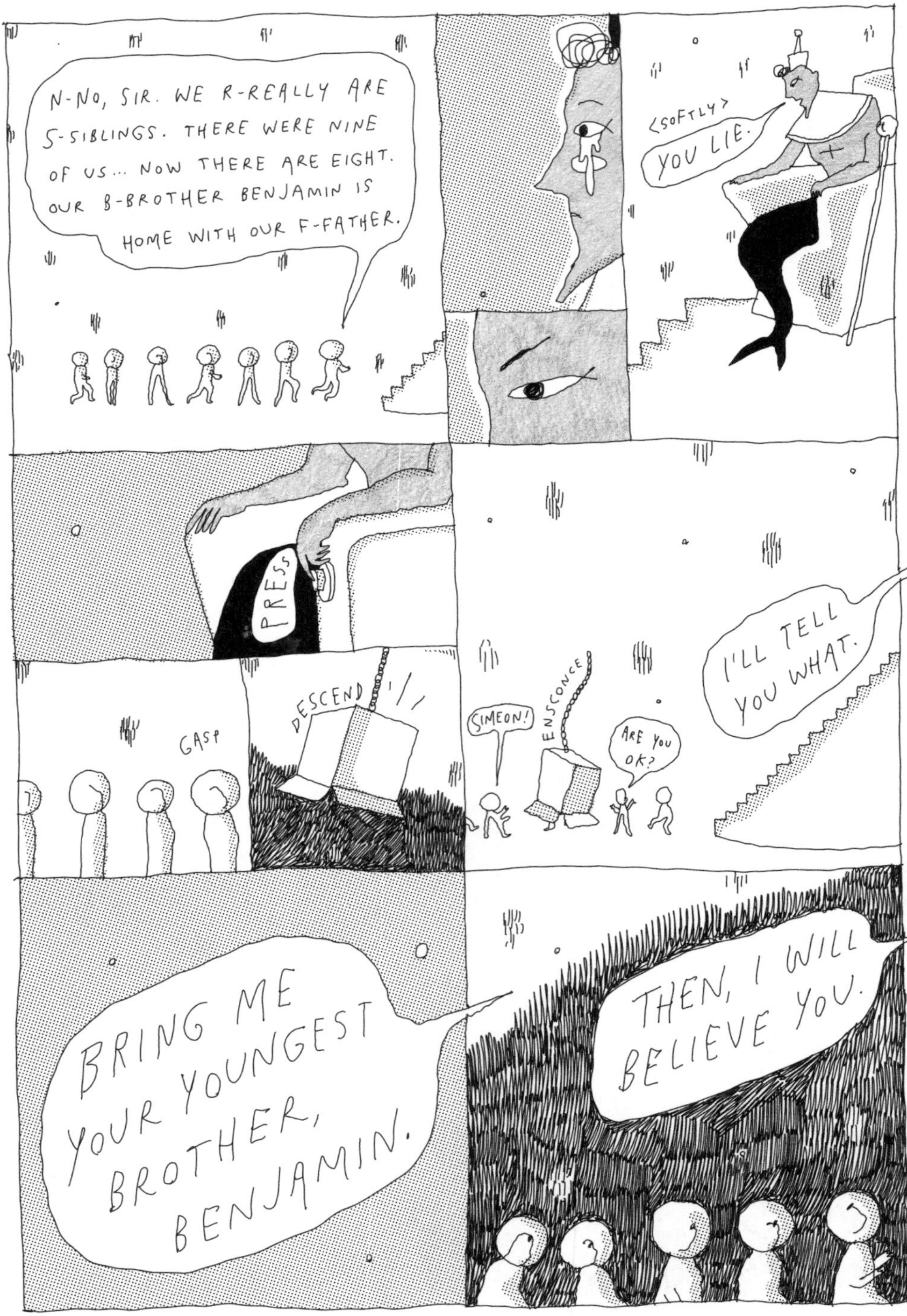
N-NO, SIR. WE R-REALLY ARE S-SIBLINGS. THERE WERE NINE OF US... NOW THERE ARE EIGHT. OUR B-BROTHER BENJAMIN IS HOME WITH OUR F-FATHER.
<SOFTLY>
YOU LIE.
PRESS
GASP
DESCEND
SIMEON!
ENSCONCE
ARE YOU OK?
I'LL TELL YOU WHAT.
BRING ME YOUR YOUNGEST BROTHER, BENJAMIN.
THEN, I WILL BELIEVE YOU.

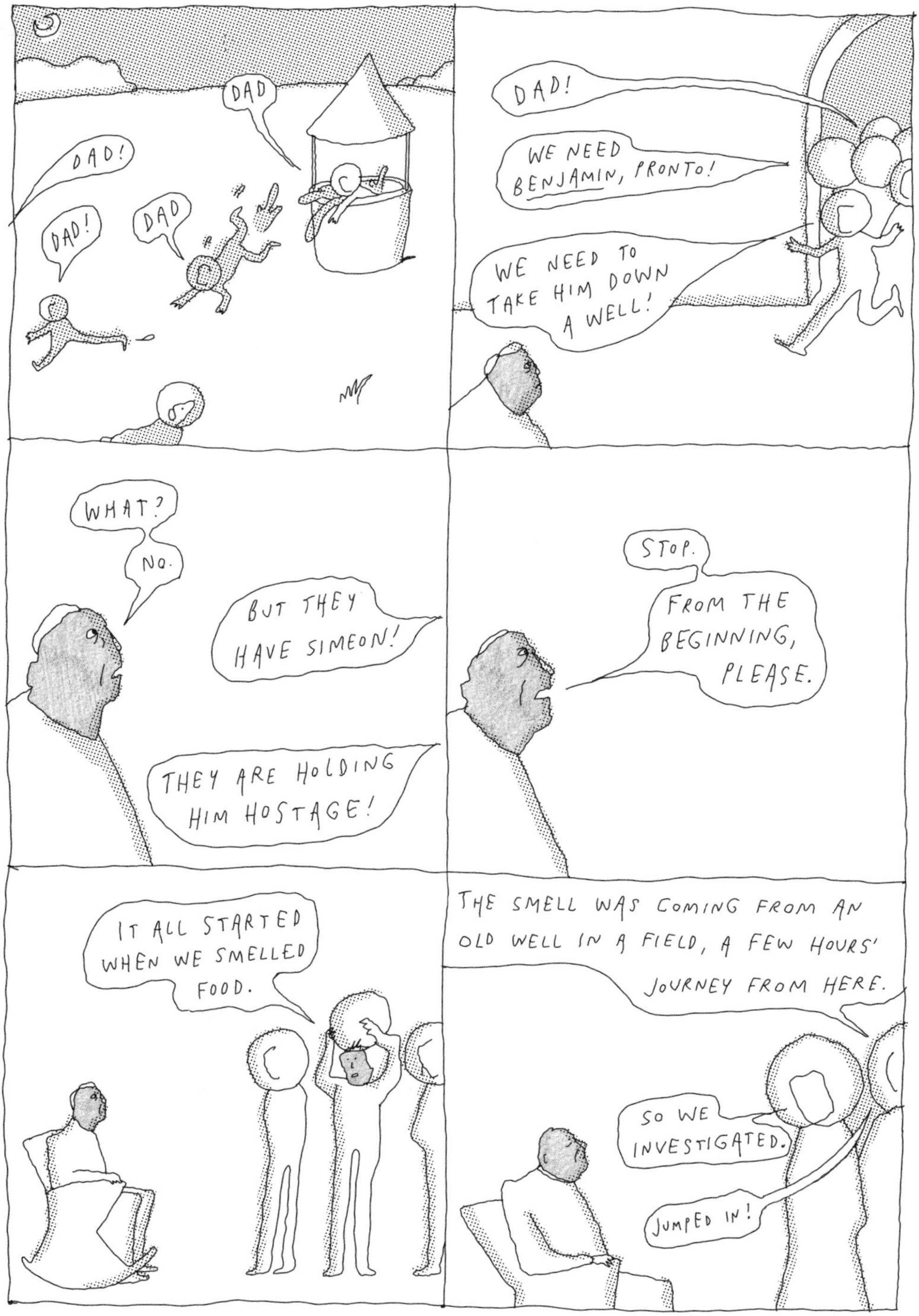
DAD
DAD!
DAD!
DAD
DAD!
WE NEED BENJAMIN, PRONTO!
WE NEED TO TAKE HIM DOWN A WELL!
WHAT?
NO.
BUT THEY HAVE SIMEON!
THEY ARE HOLDING HIM HOSTAGE!
STOP.
FROM THE BEGINNING, PLEASE.
IT ALL STARTED WHEN WE SMELLED FOOD.
THE SMELL WAS COMING FROM AN OLD WELL IN A FIELD, A FEW HOURS' JOURNEY FROM HERE.
SO WE INVESTIGATED.
JUMPED IN!

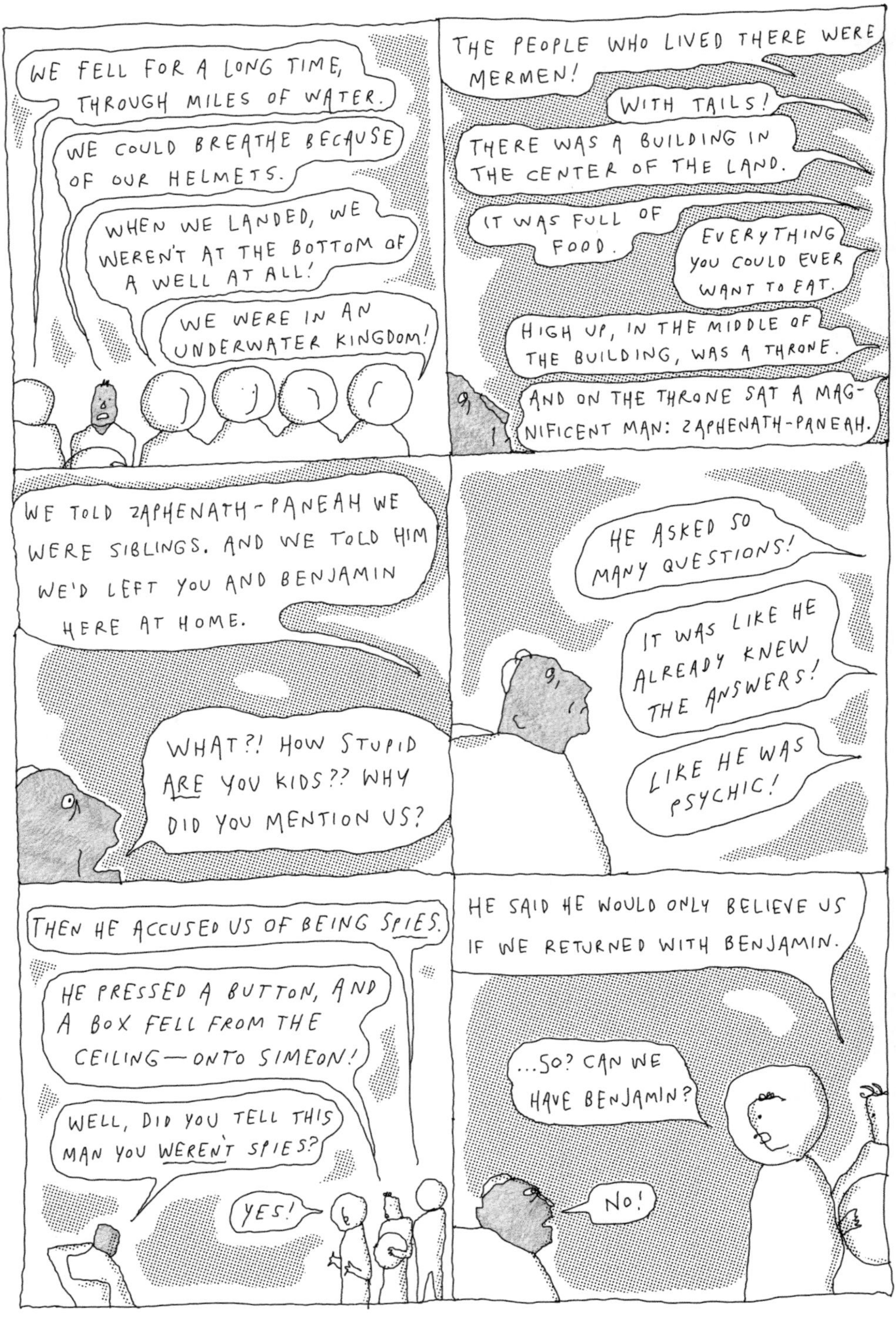
WE FELL FOR A LONG TIME, THROUGH MILES OF WATER.
WE COULD BREATHE BECAUSE OF OUR HELMETS.
WHEN WE LANDED, WE WEREN'T AT THE BOTTOM OF A WELL AT ALL!
WE WERE IN AN UNDERWATER KINGDOM!
THE PEOPLE WHO LIVED THERE WERE MERMEN!
WITH TAILS!
THERE WAS A BUILDING IN THE CENTER OF THE LAND.
IT WAS FULL OF FOOD.
EVERYTHING YOU COULD EVER WANT TO EAT.
HIGH UP, IN THE MIDDLE OF THE BUILDING, WAS A THRONE.
AND ON THE THRONE SAT A MAGNIFICENT MAN: ZAPHENATH-PANEAH.
WE TOLD ZAPHENATH-PANEAH WE WERE SIBLINGS. AND WE TOLD HIM WE'D LEFT YOU AND BENJAMIN HERE AT HOME.
WHAT?! HOW STUPID ARE YOU KIDS?? WHY DID YOU MENTION US?
HE ASKED SO MANY QUESTIONS!
IT WAS LIKE HE ALREADY KNEW THE ANSWERS!
LIKE HE WAS PSYCHIC!
THEN HE ACCUSED US OF BEING SPIES.
HE PRESSED A BUTTON, AND A BOX FELL FROM THE CEILING—ONTO SIMEON!
WELL, DID YOU TELL THIS MAN YOU WEREN'T SPIES?
YES!
HE SAID HE WOULD ONLY BELIEVE US IF WE RETURNED WITH BENJAMIN.
...SO? CAN WE HAVE BENJAMIN?
NO!

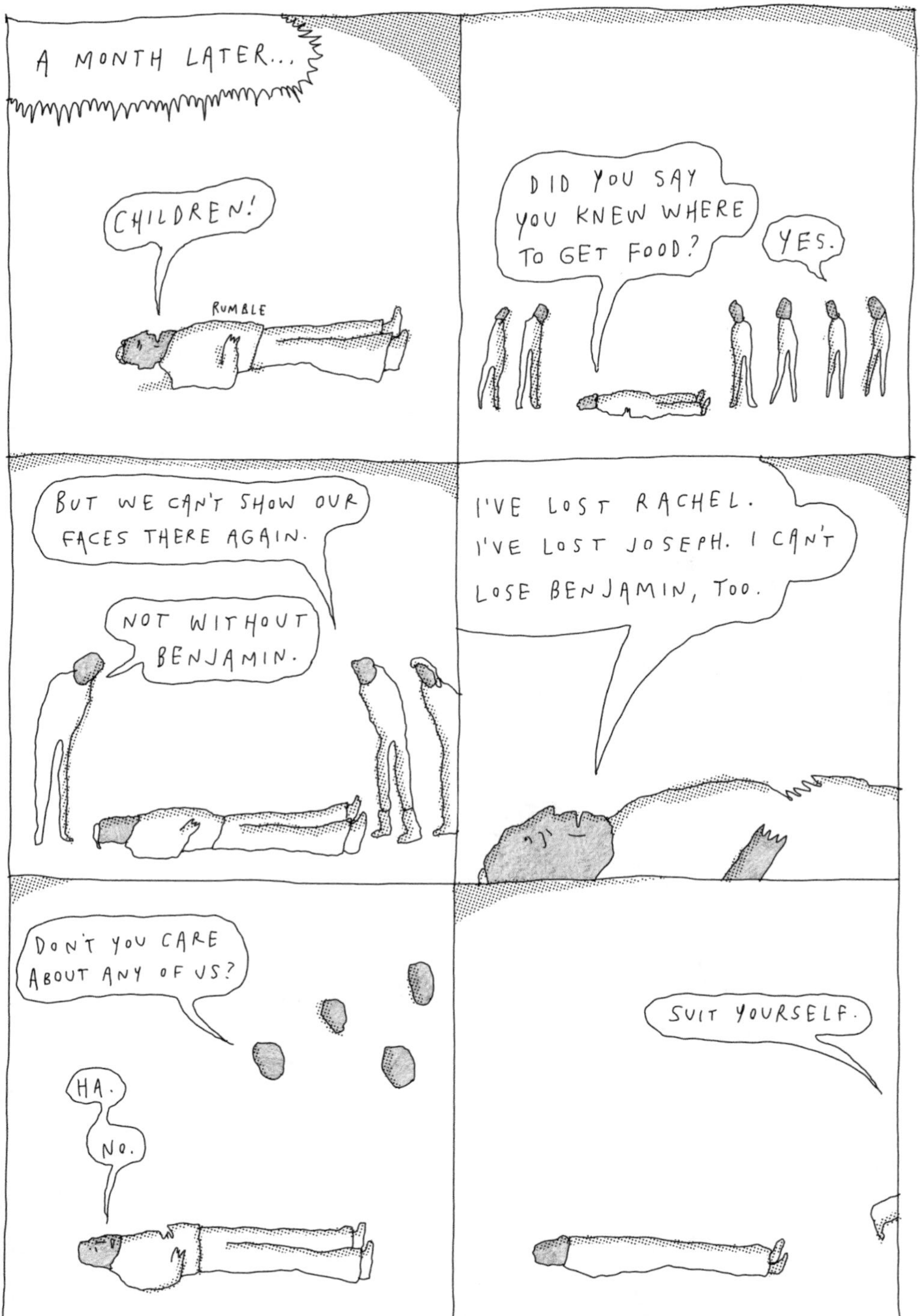
A MONTH LATER...
CHILDREN!
RUMBLE
DID YOU SAY YOU KNEW WHERE TO GET FOOD?
YES.
BUT WE CAN'T SHOW OUR FACES THERE AGAIN.
NOT WITHOUT BENJAMIN.
I'VE LOST RACHEL. I'VE LOST JOSEPH. I CAN'T LOSE BENJAMIN, TOO.
DON'T YOU CARE ABOUT ANY OF US?
HA.
NO.
SUIT YOURSELF.

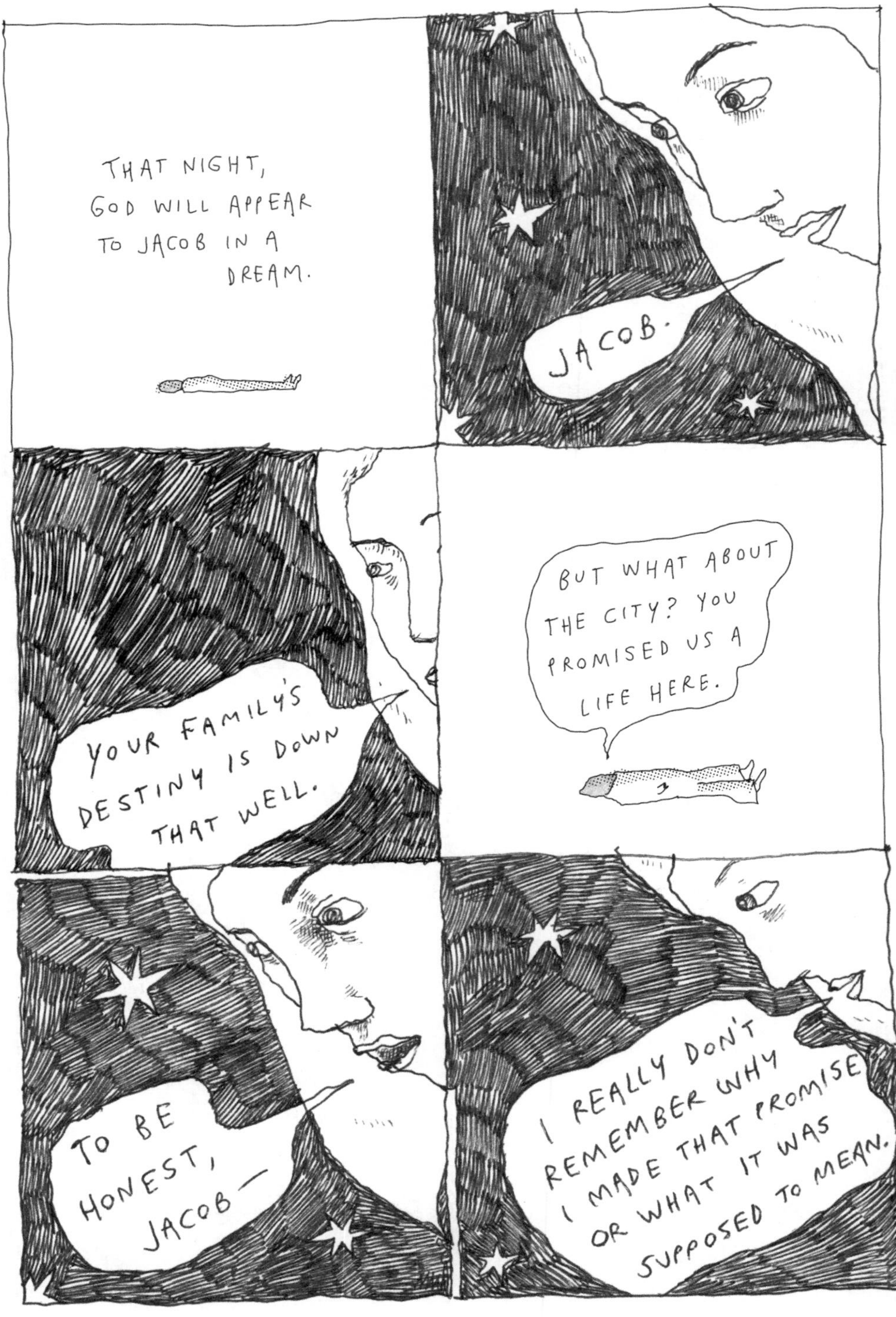
THAT NIGHT, GOD WILL APPEAR TO JACOB IN A DREAM.
JACOB.
YOUR FAMILY'S DESTINY IS DOWN THAT WELL.
BUT WHAT ABOUT THE CITY? YOU PROMISED US A LIFE HERE.
TO BE HONEST, JACOB—
I REALLY DON'T REMEMBER WHY I MADE THAT PROMISE OR WHAT IT WAS SUPPOSED TO MEAN.

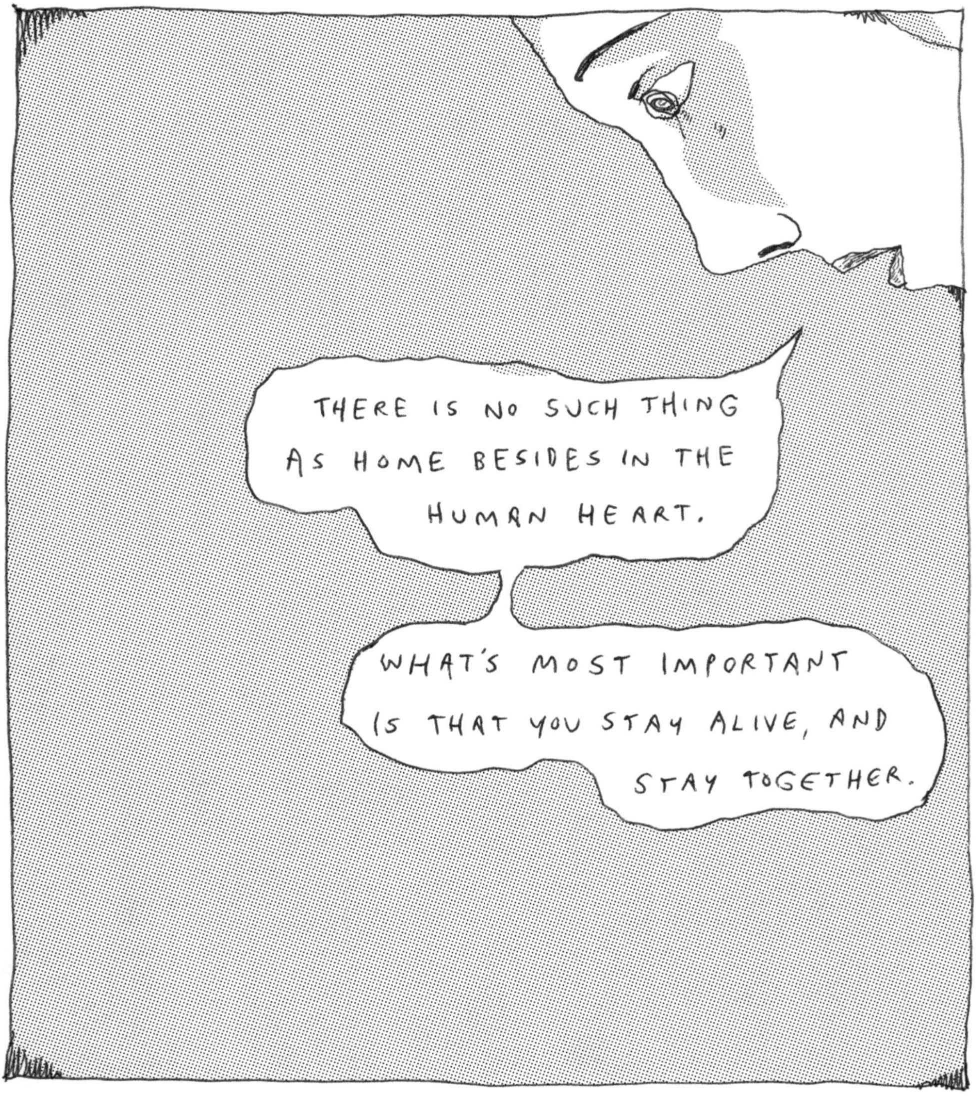
THERE IS NO SUCH THING AS HOME BESIDES IN THE HUMAN HEART.
WHAT'S MOST IMPORTANT IS THAT YOU STAY ALIVE, AND STAY TOGETHER.

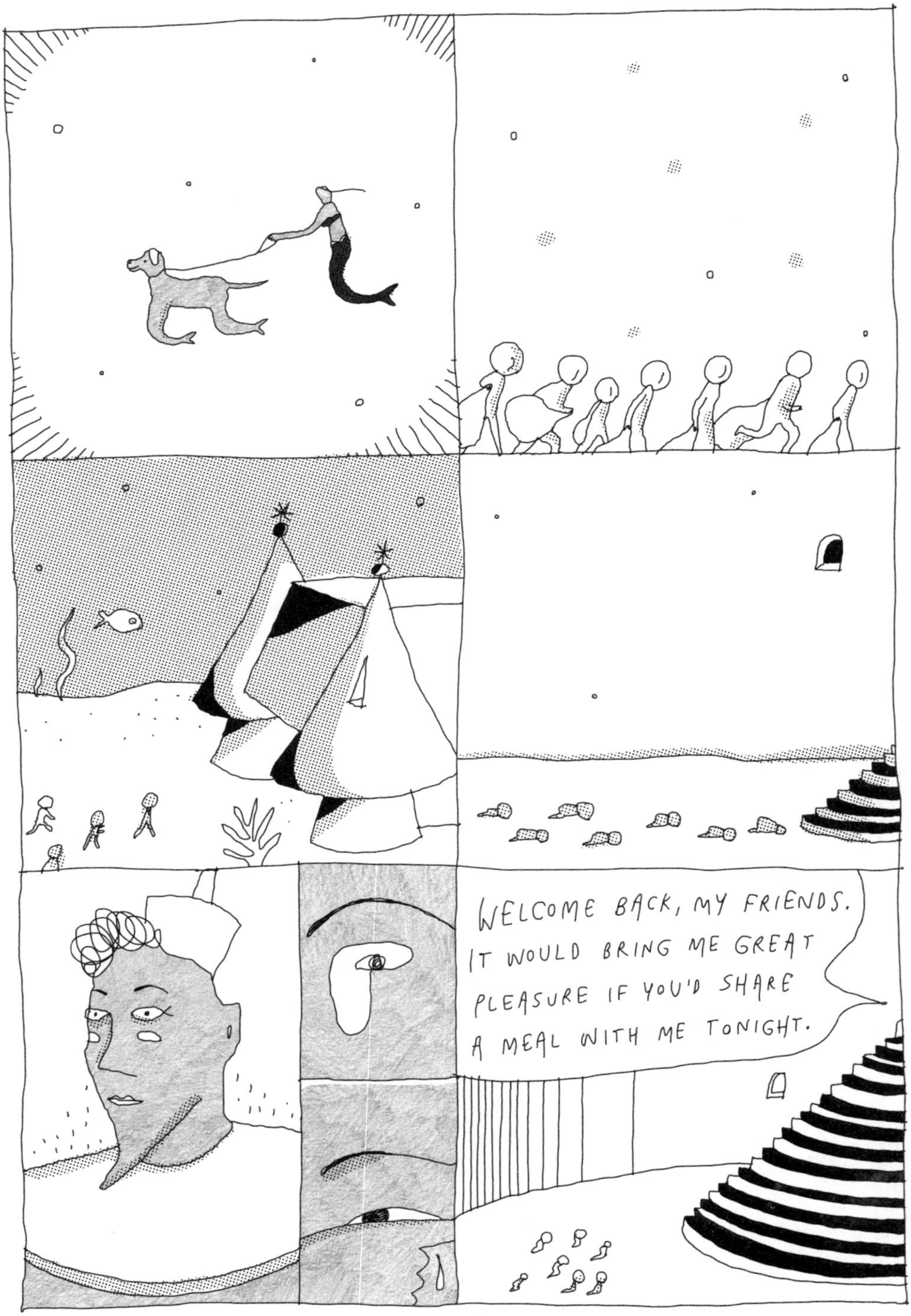
WELCOME BACK, MY FRIENDS. IT WOULD BRING ME GREAT PLEASURE IF YOU'D SHARE A MEAL WITH ME TONIGHT.

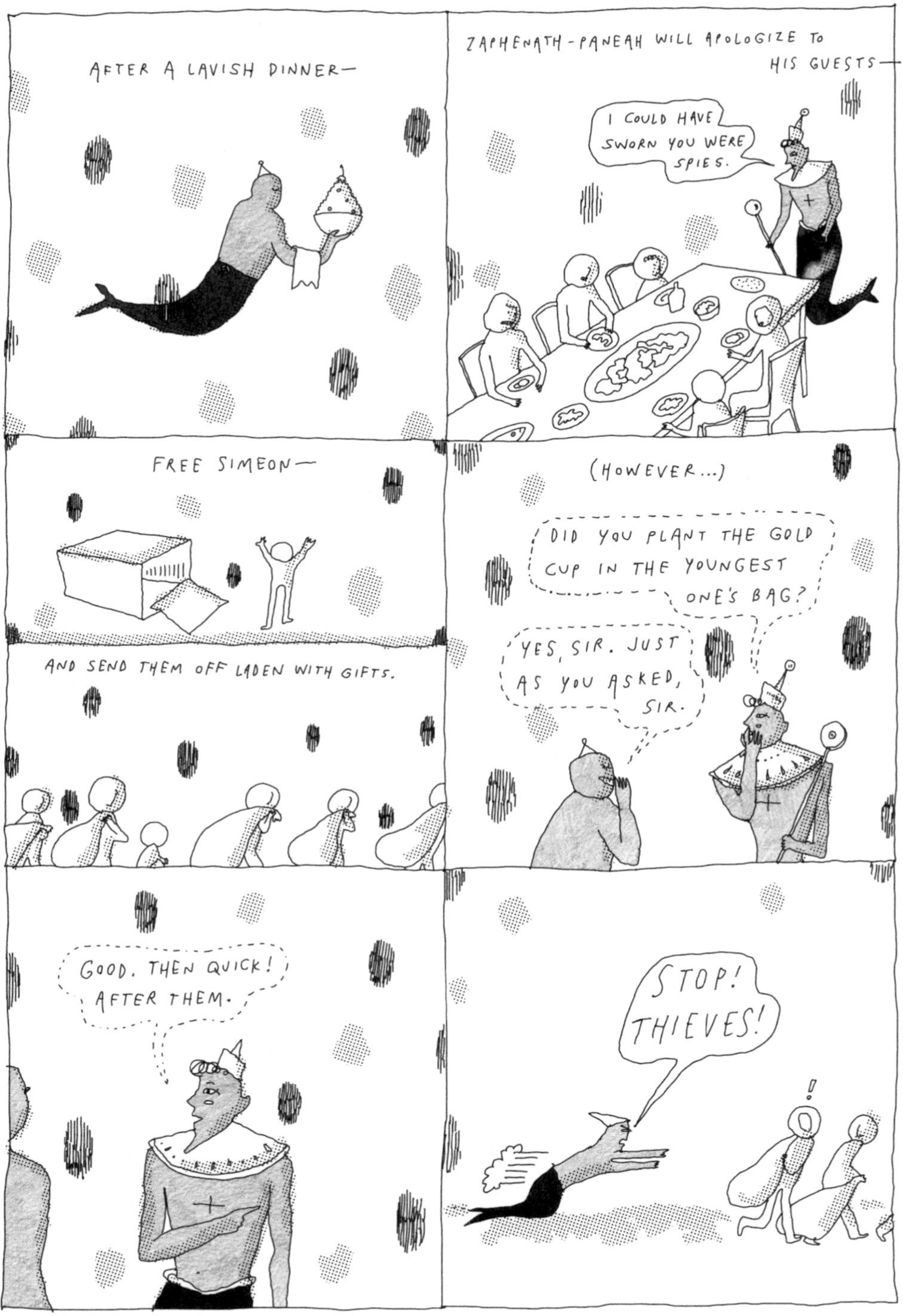

AFTER A LAVISH DINNER—
ZAPHENATH-PANEAH WILL APOLOGIZE TO HIS GUESTS—
I COULD HAVE SWORN YOU WERE SPIES.
FREE SIMEON—
AND SEND THEM OFF LADEN WITH GIFTS.
(HOWEVER...)
DID YOU PLANT THE GOLD CUP IN THE YOUNGEST ONE'S BAG?
YES, SIR. JUST AS YOU ASKED, SIR.
GOOD. THEN QUICK! AFTER THEM.
STOP! THIEVES!
!

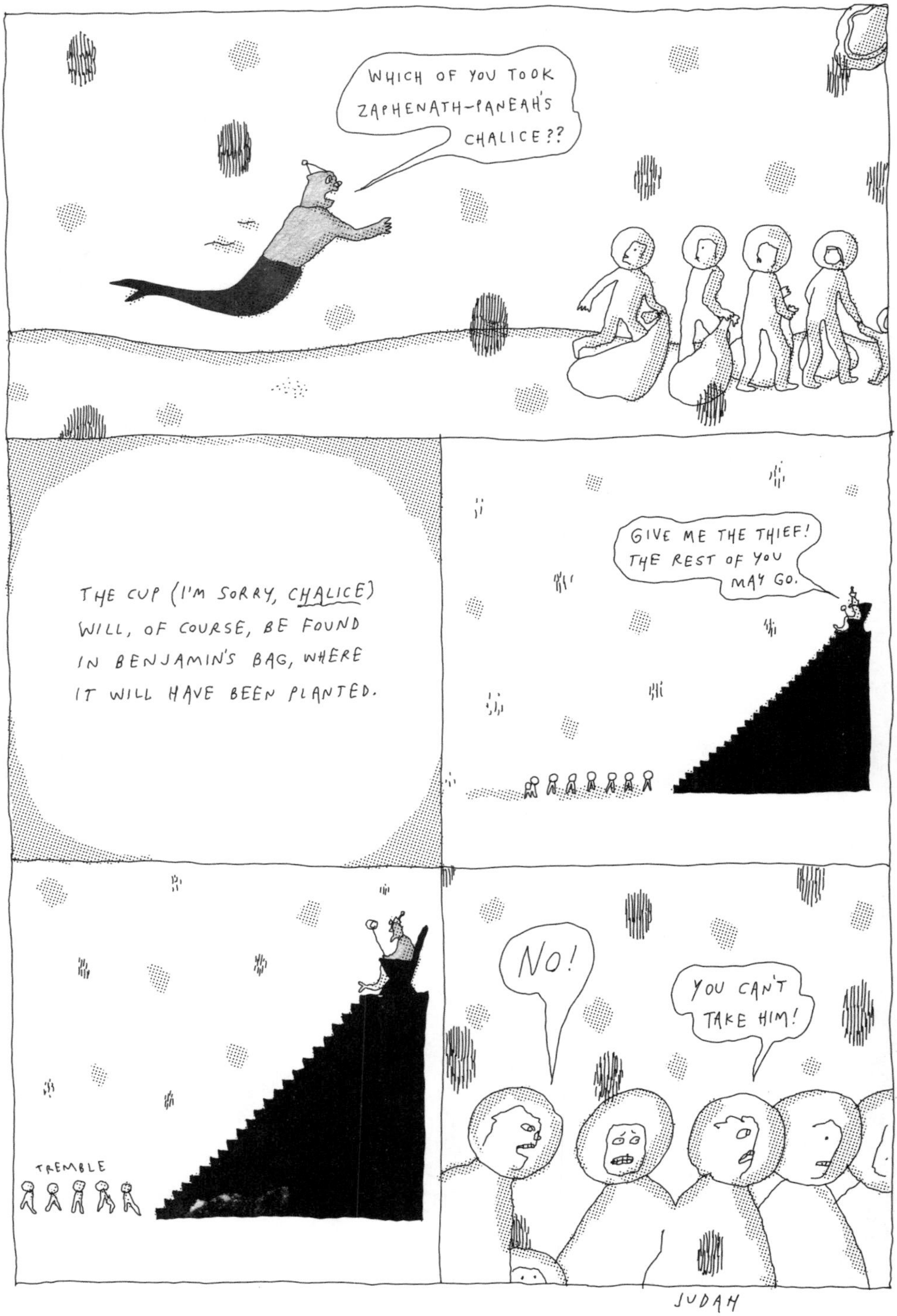
WHICH OF YOU TOOK ZAPHENATH-PANEAH'S CHALICE??
THE CUP (I'M SORRY, CHALICE) WILL, OF COURSE, BE FOUND IN BENJAMIN'S BAG, WHERE IT WILL HAVE BEEN PLANTED.
GIVE ME THE THIEF! THE REST OF YOU MAY GO.
TREMBLE
NO!
YOU CAN'T TAKE HIM!
JUDAH

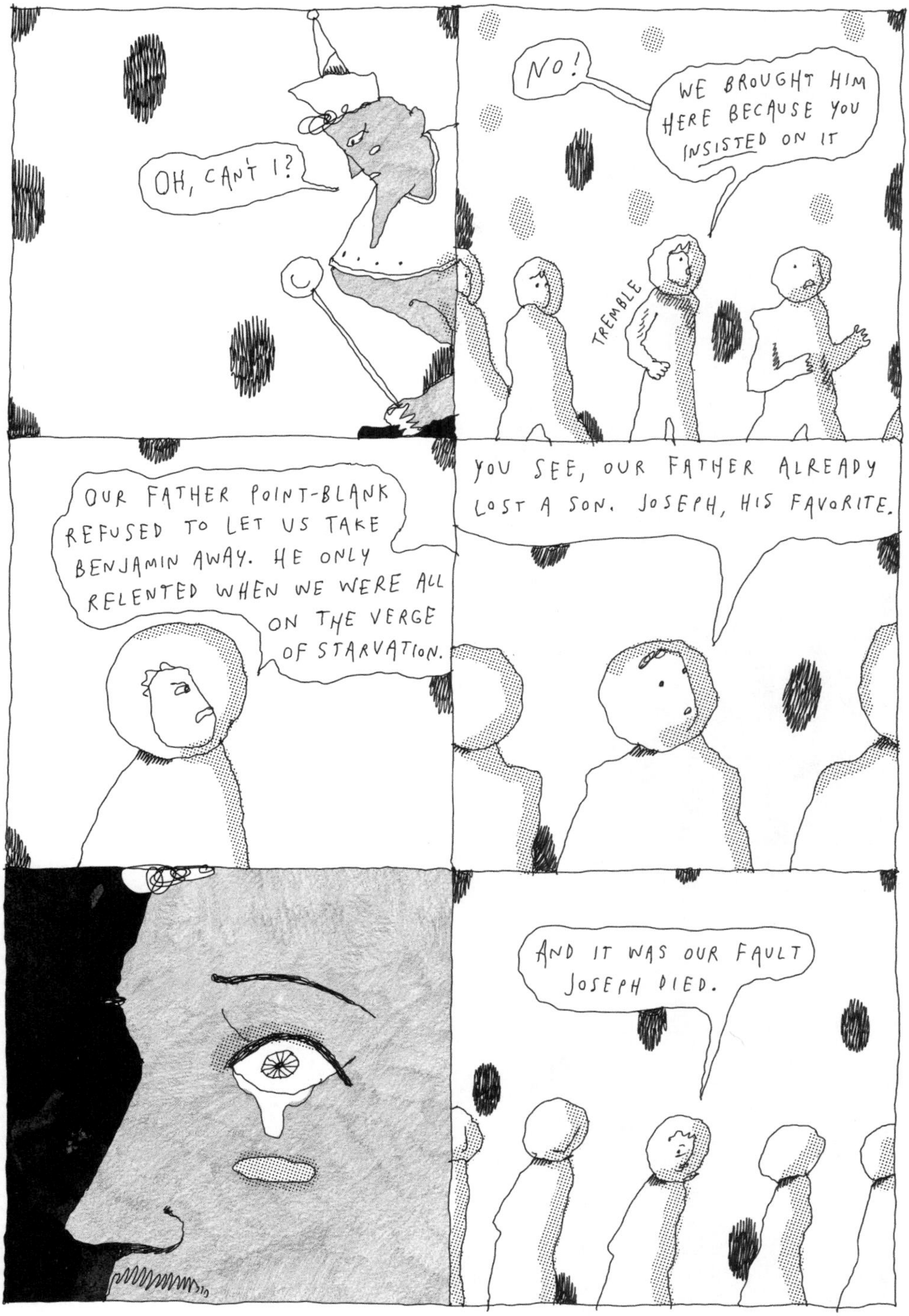
OH, CAN'T I?
NO!
WE BROUGHT HIM HERE BECAUSE YOU INSISTED ON IT
TREMBLE
OUR FATHER POINT-BLANK REFUSED TO LET US TAKE BENJAMIN AWAY. HE ONLY RELENTED WHEN WE WERE ALL ON THE VERGE OF STARVATION.
YOU SEE, OUR FATHER ALREADY LOST A SON. JOSEPH, HIS FAVORITE.
AND IT WAS OUR FAULT JOSEPH DIED.

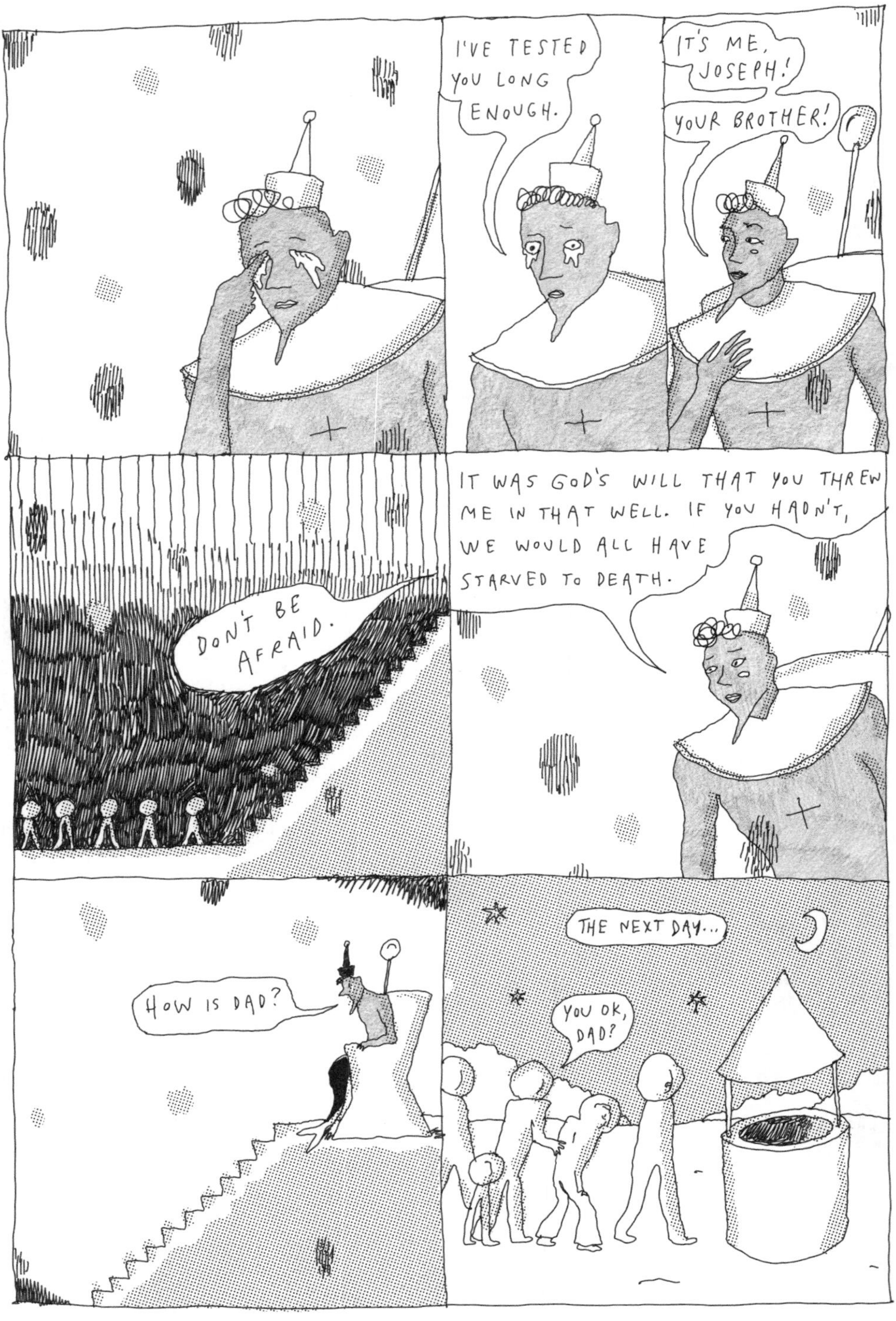
I'VE TESTED YOU LONG ENOUGH.
IT'S ME, JOSEPH!
YOUR BROTHER!
DON'T BE AFRAID.
IT WAS GOD'S WILL THAT YOU THREW ME IN THAT WELL. IF YOU HADN'T, WE WOULD ALL HAVE STARVED TO DEATH.
HOW IS DAD?
THE NEXT DAY...
YOU OK, DAD?

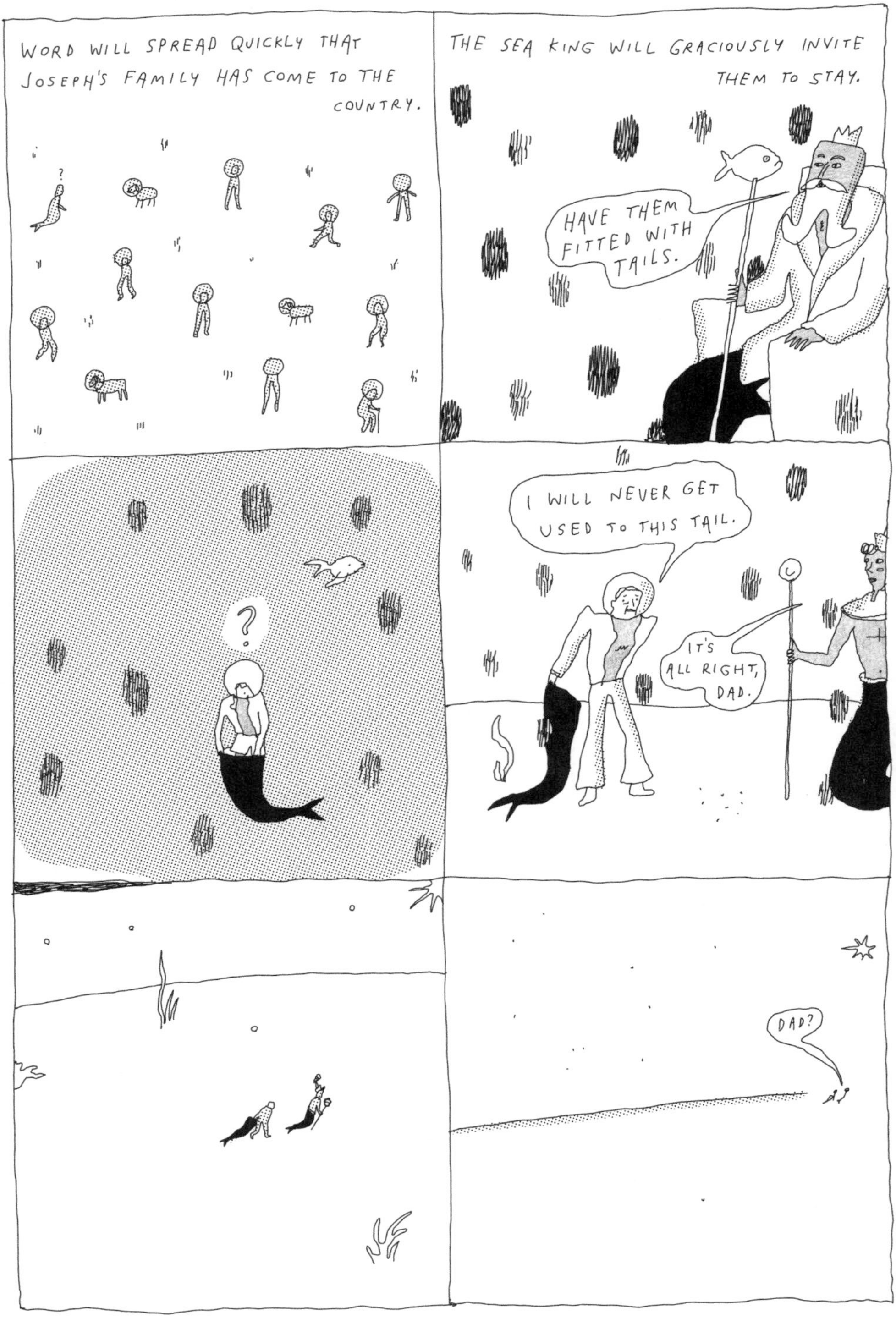
WORD WILL SPREAD QUICKLY THAT JOSEPH'S FAMILY HAS COME TO THE COUNTRY.
THE SEA KING WILL GRACIOUSLY INVITE THEM TO STAY.
HAVE THEM FITTED WITH TAILS.
I WILL NEVER GET USED TO THIS TAIL.
IT'S ALL RIGHT, DAD.
DAD?

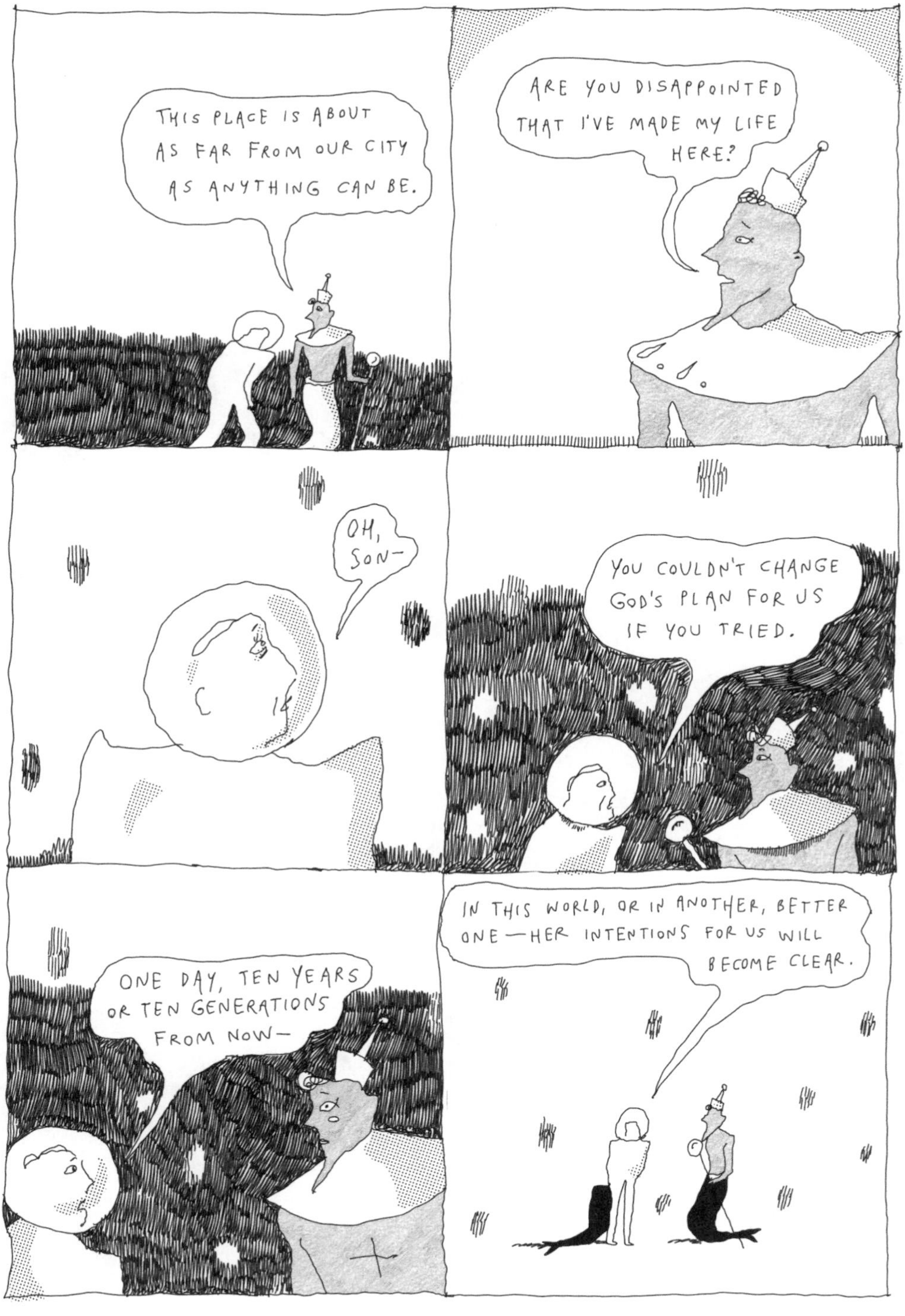
THIS PLACE IS ABOUT AS FAR FROM OUR CITY AS ANYTHING CAN BE.
ARE YOU DISAPPOINTED THAT I'VE MADE MY LIFE HERE?
OH, SON—
YOU COULDN'T CHANGE GOD'S PLAN FOR US IF YOU TRIED.
ONE DAY, TEN YEARS OR TEN GENERATIONS FROM NOW—
IN THIS WORLD, OR IN ANOTHER, BETTER ONE—HER INTENTIONS FOR US WILL BECOME CLEAR.

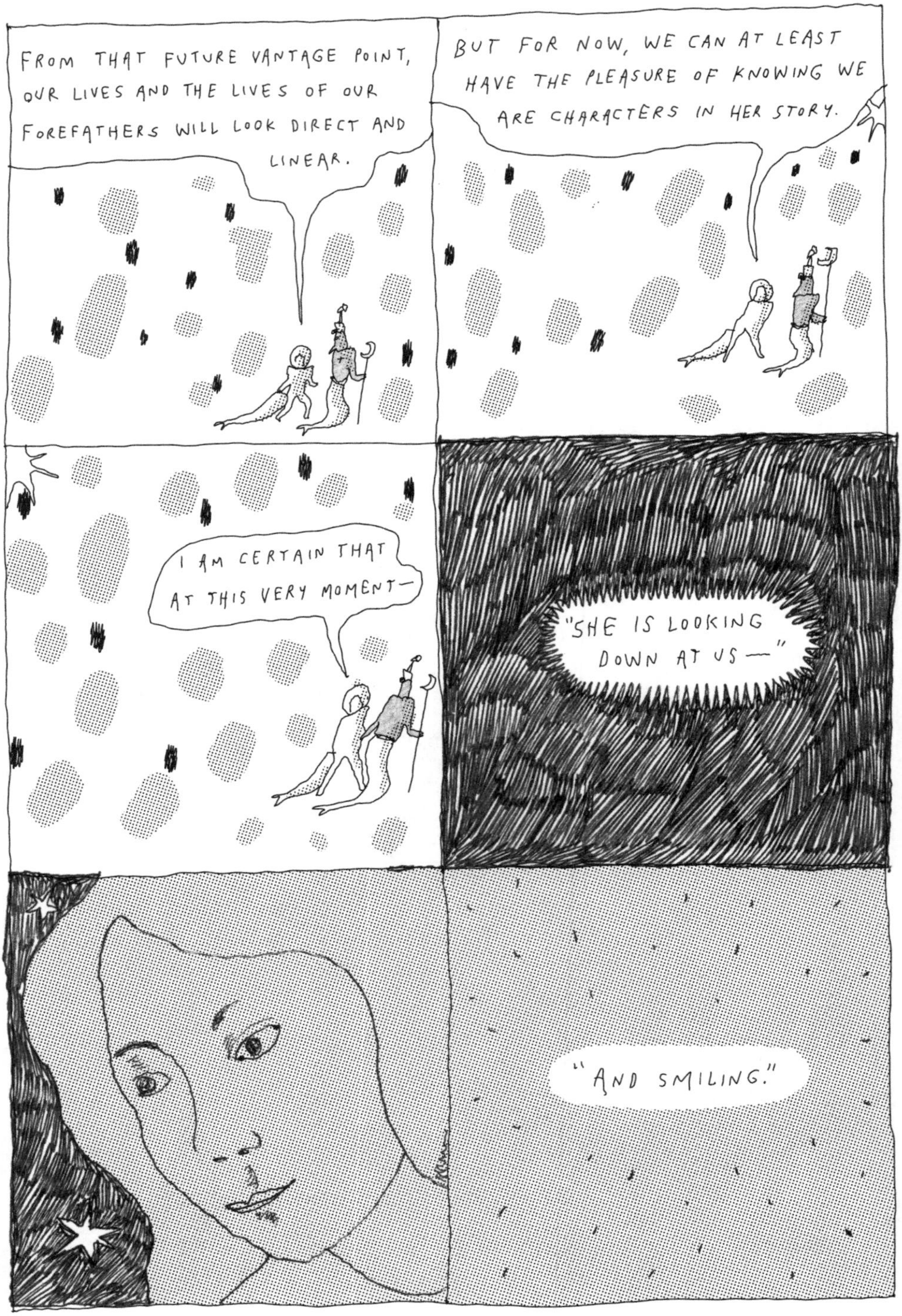
FROM THAT FUTURE VANTAGE POINT, OUR LIVES AND THE LIVES OF OUR FOREFATHERS WILL LOOK DIRECT AND LINEAR.
BUT FOR NOW, WE CAN AT LEAST HAVE THE PLEASURE OF KNOWING WE ARE CHARACTERS IN HER STORY.
I AM CERTAIN THAT AT THIS VERY MOMENT—
"SHE IS LOOKING DOWN AT US—"
"AND SMILING."

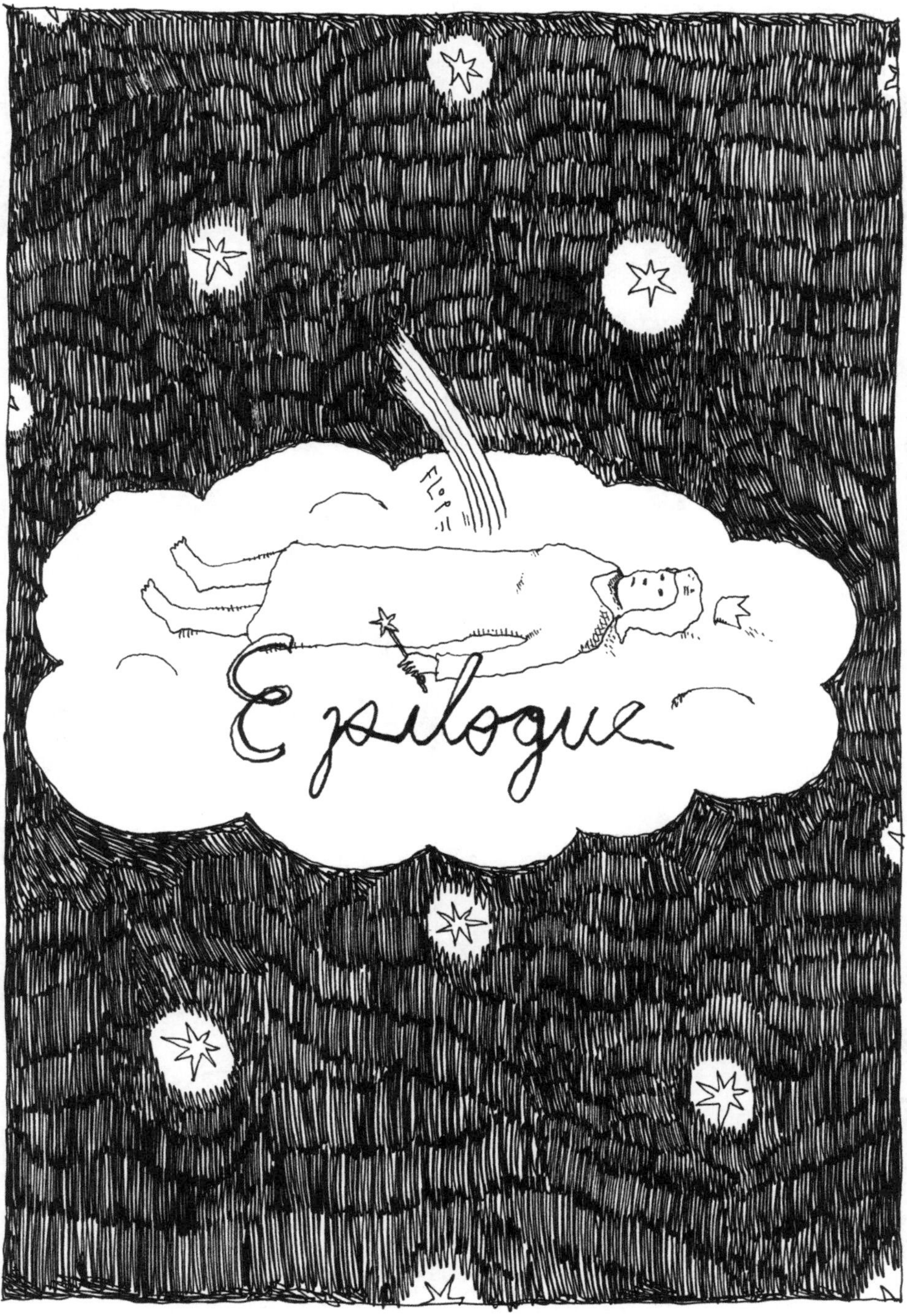
FLOP!
Epilogue

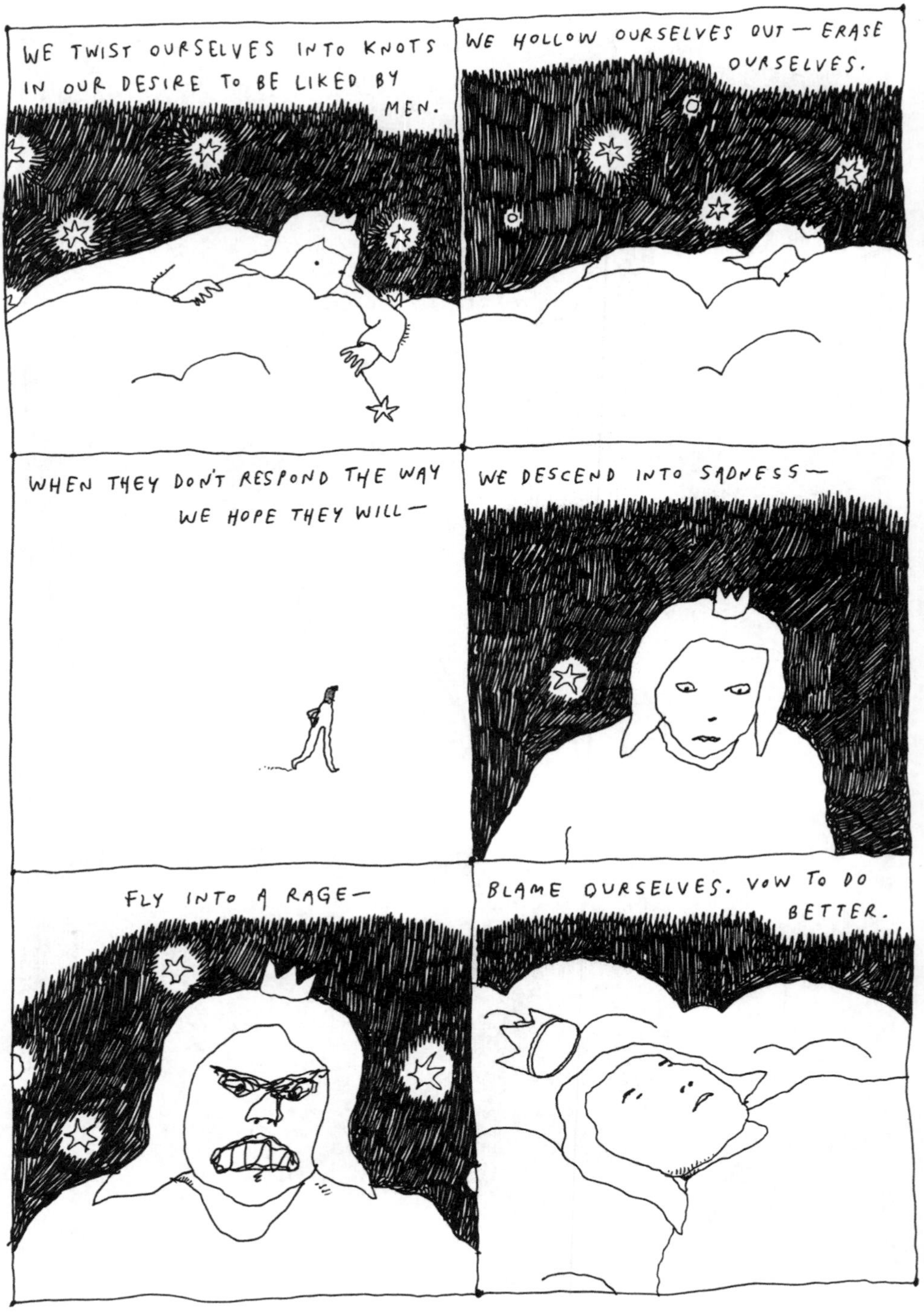
WE TWIST OURSELVES INTO KNOTS IN OUR DESIRE TO BE LIKED BY MEN.
WE HOLLOW OURSELVES OUT — ERASE OURSELVES.
WHEN THEY DON'T RESPOND THE WAY WE HOPE THEY WILL —
WE DESCEND INTO SADNESS —
FLY INTO A RAGE —
BLAME OURSELVES. VOW TO DO BETTER.

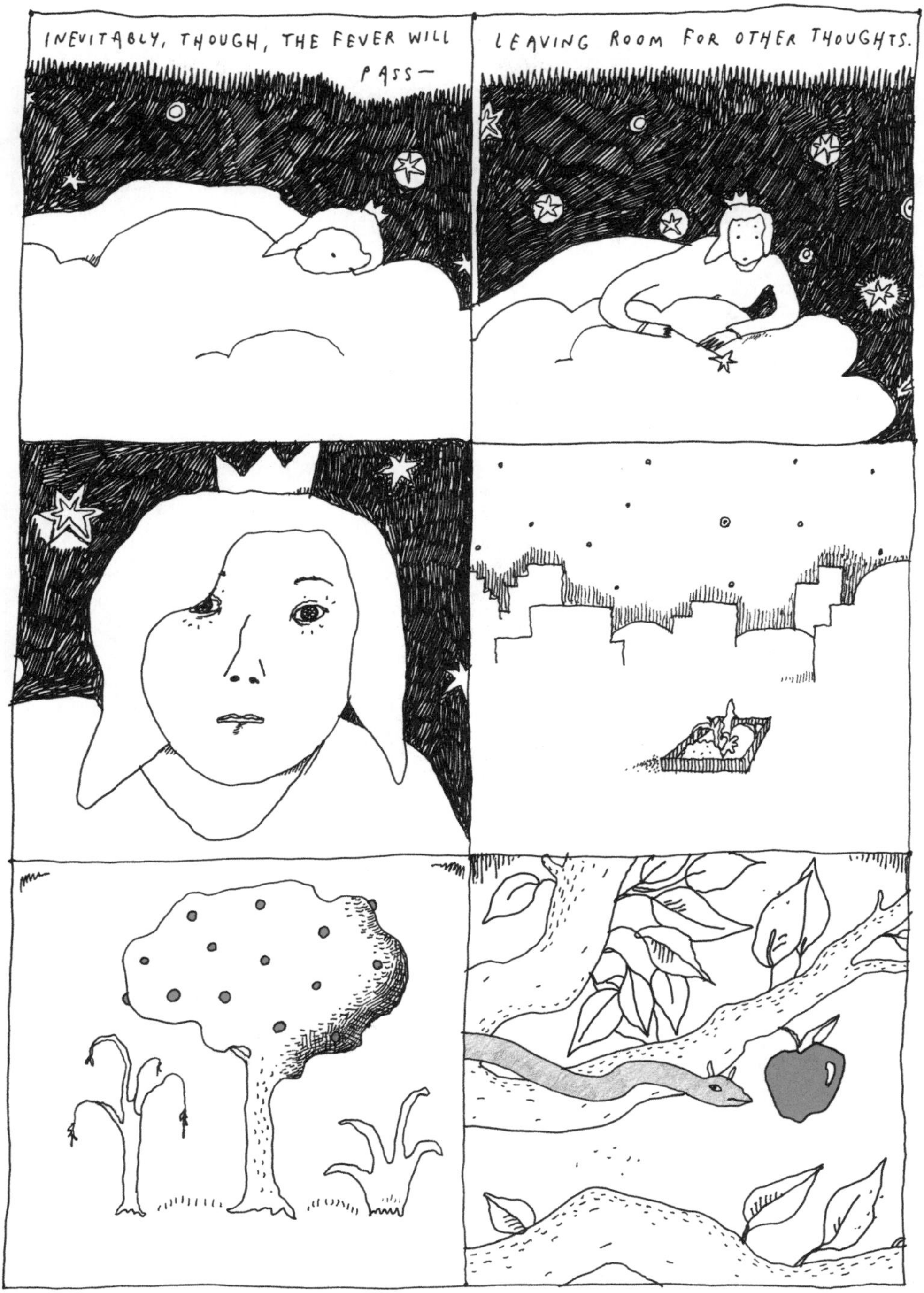
INEVITABLY, THOUGH, THE FEVER WILL PASS—
LEAVING ROOM FOR OTHER THOUGHTS.

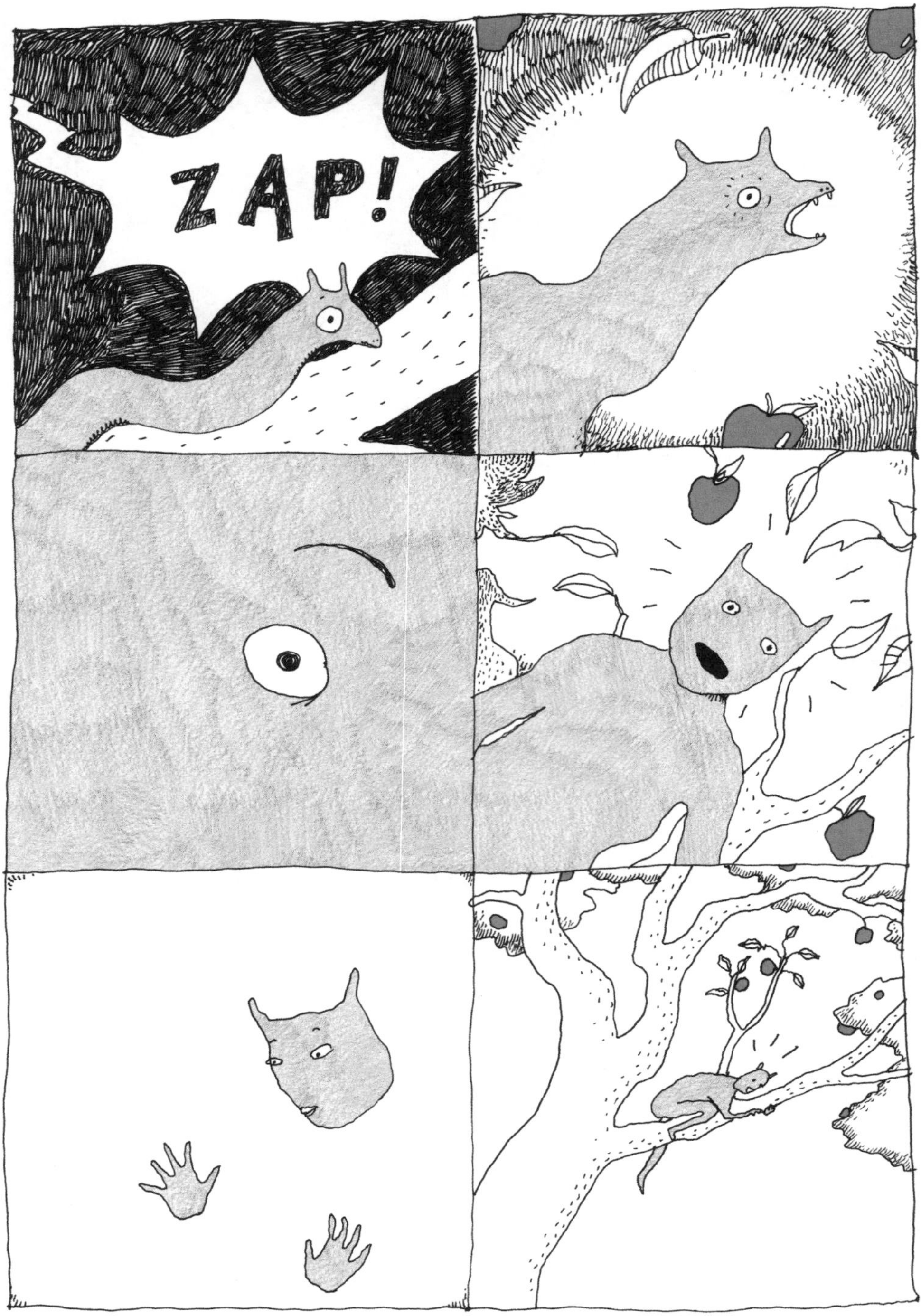
ZAP!

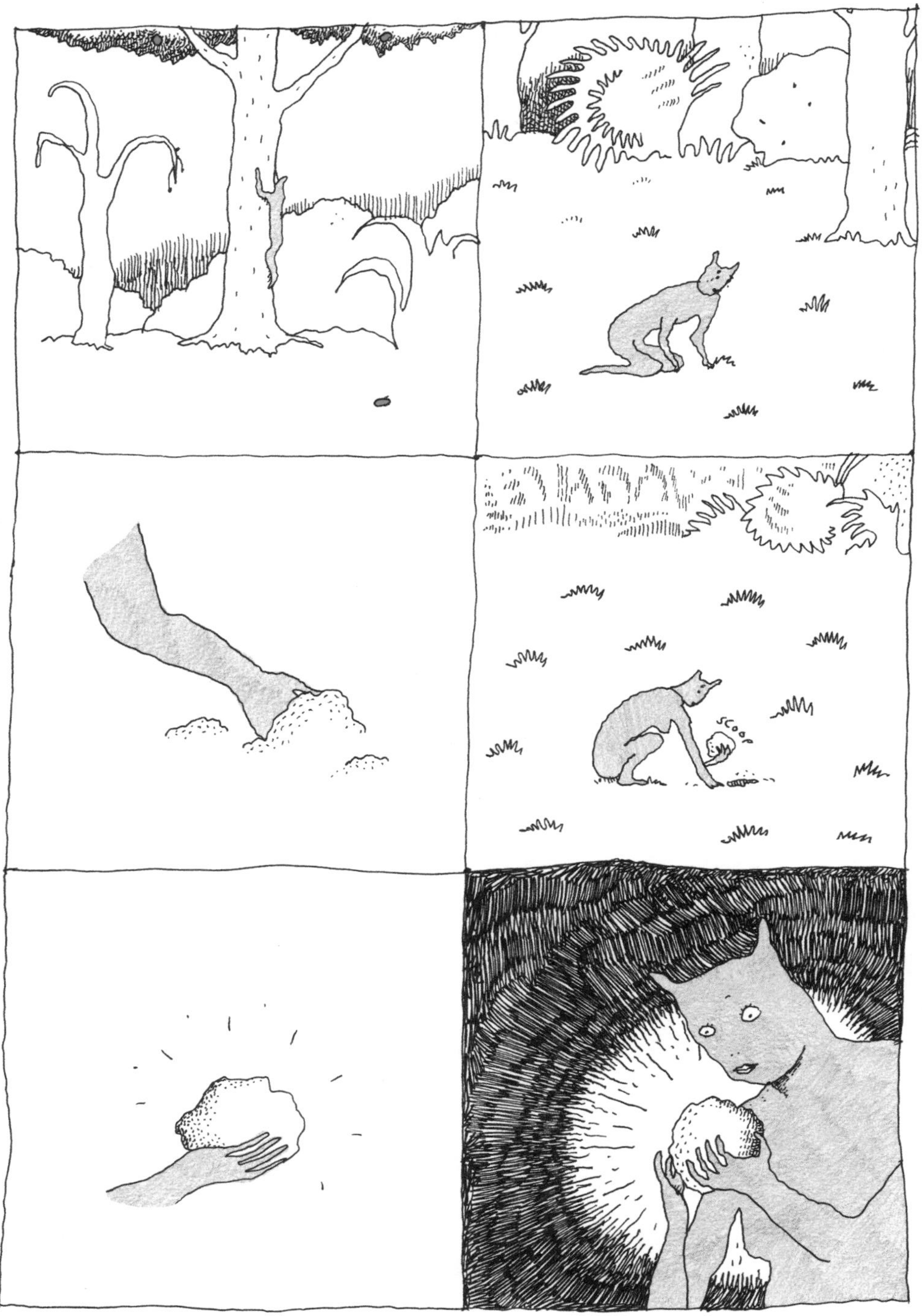
SCOOP

AUTHOR'S NOTE

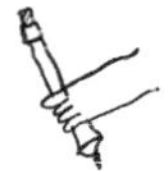

THE BOOK OF GENESIS IS A PATCHWORK OF VERY OLD AND EVEN OLDER TEXTS. IT EXPLAINS THE WAYS OF THE WORLD, ACCORDING TO ITS ANCIENT WRITERS: HOW THE UNIVERSE CAME INTO BEING, WHAT SETS HUMANS APART FROM ANIMALS, AND HOW THE DIFFERENT NATIONS CAME TO EXIST.

GENESIS CONTAINS MANY THINGS THAT ARE TIMELESS — THE CREATION OF THE WORLD IN SEVEN DAYS ISN'T OUR CURRENT CREATION STORY, BUT THE DESIRE TO EXPLAIN THE BEGINNING OF EVERYTHING IS AS URGENT A HUMAN NEED NOW AS IT WAS WHEN THE TORAH WAS FIRST PUT INTO WRITING. THERE IS A LOT OF DELICIOUS DRAMA, TOO — JEALOUSY BETWEEN SISTERS, A WILY NEPHEW GETTING THE BEST OF A CHEATING UNCLE, AN EGOTISTICAL BOY WHOSE DREAMS OF RULING OVER HIS BROTHERS END UP COMING TRUE. THERE ARE ALSO SOME THINGS THAT ARE HORRIFYING TO A READER TODAY — THE CASUALLY ACCEPTED INSTANCES OF SLAVERY AND RAPE — AND SOME THAT ARE BEWILDERING — THE EXTREME FAVORITISM OF ONE CHILD OVER ANOTHER.

I'VE NEVER HAD TROUBLE RECONCILING THE TIMELESS PARTS OF GENESIS WITH THE HORRIFIC PARTS. THIS MIGHT BE BECAUSE I DON'T HAVE A PARTICULARLY RELIGIOUS SOUL. I'VE ALWAYS SEEN THIS PART OF THE TORAH AS A MARVELOUS, AMORAL, MILLENNIA-OLD PIECE OF LITERATURE, LIKE THE EPIC OF GILGAMESH AND THE ODYSSEY, RATHER THAN SOMETHING THAT SHOULD BE TRUSTED AND FOLLOWED AS LAW. ONCE YOU SCRATCH THE SURFACE OF THE STORIES, YOU FIND ALL KINDS OF HIDDEN AGENDAS: EVE EATS THE FRUIT OF THE TREE OF KNOWLEDGE, AND THAT'S WHY A WOMAN MUST ALWAYS SERVE HER HUSBAND. ONE OF NOAH'S SONS, HAM, WAS DISRESPECTFUL TO HIS FATHER; THEREFORE IT'S OK FOR HIS BROTHER SHEM'S DESCENDANTS, THE ISRAELITES, TO DOMINATE HAM'S, THE CANAANITES. THE STORY IN GENESIS THAT SEEMS TO ME MOST INFUSED WITH ULTERIOR MOTIVE IS THE STORY OF DINAH, JACOB'S ONLY DAUGHTER, WHOSE RAPE BY A MAN NAMED SHECHEM PROMPTS TWO OF JACOB'S SONS, SIMEON AND LEVI, TO MURDER SHECHEM'S

WHOLE TRIBE. THIS STORY SEEMS TO HAVE BEEN PUT INTO THE TEXT ONLY TO EXPLAIN WHY SIMEON'S AND LEVI'S OFFSPRING WERE DWINDLING AT THE TIME THE TORAH WAS BEING WRITTEN. THE PARTS OF THE BOOK OF GENESIS WITH BLATANT AGENDAS WERE THE PARTS I CHANGED MOST. IN MY VERSION, I MADE DINAH JUST ONE OF THE GUYS — A SHEPHERD WITH HER BROTHERS. MY OWN WISHFUL REWRITING OF THE NARRATIVE. THE STORY OF HAGAR — AN ENSLAVED PERSON OWNED BY SARAI AND THE MOTHER OF ABRAM'S FIRST AND LESS LOVED SON, ISHMAEL — WAS ONE OF THE ELEMENTS THAT GOT CUT OUT OF MY ADAPTATION. I HAD TRIED TO TELL HAGAR'S STORY AS A SMALL PART OF ABRAM'S STRING OF ADVENTURES, THE WAY IT'S PRESENTED IN THE TORAH, BUT I COULDN'T DO IT JUSTICE THAT WAY. HAGAR NEEDS MORE SPACE AND THOUGHT THAN THE REST OF ABRAM'S ADVENTURES PUT TOGETHER. OTHERWISE, HER STORY MAKES NO SENSE.

STUDYING THE TORAH AT HEBREW DAY SCHOOL, I THOUGHT OF IT MOSTLY AS A PORTRAIT OF ONE CHILDLIKE (AND THEREFORE RELATABLE) CHARACTER FULL OF FEELINGS AND DESIRES: GOD. I'VE NEVER REALLY ASKED MYSELF IF I BELIEVE IN GOD, BUT I'VE ALWAYS BEEN ENCHANTED BY HER, THE WAY I AM BY MY FAVORITE CHARACTERS IN STORIES. THIS BOOK IS AN ATTEMPT TO DRAW OUT THAT CHARACTER AS I SAW HER (SINCE I STARTED WRITING THIS BOOK, IT HURTS TO CALL GOD "HIM") WHEN I WAS YOUNG. GIVING GOD A NEW GENDER — MY OWN — WAS MY FIRST STEP TOWARD RECLAIMING THIS WORK OF LITERATURE FOR MYSELF.

I HOPE THE GOD I'VE CREATED IN THIS BOOK IS RELATABLE IN SOME WAYS TO SOME PEOPLE, OR THAT SHE'S AT LEAST A FUN CHARACTER TO READ ABOUT. BUT MY REAL AIM IN MAKING THIS BOOK IS TO DEMONSTRATE THAT EACH OF US IS ALLOWED TO CREATE GOD (OR GODS) IN OUR OWN IMAGE. AND THAT WE MUST RESHAPE THE LARGER STORIES THAT ARE HANDED DOWN TO US — FAMILY STORIES, RELIGIOUS AND CULTURAL STORIES, OUR INDIVIDUAL AND COLLECTIVE PASTS — AND TELL THEM IN A WAY THAT FEELS HONEST TO US. STORIES NEED TO BE TOLD AND RETOLD IN DIFFERENT VOICES. THAT IS HOW THEY BREATHE.

ACKNOWLEDGMENTS

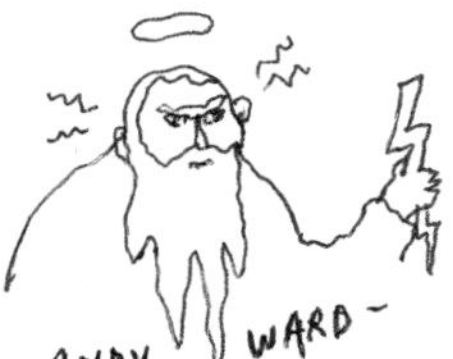

ANDY WARD – MY WISE, COMPASSIONATE, AND EXTREMELY DEDICATED EDITOR; NOT ACTUALLY ZEUS-LIKE

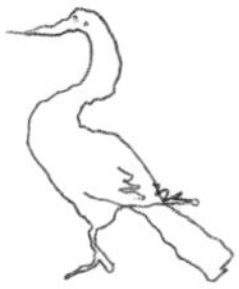

MY AGENT, **MEREDITH KAFFEL SIMONOFF**, WHO IS A SMART & PERCEPTIVE READER & BIG-PICTURE-SEER

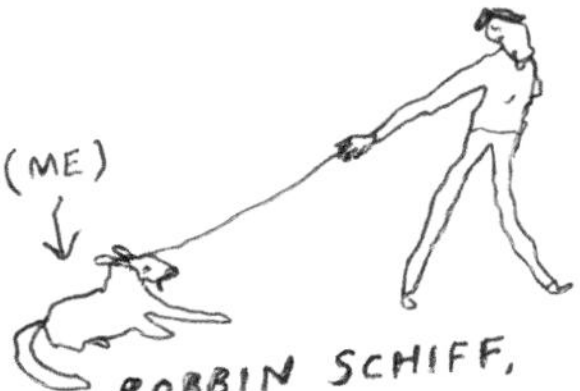
(ME)

ROBBIN SCHIFF, ART DIRECTOR, FOR ALLLL THE PATIENT GUIDANCE & COAXING WITH THIS COVER

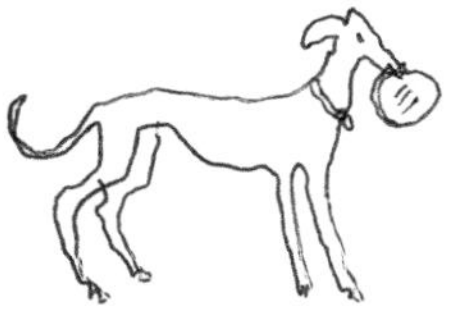

ERIN RICHARDS, DEAR & EXCELLENT PUBLICIST

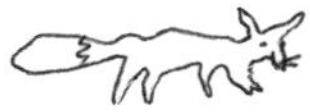

SUSAN BROWN, COPY EDITOR, FOR THE VERY GOOD CATCHES

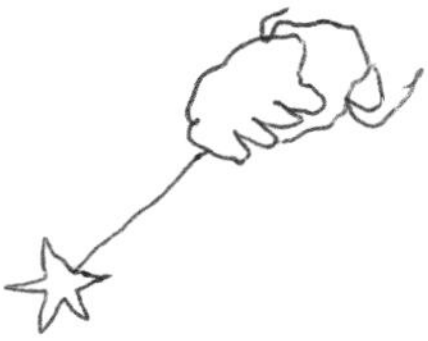

THE NEW YORKER (FEATURING **EMMA ALLEN, COLIN STOKES, & DAVID REMNICK**) FOR ENABLING ME TO SUPPORT MYSELF (WITH A DREAM JOB) WHILE WORKING ON THIS BOOK. ETERNAL GRATITUDE.

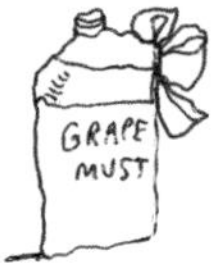
GRAPE
MUST

SARAH FEIGHTNER AND **ADA YONENAKA**, PRODUCTION TEAM, WHO HAVE MADE MY BOOKS TURN OUT WELL-PRINTED AND BEAUTIFUL

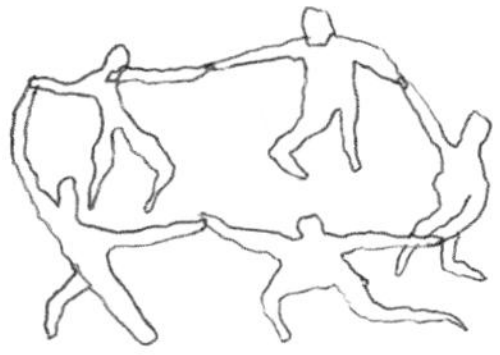

THE REST OF THE TEAM AT RANDOM HOUSE: **KAELI SUBBERWAL, MADISON DETTLINGER, REBECCA BERLANT, TOM PERRY & MARIE PANTOJAN**

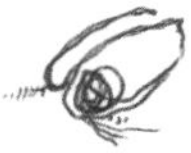

READERS & ADVICE GIVERS INCLUDING BUT NOT LIMITED TO **TAHNEER OKSMAN, GABRIELLE BELL, ROZ CHAST, JULIANA WANG, AGNES BORINSKY, RODRIGO CORRAL, ROMAN MURADOV, SCOTT GOODMAN, & HARRIET, MICHAEL & GIDEON FINCK**

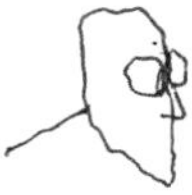

JORGE COLOMBO FOR LETTING ME USE HIS IPAD PROCREATE BRUSHES FOR THIS BOOK & BOOK COVER, AND FOR ALL THE COVER FEEDBACK

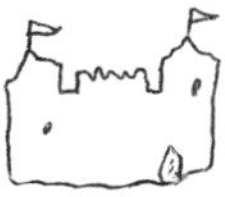

WILLAPA BAY AiR AND **HEADLANDS CENTER FOR THE ARTS** FOR THE RESIDENCIES WHILE I WORKED ON THIS BOOK

ABOUT THE AUTHOR

RECIPIENT

LIANA FINCK IS THE AUTHOR OF PASSING FOR HUMAN AND EXCUSE ME AND A REGULAR CONTRIBUTOR TO THE NEW YORKER. SHE IS A RECIPIENT OF A FULBRIGHT FELLOWSHIP, A NEW YORK FOUNDATION FOR THE ARTS ARTIST FELLOWSHIP, AND A SIX POINTS FELLOWSHIP FOR EMERGING JEWISH ARTISTS. SHE HAS HAD ARTIST RESIDENCIES WITH MACDOWELL, YADDO, AND THE LOWER MANHATTAN CULTURAL COUNCIL.

APPLAUSE!

ABOUT THE TYPE: N|A